DATE DUE

	WITHDRAWN		

Demco, Inc. 38-293

JUN 29 2011

A

Philip E. Lilienthal

B O O K

The Philip E. Lilienthal imprint
honors special books
in commemoration of a man whose work
at University of California Press from 1954 to 1979
was marked by dedication to young authors
and to high standards in the field of Asian Studies.
Friends, family, authors, and foundations have together
endowed the Lilienthal Fund, which enables UC Press
to publish under this imprint selected books
in a way that reflects the taste and judgment
of a great and beloved editor.

The publisher gratefully acknowledges the generous
contribution to this book provided by the Philip E. Lilienthal Asian Studies
Endowment Fund of the University of California Press Foundation,
which is supported by a major gift from Sally Lilienthal.

Vietnam 1946

FROM INDOCHINA TO VIETNAM:
REVOLUTION AND WAR IN A GLOBAL PERSPECTIVE

Edited by Fredrik Logevall and Christopher E. Goscha

Vietnam 1946

How the War Began

Stein Tønnesson

With a foreword by Philippe Devillers

UNIVERSITY OF CALIFORNIA PRESS

Berkeley   Los Angeles   London

Portions of this book were published in earlier forms in Stein Tønnesson, *The Outbreak of the War in Indochina, 1946*, PRIO Report no. 3 (International Peace Research Institute, Oslo, 1984); *1946: Déclenchement de la guerre d'Indochine. Les vêpres tonkinoises du 19 décembre* (Paris: L'Harmattan, 1987); "A French Decision for War: French and Vietnamese Decision-Making before the Outbreak of the War in Indochina, December 1946," *Vietnam Forum*, no. 12 (Summer–Fall 1988): 112–35; and "La paix imposée par la Chine: L'accord franco-vietnamien du 6 mars 1946," *Cahiers de l'Institut d'histoire du temps présent*, no. 34 (1996): 35–56, and are reproduced here by permission of the International Peace Research Institute, Oslo (PRIO), L'Harmattan, the Institut de l'histoire du temps présent, and *Vietnam Forum*, Council on Southeast Asia Studies, Yale University.

University of California Press, one of the most distinguished university presses in the United States, enriches lives around the world by advancing scholarship in the humanities, social sciences, and natural sciences. Its activities are supported by the UC Press Foundation and by philanthropic contributions from individuals and institutions. For more information, visit www.ucpress.edu.

University of California Press
Berkeley and Los Angeles, California

University of California Press, Ltd.
London, England

Library of Congress Cataloging-in-Publication Data

Tønnesson, Stein.
    Vietnam 1946 : how the war began / Stein Tønnesson.
        p.   cm. — (From Indochina to Vietnam : revolution and war
    in a global perspective ; 3)
    Includes bibliographical references and index.
    ISBN 978-0-520-25602-6 (cloth : alk. paper)
    1. Indochinese War, 1946–1954.   2. Indochinese War, 1946–1954—
Causes.   3. Vietnam—History—1946–1975.   4. France—Relations—
Vietnam.   5. Vietnam—Relations—France.   6. China—Relations—
Vietnam.   7. Vietnam—Relations—China.   I. Title.
DS553.1.T67   2010
959.704'11—dc22   2009011530

Manufactured in the United States of America

18   17   16   15   14   13   12   11   10
11   10   9   8   7   6   5   4   3   2

This book is printed on Natures Book, which contains 30% postconsumer waste and meets the minimum requirements of ANSI/NISO Z39.48–1992 (R 1997) *(Permanence of Paper).*

For Philippe Devillers, who was there in 1946,
published his Histoire du Viêt-Nam *in 1952, came to Oslo to speak*
up against the American Vietnam War in 1968, has inspired and
reviewed my writings since he sent me to the archives in 1981,
published Paris-Saigon-Hanoi *in 1988, and still wonders*
what really happened that December 19.

CONTENTS

ILLUSTRATIONS

Historians have written scores of books in English on the events leading the Americans into war in Vietnam in the early 1960s. And many more are now appearing on the Vietnamese side. Strangely enough, remarkably few scholars have examined the outbreak of the first war in Indochina in 1945–46 between the French and the same Vietnamese, despite the fact that combined the two wars constituted one of the longest, most important, and violent conflicts of the Cold War. Hence the importance of Stein Tønnesson's incisive study of the start of the war for Vietnam in 1945–46, *Vietnam 1946: How the War Began*. In this path-breaking book, Tønnesson provides the first detailed account of the events, decisions, and people who led France in particular into its first of two long wars of decolonization.

As early as 1952, French scholar Philippe Devillers had first suggested that the official French explanations for the outbreak of the war, which pinned the blame exclusively on the Democratic Republic of Vietnam (DRV), were flawed. The French, especially local officials in charge in Indochina, also were responsible. Devillers based much of his argument on research in Vietnam in 1945–46, on interviews with scores of French and Vietnamese decision-makers, and on his access to internal documents in Paris.

There matters in large part rested until the 1980s. With the opening of the relevant files in the archives in France, Britain, and the United States, Stein Tønnesson not only could confirm many of Devillers's findings, but go much further.[1] In re-

---

1. Devillers published a collection of internal documents demonstrating, in his view, French responsibility for the outbreak of the war. Philippe Devillers, *Paris-Saigon-Hanoi: les archives de la guerre 1944–1947* (Paris: Gallimard/Julliard, 1988).

search spanning more than two decades, Tønnesson has meticulously examined the extensive archival holdings on the outbreak of the war held in the Service historique de la défense, the Ministère des Affaires étrangères, and especially at the Centre des Archives d'Outre-mer. He has also worked, albeit with more limitations, in the Vietnamese archives in Hanoi and has made use of important Vietnamese primary and secondary sources. Throughout, he has published cutting-edge, multiarchival scholarship based on this research, in the French as well as the English language.[2] *Vietnam 1946: How the War Began* draws on newly available material in several countries to present an original and matchlessly authoritative study of the origins of the first Indochina War, which set the stage for the American one.

Tønnesson shows the degree to which local French authorities in Indochina, determined to roll back the sovereignty of the DRV, ignored entreaties to negotiate and intentionally pushed the Vietnamese into a corner, if not a trap. Their secret hope was that the Vietnamese would lash out, thereby providing local French authorities the pretext they needed to take France into war. Local officials got their wish on December 19, 1946, when the Vietnamese attacked. Important questions remain about Vietnamese decision-making in the crucial weeks leading up to war, the answers to which are dependent on archival materials that remain under lock and key. In the meantime, however, Tønnesson has provided us with the first serious scholarly account of what happened during those perilous ten months between February and December 1946.

This book will be of great interest to readers interested in Vietnamese, French, international, colonial, postcolonial, decolonization, and Vietnam War studies. After all, the outbreak of the war in 1946 was all about the transition "from Indochina to Vietnam," from a colonial state to a national one. The long and bloody struggle that commenced on that December day also had, from the start, a global dimension, drawing in superpowers and regional actors alike. *Vietnam 1946* shows, like no other, how it came to be.

Christopher Goscha, Université du Québec à Montréal
Fredrik Logevall, Cornell University

2. See especially Stein Tønnesson, *1946: Déclenchement de la guerre d'Indochine: Les vêpres tonkinoises du 19 décembre* (Paris: L'Harmattan, 1987) and *The Vietnamese Revolution of 1945* (London: SAGE, 1991).

In a memorable lecture delivered in April 1965 at Johns Hopkins University, U.S. Senator J. William Fulbright opposed what he called the Johnson administration's new and dangerous "arrogance of power." President Lyndon B. Johnson had just started to bomb North Vietnam in the hope of deterring Hanoi from fighting for the unification of Vietnam. "Arrogance of Power" could have been the title of this book, which documents similar French behavior in 1946—the first French experience of "decolonization."

In August 1945, after Japan surrendered, and following the American reoccupation of the Philippines and the British recovery of Burma, the French government pledged immediately to restore French sovereignty over Indochina, a country the Japanese had seized six months earlier. Neither London nor Chongqing nor Washington challenged this claim at the time. General Philippe Leclerc was appointed to lead a French expeditionary force to do the job, and Admiral Georges Thierry d'Argenlieu was made high commissioner. Paris would decide later what to do with Indochina.

Under Japan's sponsorship, on March 11, 1945, Vietnam had "reaffirmed its right to independence." On the day of the Japanese capitulation, September 2, 1945, Ho Chi Minh, standing in front of a mass meeting in Hanoi, proclaimed that "Vietnam has the right to be a free and independent country" and was determined to "safeguard its right to liberty and independence," although China and Britain must for a few weeks be allowed to ensure the repatriation of Japanese forces. In a moving message on August 20, the emperor of Vietnam, Bao Dai, had just warned France's leader Charles de Gaulle: "I beg you to understand that the only means of safeguarding French interests and the spiritual influence of France in Indochina is to recognize the independence of Vietnam unreservedly and to renounce any idea of reestablishing French sovereignty or rule here in any form. . . . Even if you were to reestablish the French administration here, it would not be obeyed, and each village would be a nest of resistance. . . . We would be able to understand each other so easily and become friends if you would stop hoping to become our masters again."

This warning fell on deaf ears. The French returned and, with British support, reconquered the south of Vietnam in three months. But how were they to go about retaking the north, still under Chinese military occupation? Expecting that the Chinese troops would soon withdraw, the French prepared "Opération Bentré," a favorite subject of Stein Tønnesson's. Having learned from his experience of guerrilla war in Cochinchina, however, General Leclerc opted to make only a show of force. He would land in Haiphong with his troops, while Jean Sainteny would negotiate in Hanoi as commissioner of the French Republic to elicit a "peaceful surrender" from Ho. Leclerc's gamble failed. The Chinese generals chose to stay put, saving Ho from having to choose between surrender and withdrawal to the rural hinterland. This also opened the way to a compromise agreement, which could have inaugurated the peaceful decolonization of Vietnam. Stein Tønnesson tells and interprets this story in the first part of his book.

French leaders did not accept this relative failure. They wanted Ho Chi Minh's republic to remain in a state of political and economic dependence on France, and they especially rejected any unification of Vietnam under a communist regime. Hoping that Ho Chi Minh could be persuaded to give up his bid for Cochinchina, d'Argenlieu called for a four-state Indochinese Federation, aiming to contain the Ho Chi Minh government in the north, and get rid of it as soon as the last Chinese troops departed. The modus vivendi agreement that Minister for Overseas France Marius Moutet had signed with Ho Chi Minh in September gave the guerrillas such control of the Cochinchinese villages/rural areas that d'Argenlieu, facing a collapse of the Saigon regime, decided to strike in the north, the center of Viet Minh power. However, he had to act quickly. He believed, as did his generals, that the war in the north would be won in two months.

The same scenario was played out twenty years later. Facing a political debacle in Saigon, and refusing to allow a communist takeover of the south, President Johnson decided in March 1965 to bomb North Vietnam. I was in Massachusetts at the time. On a plane, I heard someone tell a friend: "Hanoi'll be on its knees and surrender in six weeks!"

France and later the United States went to war in Vietnam confident of rapid victory but ultimately lost, after millions of men, women, and children had died. Bao Dai's warning to de Gaulle was prophetic.

The main revelation of this book is the failure of the intelligence services. Most of the reports of the French Deuxième Bureau (military intelligence) and other services were reliable as far as the Viet Minh's structures, personnel, and even resources were concerned. However, they never understood the nature and the depth of Vietnamese nationalism and determination. Stein Tønnesson's book, the fruit of years of research in French, British, and American archives, and of interviews with surviving participants, leaves no doubt as to the French role in these terrible events. I met Stein twenty-seven years ago, and I am happy to have helped him find his way through this labyrinth. He has produced a remarkable piece of scholarship. His deciphering of complex situations, his capacity to make sense of thousands of pages of archival documents, and to do so in such clear prose, has won my admiration. It's a breathtaking story. May the reader share the experience.

Philippe Devillers
Paris, December 19, 2008

ACKNOWLEDGMENTS

The present book has come about in three stages. I first wrote an MA thesis at the University of Oslo in 1981–82, which I published as a report of the International Peace Research Institute, Oslo (PRIO), in 1984. For introducing me to archival work and historical reasoning, I want to thank my supervisor at the University of Oslo, Helge Ø. Pharo, my supervisor at PRIO, the late Marek Thee, David G. Marr, who treated me as if I were already an accomplished scholar when we first met in the French colonial archives, Alain Ruscio and Odette Vilmont, with whom I could discuss every detail of the 1946 events, and above all Philippe Devillers, who received me in Paris in October 1981, briefed me on his own experiences and research on the 1945–46 period, and put me on the right track in the archives. Neither his nor Marr's or my work would have been possible without the wonderful help we got from the archivists. My good friends in the archives provided invaluable support both at the first and second stage. It feels natural for me to choose Lucette Vachier at the Centre des archives d'Outre Mer in Aix-en-Provence to represent all of them.

Second, I wrote a book in French on the basis of the MA thesis, which was published in Paris by l'Harmattan in 1987 under the title *1946: Déclenchement de la guerre d'Indochine: Les vêpres tonkinoises du 19 décembre*. For this period I should acknowledge the assistance I received from Bruno Metz, who not only translated the manuscript from English to French, but also contributed manifold suggestions on content and argument, as well as from my editor, Alain Forest, who reorganized much of the book and made it more readable. I would also like to thank the Research Council of Norway, who supported both the publication and me, and the Institute of Defense Studies in Oslo, who hosted me at the time. And thanks go to the late Huynh Kim Khanh, who put me in touch with l'Harmattan, after discussions with Pierre Brocheux and Daniel Hémery at the Université de Paris VII at Jussieu, and Denis Pryen at l'Harmattan, who sees no problem in allowing me to publish a new, updated English version of the book he published in 1987.

In between the second and the third stage came a long period when I worked on other subjects, the Vietnamese Revolution of 1945, nation-building in Southeast Asia in the 1940s and 1950s, and the history of the dispute in the South China Sea. In 1989, I visited Vietnam for the first time and was exceptionally well received at the Institute of International Relations, the Institute of History of the National Centre for Social Sciences, and the Department of History at the University of Hanoi. I particularly want to thank my friends at the Institute of International Relations, above all Luu Doan Huynh, Nguyen Vu Tung, Duong Quoc Thanh and Hoang Anh Tuan, who have always been ready to host and help me. I visited Vietnam multiple times after 1989, and got many chances to discuss my findings and queries on the outbreak of the Indochina War in 1946 with Vietnam's military, diplomatic, and political historians, notably Bui Dinh Thanh, Duong Kinh Quoc, Dao Hung, Duong Trung Quoc, and not least Dinh Xuan Lam, who found time, along with his own research on nineteenth-century Vietnam, to translate my French book into Vietnamese. I also had the opportunity to befriend and discuss Vietnamese history with internationally recognized Vietnam scholars such as Pierre Brocheux, Laurent Césari, William J. Duiker, Charles Fourniau, Lloyd Gardner, Daniel Hémery, Gary Hess, Robert J. McMahon, Irene Nørlund, Phan Huy Le, Alain Ruscio, Masaya Shiraishi, Anthony Short, Hugues Tertrais, the late Ralph B. Smith, Judith Stowe, Martin Stuart-Fox, and Marilyn Young, and got a chance to take part in two U.S.-Vietnamese conferences, where a team around former U.S. Secretary of Defense Robert McNamara discussed the tragedy and lessons of Vietnam with Vietnamese diplomats and military officers.

Back in 1982, David Marr, Alain Ruscio, Odette Vilmont, and I were the only historians working on the French Indochina files, while the reading rooms of the colonial archives were crowded with North African scholars working on the histories of their countries. We dealt with different worlds; in the breaks I talked so much about the French colonial administrator Léon Pignon that a French scholar on North Africa, Olivier Vergniot, started calling me Petit Pignon (Little Kernel). With the worsening intellectual climate in the 1990s, the North African scholars disappeared from the reading rooms. I missed them, but took great pleasure in witnessing a new generation of Vietnam historians from many countries filling up the reading rooms and scholarly conferences, and producing wonderful papers, theses, and books: Mark Bradley, Robert Brigham, Chen Jian, Anne Foster, Ilya Gaiduk, Gilles de Gantes, Christophe Giebel, Christopher E. Goscha, François Guillemot, Andrew Hardy, Eric Jennings, Pierre Journoux, Vladimir Kolotov, Agathe Larcher, Philippe LeFailler, Lin Hua, Fred Logevall, Shawn McHale, Nguyen Van Ky, Mari Olsen, Qiang Zhai, Sophie Quinn-Judge, Martin Shipway, Martin Thomas, Frédéric Turpin, Claire Tran Thi Lien, Benoit de Tréglodé, Daniel Varga, and Peter Zinoman, to name but some. In February 2008, Claire Tran Thi Lien organized a seminar in Paris on Vietnam 1946, with Philippe Devillers and myself as speakers. If one of the young should be mentioned in particular, it would have to be Frédéric Turpin. He is one of the few Vietnam historians whom I've never met, but I greatly admire his 666-page study *De Gaulle, les gaullistes et l'Indochine* (Paris: Les Indes savantes, 2005).

In 2001, I became director of PRIO, the same institute who hosted my work as a graduate student 1981–82 and as a doctoral student in 1988–91. When Chris Goscha and Fred Logevall contacted me in 2005, asking if I was willing to write a new book for their University of California Press series, on the basis of my 1984 report and my 1987 French book, I first thought it would be impossible to manage while at the same time fulfilling my duties at PRIO, but my deputy director, Kristian Berg Harpviken, agreed to lead PRIO during my most intense periods of work, and Chris Goscha and Fred Logevall provided such encouragement and valuable advice that I managed to surmount the third stage of this book's production, merge the two former manuscripts, translate back from French to English, add a chapter based on an article I had published on the March 6, 1946 agreement, include material published by my colleagues since the 1980s, and write a completely new introduction and conclusion. At this third stage my main gratitude goes primarily to Chris and Fred, but almost equally to Philippe Devillers and David Marr who read and commented on the manuscript. I would also like to express my gratitude to Chu Duc Tinh, director of the Ho Chi Minh Museum in Hanoi, Trieu Van Hien, director of the Museum of Revolution in Hanoi, and director of the Museum of History in Hanoi, Pham Quoc Quan, for providing me with new evidence in the summer of 2007, for allowing me to use their holdings, and for authorizing the reproduction of some of their exhibits as illustrations. My thanks go also to my relative Tor Fuglevik, who photographed the painting that is used on the cover of the book, and to Tran Kieu, a leading personality among the Norwegian Vietnamese Diaspora, as well as my friend Ha Hoang Hop in Hanoi, who both helped me to read some key Vietnamese texts, and who provided me with valuable advice.

Two important sources to Vietnamese decision-making during the wars in Vietnam are General Vo Nguyen Giap's most recent memoirs, and a new biography of Giap by the Vietnamese historian Tran Trong Trung. I would like to acknowledge my gratitude to Tran Trong Trung for our discussions in the past, and to General Giap himself for taking time to read Devillers's and my work; for having the courage to reflect on our queries in several interviews and later in his memoirs; for bluntly telling me on September 18, 1992 that "we" took the initiative in the fighting on December 19, 1946; for allowing me to attend when, on June 23, 1997, he discarded Robert McNamara's suggestion that both sides, not just the Americans, had made mistakes in the Vietnam War; and for receiving me in his villa on December 20, 2005, to express an old warrior's wish for peace.

ABBREVIATIONS

1MiF	microfilm file (AOM)
AE	Affaires économiques
AFP	Agence France-Presse
Ambafrance	Ambassade de France
AN	Archives nationales (Paris)
AOM	Centre des archives d'Outre Mer (Aix-en-Provence)
AP	Affaires politiques
app	appendix
BCR	Bureau central de renseignements d'Indochine (Saigon)
BFDOC	Bureau fédéral de documentation (Saigon)
BR	Bulletin de renseignements
C	Carton (box)
CAB	Cabinet (Secretariat)
CCS	Combined Chiefs of Staff (Washington DC)
CEFEO	Corps expéditionnaire français en Extrême-Orient
Comafeco	Commissaire fédéral aux affaires économiques (Saigon)
Comafpol	Commissaire fédéral aux affaires politiques (Saigon)
COMAR	Commandement de la Marine
Cominf	Commissaire de l'information (Saigon)
Cominindo	Comité interministériel de l'Indochine (Paris)
Comrep	Commissaire de la République (Saigon, Hue, Hanoi, Phnom Penh, Vientiane)
Cororient	Corps expéditionnaire d'Extrême-Orient (French Far Eastern Expeditionary Force)

CP	Conseiller politique (Comafpol)
d	dossier (folder)
Dai Viet	Dai Viet Quoc Dan Hoi (Great Viet Nam Nationalist Association)
DB	*division blindée* (armored division)
Defnat	*défense nationale*
DF	Central Decimal File (RG69, USNA)
DGD	Direction générale de documentation (BFDOC)
DGER	Direction générale des études et recherches (name of the French intelligence agency until January 1946, when it changed to SDECE)
DIC	*division d'infanterie coloniale*
Dircab	*directeur de cabinet* (secretariat)
Dirinfor	Direction fédérale de l'information et du tourisme (Saigon)
Dirsurfe	Direction de la Sûreté fédérale (Saigon)
DMH	Viet Nam Cach Menh Dong Minh Hoi (Vietnamese Revolutionary League)
DRV	Democratic Republic of Vietnam
EA	[Fonds] Etats associés (former file in MAE, Paris, containing most of the Comindo files. Since the research for this book was done, the EA file has been integrated into MAE's general filing system)
EMGDN	Etat-major général de la défense nationale (French Chiefs of Staff, Paris)
EMP	Etat-major particulier (of the French high commissioner, Saigon)
FNSP	Fondation nationale des sciences politiques (Paris)
FO	Foreign Office (London)
FOM	Ministère de la France d'Outre Mer (Paris)
Fransul	Consul de la France
FRUS	*Foreign Relations of the United States* (GPO publication series)
G	local time
Génésuper	Général commandant supérieur des troupes françaises en Extrême-Orient (Saigon)
GPO	U.S. Government Printing Office (Washington DC)
h	*heures* (hours)
Haussaire	Haut commissaire
HC	Haut commissariat
ICP	Indochinese Communist Party (Dong Duong Cong San Dang; see also PCI below)
Lien Viet	Hoi Lien Hiep Quoc Dan Viet Nam (League for the National Union of Viet Nam)
MAE	Ministère des affaires étrangères (Paris)

MRP	Mouvement des Républicains populaires (French political party)
n.d.	no date
OSS	Office of Strategic Services (CIA's forerunner)
PCE	Service de protection du Corps expéditionnaire
PCF	Parti communiste français
PCI	Parti communiste indochinois
Prési Paris	Présidence du Conseil (the French government office in the Hôtel Matignon, Paris, where the prime minister resides)
PRIO	International Peace Research Institute, Oslo
PRO	Public Record Office (London)
RG	Record Group (USNA)
RIC	*régiment d'infanterie coloniale*
S.Eco.	Fonds Service économique (AOM)
SACSEA	Supreme Allied Commander South East Asia (Mountbatten, Kandy, Sri Lanka)
s/d	*sous-dossier*
SDECE	Service de documentation extérieure et de contre-espionnage (Paris), name of the French intelligence service from January 1946
SEAC	South East Asia Command (Kandy, Sri Lanka)
Secstate	Secretary of State (Washington DC)
SEH	Service d'études historiques (French military intelligence agency)
SEHAN	Service d'études historiques, Hanoi
SESAG	Service d'études historiques, Saigon
sess.	session *(séance)*
SFIO	Section française de l'Internationale ouvrière (French political party)
SHAT	Service historique de l'Armée de Terre (Paris)
SHM	Service historique de la Marine (Paris)
Tel.	Fonds télégrammes (file with chronologically organized telegrams from the FOM registry, AOM)
TFEO	Troupes françaises Extrême-Orient
TFIN	Troupes françaises Indochine du Nord
TFIS	Troupes françaises Indochine du Sud
TO	*télégramme officiel*
Tong Bo	The Directorate or Political Bureau of the Viet Minh, elected by the Central Committee
Tu Ve	Militia force in Hanoi
UDOFI	Union pour la défense de l'oeuvre française en Indochine (Union for the Defense of the French Achievements in Indochina)
USNA	U.S. National Archives (Suitland, Maryland)

Viet Minh	Viet Nam Doc Lap Dong Minh (Viet Nam Independence League)
VM	Viet Minh
VN	Vietnam
VNA-I	Vietnamese National Archives (Hanoi)
VNA-II	Vietnamese National Archives (Ho Chi Minh City)
VNDCD	Viet Nam Dan Chu Dang (Vietnamese Democratic Popular Party, adhering to the Viet Minh)
VNQDD	Viet Nam Quoc Dan Dang (Viet Nam Nationalist Party)
Z	Zulu time (GMT)

Introduction

While there is battle and hatred men have eyes for nothing save the fact that the enemy is the cause of all the troubles; but long, long afterwards, when all passion has been spent, the historian often sees that it was a conflict between one half-right that was perhaps too wilful, and another half-right that was perhaps too proud; and behind even this he discerns that it was a terrible predicament, which had the effect of putting men so at cross-purposes with one another.

HERBERT BUTTERFIELD, *HISTORY AND HUMAN RELATIONS*

Butterfield calls this phenomenon "the tragic element in human conflict" and suggests that the history of any conflict acquires this structure as it becomes revised and corrected and reshaped with the passage of time.[1]

War was Vietnam's predicament for well over forty years. No other country has suffered as many war casualties since World War II. In the first five months of 1945, partly because Allied bombing disrupted transportation and partly because the French and Japanese authorities in Indochina did not prioritize the transportation of rice, famine cost the lives of some one million people in north-central and northern Vietnam.[2] This was the first of a series of man-made disasters. In the First Indochina War, from 1945 to 1954, an estimated 365,000 people were killed, 40,000 on the French side, 200,000 on the side of those fighting the French, and 125,000 civilians. To these must be added the many deaths indirectly caused by the war.[3] Between the Geneva settlement of 1954, which split Vietnam in two halves, and the beginning of the Vietnam War in 1959, tens of thousands were killed in North Vietnam's radical land reform (1954–56), in South Vietnam's repression of communists, gangsters, and religious sects, and in the fight for control of Laos.

The number of casualties in the Vietnam War (1959–75) remains contested. It is often exaggerated, but all agree that it was appallingly high. On the basis of Micheal Clodfelter's detailed study of casualties year by year and a number of other sources, Bethany Lacina has estimated the total number of battle deaths for North Vietnam and the National Liberation Front of South Vietnam (NLF) to be more than one million. South Vietnam lost an estimated 250,000 soldiers; the United States had

46,122 troops killed in action, out of a total of 58,153 deaths; and other countries fighting on the side of South Vietnam lost more than 5,000 troops in battle. In addition, the war killed an estimated 65,000 North Vietnamese civilians and 650,000 South Vietnamese. This amounts to a total of more than two million battle-related deaths, more than in any other war since 1945.[4] If we include the casualties on the Cambodian and Laotian battlefields, we must add another 500,000, equally divided between these two countries.

After the end of the Vietnam War and the unification of North and South Vietnam, only three years elapsed before Vietnam went to war again, this time against the Khmer Rouge. Vietnam's invasion of Cambodia in the last days of 1978 provoked a temporary Chinese invasion of North Vietnam from February to March 1979, in which China would claim to have killed 30,000 Vietnamese, while Vietnam claimed it had killed 26,000 Chinese. For the next ten years, the tables were turned when Vietnam waged counterinsurgency warfare in Cambodia, with the guerrilla forces of the Khmer Rouge and their allies receiving weapons, sanctuary, and other support from Thailand, China, and the United States. The guerrilla war in Cambodia from 1979 until 1989 is thought to have cost at least 150,000 lives, and some 80,000 civilians were killed by landmines, which still riddle the Cambodian landscape, killing or maiming numerous children. Yet the tragedy of the Third Indochina War (1978–89) was dwarfed by the preceding Khmer Rouge genocide, which resulted in probably more than two million deaths, out of a population of between seven and eight million.

The end of the Cold War brought peace at last to Indochina. Vietnamese troops withdrew from Cambodia in 1989, and the Paris agreement on Cambodia was signed in 1991. Four years later, Vietnam obtained normal relations with the United States and also joined the Association of Southeast Asian Nations (ASEAN), which had been established in 1967 with the partial aim of containing Vietnamese communism. As of 2009, Vietnam has been free from war for two full decades. It has engaged in commercial, cultural, and diplomatic relations with all its neighbors and all its former enemies and even joined the World Trade Organization (WTO). These past two decades of "Vietnam Peace" have significantly improved the living standards of most of the 85 million Vietnamese who now live there and resulted in more and more interaction between them and their 2.5 million compatriots overseas.[5] Vietnam's diaspora comprises resourceful individuals who fled their homes during or after Vietnam's wars, and their offspring. The overseas Vietnamese (Viet Kieu) now constitute a priceless reservoir of capital and skills needed in Vietnam's further development. Just as we need to explain the onset of Vietnam's wars, we now also need to explain and understand its peace since 1989.

Did the sequence of wars in Vietnam have a beginning? Anthony Short asked this question in *The Origins of the Vietnam War*, which he published in 1989, just as the last of the Indochina wars reached its end. He starts his account with the

French colonization (1858–85) and analyzes the nature of French colonial rule, with its reliance on rubber plantations, forced labor, the opium trade, and harsh repression of nationalist movements, while the construction of modern institutions, roads, and railways linked Indochina together. The origins of war may "be sought, in the first place, in the relationship between France and Vietnam," Short affirms.[6] Then he describes how French rule continued during the period of Japanese occupation (1941–45) and how Japan toppled the French regime in a coup on March 9, 1945. This coup resulted in a power vacuum, which in turn provided the Viet Nam Independence League (Viet Minh), led by the experienced communist Ho Chi Minh, with a chance to organize a vast network of popular organizations in much of Indochina. The Japanese surrender on August 15, 1945, became the signal for a general insurrection, led by communists in most places, and resulting in the establishment of the Democratic Republic of Vietnam (DRV). The insurrection was soon known as the "August Revolution." Its crowning event was President Ho Chi Minh's declaration of independence before a massive gathering in Hanoi on September 2, 1945. This is now Vietnam's national day. The August Revolution was swift and relatively peaceful, although a certain number of prominent conservative and Trotskyite leaders were murdered.

It is possible to argue that Vietnam's chain of wars began with the arrival of British occupation forces in Saigon in September and their decision to rearm the French prisoners of war who were then still in Japanese camps. The latter promptly staged a coup against the revolutionary government in Saigon on September 23, 1945. This provoked a massacre of French civilians at the Cité Héraud, and on September 26, Peter Dewey, the son of a famous U.S. senator, became the first American to be killed in Vietnam.[7] A pacification campaign followed, with British, French, and Japanese troops killing and disarming revolutionary nationalists in Cambodia, southern Vietnam, and southern Laos. After a short period of disarray, the local communists and other nationalists responded with guerrilla tactics and widespread use of terror against those who collaborated with the French. It makes sense to argue, as the Vietnamese general Vo Nguyen Giap does in his recent memoirs, that this campaign was the start of Vietnam's "Thirty Years' War."[8] In 1946, however, it was not a given that there would be a long-drawn-out war. In order to reestablish a French presence also in northern Indochina, which was under Chinese, not British, occupation, the French signed an agreement with Ho Chi Minh on March 6, 1946. Then followed nine months of coexistence between the representatives of the French Fourth Republic and the Democratic Republic of Vietnam. Just after midnight between September 14 and 15, Ho Chi Minh and Minister for Overseas France Marius Moutet signed a modus vivendi agreement (dated September 14), including a cease-fire in southern Vietnam, to come into force by October 31. The French historian Alain Ruscio also concludes that the war started as a series of incidents:

Rather than one event, we prefer to draw attention to a cascade of events. From March 1945 to the summer of 1947, there was a succession of occurrences, some secondary, others serious, but most of which (yet not all) were of comparable importance. This succession led little by little from the possibility of war to the probability of war, and then from this to its inevitability. Even though, almost half a century later, one or two of these occurrences seem salient, it is the combined process that we must take into consideration.[9]

This book assumes as its point of departure that the "policy of agreement" *(politique d'accord)* that the two parties sought to apply in 1946 might have been viable, that it *was possible* to prevent the war that followed, and that this remained possible until December 19, 1946. Hence, the proximate cause of Vietnam's string of wars was not the long history of French colonial rule, the Japanese coup against the French colonial regime in March 1945, the Vietnamese August Revolution, or even the violent repression carried out in southern Vietnam by French and British forces in 1945–46. Neither was it the failure of Franco-Vietnamese negotiations in the summer of 1946—they did not fail completely, but ended in a modus vivendi. Rather, the proximate cause of the Vietnam wars was the breakdown of Franco-Vietnamese cooperation during November–December 1946 and the outbreak of armed struggle in the streets of Hanoi at 2003 hours on December 19. The First Indochina War broke out that day, and this led to a sequence of wars with dreadful consequences, primarily for the Vietnamese themselves and their immediate neighbors, but also for France, the United States, and the world.

This book is not a military history but a political case study of how and why a war began. It seeks to answer two questions. Why was there no outbreak of war on March 6, 1946, when a serious crisis resolved itself through the signing of a peace agreement? And why did war break out on December 19? A concluding chapter asks who might have prevented the war from breaking out and how. The narrative covers the period from February 1946 to January 1947 but does not dwell on the long-drawn-out Franco-Vietnamese negotiations in Dalat, a small town in Vietnam's central highlands, during April–May, and at Fontainebleau, south of Paris, in July–September. Instead, it concentrates on the crises that preceded and followed these failed negotiations, one leading to the March 6 agreement, the other to the battle for Hanoi.

This book challenges two established wisdoms. The first is the widespread belief that the March 6 agreement reflected a temporary ascendancy of liberal reformers or moderate pragmatists within the French decision-making system. They are said to have perceived the need to accommodate Vietnamese nationalism and make a deal with Ho Chi Minh. This book demonstrates that the French were already prepared to wage war against the DRV in March 1946, and that they took a gigantic gamble in dispatching an invasion force to the port city of Haiphong. This was no mere show of force, but part of a seriously prepared operation to seize control of the main centers in the north, including Hanoi. Arriving at Haiphong in the morning of March 6, the French fleet sailed right into a Chinese trap. The French thought they had secured Chinese support for disembarking troops in the north in a treaty signed in Chongqing on February 28, but Chiang Kai-shek's government fooled them. When the French ships approached Haiphong harbor, the Chinese stood ready to resist the French onslaught and actually fired at the ships. Meanwhile, the Chinese were pressuring both the Vietnamese government and a French team of negotiators in Hanoi to sign a deal on behalf of their two nations. Neither the French nor the DRV could afford an open confrontation with China, so under Chinese coercion, they underwrote concessions that both parties hoped to be able to retract at a later stage. The March 6 accords were a fragile peace imposed by China.

The second piece of accepted wisdom is that the outbreak of war in Hanoi on December 19 was a premeditated Vietnamese surprise attack against the French, for which the Vietnamese government was clearly responsible, although it acted in response to the French seizure of the cities of Haiphong and Langson in November. This is how history was written by some prominent authors during the Indochina War, although there was always another school of thought, which emphasized that the Vietnamese had been provoked and hypothesized that President Ho Chi Minh and General Vo Nguyen Giap lost control of angry leaders lower down in the hierarchy that day.[10] More recently, the tendency to hold the Vietnamese responsible for the December 19 attack has been reinforced by the writings of Vietnamese historians and by Vo Nguyen Giap himself, who after a long period of ambiguity concerning December 19 came out and proudly avowed that their side indeed had taken the initiative to fight.[11] General Giap has been adamant both in his written memoirs and in conversations with the present author that he—or "we," as he says—decided to open fire first: "If we had waited any longer, the French might have attacked us," he asserted in 1992. "If any mistake was made, it was that we waited too long."

This book challenges the dominant interpretation of December 19 and holds that the outbreak of war that day could have been averted. The March 6 agreement, although signed under Chinese pressure, encouraged and strengthened those French and Vietnamese leaders who wanted to spare human lives and avoid the financial and political costs of a long-drawn-out war. President Ho himself was one. The leader of the French government at the time the war broke out, the veteran socialist Léon Blum, was also dedicated to the pursuit of peace, and Marius Moutet, the socialist minister for Overseas France, who signed the modus vivendi agreement with Ho Chi Minh on the night of September 14–15, continued to defend his "policy of accord." The main warmongers, who must bear the brunt of the responsibility, not only for the seizure of Haiphong in November, but also for the outbreak in Hanoi, were a French triumvirate in Saigon, consisting of High Commissioner Admiral Georges Thierry d'Argenlieu, Supreme Commander General Jean-Etienne Valluy, and Federal Commissioner of Political Affairs Léon Pignon, who sought a clean break with the communist-dominated Vietnamese regime. D'Argenlieu was not just inspired by instructions and orders of the French government at the time, but sought to apply the wishes of his main mentor, the former leader of the French government who had resigned in January 1946: General Charles de Gaulle. When the French conquest of Haiphong did not immediately provoke a breakdown of relations, they resorted to a tactic of escalating pressures on the Hanoi government, meant to either foment a split between "moderates" and "extremists" or provoke the Vietnamese to open hostilities. French intelligence knew that the Vietnamese had an attack plan ready and had actually bought a copy of it. The French triumvirate waited impatiently for the Vietnamese to take action. Although Paris was absorbed in a cabinet crisis and the French government had internal disagreements, the outgoing premier, Georges Bidault, made clear in a telegram to Saigon on December 12 that he was critical of the aggressive line pursued by the French locally, and a representative of the Saigon triumvirate was instructed in a meeting on December 14 that if more "incidents" occurred, the fault must not be on the French side. For three long weeks after the loss of Haiphong, the Vietnamese restrained themselves. Ho appealed repeatedly to the French, Chinese, and American governments to intervene and rescue the peace, and he would soon have received a positive reply from Léon Blum if the Vietnamese armed forces had not launched their attack in the evening of December 19.

Blum's new all-socialist government, with himself as both premier and foreign minister, won a vote of confidence in the French National Assembly on December 17. On the day he took over from his predecessor Georges Bidault, December 18, Blum decided to send Moutet on a peace mission to Hanoi. It was too late. On the afternoon of December 19, something went amiss among the Vietnamese leaders, gathered for a meeting of the Communist Party's Standing Bureau in a village outside of Hanoi. The decision they took remains a mystery, but Vo Nguyen Giap's troops had made feverish preparations to attack the French. Giap may have ordered his troops into action to preempt an attack he wrongly anticipated from the French side, or perhaps he was pushed into action by impatient cadres. He made what was perhaps the biggest mistake in his life when launching an assault just at the time when Vietnam had a chance to expose French colonial wrongdoings to a relatively sympathetic government in Paris, as well as to French and international public opinion. Now there was instead an international outcry against Vietnamese savagery. Giap walked right into the trap that the Saigon triumvirate had set for him.

This is how the sequence of wars in Vietnam began. It has not been easy to establish, and much remains to be sorted out, particularly on the Vietnamese side, where we have no access to the Communist Party's archives. The source material for the following story is primarily French, although a number of British and American documents have also been used. Since no Vietnamese archives were consulted, what is said about Vietnamese policies and decision-making relies on a combination of French intelligence reports, Vietnamese books and memoirs, primarily those of Vo Nguyen Giap, and some interviews with Vietnamese veterans and historians. Chiang Kai-shek's China plays a major role in the account, but no Chinese archives were consulted either. It is possible, however, to build on King C. Chen and Lin Hua's work. Lin Hua has done archival research in Taiwan, the People's Republic of China, and France.[12]

Students of history inquiring into political crisis management should always draw up an outline of the decision-making system in the governments under study *before* they start working in the archives. This makes it possible to start with the files of the top-level decision-making bodies and the papers of the top decision-makers, before proceeding downward in the hierarchy as far as time allows. It is important not to use the present-day filing system as the point of departure, but instead to find out where the operational files of the most important persons and institutions are located. It is normal to find copies of the same documents in several archives and in the files of many different institutions, reflecting their historical circulation. Indeed, it is often interesting to see *when* a copy of a given document was received by the various bodies of a certain government, to *whom* it was circulated, and what *comments* they made.

When the Vietnamese files are opened, it will be important to look into the papers of President Ho Chi Minh's secretaries, of General Vo Nguyen Giap's military headquarters, and of the party organization led by Secretary-General Truong Chinh. The files of the Vietnamese Foreign Ministry and Ministry of the Interior will also be of interest. Some of the DRV files were later captured by the French and are held at the Centre des archives d'outre-mer (AOM) in Aix-en-Provence (the Gouvernement de fait, or GF, file), where they have been studied by David G. Marr of the Australian National University. The fact that these files were not destroyed, but remained intact when the French took control of Hanoi, would seem to indicate that the Vietnamese attack did not follow a decision made long in advance, and that the option of continuing to run the government from the ministries in Hanoi was kept open right to the end. These files do not, however, emanate from the decision-makers at the very top. The key files were either destroyed or taken with them by the party leaders to their various headquarters during the course of the Indochina wars. Many documents have surely been lost, but when the Vietnamese Communist Party (VCP) opens its archives in Hanoi to research, they are still likely to contain some fascinating material, which has so far been available only to the party leaders themselves, who surely have no time to study it.

In France, the two highest-level operational files are those of the prime minister's office (présidence du Conseil), which were originally in the Hôtel Matignon and are now in the Archives nationales in Paris (F60 C3035). Unfortunately, they do not yield much as far as French Indochina policy in 1946 is concerned, but some interesting letters and other documents are to be found among Prime Minister Georges Bidault's private papers, which are also in the Archives nationales (457AP). The same is true of the private papers of Minister for Overseas France Marius Moutet, which are kept at AOM, Aix-en-Provence (PA28).

The most important and voluminous of the Indochina files in Paris from 1946 are those of the Comité interministériel pour l'Indochine (Cominindo), which was set up by General de Gaulle on February 15, 1945, for the specific purpose of coordinating the French government's Indochina policy, under the chairmanship of the premier himself. Its secretariat was housed close to de Gaulle's own office in the Ministry of the Armies (rue St. Dominique). When I first came to Paris to do archival work in 1981, no one seemed to know where the Cominindo files were located. I was told in the archives of the Ministry of Overseas France at 27 rue Oudinot, that they had disappeared. As a substitute, I was given access to a file with copies of all the telegrams exchanged between Saigon and the Ministry of Overseas France in Paris during 1946. To go through all of them was impossible, but the telegram file led to quite a few discoveries concerning the period of crisis from November to December, when exact timetables are of great importance. It was interesting to see which telegrams were given top priority, and how long it took for them to reach their addressees. Today, there are no longer any Indochina files at rue Oudinot. They were moved to AOM, Aix-en-Provence in 1986, so that they could be kept together with the files repatriated from Indochina after decolonization.

It appeared to me that the way to locate the Cominindo files would be to find out who took over the remit of the Cominindo after it was dissolved. In February 1947, Moutet took over as chair of the Cominindo, and the staff and files were moved from rue St. Dominique to rue Oudinot. In July 1950, however, reflecting the transformation of French Indochina in the previous year into three "associated states" (Cambodia, Laos, and Vietnam), a new Ministry of Associated States was set up, with offices on the rue de Lille, and the Cominindo file was moved once again. Three years later, the three states ceased to be associated and were recognized as fully independent. So the archives were transferred once again, this time to the Ministry of Foreign Affairs at the Quai d'Orsay. However, the Quai d'Orsay did not have enough space, and it was decided to send all documents dating from before 1945 back to rue Oudinot, where they were merged into the Indochina file of the Ministry of Overseas France, the Indochine Nouveau Fonds (INF), which was transferred to AOM, Aix-en-Provence, in 1986. For the historian, it is quite a challenge to determine whether a document or folder in the INF file from before 1945 emanates from the Ministry of Colonies (renamed the Ministry of Overseas France in January 1946) or from the files of the Cominindo. The Quai d'Orsay retained all the documents from 1945 on, which were held in a separate file, called the Fonds Etats associés (EA). It contains the bulk of the Cominindo archive, an unexplored gold mine when I dug into it in the years 1985–89, before the staff had time to go through it and classify the material. Some of the most important folders for the present study were in fact only made generally available to researchers (under a sixty-year rule) at the beginning of 2007. The EA file is the best starting point for anyone wanting to study the Indochina policy of the French government during the years 1944–47. However, the archive staff have renumbered the folders both in the EA file and in the Foreign Ministry's own Asia file (Asie-Océanie). This has had the unfortunate consequence that the reference numbers I noted down in the 1980s are no longer valid. I apologize for having been unable to renumber all the boxes and folders in the notes to this book, but my numbers can be converted to the new ones by juxtaposing the new and old finding aids in the archives, which the ever-helpful staff will make available on request.

Among the ministries and other institutions represented in the Cominindo, the most important were the Ministry of Overseas France, the Ministry of Foreign Affairs, the various Defense Ministries (Air, Navy, Army, Defense), the Chiefs of Staff, Etat-major général de la défense nationale (EMGDN), and the intelligence agency, Service de documentation extérieure et de contre-espionnage (SDECE). The SDECE files are apparently still in the hands of the central French intelligence agency and are inaccessible. The EMGDN files are kept in the Service historique de l'Armée de Terre (SHAT) at Vincennes castle in Paris. This file (4Q) contains top-level military documents concerning Indochina and has been extremely valuable for this study. Unfortunately, most students are unaware of the 4Q file or are denied access to it. They are instead directed to the enormous 10H file, which contains repatriated French army documents from Indochina.[13] When working on top-level decision-making, it is preferable to start with the 4Q file before entering the 10H file.

The repatriated civilian files from Indochina are at AOM, Aix-en-Provence. Unfortunately, they do not include many of High Commissioner Georges Thierry d'Argenlieu's files. He probably took them with him when he was replaced as high commissioner in February 1947; his *Chronique d'Indochine*, which was published posthumously in 1985, is based on a comprehensive private collection. In 1991, d'Argenlieu's family handed his papers over to the French National Archives, which completed an inventory in 2000 (Papiers Georges Thierry d'Argenlieu, 517 AP). I should have also consulted these papers for the present book, which Frédéric Turpin used in his study of de Gaulle and the Gaullists' Indochina policy,[14] but I did not find the time to do so. By far the most interesting file in Aix-en-Provence is the Conseiller politique (CP) file. D'Argenlieu's political advisor Léon Pignon (who became high commissioner himself in 1948) kept a huge file with intelligence reports, memorandums, and reports about political developments in 1946, including many of his own letters and reports. Another important actor on the French side was Jean Sainteny, born Jean Roger. As commissioner of the French Republic in Tonkin and North Annam, Sainteny led the negotiations that resulted in the March 6 Franco-Vietnamese accords. Sainteny's private papers are in the care of the Fondation nationale des sciences politiques (FNSP) in Paris. His substantial archives are extremely valuable and formed much of the basis for Philippe Devillers's annotated collection *Paris-Saigon-Hanoi: Les archives de la guerre, 1944–1947* (1988).

The result of my archival studies is a detailed, chronological account of highly complex decision-making, with an inordinate number of references to archival documents and other sources. Most of the sources are in French, and quite a few are in Vietnamese. When quoted in the text, they have been translated into English. The quotation in the original language, and also some additional commentaries, can be found in an extended set of notes, using the same note numbers as the book itself, at my web site, www.cliostein.com. The purpose of the book is not just to present new material but to correct some basic mistakes in existing narratives. An additional purpose is to disentangle the ways in which well-placed spoilers can prevent their leaders from fulfilling the most basic obligation of any government: to preserve the peace.

1

A Clash of Republics

The sequence of war in Indochina began as a collision between two new republics, the Democratic Republic of Vietnam (DRV) and the French Fourth Republic. Both were strongly influenced by socialist and communist thinking, while at the same time both strove to build a national consensus with nonsocialist nationalist groups. Both aimed at modernizing Indochina through industrialization, trade, and representative institutions. Both were positively inclined toward the idea of building a common political arena for the Viet, Lao, Khmer, and highland minority peoples, so that they could stimulate one another's quest for modernity. Both agreed that an Indochinese Federation should form a part of a new French Union and remain associated with France in a progressive family of nations.

What caused the two republics to clash was not just the question of Vietnamese national independence, although there was an acute conflict between the DRV's quest for recognition of its authority and sovereignty and the French insistence on maintaining French sovereignty—and authority—in the colonies. An equally difficult question concerned the geographical scope of the Vietnamese nation. Although the Vietnamese Revolution in August–September 1945 had its main origin in northern Indochina, in the country the French called "Tonkin," the revolutionaries were committed to the idea of a united Vietnam stretching all the way down to the point of Ca Mau. They intended to give this united Vietnam a leading role in the modernization of the whole of Indochina, as the biggest and most advanced of three nations.

The French rejected the Vietnamese national idea. They used the term "Vietnam" only reluctantly, and spoke of "Annamites" or "Annamese" instead when referring to the ethnic majority group in the protectorates of Tonkin and Annam and the colony of Cochinchina. Both Gaullist and leftist colonial reformers were adamant that a modern, democratic Indochina should not come under "Annamite" domination, but build on a balance among five separate units: Cambodia, Laos, Cochinchina, Annam, and Tonkin. To the extent that they accepted the term "Vietnam," which in the 1920s and 1930s had been the hallmark of noncommunist nationalists under Chinese inspiration, while the communists then mostly spoke of Indochina (Dong Duong), the French tended to see "Vietnam" as a new name only for Tonkin, and possibly the northern half of Annam. The French opposed the unification of the three Viet-dominated regions Bac Ky (Tonkin), Trung Ky (Annam), and Nam Ky (Cochinchina), which the Vietnamese nationalists preferred to call Bac Bo, Trung Bo, and Nam Bo; the use of the term "Bo" was a way of signaling that the north, central, and south regions belonged to the same nation. It was also a problem that in French legal terms, the most economically developed and modern of the Indochinese lands, Cochinchina, had the status of a colony under full French sovereignty, and that this status could be altered only by a decision in the French National Assembly.[1]

Cochinchina had been the first part of Indochina to be colonized by France, and it remained the cornerstone of the design made in Paris in early 1945 for a democratic Indochinese Federation under French supervision and guidance. Saigon would be at the center of Indochina's economic advancement; Hue and Hanoi were seen as more backward and subject to Chinese political influence; Phnom Penh and Vientiane were even more backward and would need French tutelage for a long time to come.

The government of the Democratic Republic of Vietnam, formed in the "August Revolution" of 1945, claimed to represent a sovereign Vietnamese nation, with a right to full independence. Its claim to independence was grounded not just in general principles, but also in recent history. Bao Dai, the French-protected emperor of Annam, with nominal authority also in Tonkin, had gained nominal independence after Japan ousted the French regime in March 1945. When he abdicated voluntarily in August 1945, he ceded his powers to the new Democratic Republic. President Ho Chi Minh did not thus declare but *confirm* Vietnam's independence in his famous address to the people in Ba Dinh square in Hanoi on September 2, 1945. Shortly before Bao Dai abdicated, his government had obtained from Japan something that France had always refused to concede: sovereignty also in Nam Ky (Cochinchina), hitherto under direct French rule, where the emperor had previously had no say. Japan changed this in early August 1945, before it surrendered to the Allies, and when the revolution took place in all the three Viet lands just after the Japanese capitulation, the revolutionary leaders in Nam Bo's capital, Saigon, did not set up a state of their own, but saw themselves as the local representatives of the new Democratic Republic of Vietnam, with Hanoi as its capital.

France did not engage with the revolutionary institutions in the south, but

FIGURE 1. The new Democratic Republic of Vietnam's defining moment. Detail from a 1979 painting by Van Tho depicting Independence Day, September 2, 1945, in Ba Dinh Square, Hanoi. A citizen holds a parasol over the head of Uncle Ho Chi Minh, as servants once did for emperors and governors-general. Ho, dressed in plain brown clothes, addresses his people through a microphone and reads his famous Declaration confirming Vietnam's independence, quoting from both the 1776 American Declaration of Independence and the 1791 French Declaration of the Rights of Man and the Citizen. The painting is reproduced here because it illustrates the importance of the Ba Dinh event in the creation of the Democratic Republic of Vietnam, not because it accurately reflects what actually happened. Oil on canvas done for the Museum of History's permanent exhibition in 1979, based on a 1945 photograph by Nguyen Ba Khoan and on documentary materials and eyewitness accounts. Courtesy Van Tho and the Museum of History, Hanoi.

intended to establish a new system with a large degree of autonomy for each of five Indochinese peoples. French politicians saw themselves as representing la France nouvelle, a New France, with a mission to regenerate, not just France itself, but its former empire as well, which would be transformed into a solidary Union française. The French mood was characterized by what one scholar has called "imperialist optimism," an expectation that metropolitan and imperial—or federalist—constitution-making would proceed hand in hand.[2] "La France nouvelle" was the term used by French socialists, communists, and Gaullists alike for the state they established after Marshal Philippe Pétain was ousted from Vichy and the Germans were driven out of Paris in the summer of 1944, which was led by General Charles de Gaulle until January 20, 1946. It remained "La France nouvelle" until the Fourth Republic had been fully established, with a constitution that came into force on December 24, 1946. Some of the most influential French politicians thought that independence should be the long-term aim for the French protectorates overseas, but in order to safeguard the French presence and prevent other foreign powers from taking over the French-ruled territories, they would not grant it immediately. They intended to secure the French presence in the Far East by setting up autonomous or self-governing units as parts of an Indochinese Federation, led by a French high commissioner. Through the introduction of a representative system, based on democratic elections, the Indochinese countries would then gradually be emancipated with a view to eventual independence.

Developments in Vietnam during 1946 were complicated by a legacy of U.S. President Franklin D. Roosevelt's promotion of a Chinese role in an international trusteeship he had hoped to set up for Indochina after the end of World War II. Roosevelt had considered Indochina a part of Generalissimo Chiang Kai-shek's military theater of operations in the war against Japan, and he hoped that Chinese troops would play the lead role in liberating Indochina. He had not been willing to let British Admiral Lord Louis Mountbatten's South East Asia Command, with its headquarters in Kandy, Ceylon (Sri Lanka), take responsibility for Allied operations in Indochina, since Mountbatten would be likely to help de Gaulle retain the colony. At the Potsdam conference in July 1945, three months after Roosevelt's death, and shortly before the Japanese surrender, a hasty compromise was reached, whereby Chiang Kai-shek got responsibility for Indochina north of the 16th parallel, and Mountbatten for the southern half. After the Japanese capitulation, which led to a temporary power vacuum, in which the Vietnamese "August Revolution" took place, British forces landed from the sea to disarm and repatriate the Japanese troops south of the 16th parallel (Cochinchina, Cambodia, the southern half of Annam, and the southernmost part of Laos), while a massive Chinese force crossed the border into the north (Tonkin, north Annam, and most of Laos) to disarm and repatriate the Japanese there.

The division of the Nguyen dynasty's Annamese heartland made it impossible

FIGURE 2. The global ambitions of the French Fourth Republic. On this map, from the back of a brochure intended to create support for the restoration of French rule in Indochina, lines run from the Cross of Lorraine, symbol of General de Gaulle's Free French movement during World War II, to the various parts of the empire, soon to be liberated. De Gaulle's government, reestablished in Paris in August 1944, planned to revive the former empire as the French Union *(Union française)*. Courtesy Annick Guénel.

to revive conservative monarchist policies in Hue after the abdication of Emperor Bao Dai on August 25, so Hue lost its historical role, and Hanoi and Saigon became the two main centers of power. The British helped the French crush the revolution in the south, and establish a new Indochinese administration centered in Saigon and led by de Gaulle's choice as high commissioner, Admiral Georges Thierry d'Argenlieu. Meanwhile the Chinese occupation authorities tolerated the continued existence of the DRV in the north, with Hanoi serving as capital both of the Vietnamese government and the Chinese occupation authorities. (Until the Vietnamese revolution, Hanoi had been the capital of the Indochinese Union as a whole.) As of January 20, 1946, when de Gaulle suddenly announced his resignation as head of the French government, the Corps expéditionnaire français en Extrême-Orient (CEFEO) he had dispatched to Indochina under the command of General Philippe Leclerc de Hautecloque was only in control of southern Indochina. In Hanoi, France was represented by the powerless Jean Sainteny, who had been flown in on an American plane from China. He tried to prepare for the arrival of French forces later, while seeking to protect French civilians against local nationalist agitators and Chinese occupation forces.

The confrontation between the DRV and the French Fourth Republic thus took different forms in north and south Vietnam. In the south, the French quickly assumed control and refused to accept any representatives of the DRV. In the north, the revolutionary Vietnamese government controlled the state apparatus and most of the provinces, but in an uneasy relationship with the Chinese military, which forced the Vietnamese communists to share power with the leaders of two China-oriented anticommunist parties, the Viet Nam Quoc Dan Dang (Viet Nam Nationalist Party), or VNQDD, and the Viet Nam Cach Menh Dong Minh Hoi (Vietnamese Revolutionary League), or DMH. Ho Chi Minh's DRV government thus formed a double aim: on the one hand, to secure the republic in the north by building political and administrative strength and developing a strong army, and, on the other, to promote the struggle against France in the south. After a series of initial defeats, the Vietnamese military forces in the south regrouped and adopted the strategy and tactics of a protracted guerrilla struggle. While seeking to repress the insurgents in the south, the French engaged in parallel talks with Chiang Kai-shek's government in Chongqing and the DRV government in Hanoi with a view to obtaining the withdrawal of all Chinese troops from northern Indochina, so that French forces could return to the only part of the French empire that had not yet been reoccupied. On October 4, 1945, the French government appointed Jean Sainteny as commissioner of the French Republic for northern Indochina (Tonkin and North Annam). He held his first important, but inconsequential, talks with Ho Chi Minh on December 1, 1945. It was assumed by everyone in Hanoi that France would at some point reestablish its military presence in northern Indochina, although this would require China's consent.

This book does not aim to analyze in any depth the arguments and positions developed by the DRV and the new French Fourth Republic in the negotiations between them in Hanoi, leading to a preliminary agreement on March 6, 1946, in the failed negotiations at Dalat in Vietnam's central highlands in April–May, or at Fontainebleau south of Paris in July–September. Neither will the book go deeply into the military aspects of the war in the south. The focus will be on the question of peace and war between France and the DRV in its northern heartland. The book dwells on two periods of crisis: February–March 1946 and November–December 1946, the first leading to a temporary peace, the second to a long-drawn-out war.

NOT YET COLD WAR

It is easy to forget that 1946 was before the real onset of the Cold War. The wartime alliance between the Western powers and the Soviet Union was still in fresh memory. Stalin was not yet generally perceived as an autocratic villain. In Paris, the Allies were haggling over the peace treaties with Italy and the Axis satellites. No one knew as yet that the Truman Doctrine and the Marshall Plan would be proclaimed the following year, and Germany was still occupied territory, divided into four occupation zones. In Asia, the United States had not committed itself to supporting Chiang Kai-shek in his war with the Chinese Red Army, but urged him to negotiate. To the extent that they had time to think about Indochina, both Harry S Truman and Chiang Kai-shek looked favorably on the recently formed DRV, hoped the French would recognize it, and that noncommunist Vietnamese nationalists would gain a greater say in its affairs. The Vietnamese communists were collaborating uneasily with a plethora of noncommunist nationalist groups, both within and outside the Viet Minh front. Back in Europe, the French Communist Party was also in government, in a coalition with the socialists (SFIO), the radicals, and Christian Democrats (MRP), and was represented on the committee that coordinated French Indochina policy. It was a period of opportunity, with open front lines.

By February 1946, the new French Republic did not yet have a constitution, although several drafts had already been considered and rejected in the one and a half years that had passed since Paris was liberated by the Free French forces of General Leclerc, an aristocrat whose original name was Philippe de Hautecloque, but who preferred to use the more popular name Leclerc. He had commanded the forces who liberated Paris in August 1944, enabling General Charles de Gaulle to install his provisional government in the French capital. De Gaulle's France demanded recognition as one of the world's four great powers, won a permanent seat on the new United Nations Security Council, and intended to play an independent role in relations with the "Anglo-Saxons" and the Soviet Union. Eager to align France with the emerging Western camp, British and American policy-makers sought to avoid measures that might offend French feelings or strengthen the French communists, as well as to help secure fundamental French interests such as the need for coal. The Russians felt a similar need to treat France with care. They wanted to keep France out of the emerging Anglo-American alliance and thus applauded some of the independent French policies in Germany.

In Asia, the Vietnamese August Revolution was a part of a nationalist wave, which in the wake of Japan's capitulation brought India, Burma, the Philippines, and Indonesia their independence. It was also a part of a communist drive that in 1949 triumphed in China, but was defeated militarily in Malaya and stalemated in Korea. These outcomes, however, could not be foreseen in 1946. The war in Indochina began long before this part of the world claimed the sustained attention of the leading statesmen in Moscow and Washington. When occasionally Vietnam was taken into account, it was seen in relation to their overall relations with France. This is why a study of the outbreak of the First Indochina War must concentrate on the bilateral Franco-Vietnamese relationship, while paying close attention to the role of the main third party, Nationalist China, and not exaggerating the importance of the roles played by the USSR and the United States.

It is time to introduce the two clashing republics, their parties, and their leaders.

THE DEMOCRATIC REPUBLIC OF VIETNAM

Although the DRV took over many buildings and personnel from the French colonial administration and from Bao Dai's State of Vietnam, it was primarily the creation of an Independence League, the Viet Nam Doc Lap Dong Minh (Viet Minh for short), and its leader Ho Chi Minh (1890–1969). "Ho Chi Minh" was a name adopted during World War II by a man who was known to most of his countrymen as Nguyen Ai Quoc (He Who Loves His Homeland). Quoc had been the founder and main exile leader of the Indochinese Communist Party (ICP), which he established in 1930. During World War II, he operated in the border region between China and Indochina, assisting the Chinese authorities, and also the American Office of Strategic Services (OSS), with intelligence from inside Indochina. His aim was to liberate Indochina from the French and Japanese "double yoke."

When local nationalist and communist groups seized power in all of Vietnam's major cities and administrative centers in August 1945, they did so under the banner of the Viet Minh, which had been organized and led by Ho Chi Minh, first in southern China and, after 1941, from secret headquarters on the Vietnamese side of the border. There was originally no central leadership of the revolution, which happened as a spontaneous chain reaction, with one city or town inspiring another, and numerous Viet Minh committees being formed, both with and without the participation of organized communists. In the days after the Japanese surrender on August 15, Viet Minh's top leaders were marching down to Hanoi from liberated areas in the mountainous region, with no means of communicating with the local revolutionary leaders elsewhere. Ho and his main collaborators were welcomed by Hanoi's local leaders when they arrived, and they then formed Vietnam's first republican government. A delegation went from Hanoi to Hue to obtain the emperor's abdication, and when he gave up his throne voluntarily, he was invited to Hanoi to serve as the new government's Supreme Advisor. With his age, experience, and personal charm, Ho Chi Minh stood out as the obvious candidate for the presidency of the new republic. He would simultaneously hold the offices of president and foreign minister. For the first time, the name Ho Chi Minh made headlines throughout the world. When Ho appeared before the masses in Hanoi on September 2, 1945, asking through a modern microphone "Can you hear me?" and getting a roar of approval in response, only a few in his audience knew for certain that he was the famous communist Nguyen Ai Quoc. Less than two months after the proclamation of the republic, the Research and Intelligence Service of the Department of State in Washington issued a 90-page intelligence survey containing biographies of sixty-nine prominent nationalist leaders in French Indochina. Ten pages were reserved for Ho Chi Minh, who was presented as "Nguyen Ai Quoc (now known as Ho Chi Minh; alias Ly-Thuy; Mr. C. M. Hoo)." The report affirmed with great certainty that Nguyen Ai Quoc was the same person as Ho Chi Minh and said he was the most experienced and intelligent of the "Annamite nationalist-communist leaders . . . with a remarkable degree of organizing ability."[3]

Nguyen Tat Thanh, the later Nguyen Ai Quoc and Ho Chi Minh, and so on, claimed to have been born in 1890. This may be true, and most authors accept it as his birth year, although the birth date given, May 19, is clearly not correct. It was chosen for him in 1946 because the republic wanted a public celebration before its president went on a high-profile visit to France. At the age of twenty-one—if we accept 1890 as his birth year—Thanh left Indochina to work his way around the world on a French ship. After having visited England and America, he went to Paris, where he took part in the foundation of the French Communist Party and argued the cause of the oppressed colonies through articles in small leftist publications. In the 1920s, he spent some time with the Comintern in Moscow and participated in the organizing of its Southeast Asian department. Then he worked with Comintern networks in China and Siam, and in 1930, he played the decisive role in uniting different factions of the Indochinese communist movement and founding the ICP.

The French Sûreté (Security Service) had been chasing him for years when he was arrested by the British in Hong Kong in 1931. They considered French requests for his extradition to Indochina, where he would surely have been executed, but decided against doing so. The international communist press provided the disinformation in 1932 that he had died from tuberculosis,[4] but the British actually released him in January 1933 and let him embark on a Chinese ship bound for Shantou. Eventually, he made his way to Moscow, where he attended the Seventh Congress of the Comintern in the summer of 1935, but not as leader of the Indochinese delegation. This was the Congress that decided to form broad popular fronts to stop fascism, a policy subsequently also adopted by the ICP, although it had settled for a more sectarian strategy at its second congress in Macao, held earlier in the year.[5] During the short period of the French socialist Léon Blum's French Popular Front Government 1936–37, the nationalist and communist parties in Indochina were permitted to work legally. Ho Chi Minh made no attempt to return to his homeland in this period, however; he got stuck in Russia until October 1938, surviving Stalin's purges, and then went to Xian in northern China.[6]

Toward the end of 1937, the ICP again came under heavy repression, and many of Ho Chi Minh's collaborators, such as Le Duan, Duong Bach Mai, and Tran Huy Lieu were arrested before the party went underground in 1939. Much of the party was destroyed when the French repressed a rebellion based in the south in 1940, but a new party leadership was constituted in the Hanoi region, where the lead ideologue of the ICP for the next forty years, Truong Chinh (Dang Xuan Khu), who had been released from prison under the French Popular Front government, and who edited the party's clandestine regional newspaper in Tonkin from 1940 on, managed to operate clandestinely throughout the whole of World War II without being captured. At a Central Committee meeting held in 1941 to reorganize the party after its leadership structure in the south had been smashed by the French, Truong Chinh was elected secretary-general, a function he would keep until 1956— and resume for a few months in 1986.[7] Others, like Pham Van Dong and Vo Nguyen Giap fled to China in 1940, where they eventually joined up with Ho Chi Minh. These two men would remain his closest confidants among the younger generation. Pham Van Dong would play a key managerial and diplomatic role and lead the Vietnamese delegation that negotiated in France in summer 1946. Vo Nguyen Giap was the founder and commander of the Vietnamese National Liberation Army and, as such, played the main role in the two crises under study here, beside Ho Chi Minh himself.

Vo Nguyen Giap was born on August 21, 1911, in Quang Binh, central Vietnam and, when these lines were written in 2009, was still occasionally receiving visitors in his villa in central Hanoi. He studied at the best French secondary schools in Hue and Hanoi, and he was already engaging in political work as a teenager. In 1937, he joined the ICP, while studying law and teaching at a private school in Hanoi. After the violent repression of the revolt instigated by the southern branch of the ICP in Cochinchina in 1940, he found life untenable in Hanoi, too, left his young bride and unborn child and went into exile in China, where he met Ho Chi Minh, and gave up an idea to visit to the Chinese communist capital Yenan. He followed Ho Chi Minh into the mountainous border region of Cao Bang province in northern Vietnam, learned the local minority languages, and formed lifelong friendships with many local leaders. In December 1944, he founded the National Liberation Army of Vietnam. In the first government formed by Ho Chi Minh after the August Revolution, Giap was minister of the interior; as of March 1946, he chaired a National Resistance Committee, headed a Vietnamese delegation that held futile negotiations with French representatives at Dalat in Vietnam's central highlands in April–May, and served as minister of defense from November.

During most of World War II, French Indochina remained a French colony, under the administration of Admiral Jean Decoux, who accepted the establishment of Japanese bases in the country and stayed loyal to Marshal Pétain in Vichy. Decoux remained in control of Indochina's internal affairs and was able to repress the activities even of pro-Japanese nationalist parties. He followed an antimodernist policy, seeking to raise the prestige of the Lao, Cambodian, and Annamese monarchs, under French protection, with strong emphasis on traditional values, and attempted to establish a basic moral affinity between Confucianism and Pétainism.[8] French Indochina's collaboration with Japan was the main reason why President Franklin D. Roosevelt could allow himself to adopt an anti-French policy in the Far East and promote the establishment of an international trusteeship to replace French colonial rule.[9] On March 9, 1945, some of the basis for this anti-French U.S. policy disappeared when Japan suddenly struck against the French colonial army and toppled Decoux's administration. The Allies had long since driven Pétain out of France, and Decoux's regime looked like an anomaly. The new French government of General de Gaulle had established secret contacts with influential elements of the Decoux administration, however, and this had not gone unnoticed. The Japanese feared a U.S. invasion of Indochina, and that the French would assist the invaders. This was why they overthrew the Decoux regime on March 9. The majority of the French colonial troops were quickly defeated and placed in concentration camps, but some French forces were able to avoid capture by fleeing to China. The Japanese then set up a puppet regime in Hue under Emperor Bao Dai. De Gaulle used the Japanese coup to push for a change in Roosevelt's Indochina policy. Then Roosevelt died, and just a few days afterward, U.S. Secretary of State Edward Stettinius promised his French counterpart to respect France's sovereignty in its Southeast Asian colonies. Still, Truman did not ask de Gaulle's advice when agreeing at the July conference in Potsdam to divide Indochina into Chinese and British military theaters, with no military role for France.[10]

Meanwhile, the Japanese coup greatly facilitated the political work of Ho Chi Minh and his Viet Minh league. Viet Minh established a "liberated zone" in the north of Vietnam and expanded its network to much of Indochina, while continuing to provide assistance to Chinese and American intelligence organizations and helping downed American pilots. Ho Chi Minh even received an American OSS mission at his headquarters in north Vietnam.[11]

The Japanese, in this late phase of the war, had little interest in fighting the Viet Minh and restricted themselves to holding the main cities and communication lines. They allowed Bao Dai's government to appoint a number of reform-oriented Vietnamese to leading administrative positions, and the Viet Minh seized the opportunity to infiltrate the public administration. Since August 1944, the Viet Minh leadership had been planning to seize power in Indochina in the final phase of the Pacific War. "We shall not even have to seize power by force, for there will be no power anymore," a document dated August 6, 1944, asserted.[12] The news of Hiroshima, Nagasaki, and the Soviet attack on Manchuria in mid-August 1945 gave the signal for the "August Revolution." Revolutionary activists seized power quickly, first in Hanoi, later in Hue and Saigon. Then Ho and Giap arrived in Hanoi, and when Bao Dai abdicated in Hue, Ho Chi Minh was able to deliver his famous declaration, confirming Vietnam's independence, on September 2, with a U.S. officer in the first row below the podium and U.S. airplanes circling in the sky above. The Japanese did not want to spill any blood in preventing the Vietnamese Revolution. The war was lost, and most of them returned to their barracks, although several thousand soldiers and officers deserted in order to serve as military instructors or even combatants in the Vietnamese Army. Those who remained in their barracks would soon receive British orders to assist in quelling the revolution in the south and dutifully carried out the task. Japanese thus fought and died on both sides.[13]

The military power vacuum that emerged after the Japanese capitulation and lasted until the arrival of British and Chinese occupation forces three weeks later made the Vietnamese Revolution possible. Ho Chi Minh could not have anticipated the Japanese surrender. He and Giap had been preparing their forces for a general uprising in support of an expected Allied invasion. The Japanese surrender took them by surprise, but the fact that they had established themselves as leaders of an Independence League and a National Liberation Army made them obvious leaders of the new republic. Truong Chinh, the ICP's secretary-general, took a more backstage role.

Bao Dai's abdication invested the DRV with essential national legitimacy, forcing those nationalist groups who looked on Ho Chi Minh with suspicion to seek a role within the framework of the new republican institutions. The alignment of forces inside Indochina was favorable to the Viet Minh's cause. A majority of the people were united in support of independence. The alignment of forces internationally, however, was not similarly beneficial. No foreign country even considered recognizing the DRV; it took many a long time even to learn of its existence. The world took French sovereignty in Indochina more or less for granted, and the Vietnamese Revolution was barely noticed in the international communist press.[14] General de Gaulle's French government left no doubt about its intention to dispatch an expeditionary force and to reestablish French rule in Indochina. De Gaulle made known immediately after the Japanese surrender that he had appointed Admiral Georges Thierry d'Argenlieu as high commissioner and General Leclerc as commander of a French expeditionary force. The Central Committee of the ICP was correct in pointing out, as its spokesman said in a speech at Ba

Dinh square in Hanoi, September 2: "the easier the seizure of power, the more difficult to preserve it."[15]

The Corps expéditionnaire français was still far away when the August Revolution took place, however, so the troops first on the spot to accept the Japanese surrender were British and Chinese, although a few French representatives parachuted in to represent the sovereign power and establish contact with French officers and soldiers in Japanese prisons and concentration camps and with the thousands of French civilians who had been living under precarious conditions since March 9. When Lord Mountbatten's British South East Asia Command had been established in 1943, no formal agreement had been reached on responsibility for Allied operations in Indochina. The British had wanted Indochina to come under Mountbatten's responsibility, along with Thailand and Burma. The Americans, under the influence of Roosevelt's trusteeship plan, had wanted it to be part of Chiang Kai-shek's theater of operations. Indochina was a matter of interallied dispute on several occasions, so when the British-American Combined Chiefs of Staff agreed at Potsdam in July 1945 on a compromise, this came as the result of a protracted quarrel. The compromise solution of splitting Indochina into two theaters had a profound and long-lasting influence on Vietnamese history.[16]

Some twenty days after the Japanese capitulation, and a week after Ho Chi Minh's independence proclamation, British troops arrived by ship in Saigon, while a huge Chinese army marched across the northern border. The British wanted to transfer power to French forces as soon as possible, but some of the Chinese commanders planned to resist French reoccupation of Tonkin and establish a China-friendly regime in Vietnam. On September 23, French soldiers from the Japanese prison camps, rearmed by the British, staged a coup in Saigon and took control of all main public buildings. This led to a wave of killings in the next days, including a massacre on French civilians at the Cité Héraud. On October 5, General Leclerc arrived in Saigon. French, British, and Japanese forces now jointly "pacified" the country, with Japanese troops used for the toughest operations. By February 1946, with British help, the French had gained control of all big towns and main communication lines and a majority of the villages south of the 16th parallel.[17] If the United States had conceded to the British at Potsdam in July and placed the whole of Indochina under Mountbatten, the French would most likely have been able to oust Ho Chi Minh's revolutionary government from Hanoi in the fall of 1945, thus immediately provoking general warfare.[18] It was the presence of a large Chinese army that allowed the Viet Minh to establish itself as the leading force in the new republic, with a legitimate claim to representing the southern part of the nation as well.

What was the Viet Minh? It was a nationalist front organization with many noncommunist members, but under communist domination, most clearly at the level of the top leadership. Before World War II, the Vietnamese communist movement had been ravaged by factional strife between internationalists who saw themselves as part of a global class struggle and nationalists who were inspired by Lenin's thesis about the right of nations to self-determination and looked to the Soviet Union for guidance in the anti-imperialist struggle. Ho Chi Minh was one of the latter and benefited during World War II from the general swing of communist parties toward accommodating national symbols and promoting national resistance against fascism, militarism, and imperialism. In the first ten years after the ICP was founded in 1930, its main leaders were based partly in exile, partly in the Saigon area, but after the southern rebellion was crushed by the French in 1940, a new leadership established itself in the north around Truong Chinh, Hoang Van Thu, and Hoang Quoc Viet. They were infrequently in contact with Ho Chi Minh's movement in the Chinese border region, which from the beginning was dominated by leading members of the ICP. After the Japanese overthrew the French colonial regime on March 9, Viet Minh groups were quickly set up in provinces and districts throughout northern Vietnam, and among the ethnic Viet in Laos as well, but southern Vietnam followed a different path. The communists there had their own front organization, the Vanguard Youth, which was tolerated by the Japanese and had no contact with Ho Chi Minh. Its leader, a freemason and medical doctor named Pham Ngoc Thach, cooperated openly with Japanese authorities, while at the same time keeping in constant touch with clandestine communist leaders.[19] The ICP as such also operated more openly in the south than in the north, and it was divided in two mutually hostile factions. In the "August Revolution," the northern Viet Minh won out. The Vanguard Youth dissolved, and the role of the ICP became more discreet in the south as well.

On November 11, 1945, at Ho Chi Minh's instigation, according to the party veteran Hoang Tung, the ICP made a move that would later expose it to serious criticism in the international communist movement: it publicly *dissolved* itself. Ho had had to plead strongly with Secretary-General Truong Chinh to get him to endorse such a heretical move, Tung recalls.[20] Vietnamese communists would always later claim, just as the French did at the time, that the dissolution was a sham. The party had simply gone underground and continued to operate in the guise of "Marxist Study Groups," or, as Truong Chinh called it, the "Organization [Doan the]." He and some other party leaders, like Hoang Quoc Viet, Nguyen Luong Bang, and Hoang Van Hoan, worked from the shadows, while others in the party's inner circle, like Ho Chi Minh, Vo Nguyen Giap, Pham Van Dong, and Hoang Huu Nam, held positions exposed to the public eye. Nguyen Luong Bang for some time served as the nominal leader of the Viet Minh front. It seems possible, although this remains to be established, that the dissolution of the ICP was more real than is generally assumed. Party work was probably neglected in 1946–47, if not by Truong Chinh, then by many of those who dedicated their time to official state functions. The French intelligence archives from this period contain heaps of captured Viet Minh and DRV documents, but very few documents emanating from any "Communist Party" or "Organization." There was no party newspaper after Truong Chinh's *Co Giai Phong* was closed down, just a theoretical monthly review, *Su That*, which was so theoretical that its real impact is likely to have been limited. If the ICP operated in disguise, the disguise must have seriously hampered the growth and functioning of the party as such, perhaps even prevented it from wielding much influence on many important decisions.[21]

The dissolution of the ICP was publicly explained in terms of an exceptional opportunity to gain national independence; the need for national unification without any class or party distinctions; the will to prove that the communists were able to make great sacrifices and to place the interests of the fatherland above those of class and party; and the desire to avoid misunderstandings both in Vietnam and abroad.[22] In reality, however, the reason was the need to reassure the Chinese occupation authorities. This was difficult, but ultimately successful. While Chiang Kaishek engaged in open warfare with the communists in China, his forces in northern Indochina tolerated the communist-dominated DRV and encouraged cooperation between it and the anticommunist parties VNQDD and Dong Minh Hoi.

From 1941 to March 1946, the Viet Minh went through several phases. First came the clandestine phase from 1941 to March 1945; then there was a second phase from March to August, when the fall of the French colonial regime created great opportunities for spreading the word and setting up Viet Minh groups in many parts of northern Indochina. Third came the phase from August 1945 to March 1946, when the Viet Minh and the institutions of the new republic overlapped. The period under study in the present book, from March to December 1946, was a fourth phase, when elaborate attempts were made to draw a line between the DRV as a state and the Viet Minh as a political front organization.[23] One reason for making the distinction between party and front was that the VNQDD and Dong Minh Hoi, whose leaders had been rivals of Ho Chi Minh's in southern China during the whole of World War II, got their share of the political power, with control of certain ministries and also certain regions, which they occupied with their own separate armies. Most of them rejected invitations to join the Viet Minh front and were considered likely traitors by the communist leaders. A broader front, the Lien Viet, was founded in order to pull them into the fold, and create a wider national consensus, but this met with only limited success, and the communist-led national liberation movement continued both nationally and internationally to go by the name Viet Minh. It included a small Socialist Party and a more influential Democratic Party, which would both continue to exist as communist "fellow travelers" right up to 1990, when these two parties were dissolved.

In the first phase, Viet Minh was organized through two parallel hierarchies, one vertical, with elected leaders, and one horizontal, with leaders appointed from above. The vertical system consisted of different types of organizations: parties, youth organizations, women's organizations, religious organizations, the army, and so on.

The horizontal system was based on a hierarchy of committees, each covering a geographic area. Politically, control from the top was rigid, but in practical matters, each committee enjoyed considerable freedom of action.

In each region, the vertical and horizontal systems were united at the top by a Viet Minh committee. Its chairman was appointed from above, but a certain number of members were elected as representatives of the vertical organizations. On the national level, the Central Committee included representatives of all the vertical organizations, representatives of each of the three Vietnamese regions, and the leaders of special organizations, such as the armed forces, the propaganda bureau, and the financial organization. Until the August Revolution, Ho Chi Minh chaired the Central Committee, but when he became president of the republic, Nguyen Luong Bang took over as chair. The Central Committee elected a Direction Committee (Tong Bo), or political bureau, which took care of the Viet Minh's day-to-day leadership. In his highly influential and generally reliable *Histoire du Viêt-Nam de 1940 à 1952* (1952), Philippe Devillers lists the following eight persons as the probable Tong Bo members in 1946: Ho Chi Minh, Truong Chinh, Vo Nguyen Giap, Pham Van Dong, Tran Huy Lieu, Hoang Quoc Viet, Ho Tung Mau, and Nguyen Luong Bang.[24]

In the second phase, after the August Revolution, the horizontal system simply replaced the old indigenous administration in the French protectorates of Annam and Tonkin, which had already been thoroughly infiltrated by communists. They now took control of the state apparatus by appointing new personnel and setting up People's Committees. This is how the Viet Minh came to overlap with the state. On January 6, 1946, Vietnam held its first national elections, but in most areas only the Viet Minh fielded candidates. Voters could choose from a number of names on the ballots, and those receiving the greatest number of votes were elected. Before the elections, the Chinese generals brokered a deal between the Viet Minh and the two China-oriented nationalist parties VNQDD and Dong Minh Hoi, allowing the latter to designate seventy unelected delegates to the National Assembly. This made the Viet Minh look more like one of three parties than an over-riding national consensus organization, yet the Viet Minh remained dominant, and although the VNQDD and DMH were awarded some nominally important positions in the government, they were never given real control.

It is of special interest to examine decision-making at the top level, and the division of roles between the ICP, or "Organization," the Tong Bo Viet Minh and the Government Council (cabinet).[25] This also interested the French intelligence services, who thought that the Tong Bo was meeting at least once a week. In addition, it had another weekly meeting with key officials in all important ministries. At this meeting, Tong Bo decisions were, according to French intelligence, "communicated for execution," although discussion of them was allowed. If this is correct, the Tong Bo must have held more power than the Government Council. It seems more likely, however, that the French confused the Tong Bo with the Standing Bureau of the

Communist Party. In French intelligence reports, there are few mentions of the ICP, and none of any Central Committee, whereas later Vietnamese historiography claims that all strategic decisions were taken by the party. This may indicate that a historical reinterpretation has taken place, where party meetings have been invented, but it seems more likely that the French were fooled. It is difficult to ascertain to what extent the party was able to uphold its basic functions after its formal dissolution, but one particular document, to which we shall return in a later chapter, is of particular importance for what it reveals about the party. This is an organizational directive conceived by Truong Chinh and formally issued on December 22, 1946, three days after the outbreak of war in Hanoi. The front page of the directive carries only the title of the document and no name of any organization. But the second page starts with the greeting "Comrades C.S.," with "C.S." meaning "Cong San" (communists), and has a foreword signed "T.V.T.U.D.C.S.D.D.," which any Vietnamese communist would recognize as "Standing Bureau of the Central Committee of the Indochinese Communist Party."[26] This proves that Truong Chinh's Standing Bureau did exist.

The relationship between the "moderate" and "extremist" tendencies within the Vietnamese leadership fascinated the French intelligence services. Their informers claimed there were two factions vying for power, and this prompted the French to try to provoke a split. Ho Chi Minh was seen as moderate. The special services knew that he worked closely with two other moderates, his party comrade Hoang Huu Nam and the socialist Hoang Minh Giam. The intelligence services disagreed among themselves on the role of Vo Nguyen Giap, but most saw him as a leading extremist. If the French were right to point to internal differences among the Viet Minh leaders, their attempts to sow dissension were always futile. The cohesion and discipline of the Vietnamese communists, enhanced by loyalty to Ho Chi Minh, proved to be extremely solid.

As of February 1946, Ho had been president of the DRV for five months. It had required great personal skill to remain in power. He continually had to negotiate with opposing nationalist parties, Chinese generals and advisors, the remaining Japanese officers, and French representatives arriving by plane or by parachute. Ho's charm and talent for gaining the friendship of his adversaries played an essential part in the Vietnamese effort to deal with China and France. General Leclerc, Commissioner Jean Sainteny, Minister Marius Moutet, and Prime Minister Georges Bidault, if not Admiral d'Argenlieu, were all addressed as "Dear friend" in Ho's letters, and he surely must have found the proper terms to ingratiate himself with the Chinese generals as well. Those who met the communist veteran with the long, white beard often testified to the profound impression he left on them. "An autodidact of great intelligence, having acquired through dedicated work a vast culture, certainly sincere in his convictions, absolutely incorruptible, [and an] ardent patriot, Ho Chi Minh is undisputedly a powerful character," a French officer wrote in 1947. "His tenacity, his energy, his devious abilities, [and] his long experience with Bolshevik methods make him a dangerous revolutionary chief, who, in order to attain his aim, the unlimited independence of Vietnam, will not retreat before any of the means employed to stop him."[27]

In his memoirs, Jean Sainteny likewise evokes Ho's "vast culture, his intelligence, his incredible level of activity, his asceticism and his absolute incorruptibility." Professor Paul Mus, one of the best-informed French specialists on Vietnam, who had played a role in French "psychological warfare" during World War II,[28] told a contact in 1947 that Ho was an "actor of genius," and, like any such genius, could act only on the basis of his sincerity. In his memoirs, Vo Nguyen Giap, himself more cold and calculating, notes the fabulously persuasive force of his master. But Giap does not see the importance of Ho's sincerity. In Giap's rational brain, Ho's charm is reduced to a tool: "Uncle Ho had an extraordinary flair for detecting the thoughts and feelings of the enemy. With great shrewdness, he worked out a concrete treatment for each type and each individual. . . . Even his enemies, men who were notoriously anti-communist, showed respect for him. They seemed to lose some of their aggressiveness when they were in his presence."[29] Giap stirred awe and admiration, but Ho inspired devotion.

During the high tide of world communism in the mid twentieth century, Ho Chi Minh was ranked among the world's outstanding communist leaders: Lenin, Stalin, Mao, Kim Il Sung, and Castro. From the vantage point of 2009, he seems the only one to stand a chance of surviving the test of history without being morally discredited. Even the dull historian whose favorite pastime is to page through dusty documents cannot escape Ho's magnetism. His letters and telegrams are always out of the ordinary. So among those who have been struck by Ho Chi Minh's shrewd charm, one must also count the historian.

THE NEW FRANCE

La France nouvelle did not have any similarly cohesive leadership. Until January 20, 1946, it was led by the towering figure of General Charles de Gaulle, whose lifespan (1890–1970), overlaps almost exactly with that of Ho Chi Minh (1890–1969). De Gaulle played an essential role in designing the decision-making system for Indochina that remained in place through the whole of 1946. When he resigned as prime minister (*président du Conseil*) on January 20 and withdrew to his native Colombey-les-Deux-Eglises, the Fourth Republic went through a difficult period of constitution-making, with four successive coalition governments in less than one year. Two persons stand out, however, as particularly important in seeking to lay the foundation for a viable French Union and a reformed French Indochina: the socialist Marius Moutet (1876–1968) and the Christian Democrat Georges Bidault (1899–1983).

In a speech to the French National Assembly on March 18, 1947, Minister for

Overseas France Marius Moutet looked back on the previous year, and admitted that he had been convinced that Ho Chi Minh was sincere in his wish to cooperate with France: "I am a man who is accustomed to his kind. I am old enough to know them," he claimed. He was sufficiently experienced to know that what a "Far Easterner" says should never be accepted as if it were "words from the Gospel." Still, he was sure that Ho had been impressed by France, which had treated him as a "real head of state."[30]

Marius Moutet was fourteen years older than Ho. He was elected for the first time to the French National Assembly in 1914, with strong support from the socialist pioneer Jean Jaurès. After the war, he specialized in the colonial question and called for a generous policy of assimilation, denouncing the practice of brutal repression in the colonies and advocating respect for democratic liberties. When the socialist Léon Blum formed his Popular Front government on June 4, 1936, he chose Moutet as minister of colonies, a portfolio he kept until April 10, 1938. At his instigation, France banned the use of forced labor in all the colonies and carried out a number of legal reforms protecting social and democratic rights. Moutet was the first French colonial minister to appoint a black person, Félix Eboué, to an important post in the colonial administration, as governor first of Guadeloupe, later of French Equatorial Africa. In 1940, after the French defeat by Hitler's army, Moutet was one of ninety members of the French National Assembly who voted against the motion to yield full powers to Marshal Pétain. Then he went underground. After the Liberation, Moutet was elected to the Constitutive Assembly and took charge of the Ministry of Overseas France on January 22, 1946, after de Gaulle had resigned. Moutet had actively opposed de Gaulle's wish for a "presidential republic" with a strong executive. Like most other veterans of the French Third Republic, Moutet wanted a constitution with a powerful National Assembly that could effectively control the executive.

During World War II, de Gaulle's and Vichy's colonial policies were actually quite similar. While Vichy sought to strengthen its overseas empire to compensate for its limited power in Europe, de Gaulle wanted to use the colonies as a base for making a contribution to the Allied cause. They thus had a common interest in maintaining the firmest possible foothold in the colonies, yet Pétainists and Gaullists fought each other bitterly in the colonies during the war, and Governor-General Jean Decoux eagerly purged the Indochinese administration of Gaullists. While Pétain and Decoux openly expressed an authoritarian ideology, de Gaulle worked closely with representatives of the political Left and Center, communists, socialists, radicals, and Christian Democrats. After the war, when Admiral Decoux was received by de Gaulle in Paris for a brief encounter, the general was in Decoux's words "more than cold; he was glacial, as it suits the 'First Resistant of France' when receiving a common governor-general from the abhorred Vichy regime."[31] At that time, Moutet did not yet wield much influence on French colonial policy, but pro-

gressive thinkers in the Ministry of Colonies, led by the liberal Gaullist Henri Laurentie, were working out recipes for major colonial reforms, replacing the "Empire"
with a "Union," the "protectorates" with "federated" or "associated states," and
"colonies" with "autonomous" or "self-governing" countries.[32]

Decoux's collaboration with the Japanese had made it difficult for de Gaulle to
seek American recognition of French sovereignty in Indochina, and de Gaulle had
no means of sending troops to the Far East without access to Allied shipping. He
sought to build a resistance movement among French civilians and military personnel in Indochina, without Decoux's knowledge, and intended, just like Ho Chi
Minh, to lend effective assistance to the Allied war effort once American or British
forces were ready to take Indochina from Japan. At the news of the Japanese coup
on March 9, 1945, de Gaulle took immediate diplomatic action. He demanded Allied help for French "resistance groups" in Indochina, transportation of a French
expeditionary force to participate in the war against Japan, and Allied recognition
of French sovereignty. When the United States bickered, based on Roosevelt's well-
known prohibition against doing anything in support of the French cause in Indochina, de Gaulle asked U.S. Ambassador Jefferson Caffery what the United States
was "driving at." Did it want to push France into becoming "one of the federated
states under the Russian aegis"?[33] Subsequently, those French troops who had been
able to avoid Japanese capture and escape to China did receive some belated air drops
from U.S. General Claire Chennault's 14th Air Command in China.

On March 24, 1945, de Gaulle issued a governmental declaration, which had been
prepared for more than a year in the Ministry of Colonies, in particular by the brilliant colonial administrator Léon Pignon, who had served his first stint in Indochina
during 1933–36. This declaration laid the foundation for French postwar Indochina
policy. It aimed at the creation of an Indochinese Federation with a significant degree of autonomy for each of its five parts.[34] The declaration stated that Tonkin, Annam, Cochinchina, Cambodia, and Laos were separated by "civilization, race and
tradition." A French governor-general (the title soon changed to high commissioner)
would head the Federation and serve as the "arbiter of all."[35] The March 24 declaration was at first considered to be liberal, and the first comment on it in the Viet
Minh's main clandestine newspaper was actually positive.[36] However, most Vietnamese commentators, both in Indochina and France, reacted against the declaration for refusing to recognize Vietnam's national unity.

Once learning of the Japanese capitulation on August 15, de Gaulle appointed
his trusted officers General Leclerc as commander in chief of the Corps expéditionnaire français en Extrême-Orient and Admiral d'Argenlieu as high commissioner for Indochina. Leclerc left first, to secure the British occupation forces' respect for French sovereignty and a quick transfer of responsibility from the British
commander in Saigon, General Douglas Gracey. D'Argenlieu took more time to prepare, and set out systematically to implement the March 24 declaration. Thus, when

de Gaulle resigned on January 20, leaving state affairs in the hands of the party politicians, a military and Gaullist-oriented hierarchy had been firmly established in Indochina. The new French government under the socialist Félix Gouin (January 23–
June 12, 1946) had other things to do than change the system and replace the
personnel that de Gaulle had put in place in the colonies. This meant that the New
France was represented in Indochina by two general officers whose views were significantly less progressive than those of mainstream French politicians. Leclerc and
d'Argenlieu were torn from the outset between their loyalty to de Gaulle, their concern about the racist attitudes of French settlers who had suffered from Japanese
and Annamite mistreatment, and their uneasy relationship to modernizing, progressive impulses emanating from the metropole. The modernizers were supported
by many of the young officers and civil servants who went out after the German capitulation to serve in Indochina.

De Gaulle had dominated French foreign policy at the expense of the former
leader of the French internal resistance movement, Foreign Minister Georges
Bidault. Bidault always felt that he lived in the shadow of the tall general, and he
would later confide that the day de Gaulle left office had been "the most beautiful
day" in his life.[37] For later generations, the rivalry between Bidault and de Gaulle
looks like one between a dwarf and a giant, and this was certainly de Gaulle's own
view, but not all French were Gaullists, and many sympathized with Bidault. Just
like de Gaulle, he saw himself as more than an ordinary politician. He had a national mission. Bidault hated de Gaulle's guts, and the general responded in kind.
A famous photograph from the victory parade after the reoccupation of Paris in
August 1944 shows the tall, imposing general overshadowing the featureless Bidault,
who was gently told to march one step behind.

While de Gaulle had to wait twelve years from January 1946 before the nation
called on him again, Bidault enjoyed some of the most influential positions in the
French Fourth Republic. He was foreign minister from September 1944 to July 1948,
with the exception of a brief—but in our context essential—interlude from December 18, 1946, to January 22, 1947. While Bidault enjoyed little freedom of action as long as de Gaulle held the premiership, he exerted considerable authority
once Félix Gouin took over. Then, in June 1946, when Gouin resigned, amid heated
constitutional debates, Bidault assumed the premiership himself, in addition to
continuing to serve as foreign minister. Hence he became France's most powerful
political leader. Bidault exemplifies an important aspect of French foreign policy
decision-making in the Fourth Republic: consistency. This may surprise those who
know that the country had no fewer than twenty-five governments between the formation of de Gaulle's first in 1944 and his return to power in 1958, but a few key
politicians, notably Georges Bidault and Robert Schuman of the Christian Democratic party (MRP), occupied either the Quai d'Orsay (Foreign Ministry) or the Hôtel Matignon (the prime minister's office) almost continuously. The governments

they took part in developed consistent strategies of economic reconstruction and European integration, and showed consistency also in their doomed attempt to reform and hold on to the French empire.[38]

The "most beautiful day" in Bidault's life, January 20, 1946, also heralded the return of Marius Moutet to the Ministry of Colonies at 27 rue Oudinot. He now got a new title, minister for Overseas France. One month earlier, he had written several programmatic articles on Indochina for the socialist daily *Le Populaire,* stating that France must retain its presence in both Asia and Africa, but not against the will of the local populations. France had made a considerable effort on behalf of the Indochinese people, but had not done enough. More was needed to invest the word "colonialism" with positive new connotations.[39] According to Moutet, American or Russian domination would not be any better than French colonialism, and he took a clear stand on two core issues in the emerging clash with the DRV, unity and independence. He stated, in consonance with de Gaulle's declaration of March 24, that "geographically, ethnically, politically, the main characteristic of Indochina is diversity. It consists of five countries: Tonkin, Annam, Cambodia, Laos, and Cochinchina."[40] He did not attribute any legal status to Ho Chi Minh's revolutionary government, even if he believed it might be possible to come to terms with some of the Viet Minh leaders. He denounced the Viet Minh for its opposition to French authority and for "believing [itself] to have constituted" a government: "One does not improvise a government, a legislation, an administration in a heterogeneous country where the public is not yet capable of knowingly [*consciemment*] expressing its preferences."[41]

This statement provides a key to his thinking: Moutet conceived of colonialism as emancipation of uneducated peoples. He expanded on it in August before a socialist gathering in the city of La Rochelle, on France's Atlantic coast: "As a young socialist militant, I called for the liberation of the working class. Today, the French working class has the means to liberate itself: it has conquered political and social rights. It is now our task to widen this liberation by fighting for the peoples that we are to educate and to support. It was to this need for liberation and emancipation that I devoted myself already in 1936 as minister in the Popular Front government."[42]

This idea of educating other peoples was written into the foreword of the French constitution that was adopted in a referendum on October 13, 1946: "Faithful to her traditional mission, France intends to lead the peoples whom she has taken care of to the freedom to administer themselves and democratically manage their own affairs."[43] In this constitution, which had been long in the making and entered into force only on December 24, 1946, the idea of emancipating other peoples so that they could become autonomous and eventually perhaps independent was juxtaposed with rival ideas of assimilating elites from the colonies into French culture to the point where they could be accepted as full French citizens. French debates over colonial issues had often been battles between those who saw the colonial relationship as a nexus between one developed and a number of undeveloped peoples and territories, and those who regarded it as a bond linking the metropole to its citizens around the world. Yet this conflict had little impact in the process of colonial reform following World War II. It was generally agreed that some colonies would develop into independent nations, while others would be integrated in France through assimilation. When the colonized peoples demanded total and immediate independence, the assimilationists and the emancipators rejected it in unison. The Catholic nationalist Bidault and the socialist emancipator Moutet agreed on the crucial aspects of French colonial policy in 1946.

Marius Moutet has been considered a weak leader betraying his own and his party's peaceful socialist ends by giving in to the influence of Bidault and the admiral de Gaulle had sent to Indochina.[44] This is only partially true. Moutet was easily influenced by others, and loath to take political risks. There are, however, two factors that tend to modify the image of the "weak leader." First, Moutet never expressed the anticolonial attitudes that were held by many other French socialists in 1946–47, notably by the party's young secretary-general, Guy Mollet. Moutet never wished to give in to Vietnamese demands for independence and unity, and in fact supported the main aspects of High Commissioner d'Argenlieu's Gaullist policy. Moutet's actions were thus more consistent with his views than has sometimes been assumed. Second, it was not just his personal leadership that was weak. His position in the decision-making system that de Gaulle had created for Indochinese affairs was weak as well. It benefited Bidault, not Moutet.

The Ministry of Overseas France was directly responsible for most French overseas territories, but not for Indochina. Moutet wanted to direct French Indochina policy himself—any minister wants real control—but by decree of February 21, 1945, de Gaulle had set up an independent body to coordinate the reoccupation of Indochina called the Comité interministériel de l'Indochine (Interministerial Committee for Indochina; hereafter, Comonindo). Gouin and Bidault preserved the Cominindo, and chaired it themselves, just as de Gaulle had done. Gouin, however, let Moutet take the real decisions, while Bidault wanted to steer French Indochina policy in the same way that de Gaulle had done.[45] The Cominindo members were the prime minister and minister of foreign affairs (Georges Bidault); minister for Overseas France (Marius Moutet); minister of the army (Edmond Michelet); minister of aviation (Charles Tillon); minister of finance (Robert Schuman); the chief of staff (General Alphonse Juin), and the chief of intelligence (Henri Ribière). Moutet was the only socialist and Tillon the only communist among them. The other three political appointees belonged to the MRP, whose views tended to dominate the committee. The Cominindo had the right to summon other key persons for its sessions, and this gave a minister without portfolio, Alexandre Varenne, a Radical politician who had been governor-general of Indochina in 1925–27 and served as chairman of the Union pour la défense de l'oeuvre française en Indochine (Union for the Defense of French Achievements in Indochina; UDOFI), an almost permanent presence in the meetings. The Cominindo had its office in the Ministry of War at 16 rue St. Dominique. As many as twenty-six persons were employed there at the most, and the office was headed by a secretary-general, who was better informed about Indochinese developments on a daily basis than anyone in the Ministry of Overseas France. The only other branches of government that were in direct communication with Saigon were General Juin's Chiefs of Staff (EMGDN) and Ribière's intelligence service (SDECE).

All nonmilitary dispatches and cables to and from Indochina went through the office of the Cominindo. Its secretary-general decided on the distribution of information to the ministries, organized the weekly advisory meetings of representatives from the same ministries, and summoned the ministers themselves when important decisions needed to be made. Under de Gaulle, this position was held by François de Langlade, a businessman with experience in Indochina and as plantation owner in British Malaya. In 1946, after an interim period with a secretary-general who did not leave any mark on French policy, the young Pierre Messmer took over.[46] Although a Gaullist more than a leftist, he was a typical representative of the New France, eager to adjust to changing times. (Messmer would serve as French prime minister in the years 1972–74.) After the Japanese surrender in August 1945, de Gaulle had designated Messmer as commissioner of the Republic for Tonkin, where he would seek to defend French interests in the face of Chinese occupation, but when Messmer parachuted into Tonkin, he was captured by the Viet Minh and held prisoner until he was able to escape. By that time, the young businessman Jean Roger, son-in-law of the second most important of all French governors-general in Indochina, Albert Sarraut (1911–14, 1917–19), and whose code name in the French Resistance was Jean Sainteny, had on his own initiative assumed the role de Gaulle had assigned Messmer. Sainteny had led a French intelligence mission in south China and got himself to Hanoi on board an American airplane. In September 1945, he was received by Ho Chi Minh, and the two men established a lifelong relationship, which Ho shrewdly and charmingly turned into a friendship. Sainteny was assisted by a local French socialist, Louis Caput; a dubious character, Jacques Bousquet; and also by the highly experienced colonial administrator Léon Pignon, who had come to Hanoi after drafting the declaration of March 24, 1945, to serve as assistant to General Marcel Alessandri, commander of the French troops who stayed in China after their escape from Tonkin in March–April 1945. When assisting Sainteny, Pignon seems to have preferred a rather discreet backstage role. Perhaps his task was to make sure that Sainteny keep in line with French policy. After some hesitation in Paris, Sainteny was formally appointed commissioner of the French Republic for Tonkin and North Annam, the function that had been intended for Messmer before he was captured by the Viet Minh. In spite of this unpleasant experience, Messmer did not become a hard-liner. In March 1946, before taking over as secretary-general of the Cominindo, he published an article advocating a liberal policy in Indochina, going as far as to "understand" the Vietnamese arguments for unification of north and south, and urging France to adopt a neutral position so that the local population could decide.[47] In April, he would annoy French authorities in Indochina by using the familiar *tu* and allowing General Vo Nguyen Giap to do the same when they were chatting with each other at a Franco-Vietnamese conference in the central highland town of Dalat.[48]

The secretary-general of the Cominindo occupied a central, but not a powerful position. It was the politicians who decided, and when they did not, the decisions were made in Saigon instead of Paris. The young Messmer could not impose any policy on Saigon without basis in a formal Cominindo decision, and while Gouin and Bidault chaired the committee, it tended to avoid making decisions. When it did, it mostly approved what the high commissioner in Saigon had done. Gouin and Bidault were so preoccupied with other matters that they were unable to closely follow events in Indochina. Bidault also seems to have preferred to leave the initiative to the high commissioner rather than to permit the minister for Overseas France to direct French policy.

In 1945, the official rationale for setting up the Cominindo had been that the military aspects of Indochina's reoccupation could not be handled under the authority of the minister of colonies.[49] When the southern half of Indochina had been reoccupied, and France entered into an agreement with Ho Chi Minh on March 6, 1946, the Cominindo lost much of its raison d'être, and Moutet's ministry took over some of its functions. In September 1946, its staff was reduced to seventeen. The Cominindo was, however, preserved, and its secretariat in the War Ministry continued to centralize official communications with Saigon. Moutet would state later that the interministerial system had led to a "dispersion of responsibilities that has been harmful to sound administrative management." He had found himself deprived of his normal functions and the "means of action that he should have at his disposal."[50] Since the prime minister did not actively use his authority, the main effect of the Cominindo system was to strengthen the autonomous power of the high commissioner in Saigon.

THE PENTAGONAL FEDERATION

Admiral Georges Thierry d'Argenlieu, high commissioner in Indochina from August 1945 to February 1947, was not born or brought up to assume political functions in the twentieth century. His aristocratic manners, pompous speeches, love of ritual, rigid principles, and badly hidden disdain for the politicians who succeeded his hero General de Gaulle made him the prime mover of French intransigence vis-à-vis Vietnam, in the eyes of both contemporary observers and later historians. D'Argenlieu belonged to the New France only to the extent that its principles had been laid down by de Gaulle, and he certainly bears much of the responsibility for the policies that led to the French Indochina War, but he also served as a scapegoat for the actions and inaction of Bidault.

D'Argenlieu had served in the French Navy during World War I, then been a monk in a Carmelite monastery in the interwar period. He was mobilized as a Navy reserve officer in 1939 and subsequently rose to high rank in de Gaulle's Free French Naval Forces. His admiration for de Gaulle was so great that the general could trust in his loyalty unreservedly. This became a problem when de Gaulle resigned. As will be evident to any reader of d'Argenlieu's posthumously published *Chronique d'Indochine* (1985), he continued to regard de Gaulle—and not the party politicians temporarily occupying government offices in Paris—as the genuine embodiment of France. D'Argenlieu would return to his monastery in 1947.

The Vietnamese saw d'Argenlieu as the archetypal reactionary colonialist. Giap has described him as a "defrocked priest" with "small, wily eyes under a wrinkled forehead and [with] thin lips." After having spent some time with him, Giap retained the memory of an "experienced, cunning, arrogant and mean man."[51] It was said of d'Argenlieu in France that he possessed one of the most brilliant minds of the twelfth century. General Jean-Etienne Valluy, who succeeded General Leclerc as commander of the CEFEO in July 1946, was more indulgent in describing the admiral as "not at all haughty, although a little formal and distant." D'Argenlieu was among the few on whom Ho Chi Minh's charms did not work. In one of their meetings, Ho said to him: *"Mon amiral,* I appeal to your Christian sentiments . . . "The monk cut the communist short: *"Monsieur le Président,* please excuse me, but we are here to discuss serious matters." The most serious matter that d'Argenlieu could imagine was the Indochinese Federation. D'Argenlieu, Valluy later declared, was passionately attached to his "pentagonal [five-country] federation," as prescribed in de Gaulle's governmental declaration of March 24, 1945.[52]

In d'Argenlieu's conception, the Federation would be controlled by a council consisting of ten representatives from France and ten from each of the five member states.[53] The main attributions of the federal council would be to vote the federal budget, decide on taxes, and pass laws proposed by the Federal government. This government would be headed by the high commissioner himself, assisted by commissioners with the same attributions as ministers in an independent state. There would be commissioners of political affairs, finance, foreign affairs, justice, education, health, information, and so on. The commissioners would hold weekly cabinet meetings, chaired by the high commissioner, with the commander in chief (Leclerc, later Valluy) as his deputy.[54] The commissioners would have all important governmental services under their authority: army, police, customs service, post, radio, and so on. This did not leave much room for the autonomy of each constituent state, but d'Argenlieu wanted to sign written conventions with each of the five in order to define their places within the Federation. He was particularly eager to develop an autonomous Cochinchina, since it had the biggest economy and also the greatest number of French residents *(colons)*. In Cochinchina, a certain number of rich and educated locals had already acquired French citizenship through assimilation. As soon as the local revolutionaries had been driven out of Saigon's public buildings on September 23, 1945, the question of institutionalized cooperation between the French residents and members of the indigenous establishment came up. The declaration of March 24 said the local governments in each of the five Indochinese countries should be developed or reformed, and that appointments should be open to all citizens. On the French side, the closest collaborators of former Governor General Decoux in the Vichy period had to go back to France, but those who could claim some kind of "Resistance" background were welcome to serve as civil servants along with new young administrators from France.

In 1946, the number of French civil servants in Indochina rose to 14,000. In 1939, there had been some 3,500.[55] One reason for the rise was that the revolution had removed the old mandarinate; another was that many among the local educated classes supported the Viet Minh. D'Argenlieu frequently complained of lack of personnel.[56] The French *colons* and some members of the local indigenous elite jointly established a Consultative Council. The leading figure on the local side was Dr. Nguyen Van Thinh, president of the Democratic Party (not the same Democratic Party as the one that was part of the Viet Minh), a passionate antirevolutionary and influential with the local elite of landowners. He found it difficult, however, to induce other upper-class Cochinchinese to join his council. They feared being stigmatized as collaborators. Yet on February 12, 1946, the Consultative Council formally constituted itself, with four French members and eight "notables." The French members wanted to integrate Cochinchina into France as a *département*. The Cochinchinese members disagreed, however, preferring autonomy.[57] Both the old and the new French civil servants, and also some indigenous French citizens, felt threatened by the prospect of Cochinchina being merged with Vietnam. They also feared the social changes that the communists might bring about.

Ho Chi Minh was once asked for his view on the planned Indochinese Federation. He replied that Vietnam would willingly accept a federation of an essentially economic nature, but was determined to prevent the prewar French Gouvernement général from resurfacing in the guise of a federation.[58] This was a rather precise description of d'Argenlieu's aim, although there was one important difference between the prewar governor-general and the postwar high commissioner: The fact that the Cominindo was chaired by the premier and not by the minister for Overseas France made the high commissioner more independent of Paris than the governors-general had been.

De Gaulle's resignation in January 1946 came as a shock to most Frenchmen in Indochina.[59] They felt the general was leaving his troops before they had fulfilled their mission to liberate all French territories. D'Argenlieu and Leclerc had come a good part of the way. A revolutionary government in Cambodia had been taken into custody, so the young King Norodom Sihanouk could once more receive sound French advice. Cochinchina and southern Annam had been reoccupied, and the local rebels there been almost crushed. Only the southernmost part of Laos had been reoccupied; most of the country was under Chinese occupation, but the French had good reason to believe that their traditional relationship with the king of Luang Phrabang would enable them to reestablish their presence in the central and northern parts of Laos as well. The situation in Chinese-occupied Tonkin and northern Annam caused more worry. The DRV government had even organized so-called national elections on January 6, and Frenchmen in Saigon worried that a government without de Gaulle might not have the fortitude to reoccupy northern Indochina and get rid of the Chinese occupation forces. Would a government led by the socialist Félix Gouin be strong and decisive enough for the delicate task of reestablishing a French presence in a country engulfed in revolution, under Chinese occupation, and controlled by communist nationalists? A three-pronged approach would be needed: negotiations with the DRV; preparation of a military operation, and negotiations with China.

2

The Chinese Trap

In the fall of 1946, before the world learned of the crisis leading to the Indochina War, Indonesian Prime Minister Sutan Sjahrir complained to the French consul in Jakarta about the narrow-minded policies of the Dutch and the British, who had joined forces in preventing his country from gaining independence. They should follow the good French example, said Sjahrir, who envied Ho Chi Minh that he could deal with such enlightened French officials, full of "kindness" and "understanding." French High Commissioner d'Argenlieu was simply a "genius." No one could expect Holland to send anyone with a similar broadness of mind to Indonesia—"one cannot after all demand the impossible"—but if at least they could send someone with a minimum of "good will."[1]

It is easily forgotten that France, for a brief interval in 1946, was seen as a model of decolonization in Asia.[2] The reason was the Franco-Vietnamese Convention that was signed in Hanoi on March 6, 1946, in the presence of British, American, and Chinese observers, which led to a period of détente between France and the young Vietnamese Republic, and allowed Ho Chi Minh to travel to France as a statesman that summer.

THE MARCH 6 AGREEMENT

France made three major concessions in the March 6 Franco-Vietnamese Convention. First, it recognized the Vietnamese Republic as a free state *(Etat libre)*, with its own government, parliament, army, and finances, although it would be integrated into the Indochinese Federation, which in turn would be a part of the French Union. The term "free" was a compromise between the Vietnamese demand for "independence" and the French offer of "autonomy" or "self-government," and the question of full independence was left to the future. The second concession was to promise a referendum among the "populations" to resolve the question of the unity of the three Vietnamese lands, Tonkin, Annam, and Cochinchina—often referred to as the three *ky* or *bo*.[3] And the third was to accept, in a military appendix to the main agreement, that the French military presence north of the 16th parallel would be limited to 15,000 troops, and to a period of five years. The military appendix, which caused an uproar in the French government when it learned about it on March 12, was negotiated in Hanoi during the night of March 5–6 and signed along with the convention the following day. It stipulated the number of French troops that could be stationed in each and every location. These were major concessions indeed, and if they had been followed up in practice, then the praise heaped on France would have been deserved.

The March 6 agreement, which is presented and discussed in virtually all of the literature on the wars in Vietnam, is most often seen as a sign of a temporary French moderation that, with tragic consequences, was subsequently abandoned. The assumption is that the agreement resulted from a genuine willingness to compromise due to French realization that a long-drawn-out war against a Vietnamese resistance movement, led by the Viet Minh, would be a catastrophe. Jean Sainteny, the chief negotiator in Hanoi, and General Philippe Leclerc, commander of the Corps expéditionnaire d'Extrême-Orient, are seen as pragmatists who, with support from the socialist minister for Overseas France, Marius Moutet, pursued a policy of accord in March 1946, notwithstanding the opposition of High Commissioner d'Argenlieu and other hard-liners. Sainteny and Leclerc have been given much of the credit for the fact that an agreement was reached.[4] Unfortunately, however, the convention did not result from any temporary ascendancy of French liberalism, pragmatism, or moderation. From Leclerc's perspective, the main function of Sainteny's negotiations in Hanoi was to provide diplomatic "cover" for the French reoccupation of the north. It was seen as essential to prevent Ho Chi Minh's government from leaving the capital before the French arrived and launching a resistance struggle from guerrilla bases in the hinterland, since this would force France to undertake a costly, protracted anti-insurgency campaign. Leclerc did not necessarily see a need to sign an agreement with Ho Chi Minh *before* the French troops landed. He wanted a show of force and hoped this would lead Ho Chi Minh to accept an agreement on French terms. Leclerc's intention was to first launch his military reoccupation, with Chinese assistance, and *then* persuade Ho to comply. What happened instead was that France fell into a Chinese trap. The Chinese refused to allow any landing of French troops until an agreement had been signed with Ho. They threatened to resist the French landing militarily, and they actually fired on the French ships when they arrived. The large number of troops being transported by the French armada needed water, and in any case, to give up the invasion at this point, turn around, and sail south was simply not an option, because it would mean a colossal loss of face. Hence the Chinese threat made it compelling for Leclerc to arrive at an agreement almost at any cost before his troops started to disembark. The alternative might be war with China. What happened was simply that France and Vietnam were forced by China to make peace.[5] The main credit for the March 6 accords should therefore go to the government of Chiang Kai-shek.

The agreement came out of several rounds of negotiations between Ho Chi Minh and Jean Sainteny, with background in talks that had started as early as December 1, 1945.[6] The power play surrounding these talks was triangular. China wanted to extract French concessions in exchange for withdrawing its occupation troops. France wanted to reestablish its presence without making too many concessions to Vietnamese nationalism. And the DRV wished to get rid of the Chinese occupation while obtaining French recognition. The French and the Vietnamese were playing for high stakes and both were willing to risk an armed confrontation with the other, but not with the Chinese. The Chinese were determined to prevent any armed conflict as long as they themselves were in the country and to reap as much profit as possible from their temporary presence. Until February 28, France conducted simultaneous negotiations with China in Chongqing and with the DRV in Hanoi. At this stage, while China had not yet given its formal consent to a French return to northern Indochina, Leclerc was eager to obtain an agreement with Ho Chi Minh that would make it possible to land in the north without meeting Vietnamese resistance. He thus urged the French government to make new promises and even hold out the promise of "independence." However, on February 28, 1946, China signed a treaty with France in Chongqing that transferred the responsibility for occupying northern Indochina from China to France. It even stipulated that the French forces could arrive in the first half of March. This diplomatic victory led Leclerc and d'Argenlieu in Saigon to decide to launch a huge military operation immediately, sending 21,000 troops north on ships with the mission of landing in Haiphong and taking possession of the last French territory that had not yet been reoccupied after World War II. At this stage the French did not see it as necessary to reach an agreement with Ho Chi Minh before the landing, since they expected the Chinese forces in the north to support the reoccupation. However, the Chinese feared being caught in the middle of a Franco-Vietnamese war and made it a condition for their cooperation that France and the DRV first sign an agreement. They also engineered a reconciliation between the Viet Minh and the Vietnamese opposition parties, which formed a government of national union on March 2. So when the Vietnamese and French negotiators in Hanoi reached the March 6 agreement, while Leclerc sailed into Haiphong with his battle-trained forces, this happened under the watchful eye of Chinese officers in Hanoi. Sainteny and Ho Chi Minh reached their accord only on the night of March 5–6, and signed it only in the late afternoon on March 6, together with the leader of one of Vietnam's China-oriented opposition parties, Vu Hong Khanh. When the new government of national unity had been formed and confirmed by the Vietnamese National Assembly four days earlier, Khanh had become vice-president of a National Resistance Committee, chaired by Vo Nguyen Giap. From Giap and Ho's perspective, it was essential that the opposition share responsibility for their compromise with France. Both the French and the Vietnamese acted under constraint. This element of constraint, and the dramatic circumstances under which the convention was negotiated, will be narrated here on the basis of sources in French, British, and American archives, Philippe Devillers's classic account, Frédéric Turpin's recent analysis, and three other important publications, one of which is based on Chinese sources. Unfortunately, the author has not had access to Vietnamese records throwing light on Ho Chi Minh's struggle for political survival during the February–March crisis. The story of his complex dealings with Sainteny, Chinese Guomindang officers representing the Allied forces of occupation, pro-Chinese Vietnamese nationalists, and his own impatient Viet Minh cadres remains to be written from a Vietnamese perspective.[7]

To understand the background and causes of the March 6 agreement, the best starting point is, not the French government's thinking about colonial reform, but its urge—indeed, it perceived it as a necessity—to reassert its sovereignty and reoccupy the last remaining territory of its prewar empire.

OPÉRATION BENTRÉ

The code name for the French reoccupation of Indochina north of the 16th parallel was Opération Bentré (the name of a town and province at the mouth of the Mekong River, south of Saigon). When Sainteny signed the March 6 agreement with Ho Chi Minh and Vu Hong Khanh, nine hours after the first French occupation forces had sailed into the port of Haiphong and been met by Chinese artillery fire, the immediate French aim was to prevent an outbreak of international war. March 6 was the day that France did not go to war against China. If it had not been for the agreement, history books would have said that the First Indochina War started on March 6, 1946, with direct Chinese involvement on the side of Vietnam.

Opération Bentré had been prepared, over the previous months, in the Third Bureau of General Leclerc's headquarters.[8] This was done without informing British Admiral Lord Louis Mountbatten. Most of his British troops had left Indochina at the end of January, along with their local commander, General Douglas Gracey, but a small British "interservice mission" remained in Saigon, and as Supreme Allied Commander Southeast Asia, Mountbatten remained formally responsible to the Combined Chiefs of Staff in Washington for the Allied occupation of the southern half of Indochina. The French had also not, of course, informed General Lu Han, who was responsible to the Allies for the occupation of the northern half.

The author of the Bentré plan was Lieutenant Colonel Jean Lecomte. His plan was approved, not just by Leclerc, but by High Commissioner d'Argenlieu as well, and the operation was cleared in a meeting of the Interministerial Committee for Indochina (Comonindo) in Paris on February 20, 1946, in the presence of the high commissioner. On the day the meeting was held, General Leclerc insisted in a cable to the French chief of staff, General Alphonse Juin, that Opération Bentré was absolutely necessary. It was only because France had used force in the south, he claimed, that it had obtained such excellent results. If the French government should think that the signing of an agreement with the Vietnamese government made a show of force redundant, then much would be lost. A demonstration of French superiority would "bring the pseudo-government to capitulate." Then would be the time to be generous and conclude negotiations with Ho Chi Minh, not earlier.[9] In instructions given to Sainteny on February 22, Leclerc emphasized: "No matter how the negotiations go, I will arrive at the fixed date."[10] On the basis of Leclerc's telegram exchanges in the run-up to Opération Bentré, a three-pronged strategy can be discerned:

- The Vietnamese government had to stay put in Hanoi rather than withdraw to the hinterland, since the launching of a long-drawn-out war of resistance by an intact Vietnamese government might have disastrous future consequences. Sainteny's task was to keep Ho Chi Minh in place in Hanoi. The French government should contribute to reassuring Vietnamese public opinion by publicly stating its generous intentions.
- Opération Bentré had to be carried out with a massive display of force.
- An agreement should be signed with Ho Chi Minh once France could speak to him from a position of strength. Leclerc was confident that Ho Chi Minh would "capitulate" when he saw how strong the French forces were and sign an agreement on French terms.

Members of Leclerc's staff, such as Colonel Repiton-Préneuf, head of Leclerc's Second Bureau, surely understood how risky this strategy was, particularly at this stage, when China had not yet given its formal consent to the French reoccupation. They no doubt hoped to reach a deal with Ho Chi Minh before the planned landing in the north.[11] Leclerc also told Sainteny on February 22 that he should seek Ho Chi Minh's written agreement to the French landing and get him to remove his troops from the Haiphong–Hanoi road. However, Leclerc shared General de Gaulle's belief in the need to first *show force* and only then negotiate. A few weeks later, after the March 6 accord had been signed, Leclerc came under criticism for his role in making huge concessions to the Vietnamese government. It was clear that d'Argenlieu disliked what he had done. On March 27, Leclerc thus justified the March 6 agreement in a letter to General de Gaulle, making a virtue of necessity. It had been absolutely necessary to sign the agreement, he argued, because a military conquest of Tonkin would have been impossible:

if we had found, in addition to the Chinese, a country rising against us or simply in disorder, we could evidently have landed in Haiphong, but—I affirm this categorically—the reconquest of Tonkin, even partially, was impossible. One does not conquer an armed, overwrought country two-thirds the size of France with a small force—at least not in 1946. In addition, the problem would soon have taken on an international dimension. This is why it is impossible to underline sufficiently the importance of the accords that have been reached.[12]

Jean Sainteny in his memoirs, and later historians as well, have seen this letter as evidence that this was also Leclerc's thinking before March 6.[13] They have probably been misled. If Leclerc had been determined to reach an agreement with the Vietnamese government before disembarking his troops, then he would not have put himself in a position that required the landing to take place on one specific date, which he did; the date was dictated by the high tide in the port of Haiphong. If he had intended to obtain the DRV's agreement before landing, he would also most likely have informed his government of this when he set Opération Bentré in motion, but he actually said the opposite. What he told the Comenindo was that an effective landing, followed by a rapid advance toward Hanoi, was likely to make Ho Chi Minh "capitulate" and sign an agreement on French terms. Also, if Leclerc's intention had been to sign first and then land, he would not have needed to put pressure on the Chinese to assist him in providing arms to the French colonial army soldiers interned in the Hanoi Citadel, or demand of the Chinese that they facilitate the arrival of airborne troops at Hanoi's airfield, which—as we shall soon see—he also did. Leclerc was given carte blanche by High Commissioner d'Argenlieu to carry out the operation as he saw fit. On March 1, when Leclerc ordered his troops to embark on ships bound north, he took an enormous gamble. And the gamble was not primarily that Ho would sign on to an agreement before the troops arrived. The main French gamble was that the Chinese would allow his troops to come ashore without permission from the Vietnamese government and assist him in moving toward Hanoi. When this gamble failed, Leclerc was forced to authorize the signing of an agreement on terms that under normal circumstances would have been unacceptable to the French government. He drew France into a trap in the hope or belief that China would not make use of it, but help France out instead. China then used its sudden leverage to force France and Vietnam to sign an agreement.

The great French hero General Philippe Leclerc, the liberator of Paris in August 1944, who was made a Marshal posthumously after he died in an airplane accident in Africa in 1947, has been treated kindly by historians, and has often been favorably compared with Admiral d'Argenlieu. They had similar aristocratic backgrounds. Both were Catholics. Both joined de Gaulle in fighting Pétain's Armistice from the lonely beginnings in the fall of 1940. They were appointed to the two highest positions in Indochina knowing nothing about the country. With d'Argenlieu taking charge of the civilian administration and Leclerc commanding the military forces, neither was placed above the other, but in matters of policy, d'Argenlieu had the final word. Leclerc is normally regarded as the more moderate or pragmatic of the two, insisting that the Vietnam problem could only be resolved politically, while d'Argenlieu is said to have preferred the use of force.[14] The difference was not so obvious at the time. On February 4, 1946, struck by Leclerc's "pacification" of southern Indochina, the U.S. Secretary of State told his ambassador in Paris that the State Department would appreciate information as to who had the French government's backing: "Leclerc, the intransigent and uncompromising colonial-minded or d'Argenlieu the conciliatory and moderate."[15] This was not a mere misunderstanding. The later conflict between the two Gaullists has often been misunderstood. It was more of a personal rivalry and of a difference in tactical approach than of diverging principles or strategies. Jean Sainteny stated in 1973 that the two held basically similar views, but that d'Argenlieu was too strongly influenced by the false optimism in Saigon. Leclerc had a better understanding of the situation in the north, but d'Argenlieu enjoyed the backing of the French government.[16] The military historians Gilbert Bodinier and Philippe Duplay have described how Leclerc, like de Gaulle, believed in the show of force as a prelude to entering into agreements, quoting a statement made by Leclerc with regard to southern Indochina in October 1945: "It would be a complete mistake to negotiate in a generous fashion with representatives of the Viet Minh before having shown our force. . . . It is certainly a question of reconquest, since negotiation with 'yellows' is pure smoke."[17] One of the most nuanced comparisons of the two Gaullist commanders was made by General Jean-Etienne Valluy, who took over Leclerc's command in July 1946 and also served as deputy high commissioner under d'Argenlieu. Valluy affirms that the admiral and the general were antithetical by nature and in ideas. D'Argenlieu always sought to demonstrate his patriotism and pursue a policy of almost architectural coherence. Leclerc, on the contrary, was an inimitable tactician, but inconsistent in politics. D'Argenlieu's actions were always consistent with the long-range objective of implementing the principles that had been laid down by his great master Charles de Gaulle on March 24, 1945.[18] More recently, Frédéric Turpin has provided an in-depth study of the relationship between Leclerc and d'Argenlieu, showing that it was the latter who always got de Gaulle's support. In the run-up to March 6, Turpin says, d'Argenlieu and the French government "imprudently gave the green light for launching Opération 'Bentré,' while Leclerc . . . shone more in terms of impulsiveness than of wise moderation."[19]

It was immediately after the Comnindo meeting on February 20, which discussed the reoccupation of northern Indochina, that d'Argenlieu gave Leclerc the green light for Opération Bentré on behalf of the French government. The French 9th Division of Colonial Infantry (9ᵉ DIC) and 2nd Armored Division (2ᵉ DB), which had just about completed the pacification of southern Indochina, boarded French warships between February 27 and March 1, just after d'Argenlieu had returned to Indochina; and on March 1, a proud fleet of thirty-five ships left Saigon to sail north along the coast. General Leclerc himself boarded the *Emile Bertin* on March 3, and from then on could communicate with Hanoi and Saigon only by radio.[20] The stated aim of the operation was to relieve the Chinese troops of their occupation duties and obtain their departure before the end of March.[21] Why March? Because the French needed time to, if necessary, repress any possible indigenous resistance before the rainy season: "Given our uncertainty concerning the attitude of the Annamite population vis-à-vis the French population in northern Indochina, we should get to the big centers as rapidly as possible so as to ensure [their] protection."[22] The big centers where French nationals had been surviving under precarious circumstances since March 9, 1945, under Japanese, Vietnamese, and Chinese rule, were Haiphong, Hon Gai, Nam Dinh, Vinh, Hue, and Hanoi. In Hanoi, there were not just French civilians, but also 3,000 unarmed troops and officers of the French colonial army interned in the Citadel, where they had been since the Japanese disarmed and interned them.

Opération Bentré would be executed by:

- A main landing force consisting of the 9e DIC under General Jean-Etienne Valluy and the Groupement Massu of the 2e DB, altogether 21,000 men. They would go by sea from Saigon and disembark in Haiphong. This landing would have to happen on either March 4, 5, or 6, because these were the only days (until 16, 17, and 18 March) when the tide would allow ships of a certain size to pass over the barrier separating the sea from the river and drop anchor in the port, twenty kilometers inland from the sea.[23]
- Coastal forces already stationed in Ha Long Bay, north of Haiphong.
- Troops that had remained in China since they fled the Japanese onslaught in March 1945. They had received only reluctant and half-hearted support from the Chinese nationalists and U.S. services in China, but had been given ample time to cultivate their anger against Asians in general over the way they had been treated, not least by the "Annamites" who had deserted them in March–April 1945. These troops, who had retained their old weapons and obtained some new ones, were serving under the command of Lieutenant Colonel Robert Quilichini. Some of them had already crossed the border into Tonkin and taken control of the border town of Lai Chau. The plan was that they should move down the western side of the Red River. (After the signing of the March 6 agreement, they moved into Laos instead.)
- A force arriving by plane at the airfield outside Hanoi, with the special mission of rearming the 3,000 French soldiers in the Hanoi Citadel. They were under the command of Lieutenant Colonel Lefèbvre d'Argence, who took his orders from General Raoul Salan. Salan, who had been made commander of the French troops in northern Indochina, was already in Hanoi, where he would

command the planned strike against the Vietnamese government. He now served as part of Sainteny's negotiating team. Salan would direct French military operations in Hanoi, while at the same time negotiating the takeover of occupation duties from the local Chinese troops.[24]

The principal aim of Opération Bentré was retaking Hanoi from the "Revolutionary Annamite Government," as the French called it. This government, like the Chinese occupation troops, was deeply resented by the French in Hanoi, civilian and military alike, many of whom looked forward to the day when they could take revenge for all their suffering since March 9, 1945. After the March 6, 1946, convention was announced, many French in Hanoi were disappointed, the soldiers above all. A report from the French Sûreté, dated March 17, said they were dissatisfied because, "since March 9, they had never lost hope of revenge, at least for the incalculable harassments and snubs they had been angrily enduring from the Annamites. Notably, the majority of the troops did not look kindly on being deprived [by the March 6 accord], from one day to the next, of the satisfactions of all kinds that they had been expecting from a 'repression.'"[25]

The French troops in the Citadel had good reason to envy their comrades in Saigon, who had already been rearmed by the British in September 1945 so that they could carry out their counterrevolutionary coup, oust the revolutionaries from all public buildings, and resume control of the colony. A key element in Opération Bentré was secretly to rearm as many as possible of the 3,000 vengeance-seekers in the Hanoi Citadel, after the French troops had landed in Haiphong, but before they arrived in Hanoi. This would allow the former prisoners of war to defend themselves, and also to protect French civilians, and take up strategic positions before the occupation troops arrived. At first the French considered the possibility of parachuting weapons down over the Citadel, but this was deemed too risky. The Annamites would discover what was happening, and guns might fall into the wrong hands. Instead, it was decided to send twelve Dakotas loaded with arms from Saigon to Gia Lam airfield outside Hanoi, load the arms secretly on trucks and drive them into the city. The documents do not say where the trucks would come from, but they had probably been procured in Hanoi.[26]

Hanoi's reoccupation would be undertaken by three main units: (1) the forces in the Citadel, divided into battalions, with responsibility for maintaining order in predefined zones;[27] (2) a special airborne force (Opération Ponchardier); and (3) the Groupement Massu (named after its commander, Colonel Jacques Massu), which, immediately after disembarking in Haiphong, would push toward Hanoi on Route coloniale 5, or, if blocked, by one of two available canals in order to get into the Red River, sail up it, and penetrate the city of Hanoi on ramps laid out in advance.

Commissioner of the Republic Jean Sainteny had received a supply of posters announcing martial law, on which the French had printed the signature of General

Lu Han, commander of the Chinese occupation troops, on the assumption that he would consent.[28] It is perhaps unnecessary to add that the plans for Opération Bentré insisted on the element of surprise.[29]

Some readers may already have asked themselves: "How was this possible?" And they are right to ask. Opération Bentré was extremely risky. It would most probably have led to a disaster. To rearm 3,000 troops unnoticed in the middle of a city where both the Chinese and Vietnamese knew there was an acute crisis was hardly possible at all, even if the Chinese had gone along with it. To push a unit with armored vehicles from Haiphong to Hanoi without alerting the Vietnamese leaders to the danger was certainly impossible. Still the plan was made and, in the days leading up to March 6, everything was done to prepare for its execution. An alternative peaceful version of Opération Bentré, meant to be executed in case the Vietnamese government should concede to the French reoccupation, was codenamed Bouquet.[30]

A formal problem remained: Indochina south of the 16th parallel was part of the British South-East Asia Command (SEAC), so the French expeditionary force needed Mountbatten's endorsement of any military operation. If forces in Mountbatten's area of responsibility moved into Chiang Kai-shek's area of responsibility, the United Kingdom might get into trouble with China. Mountbatten had in January 1946 withdrawn all British troops from Indochina and left the southern half in French control as far as all practical matters were concerned. He effectively delegated his powers to General Leclerc. In January 1946, Britain had asked the Combined Chiefs of Staff in Washington for permission to let France take full formal responsibility as well, but on February 1, the Americans refused.[31] The British were keen to stay out of trouble,[32] so Mountbatten was shocked to learn, three weeks later, that Leclerc had been preparing a major operation without informing him. He complained and asked Leclerc to give a full report of what was going on. First, the Frenchman answered evasively, but he then provided the information required, except the plan for the reoccupation of Hanoi. Mountbatten smelled a rat and decided to wash his hands of the French immediately. He got his government to negotiate a compromise in Washington as quickly as possible whereby France took full responsibility for southern Indochina, with just one exception: Britain would remain in charge of repatriating Japanese prisoners of war. Since Leclerc had indicated that the French troops would disembark in Haiphong on March 5, Mountbatten specified that responsibility for southern Indochina would formally revert to France on the night of March 4–5, although the last British battalion would in fact only leave Saigon on March 29.[33] Mountbatten's main concern was to ensure that Britain not be implicated in any French conflict with China.[34] The British consul in Saigon had reported on February 21 that General Salan, although optimistic, was foreseeing a pacification campaign in northern Indochina that might last a year or more: "According to a most reliable source in Hanoi General Salan who will command French forces is most optimistic as to the result of operation and he has expressed the opinion that clearing of main centers such as Hanoi, Haiphong, Hue, etc. is likely to take place quickly without meeting any very serious Annamite resistance. He realizes however that Annamite forces will retire to the hills and final pacification of the territory cannot be expected for a year or more."[35] Mountbatten's main concern, however, was to know how France intended to avoid conflict with China.

The French were, of course, aware that the principal weakness of Opération Bentré was its dependence on China's willingness, not merely to tolerate, but actually to facilitate the French reoccupation. China, to be sure, was legally bound to do so, since it recognized French sovereignty, but allowing a French reoccupation by force had the potential to create political problems at home for Chiang Kai-shek's government and might also lead to Vietnamese reprisals against Chinese nationals living in Indochina.[36]

NEGOTIATIONS WITH CHINA

It is generally unwise to set an invasion in motion and place oneself in a situation of no-return if one is not prepared, under any circumstance, to accept the consequences. France was ready to confront the Viet Minh if Ho Chi Minh refused to sign an agreement, but not if this meant war with China as well. Still, in the days from February 27 to March 1, before he could know how the Chinese were going to react, Leclerc sent north what Admiral d'Argenlieu in his memoirs calls "a little armada." As mentioned, it could not turn around since there was not enough drinking water for the troops to stay on board much longer, and the tide made it necessary for the ships to enter Haiphong harbor on March 4, 5, or 6. The French decision-makers were hoping that the arrival of the troops would lead Ho Chi Minh to sign an agreement on French terms, and that the Chinese would offer their support.[37] However, the Chinese and Vietnamese both realized that France was putting its own forces and prestige at risk. This weakened the hand of the French, and they almost panicked when they discovered that the Chinese were not after all willing to cooperate, although they were legally obliged to do so in the February 28 treaty of Chongqing, and although some of the Chinese general officers had been given huge bribes.

General Leclerc realized the risk, and this is why he had tried to get the French government to make a declaration using the term "independence." This, he thought, would make it easier for Sainteny to induce Ho Chi Minh to stay on in Hanoi until the French arrived. Leclerc had also insisted that he get a direct order from the new French government, not just from d'Argenlieu, before setting Opération Bentré in motion. During the period when Leclerc was undertaking the "pacification" of southern Indochina, there had not been much tension between the admiral and the general, but in the run-up to Opération Bentré, their relationship soured. In late January or early February, d'Argenlieu sent the commander of the 9ᵉ DIC, General Jean-Etienne Valluy, to Paris in order to ask urgently for a government order. Valluy presented the Comenindo, which met on January 26 (less than a week after de Gaulle's resignation), with a memorandum, which he later also sent to Foreign Minister Georges Bidault, listing three requirements for a successful reinstallation of French power in the north: (1) military action, (2) diplomatic action vis-à-vis the Chinese, and (3) political action vis-à-vis the "Annamites." He also said there was no time for delay, since the "climatic conditions" for the landing of troops were best in late February or early March. Valluy argued that a purely military operation was undesirable, for four main reasons: (1) it would be met simultaneously with both Chinese and "Annamite" resistance; (2) it might provoke a massacre on the French population in the north; (3) it would increase the risk of protracted guerrilla warfare; and (4) reactions both at home and abroad would be hostile. Military action therefore had to be "covered" by diplomatic and political action. According to Valluy, Ho Chi Minh could be expected to behave reasonably now that he knew the game in Cochinchina was lost.[38] Valluy does not seem to have obtained the order he sought.

On February 13, d'Argenlieu went to Paris himself, leaving Leclerc behind as interim high commissioner. In this capacity, Leclerc would report to d'Argenlieu. Leclerc now feared seeing d'Argenlieu interpose himself between the government and himself, interpreting French Indochina policy in ways that were not necessarily in consonance with the views of the responsible ministers. D'Argenlieu would later characterize Leclerc's efforts to contact the government directly, instead of through him, as "ridiculous."[39] It was on February 14, the day after d'Argenlieu's departure from Saigon, that Leclerc dispatched his message to Paris advising the government to make a public statement promising "independence." The Vietnamese would accept this to mean what the French understood by "autonomy," Leclerc claimed. He strongly urged the government to make this declaration before the French landings in Tonkin.[40] This does not mean that Leclerc wanted to make the landing in the north depend on an agreement with Ho Chi Minh. He wanted a government declaration that would entice Ho to remain in Hanoi and negotiate until *and after* the French troops had landed. This would allow France to negotiate from a position of strength. For Leclerc, words counted less than deeds, and what really counted was to show one's force and determination. The purpose of making a promise was not so much to bind the future as to affect the adversary's immediate behavior. If only France could establish a forceful presence in the north, the rest could be arranged more easily.

It seems possible that Paris would have followed Leclerc's advice to use the term "independence"—against d'Argenlieu's objections—if Sainteny had not reported from a meeting with Ho on February 16 that the Vietnamese might accept something less. Sainteny received a reply from the French government, drafted by d'Argenlieu and approved by the Cominindo, authorizing him to sign an agreement with Vietnam on the basis of "self-government" (the English word was used). D'Argenlieu insisted, however, that nothing should be included in the agreement that would indicate French acceptance of a union of the three *ky*. "President Ho Chi Minh will certainly admit that it would be contrary to democratic principles to adopt a solution on this point without first allowing the peoples concerned to make known their opinion in full liberty and in full independence," the admiral cabled Sainteny.[41] This was a miscalculation. D'Argenlieu probably meant it as an argument against making any kind of concession as far as Cochinchina was concerned. His plan was to develop separate institutions in Cochinchina that would gradually prepare the ground for an expression of popular opinion. However, when Sainteny put forward d'Argenlieu's argument in a talk with Ho Chi Minh, he seems to have used it as a basis for suggesting a referendum. Ho at first balked, but he later accepted. A referendum could not be easily dismissed by someone purporting to represent a democracy, so Sainteny made a promise that d'Argenlieu would later see as disastrous: France would respect the decision of the "populations" of the three *ky*, consulted in a referendum.[42] Sainteny broke the rule that one should only hold a referendum on a matter considered to be vital if one can trust that the result will be acceptable. Ho did not break this rule, since he was sure that a majority would vote in favor of national unity, but Sainteny promised to hold a referendum in Cochinchina, a territory that from the French legal perspective was under total French sovereignty. This promise went beyond what France was prepared to do.

During his stay in Paris from February 17 to 25, the admiral does not seem to have wanted to discuss the risk of war. He assured the government that everything was going well with the negotiations both in Chongqing and Hanoi. When the Cominindo met on February 20, he said that both Franco-Chinese and Franco-Annamite agreements were on the verge of being signed. This must have pleased Minister for Overseas France Marius Moutet, but he wanted to be sure, and at the beginning of March, he asked the high commissioner to "clarify if you will wait to take over from the Chinese troops until you have concluded an agreement with Ho Chi Minh. Our wish is that you seek to obtain the agreement in advance." Moutet also expressed some reticence as far as the plan to rearm the troops interned in the Citadel was concerned: "I add that to prevent incidents similar to the ones that took place in Saigon at the time when the local regiments were rearmed [September 1945] the conditions under which the rearming of the Hanoi Citadel will be undertaken should be vested with the necessary guarantees."[43] And the following cryptic sentence reveals that the minister was not sure of being obeyed: "It is essential for the commanders to understand that the Army cannot but be the instrument of a policy. That we must strive to get results by political means so as to avoid military operations. The soldiers cannot make themselves the judges of this policy, which does not seem to have the support of some of them."[44]

Since January 8, a team of French negotiators led by General Salan had been negotiating with the Chinese government in Chongqing over the terms under which the Chinese occupation army in northern Indochina would be relieved by French forces. These negotiations were linked to larger diplomatic negotiations, not only about Indochina, but also about French extraterritorial rights in China, about trade, and about the territory that France had been leasing at Zhanjiang (also spelled Guangzhouwan or Kwangchowan) on the Leizhou Peninsula north of Hainan Island. In the treaty signed in Chongqing on February 28, the French gave up Zhanjiang as well as all their extraterritorial rights in Shanghai, Tianjin, Hangzhou, and Guangzhou, and promised that Haiphong would be a free port as far as Chinese trade was concerned.[45] In return, France wanted a rapid Chinese withdrawal from Indochina, coordinated with the arrival of French troops. However, when the French troops started to embark in Saigon on February 27, the French negotiators in Chongqing and Hanoi had not yet told their Chinese counterparts that the landing was imminent and would be in force. The Sino-French treaty included a point saying that French troops would take over occupation duties in northern Indochina as early as the second half of March, but it spoke of a "relief" (relève), not of a massive occupation. And the French negotiators had not said anything about what they intended to do with the Vietnamese government.[46]

Immediately after the signing of the bilateral treaty in Chongqing, the French informed Chiang Kai-shek's chiefs of staff that a French landing force was well on its way to Haiphong and would arrive in early March. This did not please the Chinese, and they were even less pleased to learn that the French also wanted their help in rearming the French troops in the Hanoi Citadel.[47] On March 1, the French negotiators thought they had obtained China's agreement to help out with the imminent landing. Colonel Jean Crépin, the main French military negotiator in Chongqing, serving under General Salan, cabled Leclerc: "Agreement reached. The fleet can sail." However, when the French demanded that the Chinese speedily clean up the quays in Haiphong, secure the road from Haiphong to Hanoi, facilitate the landing of twelve planes at Gia Lam airfield outside Hanoi, and provide security on the road from Gia Lam to the Citadel, the Chinese refused. The French insisted that the Chinese military command send the necessary instructions to Hanoi on the very evening of March 1. The Chinese negotiators balked, expressing their reluctance and their fear of Vietnamese reprisals against Chinese nationals in Tonkin, and they found multiple excuses during the next few days for being unable to meet the French wishes.[48] The dispute had to be resolved by Generalissimo Chiang Kai-shek himself, just as he was busy with the Second Plenum of the Sixth Congress of the Guomindang party, where the conservative faction criticized him for handing Vietnam back to the French colonialists. As a last resort, the French asked the British ambassador to China, Sir Adrian Carton de Wiart, to help convince his friend the Generalissimo, but this initiative (made without Mountbatten's knowledge) also failed:

"French Ambassador sent his Counsellor to see me today. Very worried because Leclerc has started his ships off from Saigon to arrive at Haiphong on the 5th. Leclerc thought the agreement was to have been signed already but it has not been. . . . The French want me to help and all I can do is to ask the Generalissimo if he will let them land or not. I am telling him that if he does not it will create a very unpleasant situation," de Wiart wrote Mountbatten.[49]

A month earlier, when General Valluy had presented the plans for the reoccupation of Tonkin to the Cominindo, he had insisted that the operation must not assume a purely military form, but should be "covered" by diplomatic action in relation both to the Chinese government and to the "Annamite leaders."[50] It was this "cover" that failed in Chongqing in the first days of March, but when negotiations fail on the central level, one has to try locally. General Salan now tried to persuade the Chinese commanders in Hanoi to facilitate the coming of the French troops. Salan's task was not easy, for both the commander of the Chinese occupation troops, General Lu Han, and the commander of the Chinese Fifty-third Army, General Zhou Fucheng, were in Chongqing at the Guomindang party plenum. General Salan therefore had to deal with second-rank commanders, General Ma Ying and General Zhao Zhenfan, as well as to negotiate with the head of the Chinese government's consultative delegation to Vietnam, Shao Baichang. On March 3, Salan addressed a letter to General Lu Han, fixing the date for the landing to March 6, explaining how the Citadel would be rearmed, and requesting free access to all airfields in northern Indochina and free use of the road from Haiphong to Hanoi.[51] He soon ran into problems with his interlocutors, who needed to discuss the matter among themselves and then make sure that they were acting in accordance with instructions from Chongqing. For the moment, Salan therefore had to give up his effort to obtain support for rearming the Citadel and concentrate on the even more urgent issue of securing the French landing in Haiphong. After having pressured the Chinese during a meeting that started on March 4 and lasted well into the morning of March 5, Salan obtained permission for the French vessels to "present" themselves in Haiphong on March 6, but not to disembark any troops. Even this agreement, however, was thrown into doubt again later in the day, when new orders arrived from Chongqing. So Salan had to start again from scratch. On the night of March 5–6, he once again reached an agreement with the aim of preventing a Sino-French clash in Haiphong. Yet when the French vessels arrived in the morning of March 6, the Chinese batteries opened fire.

Salan's negotiations with the Chinese officers and the chain of events leading to the so-called "Haiphong incident" have been well described in Lin Hua's book *Chiang Kai-shek, de Gaulle contre Hô Chi Minh* and in Frédéric Turpin's *De Gaulle, les gaullistes et l'Indochine, 1940–1956*. Turpin calls the incident "dramatic and stupid" and holds General Leclerc at least partially responsible, since he had been amply informed about the situation and hence knew that an attempt to disembark would entail a serious risk of incidents.[52] What Leclerc and his staff knew at the time and Lin Hua and Turpin have demonstrated in detail, is that the Sino-French incident in Haiphong did not result from any misunderstanding, or from a decision by local Chinese commanders at variance with orders from Chongqing. Although the central Chinese government and the Chinese military commanders in Indochina certainly had different perspectives,[53] they agreed on the need to prevent the French from going to war against Vietnam. So when the Chinese batteries in Haiphong opened fire on the French ships entering the harbor, they were seeking to defend their own and the Asian interest against a European invasion force. The operation was directed by the Manchu General Wang Lihuan, commander of the 130th Division of the Chinese Fifty-third Army, whose order to open fire was based on his best interpretation of the instructions he had received from Chongqing.[54] At the time he gave his order, he did not yet know that a Franco-Vietnamese agreement was about to be finalized in Hanoi; when he learned this, the fighting stopped, at 11 a.m., just as the final negotiations between Sainteny and Ho Chi Minh were ending and preparations were being made for the signing ceremony. If the negotiators had not reached an agreement at that point, then General Wang would probably have continued to resist the French onslaught in cooperation with Vo Nguyen Giap's Vietnamese forces and with tactical advice from Japanese officers still in his custody.[55] The Chinese actions were not as undisciplined as some historians have pretended. They were premeditated, conscious blackmail, aimed at forcing the French and Vietnamese to reach agreement. The Chinese did not want to be caught up in a Franco-Vietnamese war, so they did their best to impose peace. And they succeeded.

Within the Guomindang a strongly nationalist right wing had long been advancing a policy of helping the Vietnamese to liberate themselves from France. It sought to promote the influence of the pro-Chinese Vietnamese opposition parties, who were far more anti-French than the communists. Guomindang nationalist conservatives were represented among the Chinese officers and advisors in Vietnam. However, Chiang Kai-shek's own main concern was his struggle with Mao Zedong's Red Army in northeastern China, which was resuming in February 1946, after a period of détente brokered by the Americans. Chiang feared that Soviet forces would withdraw from Manchuria and leave it in the hands of the Chinese communists. In southeastern China (Yunnan, Guangxi, Guangdong), Chiang just wanted to secure and deepen his control and get the local generals to provide troops for his war in the north. He neither wanted to be embroiled in a Vietnamese war of liberation nor to be seen as someone who helped France repress a fellow Asian people. Chiang Kai-shek wanted peace on his southern flank while focusing on his struggle for Manchuria. He planned to move the Chinese Sixtieth Army, consisting of troops from Yunnan, to the Vietnamese ports of Haiphong and Hongai, so that they could be shipped to the Manchurian front. For this to be done, it was essential to prevent armed conflict between Vietnam and France. China signed the February 28 treaty, not only to obtain an end to all French extraterritorial rights in China, or in return for a large payment, but also because China's recognition of French sovereignty in Indochina might help secure acceptance internationally of China's sovereignty in Manchuria, which the Japanese had separated from China and made into the independent state of Manchukuo. This was one of the reasons why Chiang promised to withdraw the Chinese troops rather than pursuing Roosevelt's plan to liberate Indochina from France.

In February, before signing the treaty with France, China made a real effort to improve the relationship between its army of occupation and the French representatives in Tonkin, who had complained continually since September 1945 that the Chinese forces were pillaging the country, that they were not respecting French sovereignty, and were doing too little to protect French civilians. The destitute Yunnanese armies, who were certainly lacking in discipline, had in part been withdrawn to China and in part been concentrated in the Haiphong-Hongai coastal region, from which they had expelled the Vietnamese army. Elsewhere, they had been replaced by the better-disciplined Fifty-third Army, which reported directly to the central Chinese government. From February 9 to 26, General Lu Han, governor of Yunnan and supreme commander of the Chinese occupation forces, was in Hanoi, where he did his best to comply with the pro-French policy of his government. In return, he accepted a "precious gift" from France and, according to the French consul in Kunming, advised Ho Chi Minh to come to an agreement with the former colonial power.[56]

NEGOTIATIONS WITH VIETNAM

Jean Sainteny's task as commissioner for Tonkin and north Annam was not easy. He represented his country in an area where French citizens continued to live in semi-captivity, while the Japanese troops were being disarmed by the Chinese. Sainteny tried to protect French civilians as well as the interned soldiers and to forge a relationship with Ho Chi Minh as the president of the "Revolutionary Annamite Government." The two of them met at irregular intervals from October 1945 on, with an important round of talks on December 1, 1945. Sainteny was assisted by Léon Pignon and a French socialist, Louis Caput, and Ho Chi Minh by Vo Nguyen Giap and Hoang Minh Giam. The talks between Sainteny and Ho took on more substance after the January 6 national elections, which bolstered the legitimacy of the DRV. The two main issues were the question of Vietnam's national independence, and the status of the country's southern region, Cochinchina. Sainteny was not prepared to use the word "independence" or to endow the Vietnamese government with any kind of authority in Cochinchina, economically the most important part of Indochina.

February 16 was a decisive day. Ho Chi Minh was in a tough political situation, in the run-up to the first session of the recently elected National Assembly, and with the nationalist parties demanding his resignation, apparently with backing from Chinese occupation authorities. They accused him of preparing to sell out to France. Amid this crisis, which happened before the Vietnamese knew that France was assembling an invasion force, Ho Chi Minh turned to Sainteny and hinted that he might not insist on immediate "independence," but might settle for "self-government," with independence as the ultimate goal. As mentioned above, this happened just as Leclerc had asked the French government to make a public statement that did include the term "independence." Ho Chi Minh's sudden moderation relieved the French government of the need to use the dangerous term and created a temporary illusion among the French that they were about to get a good deal. They would soon be disappointed.

After his apparent breakthrough, Sainteny went to Saigon to receive Leclerc's instructions. He returned to Hanoi on February 19, a day on which there were anticommunist nationalist demonstrations in the streets. The opposition knew that Ho was negotiating, accused him of preparing to sell out national independence, and demanded that he step back and leave the presidency in the hands of the former emperor, Bao Dai. On the morning of February 22, Ho was sufficiently exasperated by the political situation, and by China's support of his rivals, to actually ask Supreme Advisor Bao Dai to take over, but that same evening he reversed himself and withdrew the suggestion. He now entered into active negotiations with both Chinese representatives and local nationalist politicians, which resulted in an agreement on February 24 to form a new government of national union. This provided Ho with renewed authority, and he now returned to a tougher line in his talks with Sainteny.

In the following days, there were several meetings between the two, but no progress on substance. Then came the news that the Sino-French treaty had been signed in Chongqing, and that it provided for a French relief of the Chinese occupation forces. This led to a new sense of urgency on the Vietnamese side, although the first priority of the Vietnamese government was not to reach an agreement with France but to rally all parties behind the government so that they would join forces in the coming war of national resistance. For this reason, the planned opening of Vietnam's first National Assembly was advanced from March 3 to March 2.

On that day, the National Assembly met for the first time under the impression of the menace of a French invasion. In a brief meeting, with 242 delegates present, it made a number of decisions and unanimously approved of Ho Chi Minh's new coalition government of "Union and Resistance." One of the main nationalist leaders, Nguyen Hai Than, became vice president and another, Nguyen Tuong Tam, foreign minister. A third, Vu Hong Khanh, was—as mentioned earlier—elected vice president of a National Resistance Committee, led by Ho's close confidant Vo

Nguyen Giap. The session of the National Assembly had originally been meant to last several days, but for security reasons, it was shortened to just four hours. The reason may have been that Ho and Giap expected the French troops to arrive at any moment. Since there had not yet been any further progress in the talks between Ho and Sainteny, the Vietnamese leadership probably expected that the French landing would lead to an all-out confrontation. The Chinese saw the danger too and started to apply heavy pressure on both sides to make peace.

BLACKMAIL FOR PEACE

It has not been possible to establish exactly the role of Chiang Kai-shek himself in the events that followed. Hence it is possible that his generals acted independently of him when refusing to go along with the French demands that they support Opéra-tion Bentré.[57] But it seems more likely that the Generalissimo agreed with his generals, indeed instructed them to resist the French landing until a Franco-Vietnamese agreement had been signed. On the internal Chinese level, the policy of blackmail had its basis in recommendations made in a February 6 report by Yuan Zijian, the political advisor to General Lu Han, commander of the Chinese forces of occupation in northern Indochina: "Right now, France's hands are tied with regard to Vietnam, and we hold the key to the situation," Yuan Zijian said. He concluded that the only way to avoid a series of disasters was to pressure the French to reach some kind of equitable understanding with the Vietnamese, including agreement on Vietnam's political status.[58]

So let us unfold, chronologically, the story of the four decisive days of Chinese blackmail:

March 3: A French liaison officer in Hanoi asked his Chinese counterpart if, in the event that the French disembarked without having signed an agreement, the Chinese would open fire. The answer was yes, but the Chinese were putting strong pressure on the various Annamite parties to unite. It would be preferable to wait for the Vietnamese to unite in a sincere entente. The French troops ought not to arrive before this entente had been realized.[59] The formation of Ho Chi Minh's new national union government had actually been cleared in the National Assembly the day before, but the new government of Union and Resistance did not meet till March 4.

March 4: During a long Franco-Chinese meeting in Hanoi, General Ma Ying mentioned the possibility of "complications with the Annamite elements. If there is a fight *[bagarre]*, there will be trouble, [and] order and security will be compromised; it is preferable to seek a solution to fend off the difficulties that may arise in case of disturbances." Salan first answered that there was "indeed a possibility of fighting, but as our arrival proceeds, we shall take responsibility for order and security, and at that time, we shall ensure order and security with all our means. There will perhaps be some wavering in the beginning, but it will disappear rapidly, and there is no reason to expect any major difficulties." A little later, Salan added: "Moreover there are talks with the Annamite government and it is not impossible that we shall become friends with them. . . . When you leave, the agreement with the Annamites will most likely be signed, and in this way the situation will be clarified." The Chinese said they preferred the affair to be resolved politically before the arrival of the French troops. Salan replied: "We are working actively on this."[60]

Ho Chi Minh's new coalition government held its first meeting that day and authorized him to continue the negotiations. Meanwhile, the Cominindo asked the high commissioner if he intended to wait with the military operation till after an agreement had been concluded with Ho Chi Minh, saying: "Our desire is that you strive to obtain the agreement first."[61] D'Argenlieu informed Leclerc that the French government had expressed a wish to see an agreement signed with Ho Chi Minh *before* the "relief operation," but added that he personally was well aware of the plan to disembark at Haiphong and Hongay and to launch an operation in Hanoi. "In the end you must decide yourself," he said.[62] What this means is probably that d'Argenlieu, in spite of the government's desire, envisaged a landing without any prior agreement, and assumed that Leclerc did the same. In order to make sure that the French government would not disavow them, d'Argenlieu warned Marius Moutet against the Chinese maneuvers and "a hidden understanding" *(accord occulte)* between the Annamites and the local Chinese command, which could lead to military conflict. Since d'Argenlieu probably did not want to be too explicit about the danger, his own words were also somewhat cryptic: "If, and this is the main factor, the government continues to support us, we shall succeed in crossing this bridge . . . it seems to me appropriate to allow all and sundry a few days to assess the action to which we are now committed. Don't be surprised therefore if my announcements remain strictly cool and objective."[63] These were the words of a man who knew that his decisions might lead to open warfare, and that his government would dislike it, but also would not have the guts to disavow him, notably since he enjoyed the support of General de Gaulle.

March 5: In the morning, the commander of the Chinese Fifty-third Army sent a cable from Chongqing to Hanoi saying: "Push Ho Chi Minh to sign with the French. . . . Order the 130th Division of the Fifty-third Army to prevent the French from landing before the completion of the Franco-Vietnamese negotiations."[64] Salan also informed Leclerc that the Chinese had promised to exert strong pressure on Ho Chi Minh during the night in order to obtain an agreement.[65]

In Hanoi, the discussions between Salan and the Chinese generals now touched directly on the negotiations between Sainteny and Ho Chi Minh. The Chinese pointed out that the Vietnamese were accusing the Chinese of having sold them out to foreigners. Salan countered: "The Annamites are cunning. Ho Chi Minh is playing a double game. He even goes as far as to make his men demonstrate in the streets to impress [us]. The matter is urgent; there is a knife to our throats: there are our men, there are our ships. I wish General Zhao could come and see what our fleet looks like tomorrow, then he would quickly understand."

General Zhao Zhenfan did not let himself be intimidated, but insisted: "Unlike you, I reckon that there will be serious incidents. There will be attacks on French as well as Chinese by the Annamites. In case of an attack, we must take up defensive positions and disregard the protection of French nationals." Salan then repeated a promise he had given the previous day to take personal responsibility for any incidents: "There may be murders, but no one can prevent this. With your way of reasoning, the French will never disembark. . . . What I ask is simply that the Chinese do not fire on the French, that there be no incidents between the French and the Chinese, that the Chinese make it possible for us to land. We are responsible for the affair."

The Chinese turned a deaf ear to this demand and returned to the necessity of first signing an agreement with Ho Chi Minh. Salan protested: "one cannot reach any understanding with him. He changes constantly. . . . Ho Chi Minh is playing a double game. Once we are on the quay, the matter will be settled here."[66]

Meanwhile the author of the Bentré plan, Lieutenant Colonel Lecomte, realized that France had got itself into a trap. He was in Hanoi, communicating with Leclerc over the radio, and he now wrote a handwritten note to Sainteny that would later become famous, saying:

> Since it is now physically impossible to modify our plan, we risk bloody incidents with the Chinese, with the international consequences that such events entail. The only hope we have of modifying the Chinese attitude is to inform them that an agreement between ourselves and the Annamite government has been signed. Given the seriousness of the situation and the scope of the possible conflict, I ask in the name of General Leclerc, who has given me the authority to tell you this, that you instantly do all that is in your power to arrive at an agreement as soon as possible, even if this should be at the price of initiatives that may later be repudiated.[67]

So at this point Ho Chi Minh could have obtained almost anything he wanted, at least on paper. But then, of course, the Chinese were not only blackmailing the French. They put pressure on the Vietnamese as well. Historians have not, unfortunately, had access to any records of conversations between Ho Chi Minh and the Chinese generals. In the evening of March 5, General Zhao met with Ho Chi Minh and then personally carried Ho's proposals to the French negotiators.[68] At this late stage, the Vietnamese negotiators suddenly brought up an explosive new issue, namely, the need to fix the number of troops the French could have in the north, how long they could stay, and where they would be allowed to have their garrisons. Well into the small hours of March 6, the Vietnamese insisted that no French troops should be allowed to enter Hanoi and demanded that the troops in the Hanoi Citadel be repatriated. It was in this situation, with no time to lose and no chance

FIGURE 3. Vietnamese painting showing Ho Chi Minh, smoking his trademark American cigarette, on the night of March 5–6, 1946, pondering whether or not to sign a compromise agreement with France. Chinese and French demons loom behind him. Museum of the Revolution, Hanoi.

to seek advice from Saigon or Paris, that Sainteny and Salan signed on to obligations that their government would find it difficult to respect. These were written into a military appendix to the political agreement, the text of which had already been finalized.[69]

March 6: In the early morning, the first French ships reached Haiphong, where they were met with heavy Chinese fire. At first, the French did not respond, although they suffered many casualties, but when the Chinese continued to fire, the French bombarded the Chinese positions and hit an ammunition dump, which blew up in a thunderous explosion. The fighting went on until 11 a.m., while the negotiators in Hanoi continued to wrangle over the final details of the military appendix to the convention. The text had been more or less ready when they restarted negotiations at 6 a.m., but the talks about the appendix lasted until 11 a.m., and General Salan was only given a short time to look at it at 4 p.m. before the accords as a whole, including the appendix, were signed in a ceremony at 5 p.m.[70]

A French intelligence report confirmed the crucial role of the Chinese in advising Ho during the final phase of the negotiations: "the Chinese authorities were kept informed minute by minute [by the Vietnamese negotiators] during the negotiations."[71] The Chinese were probably also instrumental in ensuring that not only the president, but also the vice president of the Resistance Committee, Vu Hong Khanh, signed the convention, together with Sainteny.[72] This was fortunate for Ho and the Viet Minh, since it prevented Vu Hong Khanh and his party from accusing the Viet Minh of having sold out to France.

That evening, d'Argenlieu explained to the French government why he had permitted the agreement to be signed: "The change in the attitude of the chiefs of staff in Chongqing and the desire of the local Chinese military to see us conclude an agreement with the Annamite government in Hanoi before the imminent landing of our troops led us to hasten its conclusion."[73]

AFTERMATH

Although there was no more shooting in Haiphong after 11 a.m., no French soldier had yet been able to disembark. Only a symbolic company was allowed to disembark that afternoon. More troops were permitted to come ashore on March 7, after two representatives of the Vietnamese government had greeted Leclerc on board the *Sénégalais.* Leclerc told them bluntly that he would have arrived "with or without your agreement."[74] The Chinese designated a zone where the French would be allowed to stay. The first significant contingent of troops disembarked the following day and stayed within the zone. Over the next two weeks, it was not at all a given that the March 6 agreement would hold. The reaction of the Vietnamese public was at first uncertain. Although Vu Hong Khanh had signed together with Ho, other nationalist opponents of the Viet Minh accused the government of having sold out, and it convened a big meeting in Hanoi in the evening of March 7 to defend itself. Giap, Khanh, and Ho spoke, explaining the need for an entente with France, and the crowd cheered. Giap said three options had been open: a long-drawn-out resistance, a short resistance, or a negotiated deal. The first would have caused enormous suffering, without certainty of success, because of unfavorable international circumstances. The second would have led to defeat, since France had ample access to modern arms. The third option had therefore been chosen. It would allow Vietnam to build both economic strength and military force. Giap compared the March 6 agreement to the agreement made by Lenin's revolutionary government with Germany at Brest-Litovsk in 1918: "Did not Russia, thanks to this agreement, become very strong? The dominant idea, the goal of the government, is peace for progress. The road that has been opened by the convention leads to total independence in the future, and this remains our goal."[75] Giap and Ho's speeches took the sting out of the opposition and paved the way for allowing Leclerc's forces to march from Haiphong to Hanoi and enter the Vietnamese capital on March 18. In official Vietnamese historiography, the March 6 agreement is considered to have been an astute maneuver, allowing the Vietnamese government to avoid having to fight both the Chinese and French at the same time. The government "sought a compromise with the French so as to put an end to the country's occupation by Chiang Kai-shek's forces and to buy time."[76] Time was needed in order to get rid, not only of the Chinese occupation, but also of "reactionary" Vietnamese groups supported by the Chinese, and to build and prepare the Vietnamese Army for a long war of resistance.

It was also not certain that the French would respect the agreement. The French colonial soldiers in the Hanoi Citadel had not given up all hope of revenging themselves, and the French expeditionary force remained ready to carry out Opération Bentré. On March 8, d'Argenlieu complained in private to General Valluy: "I marvel, yes, *Mon Général*, that is the right word, I marvel at France having such a fine expeditionary force in Indochina, and that its commanders prefer to talk rather than fight."[77] On the following day, he made a speech in commemoration of those who had resisted the Japanese coup on March 9 one year earlier. He declared that he would accept the March 6 convention, which was "good,"[78] but referred to the Vietnamese government only as "the Hanoi government," and he compared the status of Vietnam to that of Cambodia, with which France had already signed a convention on January 7.[79] Meanwhile, the French troops and officers in Haiphong were impatient to move on to Hanoi. The Chinese stalled for fear of disturbances, but the French reminded them that they were obliged by treaty to hand over all authority to them before the end of March. The French now also reopened their request to secretly rearm the troops in the Hanoi Citadel. Reluctantly, the Chinese gave their permission, and ten aircraft took off from Tan Son Nhut airfield outside Saigon loaded with arms, to be transported secretly on trucks from Gia Lam airfield into

FIGURE 4. A quintet of French decision-makers in Indochina. Photograph taken just after the March 6, 1946, Franco-Vietnamese accords were signed in Hanoi. From the left: Procurator-General Maurice Walrand, Federal Commissioner of Political Affairs Léon Pignon, General Jean-Etienne Valluy, General Jean-Philippe Leclerc, and Commissioner of the French Republic Jean Sainteny. Reproduced from Jean Sainteny, *Histoire d'une paix manquée: Indochine, 1945–1947* (1953).

Hanoi. Then the Chinese backtracked, and General Salan was forced to order the aircraft to turn around and land at Pakse in Laos instead. The guns arrived only on March 21 or 22, three or four days after Leclerc's forces had marched into the city, without a shot being fired.[80]

No one has applauded the Chinese role in obtaining the March 6 agreement and in securing respect for it in the ensuing critical weeks. Chiang Kai-shek's army of 200,000 men, particularly the Yunnanese troops, had been pillaging and living off the land. They were despised by French and Vietnamese alike. Almost exactly at the same time as the March 6 accord was signed in Hanoi, the former British prime minister Winston Churchill made a famous speech in Fulton, Missouri, in which he said: "From Stettin in the Baltic to Trieste in the Adriatic an iron curtain has descended across the [European] Continent. Behind that line lie all the capitals of the ancient states of Central and Eastern Europe. Warsaw, Berlin, Prague, Vienna, Budapest, Belgrade, Bucharest and Sofia. . . . The outlook is also anxious in the Far East and especially in Manchuria." Stalin had just decided to withdraw the Soviet occupation troops from Manchuria before Chiang Kai-shek was able to replace them with sufficiently strong forces to prevent a takeover by the Chinese communists. By June 1946, the Chinese civil war broke out in earnest, and three years later, Chiang Kai-shek was forced to flee to Taiwan. In 1950, some of the same Chinese officers who had served Chiang Kai-shek in Vietnam during 1945–46 would be sent by Mao Zedong to the "liberated areas" of northern Indochina as advisors, instructors, and road builders in the service of the Viet Minh.[81] The People's Republic of China felt no urge to boast of China's pacifying role during 1945–46, but when we look carefully into the events of February–March 1946, it is clear that the short and fragile Franco-Vietnamese "peace" from March to November, which allowed Ho Chi Minh to visit France and step onto the world stage as a statesman, and made it possible for Giap to build up his army, was *a peace imposed by China*. China played on the fact that neither the French nor the Viet Minh was willing to risk a two-front war. General Valluy had made it clear to the French prime minister at the beginning of February that a two-front war was unacceptable: "Tonkin cannot wait more than one or two months for a solution . . . this must not at any rate take on the appearance of a purely military action, because this would lead to a simultaneous confrontation with the Chinese and Annamites." The Viet Minh leaders made the same point internally shortly before they decided to sign the March 6 agreement: "If France accepts Vietnamese sovereignty, we can make peace. Peace in order to annihilate the ambitious white Chinese, the Vietnamese reactionaries, and the remaining French fascists. Otherwise, we would be isolated and forced to fight two adversaries at the same time, which could lead to defeat."[82]

How long did China continue to impose its peace? Arguably, until September 18, when the last Chinese unit pulled out of Haiphong. As long as at least some Chinese occupation troops were present in northern Indochina, an outbreak of open hostilities between France and Vietnam risked having international repercussions. The triangular power structure, with three armies present on the same territory, tended to preserve the peace. The result was a kind of informal modus vivendi, with the French and the Vietnamese finding ways of coping with each other, without ever agreeing. Just three days before the end of the Chinese occupation on September 18, however, Ho Chi Minh and Marius Moutet decided on their own modus vivendi.

3

Modus Vivendi

Late in the evening of September 14, 1946, Ho Chi Minh went to see Marius Moutet in his Paris apartment. Ho had been in France through the summer, giving interviews and making an indelible personal impression on many French and foreign figures, but the formal Franco-Vietnamese negotiations at Fontainebleau, at a safe distance from the Paris melting pot, had not led to any agreement. The main stumbling blocks were still the questions of national independence and uniting the Vietnamese *ky*. France had not been willing to grant independence, and the Vietnamese had not been willing to settle for less, except as a transitory arrangement. And, even more important, France had refused to fix a time for the referendum on Vietnamese unity, and the Vietnamese would not sign onto any agreement unless they could mark a date for such a referendum in their calendars.

The day before, the Vietnamese negotiators—aside from Ho himself, who remained in Paris—had left Fontainebleau to board the ship *Pasteur* at Marseille and sail home, leaving unfinished business behind them. Ho had lunch with Moutet, and they agreed that it was unacceptable for the president of Vietnam to go home empty-handed. Drafts were exchanged for a new preliminary agreement, reconfirming the March 6 Convention, adding a few points, and fixing a definitive round of negotiations for January 1947. Moutet received Ho at home in the evening, and after midnight on September 15, they signed the agreement in the minister's bedroom.[1] On the way back to his hotel, Ho Chi Minh pondered the possible reactions in Vietnam to the disappointing outcome of his long stay abroad since May. He is said to have murmured: "I have just signed my death sentence."[2]

Ho was not, however, condemned by his compatriots. The DRV benefited significantly from the modus vivendi agreement, which in fact weakened the French position, particularly in Cochinchina. The most important point in the agreement was a cease-fire in southern Indochina, where the Viet Minh guerrillas had become increasingly active since the best and most experienced French forces had left for the north in March. The cease-fire agreement meant de facto recognition of the guerrilla forces and made it difficult for the French to continue denouncing them as terrorists. The modus vivendi contained eleven articles, outlining the conditions for Franco-Vietnamese cooperation in the economic, cultural, diplomatic, and military fields, but apart from the cease-fire and a promise from both sides to respect democratic liberties, it did not include new concessions. It stipulated that a definitive round of negotiations should be organized once the institutions of the French Fourth Republic had been put in place by January 1947.

Why did France and Vietnam fail to reach a genuine agreement in the spring and summer of 1946? Why did they have to satisfy themselves with a modus vivendi? Before analyzing the implementation of the preliminary agreement, we must seek answers to these questions. Three possible reasons will be considered: (1) the continued presence of the Chinese occupation forces in northern Indochina; (2) the fact that neither side was satisfied with the March 6 accords—rather, each saw them as a stepping-stone to advancing its own position; and (3) the unclear political situation in France: the Fourth Republic did not yet have a constitution and the lines of governmental authority were blurred.

THE SLOW CHINESE WITHDRAWAL

The continued Chinese presence in the north was a nuisance for both the French and the Vietnamese. While the French expected the Vietnamese to be more forthcoming once they had lost their Chinese "protection," the Viet Minh leaders looked forward to the day when they could oust the pro-Chinese anticommunist nationalists from the government and from the provinces they controlled militarily along the Chinese border. In April, the Vietnamese coalition government agreed to ask the Chinese Fifty-third Army to stay in Tonkin until a definitive agreement had been concluded with France, but this was at the instigation of the VNQDD, whose leader Nguyen Tuong Tam was foreign minister.[3]

The Chinese presence in the north was one of the reasons why the French government decided to invite Ho to France. Leclerc and Sainteny wanted to get him out of reach of Chinese influence. On March 15, Leclerc sent a telegram to d'Argenlieu warning against a possible Chinese scheme to disrupt the newly established Franco-Vietnamese cooperation: "In order to frustrate this scheme, we must break the Sino-Annamite collusion and as soon as possible remove the Viet Minh government from the influence of the Chinese and the extremist Annamite parties."[4] Leclerc favored immediate negotiations in France and instructed General Salan to tell Ho there would be a conference in Paris.[5] This was just before Leclerc made his entry into Hanoi. His promise had not been cleared with d'Argenlieu, who in fact had told the French government a week earlier that it would be a serious mistake to negotiate in Paris, since this would reduce the authority of the high commissioner and give Tonkin better treatment than the other members of the Indochinese Federation. He also no doubt disliked the prospect of Ho meddling in French politics, given his record as a veteran of communist proselytizing and his numerous contacts in France. D'Argenlieu agreed that the Annamite representatives should be extricated from the unhealthy atmosphere in Hanoi, but from his Gaullist perspective, Paris would be even worse. The best place to negotiate, he thought, was the small highland town of Dalat, whose cooler climate had made it a preferred resort in the hot season for French colonial administrators; d'Argenlieu was even working on a long-held plan to make Dalat the new capital of the Indochinese Federation. Talks there would not be disturbed by "spontaneous or organized mass demonstrations."[6] On March 24, he invited Ho Chi Minh to meet him on board one of his warships in Ha Long Bay north of Haiphong, but did not invite Leclerc. At this meeting, d'Argenlieu rejected Ho's demand for immediate negotiations in Paris, thus contradicting Leclerc, who became extremely angry.[7]

Leclerc's arguments in the March 15 telegram show that the principal motive for his more conciliatory attitude was the fear of a simultaneous conflict with the Chinese and the Viet Minh. He based his judgment on the situation in the north. D'Argenlieu took a longer view and mainly feared the concessions that Ho might extract from the left-leaning French government after de Gaulle had left power. On March 27, Leclerc defended the March 6 agreement in his long, previously mentioned report, which he sent informally to de Gaulle.[8] If his forces had been engaged in serious combat both with the Annamites and the Chinese, he said, "the reconquest of Tonkin, even partially, would have been impossible." He criticized d'Argenlieu (without naming him) for not having informed the French government properly of this danger. According to Leclerc, France had won the first round. The second would have to be won by means of politics and negotiations. As soon as the Chinese had left, he thought, the problems would be a lot easier to resolve, since the French would then be in a stronger position.[9]

Leclerc was wrong to think that the Chinese influence made the Vietnamese less reasonable. As we have seen, the Chinese actually wanted the Vietnamese government to cooperate with France. To some extent, the Viet Minh also needed the French to counterbalance China; once the Chinese were gone, the Viet Minh would be in better control internally, have better prospects of being able to fight a protracted resistance struggle, and hence be less willing to compromise. This was well understood by the key French policy-maker Léon Pignon, who had assisted Sainteny in the talks leading up to the March 6 agreement, played a significant role in the French delegation to the Fontainebleau conference from July to September 1946, and joined d'Argenlieu in Saigon as his main political advisor on October 2. Pignon was a brilliant

FIGURE 5. Ho Chi Minh with Admiral Georges Thierry d'Argenlieu, high commissioner of French Indochina, on board the French Navy ship *Emile Bertin* in Ha Long Bay, north of Ha Long, March 24, 1946. D'Argenlieu, an admiral, preferred such naval encounters as a way of displaying French power. Courtesy Philippe Devillers.

student from the French Ecole coloniale and the "Machiavelli" of the French administration. No ideology except the national interest counted for him. In Indochina, it was in the interest of France to divide and rule.[10] In early 1946, when the influence of China and the China-oriented Vietnamese parties was strong and growing, Pignon wanted to pull the Viet Minh away from China and toward France. Hence he eagerly assisted Sainteny in his talks with Ho Chi Minh. After March 6, Pignon quickly realized that the Viet Minh was France's most formidable enemy, and then developed a positive interest in former Emperor Bao Dai, as well as the leaders of the pro-Chinese nationalist parties, as counterbalancing forces to the Viet Minh. The Chinese troops were detested by the Vietnamese and French populations alike, but it was their presence that made it necessary for both the French and the Vietnamese to manage their problems without resorting to violence. Once the Chinese had left, neither side would have to fear a two-front war. Pignon and d'Argenlieu, with their more long-term view, understood this better than the shortsighted Leclerc.

Leclerc continued to entertain the illusion that the Viet Minh would turn more reasonable once the Chinese had left. When most of the Chinese troops had gone home at the beginning of June, he wrote to the MRP's chairman, Maurice Schumann, saying that there was no longer any need to make concessions to Vietnam. France now held all the vital points in Indochina, Leclerc asserted, thus all the trumps: "I think, under these circumstances, that it would be very dangerous for the French representatives at the negotiations to let themselves be duped by the deceptive language (democracy, resistance, the New France) that Ho Chi Minh and his team have mastered to perfection."[11] Schumann forwarded the letter to Prime Minister Georges Bidault.

Leclerc's position had hardened, but he had not changed his general attitude. It was merely common sense, from his perspective, that the essential thing was to have forces on the ground. Once the French military presence had been solidified, France could decide how generous it wanted to be. When Leclerc left his command and returned to Paris, he told a group of influential newsmen that a firm French attitude would help make the Vietnamese more conciliatory. In the event of conflict, the Vietnamese government would have to withdraw to the interior of the country. And if that should happen, then French control of rich Cochinchina and of key locations in the north would, after a while, force the Vietnamese to change their attitude.[12] Leclerc left his command on July 18. He was replaced by General Jean-Etienne Valluy, who until then had commanded the French forces in northern Indochina. This was while the Fontainebleau conference was going on, with several committees working on the various chapters of a proposed treaty. With the prospect of improving their position in the wake of the Chinese departure, the French did not have any strong incentive to compromise. In Leclerc's final report from his mission, he pointed out as a problem that the French garrisons in the north were "almost prisoners"; they had no room to move. This actually resulted from the military appendix to the March 6 agreement, and a follow-up military convention ("Conférence d'Etat-major") that General Salan signed on April 3.[13] The March 6 convention itself stipulated that a force of 10,000 Vietnamese and 15,000 French troops were to relieve the Chinese occupation army north of the 16th parallel. The number of French and Vietnamese troops in each garrison was also fixed. Vietnamese troops would remain under Vietnamese control but were to be at the disposal of the French commander. French forces in the north were explicitly not to exceed 15,000, while no ceiling was established for the Vietnamese army outside of the "forces of relief." A permanent Vietnamese delegation would be accredited to the French commander, and in order to prevent local incidents, the Vietnamese were to be informed forty-eight hours in advance of any French troop movements. There were to be mixed liaison commissions on all important levels. When Valluy left the north to take overall command in Saigon, the troops in the north got a new commander, Colonel Jean Crépin, who served for only a month, during which a serious incident occurred at Bac Ninh, just north of Hanoi. Shortly afterward, Louis-Constant Morlière, a three-star general, took over the northern command. All these commanders had to worry as much about their relations with the Chinese occupation army as with the government of Vietnam, and the Chinese presence made it essential to prevent incidents such as the one at Bac Ninh from escalating.

As long as the Chinese troops were there, it was difficult for both France and the Viet Minh to improve their positions. The Viet Minh wanted to get rid of the pro-Chinese nationalist parties, whose armies had ousted the Viet Minh from certain areas with Chinese support. Cooperation in the coalition government was uneasy at best. The Viet Minh were eager to get the Chinese to leave, and the French could not wait for them to go. The Chinese continued to blackmail the French, however, and made their departure contingent on substantial further payments. The Chinese promised over and over again to live up to their obligation in the February 28 Chongqing treaty and leave French Indochina. Still, it took until June before the bulk of the troops pulled out, and even then a few important Yunnanese units remained in the strategic city of Haiphong. It was they who sailed out of the harbor on September 18 in order to play their part in the Chinese Civil War, which had broken out in Manchuria in June. Thus the stabilizing triangular power structure in northern Indochina gave way to a bipolar conflict between two parties, the French and the Viet Minh, who had both been waiting for a chance to push their positions forward in relation to the compromise they had been forced to make on March 6.

TWO ADVANCING FORCES

The second reason why France and Vietnam did not reach any new agreement after March 6, except for a modus vivendi, was that neither the French nor the Vietnamese government really valued the accord. They saw it as a stepping-stone to advance their own positions rather than the beginning of a road to further compromise or win-win solutions. Instead of preparing themselves mentally and practically to move forward together, they both sought to make changes on the ground so as to improve their positions before the next round of negotiations.

There might have been room for compromise. The DRV could have opted to concentrate on building an independent state in the north, refrain from waging armed struggle in the south, and postpone national unification to a later stage. Alternatively, it could have accepted something less than independence, subject to France allowing a referendum on national unification. The French could have let the north go its own way, and concentrated on modernizing Cochinchina, Cambodia, and Laos. Or they could have tolerated a development in the direction of Vietnamese unity, while insisting on a certain number of French prerogatives and a sustained French military presence in all of Indochina. The March 6 agreement did not bring the parties much closer to a compromise of either kind, since instead of trading sovereignty for unity or vice versa, it met both of the two main national demands halfway. "Freedom" was not quite the same as independence but could be interpreted that way. A referendum was not quite national unity but could be expected to bring it about.

When Sainteny told Ho Chi Minh, after signing the March 6 convention, how satisfied he was that war had been averted, Ho answered: "And it grieves me, because basically you are the one who have won. You know very well that I wanted more than that. . . . But after all I also understand that one cannot get everything in one day."[14] Compromises are easier to reach when one party is advancing and the other retreating than when both are advancing, or think they are. The Vietnamese sought to solidify their republican institutions in the north and to consolidate control of the whole of Tonkin/Bac Bo as soon as the Chinese forces left. They also wanted to use this occasion to rid themselves of their coalition partners in the government of Union and Resistance, who had been dreaming of replacing French domination with Sino-American influence. And in Cochinchina/Nam Bo, the Vietnamese government backed an increasingly active guerrilla campaign meant to dissuade anyone from collaborating with France as long as no agreement had been reached. The French for their part put major emphasis on seeking to establish a local, autonomous, progressive, and pro-French government in Cochinchina and to build Laos and Cambodia into solid components of the Indochinese Federation. While this was being done, they preferred not to make any dramatic new deals with the Hanoi government, which they saw as representing only Tonkin. The French hope was to build strong federal institutions and then cope with the Hanoi government as representing just one of five units. In the long run, the Vietnamese were no more inclined to tolerate French military presence than the French were to accept a state controlled by the Viet Minh. The French intended under no circumstances to let Hanoi control the south, while the primary Vietnamese goal was north-south national unification.

All this meant that the Franco-Vietnamese preparatory talks in Dalat (d'Argenlieu's preferred location) from April 17 to May 11, and at Fontainebleau from July 6 to September 10, were doomed almost from the outset. Both sides had prepared themselves well, and they held a number of interesting discussions, but the stumbling block that prevented any negotiated agreement was the referendum on Vietnamese national unity that had been promised on March 6. The Vietnamese insisted that the French set a date, and were sure of winning the popular vote. The French, well aware that even the prospect of a referendum would kill all hope of persuading the Cochinchinese to establish viable autonomous institutions, consistently refused to set a date. This sealed the fate of the negotiations.

In April, at Dalat, the two main negotiators were Max André, a Christian Democratic party (MRP) member of the French National Assembly, and Vietnam's foreign minister, Nguyen Tuong Tam (VNQDD), while d'Argenlieu, as head of the Indochinese Federation, tried to play the role of a neutral host. Because of his status as a foreign minister, Tam did not engage directly in the negotiations, so in practice the Vietnamese delegation was led by Vo Nguyen Giap. The tone was not good. When the conference broke down, d'Argenlieu felt it was time to concentrate on building the rest of the Federation and leave Tonkin to its own fate for the time being. He reported to Paris that the Chinese presence made it necessary to continue to tread cautiously in the north, but if France concentrated on building up the Federation's other components, the "free state in the north" would probably want to join it at a later stage, at least militarily, economically and culturally. A breakdown of the Franco-Vietnamese conference in France, which was then just on the planning stage, would do no harm, d'Argenlieu affirmed. It would give Laos, Cambodia, Cochinchina, and southern Annam—not to mention France—"total freedom of action."[15] In May, he proposed that representatives of the other federated states be invited to Paris at the same time as the delegation from Hanoi. When the French government rejected this proposal, he instead summoned representatives of the other "countries" to Dalat for what would be called the "second Dalat conference."[16]

Rather than digging into the files of the futile negotiations,[17] we should look at the attempts made by each side to advance their positions while the talks were going on, and while waiting for the Chinese troops to leave. The French experimented with Cochinchinese autonomy and set up federal institutions to govern all five parts of Indochina; the guerrilla movement in the south sought to undermine these French experiments; and the Viet Minh endeavored to take full internal control in the north, while building up armed forces to prepare for a protracted war. These actions may explain the absence of an agreement better than anything that was being said in Dalat or Fontainebleau.

In Saigon, French authorities established a provisional Cochinchinese government, but inasmuch as an overwhelming majority of southerners favored national unification,[18] the provisional government only represented a tiny, wealthy, pro-French minority. It faced a hostile public opinion and an increasingly powerful guerrilla movement, led by the Viet Minh in cooperation with the powerful religious sects. The French never trusted the Cochinchinese government enough to give it real power. The experiment with Cochinchinese autonomy thus proved a failure.

The linchpin of d'Argenlieu's Federation was Cochinchina. One week after the March 6 accord, the Cochinchinese Council demanded the same status as the Vietnamese government. It also wanted to be a "free state." The commissioner of the French Republic for Cochinchina, Jean Cédile, declared that the March 6 agreement was only a local convention for the north, and that the referendum mentioned in the convention would be held only when order had been completely restored.[19] On March 26, the Cochinchinese Council had designated Dr. Nguyen Van Thinh as president of a new provisional government of the Cochinchinese Republic, but it took until June 1 before he was formally recognized as such by the high commissioner. The March 26 decision provoked a wave of assassinations of "traitors" and stepped up an already ongoing propaganda war between "unionists" and "separatists" in the south. In April, a Cochinchinese mission visited Paris, and d'Argenlieu asked the French government to reach a decision as soon as possible. The government stalled. Then d'Argenlieu proceeded to allow the official proclamation of the Cochinchinese Republic on June 1, 1946. Two days later, a Franco-Cochinchinese Convention was signed by Commissioner Cédile and Dr. Thinh. The Cochinchinese Council was subsequently enlarged to ninety-two members, all designated by the high commissioner. There was much speculation as to the probable outcome of a referendum on national unity. Devillers quotes one of the French members of the Council as saying in September 1946 that it would be sheer folly to hold a referendum, because it would be interpreted as a vote for or against France, and 90 percent would be "against us."[20] The American consul in Saigon, Charles Reed, thought that 65–70 percent would vote for inclusion in Vietnam, pointing out that the unionist press by far outnumbered the separatist newspapers.[21] The new Cochinchinese Republic enjoyed very limited support.

On May 31, Ho Chi Minh and the Vietnamese negotiating team for the upcoming conference at Fontainebleau left Vietnam on a French plane. They arrived in France just after the French elections on June 2, which led to a cabinet crisis. The leader of the Vietnamese negotiating team, Pham Van Dong, was already in France, where he had led a friendship visit since April 26. Due to a lack of preparations, to the cabinet crisis, and to the fact that d'Argenlieu had been opposed to having negotiations on French soil, the opening of the Fontainebleau conference was delayed by several weeks. Ho Chi Minh and the Vietnamese negotiators were therefore idle during the first part of their stay. Ho was sent to Biarritz on the French Atlantic coast, far away from the French political scene, on a kind of vacation. From June 22 to July 4, however, he was received as an official guest of the French government in Paris, where he stayed while the Vietnamese negotiators met their French counterparts at Fontainebleau. When the conference finally opened, on July 6, it immediately ran into difficulties, with the Vietnamese denouncing the unilateral declaration of a French-sponsored Cochinchinese Republic one month earlier. The conference dragged on without bringing clarification to the questions of either independence or unity. In late July, the Vietnamese delegation learned that d'Argenlieu had summoned a second Dalat conference to begin on August 1, without inviting the DRV and with handpicked delegates from some areas that the DRV considered to be under its sovereignty. This prompted the Vietnamese to temporarily break off the negotiations. D'Argenlieu had not informed Moutet in advance that the Dalat conference was about to start, so the minister for Overseas France also reacted strongly, although only against the inappropriate timing. Moutet was in general agreement with the principle of building a five-state Indochinese Federation with a powerful French-controlled executive.

At the second Dalat conference in August, which took place while the Fontainebleau conference was in recess, Cochinchinese representatives met with delegates from Laos and Cambodia and observers from southern Annam and some highland minority areas. In d'Argenlieu's conception, the March 6 agreement concerned only Tonkin, and he intended to create a system of similar agreements with all five federated states. The first agreement had been signed with Cambodia as early as January 7. The March 6 agreement, seen by d'Argenlieu as applicable only to Tonkin, was the second. A third was signed with Cochinchina on June 3, and a fourth with Laos on August 27. Only Annam, which was divided by the 16th parallel, did not get any such agreement. D'Argenlieu's federal conference at Dalat proved a partial failure, as protests from the Vietnamese delegation to Fontainebleau forced the French government to instruct Saigon to postpone some of its political federation-building, and also because the Cambodian and Laotian representatives did not support a French-dominated Federation as enthusiastically as d'Argenlieu might have hoped. Yet the conference did come up with detailed proposals for the composition and attributions of Indochina's federal institutions, emphasizing that Dalat should be its capital. D'Argenlieu prepared to move his own headquarters from Saigon to Dalat and ordered large amounts of equipment from France for the purpose. When the equipment did not arrive on time, d'Argenlieu complained.[22]

The main reason cited by the French for refusing to set a date for the referendum was the ongoing "terrorist" campaign in the south. In Leclerc's end-of-mission report in June 1946, he pointed out that the government in Hanoi was simultaneously negotiating with France and supporting a war against the French in the south. "Like Janus, this government has two faces." This was true, but it was not something the Vietnamese government was shy about. It claimed sovereignty over the whole of "Vietnam" and saw the guerrilla struggle in the south as a way of underpinning that claim. At the time of the August Revolution in 1945, the Viet Minh had dominated the north to a much greater extent than the south. In Nam Bo, the two religious sects Hoa Hao and Cao Dai had considerable backing in the countryside, and the Trotskyites were strong in the cities. The communist movement in the south was led by theoretically inclined intellectuals who were less tactically and diplomatically skilled than their comrades in the north. The contentious character of the nationalist movement in the south facilitated Leclerc's "pacification campaign" at the end of 1945 and the beginning of 1946. He took on the armies of the Hoa Hao, the Cao Dai, and the Viet Minh one after the other. At first, he seemed to score a resounding military success. Many Caodaists rallied to the French. By March, Leclerc estimated that his troops controlled, not just the cities, but also 80 percent of the villages.[23] Politically, however, France had confronted and alienated much of the population, and when the Viet Minh reorganized its forces and started to cooperate more systematically with the religious sects, guerrilla activity resurfaced in most of the areas the French thought they had pacified. Leclerc had placed small French units at many minor posts. When the guerrillas started their nightly attacks, these posts proved untenable, and the French had to concentrate their troops. According to a later report from Leclerc, only 10 percent of the villages in Cochinchina were under French control by January 1947.[24] It was not, of course, that the proportion of French-controlled villages had sunk from 80 to 10 percent in a matter of less than a year. Rather, Leclerc's successes in January–February were hollow, although this was not immediately apparent. The Vietnamese resistance needed to regroup after the massive repression it had experienced since September 1945. Not only the French 9ᵉ DIC and 2ᵉ DB had been active in the repression; British Gurkha forces were involved as well, and some of the bloodiest operations were carried out by Japanese troops serving under British orders after they surrendered. According to a British report, among the soldiers killed in southern Indochina from the time the trouble started in October 1945 until order seemed to have been established on January 13, 1946, there were three Britons, 37 Gurkhas, 85 French, 129 Japanese, and one American (Lt. Col. Peter Dewey). Of the Vietnamese casualties, 641 were killed by British-Indian, 1,565 by French, and 2,756 by Japanese troops.[25] The Japanese killed and wounded more and took more prisoners than the British and French taken together. The British commanders were amazed at the discipline with which the Japanese troops fought for a cause that was not theirs. When the Viet Minh reorganized the resistance forces and started its guerrilla campaign in the south, the British troops had left, the Japanese were in the process of being repatriated, and the battle-hardened French 9ᵉ DIC and 2ᵉ DB had gone north. The less experienced 3ᵉ DIC was left to control Cochinchina, southern Annam and Cambodia. No wonder Nguyen Binh, the new guerrilla commander who had come down from the north to take charge, found it easier to organize the resistance than his predecessor had done.

The reorganization of the guerrilla forces in the south was not carried out by the Viet Minh's southern leadership, but by Nguyen Binh, a former VNQDD activist turned communist, who was soon playing a role in the south similar to Vo Nguyen Giap's in the north. He came as the central government's military delegate to the south, took direct command of the eastern military zone, including Saigon-Cholon, and, in addition, took responsibility for coordinating all three southern war zones. Nguyen Binh rose to become a legendary leader and was extremely popular among the anticolonial fighters. Until March 1946, he concentrated on organizing his network and command structure and did not engage his troops in serious fighting. In the beginning of March, when the bulk of the French forces went north, he judged that the time was ripe for action. This was when the provisional Cochinchinese government was established. Now any local leader supporting the new Cochinchina or otherwise collaborating with France risked assassination. The number of political murders increased exponentially, and guerrilla units began to harass isolated French units. A National United Front was founded under Nguyen Binh on April 10, including adherents of the religious sects Cao Dai and Hoa Hao and other anticolonial groups. On April 19, Nguyen Binh ordered a general offensive to "support" the first Dalat conference.[26] The guerrilla war in the south dragged on through May–August, and when the French troops concentrated in large units, pro-French village leaders (notables) were left without protection. In Pignon's words, the concentration of the French military forces was "militarily indispensable, but politically a catastrophe."[27] During the Fontainebleau conference, he denounced French military authorities for their "extreme naïveté."[28] In September–October, in the run-up to the effectuation of the modus vivendi cease-fire, Nguyen Binh further intensified his guerrilla struggle.[29]

The methods used by the guerrillas were established in general instructions from Hanoi, signed by Tran Huy Lieu, another communist who had started out as a VNQDD activist but had crossed over while in prison in the early 1930s, after having recruited Nguyen Binh to the VNQDD. The two of them were friends, and Binh was now practicing in the south what Lieu was prescribing verbally from the north. Tran Huy Lieu had served as minister of communications and propaganda in the DRV's first government, and had headed the delegation that received Bao Dai's abdication in Hue late August 1945. In Vietnamese historiography, the teaching of guerrilla principles is normally associated with Communist Party Secretary-General Truong Chinh and Commander in Chief Vo Nguyen Giap. But in this early phase, the textbook was written by Tran Huy Lieu, who a few years later, after he had succumbed to "voluntarism" and committed some serious mistakes, suffered the tragic fate of being condemned to a life as a professional historian. Regardless of Lieu's later fate, his instructions from 1946 give a lively description of the tactics that the Vietnamese "tiger" would be using for nearly thirty years in its struggle against the Western "elephants." The guerrillas, he said,

> operate in a familiar atmosphere. Secrecy and surprise are the general conditions for their success in confrontations with an awkward adversary who is badly informed and operates in an unfavorable climate.
>
> The miracle of guerrilla war is that the whole population takes part. The soldier is the inhabitant, and the inhabitant is the soldier. . . . The tactics consist in avoiding well-guarded positions, attacking posts where the garrison is weak, advancing if the enemy retreats and retreating if the enemy advances, organizing ambushes where the enemy will be overcome by numbers in spite of his valor. . . . One of the guerrilla tactics consists in making the enemy "blind." Our soldiers do not wear uniforms, they don't concentrate in barracks, and they slip through crowds, which hide them if necessary. In that way, the French soldiers are incapable of detecting their presence. . . . Another of the guerrilla tactics consists in making the enemy "deaf."[30]

These were only a small part of Tran Huy Lieu's instructions. They show that the Vietnamese were already familiar with the principles of guerrilla warfare.

The telegrams from Saigon to Paris in September–October reported an increasing number of clashes between French and "rebel" forces. Details and assessments of the gravity of the insurgency differed, but all reports cited a higher number of "rebels" than Frenchmen killed.[31] A report from October 7 serves to illustrate: "An ambush region Tanan costs us one dead, 2 injured. Rebel losses serious."[32] "Partisans"—that is, Vietnamese fighting on the French side—were often among those killed. The French strove to establish a "partisan army." Thus on September 19, the high commissioner asked Paris for equipment for 9,300 "partisan" troops in Cochinchina and 1,200 in south Annam.[33] The "partisans" seem to have been used to guard the most dangerous outposts. That same September 19, Saigon reported: "In region Hocmon, Thudaumot, favorable activity of our patrols: 6 rebels killed, 3 injured, 23 prisoners, of whom several members assassination committee. Same region partisans have evacuated a post under pressure rebels and lost 2 dead, 1 disappeared."[34] The one who disappeared may well have reappeared as a "rebel" later.

During the last weeks before the cease-fire prescribed in the modus vivendi agreement entered into force on October 30, the Viet Minh launched a military offensive. On October 26, d'Argenlieu reported a serious attack on the city of My Tho, southwest of Saigon.[35] By the end of October, Devillers affirms, the Viet Minh held practically three-quarters of Cochinchina.[36]

So what we see in the south is two sides both trying to advance their positions, France by establishing new autonomous institutions in defiance of the promise made in the March 6 accords, and the Viet Minh by mounting an increasingly effective insurgency. The same picture, two parties each trying to advance at the expense of the other, is also to be found in the north. After long delays, the Chinese troops finally withdrew from Hanoi, and the Viet Minh was able to gradually eliminate the political influence of the pro-Chinese parties.

When the Chinese troops left, the government quickly reoccupied most of those provinces that the Chinese had left to the pro-Chinese parties and their militias. The most important leaders of the Dong Minh Hoi and Viet Nam Quoc Dan Dang (VNQDD) took refuge in China or in a few remaining strongholds near the Chinese border. In July, their Hanoi headquarters were searched by a commando unit of the Vietnamese police. Corpses of tortured and killed French soldiers were found, and seen as proof that the pro-Chinese parties were guilty of kidnapping French citizens.[37] From a local French perspective, the Viet Minh was actually quite moderate in comparison with the VNQDD and Dong Minh Hoi. The Viet Minh was thus able to suppress the opposition and monopolize political power in the north without provoking French hostility. It was difficult for the French to protest when the Vietnamese authorities arrested someone accused of having organized the kidnapping or killing of French civilians, or when they intervened to prevent opposition newspapers from launching incendiary campaigns against France. Still, the suppression of the only organized political opposition existing in the north was observed with dismay by the French authorities in Saigon, notably by Léon Pignon, who had become d'Argenlieu's principal political advisor as commissioner for political affairs. He was able to see the larger strategic picture and would have preferred to see the Viet Minh weakened by internal power struggles and real challenges from any kind of opposition, no matter what its attitude to France. Pignon knew that politics is more about power than about attitudes, and that the latter may well change with shifts of power. In 1973, Pignon admitted that when he returned from the Fontainebleau conference, he had already lost hope of a peaceful solution, mainly because the Viet Minh had liquidated the nationalist groups in the north, so France had to face a monolithic national bloc.[38]

So both in the south and the north, the Viet Minh was strengthening its position. During the July–September period, the same was not the case with the French. They had established garrisons in the north by virtue of the March 6 agreement, but did not now push their positions much forward. The military units in the north had, however, drawn up plans for how to use any emergency to enhance their control of the towns where they had been deployed. The attempts to establish mutual confidence and cooperation between the French and Vietnamese armies had only very limited success.

When an agreement has been forced on two parties who are both dissatisfied with it, then it may still be possible to make a virtue of it, and start defending the need for peace, confidence, and further compromise. The March 6 agreement did take on a positive value, not just internationally, but in France as well. Georges Bidault told the MRP's Grand Council, which met on March 8–10, that Indochina had just "been saved."[39] The French leftist parties were much relieved to learn that the Gaullist commanders in Indochina had agreed to accommodate the national aspirations of the Vietnamese, and many French leftists took good care of President Ho while he was in France. "Peace" was a dominant value in postwar Europe, and there was much opposition to the prospect of embarking on new colonial wars. Perhaps there might therefore have been a chance for the agreement to be more faithfully applied after all, and for new, more fruitful negotiations to take place. But this would probably have required a change of leaders on one or both of the sides, primarily the French. Although it defended and even boasted of the March 6 agreement rhetorically, the French government did not put pressure on d'Argenlieu to apply it faithfully; instead, it allowed him to organize and build his anti–Viet Minh— if not anti-Vietnamese—Indochinese Federation. One explanation for this may be that the uncertainty of the political situation in France prevented the French government from adopting a more consistent policy of accords.

THE UNACCOMPLISHED FRENCH REPUBLIC

Whereas the victors of World War II negotiated the European peace treaties in the heart of Paris, the Vietnamese negotiators were asked to carry out their negotiations in the small town of Fontainebleau, some sixty-five kilometers southeast of Paris. And a second-rate politician, Max André, was appointed to lead the French delegation. Pham Van Dong's Vietnamese delegation hammered throughout July, August, and early September 1946 on the two principal Vietnamese demands: independence and unity. Meanwhile, Ho pleaded the Vietnamese cause in Paris itself. But all in vain. The French delegation rejected the primary Vietnamese demands. Was this because of the general confusion in French politics, the failure of French politicians to adopt a new constitution, and the general difficulties of working out clear policies in a coalition government engaged in setting up a new republic?

Like the DRV, the French Fourth Republic did not yet have a constitution. A commission had drafted a proposal that was supported by the communists and socialists, but it was rejected in a French referendum on May 5, after the MRP had joined de Gaulle in opposing it. A new text therefore had to be worked out, while France prepared to elect a new Constitutive National Assembly on June 2. The MRP did well in these elections. Bidault formed a new government, and the MRP played a decisive role in modifying the constitution so that it could be approved in a second referendum, to be held in October. The new constitution notably reduced the degree of autonomy allowed for colonial territories with membership and representation in the French Union.[40] Constitutional squabbles took up much of the government's attention during the summer and fall of 1946, and, in his capacity as foreign minister, Bidault was greatly preoccupied with the Paris Peace Conference, where the victorious Allies took a long time to work out complex agreements with the defeated states in Europe.

The dispersion of responsibilities in the French decision-making system is clearly shown in the lack of coordination between the high commissioner's actions to foster an autonomous Cochinchina and the French government's attempts to negotiate with Vietnam in Fontainebleau. On March 29, 1946, Bidault told d'Argenlieu that if Cochinchina, "the richest and most densely populated province in Indochina," were united with Vietnam, France would lose one of her greatest "trumps."[41] During the abortive conference at Dalat in April, however, Minister for Overseas France Moutet told d'Argenlieu that it would be considered a French "maneuver" if France permitted an autonomous Cochinchinese government to be constituted after having promised in the March 6 agreement to respect the result of a referendum on the question of Vietnamese unity. It would lead to Vietnamese protests and put the French government in a "difficult situation" if a delegation of Cochinchinese representatives were sent to Paris while France was expecting a delegation from Vietnam.[42] Yet again, as mentioned, a delegation of the sort did go to Paris, and d'Argenlieu continued his preparations to formally endorse the provisional Cochinchinese government.[43]

When the first Dalat conference broke up without having yielded any results on May 11, the reason was that the French refused even to discuss plans for the agreed referendum. The Vietnamese were dismayed, particularly in the light of the ongoing French attempts to promote the establishment of an autonomous Cochinchina. Four days after the failure at Dalat, the secretary-general of the French Interministerial Committee for Indochina (Cominindo) warned d'Argenlieu that it was not government policy to undermine the March 6 accord. The government had decided to keep strictly to the clause of the March 6 convention stipulating that a referendum would fix the status of Cochinchina, he said.[44]

On the same day as d'Argenlieu got these disconcerting instructions, however, Moutet transmitted a message to him from former Governor-General Alexandre Varenne, who advised Saigon to postpone the referendum until the situation had been completely normalized, and to constitute a provisional "Annamite" government in Cochinchina, with a prestige comparable to that of the Vietnamese government, without delay. Moutet specified that this was just Varenne's opinion, and that he would express his own later.[45] It was enough, however, for d'Argenlieu to act. While Ho was en route to France by air, d'Argenlieu authorized the proclamation of the Cochinchinese Republic on June 1. D'Argenlieu thus went ahead, based on mixed signals, although Paris had yet not consented formally to the move. On June 4, the Cominindo approved what d'Argenlieu had done. The pattern is clear: d'Argenlieu acted as soon as he thought he could do so without being disavowed; Cominindo—after some delay—approved.

On June 19, 1946, when Ho Chi Minh was already in France, Bidault had taken over from Félix Gouin as French premier. Bidault did not want to leave responsibility for Indochina to Moutet, as his predecessor had done. Nor did Bidault have the capacity to direct French Indochina policy himself. He was unable to follow Indochinese affairs regularly, so his solution was to leave the initiative to the high commissioner. During Bidault's time as premier, the Cominindo was not used the way de Gaulle had intended. It usually endorsed what the high commissioner had already done. The main effect of Bidault's blocking of the Cominindo's authority was to strengthen the leverage and autonomy of High Commissioner Thierry d'Argenlieu.

On July 25, with the delegations at Fontainebleau struggling to find something useful to talk about, while avoiding the most divisive issues, d'Argenlieu announced that he would convene his second Dalat conference. The Vietnamese negotiators in Paris thought they were negotiating on behalf of the whole of Vietnam, so when d'Argenlieu started negotiations on Vietnamese territory with hand-picked representatives from areas that the Vietnamese government considered to be under its authority, this constituted a slap in the face. Once again, d'Argenlieu had not been explicitly authorized by Paris to do what he did,[46] and when the news arrived, the French representatives at Fontainebleau were embarrassed. The chief Vietnamese negotiator, Pham Van Dong, accused France of violating the March 6 agreement and delivered a formal note of protest. Moutet drafted a reassuring reply and tried to persuade Bidault to make an urgent decision. Bidault said he was too preoccupied with the Paris Peace Conference, and he asked Moutet not to bring the matter up in the cabinet's first meeting, since he had not had time to read the documents. When, by August 1, the Vietnamese had yet not received any reply, they broke off the negotiations. D'Argenlieu now advised the government to suspend the Fontainebleau conference once and for all.[47] This infuriated Moutet, who was rumored to have demanded of Bidault that d'Argenlieu be replaced as high commissioner. Bidault, according to the same rumors, refused.[48] The head of the Asian Department in the French Foreign Ministry would say later that this had come close to provoking a cabinet crisis.[49]

After having resolved their differences to Bidault's satisfaction, both Moutet and Bidault assured d'Argenlieu of their confidence.[50] Moutet's assurance was more reserved than Bidault's. He would tell Agence France-Presse (AFP) later that the disagreements in August had been "tactical." The "policy of accords" had always been practiced with the total consent of Admiral d'Argenlieu and of General Leclerc and his successor Valluy.[51] We may conclude from the evidence of July–August, however, that d'Argenlieu did not enjoy Moutet's full support, but was protected by Bidault.

After Pham Van Dong had broken off negotiations at Fontainebleau to protest the convening of the second Dalat conference, the Vietnamese packed their bags. Now the French government needed a face-saving operation. On August 9, the leader of the French delegation, Max André, assured Pham Van Dong that the Dalat conference would take no decisions, and would serve only as a sounding board. On this basis, Dong agreed to reopen the talks at Fontainebleau. The crisis also led to open debate in the French press about the Vietnamese demands. Moutet criticized the French Communist Party for failing to oppose the merger of Cochinchina with Vietnam, which would be "a serious mistake."[52] The Comanindo met on August 10 and 12 and decided to work out a proposal for a preliminary agreement, while leaving aside the two main issues of independence and unity.[53] Moutet criticized d'Argenlieu in a personal letter on August 19 for having convened the Dalat conference without informing Paris properly, but assured him that if there were disagreement between the two of them, it was not on the essence, merely on the form.[54]

What d'Argenlieu feared most of all was that the French delegation to Fontainebleau would agree to set a date for the referendum. This would ruin his policy for Cochinchinese autonomy. D'Argenlieu had wished to demonstrate clearly that the Vietnamese government only represented the north; this was one of his reasons for summoning the conference at Dalat. On the first day of that conference, he sent a long memo to Paris suggesting that the negotiations at Fontainebleau be suspended in order to give the other federated states more time to build up their institutions.[55] Moutet did not care for this advice; although he fully agreed with the policy of encouraging Cochinchinese autonomy, he did not want a confrontation with the Vietnamese government. Now he conceded that the time was not ripe to fix a date for the referendum. He realized that this would make it impossible to reach an overall agreement at Fontainebleau, but he considered it necessary to win time. Before the referendum, local authorities should be established in Cochinchina and a great effort should be made to mobilize popular support for them. The population should be given a sense of freedom, without which a majority would no doubt express itself in favor of a united Vietnam. Much had to be done in order to "obtain a referendum favorable to autonomy." Moutet thought that "authentic Cochinchinese" should take care of the propaganda effort, and that groups should be created in every locality, secretly at first, to work for autonomy. A program of social and agrarian reform would also be necessary.[56] The evolution of Cochinchinese autonomy was clearly not just d'Argenlieu's personal policy. It had the full backing of the minister for Overseas France.

The contention that their disagreement was tactical thus does not seem to have been untrue. As of August 1946, Moutet and d'Argenlieu agreed on the need to promote Cochinchinese autonomy, but disagreed on the timing of certain public initiatives, and on the decision-making authority of the high commissioner and the minister for Overseas France. D'Argenlieu took important decisions on his own as soon as he thought he could do so without the risk of being disavowed. Moutet was hesitant and not in a position to make important commitments without clear support from the prime minister or a meeting in the cabinet or the Cominindo. Bidault, who was formally responsible but preoccupied with other matters, willingly left the field to d'Argenlieu. After the Fontainebleau conference, Bidault thanked d'Argenlieu in a personal telegram for his efforts on behalf of France and assured him of his full confidence and friendship.[57]

Since French politics was so chaotic, it is tempting to explain the failure of the Franco-Vietnamese negotiations as a result of the inability of the French coalition government to reach clear-cut decisions. However, this explanation is not convincing for the very reason just pointed out. With the timid exception of the Parti communiste français (PCF), the main political forces in France agreed that Vietnam should not be given full independence, and that the Viet Minh should under no circumstance be allowed to take control of Cochinchina. This latter point was almost an obsession for Moutet, the main socialist decision-maker on Indochina. There was a clear governmental majority behind France's determination not to yield on the two main issues on the agenda. This would be confirmed in November–December when France finally got its new constitution (adopted with a 53 percent majority in a referendum on October 13), when the first regular elections of the French Fourth Republic were held on November 10, and when Bidault's government, operating in a caretaker capacity pending the formation of a new French cabinet, was finally able to agree on a set of instructions for the high commissioner on December 10. The French government made it clear that if Vietnam got full independence, the French presence in Indochina as a whole would be threatened. On the question of uniting the three *ky*, the French position was only slightly less firm. With the exception of the timid communists, the only French decision-makers who argued in favor of Vietnamese unity were those who envisaged setting up a non-communist and more controllable national alternative to the Viet Minh. Here again, the French government's attitude did not leave room for any genuine compromise with Ho Chi Minh.

The main reason for the failure of the Franco-Vietnamese negotiations was thus not the confusion or incapacity of the French government, and the slow withdrawal of the Chinese forces merely delayed the clarification of Franco-Vietnamese relations in the north. The main reason was that both parties saw the March 6 agreement as a stepping-stone to further advancing their positions, instead of looking for a genuine compromise. However, an earnest attempt was made by both sides to at least establish a modus vivendi, a preliminary agreement that could prevent open confrontation.

THE SEPTEMBER 14 AGREEMENT

In the first days of September, the Vietnamese and French representatives at Fontainebleau realized that they would not reach any comprehensive agreement. Each side then worked out a draft for a preliminary agreement, skirting the two principal problems, independence and unity. The text was ready on the morning of September 10, but in the afternoon, Pham Van Dong made a last attempt to get the French government to yield, saying that he would only sign if the French agreed to a date and procedure for the referendum in Nam Bo (Cochinchina). France had consistently refused to do so, arguing that as long as "terrorist" activity was going on in the south, it was impossible to organize a free and fair referendum, and the French negotiators stuck to this line. Most of the Vietnamese negotiators, including Dong himself, then left Paris on September 13. President Ho and the two Vietnamese negotiators Duong Bach Mai and Hoang Minh Giam stayed behind. During a lunch on September 11, as we have seen, Moutet and Ho had agreed that a total deadlock was unacceptable. Ho entreated the French not to let him return empty-handed. "You won't regret it if you strengthen my hand against those who intend to supplant me," he said. "If we have to fight, we'll fight. You'll kill ten of us, but we'll kill one of you, and in the end, you'll tire first."[58]

That same evening, a meeting was organized between three French representatives and two Vietnamese, whereupon Ho Chi Minh wrote a new draft. He received a French counterproposal on September 14, which he possibly discussed in the afternoon with Prime Minister Bidault.[59] And then he went to Moutet's home to sign. What was the content of the so-called modus vivendi agreement?[60] The introduction to its eleven articles confirmed that the March 6 agreement would continue to be in force. This meant for one thing that there would still be a limit to the number of French troops north of the 16th parallel, for another, that France maintained its promise to respect the result of a referendum on national unity. In article 10, the contracting parties agreed that negotiations for a definitive treaty should begin no later than January 1947. The modus vivendi agreement was to come into force on October 30, 1946 (article 11).

The first eight articles were formulated as reciprocal engagements, but in fact they were a list of Vietnamese concessions to French interests in the territories controlled by the DRV. Ho Chi Minh promised to:

- let French nationals enjoy the same freedoms in Vietnam as Vietnamese nationals, above all, freedom to set up a business (article 1)
- not make any change in the status of French property and companies in Vietnam without a preliminary agreement with France (article 2)
- make restitution to its owners of all French property requisitioned by the Vietnamese government (article 2)
- permit French educational and scientific institutions to work freely in Vietnam under French programs and return the Pasteur Institute in Hanoi to the French (article 3)
- guarantee absolute priority to French nationals whenever Vietnam needed advisors, technicians, or experts (article 4)
- respect the French-controlled Indochinese piaster as the sole currency for all of Indochina (article 5)
- form a Customs Union with the other members of the Indochinese Federation (article 6)

It was agreed to establish five mixed commissions. The most important were:

- a coordinating committee for customs, foreign trade, and currency, which would organize the Indochinese customs service (article 6)
- a coordinating committee for communications throughout Indochina (article 7)
- a commission to determine arrangements for Vietnamese consular representation in neighboring countries and for relations with foreign consuls (article 8)

These eight articles reflected the degree to which Ho Chi Minh was prepared to compromise on actual Vietnamese independence. Article 9 mainly concerned French-controlled Cochinchina and southern Annam, stipulating that a general cease-fire would enter into force here on October 30. The French and the Vietnamese general staffs were to arrange the "conditions of application and supervision of measures decided in common." The two sides would interpret this cryptic sentence quite differently.

The enjoyment of democratic freedoms was to be reciprocally guaranteed. Unfriendly propaganda should be terminated on both sides. A person designated by the Vietnamese government should be accredited to the high commissioner to establish the necessary cooperation in implementing the agreement.

For the Vietnamese, it was important that the French government agreed with the Vietnamese government on a cease-fire in Cochinchina and south Annam, since this could be seen as an implicit recognition of Vietnamese institutions south of the 16th parallel. By contrast, the French authorities in Saigon interpreted the cease-fire as a prelude to the disarming or withdrawal of all Vietnamese military forces from the south.

Ho Chi Minh had asked for a period of as much as six weeks between the signing of the modus vivendi agreement and its application. Both sides therefore had a good while to prepare their interpretations and develop strategies for using the agreement for their own ends. The interpretations would be different indeed, and little of the modus vivendi agreement was ever applied.

HO RETURNS TO HANOI

Just hours before the modus vivendi agreement was signed, the twenty-five members of the Vietnamese delegation to Fontainebleau left Marseille on board the *Pasteur*.[61] Curiously, they made no mention of the modus vivendi agreement in their first public statement at home after they arrived in Haiphong on October 3. On one of their first days at sea, they had received two short telegrams from Ho Chi Minh informing them that it had been signed.[62] Pham Van Dong cabled Hoang Minh Giam, who had stayed in Paris as Vietnamese representative to France, that he would like to see the text.[63] However, the Cominindo instructed Saigon to give the Vietnamese delegation a copy when the *Pasteur* arrived at Cap St. Jacques (Vung Tau) in the far south of Vietnam.[64] The delegation to Fontainebleau thus had to wait two weeks before learning the result of its negotiations.

While in France, the Vietnamese delegation had not just negotiated. It had also been shopping and had brought six tons of luggage, mainly radio equipment. At Marseille, the luggage was "in error" marked "Saigon" instead of "Haiphong." The Cominindo told Saigon that this "error" would create a "pretext" *(sic)* for disembarking the luggage at Cap St. Jacques and holding it there for a while.[65] When the *Pasteur* arrived in Haiphong, much of the luggage had been damaged.[66]

On the delegation's return to Hanoi, the Vietnamese government got its first confidential reports on the Fontainebleau negotiations. Preparations to apply the modus vivendi agreement could therefore only begin three weeks after the agreement had been concluded.[67] The French high commissioner had been promptly and thoroughly briefed by his collaborators Léon Pignon, Albert Torel, and the financial advisor Gonon, who left Paris on a flight for Saigon on September 24.

Ho Chi Minh left France four days after the modus vivendi agreement had been signed on board the French warship *Dumont d'Urville*, and arrived in Haiphong on October 20, ten days before the agreement was to enter into force. En route, Ho learned that the new French constitution, which despite the MRP's amendments received strong support from the French communists and socialists, had been approved by referendum on October 13. Ho may also have learned that the results of the referendum had been less positive in Indochina. For, although the population in Nam Bo were not permitted to have their referendum on national unity, all French citizens in Cochinchina, both the *colons* and the tiny number of indigenous French citizens, were allowed to participate in the French constitutional referendum. There were 34,292 French citizens in Indochina who were eligible to vote, and of the 18,213 who did so, only 3,559 voted yes on the constitution, as against the 14,456 who followed General de Gaulle's advice and voted no.[68] The American consul explained this as a "possible Fascist reaction."[69] The Vietnamese government protested against the holding of a French referendum on Vietnamese soil.[70] The French leftist newspaper *Franc-Tireur* commented: "The 'colons' have voted no. The people were not permitted to speak."[71]

Ho Chi Minh was still at sea when the referendum was held. Giap writes in his memoirs that the *Dumont d'Urville* sailed at a rather leisurely pace and that the French seemed to be deliberately delaying the return of the president.[72] Why didn't he take a plane, as he had when he traveled to France? Jean Sainteny, who accompanied Ho Chi Minh during his stay in France, says that Ho refused a French offer of a plane, using his health as pretext.[73] Giap writes that the Hanoi government feared that the French might try to obstruct the return of Ho Chi Minh and the Vietnamese delegation.[74] Ngo Dinh Diem later suggested that Ho Chi Minh had signed the modus vivendi agreement in order to be sure that the French would let him return at all.[75] All this is pure speculation.

It is difficult to understand why Ho Chi Minh preferred a long sea voyage. One possibility is that he wanted to allow time for Giap to strengthen the Viet Minh in the north and Nguyen Binh to build up his forces in the south; when the president returned, he would have to play his role as a responsible, moderating force, but whatever had been done before could be excused by his absence. Another possibility is that he thought the DRV government would need time to prepare the population to accept the modus vivendi agreement.

During Ho's long journey, he could only communicate with France and Vietnam through French military cables. The French therefore knew, and we know, what Ho told Hanoi. Before leaving France, he informed the Vietnamese government of the modus vivendi agreement, adding that a copy would be sent to Hanoi by air.[76] From on board the ship, he instructed Hanoi to explain the terms of the modus vivendi agreement to the people and to start implementing its clauses, and he asked for information on the situation back home.[77] On the ship, Ho Chi Minh acted the part of friendly and moderate national leader and established warm relations with the French crew, who admired him for his asceticism. In contrast to the delegation on the *Pasteur*, Ho brought no luggage with him, and he impressed the crew by washing his own clothes.[78] The French captain would praise Ho for his intelligence and charm, but added that he seemed to bow easily to advice from those in whom he had confidence.[79]

On the first day of his journey, Ho assured Moutet of his friendship and said he counted on his good faith in applying their agreement.[80] About one week later, he received a courteous, but apolitical, telegram from Bidault. Having received the first reports from Vietnam, Ho replied thanking Bidault for his friendly message and remarking: "Modus vivendi has not satisfied population Vietnam. That's human. Will do my best and will succeed if French friends in Cochinchina faithfully apply democratic freedom, cessation hostilities, liberation prisoners and abstain from unfriendly words and actions. I count on your active help to accomplish work in interest two countries."[81]

This message is important for two reasons. It shows that in Ho Chi Minh's view, faithful Vietnamese application of the modus vivendi agreement depended on a change in French Cochinchina policy; and it represents an attempt to establish direct contact between the Vietnamese president and the French premier. For Ho Chi Minh, it must have been important to have a link to Bidault. He was the most influential of the French politicians, and if Ho could have direct contact with him, the Franco-Vietnamese relationship would be based on equality. Bidault sensed this immediately and never answered. Considering the message to be of political nature, he thought that it should be answered by the high commissioner, not by the French premier or the minister for Overseas France. In the beginning of November, he therefore forwarded Ho's telegram to d'Argenlieu.[82] Ho Chi Minh had also left his close collaborator Hoang Minh Giam behind in Paris as head of a permanent four-member Vietnamese delegation. On learning this, d'Argenlieu cabled Paris that this delegation was not part of the modus vivendi agreement and asked for an explanation. On October 5, Paris replied that the Giam mission had no official status and that a letter had been sent to the Vietnamese president expressing the "inappropriateness" of the delegation. Paris was not prepared, however, to deny the members of the Vietnamese delegation the right to stay in a private capacity. D'Argenlieu was not satisfied and asked Moutet to send the four Vietnamese packing.[83] His demand was not met, but Hoang Minh Giam did not get any appointments and soon realized that he was wasting his time. In November, he therefore returned to Hanoi. He was replaced in Paris by Tran Ngoc Danh, who had a lower profile.[84] After Ho's return to Hanoi, while the two sides were trying to implement the modus vivendi agreement, d'Argenlieu enclosed a comment to a message he forwarded from the Vietnamese to the French government: "It may be acceptable for messages of a purely formal and conventional nature to be addressed directly by Ho Chi Minh to the French premier, but this should not be the case with messages of a political nature."[85] To support his monopoly of political communication with Hanoi at a time when it seemed that Bidault might have to resign, d'Argenlieu later cited Bidault's decision in October not to answer Ho's message from the *Dumont d'Urville*.[86]

During the absence of Ho Chi Minh, the Viet Minh had strengthened its position considerably. The main Dong Minh Hoi leaders had disappeared from the scene, and the VNQDD had also been weakened. The modus vivendi agreement was probably unpopular with many young Vietnamese activists, but the Tong Bo undertook measures to prohibit any public criticism of President Ho.[87] The French searched in vain for attacks against him in the Vietnamese press. The only negative comment they found was in the Viet Minh mouthpiece *Cuu Quoc,* affirming that the Vietnamese people had not been satisfied and that the concessions made had been too extensive. This criticism may have formed the background for the telegram from Ho to Bidault saying this reaction was "human." A typical reaction to the modus vivendi agreement was reported by a French intelligence unit in Hue, where a provincial-level directive had justified the accord in terms of Vietnam's need to obtain support from great powers such as the United States, the United Kingdom, Russia, and China (listed in that order). Vietnam was not strong enough to enter into a military struggle; it was thus necessary to make use of the modus vivendi agreement as best one could. Local Viet Minh institutions received orders to convince people that everything done by "our old president" had always been for the best of the nation.

When the *Dumont d'Urville* sailed into Cam Ranh Bay on the southeastern coast of Indochina, Admiral d'Argenlieu was there to meet the Vietnamese president and to demonstrate that in the future, it was he who would represent France in relations with Vietnam. Ho Chi Minh and d'Argenlieu met twice on board the admiral's ships in 1946, on the *Emile Bertin* in Ha Long Bay on March 24 and on the *Suffren* in Cam Ranh Bay on October 18. The admiral favored these naval meetings because they could be held in an atmosphere of French force. In March, d'Argenlieu had received Ho Chi Minh with "much pomp and ceremony." Ho reacted to this by strengthening his "ultra-simple" features.[88] In his report from the March 24 meeting, d'Argenlieu said that the parade and the naval review seemed to make a great impression on the Vietnamese president.[89] Ho Chi Minh told General Salan, who accompanied him back to Hanoi, that the admiral's ships could not sail up the Vietnamese rivers.[90] On October 18, the subject for discussion was the application of the modus vivendi agreement. Franco-Vietnamese relations in the south after the cease-fire were the sticking point. Ho promised to choose an official representative to Saigon who would permit the "exchange of friendly views." They agreed to start talks to fix the principles for the cessation of hostilities in the different sectors, and when d'Argenlieu denounced terrorist activity in Cochinchina and southern Annam, Ho Chi Minh answered by disclaiming it.[91] When d'Argenlieu demanded the withdrawal (he called it "repatriation") of all Vietnamese troops from the south, and said he had received "the most formal instructions" on this matter, however, Ho was "absolutely intransigent."[92] Yet d'Argenlieu had the impression that Ho Chi Minh sincerely desired an understanding with France and commented that the actions of the president upon his return to Hanoi would show if he really meant to apply the modus vivendi agreement. The proof of the pudding would be in the eating. D'Argenlieu said he sensed that Ho Chi Minh was anxious about the situation he would find on his return. This was obviously true. Ho had been away for over four months, and during the last month, his sole contacts with the outside world had been through French cables. Now he would meet Giap and other close collaborators of his and be able to ask them in full confidence what had happened since he left on May 31.

The *Dumont d'Urville* sailed into Haiphong harbor on October 20, and on the following day Ho traveled to Hanoi by special train. According to the American vice-consul, 80,000 people were assembled in the capital to greet him.[93] The suppression of the nationalist parties had eliminated the only organized opposition to Viet Minh rule. There were no longer any political channels for the probably widespread discontent with the modus vivendi agreement, and Ho could forget his fears of being outflanked by aggressive elements outside the Viet Minh. On October 23, he made a declaration to the people defending the concessions made and trying to prepare for the application of the cease-fire by forbidding any violent action in the south: "Toward the French Army, we must be correct. Toward the French residents, we must be moderate, so that the provocateurs who intend to divide us may find themselves with no pretext, and our [bid for] unity and independence will soon succeed." Ho promised his compatriots in the south that unity would come: "No one can divide Vietnam." But to obtain this, it was necessary to respect the agreement: "The Vietnamese Army and the French Army must simultaneously stop fighting. . . . Violent actions are absolutely forbidden."[94]

This warning concerned the south, where it was important for the DRV to display authority over Nguyen Binh's forces. Meanwhile, the Viet Minh was consolidating its position in the north, where the opposition parties could no longer count on Chinese protection. From October 23 to 27, shortly before the second session of the Vietnamese National Assembly, the remains of the opposition parties carried out a political campaign against the government's collaboration with France, and the government responded with repression. The French estimated that 200 arrests were made by Vietnamese authorities in each of two different raids.[95]

By this time, the Viet Minh was in control of an administration under the authority of people's committees on all levels, one hundred and twenty newspapers, one national radio station, as well as several local ones, and a growing army. The biggest problem was to finance the new state, for the economy was a shambles.[96]

THE UNACCOMPLISHED VIETNAMESE REPUBLIC

The second session of the DRV's National Assembly convened on October 28. This was the same assembly that had been elected on January 6, where the opposition parties had taken up seventy unelected seats, and that had met for its first short session on March 2. Most of the seventy non–Viet Minh members had been present in March. When the second session opened, only thirty-seven of them showed up. When it convened, the National Assembly still followed the French model of placing Marxists and socialists on the left, Christian Democrats in the center, and conservative groups on the right, but this artificial division was soon abandoned.

The Vietnamese cabinet that had been formed during the crisis in February–March was a broad coalition, with unaffiliated personalities as well as prominent members of the pro-Chinese parties taking over important ministries—at least formally; the noncommunist ministers tended to be provided with communist deputies, who in practice held much of the power. Some of the ministers fled to China before the cabinet was dissolved on October 29, and on November 3, Ho Chi Minh announced the formation of a new government, whose composition was more in consonance with real power. Viet Minh took all the key portfolios. Ho Chi Minh remained president, while also taking responsibility for foreign affairs, with Hoang Minh Giam as state secretary. Vo Nguyen Giap became minister of defense, while Minister of the Interior Huynh Thuc Khang, an aging unaffiliated personality who had ensured the interim of the presidency while Ho Chi Minh was away, retained his portfolio, with Hoang Huu Nam as state secretary. Nam also ran the Liaison Office (Lien Kiem) with the French military. Pham Van Dong took up the position as state secretary in the Ministry of National Economy. Here the post as minister was kept vacant so that it could be filled later on by someone from the south; Pham Van Dong would actually soon go south himself. With the formation of this cabinet, the communists took firm control of the government apparatus in anticipation of a new crisis. The French were obviously disappointed. Before leaving for France, Ho had let the French understand ("promised," Pignon says) that he would enlarge his government so as to include more moderate personalities. Now the opposite happened.[97]

On November 8, the National Assembly approved a new democratic constitution. "The constitution that you have just approved is the Vietnamese people's first constitution. Even though it is not 100 percent perfect, it is still satisfactory and appropriate for our young nation. It condones the establishment of the republican and democratic regime," President Ho Chi Minh told Vietnam's first National Assembly on November 9, just after it had approved the constitution, with 240 votes to 2.[98]

The Vietnamese constitution of 1946 consists of seventy paragraphs, divided into seven chapters. It starts out by defining the Vietnamese state as a Democratic Republic. The republican regime was unanimously approved by the Assembly. Then the constitution goes on to assign sovereignty to the "popular community," without any distinctions made as to race, gender, prosperity, class, or religion. It states that Vietnam is a united territory of the northern, central, and southern regions, which cannot be divided, and specifies Hanoi as the shared capital.[99]

Chapter 3 deals with the main expression of popular sovereignty, the National Assembly, which would consist of just one chamber. It would be the highest authority in the DRV. There would be national elections every three years.[100] The government (chapter 4) would be led by the president of the Republic who was to be elected by the National Assembly for five-year terms.

Why has not Ho Chi Minh's first constitution received a more prominent role in Vietnamese historical memory? First there are the inherent weaknesses in the text as such, perhaps what Ho Chi Minh meant when he said that it was not 100 percent perfect. As a constitution, it was deeply "Rousseauist," in that it embodied all sovereignty in the people as such, represented by the National Assembly and its Standing Committee. There were no provisions for a division of power between legislative, executive, and judicial branches, except for a statement that the government should not put pressure on the courts.

The most powerful political organization in the DRV was the Viet Minh and its Central Committee (Tong Bo), and behind it, the formally dissolved, but clandestinely operating communist party "Organization," but they had no place in the constitution. The Tong Bo remained a power, behind the scenes, and the ICP even more so. In the discussions leading up to the adoption of the constitution, the Viet Minh was treated more or less like any other party, although in reality it was a state within the state.

Let us immediately proceed, however, to the second explanation for the weak position of the 1946 constitution in Vietnamese national memory, namely, the limited role that the constitution-making process had played in Vietnam's political life. A successful and important constitution normally comes into being as the result of a thorough process of bargaining and consensus-building. This did not happen in Vietnam in 1946. When the National Assembly met for its first brief session on March 2, it elected a commission to work out a constitution on the basis of a draft that had already been written in November. The commission had seven Viet Minh members, three Dong Minh Hoi, and one VNQDD.[101] They deliberated during the summer and autumn, but their work did not receive much public attention. In September, the government, which during Ho's absence was led effectively by Vo Nguyen Giap, attempted to integrate the Dong Minh Hoi and the VNQDD in a new Viet Minh–dominated national bloc (Lien Viet) through a combination of pressures and offers. The main recalcitrant leaders of the two opposition parties were arrested or driven into Chinese exile, while others agreed to work with the Viet Minh. The integration effort was most successful in relation to the Dong Minh Hoi. In the constitutional committee, the three Dong Minh Hoi members went along with the majority, whereas the one VNQDD member, Pham Gia Do, held to his own independent opinion, favoring a two-chamber system with more checks and balances.

When the National Assembly met on October 28, Pham Gia Do continued to dissent and was condemned by other members for breaking national unity and failing to support the government's struggle for national independence. He was on one occasion prevented from voicing his opinion, and he was one of the two who voted against the constitution on November 9. The Assembly members were grouped into a number of factions: Marxists, socialists, democrats, Viet Minh, Dong Minh Hoi, and VNQDD. All of these had different priorities, but apart from the VNQDD, they all formed a part of a national bloc. The process was an inter-esting attempt to develop a kind of multifactional politics, within the framework of overall national unity, in support of Ho Chi Minh and the Viet Minh front, but it suffered from the fact that the National Assembly did not meet between March 2 and October 28.

The Vietnamese and French constitution making went on in parallel, within al-most exactly the same time frame. The first drafts were written already in fall 1945 and the final versions were adopted one year later, but whereas the communist pro-posal for a unicameral system was rejected in France, it was accepted by a massive majority in Vietnam. When Pham Van Dong presided over the deliberations of the Vietnamese National Assembly in October–November 1946, he had a copy of the just-adopted French constitution on the table before him.[102] It may be added that Vietnam was not alone in adopting a French-inspired constitution in this period. The Laotians and Cambodians also acquired new constitutions conceived in the French language and translated into the vernacular.

One of the most controversial matters in the French constitution was not men-tioned in the Vietnamese one. This was colonial reform. The new constitution of the Fourth Republic replaced the French Empire with the French Union, which was to have its own assembly, consisting of representatives from France, both metro-politan and overseas. Vietnam was supposed to be a member of the French Union through its membership in the Indochinese Federation. This was provided for in the French constitution but not at all reflected in the Vietnamese, which did not even mention the existence of France, the French Union, or the Indochinese Fed-eration. The Vietnamese constitution treated France as if it had no privileged role to play at all. This may have been a Solomonic solution, given that the Vietnamese and French negotiators at Fontainebleau had not been able to agree on the terms of Vietnam's membership in the French Union, but it also meant that the constitu-tion acquired an unrealistic aura. It ignored both the existence of the Viet Minh and of the French. It was therefore clear to everyone concerned that if France and the DRV were to reach an agreement during their next round of negotiations, Viet-nam's new constitution would have to be modified.

Because of the crisis, and perhaps also because of a general lack of resources, the Vietnamese National Assembly decided immediately after adopting the constitu-tion that it should not yet be promulgated, since this would oblige the government to call a national referendum and elect a new National Assembly before the con-stitution could enter into force, just as France had been doing. The assembly elected on January 6, 1946 would then be seen as a Constitutive Assembly, and a new as-sembly would become the first genuine National Assembly under the new consti-tution. Instead the "Constitutive Assembly" decided to prolong its existence, while letting the new constitution enter into force without being promulgated. Formally, this meant that the National Assembly violated the terms of the constitution immediately after having voted on it. There were few protests against this, since the crisis called for general pragmatism, but as a legal document, the constitution was handicapped from the start.

MOUTET'S STRATEGY

Marius Moutet was deeply engaged in French constitution-making and not overly concerned by political developments in Hanoi. His main concern was Cochinchina, the richest and most modern part of the French colony. A week after the modus vivendi agreement was signed in September, he emphasized in a set of instructions to d'Argenlieu that Cochinchina was the axis of French Indochina policy. The modus vivendi agreement represented a notable French advance in relation to the provisional agreement of March 6, he affirmed. The French position north of the 16th parallel had been appreciably improved, and the high commissioner was instructed to use all his authority to ensure that the Vietnamese government fulfilled its obligations with a "maximum of precision." France for its part would also have to apply the agreement faithfully in order to create a détente. He instructed d'Argenlieu to avoid any action that might worsen Franco-Vietnamese relations before the date when the agreement would enter into force: October 30. It would even be advisable for French authorities to take the first steps toward détente by establishing democratic rights in Cochinchina. The government had become convinced that Cochinchina was "the very pivot of our whole Indochina policy." France had to succeed quickly in Cochinchina, because the future French presence in Indochina as a whole would almost exclusively depend on the success of the Cochinchina policy.[103]

When he received Moutet's instructions, the high commissioner was planning to hold municipal elections in Cochinchina as a way of testing the waters. In late September, he toured parts of the Cochinchinese countryside with Colonel Nguyen Van Xuan, vice president of the Cochinchinese Council. Saigon cabled Paris that d'Argenlieu was everywhere received by an enthusiastic population, and quoted from his speech: "Cochinchina has now been liberated thanks to the French forces, who after having liberated France did not regard their task as accomplished as long as the Japanese enemy still held Indochina." The audience must have known that French forces had not liberated France all by themselves, that the Japanese had capitulated before de Gaulle's forces arrived in Indochina, and that the French had not "liberated" Cochinchina from the Japanese, but from an indigenous revolution with the help of Japanese troops. D'Argenlieu continued his speech in the same vein and soon ran into a paradox that merits quotation: "We wish Cochinchina to be free, and we do not permit that anyone in the name of this freedom make you their slaves. France is at your disposal, and it is important that no one should forget this."[104] This was a warning against supporting the guerrillas. The municipal elections were held in a few places, but lack of success and Viet Minh reprisals against those who were elected forced the French to give up their attempts to establish democracy.

Moutet's instructions of September 21 also pointed at the need to enlarge the Cochinchinese cabinet of Dr. Thinh, with the aim of creating a government that would represent the majority of the people. D'Argenlieu should not be afraid to let advocates of Vietnamese unity join Dr. Thinh's government, Moutet said. The French government did not fear the evolution of a "sincere democracy" in Cochinchina, even if this eventually led to the three *ky* being unified in one form or another, although not on Viet Minh terms. This last instruction was probably meant to pave the way for Nguyen Van Xuan. He had led a Cochinchinese delegation to Paris and had kept in close contact with French socialist leaders. He was not an easily controllable person, but he was hostile to the Viet Minh and had declared to French journalists during the second Dalat conference on August 4 that nothing would have prevented the unification of the three *ky* if the Hanoi government had been less leftist.[105]

The instructions from Moutet to d'Argenlieu show that Moutet held the same view. The policy of Cochinchinese autonomy was not a matter of principle. Moutet feared war with the Viet Minh. He stated in his letter to d'Argenlieu that a "policy of force" would almost certainly be unsuccessful, because French military means were and would remain limited.[106] On the other hand, Moutet also feared the unification of Vietnam under Viet Minh's dominance. His way out of the dilemma was to build a political force in the south that could counterbalance the Viet Minh's power in the north. This political strategy was, however, more or less impossible to bring to fruition, since any genuine attempt to let the southerners decide on their own would most likely lead to unification with the north, with the Viet Minh assuming a dominant role. And now the cease-fire had deprived the French of the opportunity to use military means to back up their strategy.

THE APPLICATION OF THE AGREEMENT

As of October 30, 1946, the Vietnamese and French authorities were obliged by their modus vivendi agreement to:

- liberate all political prisoners, respect democratic liberties, such as freedom of press and organization, and terminate all hostile propaganda
- cease all acts of hostility
- establish mixed commissions to prepare a durable military arrangement for the south, and the conditions for economic cooperation in the north, including the restitution of French property to its owners

To what extent did the two sides meet their obligations? There is no indication that the modus vivendi agreement induced the government in Hanoi to liberate any of its prisoners. Actually, French intelligence later laid hands on a top secret Vietnamese circular, dated October 28, 1946, instructing municipal and provincial authorities to make a list of executed or imprisoned "reactionary traitors" and fabricate documents to prove that they had been killed trying to escape, or were in prison for collaborating with the Japanese or for counterfeiting.[107] The Vietnamese did not have to present any lists to the French, however, for French authorities only began to prepare demands for the release of prisoners on November 21, when the situation in the port city of Haiphong was on the brink of open warfare.[108]

Only a short time before the order to forge evidence was issued, the Vietnamese press started a campaign against French oppression in the south. They attacked the French for having arrested the well-known engineer Nguyen Ngoc Bich and for having executed five identified Vietnamese patriots. D'Argenlieu informed Paris that three of them had been mortally wounded trying to escape. The fourth had died in hospital from battle wounds. The fifth was not dead at all, but was under arrest in Saigon. D'Argenlieu asked Paris to use this information and preclude new attacks from Hanoi propaganda and "its extensions in France, which constitute the most important arm that the Vietnamese government counts on."[109]

The Vietnamese error of including on their list of executions the name of a man who was still alive furnished d'Argenlieu with a propaganda opportunity. Already before the return of Ho Chi Minh, he had liberated ten well-known political prisoners, including both the man believed dead and the engineer who had been identified in the Vietnamese press. Nine of the liberated prisoners were sent to the north, while Nguyen Ngoc Bich, no doubt because of his technical expertise, was taken to Paris so he could be kept away from "local influence." The high commissioner secured wide publicity for this gesture before the return of the Vietnamese president and used it in his talks with Ho at Cam Ranh Bay.[110] The 10 belonged to a group of 85, who were released before Ho's return from France. On October 31, another 150 were released, so altogether, Saigon released 235 political prisoners.[111]

The sources for this book include only scarce information on the freedom of press in the north.[112] Yet it is clear that when the China-oriented opposition was suppressed, its (violently anti-French) press was either closed down or put under Viet Minh control. There seems to have been an effective Vietnamese censorship, which was used both to hinder criticism of the Viet Minh and to quell the most violently anti-French outbursts. Just after Ho's return to Hanoi, the interim French commissioner of the Republic during Sainteny's absence, General Morlière, reported that the president had chided the Vietnamese director of information, Tran Huy Lieu, for having permitted an anti-French campaign in the press while he himself was in France.[113]

French censorship in the south was lessened as a result of the modus vivendi agreement. This permitted the unionist press to demonstrate how little support there was for Dr. Thinh's "pseudo-government." The French later evoked the freedom of the press as one of the reasons for the failure of Cochinchinese separatism. In mid-

November, the French Marxist paper *Lendemains* published an interview with the chairman of the Administrative Committee for Nam Bo, who had been appointed by the DRV government in Hanoi. The interview was reproduced in four Vietnamese-language newspapers. This was too much for the French authorities, who decided to suspend the publication of *Lendemains* for one month and the four unionist newspapers for four days. In explaining this to Paris, Pignon argued that the population would have the impression that the French cause was essentially bad if those responsible for its defense permitted themselves to be openly and publicly held up to ridicule.[114]

One week before the crucial date when the cease-fire entered into force, the Vietnamese press reported that the commissar for the Vietnamese armies in Nam Bo had ordered all units to terminate hostilities from the night of October 29–30.[115] This order was faithfully observed. The daily French military bulletins reported several attacks in the days preceding October 30, but the November 1 bulletin read: "Cochinchina—Since October 30, 0-time, situation calm on all sectors."[116] A similar message was sent to Paris two days later: "Nearly absolute calm and cessation terrorist activity signaled in all Cochinchinese provinces."[117]

The truce seems to have been observed for a little over a week, but on November 9, the Cochinchinese Council complained in a cable to Paris of Vietnamese attacks on partisan posts and of attempts on the life of a Cochinchina Council member, all in violation of the modus vivendi agreement.[118] A few days later, the first protests against French violations were sent from Hanoi,[119] and on November 23, d'Argenlieu presented the Cominindo with a table of kidnappings, assassinations, desertions, sabotage, and skirmishes showing that the truce had only been effective for a week, and that on November 20, the activity of the "rebels" was back to normal.[120]

Why did the Vietnamese adhere so strictly to the cease-fire in the first days, and who was responsible for its breakdown? The observance of the truce on the day and time fixed by Nguyen Binh showed that Vietnamese authorities had full control of their troops. This was probably why they strictly avoided all incidents in the first days of November.[121] The responsibility for the breakdown is more difficult to establish, but the Vietnamese and French interpreted the cease-fire differently. The Vietnamese maintained that all troops should hold their positions and not move into territory controlled by the adversary. The commander of the French forces in the south, General Georges Nyo, saw this differently. On October 30, he ordered French troops to secure the maintenance of law and order throughout the whole territory and to react immediately against any "rebel element" fomenting trouble. The local commanders were also told to prepare for larger operations against inactive "armed bands," although such operations should only start on the explicit order of the general himself.[122] Given the nature of these instructions, it seems probable that the clashes in November occurred when French troops moved into territory that the guerrilla leaders considered to be theirs.

In a private conversation in late October, Ho Chi Minh told U.S. Vice-Consul James O'Sullivan that the effectiveness of the modus vivendi agreement would depend upon French actions in Cochinchina. If they kept their promise to respect civil liberties, release political prisoners, and stop attacking Vietnamese forces, things would go well for them also in Tonkin. Otherwise, the mixed commissions would not accomplish much.[123] On October 30, Hanoi instructed the liaison officers in eleven towns north of the 16th parallel not to start applying the modus vivendi agreement before they had received a specific order from the government.[124]

This meant that the application of the modus vivendi agreement in the north would depend on a successful cease-fire in the south, which in turn would depend on some kind of recognition of the Vietnamese institutions in Nam Bo. The Vietnamese were only willing to start meeting their obligations in the north if the French would accept Vietnamese institutions as partners in a political and military solution for the south. Much would depend on the so-called Nyo talks, which aimed at finding a military solution.

In the last phase of the Fontainebleau conference, the French had proposed that the cease-fire be followed by the withdrawal of all Vietnamese forces from the south. Ho Chi Minh refused to let this become part of the modus vivendi agreement he signed in the early hours of September 15.[125] Hence the agreement gave no details on the implementation of the cease-fire. It only stated: "Agreements of the French and Viet Nam General Staff should arrange the conditions of application and supervision of measures decided in common" (article 9b). The French Ministry of National Defense prepared internal instructions for the interpretation of the military clauses of the modus vivendi agreement, which were sent to Saigon on October 1.[126] They directed the high commissioner to demand the withdrawal and disarming of all Vietnamese forces in the south. On October 31, d'Argenlieu assured Paris that the fundamental issue in the military negotiations would be the "repatriation" of regular troops that had come to the south from the north, and the disarming of the "rebels" in the south. The retention of these troops in Cochinchina and southern Annam would "be tantamount to recognition of Hanoi's sovereignty over these territories." D'Argenlieu had therefore instructed General Nyo to make these demands at the very start of the military negotiations.[127]

When the talks opened in Hanoi on November 3, just as the new Vietnamese government was being approved by the National Assembly, the Vietnamese categorically rejected Nyo's demands. It was not Giap but Hoang Huu Nam who conducted the talks on the Vietnamese side, in his capacity as a delegate from the National Resistance Committee. He was assisted, however, by Giap's chief of staff, according to a French report a "mute personality" who continuously passed little handwritten notes to Nam "prescribing the imperative point of view of the Army and Giap." Since neither of the two sides wanted to take responsibility for a rupture, the talks continued until war broke out in Hanoi. The Vietnamese delegation tried to propose a preliminary agreement to prevent any hostile actions. The French were not completely against it, but let the negotiations drag on. "The French Commission was up against a difficult task, since it was expected to engage in military accords that must inevitably concern problems that were basically political, and that had been resolved neither by the accords of March 6 nor at Dalat or Fontainebleau," Nyo concluded on December 23.[128]

When the talks began in Hanoi on November 3, the Vietnamese rejected Nyo's demands out of hand. Neither party was willing to compromise, but both were ready to continue negotiating.[129] The Vietnamese delegation tried to get Nyo to accept a preliminary agreement to avoid any hostility until a definitive agreement could be reached. The French did not refuse explicitly, but no agreement was reached.[130]

The Vietnamese had also hoped that the French would agree to deal with their regional leaders in the south. On September 13, the Resistance Committee for the Southern Region had been reorganized, and on September 22, the provisional Administrative Committee for Nam Bo, which had been set up during the August Revolution in 1945, issued a proclamation claiming to be the sole legal authority in Nam Bo.[131] The Administrative Committee was now chaired by Pham Van Bach, and Nguyen Binh was commissar for military affairs. On October 17, the Administrative Committee sent instructions to the provincial committees explaining why the modus vivendi agreement had been signed and how it could be used to make progress in the struggle for unity and independence: faithful French application of the clauses would mean recognizing the authority of the Vietnamese government in the south. Therefore: "We must show the French and the foreign powers that we are well disciplined, that we obey the orders of the government, and that we respect the signature of Ho Chi Minh."[132] The modus vivendi agreement prescribed that a person designated by the Vietnamese government and approved by the French government should be accredited to the high commissioner in Saigon. In late October, the Vietnamese government designated Pham Van Bach to fill this function, thus hoping for an indirect French recognition of the Administrative Committee. D'Argenlieu was not to be fooled and asked the French government for authorization to inform Ho Chi Minh that the designation of Pham Van Bach could not be approved. At the same time, he cabled Ho that "nothing was less probable" than an approval from Paris.[133] Moutet replied to d'Argenlieu instead of writing directly to Ho Chi Minh, instructing the high commissioner to formally protest the existence of the Administrative Committee for the Southern Region.[134] Ho Chi Minh asked several times for an answer from the French government. Its formal refusal to accept Pham Van Bach arrived on November 25.[135] By then focus was no longer on the south.

The French were not content just to disapprove of Pham Van Bach's designation. They wanted Ho to disavow the so-called Resistance in the south. On November 2, Moutet wanted to know if the French commissioner in Hanoi (Morlière) had made "the necessary representations" to the Vietnamese government with regard to the setting up of the Resistance Committee for the Southern Region.[136] In reality, that Resistance Committee had existed for a long time, but the French challenged the legality of a decree that had reorganized it on September 13. Moutet's request provoked an exchange of notes between d'Argenlieu and Ho on the legality of the Administrative Committee for Nam Bo. D'Argenlieu's first protest reached Ho on November 7. The activities of the committee were asserted to be in contradiction with both the March 6 and September 14 agreements, and Ho Chi Minh was asked to halt all activities by institutions in Cochinchina representing the Vietnamese government.[137]

Ho retorted that the Administrative Committee had existed since August 25, 1945, and that both the March 6 and September 14 agreements were based on the preservation of status quo until the referendum could be held.[138] D'Argenlieu replied that this interpretation of the March 6 and September 14 agreements lacked any juridical foundation. Cochinchina was French territory, and its status could only be changed by a decision of the French parliament, which would ratify the wish of the population, consulted in a referendum. He warned that if Ho persisted in his interpretation, it would affect the very basis of the current negotiations.[139] On November 14, Ho Chi Minh answered that article 9 of the modus vivendi agreement was incompatible with the thesis that denied the existence of Vietnamese administrative and military institutions in Cochinchina. Cochinchina was a part of Vietnam where there was a special de facto situation due to the presence of French military forces. He warned the high commissioner against resorting to violence, since that could lead to a suspension of the application of the modus vivendi agreement. In that case, the Vietnamese government would decline all responsibility.[140] The prospect of a suspension was not something d'Argenlieu feared. He had long wanted this to happen.[141] On November 13, he had left Saigon for Paris, determined to ask the Comonindo to suspend the agreement that Moutet had signed two months earlier. In d'Argenlieu's absence, it was the interim high commissioner, General Valluy, who closed the correspondence with Ho Chi Minh on November 20. He confirmed what had been said in the previous letters and added that article 9 of the modus vivendi agreement referred to the existence of armed hostilities, which it was meant to terminate, and not to any de jure situation.[142]

The correspondence on the status of Nam Bo/Cochinchina was the final demarcation of two incompatible positions. At Fontainebleau, the French had refused to fix a date for the referendum, because they needed time to whip up support for Cochinchinese autonomy. When the press was let free and the "rebels" were permitted to show their loyalty to Hanoi by strictly observing the cease-fire, the protagonists of Vietnamese unity made their views heard in the Saigon media. In light of this development, the instructions from Paris to obtain the withdrawal of Vietnamese forces from the south were totally inapplicable. But in the Nyo talks, France avoided any concession to the principle of an official Vietnamese presence in the south. At the same time, d'Argenlieu, incited by a request from Moutet, chose to accentuate the most delicate of all topics by demanding that the DRV institutions in the south be abolished. The conflict over the status of Nam Bo sealed the fate of the modus vivendi agreement.

Only one single clause in the agreement was fully implemented: on October 31, the Vietnamese handed the Pasteur Institute in Hanoi back to the French. French intelligence reported on November 7 that Vietnamese authorities had decided not to resolve anything else as long as there was no progress in the Nyo talks.[143] This does not mean that the Vietnamese did not take the mixed commissions seriously. They prepared themselves for hard, protracted negotiations on every issue.[144] The Vietnamese preparations were of no use, however, as it proved impossible to agree even on a location for the talks. The mixed commissions were thus never established. Ho Chi Minh insisted that they meet in Hanoi,[145] while d'Argenlieu maintained that the site for the most important commissions should be Dalat. He explained to Paris that as a matter of principle, matters of concern to the whole of the Indochinese Federation should be discussed in Dalat. Moreover, it was necessary to get the Vietnamese negotiators away from Hanoi, where they would spend all their time on political agitation instead of negotiating sincerely.[146]

Some days after d'Argenlieu's departure for Paris, Saigon decided that the disagreement on where to locate the commissions should not be allowed to delay the promised restitution of French property. The chief economic negotiator, Ladreit de Lacharrière, went to Hanoi in order to establish the commissions supposed to take care of the restitution. Valluy called this a "gesture of reconciliation."[147] When d'Argenlieu saw this in a telegram he received in Paris, he feared that Valluy had gone soft, and he hastened to express his hope that de Lacharrière's mission was inspired by the need to make Hanoi meet its obligations rather than a wish to make excessive gestures of reconciliation.[148]

Just after de Lacharrière arrived in Hanoi, a serious incident occurred in Haiphong as the result of a customs conflict. De Lacharrière obtained a promise from Ho to establish the commissions for the restitution of French property immediately, but in return, Ho wanted a special mixed commission to find an urgent provisional solution to the customs conflict in Haiphong. De Lacharrière discussed this with Commissioner of the Republic Morlière and his delegate for economic affairs, Robert Davée. They all agreed that Ho's proposal should be accepted and said so in a cable to Saigon.[149]

Valluy refused, however, arguing that the creation of a special mixed commission would give the impression that France had modified its position and bowed to Vietnamese pressure.[150] When cabling his refusal to Hanoi on November 23, Valluy had already ordered French forces in Haiphong into action. The battle of Haiphong put an end to all hope of a modus vivendi.

PANIC IN SAIGON

The Vietnamese government had a clear strategy for how to utilize the modus vivendi agreement. It wanted to exploit article 9 to the full and delay the application of the other clauses till the French had been forced to deal with its representatives in the south. French strategy was more wavering, due to the fact that the agreement had been signed by Moutet against the wish of d'Argenlieu. D'Argenlieu had no faith in the modus vivendi agreement and especially disliked article 9. Yet his first reports on the effective cease-fire indicate that there was a moment of relative optimism in Saigon. However, with the abortive Nyo talks, numerous reports of defections by village notables, and an acute crisis in the Cochinchinese Council, the French in Saigon felt that the ground was giving way under their feet. By mid-November, they were convinced that the only way to safeguard French prestige and power would be to take drastic action and teach the Vietnamese a lesson.

As early as October 15, three days before Ho's return, d'Argenlieu had regretted that a vicious campaign was under way to oblige the French to accept the Vietnamese view with regard to Cochinchina. The French were giving only moderate answers to the Vietnamese "calumnies," because otherwise the favorable climate for the application of the modus vivendi agreement might be disturbed; however, the French might soon find themselves in an inferior position if they maintained this modest attitude confronted with an "adversary with no scruples," d'Argenlieu said. In any case, the Vietnamese campaign would cease if Ho wanted it to: "We shall be enlightened as to the real intentions of V.N. when the president has resumed the reins of power."[151] Two days later, on October 17, while preparing to receive the Vietnamese president the following day on the *Suffren,* d'Argenlieu received a succinct note from his new political advisor, Federal Commissioner for Political Affairs Léon Pignon. He was certain that Ho aimed to "eliminate France from Indochina." France had three main options, of which only the third was allowed for the time being: (1) a military coup in Tonkin against the Vietnamese government; (2) a strategic withdrawal to established economic and cultural positions, with recognition of Vietnam's independence; and (3) political and military action to get the Vietnamese government to start dealing seriously with France and effect real change, not just modify its façade.[152]

After meeting Ho at Cam Ranh Bay on October 18, d'Argenlieu cabled Paris a quite optimistic report, a testimony to Ho's personal and diplomatic skills. The admiral was now under the impression that Ho wanted, at least for a while, to consolidate the results he had gained by seeking détente with France. But d'Argenlieu was also convinced that Ho would try, by "mixing kindness and friendly declarations with blackmail and intimidation," to improve his position in Cochinchina, even beyond the substantial gains he had achieved through article 9 of the modus vivendi agreement.[153] At the same time, however, d'Argenlieu warned the French chiefs of staff that the possibility of Vietnamese military action against the French in the north could not be excluded, and that France needed to prepare itself to respond immediately in both "Hanoi and Annam." The government should therefore not just maintain 75,000 French troops in Indochina but dispatch reinforcements.[154] A few days later, d'Argenlieu dutifully forwarded friendly messages to Paris from the Vietnamese president, who courteously greeted Bidault, Moutet, and also the communist minister of reconstruction, François Billoux. The telegram to Bidault was strongest on substance ("faithful application of the modus vivendi agreement"), the one to Billoux on intimacy ("kisses to the kids").[155]

D'Argenlieu did not like such telegrams. On October 26, he complained to Paris of the false impression made by "official courtesy." He spoke of Hanoi's "double game"; Ho Chi Minh was a shrewd politician who could officially disavow his subordinates when their actions were too defiant, while at the same time letting his government fuel the underground groups in the south with instructions to keep up their terrorist activity. D'Argenlieu quoted a sample of such instructions, captured by French intelligence. He concluded that the Vietnamese were exploiting article 9 in an effort to unravel a year of French efforts in Cochinchina. The modus vivendi agreement would transform those who were legally and legitimately considered rebels into regular troops of a member country of the French Union. D'Argenlieu warned that it could become necessary to overthrow a scheme so minutely contrived by an "implacable adversary." If this proved to be the case, it would be best to inform Ho Chi Minh that the date of the entry into force of the cease-fire would have to be postponed.[156]

This was in fact an attack on Moutet for having signed the modus vivendi agreement. D'Argenlieu did not, however, put his threat to postpone the application into effect. On October 30, he instead gave the lengthy speech quoted above, denouncing terrorist activity in the south, assuring the Cochinchinese provisional government of French support, and expressing his doubts that Vietnam would comply with all its obligations.[157] Then the successful implementation of the cease-fire produced brief euphoria. On November 1, d'Argenlieu told Paris that Ho seemed to be refraining from the kind of actions that would justify postponing the application of the modus vivendi agreement.[158] And on November 3, he described the situation in the south as "seriously improving" and said that the talks in Hanoi were developing favorably.[159]

These telegrams show that High Commissioner d'Argenlieu was wavering. The factor he was most uncertain about was Ho's personal power. He seems to have been relying on secret intelligence from Hanoi. On November 6, he told Moutet that his information on Ho's desire to avoid a rupture stemmed from an absolutely reliable source, saying that Ho was in control of the situation. The anticommunist opposition in the north, whose only weapon was to outbid the Viet Minh in terms of xenophobia, was now incapable of expressing its views publicly, because the Vietnamese security forces were both numerous and efficient. The opposition now longed for Emperor Bao Dai's return, d'Argenlieu claimed. Some hoped that France, others that the United States, would bring him back from China.[160]

There is a remarkable contrast between these conciliatory cables in the first days of November and the hard words d'Argenlieu had used in his October 26 message. This may reflect a temporary optimism in Saigon, caused by the success of the cease-fire. It is also conceivable that d'Argenlieu, knowing full well that Moutet had invested his personal prestige in the modus vivendi agreement, was concealing his real view and waiting for a better opportunity to unravel the gains made by the adversary. By November 13, when d'Argenlieu went to Paris, there was nothing left of the early November optimism.

As soon as d'Argenlieu had left, the cables from Deputy High Commissioner Valluy began resorting to the same themes that d'Argenlieu had expressed in the first half of October. Valluy blamed the worsening situation in Cochinchina on France's "tacit recognition" of the Vietnamese claims on the region.[161] On November 19, he warned the French government that the French position in Cochinchina, as well as in the rest of Indochina, was being compromised. French "unilateral application" was more and more detrimental, and an all-out effort using "all available means" was therefore being planned. Valluy insisted that this effort be supported by a solemn governmental declaration affirming French sovereignty in Cochinchina.[162]

In itself, the modus vivendi agreement had seemed like a French victory. France obtained significant long-term concessions from the Vietnamese without giving in to their demands for independence and union. However, the effective execution of the cease-fire and the demonstration of popular support in the south for the cause of national unity turned the application of the agreement into a political victory for Ho Chi Minh. This pushed the French into a mental state of crisis. Until November, they had hoped to have their cake and eat it too: control of Cochinchina and peace with Vietnam. The increase in guerrilla activity, the political strength of the unionists, the French reluctance to let Dr. Thinh have real power, and signs that the French authorities might abandon their support for the separatists—all these factors combined to generate a severe crisis in the Cochinchinese Council and government, precisely at the time when the modus vivendi agreement entered into force.

The French and indigenous members of the Cochinchinese Council (which was meant to serve as precursor for an elected parliament) blamed Dr. Thinh's government for the crisis and on October 31 demanded a cabinet reshuffle. One week later, when unable to present the council with a new government, Dr. Thinh came under attack. His main critic, Dr. Le Van Hoach, declared: "A government resembles a sports team. The premier is the captain. The rest of us, the Assembly members, are the supporters. The present team has been engaged in tough matches against other teams. It has lost because of lack of cohesion among the members. We, the supporters, demand a reshuffle of the team, discarding the incapable and selecting new players who are more on top of things."[163]

President Thinh who already in August had complained in private that the French administration seemed bent on "demonstrating to the Viet Minh that we are their puppets," replied:

> All the insufficiencies that I'm being reproached with derive from the hybrid political regime that has been given to Cochinchina. Is it a Colony or a Republic? Our government suffers from this situation and does not have the means to act. The implementation of the modus vivendi [agreement] in Cochinchina places us in a delicate situation. Are we going to be relieved by the new Nam Bo government? Cochinchina is having a hard time at the moment. You asked me the other day to change my governing team, [and] I'm ready to do so. But I first had to ask Monsieur the commissioner of the Republic, whom I need to consult on such issues. It is also for this reason that I have asked him to come and take part in the session this evening. Rest assured, however, that the government reshuffle you want will be accomplished with the shortest possible delay.[164]

Dr. Thinh promised the council to present it with a new cabinet before November 15, but on November 10, his body was found hanging from the bolt of his window.[165] Those remembering the French colonization of Cochinchina eighty years earlier would recall how the mandarin Phan Thanh Gian, after having tried to collaborate with the new foreign masters, had also resolved his impossible situation by taking his own life.[166] D'Argenlieu immediately informed Paris, asserting that Dr. Thinh's suicide must have been motivated by a desire to expose the injustice of the attacks directed against him by groups influenced by the Hanoi government—attacks to which "the modus vivendi [agreement] had given all the more liberty of expression."[167] Dr. Thinh's suicide put an end to the French hopes of creating a strong, loyal, and autonomous Cochinchina as the cornerstone of the Indochinese Federation. Yet the Cochinchinese experiment continued. Shortly before his departure on November 13, d'Argenlieu called his advisors together to seek a way out of this blind alley. They started by conceding defeat. Then Albert Torel, the new (first interim) French commissioner for Cochinchina, who had been skeptical to the idea of Cochinchinese separatism and rather preferred to reinstate a monarchic solution for the whole of Annam (Vietnam), gave his less than enthusiastic appreciation of the candidates to succeed Dr. Thinh. He concluded that it was difficult to find the right man and proposed replacing the Cochinchinese government with a provisional administrative committee, so that "the conflict could be localized between France and Vietnam." Pignon did not agree. "In a first phase," he said, we must "play according to the rules of the game and honor our pledges." D'Argenlieu consented: "The Cochinchinese government must remain in place," but in the choice of personalities, one should seek out "genuine noncommunist unionists" (protagonists of unifying the three ky). After some weeks of prevarication, the two main candidates for the presidency, the ultra-separatist Tran Van Ty and the unionist Nguyen Van Xuan, were obliged to withdraw their candidatures, and on December 6, the sporty but otherwise unremarkable Le Van Hoach was elected president.[168]

In France, the news of Dr. Thinh's suicide arrived at the same time as the first results of the French general elections, but the socialist mouthpiece Le Populaire had enough space for a comment that was probably more to the point than the explanation given by d'Argenlieu: "The faithful application by both sides of the 'modus vivendi' [agreement] signed by Mr. Ho Chi Minh and Marius Moutet, is little by little stripping this pseudo-government of all 'raison d'être' and authority. The suicide of its president will, no doubt, hasten its demise."[169]

In the week before the suicide, the cease-fire in Nam Bo had remained quite effective, and this further reinforced the prestige of the Vietnamese government in the south. The Viet Minh simply won the propaganda war. Its political success and the French and autonomist failure became only too evident. Such situations have historically been among the most dangerous. When the powerful see the basis for their power eroding, they sometimes embark on risky, even reckless, actions. The risk that the communist advance in the French parliamentary elections on November 10 would lead to the formation of a cabinet favoring concessions to Vietnam contributed to the panic, which provoked a strategic shift in Saigon. The option of shifting to a strategy of open confrontation had been discussed before, but only on a tentative basis. Until now the strategy had been designed to avoid any large-scale military conflict in the north, while concentrating on building up French control of Cochinchina, southern Annam, Cambodia, and Laos. It was believed that a successful application of this strategy would eventually oblige Hanoi to accept more or less the same terms as those offered to the governments in Vientiane, Phnom Penh, and Saigon. The French decision-makers in Saigon now feared that a new French government would make additional concessions to Hanoi, and perhaps give Vietnam the status of an "associated state"—a new legal category of semi-independent states included in the French constitution just adopted.[170] This convinced d'Argenlieu and his team that a new strategy was needed, and that they had to take the initiative without waiting for new government instructions. Something dramatic had to be done to demonstrate the firm intent of France to defend its presence in Asia. The decision to seek a confrontation in the north was probably made on November 12 or 13, just before d'Argenlieu departed for Paris. He left behind him instructions for Valluy to regroup the French forces in the north in order to prepare for the eventuality of France being obliged to resort to "direct forcible action against the Hanoi government."[171] It is important to note that the principal purpose of this decision was to secure French control of the south, not to conquer the north. D'Argenlieu and his team believed that a rupture in the north would have a favorable effect on the attitude of the population in the south.

4

Massacre

The mission of the Navy has been perfectly executed, notably Savorgna de Brazza firing at Kien An and a designated village.

NAVY COMMAND, HAIPHONG, NOVEMBER 23, 1946

The deaths of thousands of human beings are concealed behind this terse telegram. When exploring the origins of the Vietnamese wars, it is easy to become absorbed in the actions of the presidents, ministers, commissioners, admirals, generals, and colonels—all men—and forget the millions of people—men, women, and children—who were wounded, who died, or who lost their closest kin. Sometimes, however, the archives of the decision-makers reveal evidence of the suffering. Jean Sainteny, the man who made peace on March 6, inspected the ruins of Haiphong on December 3, and noted, not only that the military action had been "very brilliant," but also that it had been "very brutal."[1]

SAIGON'S DECISION

The key decisions leading to the Haiphong massacre were taken by High Commissioner d'Argenlieu between November 11 and 13, 1946, when he attended Dr. Thinh's funeral and learned that the French general election had made the Parti communiste français the biggest party in the National Assembly. On November 13, he left dramatic instructions behind for General Valluy, who was to stand in for him while he was lobbying in Paris and visiting de Gaulle at his home in Colombey-les-Deux-Églises. Just as in February, the French and Vietnamese adversaries were preparing themselves for a showdown in the north. Meanwhile, the insurgency gradually resumed in the south, just as it had in March, but this time the southern guerrilla leaders were either unable or unwilling, after their effective implementation of the cease-fire, to mount any serious offensive.[2] In the north, there was no longer a Chinese army to enforce the peace. The port city of Haiphong and the capital Hanoi were once again in focus, with a sideshow going on in Langson, a town strategically placed on the most important railroad to China.

The SFIO's Indochina slogan—"Neither abandonment, nor conquest"—was meant to reconcile peace with French greatness. D'Argenlieu had convinced himself that the two were not compatible, and he naturally opted for *greatness (grandeur)*. The socialist concept in fact implied a two-pronged strategy, which had dominated French thinking in 1945–46, but was now abandoned in Saigon. The losing strategy had consisted in letting the Viet Minh dominate the north for the time being. The men behind this strategy may well have expected that when French control of the south had been secured, and its economic life had resumed, the regime in the north would come to terms, since it depended economically on the south. Having failed to generate local support in the south, d'Argenlieu and his collaborators scrapped the two-pronged strategy, and gambled on a hope that if the Viet Minh's main power base in the north could be made to collapse, then either Ho Chi Minh would reduce his ambitions or France would find more reasonable partners. This would in turn leave room for establishing a constructive relationship with the south-based elites.

By mid-October, when Ho Chi Minh was on his way back on the *Dumont d'Urville*, d'Argenlieu had already mentioned the possibility that the French might, as a considered countermeasure to a likely enemy attack, have to resort to a coup in Tonkin. "I consider that the hypothesis of forceful action by the Hanoi government under the most diverse pretexts, born of the exploitation of the modus vivendi [agreement], cannot be excluded. . . . If the government recognizes the probability of this hypothesis, we need to start getting ready to deal with it. An immediate response both in Hanoi and in Annam would then be necessary," d'Argenlieu secretly wired Bidault and General Juin on October 19. He asked that they make reinforcements available. Juin supported d'Argenlieu's proposal at a meeting of the Cominindo on October 23, the day Ho Chi Minh was welcomed home by cheering masses in Hanoi. In view of the possibility of a "very serious crisis in Indochina," Juin held it necessary to put reinforcements at the disposal of the high commissioner as quickly as possible.[3] Two days afterward, d'Argenlieu told his staff in Saigon that they should prepare to take advantage of renewed hostilities, which could break out as early as January 1947, to launch an offensive of their own with the aim of politically and morally neutralizing the Hanoi government so as to facilitate the pacification of the south.[4]

In reality, d'Argenlieu was not really waiting for an initiative from the adversary, merely for an occasion to act himself. He now asked Valluy to plan a *coup de force* in Tonkin. A preliminary study was undertaken by the 3^e Bureau in Saigon and sent to the admiral on November 9. Two options were considered: occupying Hanoi or abandoning it. In both cases, it would be advisable to evacuate the French garrisons in the important cities of Nam Dinh and Langson, as well as Phu Lang Thuong and

Bac Ninh. The essential point for Valluy, who had long complained that his troops were too dispersed, was to hold Haiphong, the port that commanded the coast. By controlling the sea and the principal ports, France could, he thought optimistically, "put the Tonkinese authorities and population at our mercy by choking the country's economy." From a military point of view, Valluy leaned toward abandoning Hanoi, but he admitted that this might be inconvenient from a political and economic viewpoint, because it would look like a retreat, and perhaps even be interpreted as signaling a French exit. In the first phase of the operations, before pulling out troops and civilians, the French forces should carry out a "coup d'état" in each city and seize important personalities. It was necessary to "neutralize the current Vietnamese government in Hanoi through a forceful action." Such "coups," however, could only succeed if they were kept completely secret, even from the "highest [French] political and administrative personalities . . . we shall have no scruples in preparing the military action through any kind of profitable diplomatic maneuver."[5]

The admiral studied this proposal in light of Dr. Thinh's suicide and the outcome of the general election in France. While appreciating the coup aspect of the plan he no doubt regarded withdrawing from so many places as excessively cautious. On November 12 or 13, just before his departure, he gave draconian instructions to Valluy:

> If, in spite of the efforts of the French government to arrive at a satisfactory agreement with the Hanoi government, hostilities should resume in the various operational theaters in Indochina, it is important that our troops be capable, not just of enduring a sudden attack from the adversary, but in addition of responding with decisive forceful action. . . . We must hence foresee the hypothesis under which the French government, after having exhausted all of its conciliatory resources, views itself as obliged, in order to retaliate against a resumption of hostilities, to resort to a forceful action against the Hanoi government.[6]

The high commissioner prescribed regrouping the forces deployed in the south, by "abandoning the excessive number of small posts, reorganizing the Cochinchinese Garde civile, and creating mobile units that can support the Army in certain important police tasks," all of this in order to deploy the most effective forces in the north. He accepted substantially reducing the strength of certain garrisons in the north (Bac Ninh, Phu Lang Thuong, Nam Dinh, and Langson) in order to concentrate the effort on the "strategic coastal base" from Haiphong to Ha Long Bay. He still wanted to "leave a symbolic garrison in Langson until further orders," and he did not in any way consider abandoning the "air-ground base of Hanoi, which constitutes the advanced starting point for the forceful actions that aim, in case of conflict, to neutralize the Hanoi government and destroy the military centers in Ha Dong, Sontay-Tong, and possibly Hoa Binh." He also asked Valluy to secure communications between Haiphong and Hanoi, at least temporarily.

Admiral d'Argenlieu's instructions thus went further than General Valluy's proposals, but they would soon themselves be overtaken by the actions of the local commanders. And much sooner than the admiral thought. He did not expect Valluy to carry out the coup during his absence, just to prepare for it, so that it could be implemented later, perhaps "already in January 1947."[7] D'Argenlieu's instructions represented a complete reversal of Valluy's previous strategy, which the French chiefs of staff had approved in August, and d'Argenlieu's reasoning was based on an analysis of the situation, not in Tonkin, but in Cochinchina. It was the failure in the south that led d'Argenlieu to reconsider the policy of détente in the north. He had seen the problems coming in October, then vacillated for some time after meeting Ho Chi Minh on October 18 and seeing how scrupulously the adversary adhered to the cease-fire agreement in the first days after its entry into force on October 30. On November 5, however, d'Argenlieu wrote a letter to de Gaulle, announcing his forthcoming visit to France and complaining about the French government's inability to see matters as they really were. He expressed his wish that the French electorate had heard and understood de Gaulle's latest pronouncement.[8] Shortly afterward, the admiral was deeply shaken by Dr. Thinh's suicide and the way it was exploited in the media. There was no way he could stop the unionist press, since this would violate the political freedoms promised in the modus vivendi agreement. There was also no way he could act decisively against the guerrillas, since they were not now active militarily, but relying on political means and on demonstrating their obedience to the Vietnamese government's orders. The Viet Minh continued to expand its political control in the countryside under cover of the modus vivendi agreement. D'Argenlieu understood that the political situation in Paris made it impossible for him to get any approval for a clean break with the Viet Minh. This was something he could at best hope to discuss confidentially with Prime Minister Bidault and Chief of Staff Juin. His intention in going to Paris was no doubt to explain the southern debacle to the members of the Cominindo, obtain a suspension of the cease-fire from them, and then start talking about the need to act in the north.

He asked Valluy to prepare the necessary material on the south, and on November 19 and 22, Valluy submitted two reports to Paris on southern developments. The application of the cease-fire was increasingly worsening the French position, he claimed. An energetic effort "with all the means at our disposal" was now under way.[9] The strict execution of the cease-fire on the day and time fixed by the "rebel leaders" had given proof of the rebel bands' discipline. At the very moment of the cease-fire, an intense, insidious and well-prepared political campaign had been launched in all the southern provinces, and the population had understood this as a stage on the way to national unification. The Viet Minh was gaining ground every day, the local chiefs were turning away from the French, and there had been 200 desertions from the partisan troops. In spite of great efforts, the French lacked the means to counteract the political progress of the rebels: "There is no reason to believe that it is possible to arrive at an agreement on an armistice in Hanoi on the conditions that have been elaborated by Paris. On the other hand, we cannot give Hanoi the moral advantage it would have if the rupture came from us. I estimate the situation to be difficult; it may be reparable in some details and in certain places, but it is essentially serious and certainly not favorable, as people seem pleased to say in some Parisian circles."[10]

D'Argenlieu had long wished to present his views personally to the French government, and on October 17, Bidault had given him the green light to come to Paris after the November 10 elections.[11] When the admiral took off for Paris on November 13, U.S. Consul Charles Reed expressed doubts that he would ever return if "leftist elements unite for political control."[12] The French press had just printed a news bulletin from Agence France-Presse (AFP) saying that d'Argenlieu would probably rejoin his monastery.[13] Valluy reacted by demanding the AFP director's dismissal.[14] During the next month, the question of whether or not d'Argenlieu should be kept on as high commissioner was a hot issue in Paris. The socialist and communist press demanded his dismissal, although they did not have any inkling of what he was up to just then. Undisturbed by these leftist noises, d'Argenlieu lobbied effectively in the political establishment for reinforcements and political support, while sending reassuring messages back to Valluy in Saigon.

Before flying to Paris, d'Argenlieu had fixed the lines of responsibility for his collaborators. Valluy was to be interim high commissioner, and the two "federal ministers" Pignon (political affairs) and Gonon (finance) would have the authority along with Valluy to act in d'Argenlieu's name. A triumvirate would thus govern Indochina, the U.S. consul remarked.[15] It was this triumvirate, led by Valluy, who took all of Saigon's fateful decisions until d'Argenlieu returned, with new government instructions, on December 23.

PLANNING FOR A COUP D'ETAT

D'Argenlieu's instructions forced Valluy to scrap the prudent strategy he had developed in July–August and dig up from his files the offensive plans devised in connection with Operation Bentré. In March–April, when it was not yet certain that the March 6 accords would hold, optional plans for "coups d'état" in the northern centers had been worked out, but since May, these had just been kept on file. Immediately after having approved the April 3 military convention, which fixed the number of French and Vietnamese troops to take joint responsibility for relieving the Japanese of their duties in the various parts of Tonkin, General Leclerc had issued a general order, "Directives No. 1," defining the task of the French northern garrisons as defending French interests by "the slow method, marking some little progress every day, without growing weary; by force when necessary."[16] Leclerc's order was not very precise, but it shows that he considered the March 6 agreements as a step on the way to increasing French control, not vice versa. The military aspects of the March 6 agreement had first been specified in an appendix to the accord itself and later in more detail in a specific convention signed on April 3, which set limits for the number of French troops to be stationed in the north, specified where the garrisons would be located, and established structures for military cooperation between the French and the Vietnamese.

General Raoul Salan signed this April 3 convention on behalf of France just before he left the northern command to General Valluy, who served in this function until succeeding Leclerc as commander of all French Far Eastern forces on July 17.[17] On April 10, Valluy specified Leclerc's "slow method" in follow-up "Directives No. 2." He emphasized the instability of a situation in which the French were threatened both by a hostile population and by Chinese troops. Thus in every garrison, the commander must draw up a security plan, which should include prescriptions for the permanent protection of the military quarters, as well as for the seizure of the town in an emergency. In addition to elaborating local plans for "neutralizing" the enemy and occupying "sensitive points," methods should be elaborated for modifying the military occupation and finally switching from a purely military operation to a "coup d'état."[18] This was, of course, conceived as a contingency plan to be implemented in the eventuality that the cooperation prescribed in the April 3 convention broke down.

As an indication of appropriate methods, the general order prescribed effective intelligence, teams of specialists (possibly in disguise) charged with the "neutralization" of local leaders, and absolute secrecy. We may assume that such plans were dutifully drawn up by the commanders of the various French garrisons, but they were not used until November. On April 27, after a trip to Hanoi, U.S. Consul Reed reported that there might be ulterior motives behind the French insistence on a rapid withdrawal of the Chinese troops, because the French might stage a military coup once the Chinese were gone.[19] If the French had done so when the majority of Chinese forces left in June, however, this would have coincided with the Paris negotiations. Saigon could not be sure of Paris's backing if the French forces in Indochina appeared to be the aggressors. Moreover, in the first period after the Chinese withdrawal, French and Vietnamese forces rubbed along in the north, notwithstanding a few incidents. The worst of these, which might in fact have escalated, occurred at Bac Ninh north of Hanoi in early August, with twelve French soldiers killed and many wounded. This led to an exchange of protests in Paris, where the Fontainebleau conference had been temporarily broken off when the Vietnamese delegation learned of d'Argenlieu's "second Dalat conference."[20]

The French moderation in the north from August to October was due to the delay in the Chinese withdrawal, the ongoing negotiations at Fontainebleau, and especially the agreed French focus on Cochinchina. A brief look back at Valluy's thinking in August will demonstrate the extent to which his strategy was later turned up-side down. At the end of August, he told the French chiefs of staff that "it is in Cochinchina and southern Annam that the future of France in Indochina and the Far East will be determined." He wanted reinforcements in Cochinchina, Cambodia (where France had provoked a military incident with Thai forces in May to demonstrate its determination to win back the Cambodian and Laotian provinces that Phnom Penh had annexed in 1941), and "perhaps" Laos. By August, however, he saw no need to further strengthen the forces in Tonkin and northern Annam. His strategic priority was to lock down Cochinchina in a closed combat area (*champs clos*) into which it would be impossible to infiltrate external aid, and then, in a second phase, destroy Nguyen Binh's guerrillas.[21]

The chiefs of staff approved this strategy, and until the signing of the modus vivendi agreement, Valluy saw no need to revise it. He even admitted, as late as September 10, that it would have been best if France had not moved its forces into Tonkin at all; they could have been put to much better use in the south: "We have laid hands on the whole country. We hold on to it by our fingertips."[22] With his south-based strategy, Valluy did not need a vigorous French commander in the north. This may explain d'Argenlieu and Valluy's choice of General Louis Constant Morlière for this position.[23] Morlière had done three stints in Indochina before World War II (1921–23, 1929–32, 1934–39), where he had come to like the natives. Born in 1897, Morlière was two years older than General Valluy, so under normal circumstances, it would have been Valluy who served under Morlière, not vice versa. However, in the French Army in the immediate postwar period, one criterion counted more than seniority: how early one had rallied to de Gaulle. Leclerc, d'Argenlieu, and Valluy had been with the Free French forces from the first days in London. Morlière had served Vichy in North Africa until de Gaulle arrived there with the Americans in 1942. In 1944, while fighting the Germans in France, Morlière was replaced as commander of the 9e DIC by Valluy. Such things are not easily forgotten. In August 1946, Morlière swallowed another bitter pill in acquiescing to d'Argenlieu's request that he serve under Valluy in the colony he knew so well from the 1920s and 1930s.

Morlière was a cautious, peaceable officer with a brilliant examination record and a paternalistic empathy for the natives. Leclerc, Valluy, and Salan saw him as an "office man," not a real soldier. Giap describes Morlière with the same kind of soldierly contempt, recounting in his memoirs how this Frenchman had manifested his compassion for the Vietnamese people by "heaping praise on one of his servants who was a very skilful and honest cook." In February 1947, after Valluy had obtained Morlière's dismissal, the latter prided himself that on his watch in Hanoi, from the settlement of the Bac Ninh incident in early August until the battle for Haiphong in late November, Tonkin had been almost completely calm.[24]

The local commander in Haiphong, 46-year-old Colonel Pierre-Louis Dèbes, who reported to Morlière in the chain of command, had served in the European campaign as chief of staff to the commander of the 9ᵉ DIC, first under Morlière, then under Valluy. He was at first sympathetic to Morlière, although he himself was a very different type—a man of action who, like d'Argenlieu, did not care much for the Vietnamese. Dèbes disliked seeing Morlière having to take orders from Valluy, and he preferred to keep at arm's length from both generals by staying on in Haiphong until he got a chance to be repatriated. Dèbes was weary of Valluy, who on past occasions had sought to give him the most arduous tasks imaginable. Dèbes had refused Valluy's request that he lead the assault on and occupation of Marseille. In October 1946, however, in view of the prospect of a possible showdown with the Vietnamese army, Dèbes loyally implemented Valluy's "Directives No. 2" by issuing detailed orders to all unit commanders in Haiphong on what they should do in an emergency. The orders were distributed in sealed envelopes that were only to be opened on Dèbes's specific order.[25] Just four weeks later, he ordered the seals to be broken. During the ensuing battle for Haiphong, copies of the instructions and also of Valluy's coup d'état directive fell into Vietnamese hands and were widely disseminated. This led the Vietnamese to believe that a similar coup was being planned for Hanoi. Dèbes's unit order prescribed the use of armored cars and artillery to gain complete control of Haiphong: "As the situation is still unstable, we can at any moment be led to intervene very fast on our own initiative. For this possibility, there must be an offensive plan."[26]

A key element in the offensive plans prepared since Operation Bentré was what the documents called "coup d'état." Such coups do not just demand military action, but also involve a political element. This was Léon Pignon's domain. Jean Sainteny could also claim some expertise in the matter, although he was primarily a businessman. *Après coup*, in January 1947, Sainteny summarized the thinking behind French actions since November: "The conclusion . . . can only be reached in Tonkin, where the head of the Resistance is located. To limit one's action to removing the southern extremities of the Viet Minh Hydra's tentacles is illusionary and means forgetting that they will regrow again in the future, as they have done repeatedly since fall 1945, as long as the main body, established in the north, has not been eliminated."[27] He might have added that it would not be enough just to kill the Hydra. One also needed to identify a beast to replace it, one that would lend itself more easily to domestication.

THE BAO DAI ILLUSION

By the time of Dr. Thinh's suicide, the French had already for some time been looking for groups and personalities who could serve as a credible alternative to the Viet Minh and also to the incompetent Cochinchinese separatists.[28] Commissioner Jean Cédile, a representative of the "New France" who had come to Indochina after the "liberation" had been the most ardent supporter of the separatist cause in Cochinchina. He left Saigon in October and was replaced as commissioner in Cochinchina by Albert Torel, an old colonial hand who was more inclined to favor a monarchical solution with a basis in the traditional court in Hue than the modernizing commercial elite in Saigon.[29] It is striking that the most conservative French decision-makers were those who were most inclined to satisfy the Vietnamese aspiration for national unity.

Since the August Revolution, which happened shortly after Japan had conceded the integration of Cochinchina into Bao Dai's Vietnamese monarchy, the Viet Minh had been the main defender of the principle of national unity, which was widely popular among the population in all of the three *ky*. At the end of September, the French made the first contact with Bao Dai, now resident in Hong Kong, fully aware that if he were to make a royal comeback, he would need to be given what France was denying Ho Chi Minh: sovereignty over the whole of "Vietnam," right down to Ca Mau Point.

As emperor of Annam from the age of twelve in 1925, Bao Dai had never wielded real power. He was a French puppet, and when he declared Vietnam independent on March 11, 1945, at the instigation of Japan, this did not much change his situation. The Japanese simply replaced his French advisors with their own, to the extent that they had sufficient manpower, and in many places they simply left a power vacuum, which was eventually filled by the Viet Minh. On August 25, Bao Dai announced his abdication, resumed using his civil name, Vinh Thuy, and was invited to serve as Supreme Advisor to Ho Chi Minh's government. He attended cabinet meetings, and in January 1946, he was elected as a member of the National Assembly from Thanh Hoa, his dynasty's ancestral home.[30] When the new government of Union and Resistance was formed and confirmed by the National Assembly on March 2, 1946, Vinh Thuy kept his advisory role, and he was sent, the following month, on a mission to Chongqing, to secure support from Chiang Kai-shek. His mission failed, to the disappointment of Vietnam's foreign minister, the VNQDD leader Nguyen Tuong Tam. Chiang Kai-shek stuck to his treaty with France and withdrew his troops from Indochina. Vinh Thuy then elected to live in exile in Hong Kong. As emperor he had acquired substantial personal needs, however, and when the French contacted him in September, they had with them both gold and money. "Many eyes are still surely turned toward him . . . but he does not at the moment represent an assured success factor," said d'Argenlieu, who felt that Bao Dai might like to go and live in Cannes on the French Riviera, in an environment that he held "dear."[31] Instead, the French invited Bao Dai on a trip to North Africa, where he could be held in reserve. He considered the offer seriously, but eventually decided to stay in Hong Kong and await developments.[32]

The French, Léon Pignon in particular, also looked into the possibility of building an alliance of convenience with conservative groups in Annam and pro-Chinese opposition groups in Tonkin. Pignon analyzed them, but found that the influence of the old mandarins did not extend beyond the city of Hue, and that virtually all of them had compromised themselves with the Japanese. It was also difficult to envisage any overt partnership with the VNQDD and Dong Minh Hoi, since they were cultivating the image of being even more anti-French and "xenophobic" than the Viet Minh. And the Vietnamese Catholic community was divided between men like Nguyen Manh Ha, who were cooperating with the Viet Minh and the friends of Ngo Dinh Diem, who had resigned in protest from Bao Dai's government in 1932 and remained fiercely anti-French. In this rather discouraging situation, the French decision-makers in Saigon seem to have placed their hopes in the creation, through some kind of decisive action, of something they repeatedly referred to as a "psychological shock." A shock might create room for new leaders to emerge under the guise of a "Bao Dai solution."

Léon Pignon knew of course how difficult it would be to convince the socialist and communist politicians in France to put an abdicated emperor back on the throne. It would have been easier with de Gaulle, who had planned to use another former emperor, Duy Tan (or Vinh San), deposed by the French and exiled to the island of Réunion in 1916, but he had died when his aircraft crashed in Central Africa in November 1945 before he could get back his throne.[33] Marius Moutet, socialist minister for Overseas France from January 20, 1946, warned repeatedly against any kind of royal restoration. He wished, with support from his director of political affairs, Henri Laurentie, to see a modernizing Cochinchinese republic, free of conservatism and, if possible, also from communism. But he cautioned during the Fontainebleau conference that if Ho Chi Minh were sidelined, "the party that replaces him will be even more extreme in its nationalism." It would probably also receive support from foreign powers, he said, and not just China.[34]

Pignon nonetheless continued to explore a monarchic solution. On October 5, he sent the Comanindo the opinion of an anonymous Annamite journalist who "admitted" that the opposition parties were still actually looking to France for support against their common enemy, the Viet Minh. This Mr. X ventured the idea that the French socialists should launch a propaganda campaign against the repression of democratic liberties in the DRV. Three weeks later, Pignon was more explicit in a letter he sent to the Comanindo and the Ministry of Overseas France: "Everything confirms that the only alternative to Ho Chi Minh and the Viet Minh is a unionist democratic monarchy. Will the metropole allow us to play this card?"[35] It would not. Laurentie was aware of the crisis in Cochinchina and the failure of the autonomous government of Dr. Thinh, but he thought the solution was to broaden the political basis of the government in Cochinchina. On October 21, a few days before receiving Pignon's letter, he had warned Marius Moutet of the upcoming Cochinchinese crisis: "Our position in Indochina has, for a few months, become dangerous . . . one essential factor works so completely against us that it threatens all our chances. This is the situation in Cochinchina; unless there is a quick recovery, we shall have no other way of reestablishing order than to introduce Ho Chi Minh there. This would be a defeat for France of incalculable consequences. A government allowing it to suffer such a defeat would never be forgiven by either public opinion or history." The only solution to this dilemma was the establishment of a Cochinchinese government, "if need be marked by unionism, which would probably be anticommunist, but which should not be only that and would draw fundamental authority from its social and national principles."[36] He thought this might still be possible, and he saw no alternative. After having received Pignon's letter, Laurentie stuck to his unrealistic point of view. He did not believe that implementing the modus vivendi agreement would ameliorate the French position. Generously allowing Cochinchina a government whose principles were "close to communism, as vigorous and captivating as those of the Viet Minh," was the only answer. This was the only way to avoid having to abandon Cochinchina to the Viet Minh. At the end of November, after the Haiphong debacle, Laurentie persisted in his view that the only way forward was to reorganize Cochinchina administratively and politically.[37] Pignon took the opposite view. He thought it had been a serious error to allow the Viet Minh to suppress the conservative, pro-Chinese nationalist groups in the north. By dealing solely with the Viet Minh, France had strengthened the nationalist credentials of its main adversary.[38]

The French vacillation between a range of unimpressive personalities in Cochinchina and the equally unimpressive Bao Dai would continue for more than two years. In 1947, Pignon was sent to Phnom Penh to run the Cambodian kingdom, and Laurentie was relocated to New York to represent France at the United Nations, but in 1948, after Moutet had been ousted from the Ministry of Overseas France and the MRP had taken full control of French Indochina policy, Pignon made a comeback as high commissioner in Saigon. In 1949, he was finally able to welcome Bao Dai as head of a new Vietnamese state, defined as an "associated state" (Etat associé) by paragraph 60 of the French constitution. Now, with enthusiastic encouragement from the United Kingdom and more hesitant acceptance by the United States, Pignon would waste his great talent in seeking to convince the Vietnamese and the whole free world that Bao Dai was a magnificent national leader.[39]

ECONOMIC WARFARE

While serving as Supreme Advisor to the DRV government in Hanoi from September 1945 to April 1946, Bao Dai had been obliged to live more frugally than he was used to. He had first witnessed how the revolutionary leaders canceled the hated head tax that France had imposed on the colony, and then later overheard, to his amusement, how the cabinet ministers looked for alternative ways of financing their young republic, such as asking people to donate their gold and jewelry. Bao Dai was no doubt relieved when the government asked him to go on his mission to China.

During all of its sixteen months in Hanoi, the DRV government struggled to build a national economy in a country that had just been through a terrible famine, and was forced to feed a huge number of Chinese occupation troops. It issued its own money, "Ho Chi Minh banknotes," which quickly depreciated, and did its best to find ways of procuring arms. After March 6, with the prospect of détente with France, government officials laid ambitious plans for developing the national economy, with industry, trade, and the construction of new infrastructure. The negotiators at Dalat and Fontainebleau prepared to discuss economic modernization plans with French specialists, and Ho Chi Minh eagerly emphasized that he wanted French businessmen and advisors, if he could just be relieved of the civil servants. At the end of October, when Ho had returned home to report on the provisions of the modus vivendi agreement, the French Sûreté confirmed that the Vietnamese government was more preoccupied than ever with laying plans to modernize its economy. A special trading company, Viet Tien, had been founded for the purpose of promoting exports and imports, industrialization, transport, and so on.[40] Then, just as d'Argenlieu was reorienting his policy, French intelligence suddenly reported on November 12 that the Tong Bo had decided three days earlier on a highly different program for economic self-sufficiency, based exclusively on agriculture. The economic reconstruction of the country was apparently adjourned.[41] In reality, the Viet Minh and the ICP had for a long time made parallel preparations for peace and war, with a division of labor between the leaders operating in public and those who were setting up bases and infrastructure for a long-term guerrilla struggle (Nguyen Long Bang, Hoang Van Hoan, and others). Still a shift seems to have occurred in the general outlook just when d'Argenlieu changed his overall strategy.

What could explain the change? For lack of good sources, we can only speculate. Ho Chi Minh had returned and met d'Argenlieu at Cam Ranh Bay. The Vietnamese National Assembly had convened, and the cabinet had been reshuffled to grant the Viet Minh a virtual monopoly on power. The cease-fire in the south had proved effective, but the first meeting with General Nyo had given little hope of a lasting settlement. The DRV could not agree with Saigon on the site for the mixed commissions. Ho Chi Minh had received d'Argenlieu's protest against the existence of the DRV's Administrative Committee for Nam Bo. The French had also unilaterally established import-export controls in Haiphong. These developments may have convinced some Viet Minh leaders that negotiations with Saigon would prove futile. If the French government did not intervene to correct d'Argenlieu's policy, it would soon be necessary to take up arms in a protracted resistance struggle. Such a conviction may have been reflected in the November 9 decision of the Tong Bo. This, however, remains to be explored once the Vietnamese archives become accessible.

One of the main worries was the import-export controls that the French had set up unilaterally. These controls were not put in place in order to levy any customs duty, but rather to prevent the Vietnamese from doing so. Their main dual purpose was to defend the value of the Indochinese piaster by reducing imports, and prevent the influx of arms, ammunition, and gasoline to supply the Vietnamese Army. Vietnamese finances had not got any better since Bao Dai and the Chinese troops had left. Military needs absorbed the republic's meager resources, and the main sources of revenue were the state-run trade in rice, taxes on foreign trade, and voluntary donations. If the French deprived the Vietnamese government of customs duty, it would be in even worse straits. Taxation of foreign trade had already got the Vietnamese government into conflict with the Chinese merchants in Haiphong, who had been promised in the Sino-French treaty of February 28 that this would be a free port. D'Argenlieu had delayed the implementation of this clause till the Chinese had withdrawn all their troops from Indochina.[42] Now the Chinese merchants expected an end to customs duties.

The numerous ethnic Chinese, who handled most of the foreign trade, were caught in the middle of the struggle for control of the port city. The French offered military protection and encouraged the Chinese to refuse to pay any Vietnamese duties. The Vietnamese had begun to collect customs in May, and in June–July, their customs service became steadily more efficient.[43] At first, the Chinese merchants agreed to pay, but when the rates increased, they started to grumble, and some sought French protection. Already in June, General Leclerc had found the time ripe to take full control of the port, telling Valluy to use military means if necessary.[44] At this stage, Valluy was the "dove." He informed Leclerc on July 5 that military occupation was unnecessary, since for all practical purposes the port was already in French hands. Besides, military action would lead to the loss of "indigenous specialized manpower."[45] Valluy further affirmed that French customs control in Haiphong would be inefficient, because goods would just be landed elsewhere. Efficient control could only be established through inspection at sea. On July 7, Colonel Dèbes advised the Chinese consul to instruct Chinese citizens not to pay customs duties to Vietnamese authorities. The consul was not enamored by the proposal and in fact informed the Vietnamese of what Dèbes had said.[46] As no Chinese request for protection was forthcoming, the French commander felt obliged to let the Vietnamese police the Chinese sector of the town, while French control was limited to the port and the European sector.[47]

In mid-August, a group of Chinese merchants complained to the French that Vietnamese customs officers had confiscated a quantity of piaster banknotes and a stock of cigarettes. The complaint was not supported by the Chinese consul, but the French seized this opportunity to set an example by demanding that the Vietnamese return the notes and cigarettes to their owners. The Vietnamese refused to do so, and on August 29, Dèbes's troops occupied the Vietnamese customs offices and arrested a number of policemen and customs officers. There was some fighting, but the mixed liaison commission intervened to stop it. Negotiations dragged on through the first half of September. The French would only release their prisoners if the cigarettes and banknotes were returned to their owners.[48] The Vietnamese refused once again and sent a delegate to uphold Vietnamese sovereignty. As the French forces were in full control of the port itself, his position was weak. He temporized until the modus vivendi agreement gave hope of a more satisfactory arrangement. To gain confidence, the Vietnamese now gave in and handed over the confiscated goods in return for the release of prisoners.[49] This happened on September 18, just as the last Chinese unit left Haiphong on board an American vessel.

During the customs crisis, d'Argenlieu's *chef de cabinet,* Longeaux, was on a mission to the north. He reported to d'Argenlieu that Hanoi seemed to accept French control of the port of Haiphong, even though this deprived them of customs revenues.[50] Shortly afterward, General Morlière issued instructions from Hanoi to establish a new import-export controls agency in Haiphong, starting October 15, 1946.[51] Exporters and importers were required to apply for a "federal" license. This followed a French decision at the end of August to prohibit the export of rice. Gasoline imports were at the same time restricted to the major petroleum companies, which were under French control.[52]

Some of the Vietnamese leaders felt unease at the "capitulation" in the customs conflict, and in October, the Haiphong Viet Minh daily *Dan Chu* demanded that Vietnamese control of customs should be defended "with blood."[53] When the import-export controls were established in mid-October, the Vietnamese government formally protested, arguing that this unilateral move violated the terms of the modus vivendi agreement, which said that "Vietnam shall form a Customs Union with the other countries of the Indochinese Federation," and prescribed that a coordinating committee should "prepare the organization of the Indochinese customs service." While the French claimed that they were entitled to set up a federal service, the Vietnamese held that each state should have a separate service, but with a common external tariff and no internal barriers. Since the mixed commission never met, there were no negotiations, but the French continued to build their federal controls unilaterally.

The conflict led to a state of almost constant nervousness. On October 30, the Sûreté said there were rumors among the Annamites that the French troops were waiting for a favorable moment to conquer the city.[54] This was exactly when Dèbes was distributing his closed envelopes. In late November and December, the French found much evidence that extreme apprehension had prevailed among the local Vietnamese commanders through October and November. On October 13, the chief of Haiphong military sector had told his troops that the French would launch a general attack on October 15, when setting up the new agency. This did not happen. Robert Davée, the French delegate for economic affairs in the north, signed instructions on October 14 for enforcing import-export controls from the following day, but he emphasized that the controls would be provisional pending final agreement between the parties.[55] He invited the Vietnamese to participate in organizing the new agency, but received no answer. From October 15, the French formally required that every importer/exporter of articles above a certain quantity should apply for a federal license. Davée promised at a press conference that banned imports would be replaced by goods furnished under a French plan.[56] He later admitted, however, that this was the weak point of the system: the north was deprived of certain consumer goods that used to be imported from abroad, and the authorities in Saigon refused to supply these goods from stocks in Cochinchina. The Vietnamese would call this a blockade, and Davée confirmed in a report to Saigon: "If not a blockade, at least a contraction of imports to Tonkin."[57] During the first month, however, the French authorities did not implement the controls very rigorously.

On October 21, the day that Ho Chi Minh took the train from Haiphong to Hanoi on his return from France, the Vietnamese troops in Haiphong were again ordered to prepare for an emergency. Ten days later, there were rumors that the French were preparing an attack on the Municipal Theater. The Vietnamese troops were put on the alert, although with orders to open fire only in self-defense. On November 4, Davée and Morlière asked Saigon to reconsider a decision not to ship replacements for the banned imports to the north. If this decision were not reversed, they argued, the new agency would either "provoke incidents by refusing imports," or it would have to disregard the import-export regulations and just freely issue licenses on request.[58] No trace of any answer from Saigon has been found in the archives. During its meeting on November 8, the Vietnamese National Assembly instructed the new government not to give in on the customs issue "at any price."[59] President Ho followed up on November 11 by protesting in traditional diplomatic language to the high commissioner against the "unilateral creation of a French customs office and control of foreign trade in the port of Haiphong." He warned that it would have serious consequences for the forthcoming negotiations if these measures were not revoked.[60]

On November 13, the Vietnamese command in Haiphong reported an "extremely provocative" French attitude and warned its troops that a serious incident might occur.[61] On the next day, the Vietnamese Ministry of the Interior instructed "all cities & Haiphong" to oblige French soldiers to go back to the French sector if they strolled out of their designated zones without a Vietnamese permit.[62] Then, five days later, the almost inevitable occurred. French authorities learned that a Chinese junk loaded with gasoline would be entering Haiphong shortly.[63] On November 18, Morlière warned Saigon that the new import-export rules would require confiscation of the shipment. This would further aggravate Vietnamese opposition, which remained "total and very intense," but Morlière stressed that to fail to do so would imply giving up the whole scheme.[64] Then, on the morning of November 20, the junk sailed into the port with its cargo.

What was the French motive for creating the export-import controls? By November 20, the government in Paris had not yet been consulted on the matter, and had not apparently seen fit to look into the customs dispute. Only on November 21, after the first fateful day in Haiphong, did the Saigon triumvirate find the time ripe for informing Paris of the long-ongoing customs quarrel. Their telegram denounced the DRV for protesting against these controls, which were a "simple administrative measure," made necessary by the "total incompetence" of the Vietnamese customs service. The alleged purpose was to prevent an enormous contraband trade in rice, other foodstuffs, metals, and so on, particularly with China, in order to "protect" the supplies of the Tonkinese population, as well as the value of the piaster.[65]

These were the official reasons, soon to be repeated in the French press. On November 27, Moutet based himself on information received from Saigon when declaring to a news agency that there had been an enormous contraband trade in foodstuffs from Tonkin.[66] In 1946, the memory of the terrible 1945 famine, which probably cost around a million lives, was still fresh. However, there was no danger of any similar famine in 1946, and the November 1946 rice crop was good.[67] Yet it does seem surprising that there should have been any sizable export of foodstuffs from the densely populated northern Vietnam, which normally depended on rice from the south. On the other hand the Vietnamese government was desperately looking for arms, and rice exports may have been used to finance arms purchases. If this was the case, then the Vietnamese government broke its own ban on rice exports, which had been proclaimed as early as October 1945, against the background of that year's famine.[68] Davée's report does not refer to any rice exports, but rather warns that the new controls might lead to a considerable reduction of imports. Saigon did have indications that Vietnam had been paying for weapons with opium and rice, and the French ban on gasoline imports was most probably meant to starve the Vietnamese Army of fuel.[69]

It was also important for the French to stop the depreciation of the piaster on the Hong Kong market, where it was under considerable pressure because of Indochina's negative balance of trade.[70] What Valluy failed to mention, was that support for the piaster was also part and parcel of the French effort to depreciate the "Ho Chi Minh banknotes."[71] The regulation of imports and exports in Haiphong was meant to reintegrate Tonkin into a French-controlled financial system. Its rapid implementation without any prior negotiations indicates that the French had political and military objectives in mind as well: halting supplies for the Vietnamese Army, undermining the economic foundations of the Vietnamese state, and provoking the Vietnamese government to either submit to French will or react forcibly. Pignon expressed some of these motives in a report he signed on November 23, the worst day in Haiphong's history: "If the Ho Chi Minh currency were to collapse, the whole system would fall together with it, since the government would be unable to procure the foreign currency it needs in any other way. It is actually quite likely that with the disturbances that such a fall would cause and the accumulated losses, the present government would find itself in a very bad position and would hardly be able to resist an increasingly numerous and forceful opposition, composed of the innumerable dupes of the Viet Minh regime."[72]

Davée mentioned the possibility that the purpose of the original decision to institute the import-export controls had been to "transfer the combat abandoned on the military level, to the economic level."[73] This had happened before Davée himself took responsibility for economic affairs in the north. Davée subtly argued that after Ho Chi Minh had accepted a federal customs service in the modus vivendi agreement, the controls could no longer be considered as economic warfare, just as a technical measure to protect the country's economy. But, and this disappointed Davée, the Vietnamese did not see it the same way. This had to mean, he felt, that Ho Chi Minh was the figurehead of a government dominated by extremists who wanted the "total eviction of the French." Hence France had only two options: leave Indochina or use force to restore its authority.[74]

The French scholar Paul Mus has called Haiphong "Tonkin's lung."[75] General Valluy in 1967 stated that to any perceptive commander, Haiphong was the focal point, but also the most exposed and vulnerable.[76] A French intelligence report from January 1947 confirmed that by taking control of Haiphong and expelling the Vietnamese customs service, the French had attacked a sector considered as vital, if not by the whole Vietnamese cabinet, at least by Giap and the military, although they had already instituted a system of barter trade, rationing, and payment in kind of government officials' salaries, so their state could continue to function even if Haiphong were lost.[77] The French deputy chief of staff, Admiral Pierre Barjot, the main critic in Paris of d'Argenlieu's and Valluy's new strategy, wrote a note on December 8 in which he concluded that the import-export controls had led inescapably to armed conflict.[78] These were afterthoughts, but, as we have seen, Morlière had warned in advance that incidents were likely. There is little doubt that Saigon sought to provoke incidents in order to undermine the modus vivendi agreement. When an incident finally occurred, Ho Chi Minh asked the French to agree to immediately establish a mixed commission to prepare a preliminary customs agreement. Davée and Morlière wanted to accept the proposal, but the triumvirate in Saigon said no.

NOVEMBER 20

There are five main sources to the events in Haiphong on November 20. Colonel Dèbes wrote a detailed report the same evening. The head of the 2e Bureau of the Navy in Tonkin, *Lieutenant de vaisseau* Nougarède, wrote his report the next day, and his boss, *Capitaine de vaisseau* Barrière, also wrote one of his own. On the Vietnamese side, Captain Le Van My, a liaison officer, wrote a report to General Giap immediately after the events. There is also a public Vietnamese account in French, printed in the French-language local newspaper *Le Peuple* on November 23. In addition, the Vietnamese government included an account as one of 76 appendices in a memorandum, which Ho Chi Minh tried to hand over to Marius Moutet when he visited Hanoi in late December.[79] The French sources are independent of the two Vietnamese, but the authors of Le Peuple's and the Ho Chi Minh memo versions had probably read Le Van My's report. All later accounts rely directly or indirectly on either Dèbes's report or the Vietnamese version.[80] The events are reconstructed here on the basis of these sources, which will be referred to only when they differ.

In the early morning of November 20, the unloading of gasoline from the Chinese junk had already begun when a French landing craft approached it and took the junk in tow. Three security officers, led by Lieutenant Jumeau,[81] seized what had already been unloaded. Vietnamese police and soldiers arrived on the spot. At this point, the reports part company. According to the Vietnamese, the French landing craft opened fire and the French soldiers guarding the gasoline attacked the local policemen, killing one. According to Dèbes, the Vietnamese soldiers fired on the French boat, and Jumeau, far from killing anyone, discussed the matter with a Vietnamese police officer, who conceded that the affair was a Franco-Chinese matter and did not concern the Vietnamese. Barrière gives another story, based on an oral report from Jumeau, which was confirmed by a French naval officer: Jumeau had been attacked (pris à partie) by a Vietnamese patrol that arrived in a truck. They fired on the French landing craft, which returned fire with its machine guns. Barrière adds that this exchange of fire was "without result," but that a Vietnamese civilian was killed, "very certainly by Vietnamese bullets."

The Dèbes and Barrière versions do not seem reliable. Jumeau was not just an ordinary officer. His "military security" group was the Haiphong branch of a new special service, the Bureau fédéral de documentation (Federal Bureau of Documentation), or BFDOC. Morlière would later reveal that Jumeau and his two companions were working for an agency that "constantly caused trouble."[82] In April 1951, Jumeau—still a lieutenant—became infamous when he ordered the massacre of twenty Vietnamese hostages at Cam Ly near Dalat.[83] On the other hand, since the landing craft had the junk in tow, it had little reason to open fire, so the Vietnamese claim that it fired first seems doubtful. It would make more sense for the soldiers on the shore to open fire in order to take back the confiscated junk. Then again, the Dèbes report says that no one was hit on the boat. Perhaps the Vietnamese fired warning shots. Dèbes's allegation that a Vietnamese police officer admitted that this was none of his business is hardly credible. Le Van My claims more convincingly that it was the French liaison officer who remarked, when the Vietnamese proposed to intervene jointly, that this was a Franco-Chinese affair of no concern to the Vietnamese.

After this initial incident, the Vietnamese sent a stronger force to the place where the French had stored the gasoline. They disarmed the Jumeau group and took them to a police station. Then the liaison intervened, and Le Van My accepted a French demand for the Jumeau group's immediate release. The car sent to pick them up, however, was fired upon. Two gunners were injured, while the driver saved himself by pretending to be dead.[84] This Vietnamese blunder provided Dèbes with a pretext for ordering armored vehicles to the scene. Approaching the police station, they drew hostile fire, and returned it with canons and machine guns, taking up position in front of the City Theater. The liaison officers intervened again, and the captured French officers were released around noon.

This could have been the end of the affair,[85] but Dèbes refused to withdraw the armored vehicles and demanded that the Vietnamese pull out of the Chinese quarter and dismantle all the barricades they had set up there. According to Dèbes these demands were accepted by the Vietnamese authorities, but when he sent a bulldozer to undertake the removal, someone shot at it. In the Vietnamese version, the demands were not accepted, and Dèbes then launched a general offensive, which lasted until late in the evening. Dèbes also describes this offensive, in which French troops occupied the City Theater (except the top floor) and other strategic points in the city. During the combat at the Theater, the chief of the French liaison office, *Commandant* Camoin, was killed when approaching the Vietnamese lines carrying a white flag.

Who was to blame for the incident and its escalation? Although the facts related in Dèbes's report show that the Vietnamese Army and self-defense groups acted nervously and were only loosely controlled by their commanders, he claimed that Vietnamese *authorities* had provoked the incident.[86] Vo Nguyen Giap asserted that the hostilities had been premeditated by the French, who had taken the initiative and bore full responsibility.[87] It is impossible to establish with certainty if it was the French or the Vietnamese who opened fire first when the junk was seized. Both were prepared to use force, the Vietnamese in order to protect their customs service, the French to defend their import-export controls. As Morlière had told Saigon earlier, violent incidents would almost inevitably result from the parallel existence of two rival services. It is not clear that the incident had been planned by either party, but it does seem suspicious that the BFDOC group was involved. The BFDOC had been established in July, under the direction of *Commandant* Schlumberger, to operate independently of the various military units' 2ᵉ Bureaus. It reported directly to d'Argenlieu, who gave it the task of collecting and distilling intelligence from the various French intelligence services. From the beginning, the BFDOC also had local agents of its own.[88]

The Vietnamese had far more to lose from the affair than the French, who were militarily superior. Events show that the Vietnamese authorities did their best to stop the fighting, while Dèbes sought to use the incident to advance his positions. He refused to withdraw from the strategically important City Theater or from any of the other points that had been occupied.[89]

It was not till late in the afternoon that the center of French decision-making moved from Haiphong to the more conciliatory Hanoi level. Vietnamese liaison officers in Hanoi had approached their French colleagues on the matter at 1430 hours, but Morlière's headquarters had not yet been briefed from Haiphong. Morlière got a short telegram from Dèbes at 1600 hours, saying that a car had been attacked and two gunners had been injured.[90] Dèbes does not seem to have wanted any interference from Hanoi. Morlière now managed to contact Dèbes on the telephone. At this point, Morlière claimed later, Dèbes was getting ready to employ his artillery. Morlière instructed him to avoid going on the attack and instead prevent further incidents.[91] It was after having received these instructions that Dèbes managed to capture the City Theater.

Morlière now sent his political advisor, Colonel Lami, to meet with Hoang Huu Nam, undersecretary of the interior and deputy secretary of the Vietnamese Committee of National Defense, one of Giap's closest collaborators. At 5:40 p.m., they agreed on an immediate cease-fire and settled that troops on both sides should in principle return to their respective positions. A mixed commission would go to Haiphong in the morning to make sure that the cease-fire was respected. The agreement was communicated to Haiphong by telephone. When Dèbes demanded that Morlière allow the French troops to remain in control of the City Theater, this contravened the Lami-Nam agreement, which Morlière had explicitly endorsed.

While Lami negotiated with Nam, Morlière informed Saigon that he had instructed Dèbes to avoid attacking and put a stop to the incidents.[92] This must have annoyed General Valluy unimaginably and made clear to him what a terrible mistake it had been to put Morlière in charge in the north. Morlière's appointment had been made at a time when the south was what mattered. Now everyone focused on the north. The next day, the center of French decision-making moved one further step up the ladder, from conciliatory Hanoi to impatient Saigon.

NOVEMBER 21

The train carrying the mixed commission from Hanoi had to stop outside Haiphong when someone shot at it. The French said it was Vietnamese fire, and the Vietnamese, that it came from the French-occupied railway station. The commission drove into the city in jeeps and armored cars. After a brief meeting, its Vietnamese members went into the line of fire in order to stop it. They succeeded, but only after several hours' efforts.[93] The French would later praise Nam, who risked his life. On their side, the French members had a heated discussion with Dèbes, who did not take part when the mixed commission met. At 1645 hours a new agreement was signed by Major Herckel for the French and Nam for the Vietnamese. All fire was prohibited under any pretext whatsoever, and the French armored cars were to withdraw immediately.[94] Lami later explained why he had not himself signed on to this agreement, but left the signing to Herckel: "Already at my arrival in Haiphong,

I realized that the attitude of Colonel Dèbes was not of a kind that would facilitate my task and that there was little chance he would consent to implementing the agreement. . . . I thought it best to abstain from signing . . . in order not to give the Vietnamese government the impression that the French civilian authorities . . . were unable to make the Army commander in Haiphong respect their signature."[95]

The evening of November 21 was calm in Haiphong, and in spite of Lami's premonitions, Dèbes might after all have complied with the Nam-Herckel agreement if Morlière had not been so eager to tell Saigon the happy news. When Valluy was informed of the Nam-Herckel agreement, he felt that an excellent opportunity for teaching Vietnam a lesson was being lost. At 1752 hours on November 21, Valluy sent a telegram directly to Dèbes, a procedure that, in Morlière's words, was "contrary to all rules of hierarchy."[96] This telegram said that it was "absolutely necessary to take advantage of the incident and ameliorate our position in Haiphong." Valluy told Dèbes that he had instructed Morlière to demand the evacuation of all Vietnamese forces from Haiphong and to obtain this by force after having undertaken "a preliminary inquiry." Valluy sent these instructions to Morlière too, and also a separate cable telling him to react immediately and vigorously against the Vietnamese provocations; he should not refrain from "capturing, disarming, and even destroying the local Vietnamese regular garrisons."[97]

That same evening, Saigon informed Paris of the events, saying Morlière's order to cease hostilities had resulted from an "extreme mood of conciliation."[98] Valluy also informed Paris of his harsh instructions to Morlière,[99] but the center of French decision-making did not shift to Paris. The French government let it stay in Saigon.

NOVEMBER 22

Valluy's instructions went beyond what Dèbes had asked for, Morlière realized, when he mulled over Valluy's orders in the night from November 21 to 22. He decided to accept what Dèbes had demanded, and thus break the Nam-Herckel agreement, but to try and make Valluy modify his most excessive orders. At 0845 in the morning, he sent a telegram to Haiphong approving the conclusions of Dèbes's report and ordering him to hold on to the City Theater.[100] An hour later, he signed a message to Valluy, in which he repeated the instructions he had just given Dèbes and added: "To demand complete evacuation of Haiphong would mean to decide with absolute certainty—I repeat, with absolute certainty—the conquest of this city, which must be preceded, if one is to avoid great losses, by its partial destruction by artillery. This would lead to a complete rupture with the March 6 agreement and the modus vivendi [agreement], and almost certainly to the spread of combat to all our garrisons in Tonkin."[101] By the time the warning arrived in Saigon, Valluy had already sent draconian new orders to Morlière and Dèbes simultaneously: "It is clear that we are faced with premeditated aggression, carefully prepared by the regular

Vietnamese Army, which does not seem to obey its government any longer. In the circumstances, your honorable attempts at conciliation and sharing out of military quarters *[répartition des cantonnements]*, as well as the inquiry I have prescribed, are now out of place. The moment has come to teach those who have treacherously attacked us a severe lesson. By all the means at your disposal, you must gain complete control of Haiphong and make the Vietnamese Army and government regret their mistakes."[102]

Morlière's warning, arriving on Valluy's desk shortly after he had sent his fateful telegram, did not have any impact. Valluy repeated to Morlière that it was necessary to exploit any possibility of improving the French position by driving all Vietnamese forces from Haiphong and its neighborhood. He added, in a moment of caution, that artillery should only be used as the last resort, but he authorized its use if necessary.[103]

November 22 was relatively calm in Haiphong. Dèbes was preparing to present the Vietnamese with an ultimatum. Lami urged him not to do so and gave the colonel a formal warning letter before departing Haiphong: "We must do everything to avoid the outbreak of a conflict, which will be generalized immediately and will endanger, not only the isolated French posts in Hai Duong and Vinh, but even more the civilian population in Hanoi. Neither the high commissioner nor the French government want such a conflict. I consequently think that the ultimatum must be presented to local Haiphong authorities only after confirmation coming from Hanoi."[104] Dèbes, however, took his orders from Saigon, and he decided to hand over the ultimatum in the morning.

NOVEMBER 23

Dèbes justified his ultimatum by alleged Vietnamese troop movements and concentrations in the Chinese quarter, a section of the town near the station, and the village Lac Vien, contrary to the November 21 agreement, and he demanded Vietnamese withdrawal from the whole Chinese quarter. He also demanded that all Vietnamese civilians in these areas be disarmed. Dèbes then tied Valluy's hands by adding that he was making these demands on instructions from the high commissioner. He concluded: "I demand pure and simple acceptance of these conditions before November 23, at nine hours, otherwise I reserve the right to take all measures that the situation requires."[105]

The Vietnamese received the ultimatum at 6 a.m., so they had three hours to reply. The chairman of the Administrative Committee in Haiphong, whose name our sources give just as Nguyen, replied immediately that the ultimatum violated earlier agreements. He dismissed the allegation that Vietnamese troops had moved. They were not massed in the Chinese quarter, as alleged: "We are astonished to receive your aforementioned letter with demands that we judge inopportune to say the least. At any rate, we make it our duty to refer to our central government in Hanoi and ask it to provide us with a reply." Dèbes immediately repeated his ultimatum, while adding another knot on the rope he was using to tie Valluy's hands: "It is up to you as representative in Haiphong of the government of the Republic of Vietnam to take responsibility for refusing or accepting these demands. They come from the high commissioner of the [French] Republic in Saigon, who sent them by telegraph last night. I draw your attention one last time to the extremely serious consequences that a refusal would entail. I await your reply at 0945." He got the reply even sooner: "I cannot but refer to my central government in Hanoi to decide on the acceptance or refusal of your demands. As far as the Administrative Committee in Haiphong is concerned, I take upon myself the responsibility for executing punctually and faithfully the two clauses of the agreement signed on November 21, 1946, in the evening, between Mr. Nam, undersecretary of state, and Colonel Herckel, representing the military authorities of the high commissioner of the French Republic in Hanoi." Contact had again been established between the liaison officers in Hanoi when the deadline expired and Dèbes gave his order for a general attack, supported by artillery. The bombardment started at 1005 hours.[106]

This is not a military history, but a political case study of how and why the war began. It is superfluous therefore to relate the details of the five-day battle for Haiphong, the French attack, a Vietnamese attempt at counterattack, the heavy use of artillery, and the French conquest of the whole region around this port city. But the horror of the Vietnamese population at the sight and sound of French naval guns, army artillery, and aircraft razing large parts of the Vietnamese quarters in Haiphong, and killing thousands, fueled the determination of many young Vietnamese to join Giap's Vietnamese Army and fight a protracted resistance struggle from base areas in the interior. They knew what President Ho had told General Salan in March: French ships could not sail up the Vietnamese rivers.

LANGSON

Langson was far from the coast, and Valluy had found it militarily advisable, back in August, to withdraw the French garrison there, while even d'Argenlieu envisaged the retention of just a symbolic force. Events would decide otherwise. In January 1947, *Le Figaro* affirmed with pleasure that the two "gateways" to Tonkin, by land at Langson and from the sea at Haiphong, had been closed. The Viet Minh had thus been deprived of any hope of easily obtaining supplies.[107] This illustrates the issue at hand in the battles of Haiphong and Langson. Hanoi lost control of its port and of one of its two rail links to China, and also of an important junction on the road along the Chinese border to the Gulf of Tonkin.

The bombing of Haiphong and the occupation of Langson took place at virtually the same time, but this does not mean they resulted from a coordinated plan. The population in the province of Langson was not as loyal to the Vietnamese government as elsewhere. The region had recently been controlled by the pro-Chinese Dong Minh Hoi. Out of 170,000 inhabitants, only some 9,000 belonged to the ethnic majority Viet (Kinh). About 5,000 were Chinese, 4,000 Man, 72,000 Tho, and 80,000 Nung.[108] When the Chinese Army left in June, Vietnamese government troops took over the city from the Dong Minh Hoi, but just a few days later, on July 8, the first French units arrived. They came with the blessing of the Vietnamese command in Hanoi, but the Vietnamese asked them to occupy a designated zone. The French troops began almost immediately to move out to nearby towns and villages, and this led to protests and small incidents. The Bac Ninh incident in early August began with a clash between Vietnamese troops and a convoy of French reinforcements for Langson.[109]

Tension between Vietnamese and French forces in the Langson area built up, and on October 12, Ho Chi Minh protested formally against confiscations, kidnappings, murders, interference with the local administration, hostile propaganda, and the incorporation of Chinese bandits and pro-Japanese Vietnamese citizens into the French forces. The French refuted the charges and expressed their regrets that it had not been possible to establish trust and cooperation with the Vietnamese Army in the border area. The mission of the French troops in Langson was to "supervise the border in cooperation, if possible, with Vietnamese troops."[110] Exactly one month later, this lack of cooperation led to open conflict.

There are several sources on what happened in Langson on November 21 and the following days. Giap composed a letter to Morlière that same evening, and the Vietnamese later prepared a memorandum covering the ten days from November 15 to 25.[111] Lieutenant Colonel Sizaire, commander of the Langson sector, wrote a report forming a basis for the French version.[112] There is also in the French archives a folder with telegrams exchanged between Sizaire, Morlière, and Valluy, and with French translations of captured Vietnamese documents.[113]

The French were preparing to hold a ceremony on November 24 in commemoration of the French soldiers and officers who had been killed and murdered by the Japanese in September 1940 and March 1945. On the latter occasion, because the French garrison in Langson had resisted so fiercely, the Japanese had executed virtually all the soldiers who surrendered. Sizaire now wanted to dig up as many French corpses as possible before the ceremony, and he wished to organize the event in the Citadel, which now served as Vietnamese military headquarters. The Vietnamese saw the planned ceremony as a pretext for preparing an attack. The Committee for the Protection of Langson City met on November 15 and decided that, in case of conflict, it would change its name to the Resistance Committee. It also decided to steer clear of any provocation and to do its best to avoid being involved in any incidents. These decisions were approved from Hanoi in a message the committee received on November 19, which said: "D'Argenlieu may soon be dismissed, so keep clear of provocations at any price. For the moment, the French are seeking to create a provocative movement, mainly in Haiphong, in the hope of protecting the terrorist policy of d'Argenlieu. Pay close attention."[114]

On November 20, the French began to dig up corpses close to the Citadel and removed some Vietnamese defense works that hampered access to the graves. In the Vietnamese version, the French forces used the opening of the graves as a pretext for military reconnaissance, attached to a plan for a *coup de force*. In the evening, Vietnamese authorities set up new headquarters outside Langson. When the French arrived in the morning to continue their grave-digging, the barrier had been reconstructed and mined. The French began to dismantle it again, and at this point, the Vietnamese do not seem to have been able to restrain themselves, at least if the French account is to be believed. Sizaire says they opened fire from positions both behind and in front of the barrier. In the Vietnamese version, they just issued a warning, and the French opened fire. A report from Hanoi to Saigon says that after the Vietnamese opened fire, two French soldiers were killed by landmines. Then the French authorities reacted rapidly.[115]

After a few hours fighting, the liaison officers intervened, and a cease-fire agreement was concluded. After the cease-fire, French troops occupied the railroad station and the post office, arguing that someone had been shooting from these buildings in violation of the agreement. Sizaire names nine dead and nine wounded on the French side and estimates the enemy's losses at fifty. The French immediately dubbed the incident a "premeditated ambush," while Giap affirmed that the well-intentioned Vietnamese forces had been the victims of a "long-premeditated" plan.[116]

During the night to November 22, the Vietnamese built several barricades, but not much fighting ensued, and in the evening the chairman of the Administrative Committee and Sizaire held a meeting. Sizaire demanded the removal of the barricades, but he would not accept a Vietnamese counterdemand that the French troops evacuate the buildings they had occupied on November 21, so no agreement was reached.[117] Sizaire was not as eager to fight as Dèbes, and he does not seem to have either sought or got any direct orders to do so from Saigon. He had informed Hanoi of the situation and was waiting for Morlière's instructions. In the Langson affair, Morlière was actually the real decision-maker. At noon on November 21, Sizaire learned from Vietnamese radio about the Haiphong incident and immediately asked Morlière if he thought there was a relationship between the Haiphong and Langson events. Morlière replied, at 1735 hours, that it was difficult to say, but recommended that Sizaire "refrain from any measure that could aggravate, widen or prolong the incident." Morlière thus followed his normal inclination, but on the morning of November 23, in light of the draconian orders he had received from Valluy concerning Haiphong, he changed tack and told Sizaire not to hesitate if he found it advisable to attack the Langson Citadel.[118] Morlière and Sizaire may not have been aware that Valluy had been planning to pull out of exposed Langson, while putting great emphasis on controlling Haiphong.

Later in the day, while Dèbes bombed Haiphong, Sizaire met his Vietnamese counterpart once more, and demanded the release of two French soldiers and ten Chinese civilians who had been arrested by the Vietnamese forces. The Vietnamese released the two Frenchmen, but not the Chinese. November 24 was calm, while Sizaire made up his mind to take full control of the city the following day if his demands were not fully accepted. In the morning of November 25, the Vietnamese refused once again to release the ten Chinese prisoners. Hence Sizaire launched a full-scale attack in accordance with a modified version of a contingency plan from July. After the defenders had been machine-gunned from an airplane and a howitzer had made a breach in the wall, the French forces overran the Citadel in less than three hours. Before dusk the center of the town was also in French hands. The outskirts were kept under artillery fire, and while the French only counted three dead and seventeen injured, Sizaire estimated Vietnamese losses to be heavy. Sizaire concluded his November 30 report by saying that the rapid Vietnamese defeat and the spontaneous joy of the "partisans" showed how frail and artificial the Vietnamese fabric was, constructed with the help of propaganda and menaces in a country where the Viet Minh had never really established its authority. A skeptical staff member in Pignon's office scribbled in the margin of Sizaire's optimistic finale: "Conclusion valid for the region from Langson to Moncay, but not for Cao Bang."[119]

This reveals what would soon become a serious problem: what should one do with the occupied areas? Would it be wise to exploit the anti-Vietnamese sentiments of ethnic minorities and establish a durable political fabric in regions where these formed a majority, or would this entail protective obligations that would later be hard to live up to? The French do not seem to have had any plan for how to resolve this. Soon after the conquest of Langson, Giap asked Morlière what the French intended to do with the occupied areas. Morlière had no answer. He cabled Saigon for instructions, but said it would be impossible to let the Vietnamese Administrative Committee return to Langson, since that would damage French "prestige with the natives" and expose them to reprisals from the Viet. Morlière proposed to grant the Hanoi government formal "suzerainty," but let the minority people maintain their own local administrations. The French garrison could supervise the area militarily in cooperation with a "provincial militia."[120] Perhaps inspired by the successful capture of Haiphong, Valluy now abandoned his more cautious strategy of just a few weeks earlier. He instructed Morlière to demand control, not just of Langson itself, but of the whole border area eastward to the Gulf of Tonkin (except, for the time being, of the city of Mong Cai). The rationale behind this order was to open an alternative way to provision the Langson Citadel, so that the French would not have to secure the exposed road from Hanoi to Langson. The security of a road along the border would depend, not only on the attitude of the local minority peoples, but also on the existence of a friendly government in China, a condition that would hold for only three years. Valluy promised that instructions regarding political and administrative measures would be forthcoming. This, of course, was up to Pignon. Sizaire received the formal order to occupy the whole region between Langson and the sea on November 30.[121]

Pignon followed up by drawing up an ambitious plan for an autonomous Tho and Nung region along the Chinese border under French "high protection." Loc Binh, Dinh Lap, and Mong Cai should all be occupied. The Vietnamese government could be invited to participate in a mixed commission, which from time to time would carry out inspections. Pignon ended his proposal by warning against trying to implement it if the French government was not "firmly determined to stay in Tonkin." To start executing the plan only to give it up again later would "finally convince the population of our impotence and irresolution."[122] Pignon's proposal would receive warm support from Sainteny, who claimed that the occupation of the "mountainous arch" around the delta, where most of the population were non-Annamites was an "absolute necessity": "Often paralyzed by an inferiority complex in relation to the men from the delta, they need to feel solidly supported before finding the necessary audacity to make them into effective auxiliaries of the French cause."[123] Neither Sainteny nor Pignon reflected that a policy based on wooing ethnic minorities might damage the relationship between the minorities and the majority population, and also thrust a wedge between the majority population and the colonial power. They also did not take into consideration the considerable military resources that such a strategy demanded. France did establish a solid military presence in the border region with China, but in October 1950 a French column trying to retreat from Cao Bang to Langson was ambushed, the worst French defeat until Dien Bien Phu in 1954. The French suffered over 4,800 dead and missing, and subsequently evacuated Langson without a fight, after which they were squeezed out of the whole border region with China.[124]

Were the French attacks in Haiphong and Langson in 1946 coordinated, or was it a coincidence that they happened at the same time? The answer is a double "no." For strategic reasons, Valluy had wanted to take full control of Haiphong, not Langson. He did not premeditate and coordinate the two attacks. But it was no coincidence that the one followed the other. Only twenty-four hours passed from the incident in Haiphong on November 20 to the opening of hostilities in Langson on November 21. Giap remarked to Morlière that this new incident came at a time when the Haiphong affair had not yet been sorted out: "This simultaneousness becomes even more troublesome when one considers that in both cases the French troops have aimed with the same careful preparation and the same determination at our public buildings and our military positions."[125] Giap feared that the two incidents were parts of a premeditated French offensive. He was right to suspect that the French operations were based on previously laid out plans, but there is no indication that the simultaneity had been planned. It was rather that Morlière and Sizaire were motivated by Valluy's orders to Dèbes.

U.S. Vice-Consul James O'Sullivan commented on the simultaneity from his position of neutrality. He accepted the French claim that the Vietnamese had opened fire in both Haiphong and Langson, and speculated that the incidents had been meant as warnings that the French could not "proceed unilaterally as they wish." However, these "warnings" appeared to have had the opposite effect on the French, "who seem now even more belligerent and confident of their power to impose whatever they wish upon the Vietnamese."[126] A report written by Colonel Lami, with a view to publication, saw the simultaneousness as proving that both incidents followed instructions from Hanoi. The French informed the public that they had discovered such instructions both in Haiphong and Langson.[127] This may well be untrue. There are many translated Vietnamese documents in the French archives, but none has been found so far that proves any Vietnamese premeditation. As shown above, some of the captured documents tend to show the opposite: Hanoi was eager to prevent its local commanders and troops from letting themselves be provoked.

If the timing of the initial incidents was coincidental, their escalations were closely connected. When Sizaire launched his attack on November 25, he knew that the conquest of Haiphong had begun two days earlier. Both the strategic conquest of Haiphong and the less than strategic capture of Langson thus followed from Valluy's order.

CASUALTIES

On November 26, all French Army and naval units in Haiphong received the following order: "The units will make known as soon as they discover it, the number of Chinese and Vietnamese corpses in their sector. Indicate the position with precision. The local command will do what is necessary to remove the bodies."[128] Colonel Dèbes's strategy consisted in smashing the Vietnamese quarter of Haiphong with heavy artillery in order not to sacrifice French lives in its conquest.[129] The Chinese quarter was spared this fate and attacked only with light artillery and troops. It was in this sector that the French suffered most of their modest losses, but the houses were spared, and most of the Chinese civilians survived. Many Vietnamese civilians had evacuated Haiphong before the bombardment, but a considerable number remained.[130] Ho Chi Minh also complained that fleeing civilians had been attacked by airplanes. French telegrams confirm that the roads leading out of Haiphong were strafed: "The firing lasted from 1000 to 1700 hours with artillery bombardment of prepared points zones F.M.F.5. Effect considerable. All defined targets were hit and even more despite particular configuration difficulties for the indigenous houses. Spitfires intervened against concentrations outside of the city."[131] Throughout the wars in Indochina, the Vietnamese strategy combined the use of regular units in uniform and guerrilla forces disguised as civilians, but regular maneuver warfare was always considered a higher form of struggle. The role of the guerrillas was to prepare for the introduction of regular units in areas under strong enemy control. The struggle for Nam Bo in 1946 was typical guerrilla warfare, and guerrilla tactics also dominated the first phase of the Indochina War, 1947–49. By concealing themselves as civilians, the guerrillas were to some extent protected, and when the adversary reacted to their attacks by killing civilians, this increased the hatred for the enemy among the population, thus facilitating recruitment and provisioning of new guerrillas. Sometimes regular forces would also mix with civilians for protection. In the Haiphong affair, the tactic of mixing soldiers and civilians did not pay off, since Dèbes did not have much inhibition against killing civilians.

Many of the civilians who managed to escape Haiphong took refuge in the nearby town of Kien An, which had already attracted French attention before the battle of Haiphong, because Chinese merchants had responded to import-export controls by redirecting their junks there. It also seems that the Vietnamese Army had established its local headquarters in Kien An.[132] General Valluy first instructed Morlière to occupy Kien An, but had second thoughts and withdrew the order. Morlière agreed that it would be unwise to attack Kien An, but by the time they learned of Morlière's and Valluy's scruples, Colonel Dèbes and his naval colleague Barrière had already bombed the village, which was full of refugees.[133] News that Kien An had been bombed was published in the Vietnamese press as early as November 24. Morlière denied it officially, but then got the chilling news from Saigon quoted as the epigraph to this chapter: the bombardment of Kien An and another "designated village" by the guns of the warship *Savorgna de Brazza* had been "perfectly executed."[134] A report from the Sûreté in Haiphong, written on November 29, says that the number of corpses found in the ruins of the Vietnamese quarters in Haiphong was not very high. Most civilians and also the Vietnamese Army had evacuated the town before its destruction. On the other hand, the Sûreté had received reports that the bombardment of Kien An and its surroundings, as well as the "strafing of the roads around the town," had resulted in many victims. Vice-Consul O'Sullivan remarked that "the immediate use of artillery fire on Kien An as well as strafing by planes in the vicinity of Haiphong also tends to support the theory that this was a terrorist measure."[135]

One might expect that Saigon would try to minimize the damage in reports to Paris, but such "minimization" had become so customary that Saigon now felt a need to do the opposite. It warned Paris against any understatements, since it had been impossible to hide the destruction to the foreign consuls. In order to prevent a poorly informed public from being confronted abruptly and without preparation with tendentious assertions blaming the French troops for the destruction, it was better to say outright that the battle had been very destructive and let the enemy take the blame. Better tell the public that the damage had been done by the Vietnamese, who set fire to their houses before evacuating. Artillery had only been used as the last resort, and not for any punitive purpose.[136]

Before the battle, there were about 100,000 inhabitants in Haiphong.[137] In the beginning of December, roughly half of them remained.[138] How many of the lacking 50,000 had been killed? There are many estimates, of which Valluy's is the lowest: 300. He must have forgotten the advice to avoid minimization when publishing his self-defense in 1967, three years before he died.[139] Most of the literature cites the figure 6,000, but this seems to stem from just one single source: Admiral Battet. He was not in Indochina in November 1946, but told Paul Mus in May 1947 that "no more than 6,000 could have been killed, as far as the fire from the cruiser on the flocks of refugees was concerned."[140] General Yves Gras remarked later that the figure 6,000 "is derived from imagination and not from observed reality; the firepower of the French forces was not sufficient to cause such a slaughter."[141] Gras seems to forget that naval guns were involved. The combined firepower of the *Savorgna de Brazza*, *Suffren*, *Chevreuil*, and *Dumont d'Urville* was impressive indeed.[142] O'Sullivan reported to Washington that after a visit to Haiphong, the chief of French military intelligence had estimated the number of Vietnamese killed and wounded during November 20–27 as somewhere between 1,500 and 2,000.[143] Pignon wrote to a friend in France that "the Vietnamese have suffered losses that are not yet known precisely, but must certainly be counted in thousands."[144] The special military intelligence agency BFDOC said 10,000 had been killed and wounded in Haiphong and Langson, most of them civilians. The BFDOC proposed to use this figure in French propaganda to expose the Vietnamese government's inability to protect its citizens, an idea no one seems to have followed up.[145]

It is difficult to assess the value of all these estimates. Vietnamese propaganda would later claim that there had been 10,000—or even 20,000—casualties, but Ho Chi Minh spoke in a letter to Léon Blum and Vincent Auriol on December 19 of the "3,000 victims of Haiphong."[146] One might consider this a maximum, since Ho Chi Minh had no interest in understating the actual number. On the other hand, Vietnamese authorities had access to only limited parts of the battlefield after the event. The French would have had an opportunity to count the bodies in the area they had occupied, but the archives have not yet revealed any accurate count. The BFDOC's figure of 10,000 includes both killed and wounded, both in Langson and Haiphong, and does not say anything about the ratio between killed and wounded. On this basis, we are forced to conclude with the same vagueness as Pignon did at the time: the casualties must be counted in thousands, and most of them were civilians. It seems reasonable to call this a massacre, which from a cynical point of view may perhaps be seen as "brilliant," since it allowed the French to take control of the main gateway to Tonkin in just five days, with very few losses to themselves.

WHO WAS TO BLAME?

The responsibility for the initial incidents in Haiphong and Langson is open to discussion, and there is good reason to think that the lack of discipline of the Vietnamese militia forces and the lower levels of the Vietnamese army played a significant role, but the blame for the calculated escalation in both Haiphong and Langson must be put squarely on the French. There is little reason to think that the Vietnamese leaders wanted a military confrontation at this stage. They needed to gain time while waiting for a new French government to be formed—and then dismiss d'Argenlieu. I shall therefore concentrate on discussing the lines of responsibility on the French side. There were four levels in the French decision-making system:

- *Haiphong:* Dèbes/Barrière; *Langson:* Sizaire
- *Hanoi:* Morlière/Lami
- *Saigon:* Valluy/Pignon/Gonon/Admiral Auboyneau
- *Paris:* Bidault/Moutet/Army Minister Michelet/Chief of Staff Juin/d'Argenlieu (visiting)

Dèbes and Valluy wanted the battle. Morlière did not and thought he was acting in consonance with the policy of his government. Morlière was not in direct contact with Paris, while Valluy constantly informed the French government and soon received reassuring replies—from d'Argenlieu.

If there had not been a conflict between Morlière and Valluy, if Morlière had not intervened against Dèbes's intention to use artillery, then Valluy might have hidden his heavy hand. He could then have relied on his local commanders' ability to act in the spirit of "the slow method" prescribed in earlier instructions. Things would have gone his way without any explicit orders, and the general public as well as the historian might have been forced to regard Dèbes and Morlière as the culprits. Morlière prevented this with his "extreme mood of conciliation." Valluy felt he had to interfere with his instructions of November 21 and November 22. Thus he condemned himself to live with the guilt. Dèbes also contributed to casting the blame on Valluy. "This magnificent soldier" made three mistakes, Valluy said later. The first was to transform the instructions he had got into an explicit ultimatum, a procedure with a "bad reputation." The second was that he did this in Valluy's name, thus implicating the highest French authority in Indochina. And the third was to give the Vietnamese only three hours to consider the demands.[147]

Valluy wrote this in 1967, just as another culprit, Robert McNamara, was having qualms and warning Lyndon B. Johnson against moving further into the Vietnam morass. It is possible that Dèbes's first and third mistakes were critical afterthoughts, but Valluy must have resented the second "mistake" deeply and immediately. By referring directly to Valluy's secret instructions in his ultimatum, Dèbes—no doubt deliberately—broke with the normal expectation of superiors operating on ethical borderlines that their wish be carried out without they themselves being implicated. This was the spirit of "the slow method." Conflicts should develop locally and be used to improve the French position without engaging the responsibility of the highest French authority.

Dèbes's errors were, of course, small in comparison with Morlière's. Soon after his arrival in Hanoi, Morlière had discovered that Dèbes's hotheadedness had played a decisive role in the August customs incident. In a report he wrote on January 10, 1947, he revealed something about both himself and Dèbes in remarking: "The least that can be said is that Dèbes does not like the Annamites." Morlière had wondered whether he should find someone to replace Dèbes, but refrained from doing so because Valluy might not allow it, and also because Dèbes's tour of duty would in any case end in late November. The battle for Haiphong delayed Dèbes's repatriation. In fact, he never got home alive. In February 1947, Morlière was sent packing instead, and Dèbes was promoted to take over the command in Hanoi.[148] Just two months later, Dèbes was killed in an air crash.

Although Valluy loyally implemented d'Argenlieu's instructions, the general cannot have been happy to have to bear all the responsibility during the crisis, while the admiral was lobbying in Paris. Before the Haiphong events, Valluy complained to Salan that he was not being sufficiently informed of the atmosphere in Paris, at a time when there was a need to generate a "psychological shock" and take "revolutionary measures." Valluy would have preferred to see d'Argenlieu, or his replacement, come and assume responsibility, he said, rather than leaving everything to him. But he had instructions, which he was prepared to apply to the letter.[149]

Concern about domestic political developments is, of course, a kind of motive that colonial decision-makers seldom put on paper, at least not the sort of paper that is later to be found in public archives. Such motives are therefore difficult to handle for historians relying entirely on written sources. Even without hard proof, it seems reasonable to assume that the domestic political situation had a crucial impact on French decision-making in Saigon. The news that the French communists and socialists had triumphed at the polls arrived just after the death of Dr. Thinh. This raised the prospect that a new French government might approach Ho Chi Minh directly and perhaps dismiss d'Argenlieu. Earlier frustrations had taught Valluy and his advisors that it was difficult to obtain clear-cut instructions from coalition governments, especially when they were outgoing or had just been formed. The decision-makers in Saigon may therefore have developed a conviction that they could and should act on their own, in the larger interest of the nation—and because de Gaulle would want them to. The November 20 incident provided an opportunity for action earlier than anyone had expected, but Valluy took a chance, solidly based on the instructions d'Argenlieu had given him on November 12. Valluy sent his fatal orders with full certainty that d'Argenlieu would support him, but he must also have known that he was creating a fait accompli for the French government.

Valluy introduced a series of self-critical articles in 1967 by acknowledging that in hindsight, he should have acted differently:

> I have never hidden my responsibility in what is called the Haiphong affair of November 1946, which is linked to personal matters. But the decisions, which today, with the knowledge of what has happened since, I consider as mistakes due to a certain impressionability—these decisions, I would say, appeared at the time and place to my civilian and military surroundings, to the great majority of Frenchmen in Indochina, and even to many Vietnamese, and also in Paris to Admiral d'Argenlieu, to the politicians and the ministers, as salutary measures imposed by the Ho Chi Minh team's policy.[150]

Now, what about the fourth and supreme level of decision-making? Paris did not intervene or issue any clear-cut instructions. This is not surprising. As a commander, Valluy had the authority to take decisions on his own in a moment of crisis. But Paris's inaction may be interpreted in several different ways. One possibility is that the government disapproved of what Valluy was doing, but was unable or did not dare to make this clear. Alternatively, the government may have approved of Valluy's actions, but preferred not to engage its own responsibility, in case something should go wrong. A third, more likely possibility, is that the key Paris decision-makers were uncertain and disagreed among themselves. It is quite difficult for the historian to resolve the question of whether Valluy and d'Argenlieu acted with some kind of tacit support from key members of the government, notably prime minister Bidault, or on their own, creating a fait accompli that neither Bidault nor anyone else in the government would have wanted. To weigh these two interpretations up against each other we must have a closer look at French party politics.

FRENCH POLITICS IN 1946

French politics in 1946 was dominated by one retired general and three political parties. General de Gaulle influenced the policy that led to war in Indochina in three ways. First, through the decision-making system he had created before resigning on January 20; the Cominindo system weakened the minister for Overseas France and gave the high commissioner great leverage. Second, through de Gaulle's influence on the officers who had served under his orders and continued to hold the top jobs in Indochina: Leclerc, d'Argenlieu, Valluy. When conflict arose between Leclerc and d'Argenlieu, for example, Leclerc asked de Gaulle for advice, rather than any responsible minister. It is not impossible that Leclerc's warnings against making concessions at the Fontainebleau conference can be traced to advice from de Gaulle. Third, de Gaulle continued to wield influence through the fear felt by leading party politicians that a failure to realize French interests in Indochina would be exploited by de Gaulle's followers to enable him to stage a comeback. The minister of armies in 1946, Edmond Michelet, would claim later that de Gaulle had urged

Bidault to make no concessions to Ho Chi Minh.[151] In his campaign against the constitution that was adopted in the French referendum of October 13, de Gaulle argued that the paragraphs on the French Union were too liberal. At a press conference in August, he stated that if France were deprived of its overseas territories, it risked no longer being a great power. These territories would then be left to be dominated by others.[152]

Under Bidault's leadership, the Christian Democratic party (Mouvement républicain populaire, or MRP) got 26 percent of the votes and 164 deputies in the National Assembly in the elections held on November 10, 1946, a setback in relation to the previous election in June. Bidault would probably have advocated a firm Indochina policy even without the pressure from de Gaulle, but the widespread respect and admiration for de Gaulle within the MRP may have contributed to uniting the party behind Bidault's intransigence.[153] The MRP grew out of the French Resistance movement and was launched as a party in 1944, in a fiercely patriotic mood. It dominated the French government in 1946 and bears most of the responsibility for the policy that led to war. Only a handful of MRP politicians took an active interest in the Indochina question, but they did not waver in their determination not to yield to any demands for independence. In 1946, Bidault was supported without qualifications by the party's chairman, Maurice Schumann, who expressed his views in the party paper L'Aube.[154]

The French Socialist Party, or SFIO (Section française de l'Internationale ouvrière), got 18 percent and 105 deputies in the November 10 elections. It was more divided than the MRP. Internal party debates fall beyond the scope of this study,[155] but it is not hard to discern the difference between the policy of Minister for Overseas France Moutet and the line of action advocated in most of the party press. While Moutet supported Cochinchinese autonomy, the socialist newspapers constantly attacked the provisional Cochinchinese government and emphasized French obligations toward Vietnam as defined in the March 6 agreement. At the SFIO's Thirty-ninth Congress in August–September 1946, a left-wing faction led by Guy Mollet and Jean Rous gained support from the majority of the delegates, and Guy Mollet was elected as new secretary-general. Franc-Tireur, mouthpiece of the Rous group, campaigned in November–December for d'Argenlieu's dismissal, and warned almost daily against the danger of a protracted war. Young left-wing socialists were far more outspoken on Indochina than the communists, and were influential in the party organization. Yet the "responsible veterans" controlled the party's policy in government.

The French Communist Party (PCF) became the largest of all the parties on November 10, with 28 percent and 170 deputies. It was the only important political force that really set its sights on cooperation with Ho Chi Minh and his government. From the outset the Communist Party was critical of the policy for Cochinchinese autonomy and supported Vietnamese claims for uniting the whole national territory (the three *ky*).[156] This surely reflected the general attitude of the communist leaders, but they showed no eagerness to make their view known or to persuade others. In fact, the Indochina policy of the French Communist Party in 1946 can be summed up in two words: Keep quiet! The party's interest in remaining a part of the French government took precedence over the urge to support its Vietnamese comrades. In the immediate postwar period, the PCF did its utmost to pose as a moderate and patriotic French force. This policy culminated in November 1946, when the party hoped to capitalize on its electoral victory and see its leader Maurice Thorez as prime minister *(président du Conseil)*. Neither the Soviet Union nor the French communists showed much enthusiasm for the Vietnamese Revolution of August 1945. When Ho Chi Minh proclaimed the DRV on September 2, 1945, almost the entire French press commented negatively. The communist mouthpiece *L'Humanité* made no comment at all; it did not mention the Vietnamese Revolution until thirteen days later, and then it just quoted a brief news bulletin from Agence France-Presse (AFP). The communists reacted favorably to the March 6 agreement, and some less influential party elders and independent fellow travelers took friendly care of Ho Chi Minh while he was in France. The PCF refrained, however, from using Charles Tillon's seat on the Cominindo or its representation in the French delegation to Fontainebleau (Henri Lozeray) to exert pressure for making concessions. When Franco-Vietnamese relations worsened in November, the communist press either withheld comment or tried to blame the incidents on some third force like the Chinese or the Americans.[157] In accordance with Moscow's Eurocentric policy at the time, the PCF preferred to sacrifice the communists in Vietnam rather than risk its own domestic popularity.

The two remaining political groups, the various Conservative elements and the Radicals (each obtaining some 11–12 percent of the vote and 40 deputies in the November 1946 elections) were both avidly colonialist and anti–Viet Minh. The analysis below of the news coverage and editorials on Indochina by six important Paris newspapers is intended as an illustration of the kind of information offered to the French public. From our perspective, the reactions to the bombardment of Haiphong and the events leading up to December 19 are of particular interest.

There were no independent newspaper correspondents in Indochina at the time. For news from Saigon, journalists relied mainly on AFP (Saulnier), which was strictly controlled by the authorities, and for news from Hanoi, on Associated Press (AP) (Moutschen).[158] D'Argenlieu had an ingrained contempt for the free press and sought to avoid giving visas to critical journalists.[159] He established such close cooperation with AFP that the press agency could be considered a branch of the administration. During the first three weeks of November, the six Paris dailies wrote little about Indochina. The effective implementation of the cease-fire and Dr. Thinh's suicide were reported, but no attempt was made to appraise the degree to which the modus vivendi agreement was being implemented. The suicide aroused criticism in the press. The Socialist Party paper *Le Populaire* predicted that the Cochinchinese government would disappear. Jacques Guérif in *Le Monde*, who felt sure that the Cochinchinese wanted autonomy, regretted that the provisional government had not been more democratic.[160] When news of the November 20 incident in Haiphong arrived, the conservative *Le Figaro*, Catholic *L'Aube*, and liberal *Le Monde* all immediately blamed it on the Vietnamese,[161] although *Le Monde* also dutifully printed the Vietnamese version.[162] The headlines in the left-wing newspapers were neutral. *Le Populaire* and the free-wheeling socialist paper *Franc-Tireur* emphasized that the incident had originated in a conflict over customs, while the communist *L'Humanité*, in a small note on page 3, hinted that the incident might have been due to a "provocation from anti-Vietnamese Chinese elements."[163] On November 23, AFP reported that Dèbes had presented the Vietnamese with an ultimatum, and this had led to a Vietnamese attack. This piece of information was faithfully reproduced by *Le Monde* and *L'Aube*. The latter even stated in its headline that the French had been attacked once again. *Le Figaro* offered a respectably factual summary of the French and Vietnamese versions. *Le Populaire* and *Franc-Tireur* expressed their disbelief in the official version, but could not offer any alternative explanation. *Le Populaire* hoped the government knew what had really happened, and *Franc-Tireur* called for d'Argenlieu's dismissal. It refuted the thesis of a "Vietnamese provocation" and asked whether "certain old-fashioned colonialists were trying to save an absurd policy through military provocations."[164] The November 26 front page of *L'Humanité*, published three days after French forces had committed a massacre in defiance of agreements signed with a government led by a communist who had taken part in the foundation of the French Communist Party, concentrated on the demand that Maurice Thorez should lead the new French government. Page 3, however, found room for news from Vietnam. Some undefined "provocative elements" were blamed for causing incidents. The article pleaded for confidence in Ho Chi Minh and demanded a termination of "equivocal methods, which always leave room for provocations." On the following day, the fact that the incident had started with an inspection of a Chinese junk was used to prove that "certain private interests, foreign to the interests of French and Vietnamese nationals, are calling the tune."[165] When the French occupation of Haiphong had been accomplished, a headline in *L'Humanité* proclaimed: "calm returns to vietnam."[166]

The use of artillery and the strafing of fleeing civilians from airplanes were only mentioned by the French press in the form of official denials, but *Le Populaire* quite correctly remarked that one of the denials in fact confirmed Vietnamese allegations that artillery had been employed.[167] Much was said about the number of French soldiers killed. In order to refute exaggerated reports in the sensational Chinese press, it was also reported that only fifty Chinese nationals had been killed. No one at the time tried to estimate the number of Vietnamese killed, and the battle or massacre in Haiphong was generally referred to as an "incident." On November 28, *Le*

Monde's Rémy Roure affirmed that from the French side, "not a single shot had been fired, except in defense."

So much for public opinion. Its ignorance and strongly nationalist sentiments should be kept in mind as we now proceed to the deliberations of the top-level decision-makers.

BIDAULT'S CABINET

Bidault's cabinet was a coalition of the three largest parties, but also included a Radical, Alexandre Varenne, who was a former governor-general of Indochina. The cabinet and Interministerial Committee for Indochina (Cominindo) were dominated by MRP ministers. Three of the Cominindo members were MRP (Bidault, Schuman, Michelet). The SFIO's only representative was Moutet; the PCF's only member Charles Tillon, a so-called aviation minister, loyally followed the party directive to keep his mouth shut. Varenne also sat in on the committee's meetings, and he spoke.[168]

A majority of these men probably hoped to avoid war in Indochina. They did not share d'Argenlieu's desire to break with Ho Chi Minh and destroy his government. The news of the Haiphong and Langson incidents arrived at a time when Paris was absorbed by a cabinet crisis. Bidault would most likely have to resign as soon as the newly elected National Assembly convened. In this situation, the outgoing ministers were unable to reach any meaningful decision on what to do about Indochina. D'Argenlieu did not get the green light he was seeking for a forceful change of policy. Neither did he get any red light. Instead the government put up a series of yellow lights. In Saigon, Valluy was waiting for the governmental decision that d'Argenlieu had gone to Paris to obtain. He got only a series of reassuring messages from d'Argenlieu himself.

D'Argenlieu arrived in Paris on the afternoon of November 15. He first saw Sainteny, whom he sent back to Indochina to resume his former function as commissioner in Hanoi. Then the admiral started lobbying. The Cominindo met on November 23, while the artillery was pounding Haiphong, to hear d'Argenlieu report on what had happened in the three preceding months. The committee wanted to hear out the high commissioner before giving the final touches to a set of new government instructions for him—or a successor—to take back to Saigon. These instructions were planned to be discussed and approved at an additional Cominindo meeting on November 29.

D'Argenlieu's report to the November 23 meeting started with the situation in Laos and Cambodia, which he declared to be satisfactory, although the local monarchs still needed to be "sensibly advised and discreetly controlled." Laotian and Cambodian politicians were observing French policies in Cochinchina and Tonkin, asking themselves whether France would show "strength and resolution or weakness and hesitation faced with the imperialist pretensions and ambitions of the Annamites." D'Argenlieu conceded that the French had failed in Cochinchina and that the suicide of Dr. Thinh was a "sign of this defeat." This was essential, since "the Annamite problem was anchored in the Cochinchinese problem." D'Argenlieu blamed the Cochinchinese failure on the French government's irresolution and the contrast between the "reserved silence" that Paris had maintained with regard to Cochinchina and the great interest shown in the Vietnamese Republic and the "person of Ho." Vietnam had exploited the general uncertainty as to what the French intentions were, and article 9 of the modus vivendi agreement (the cease-fire) had made this easier. In fact, article 9 represented a serious menace to the French "patrimony." D'Argenlieu therefore found it indispensable to suspend the application of the modus vivendi agreement. This measure would produce the "psychological shock" that was needed.[169]

Although d'Argenlieu had instructed Valluy on November 12 not to exclude a direct confrontation with the "Hanoi government," he does not seem to have mentioned the risk of a conflict in the north in his report to the Cominindo on November 23. He spoke almost exclusively of Cochinchina. Yet all the participants in the meeting, with a possible exception of Tillon, must have known about the instructions Valluy had sent Dèbes on November 21.[170] The meeting began at 3 p.m. Valluy's second set of instructions to Dèbes and Morlière, prescribing teaching the Vietnamese a severe lesson, was dated by the Paris cipher office: November 23, 1747 hours.[171] It thus seems probable that at least some of the Cominindo members received this news during or just after the meeting. D'Argenlieu's report was followed by a long discussion between Bidault, Moutet, and Michelet. According to the minutes, Tillon also said something.[172] Unfortunately, neither of the existing summaries of the November 23 discussion quote what Michelet and Tillon said. Neither Bidault nor Moutet seems to have mentioned Haiphong. Both Bidault and Moutet expressed themselves in favor of authorizing Saigon to break the cease-fire that was prescribed in article 9 of the September 14 modus vivendi agreement. Bidault emphasized that Cochinchina was a French colony and would remain so until the French National Assembly had decided otherwise. French law was valid in Cochinchina, and "the government has the duty to make all French rights respected with all means, including force."[173]

Moutet claimed that article 9 of the modus vivendi agreement had not given Vietnam any authority in Cochinchina. The only matter pertaining to Cochinchina that could be discussed with the Hanoi government was the order for the termination of hostilities. Moutet affirmed that the French command had faithfully respected the cease-fire, but French soldiers were still being attacked, and attacks were also directed against Annamites whom the French command was obliged to protect. "As a consequence it [the command] must consider it as its duty to reestablish order and quell any agitation, if need be by force."[174] Bidault's and Moutet's statements seem to have applied only to Cochinchina, but when we consider that they must have been aware of the ongoing crisis in Haiphong, they must also have understood that their statements could be interpreted as a green light for using force in the north as well. This was d'Argenlieu's understanding when he approved of everything Valluy had done in a cable to Saigon on November 25: "I totally approve of the instructions that you have given General Morlière. They are in line with the mood of the government [dispositions gouvernementales] as this can be derived from the November 23 session of the committee."[175]

Bidault's cabinet held its last meeting on November 27, and when the first National Assembly of the Fourth Republic met on the following day, Bidault announced his resignation. After the cabinet meeting on November 27, Moutet replicated Valluy's version of the Haiphong events in a statement to the press, adding that if the "policy of agreement" were sabotaged by the other party, the only option left to France was "firmness without any faltering."[176] This statement was well received by the Saigon authorities, who asked for the full text, since it might be "useful on a later occasion."[177]

To what extent should Bidault's government be blamed for the events in Indochina? Did it know what Valluy and Dèbes had done? Did Saigon inform Paris properly? Until November 21, the high commissioner does not seem to have informed Paris of the import-export controls and their possible implications.[178] But d'Argenlieu had informed Bidault and General Juin about the draconian instructions he had given Valluy on November 12. We do not unfortunately know to what extent they informed others, or what they said to d'Argenlieu about it when he came to Paris. It is clear that Valluy was not fully comfortable with the situation d'Argenlieu had placed him in, where he was implementing the admiral's policy without knowing for sure that the government was behind it. After d'Argenlieu's departure from Saigon, Valluy sent a series of telegrams to Paris with arguments in favor of a firm policy. He clearly did not wish to keep Paris out of the game and to become personally responsible for a "fait accompli."

The information sent to Paris during the fighting in Haiphong was biased and incomplete. The affair was constantly referred to as a premeditated Vietnamese provocation. Nothing was said about the number of victims, nor was Paris informed of Valluy's dispute with Morlière. Valluy did, however, inform Paris without much delay of his November 21 and November 22 instructions, quoting even the crudest words.[179] A protest from Ho Chi Minh to Bidault, asking him to order an immediate cease-fire, was also forwarded to Paris on November 27.[180]

The first reactions from Paris must have pleased Valluy. Several telegrams assured him of full governmental support,[181] but they all came from d'Argenlieu. A few days later, he received some critical questions and comments from the chiefs of staff. This made him fear that d'Argenlieu did not after all have his back covered. As we shall soon see, this fear had a profound influence on the French behavior over the next few weeks, when Valluy was dithering.

It is difficult accurately to analyze the role and responsibility of Bidault and his government in the events that led to the massacre and occupation of Haiphong and Langson. The French actions were undertaken under the authority of instructions from the high commissioner, not from the prime minister or any other minister, but the fact that d'Argenlieu informed Bidault and Juin of his November 12 instructions to Valluy before they were implemented does engage the responsibility both of the premier and the chief of staff. Although Moutet's authorization on November 23 to break the cease-fire agreement that he himself had signed in mid-September may have applied only to the south, he must soon have learned what d'Argenlieu and Valluy were doing, but did not try to stop them. It seems clear that at least some of the French ministers had sufficient knowledge to understand that their "New France" was on its way to an all-out confrontation with the Viet Minh.

However, the occupation of Haiphong and Langson did not lead to an immediate outbreak of war, as d'Argenlieu and Valluy had probably expected. The Vietnamese Army continued to prepare itself for a protracted war of resistance, but did not retaliate. A one-month stalemate ensued, during which the French government again had a chance to intervene. Ho Chi Minh desperately wanted it to do so, indeed, he begged for it, so that he could either gain more time or avoid war altogether. The French triumvirate in Saigon, however, had little time to lose. Valluy was ready to order the implementation of some of the core ingredients in the abortive Opération Bentré from February–March, starting with an offensive west from Haiphong to take control of the road to Hanoi. This would need to be done in combination with a "police action" to capture Ho Chi Minh and his government. But could the high commissioner take the responsibility for launching further offensive operations when the Vietnamese government was not reacting more forcefully? If not, then it might be preferable to find a way to induce the Viet Minh to provide a pretext. France was in need of a trap.

5

The French Trap

After November 23, Morlière expected the French seizure of Haiphong and Lang-son to lead immediately to a general conflagration, and he concentrated on preparing his forces for responding to a Vietnamese counterattack. In Haiphong, French military intelligence laid their hands on a Vietnamese plan to attack the French garrison in Hanoi, and this reinforced the expectation that the Vietnamese would take the initiative. This would then trigger the "coups d'état" that had been part of French planning since the cancellation of Opération Bentré after the March 6 accord. But the Vietnamese did not attack. Instead, they intensified their defensive preparations and put up barricades in the streets of Hanoi. The foreign consuls told Morlière that several members of the Vietnamese cabinet had expressed their desire to localize the conflict or even put an end to it.[1] Giap asked to see Morlière, and this prompted an exchange of letters. Morlière's attempts to prevent the Haiphong massacre had not become public knowledge, but the letters he now sent to the Vietnamese government, on instructions from Valluy, were publicized immediately. They led the Vietnamese to nickname Morlière "The general of ultimatums" and French leftists to accuse him of belonging to a "colonialist camarilla."[2]

Morlière agreed to see Giap at 4 p.m. on November 26. He had decided to demand that the Vietnamese government accept French control of Haiphong. A Vietnamese civilian administration and militia could be reestablished there, but the regular Vietnamese Army would have to stay in a demarcated zone outside. Morlière informed Valluy of his intention before presenting the demands to Giap, and this gave Valluy the chance to stop him. Two hours before the meeting, he instructed Morlière to postpone it.[3] Did Valluy want to capitalize on the victory in Haiphong and provoke a clean break with Ho Chi Minh? Not necessarily. Valluy and his po-

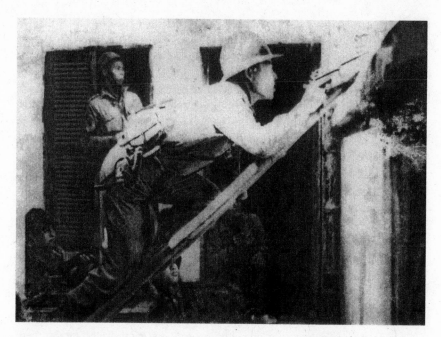

FIGURE 6. Tu Ve (militia) barricade under construction in Mai Hac De Street, Hanoi, late 1946.

litical schemer, Pignon, were both concerned that France should not appear as the aggressor. On November 23, during the battle for Haiphong, and on the same day the Cominindo met in Paris, they had refused to carry out an order from d'Argenlieu to reinstall the French commissioner in Tonkin (still Morlière, while Sainteny was away) in the former palace of the governor-general, explaining in a telegram: "Under the present circumstances, and after the very serious incidents in Haiphong and Langson, this occupation would be interpreted as a provocation indicating our wish for a rupture. In short, it is the whole policy of the French government that will be called into question by this issue, and we believe that it would be indispensable to consult it in advance."[4]

This telegram, which Valluy and Pignon sent jointly to d'Argenlieu, provides a fascinating glimpse into the relationship that had developed between the French government and its representatives in Indochina. The interim high commissioner and his political advisor did not trust that the high commissioner, although he was in Paris with access to the ministers, could correctly interpret the government's policy. They therefore defied his orders on a highly sensitive and symbolic issue.

Three days later, when Valluy got to see the demands that Morlière intended to present to Giap, he found them far too modest. He instructed Morlière, before meeting Giap, to continue the military operations and enlarge the French-controlled zone around Haiphong. Then he should present Giap with the following demands: the demarcation of a large zone around Haiphong, where no military or paramilitary Vietnamese units would have the right to stay; French control of all passage of military units and of river boats through the zone; and full freedom of movement for the French on the road from Haiphong to Do Son (a small coastal town south of Haiphong). In Langson, Morlière was to consolidate the recent gains while waiting for new orders.[5]

Morlière did not immediately obey, and he warned Valluy that it would be impossible for the Vietnamese to allow full French control of the important river traffic. Valluy, now somewhat more confident of the French government's support, since he had received word from d'Argenlieu that the instructions he had sent Morlière in connection with the occupation of Haiphong were "in line with the governmental dispositions," explained to Morlière that French control of the river traffic would only affect military transports. He refused to modify in any way the demands he had prescribed. Morlière then obligingly conveyed the demands to Giap in a meeting on November 27. He told Giap that the demands had been "approved" by Saigon, but did not reveal that they had been dictated to him.[6]

Giap proposed creating a mixed commission to discuss the question. Morlière replied that the conditions were the result of "very precise instructions" that could not be discussed. A mixed commission would therefore only be useful if its purpose were to determine how the measures demanded were to be executed. Giap retorted that the demands affected Vietnam's national sovereignty and asked Morlière to reconsider them and inform Saigon of his suggestions. Morlière reiterated that the conditions were well known by the French High Command, and that Saigon had been constantly informed of Giap's proposals.[7] Giap then let the matter drop. When U.S. Vice-Consul O'Sullivan informed Washington of Morlière's conditions, he called them an "ultimatum without deadline" and said the French seemed determined to force Vietnamese collaboration on French terms "or to crush Government."[8]

When the "ultimatum without deadline" became known in France, the socialist journal Le Populaire simply printed the news without comment. The MRP mouthpiece L'Aube focused on the Vietnamese delay in answering, and the conservative Le Figaro cited an explanation from d'Argenlieu. The communist L'Humanité thought the method of ultimatums was "no good" and that the "pseudo-policy of firmness," which had been applied earlier in Lebanon and Syria, was undermining French moral authority and "opened the door to others."[9] The leftist Franc-Tireur presented the ultimatum in blazing headlines, asked whether France was preparing for "reconquest," and demanded that a parliamentary commission be dispatched to Indochina.

Although the ruling triumvirate in Saigon may have wanted to crush the Viet-

THE FRENCH TRAP 149

namese government, the French did not do so in the first half of December, for three main reasons. First, Morlière and Valluy were concerned about the likely fate of French civilians in Hanoi and the security of the small French garrisons in Vinh, Hai Duong, Bac Ninh, and Phu Lang Thuong. Second, Valluy and Pignon continued to worry that their actions might be disavowed by the French government. And third, some of the French decision-makers thought it might be possible to impose French terms on a moderate Vietnamese faction and detach it from the extremists. Most important was the uncertainty concerning the French government's attitude. The reason why Valluy and Morlière's ultimatum set no time limit was most likely that Valluy was waiting to see the results of the next Cominindo meeting on November 29, which was expected to adopt the long-awaited government instructions.

Reporting the French ultimatum, O'Sullivan added that the Vietnamese course of action was "not yet determined." The evacuation of the great majority of the civilian Vietnamese population from Hanoi, which had started when Dèbes seized Haiphong, was continuing. The DRV government, at least in part, had also left the capital, and the population, particularly on the outskirts, was "almost in panic."[10] On November 30, Morlière also reported the continued exodus of civilians from Hanoi, but said he saw no signs of an imminent Vietnamese counterattack inside the city. In the face of the French refusal to discuss the harsh terms laid down by Valluy, and the French government's determination, the Vietnamese government still did not seem to be contemplating "aggressive action, but tries to drag things out," Morlière informed the high commissioner.[11] Each side was waiting for the other to take the next step, and for Paris to clarify its position.

A WHISTLE BLOWER

We have seen how strangely out of touch the Cominindo was on the afternoon of November 23. It discussed the situation in Cochinchina and the need to renege on the cease-fire at length, at a time when French artillery had been pounding Haiphong for a full day. None of its members sounded the alert or asked what this was all about. If the minutes are to be trusted, neither Bidault nor Moutet mentioned Haiphong at all. But one of Cominindo's deputy members blew the whistle after the meeting. He was neither a minister nor one of the colonial reformers in the Ministry of Overseas France, but France's deputy chief of staff, Admiral Pierre Barjot. And he soon got support from the prime minister's military advisor.

Valluy and Pignon had good reason to doubt d'Argenlieu's ability to interpret the policy of the French government correctly, and Valluy knew that a full-scale confrontation with the Viet Minh would require French reinforcements and mean a substantial increase in French military expenses. The chiefs of staff were acutely aware that many French politicians were looking for ways to *cut* French military spending. Demands for greater economy were a permanent source of friction between Paris and Saigon. In their electoral campaigns, the communists and socialists had made a point of promising reductions in military expenditures. Moutet had even tried to keep such electoral promises. In September, he sent an interministerial control commission, led by Inspector Georges Gayet, to Indochina to study saving options. Gayet was not exactly a welcome visitor. He and Valluy flew at each other's throats at once. They could not even agree how many troops there actually were in the Saigon area.[12] D'Argenlieu did not wait to see Gayet's conclusions before cabling Paris, on October 4, that the modus vivendi agreement by no means reduced the need for troops: "I think that at present there can be no better use for the money and for French troops than the preservation of the territories of the Union."[13] Gayet predictably took the opposite view: massive cuts in the number of European troops would be possible if the modus vivendi agreement were faithfully applied.[14] For one thing, he said, there were too many general officers in the colony. Gayet's views drew violent reactions, not only in Saigon, but also from France's chiefs of staff, the Etat-major général de la défense nationale (EMGDN). In a letter to Moutet, the EMGDN rejected all of Gayet's conclusions and supported Saigon's demand that 75,000 French troops remain in Indochina through the year 1947.[15] During the occupation of Haiphong, Valluy sent a request to Paris for reinforcements, saying: "The intentions of the Hanoi government and our new constraints in Cambodia make it impossible to affirm that our military superiority can be maintained with the same margin in the months to come."[16]

The chiefs of staff had backed d'Argenlieu and Valluy against Gayet, and Moutet does not seem to have pursued his wish for troop reductions, but the EMGDN had to think seriously about the risks France would run in other parts of the Union if too many troops were committed to Indochina, and also the additional costs that a war in Indochina would entail. It was not Chief of Staff General Alphonse Juin himself who blew the whistle, but his deputy, Admiral Barjot. He had the backing of General Humbert, Prime Minister Bidault's chief military advisor, who submitted a memorandum to Bidault on November 30 saying that it would be possible to send the reinforcements requested by Valluy if this were a temporary measure, but if it heralded a policy based on force, it was a step into the abyss, since this would go far beyond France's capabilities.[17]

Juin had left on a visit to Brazil, and Barjot represented the EMGDN when the Cominindo met on November 29. Before the meeting, he asked Saigon for more information about the occupation of Haiphong. Valluy replied, one day after the meeting, saying that he had nothing to add to what he had already said.[18] Barjot then decided to be more precise. He wanted a description of the import-export controls and the Vietnamese reactions to them, he wished to know the time and date of the Herckel-Nam agreement in relation to the time and date of Valluy's order to occupy Haiphong, and how much damage had been done to the Chinese sector of

Haiphong. He furthermore demanded an evaluation of the overall military situation in the north.[19] Barjot's questionnaire arrived in Saigon along with a demand from Moutet for an explanation of the "Dercourt coup d'état order," one of Dèbes's closed-envelope orders, which had been captured by the Vietnamese during the fighting and published in the Vietnamese press.[20] Valluy explained to Moutet that the unit commanded by Dercourt had a special mission, which was necessarily of a somewhat offensive nature even in a generally defensive context.[21] With fortunate consequences for the historian, Barjot's questionnaire was forwarded to Hanoi, where Morlière used this opportunity to scrupulously assemble all the instructions he had received and sent during the battle in Haiphong, write up a report, attach all relevant documents, and send the whole package to Saigon. This is the Morlière report of December 4, 1946, frequently cited in the notes to this book.[22]

The Morlière report did not please Valluy, who sourly told Morlière that Barjot's questions had a "journalistic" purpose and by no means constituted a governmental inquiry. Morlière's report would be sent to d'Argenlieu, who would take care of Barjot.[23] It has not been established whether or not d'Argenlieu or Morlière showed Morlière's report to anyone, but a copy was sent from the Comonindo to the French Foreign Ministry on January 3, 1947. Moutet was handed a copy by Morlière himself in Saigon on January 6.[24]

Pignon had seen the Morlière report almost a month earlier, and it must have troubled his conscience. He was working on a long report of his own on Haiphong and Langson, with seventeen documents attached to it, but none of the incriminating ones that Morlière included. How could Pignon send his own report to Paris without mentioning the facts recounted in Morlière's? Could he risk being accused of withholding information from his government? A solution was found. He cited the numbers of all the telegrams quoted by Morlière, said they had been encrypted with an operational code, and that they were very secret and could not be circulated. Competent authorities could claim the decrypted texts from Valluy's headquarters.[25] Pignon's report was sent to Paris on December 10, but not Morlière's. No one is likely to have requested the decrypted texts.

Eleven days earlier, without any support from Morlière, Barjot had written a long critical memorandum of his own, signed it on November 29, made sure Bidault got a copy, and probably brought it up in the Comonindo meeting. Barjot emphasized that the import-export controls had been established without any prior negotiations, and that Valluy's instructions to Morlière had led to renewed hostilities in Haiphong at a time when the conflict had been settled locally through the Nam-Herckel agreement:

The key to our security in Indochina is Cochinchina and not Tonkin. We cannot be everywhere at the same time and forcefully occupy all points. We must know how to choose. The choice is evident: the cornerstone of our presence in Indochina is

Cochinchina. This is where we must concentrate our forces. We have no interest in kindling military operations in the north that would lead us—and are already leading us—to transfer ships, parachutists, [and] aircraft from south to north, and thus drain Cochinchina. . . . If we wanted to reduce all the territories of northern, southern, and central Indochina by force, we wouldn't be able to do it with 10,000 or 15,000 additional troops. We'd need 250,000.

To send substantial reinforcements to Indochina would, according to Barjot, be "one of the most serious strategic mistakes" imaginable, for there would be no reserves left in the event of hostilities breaking out in French Africa (as happened in Madagascar the following March). "The view of the chiefs of staff is definite," Barjot concluded. "It is in Cochinchina that our military effort should continue to be made."[26] Valluy must have recognized in Barjot's recommendation the strategy that he himself had laid down in August.

General Leclerc read Barjot's memo in Paris and supported it. On December 5, after having discussed Indochina with Bidault on December 3, he wrote a memorandum in which he regretted that a method "essentially different" from his own had been employed in Indochina for the past few months: "They want to break the Vietnamese resistance by force, readopting methods that date from the conquest; moreover, they don't believe Ho Chi Minh and his team to be effective."[27] When Leclerc referred to methods "that date from the conquest," he doubtless meant the conquest of Tonkin in 1884–85, but he might just as well have been alluding to his own Opération Bentré, which had drained Cochinchina of troops in March, thus allowing the Viet Minh to regroup and reorganize its forces in the south so they could wage an effective guerilla struggle.

On December 8, Barjot wrote an even more critical memo, asking if the import-export controls had been intended as a way to gain control of the Vietnamese currency, and saying that "in any case, this measure had led inescapably to armed conflict." He accused Saigon of having delayed sending vital information to Paris, and criticized d'Argenlieu for his failure to carry out government instructions to obtain the withdrawal and disarming of Vietnamese troops in the south. Saigon had instead focused on Tonkin. Barjot castigated Saigon for having neglected Cochinchina. He feared that France would now have to struggle on several fronts instead of one. Barjot regarded Cochinchina as "strategic territory," the "keystone of the French presence in Indochina."[28] He had hoped that the Vietnamese government could be persuaded to withdraw its troops from the south. D'Argenlieu had enough experience to know that this was impossible. He had seen how the French position in Cochinchina was being undermined politically. On November 23, the Comonindo authorized him to break the cease-fire. Did this also give him a free hand in the north? D'Argenlieu thought it did; Barjot did not.

Barjot was unable, however, to convince General Juin, when he returned from

Brazil. D'Argenlieu protested to Juin against the circulation of Barjot's memos, claiming that they represented a "serious breach of the rules of military discipline." Juin agreed that it was none of Barjot's business to make such appraisals. He informed the Cominindo's secretary-general, Pierre Messmer, that Barjot's studies represented only the latter's personal opinion. Messmer returned the copies he had got to General Juin and assured him that he had not distributed them to any of the ministers.[29]

When Barjot realized that he had been gagged, he made a desperate attempt to influence public opinion by secretly contacting the newspaper *Franc-Tireur*, which had vigorously demanded d'Argenlieu's dismissal, and giving it copies of his memorandums. Hence, on December 20, *Franc-Tireur* was able to cite the instructions Valluy had sent to Colonel Dèbes on November 21–22. But it could not reveal its source.[30] Ten years later, when he commanded the naval forces that occupied Suez together with the British after Nasser nationalized the canal, it was Barjot's turn to lead France to a disaster.

CARETAKERS

When the Cominindo met on November 29, Bidault's coalition government had just resigned. Nobody knew for sure whether the next premier would be Maurice Thorez, Georges Bidault (again), or perhaps a socialist. Moutet opened the debate,[31] but no minutes of his statement have been found in the French archives. Alexandre Varenne, the second speaker, defended the import-export controls as necessary means to prevent the contraband trade in arms for the Vietnamese Army, which now numbered 75,000. In Varenne's view, the government ought to do two things: issue a strong statement and make it clear that the policy of accord could only continue if the other side stopped breaking the agreements.[32] Bidault pointed to a fundamental dilemma in French colonial policy. On the one hand, nothing should be done in Indochina that could be exploited by the sultan of Morocco or the bey of Tunis. On the other hand, a resort to force pure and simple might alienate both French and international public opinion. It was at any rate necessary to make it known that France would defend its presence in Indochina "with all means."[33] Bidault's rejection of "pure force" and his mention of international public opinion indicate that he did not fully support d'Argenlieu. What was said in the rest of the meeting is not known; no public declaration followed,[34] and the instructions to d'Argenlieu, which should have been adopted at the meeting, were not ready. This could mean that some kind of disagreement absorbed the Cominindo's time. Unfortunately for d'Argenlieu and Valluy, no clear guidelines emerged.

On December 3, the French National Assembly elected the socialist Vincent Auriol as its speaker, and on the following day, the Assembly voted on the candidature of the communist leader Maurice Thorez to lead the new French government. Most of the socialists voted for him, but he did not obtain a majority. On December 5, the Assembly voted even more decisively against Georges Bidault. Knowing that he would definitely have to give up the prime ministership, Bidault now sought consensus among his ministers on the new instructions for the high commissioner, and had to decide whether or not d'Argenlieu should keep his job.

Since the leaders of the two largest parties had failed to gain support from a parliamentary majority, the task of forming a new government had to be given to a socialist. On December 7, the SFIO's National Council adopted a new governmental action program, whose section on the French Union represented a victory for Moutet's procolonial approach. It criticized those who "pushed the indigenous populations toward totally autonomous regimes or independence in contradiction with their real interests" and emphasized that France would not just respect the agreements that had been reached with Vietnam, but also make these agreements respected by everyone. The high commissioner should put an end to the grievous incidents that stood in the way of reestablishing peace and order. As soon as calm had been restored, he should concentrate on settling the difficult problems of Cochinchina and the integration of the "various countries" into the Indochinese Federation and the French Union.[35] This program offered Moutet a political basis for reaching an agreement with the two MRP ministers, Bidault and Michelet, on the new instructions for the high commissioner, and renewing d'Argenlieu's mandate.

The admiral stayed in Paris during the whole cabinet crisis, except when visiting Charles de Gaulle in Colombey-les-Deux-Eglises. He had his own secretariat in Paris (AGINDO), paid out of the budget of the Indochinese Federation. D'Argenlieu was a controversial issue in French politics. For the MRP and the political right, he was a symbol of patriotism. If he were sacked, it would be a sign that France was abandoning its role as a great power. Moutet, for his part, was eager to replace d'Argenlieu and take control more directly. In November, his ministry drafted a decree defining the qualifications of a new high commissioner, who would report directly to the Ministry of Overseas France at 27 rue Oudinot.[36] Why didn't Moutet push harder? Why did he agree to keep d'Argenlieu as high commissioner? Moutet would explain later at an internal Socialist Party meeting that Prime Minister Georges Bidault had also wanted to replace d'Argenlieu in November–December, but been prevented from doing so by other MRP leaders: "Bidault was afraid of a split in his party."[37] The answer to the question of why d'Argenlieu was not sacked is no doubt to be found in the wheeling and dealing that preceded the formation of France's new socialist government on December 16, 1946. The MRP's votes were needed.[38] Moutet was the only member of the Cominindo who was likely to keep his portfolio under a socialist premier, so without his consent, the Cominindo could not have agreed on the confidential instructions that were handed over to d'Argenlieu on December 10, two days before the National Assembly was to vote on the socialist candidate for the premiership. It may seem surprising that a caretaker government would issue such important instructions rather than leave this responsibility to the next government. One reason was a sense of haste in view of the Indochina crisis. Another may have been the expectation that the next government would probably be a one-party government, whereas the outgoing coalition had broader national legitimacy. And a third possible reason, linked to the second, was that the MRP may have made its voting for a socialist premier subject to d'Argenlieu's retention as high commissioner, with a new mandate.

The ministers in Bidault's government had first agreed on a text defining the aims of the French presence in the Far East. This was drafted in Moutet's ministry, probably under the direction of Henri Laurentie, who had also been in charge when de Gaulle's March 24, 1945, declaration was written. Moutet wanted to replace that declaration with a significant new document that would focus less on lofty promises and administrative structure and more on how to define core French interests, which are listed in the introduction to the December 10, 1946, instructions. A slightly revised version was given to d'Argenlieu's successor, Emile Bollaert, in March 1947, this time with the signature of the main ministers in Paul Ramadier's coalition government, Thorez included. The communist leader thus also signed on to Moutet's definition of the French national interest. This was a key document in the history of French colonial thinking, defining the ideas that guided French colonial policy during the years between World War II and the Cold War. As emphasized in chapter 1 of this book, this was not a period characterized by colonial retreat, but one marked by attempted colonial reinvigoration and reform.[39]

The introduction defined three essential moral and material interests: the preservation and development of French cultural influence and economic interests; the protection of ethnic minorities; and the security of strategic bases. It made explicit that recognition of these interests did not allow the high commissioner to "remove, in the political domain, the upholding of a certain control of planning and of some well-defined territorial zones." This meant that France must, on the one hand, have a position as a privileged advisor of the government in each of the Indochinese states, and, on the other hand, directly control certain zones around its strategic bases. The instructions considered it possible for a "nation like the United States" (the first draft said an "essentially capitalist nation like the United States") to safeguard its investments solely by resorting to conditional economic and financial aid. France, engaged in its own reconstruction, did not have the means to practice such "liberalism" and was also opposed to it in principle. Neither could France apply the policy of the Soviet Union in its "associated territories," whose geographic proximity provided the metropole with the option of rapid intervention. After making these comparisons, the authors emphasized that if the Indochinese states "could safeguard the normal movement of French economic and cultural activities, nothing would prevent . . . abandoning all guarantees." The formulation here is probably deliberately equivocal. "Guarantees" should be understood to mean formal engagement to respect French sovereignty. If France had been in as strong a position as the United States or the Soviet Union, it could have given up its sovereignty in confidence that the lo-cals would remain under strong French influence. But based on experience dating back more than a century, say the instructions, and reinforced by recent events, "such a conclusion remains premature." To make the French Union into "a Commonwealth with purely symbolic allegiance" would rapidly sanction "the total abdication of France and the sacrifice of all its interests." The same would be the case if France were to abandon its control of strategic zones. France should thus not, in the present situation, concede to the peoples of Indochina "an unconditional independence, which would in reality be nothing but a fiction seriously prejudicial to both parties."

As shown in Mark Lawrence's study of French, British, and American Indochina policy from 1944 to 1950, the French government's decision not to grant Vietnam independence was counterproductive. The intention was to preserve French pre-eminence in Indochina. The result was dependence on other Western powers. In 1945, the French government had depended on the great powers, especially Great Britain, for help in transporting and equipping French troops to reoccupy south-ern Indochina. The French government had spent much time in this period justi-fying its policy in the eyes of its Western allies and had constantly worried that the Americans would undermine the French position. French dependence was reduced when the British left Indochina in January–March 1946. For three more months, there were huge numbers of Chinese troops in the north, some of whom needed U.S. assistance to be shipped to northern China. From June on, a more self-suffi-cient period followed for France, allowing the French government to presume that other powers would not interfere. This might have lasted if France had kept the peace with Vietnam and made the modus vivendi agreement work, but when full-scale war broke out, France again needed more troops, more ships, arms, and equipment, and again depended on support from powerful allies. The main risk was not there-fore that France might be supplanted by rivals, as the authors of the governmental instructions claimed, but that war would tie up French resources and make France depend on outside help. This did not happen immediately after December 19. Al-though the cost of the French expeditionary force increased by approximately 40 percent in the first part of 1947, the total French cost of the war would thereafter remain at the same manageable level for three years, while the economy suffered enormously in the areas controlled by the Viet Minh. As of 1949–50, however, the cost increased to an extent that made France more and more dependent on outside help and shifted decision-making power from the ministries of Defense and Over-seas France to the Ministry of Finance. French Prime Minister Pierre Mendès-France, who ended the First Indochina War in 1954, would say: "Not all problems are financial, but they eventually turn out to be."[40]

The December 10 instructions did not include any reference to "grandeur" or to a civilizing mission. They simply identified the three main French interests and con-cluded that they could not, at present, be realized if Vietnam became independent.

No differentiation was made between these interests, but it goes without saying that if the French presence were to be sustainable, the cultural and security aspects of it would have to be paid for by some kind of taxation, which in turn would depend on the colony's income-generating capacity. There had always been some Frenchmen who believed that Indochina could become profitable, and the French had striven continually for its economic development *(mise-en-valeur)*. The French *colons* owned rice fields and rubber plantations, and French companies ran mines. The Banque de l'Indochine had a hand in most sectors of Indochina's economy. The French returned in 1945 with great expectations of economic modernization. A plan for Indochina's industrialization was drawn up by Paul Bernard, who had argued in favor of a great industrial effort in two books during the 1930s. The intended budget for the industrialization plan, which was never implemented, was on the same level as the total French war expenditures in Indochina during 1945-50.[41] From late 1945 on, d'Argenlieu's various economic departments in Saigon took measures to attract French investments and develop the export of rice and rubber, as well as industrial products. There can be no doubt that the desire for a return on private and public investments, and for preparing the ground for new investments, counted in the French determination to win back and reform the colony. Paradoxically, instructions edited by the staff of the socialist Moutet, and signed by the communist leader Thorez, among others, easily lend themselves to arguments claiming that France engaged itself militarily in order to protect and develop its own material self-interest. If Gaullists or Christian Democrats had drafted the instructions, they would probably not have paid as much attention to commonplace material affairs. Bidault stated that his main reason for refusing to make concessions to Ho Chi Minh was the risk of contaminating French Africa. This reasoning resembles the "domino theory" that haunted U.S. Vietnam policy in the 1960s.

Hence the fear of contamination, and the preservation of French cultural and economic interests were the main reasons for the inflexibility of the French government in 1946-47. Valluy would share this view in 1967:

> What seems surprising today, after twenty years of retreat, is, firstly, how timid we were in applying a liberal order and that, by mid-1946, we opposed a nationalist movement, even though we had repeatedly proclaimed ourselves champions of the right of peoples to manage their own affairs, and subsequently, in contrast to the English example in India and Burma, persisted with our federal formula, in which there was scant effort to conceal the preeminence of the metropole. This was probably out of fear of creating a dangerous precedent for our African possessions, and also the fear of being economically evicted from Cochinchina, which was richly endowed with various products.[42]

The military chapter of the instructions resulted from a compromise between the chiefs of staff's wish to restrict the number of troops deployed in the Far East and d'Argenlieu's insistence that there could be no better use of French resources. D'Argenlieu wanted to engage France deeply in the border region with China. The EMGDN preferred to limit this engagement. The high commissioner simply wished to renounce the military convention of April 3. The EMGDN wanted it renegotiated. D'Argenlieu demanded considerable reinforcements. The EMGDN warned against transferring troops from Cochinchina to Tonkin. Barjot's hand can be seen in the views expressed by the EMGDN.[43]

The instructions, as signed by the ministers on December 10, did not in any way authorize the high commissioner to carry out the orders he had given to Valluy on November 12 and seek a confrontation with the Viet Minh in the north. Nor did they contain any explicit post facto approval of what had been done in Haiphong. What the military chapter did was to insist, first, on the fundamental necessity of defending the strategic bases, which "constitute the skeleton of the future military organization of the Federation." Since Haiphong was considered to be such a base, along with Cam Ranh Bay, this point may be seen as indirectly approving the conquest of the port city. Second, the instructions gave the high commissioner authority to "act efficiently to ensure respect for the clauses of the modus vivendi agreement and to maintain public order." Although this meant literally that d'Argenlieu could use force to uphold the cease-fire, in practice, it meant breaking it. D'Argenlieu would have preferred an explicit and public renunciation of the cease-fire. More concretely, the high commissioner gained the consent of the French government to enlarge the occupation of the Sino-Vietnamese border zone, which had begun with the seizure of Langson. This went against Barjot and his sound strategic considerations. The fact that it was nonetheless included in the government's instructions may have something to do with the influence of Moutet, who was more concerned with the protection of ethnic minorities than with avoiding the dispersal of troops. Back in June, Moutet had authorized the conquest of the central highlands of north Annam, in violation of the April 3 military convention, and with the goal of establishing an autonomous ethnic minority area. Barjot was responsible for the final point: no troops should be transferred from south to north. The maintenance of sufficient military forces in Cochinchina, said the directives, constituted the "keystone of the French edifice in Indochina." The primary task of the high commissioner was to get the armed Tonkinese "elements" who had been infiltrated into Cochinchina to pull out. This was as much Barjot's concern in 1946 as it would be General Westmoreland's in the 1960s. .

The general introduction to the governmental instructions faithfully reflected the thinking of the minister for Overseas France. It focused on basic French interests, but included the protection of ethnic minorities. But as far as the structural or institutional questions were concerned, Moutet did not get what he wanted. This comes out clearly if we compare the draft version prepared for the Comenindo meeting on November 29 with the final version signed on December 10. The draft version, which no doubt reflected Moutet's views, although it had probably been edited by the two "liberal Gaullists," Henri Laurentie (Moutet's director of political affairs) and Pierre Messmer (Cominindo secretary-general), scrapped the March 24, 1945, declaration's core idea of a strong Indochinese Federation, with relative autonomy from Paris. Now that France had got its new constitution and replaced the defunct empire with a future-oriented French Union, said a memo written by Moutet, it was time to reduce the powers of the federal government in Saigon *("Organe tentaculaire dont il faut limiter les pouvoirs")*. The draft instructions sought to shrink the size of the federal government in Saigon, emphasizing that the federation was "essentially administrative" and should not direct policy.[44]

This was a direct attack on d'Argenlieu and his desire to rule French Indochina with powers similar to those that U.S. General Douglas MacArthur had in Japan. Then also the federal idea found its way back into the final version of the instructions, which aimed to establish more federal services in the various Indochinese states. D'Argenlieu had thus won a victory over Moutet, most probably due to the influence of the MRP ministers and of Alexandre Varenne, who all sought to prevent too much socialist interference in French colonial policy.

D'Argenlieu's backers also managed to block another significant proposal from the Ministry of Overseas France. It had wanted to stop objecting to the unification of the three *ky*. The first draft version stated: "It is now certain that Cochinchina will be united with Vietnam sooner or later. We must therefore already now plan for this unification, which must, however, ensure the administrative and fiscal autonomy of Cochinchina." In the final version, this passage was taken out. The signed instructions said instead that France would "seek to find a local solution" in Cochinchina, while letting personalities with moderately unionist opinions participate in the Cochinchinese government. The document also made clear that this "local solution" would make "recourse to a referendum" redundant. So the French government chose finally to renounce the most important of the concessions in the March 6 accord.

It is interesting to compare the paragraph on the "local solution" with Moutet's original draft, which said: "Our military action [in Tonkin and Annam] must be accompanied by political action." Moutet probably hoped that by accepting the unification of the three *ky*, it would be possible to obtain a government reshuffle in Hanoi, with the introduction of noncommunist ministers from the south. This resembled options Pignon and Torel had been mulling over for a long time. But while Moutet probably imagined a negotiated solution, in which Ho Chi Minh would retain his role as national leader, d'Argenlieu's political advisors in Saigon envisaged creating a new noncommunist government for all of Vietnam and breaking with the Viet Minh.

D'Argenlieu had reason to be satisfied with his new instructions, although he did not obtain the suspension of the modus vivendi agreement that he had been seeking. The instructions say that "the results obtained so far, even though they disappoint the hopes we had some weeks ago, do not justify a suspension or denunciation of the modus vivendi [agreement]." The three ministers who signed the instructions (Bidault, Moutet, and Michelet) added, however, that the high commissioner should apply "a set of firm measures, with the aim of getting the Vietnamese government to realize the state of affairs considered preferable for the good of the two peoples." This was open to interpretation, for which d'Argenlieu's team in Saigon had a talent. The instructions did, however, provide two examples: the high commissioner was authorized to use force to obtain the restitution of French property if the Vietnamese government prevented it—a sure recipe for trouble. He was also authorized to make the Vietnamese government aware of its responsibility to uphold law and order. This was all that the instructions had to say about the relationship between France and the Vietnamese government, except for an affirmation in the introduction that this relationship was bad and had "no appearance of any possibility of normalization."[45]

The three ministers, when acting in unison, preferred to refrain from taking any clear position on the situation in Tonkin, and most notably did not take any initiative to establish direct contact with the Vietnamese government to resolve the crisis. Hence they left crisis management to d'Argenlieu and the men on the spot. This means that they must, perhaps with closed eyes, have accepted the risk that the recent incidents would lead to full-scale war. Moutet, however, clearly wanted to avoid such an outcome, and he was as of December 10 the only one among the three ministers in the outgoing cabinet who could expect to retain his portfolio in the next one. This gave him greater leverage than before, and his ministry knew this. The day after d'Argenlieu got his instructions, Moutet's director of political affairs, Henri Laurentie, drafted a crystal clear telegram for Moutet to sign and send to Valluy, which aimed to prevent the French effort from being diverted away from Cochinchina and to ensure that key decisions were taken by the new government in Paris, not in Saigon. The telegram warned Valluy that he could under no circumstances expect any military reinforcements, and that "France must not be placed in a situation where the alternatives are either to make an effort beyond its means or to withdraw from Indochina. This is an imperative condition for your policy." The telegram stressed, moreover, that the government rejected the idea of any initiative having "as its aim or effect to oust Ho Chi Minh personally from power." The reason cited shows how clear-sighted Laurentie was: "The consequence of this would actually be a period of second-rate competition, which would end up favoring those who have no future unless resorting to French assistance." Laurentie knew that a good adversary can be preferable to bad allies. The telegram ended by asking Valluy to persuade Ho Chi Minh to get rid of the "extremist elements in his government." If Valluy were unable to succeed on this score, then it would be *the French government*'s responsibility to determine "under which conditions and to what extent one might resort to auxiliary military action."[46]

The telegram was on the table, ready to be sent on December 11. But Moutet did not send it. There is a copy of it among Bidault's personal papers, so Moutet may have consulted the outgoing premier before deciding to let go a chance to avert war. On the following day, December 12, Bidault sent his own telegram to Valluy, commenting on a report that Valluy had submitted on December 6. Valluy had warned the government of the "almost fatal character of the rupture that the hatred and ill will of the Hanoi Government is drawing us into." Bidault commented: "I wish to point out that I was surprised by the terms of the telegram cited above, which suddenly refers to an alarming situation that nothing in your preceding communications had permitted [us] to foresee." The draft also included the following sentence, which was deleted before the cable was dispatched: "J'espère qu'il ne s'agit pas là d'une simple habileté destinée à couvrir votre responsabilité dans tous les cas" (I hope that it is not a matter here of skillfully covering up your responsibility whatever the case).[47] Even without the last sentence, this message must have had a chilling effect on Valluy. If it had also contained the omitted sentence, the general would have slept badly. Bidault did not let Valluy know that he was questioning his motives, but he let his poisonous sentence stand in the draft in the Cominindo files. So perhaps it was Bidault himself who tried to cover up his responsibility. The following day, his MRP party issued a leaflet demanding that a "unanimous French government" demonstrate its will to make the French presence in Indochina respected and, as soon as possible, implement a plan to "fight all kinds of terrorism energetically."[48]

MISSION IMPOSSIBLE

Moutet's unsent telegram asked Valluy to get Ho Chi Minh to understand that he should separate himself from his party's extremists, but said that if this failed, Valluy should not draw the conclusion himself, but refer to the government in Paris. The point about who should draw the conclusion was new, but the French endeavor to persuade Ho Chi Minh to break away from his undesirable lieutenants (notably Vo Nguyen Giap) and replace them with more moderate ministers had been going on for a couple of weeks. The man who had been instructed to undertake this impossible mission was the Frenchman who knew Ho best, Jean Sainteny, the "man of March 6."[49] He had accompanied Ho to France and organized his stay there, but did not go back together with the president. Sainteny took care of his business interests in France until he was asked, in November, to return to his assignment in Hanoi. The French Sainteny myth, as expressed on the jacket of his memoirs from 1953, is that he returned to Hanoi *too late* to prevent the outbreak of war.[50] This myth has no better foundation than the one about General Leclerc's pragmatic will for peace. When Sainteny returned to Hanoi in early December, his task, as defined in instructions from d'Argenlieu and Valluy, was to exploit his friendship with Ho

Chi Minh in order to provoke a split in the Vietnamese cabinet. Sainteny did not arrive too late in Hanoi, but his mission was impossible and his instructions were so narrow that there was no room for any rapprochement with the DRV. Sainteny had virtually nothing to offer. From December 3 to 19, he acted in Hanoi faithfully on lines set by d'Argenlieu, Valluy, and Pignon.

In the beginning of October, d'Argenlieu had praised Sainteny for his "qualities of firmness and diplomacy" and asked Moutet to reinstate him in Hanoi.[51] In reality, however, d'Argenlieu was in two minds about the handsome businessman. He feared Sainteny's tendency to seek local arrangements without considering the larger context.[52] D'Argenlieu had not quite forgiven Sainteny for having introduced the referendum and the last-minute concessions in the March 6 agreement. When it proved impossible for Sainteny to pass through Saigon before d'Argenlieu's departure from Indochina on November 13, d'Argenlieu told Sainteny to stay in Paris, so that they could have a good talk before he flew to Indochina.[53] They met on d'Argenlieu's first day in Paris, and Sainteny landed in Saigon just as Dèbes's artillery was pounding Haiphong.

D'Argenlieu now instructed Valluy to keep Sainteny in Saigon for a while in order to prepare him for his mission in Hanoi.[54] Sainteny was therefore still in the south when Valluy dictated the terms of the "ultimatum without deadline" to Morlière. Valluy thought it best to hold Sainteny in reserve until the first Vietnamese reactions to the ultimatum were known. On November 30, in the absence of a Vietnamese retaliation for the French conquest of Haiphong, Valluy found the time ripe for Sainteny to go north to remedy Morlière's failure to draw political advantages from the recent military successes. Valluy had received reports that the Vietnamese leadership was deeply divided and that one group, with Giap, wanted to evacuate the government from Hanoi and take up arms, while another was so "scared" by this prospect that it might be willing to make certain concessions. Ho Chi Minh's position in relation to those two tendencies remained "undecided." In this situation, Valluy felt that Sainteny was the only person capable of "taking political advantage of the situation."[55]

Before Sainteny left Saigon, a meeting of the most important members of the federal cabinet (and Albert Torel) laid down a set of instructions. The substance was: exploit in all fields the advantages that we have obtained in Tonkin as a result of our military successes in Haiphong and Langson, without forcing Ho Chi Minh and his cabinet to desperate solutions; take the high ground with the Vietnamese leaders to compel them to negotiate under conditions far more favorable to us; seek to get the president to repudiate and, if possible, eliminate the extremist elements; refuse to give up any of our positions, but if there is to be a rupture, be careful to let the other side take the initiative, while taking all precautions to avoid being caught by surprise.[56]

The demands that Sainteny should put forward were clearly defined. All Vietnamese troops in Cochinchina were to be repatriated to the north, leaving the French free to suppress all terrorism. In Tonkin, the French were to take control of Radio Bach Mai, the official Vietnamese radio station, obtain the release of all hostages, and ensure the resumption of economic life in its entirety. In return for Vietnamese support, Sainteny was authorized to make two offers. The first was to negotiate regarding customs duties and international trade. The second was to withdraw French troops from Bac Ninh and Phu Lang Thuong. The decision to abolish these garrisons had actually been made already, because they were too vulnerable and taking control of the road from Langson to the Gulf of Tonkin had in any case reduced the need to control the road from Hanoi through Bac Ninh and Phu Lang Thuong to Langson.[57]

The authors of the instructions must have realized that the mission they were giving Sainteny was impossible. No responsible Vietnamese leader could accept such demands, and the two carrots they allowed Sainteny to dangle before Ho were so tiny that there was next to nothing to negotiate about. The warning against forcing the Vietnamese government to take desperate measures, however, indicates that not everyone in Saigon wanted a break. Some nurtured the illusion that it might be possible to get the Vietnamese president to continue working with France and break ranks with the "extremists" surrounding him. On the day before Sainteny's arrival in Hanoi, Morlière saw Undersecretary of the Interior Hoang Huu Nam and Undersecretary of Foreign Affairs Hoang Minh Giam, who had been the two main negotiators on the Vietnamese side in the run-up to the March 6 accords. Morlière found them discouraged and in disarray. They wanted to prevent the conflict from spreading to Hanoi and did not intend to counterattack, but they were determined to defend themselves against "any new provocation."[58] Morlière also reported that Ho Chi Minh was considering the possibility of replacing two of his ministers with moderate personalities.[59] Morlière welcomed Sainteny in Hanoi on December 2, and as Sainteny said later, Morlière would now confine himself to his military duties, preparing for what "seemed to be more and more inevitable; the test of strength." Sainteny would take care of the political dimension.[60]

On his first day in Hanoi, Sainteny received a protest against French actions in Haiphong, Kien An, and Langson from the "Association Viet-Nam France," which represented the softest, most francophile faction of the Vietnamese nationalist movement.[61] The instructions Sainteny had been given in Saigon differed from the ones he had got from d'Argenlieu in Paris on one important point; d'Argenlieu wanted him to take up residence in the Governor-General's Palace in Hanoi. Sainteny had actually done this once before, after getting to Hanoi on a U.S. plane in the midst of the August 1945 Revolution, but he had been expelled from the palace by a Chinese general in October 1945. Valluy and Pignon did not, as we have seen, find it advisable to undertake such a symbolic provocation and did not therefore include this point in their instructions to him.[62]

Sainteny's main mission was to provoke a split in the Vietnamese leadership and thus prevent Ho from becoming an enemy of France. Pignon and Valluy probably realized how futile the attempt would be. Whether or not Sainteny understood it himself is more doubtful, but in their first and only meeting, Ho realized that his French friend had arrived with empty hands.[63] When being received by the president in the evening of December 3, Sainteny noticed that his host was suffering from an illness that, "even if it was not diplomatic, did not seem to be unrelated to the current events." They met in Ho's Hanoi office, although at this stage the president did not actually work there any longer, but operated from a safe house outside the city. He was discreetly driven into the city to attend meetings and out again immediately afterward.[64] On December 2, Giam and Nam were present all the time, so that Sainteny was never alone with Ho.[65]

Sainteny told the president outright that "certain elements in his entourage" had prejudiced Franco-Vietnamese reconciliation during his prolonged stay in Paris (an allusion to Giap). Instead of answering, Ho charged the French with responsibility for Haiphong and Langson, adding that it was necessary to calm tempers and proposing that the military commission and the commission for restitution of French property envisaged in the modus vivendi agreement should pursue their work. Ho also proposed establishing two joint commissions in order to settle the Haiphong affair both on the military level and with regard to customs control. He finally suggested that the French and Vietnamese military should retreat to the positions they had held before the latest incidents. Nam and Giam emphasized the vital importance of this point. Sainteny replied that establishing the joint commissions was acceptable, but that the French government would categorically reject a return to status quo ante. Vietnamese aggression would meet with French countermeasures in the future as well. The meeting resulted in a press release saying that an exchange of views had taken place in order to explore the possibilities of relaxing existing tension. Sainteny felt that Ho and his most loyal followers would do everything to avoid a rupture. He was not yet sure as to who these loyal followers were, or how much power they still held, but he felt certain that he had made them understand that France was playing its last card before the test of strength.[66]

In his first report to Valluy, Sainteny did not mention that Ho had asked him to forward an urgent message spelling out his three proposals to the French government. The Vietnamese were hoping that these proposals would make Paris intervene,[67] and in an interview with the newspaper *Paris-Saigon* on December 7, Sainteny claimed that he had dispatched the message.[68] This seems unlikely, since it has proven impossible to locate it in the French archives. The Vietnamese press wrote positively about Sainteny when he arrived, but by mid-December, the tone had changed, and Sainteny was denounced for playacting since March 6.[69]

On the morning of December 5, Sainteny informed U.S. Vice-Consul O'Sullivan that a "police action" was being planned. The Vietnamese government had become far more "terroristic" than hitherto and now represented only a minority of the population. The French would allow Ho to stay on as president, but anti-French elements would have to go. After the present cabinet had been dismantled, the people would be allowed to choose whatever cabinet they wanted, provided it was not anti-French. Sainteny denied that this would lead to the establishment of a puppet government, but O'Sullivan felt that "despite Sainteny's words," the French would be forced to set up such a government. He feared that French efforts to rid the country of the Viet Minh would take much longer than the short period Sainteny envisioned.[70] Later the same day, Sainteny saw Giam and advised him that the only alternative to the "test of strength" would be a profound cabinet reshuffle, replacing "certain ministers by clearly pro-French personalities." After a long discussion, Giam promised to present the French government with a list of potential Vietnamese ministers if the French would in return adhere strictly to the March 6 agreement. Sainteny now felt uncertain as to Giam's real power, and he complained to Saigon that he knew too little about internal power relations among the Vietnamese leaders.[71]

Sainteny may not have understood that the real power did not belong to the cabinet as such, but to the clandestine Communist Party. Hence a government reshuffle would not be of great consequence. The most important decisions were either taken informally by a group of Ho Chi Minh's closest advisors or by the secretly operating Standing Bureau of the [Communist] Party. Among Ho Chi Minh's closest advisors were the three communists Pham Van Dong, Vo Nguyen Giap, and Hoang Huu Nam and the socialist Hoang Minh Giam. The French intelligence services seem to have imagined that the Viet Minh Tong Bo was playing a significant role behind the scenes, but this does not seem to have been the case. The Tong Bo did not meet often and was not as influential as the French imagined. When the most critical decisions were made, it seems that Truong Chinh called the Standing Bureau of the Party Central Committee together. This, at least, is what today's party historians want us to believe. It is not entirely clear who belonged to the Standing Bureau at the time, but it included Truong Chinh, Ho Chi Minh, Le Duc Tho, and Vo Nguyen Giap, probably also Hoang Van Hoan and Nguyen Luong Bang, and maybe Hoang Quoc Viet, Tran Huy Lieu, and Pham Van Dong, although the latter is said to have joined the Standing Bureau only in 1949. In November–December 1946, at any rate, Pham Van Dong did not take part in Hanoi's decision-making, but went south (just after having married) to lead the resistance in south-central Vietnam. French sources do not reveal much awareness of the role played by Secretary-General of the Party Truong Chinh and the party's main figure responsible for personnel issues, Le Duc Tho, or even of the intelligence boss Tran Quoc Hoan. The French also do not seem to have been aware that the two top communists Nguyen Luong Bang and Hoang Van Hoan had been assigned the task to set up bases in the countryside to serve as headquarters in the coming war of resistance. The main decision-makers in Hanoi during the crisis thus seem to have been Ho Chi Minh, Truong Chinh, Le Duc Tho, and Vo Nguyen Giap, while Hoang Huu Nam and Hoang Minh Giam played an essentially diplomatic role vis-à-vis the French.

O'Sullivan reported to Washington that Sainteny foresaw a rapid French victory, and this is confirmed by a prophecy Sainteny sent to Saigon a week after his arrival. While the Viet Minh's victory at the interior level seemed total after the last strongholds of the China-oriented opposition had been conquered, he said, one should have no illusions as to a "unity" built so rapidly and with such violent means: "Viet Minh's edifice is still young, and as with all totalitarian regimes, it may be expected to come tumbling down at the first serious defeat" (an amazing statement for someone belonging to the generation who had watched Stalin's Soviet Union overcome the German onslaught). In his report, Sainteny ruminated on the queerness of his being able to talk man-to-man with Nam on the brink of war. He was under the impression that the Vietnamese leaders were unable to accept the reality. They would neither accept the French demands, because that would mean conceding defeat, nor would they proclaim a general insurrection. Applying "typical Far Eastern tactics," the Viet Minh preferred to act as if things would return to normal all by themselves as soon as the emergency had passed.[72] The obvious conclusion was not committed to paper, but was no less real for being held in abeyance: France would soon have to do something to help Hanoi make its choice.

General Morlière did not confine himself entirely to his military role after Sainteny's arrival. First, he compiled his voluminous report on the Haiphong and Langson incidents in response to Admiral Barjot's request. Then he wrote another report on the present situation and its possibilities, which he completed on December 12. At this stage, Morlière was still in charge militarily, and he claimed that the French "reactions" in Haiphong and Langson expressed the unanimous feelings of the troops and the French population. He saw himself as having been pushed into a dead end after having long faced a paradoxical state of affairs, with France and the Viet Minh fighting in Cochinchina while their representatives toasted one another at dinners in Tonkin. The Vietnamese government would not give in to French demands, because this would mean "self-condemnation," he affirmed, but France on its side could not accept a return to the pre-Haiphong situation, which would only lead to new incidents. The French presence as a whole was at stake. No French enterprise would be able to establish itself in Indochina or develop without French control, and this control would be illusory without the presence of French forces.[73] Such was the crux of the matter. When the mutual hatred had reached the point where even French economic activity would be threatened if the Viet Minh remained in power, even a man like Morlière was prepared to face a test of strength.[74]

Morlière stated in his report that if the Vietnamese cabinet were not reshuffled, it would have to disappear. The only thing that could make it disappear was a military defeat. Therefore, a conflict seemed "nearly inevitable." The population would certainly prefer "butter to guns," and the Vietnamese government would face numerous problems if it retreated to the interior of the country. Eventually, it would reform or dissolve itself and listen to the "voice of reason." That would be the time for France to show generosity. Morlière concluded that only a determined attitude on the part of the French government and a decision to accept and sustain a serious and prolonged effort would make it possible to save French Indochina and, with it, the rest of France's overseas territories.[75]

Under the pressure of events, Morlière had grown highly pessimistic. In the days prior to December 19, virtually all French in Hanoi seem to have regarded war as inevitable. Nevertheless, it should be noted that while Sainteny believed there would be a rapid collapse of the Viet Minh, Morlière stressed that the struggle would be long and arduous. After completing his report, Morlière gave it to Sainteny and asked him to send it to Saigon. Sainteny found the conclusions too pessimistic and added some strangely sanguine comments, based on the illusion that a nation can be forced from the outside to find itself new leaders. He said the March 6 agreement had not been signed on behalf of the Viet Minh, but on behalf of the whole people, so it would remain in force even after the eventual fall of the government. Vietnam would surely find new and better leaders: "Although France has been let down by the men she consolidated in power with the assumption that they were deserving of it, she does not for that reason renege on the position she took on March 6. If, then, when tested, the Viet Minh is unable to appear as any more than a party of agitators, then Vietnam will find another governmental team on its own. France's duty is not to oppose this, faithful to its desire to see this country administer itself through a government of its own choice."

In Saigon, Pignon was more positive. He liked Morlière's December 12 report much better than the compilation of documents he had got from him a few days earlier concerning the Haiphong affair. Before forwarding Morlière's new report to Messmer in Paris, Pignon added a strong endorsement: "For three and a half months, General Morlière has with the best of intentions sought to lay the basis for a confident cooperation with the government of the Republic of Vietnam, at the cost of extremely strong criticism from the French population in Indochina, as well as from the troops under his command. In this report, he offers a concise, well-documented, impartial and sincere summary of his failure. The report thus constitutes the least suspect and most objective analysis of the situation that has developed in Tonkin."

In January–February 1947, Morlière felt that his December 12 report had been a mistake, and he became convinced once again that a purely military solution was impossible. It was necessary to negotiate, and the sooner the better: "We are not fighting against the Viet Minh only, but against a huge majority, if not the entirety, of the population, for whom the rallying point is 'Doc Lap,' meaning 'Independence' . . . Many Annamites are hostile or indifferent to the Viet Minh, but their nationalism, their patriotism, and also the xenophobia latent in Asia make them rally without hesitation behind Ho Chi Minh, who has become the symbol of Vietnam."[76]

INTELLIGENCE

Sainteny's main asset was his personal relationship with Ho Chi Minh, but since he came empty-handed, he got just one chance to take advantage of this and failed. He then had to do with the two messengers that Ho was using in his dealings with the French, Undersecretary of the Interior Hoang Huu Nam and Undersecretary of Foreign Affairs Hoang Minh Giam. Sainteny's complaint to Saigon that he knew too little about the Viet Minh's internal affairs is actually a bit surprising. French Indochina had always been a police state, with governors relying on the Sûreté and its innumerable agents for information. And every military unit of some size had its 2ᵉ Bureau. Probably the best source on the early history of the Indochinese Communist Party is the archives of the French intelligence services, which had recruited one of Ho Chi Minh's best friends as an agent, so that everything that was said in Ho's little group in Guangzhou in the 1920s was duly reported and filed.[77] Not long afterward, this man came under suspicion by his comrades. In 1931, when Ho was arrested by the British in Hong Kong, the French agent was also arrested and sent to Vietnam, where he settled in Thai Binh province. After the August Revolution, the local leaders in Thai Binh wanted to eliminate him, but Ho did not allow this. Only in 1950, when French troops were nearby, was this French agent liquidated, out of fear that he might reestablish his French connections.[78] The Sûreté exploited children born of mixed relationships as informers and was in the habit of turning prisoners around to use them as double agents. As a young history teacher, Vo Nguyen Giap had been arrested, but his Sûreté interrogator came to admire his intelligence, arranged for his release, and also secured stipends for his further education.[79] This was a mixed blessing for Giap, who came to be suspected by some of his comrades of having made a deal. The Trotskyites accused him openly of this.

There is an impressive number of boxes in the French colonial archives with carefully typewritten excerpts of words written in confidence in private mail by all kinds of people, a gold mine indeed if someone should want to write the history of Indochinese mentalities. The person who knew most about Indochinese communism in the 1930s and first half of the 1940s was probably Louis Arnoux, intendant-general of the Indochina police until March 1945, but his loyalty to Vichy and Governor-General Jean Decoux prevented him from playing any visible role under the Fourth Republic. France had abundant intelligence, and we historians are grateful.[80] Still it was all to no avail. It is hard to find any country in the world where the communists gained more strength and prestige than in Vietnam.

When Sainteny arrived in Hanoi, some of the best brains in the French intelligence services had already been operating in the city for some time, often independently of one another. D'Argenlieu, Leclerc, and Valluy were military men who did not want to rely on the Sûreté, the instrument of Léon Pignon. And the naval high commissioner did not trust the army's 2ᵉ Bureaus, which reported to their various commanders. D'Argenlieu and Leclerc could not of course rely on each other's services, so each of them founded a secret service of his own, d'Argenlieu the Bureau fédéral de documentation (BFDOC), and Leclerc the Service d'études historiques (Historical Studies Service; SEH), with one branch in Saigon (SESAG) and one in Hanoi (SEHAN).[81]

Morlière saw the BFDOC's hand behind the initial incident in Haiphong on November 20, discussed in chapter 4, and, as we have seen, after the Haiphong massacre, the chief of the BFDOC, Commandant Schlumberger, disingenuously suggested that French propaganda should cite the high number of casualties in Haiphong as proof that the Vietnamese government was incapable of protecting its citizens. Actually, the BFDOC was not meant to be a "special service," narrowly defined, but a kind of coordinating unit distilling intelligence from all the other existing services and writing up syntheses. But Schlumberger soon established special branches in the various Indochinese centers. His agents were recruited from among the local security officers. The Vietnamese capital appears to have been a weak point in the BFDOC system, but as of December 1, 1946, it had its own branch there as well, with the task of coordinating the various secret services, centralizing all the intelligence, and transmitting it directly to the BFDOC in Saigon. One problem with this system was that the BFDOC staff lacked competence. The BFDOC's only asset seems to have been the trust of d'Argenlieu.

The French intelligence services in Indochina were never able to reestablish networks of the same quality they had enjoyed until March 9, 1945, and the reorganization of French intelligence services was far more successful in the south than in the north. The most qualified services in Hanoi were the Sûreté and the SEHAN. In Tonkin, the Sûreté was directed by the capable André Moret, who had previously directed the political section of the French police in Shanghai. The head of SEH was Lieutenant Colonel Trocard, whose advantage vis-à-vis his competitors was that he had leftist views, which facilitated communication with communist sympathizers. According to Valluy, his friend Colonel Trocard was an "eminent intelligence expert." He would be killed in an ambush in 1947. We have not found out who directed his section in Hanoi (SEHAN), but a certain Jacques Bousquet seems to have played a prominent role. Bousquet was a former official in the Vichy government who turned to communism in 1943. In the early days of March 1946, he served as the main go-between for Sainteny and Ho Chi Minh.[82] Then he became cultural advisor to the Vietnamese government, kept in touch with Vo Nguyen Giap, continued to work clandestinely for French services, and had access to considerable financial resources. He left Hanoi before the war began, and on December 20, 1946, the French Foreign Ministry tried to arrange for him, apparently on his way from Rio to Lisbon, to be put on a plane to Paris. In January 1947, the French would ask the British authorities unofficially to arrest Bousquet in Hong Kong and send him discreetly to Indochina. He was apparently under suspicion of engaging in arms trade on behalf of the Viet Minh. In April 1947, Bousquet was still—or once again—in Hong Kong, where he gave an interview to the correspondent of the Saigon-based newspaper *Sud*: "In Haiphong I witnessed their confusion; the Vietnamese ministers could not control the indiscipline of their military. They had wanted to stop the fighting. They could not. Hanoi was haunted by fear. I left the city before December 20, but I know that the Viet Minh lived in an atmosphere of panic."[83]

The SEH seems to have operated in a social environment in which procommunist Europeans fraternized with a small group of francophile Viet Minh cadres. This allowed SEHAN to collect quite detailed information about discussions among some of the main Viet Minh leaders. The value of this intelligence seems dubious, however, since it did not apparently include anything about Truong Chinh's party organization. It seems possible that the Vietnamese were using the SEH as a target for disinformation. D'Argenlieu despised the SEH and, at the end of October, complained to Paris about the "connivances that exist between certain Frenchmen and the organizations of Hanoi." According to the admiral, essential information was passed both ways. He even mentioned the possibility that he might have to proceed to "the neutralization of dangerous elements." Valluy would write in 1967 that d'Argenlieu had demanded that he get rid of his friend Colonel Trocard, who "mingled too much with the Marxists."[84]

SEH and Sûreté reports differed in content. The SEH aimed to provoke a split within the Viet Minh in order to preserve the relationship between France and Ho Chi Minh, while the Sûreté, with its network of informers among the Chinese population, as well as pro-Chinese and pro-American Vietnamese, was opting for a clean break. The relationship between the SEH and the Sûreté was characterized by mutual suspicion, and the second-rate people working for the BFDOC cannot have found it easy to coordinate them. In light of his own agency's weakness in Hanoi, d'Argenlieu probably had to rely on Pignon's Sûreté, while Sainteny and Valluy pinned their hopes on the SEH. After the outbreak of war on December 19, d'Argenlieu concluded that he and Pignon had been right all along: "To look for the individual thinking of Ho Chi Minh himself is futile. It comes down to the same thing whether one thinks that he is playing a different game from that of the active hostile elements of his party, like Vo Nguyen Giap, or that he has become their prisoner and has lost all authority after his excessively long stay in France. The idea that the command may have had of isolating Ho Chi Minh from our hard-core adversaries and building an acceptable government around him is a lost hope."[85]

Let us recapitulate the most important intelligence emanating from Moret and the SEHAN during the period October–November, without necessarily believing what it said. The main point here is not to summarize what actually happened among the Vietnamese decision-makers, but to get an idea of what the French *thought was going on*.

On October 6, the SEHAN reported that the Tong Bo had met the evening before and listened to Pham Van Dong's report from Fontainebleau, but did not say who else was present. Dong said he personally did not believe that the French had good intentions or that a sincere entente was possible. The meeting discussed military action in the event of a Franco-Vietnamese conflict. One week later, the SE-HAN quoted from a secret government order, No. 177, widening the powers of the Army Commissariat (Giap) to include all of Indochina and learned that Giap would be appointed minister of defense. In the beginning of November, the SEHAN evoked a person it called "Nhan Nhan," who did not have any official position but nonetheless took part in important meetings. This man, often referred to as secretary-general, was about forty years old, had eyeglasses, a constant smile, and a somewhat timid demeanor, and he moved frequently from one place to another. The day before Pham Van Dong left for France with Ho Chi Minh on May 31, "Nhan" had been one of four participants in an important meeting. The others were Vo Nguyen Giap, Hoang Huu Nam, and Pham Van Dong. The description of "Nhan Nhan" does not fit the party secretary-general Truong Chinh, who did not use glasses; it better fits the near-sighted Hoang Quoc Viet or Tran Huy Lieu.

The SEHAN was under the impression at the beginning of November that a conflict was about to emerge between the military command and the government. The government wanted to put brakes on the defensive measures undertaken in Hanoi, but this was prevented by the military command. The SEHAN commented on the personality of Giap and found that his nationalism and hatred of the French were becoming more important for him than his communist ideals. (In the SEHAN's view, communism was preferable to xenophobic nationalism; for Pignon and the Sûreté, it was the other way around.) Giap, concluded the SEHAN, was really the man one needed to stop. He controlled the army and was vying for power with Hoang Huu Nam and Pham Van Dong. While the fighting in Haiphong was going on, Giap had proclaimed a state of emergency throughout Vietnam. The SEHAN learned that on this occasion, there had been a serious quarrel between him and the Viet Minh propaganda chief Tran Huy Lieu, who reproached Giap for his "dictatorial" policy. The SEHAN's informer claimed to know that Giap was in favor of a total struggle (lutte à outrance), whereas Ho Chi Minh and Tran Huy Lieu wanted peace. Tran Huy Lieu was said to have asked: "What would have remained of the Vietnamese Army now if we had listened to Giap when he wanted to go to war not very long ago against the Chinese occupants?"[86] This could be disinformation. The general view is that in February–March, Tran Huy Lieu was intransigent, while Giap was more cautious, although this impression was mainly created by the aggressive tone of the Viet Minh newspaper Cuu Cuoc, which was known to represent Tran Huy Lieu's views.

Another informer claimed to know, at approximately the same time, that Giap was calling military experts from the various parts of Vietnam together in Hanoi, one of whom was General Nguyen Son, coming up from Quang Ngai in central

Vietnam. Other French intelligence services reported, at the end of November, that they had intercepted messages to Giap from the guerrilla leader in the south, Nguyen Binh, recommending the abandonment of all illusions and the adoption in the north of the same guerrilla strategy that had succeeded so well in the south.

On November 25 and 27, a Sûreté informer warned of an imminent Vietnamese attack in Hanoi. At a "reasonable" price, the Sûreté bought copies of a "Defense Plan for the Capital Hanoi," approved by Ho Chi Minh on November 24 in a restricted cabinet meeting, as well as a plan for an attack on Gia Lam airfield, approved on November 26 by a commission of military experts. The two plans had both been worked out by Giap. The Sûreté boss, Moret, affirmed that there was no reason to doubt the honesty *(bonne foi)* of the informer. Was this a case of disinformation? Perhaps. What we do know is that Morlière's staff found the plans "interesting," and that Vietnamese troop movements and construction of barricades in the period leading up to December 19 did conform with the plans.

The Hanoi defense plan spelled out the measures to be taken if there were an incident, or if the government launched the watchword BDHV *(binh dan hoc vu:* "literacy campaign"). The National Guard, aided by the Tu Ve (local militia) would encircle the Citadel, and the Tu Ve would arrest all the French civilians they could lay hands on in the city. The main French administrative buildings would be occupied immediately, except the Pasteur Institute and the Banque de l'Indochine, which would be encircled. Barricades would be put up in the area around the Citadel. All Vietnamese civilians who could not be mobilized were to be evacuated. To prevent the French from flying in reinforcements, Gia Lam airfield was to be seized, but so as not to complicate later diplomatic negotiations, destruction of equipment and fuel at the airfield was to be avoided. The plan built on the assumption that there would be diplomatic contact between the two countries during the execution of these measures. So a basic aim of the defensive measures was to gain cards to play at the negotiating table. The plan also included a withdrawal plan, however, to be executed if the situation made it necessary. This would soon prove necessary.

Whether authentic or not, the possession of these plans must have influenced French behavior in the following weeks. Morlière was able to prepare his forces for preventing their successful execution. The fact that Morlière had got hold of these plans may also have induced him to wait for the Vietnamese to attack rather than take the initiative himself. In his memoirs, however, Giap claims that he never seriously considered carrying out such a hazardous attack against the superior French forces.

Views expressed by Giap, according to the SEHAN, in meetings of the Viet Minh Struggle Front during the battle for Haiphong indicated that a Vietnamese counterattack might come soon. However, not much happened. The Vietnamese reinforced their defense works and cut off communications on the road between the capital and its port. Realizing that the Vietnamese were unlikely to take the bait and launch the attack Valluy had been waiting for, the French general decided—as we have seen—to send Sainteny to Hanoi. While Sainteny established contact with Ho Chi Minh, Valluy planned for Dèbes's forces to push gradually forward from Haiphong to Hanoi in order to reopen the road, thus increasing the pressure on the Vietnamese government. The SEHAN, and Sainteny, were meant to play crucial roles in the political exploitation of this pressure. D'Argenlieu, however, tried to prevent this. He did not want to see any repetition of March 6, and he feared that the SEH might be able to establish the basis for a new agreement with Ho. On November 28 or 29, either the day before or the same day as the Cominindo met in Paris, d'Argenlieu received a letter from Bidault in his capacity as minister of foreign affairs asking for information about the situation in Hanoi. Unfortunately, this correspondence itself has not been found in the archives, just references to it in d'Argenlieu's correspondence with Valluy. On November 29, d'Argenlieu asked Valluy to send Lieutenant Colonel Trocard and Second Lieutenant B. (no doubt Bousquet) to Paris without delay, so that they could be put at the disposal of the Ministry of the Armies. On the next day, he sent a copy of Bidault's letter to Valluy, asking him to open an inquest with the Commissioner of the Republic in Tonkin and the various special agencies operating there in order to allow d'Argenlieu to meet the request of the Minister of Foreign Affairs. The inquest was to be undertaken by the BFDOC branch. D'Argenlieu seems to have tried to deprive Valluy of his best agents right in the middle of a crisis.

Bidault may have been interested to know more about the alleged conflict between Ho and the extremists. Sainteny hoped to divide the Viet Minh, and Valluy's instructions to him show that the two of them had found the right tone. Valluy had little to lose by allowing Sainteny to try and drive a wedge between moderates and extremists on the Vietnamese side. The risk was that this could lead to open hostilities, but that risk was worth taking, since this outcome was what d'Argenlieu wanted. The high commissioner and his political advisor, Pignon, would prefer to break with the Viet Minh altogether. It would seem that Valluy failed to obey d'Argenlieu's orders. He agreed to create a BFDOC branch in Hanoi by decree of December 10, but he did not send either Trocard or Bousquet to Paris. Instead, Trocard went to Hanoi, and Bousquet left the country.

PREMEDITATION

Throughout 1947, French intelligence "proved" again and again that the Vietnamese attack in Hanoi on December 19 had been long premeditated. A great number of "proofs" were established. The reason why the French continued to unearth more and more "proofs" was that none of them were entirely convincing. Premeditation can be defined as "preplanning of an act showing intent to commit it." The French proved beyond doubt that an attack had been preplanned, but the captured documents did not tell under what circumstances the Vietnamese intended to commit the planned act.[87] The French were never able to prove that a decision to attack had been made before the final crisis. This makes it reasonable to assume that although both parties laid offensive plans, they remained undecided up to the last moment. On the brink, they both hesitated; but on the evening of December 19, they stumbled and fell into war.

After having captured and read Valluy's "Directives No. 2," as well as the plans Colonel Dèbes had laid for Haiphong, the Vietnamese convinced themselves that the French would attack in Hanoi as well. This fear must have strengthened the hand of those who thought it was time to launch the "people's war." But how should it be launched? By withdrawing from the cities and taking up a guerrilla struggle from base areas in the highlands? In the form of counterattack or through passive resistance? The advantage of the former was that the Vietnamese could choose time and place. The advantage of the second was that it would give them the moral high ground, and the French government might get a chance to dismiss d'Argenlieu. To just withdraw without a fight would not look good in the eyes of the local population, however, so although this had been the choice of the Vietnamese ancestors each time they had faced an invasion by a superior force, says Giap's memoirs, that option was quickly discarded.[88]

Defensive works like evacuation of civilians and barricade construction started in Hanoi immediately after the outbreak of hostilities in Haiphong. Not all civilians were willing to evacuate, though; some pro-French or "unreliable" persons were arrested and sent out of town.[89] Duong Trung Quoc, a leader of the Vietnamese Association of Historians, editor of *Xua & Nay* (Past and Present), as well as of a recent picture book about the beginning of the Indochina War in 1946–47,[90] and an independent member of the Vietnamese National Assembly, told me in summer 2007 that his mother and father had been living in Hanoi as a young couple when the French took Haiphong. They came from a well-to-do family with no sympathy for communism. His mother had just discovered that she was pregnant. On the advice of Quoc's grandfather, the couple moved out of Hanoi to live in the safety of Sontay province, in the house of relatives.

Many Vietnamese ministers and other top leaders spent the nights outside of the capital, while working in Hanoi during the day. Some government institutions and some of their archives were evacuated to previously prepared locations.[91] Barricades were systematically constructed in the Sino-Vietnamese section of the town, where all sorts of preparations were made for a sustained defense, like opening holes from one apartment to the next, so that snipers and other militiamen could move freely along the street without coming out into the open.

In order not to give the French an easy pretext, the free circulation of French cars in the European sector and in essential streets was not impeded.[92] Giap confirms in his memoirs that a detailed defense plan was prepared, but does not mention any attack plan. We do know, however, that such plans existed, and the concentration of troops around Hanoi was no defensive measure.[93] One army cadre, Ngo Van Chieu, confided to his diary that there was indeed an attack plan. The Tu Ve were to attack French civilians and soldiers "locally," while the army was to move in from the outside, seize the Citadel, eliminate the French there, and form a shock unit with whatever equipment they could find.[94]

On Sainteny's first day in Hanoi, the Tong Bo published a warning in *Cuu Quoc*, the Viet Minh mouthpiece, that the French reactionaries were invading Bac Bo. If this continued, the invaders would get to know the courage and force of the Vietnamese people. The Vietnamese people did not like war, but how many times had they not fought for their independence? They had drowned the Chinese soldiers of the Mongols at Bach Dang and buried alive the troops of the Qing *(Thanh)* at Dong Da: "We do not want anything excessive. We simply wish our homeland to be independent, and we are determined to sacrifice our blood and our bones to protect this independence. We are prepared." Another article, on December 5, declared: "To resist is to live, not to resist is to die." Tong Bo demanded that the government take "decisive measures."[95] This proclamation must have been meant both as a warning to the French and an assurance to the Viet Minh's many angry compatriots that it would not tolerate any further concessions. In the period after its publication, Vietnamese censorship concentrated on suppressing the most violently anti-French articles.[96]

One of the young and angry Vietnamese was the father of the historian Duong Trung Quoc. He felt it disgraceful to live in safety in Sontay outside the capital when the nation was in danger, so he asked his father for permission to join the volunteer forces in the capital. Quoc's grandfather refused, arguing that he and his wife were old and would have to rely on their only son to care for them, and that he should think of his young wife and unborn child. The angry young man did not give up, however, and finally his father said that if he could convince his mother, he could go. The son entreated his mother to let him join the fight and got her permission. So Quoc's father left his parents and young wife to enroll in the militia inside Hanoi.

On December 1, a SEHAN report claimed that Giap was planning to carry out an attack in Hanoi on the night of December 5–6. He had allegedly told someone in confidence that he preferred to see things realistically: it would take time for the French to return to reason. When they "have spilled ten or hundred times more blood than hitherto, then they will understand that they must seek détente with us." It would be better now to open fire oneself than to wait for the French to take action. Giap reportedly said that he had field guns, mortars, and 35,000 men. More of the civilian population would be evacuated, and assault sections would be formed.

Such "humint" reports, based on what could be picked up from informers in Hanoi, conformed well with French "sigint" intelligence based on intercepted radio messages between the south and north of Vietnam. On December 2, a message Nguyen Binh had sent Giap on November 28 was deciphered by the French. Binh's advice to Giap corresponded with what actually happened three weeks later: sabotage the waterworks and electric power station; destroy the bridge connecting the city to the airfield; block the streets. The French also intercepted Giap's answer, dated November 30: "In full agreement with your intentions. We are preparing ourselves. As soon as the news of the French attack on Hanoi is confirmed, all the fronts in Nam Bo should attack simultaneously."[97] A new telegram from Binh, dated December 8, again urged Giap to abandon all illusions. Binh asked if combat was continuing in Haiphong and Langson and asked for permission to start his own offensive.[98]

On December 9, the Sûreté chief reported that the Vietnamese government was feverishly preparing for the worst and was ready to use force. If the French command left the "Annamite leaders" at the current dead end, they were likely to open hostilities.[99] This was what d'Argenlieu hoped for, but other reports from Hanoi were less pleasing to the high commissioner, whose greatest fear must have been to see things drag out so long that Ho Chi Minh would manage to establish contact with a new French government. When Sainteny arrived in Hanoi, he did not detect any immediate Vietnamese plans to attack. In the following days, there were reports of possible attacks, first on December 5, then on December 12, but by mid-December, Sainteny concluded that the Annamite government did not intend to start a general conflict.[100]

Morlière's and Sainteny's impression that the Vietnamese leaders were confused and had no intention of attacking does not conform with the reports of the French intelligence services. We have no way of knowing how seriously they took the intelligence, or which service they most relied on. The 2e Bureau in Saigon characterized the attitudes of the main Vietnamese leaders on December 6: "Mr. Giap has taken all precautions to avoid being surprised in case of a rupture. Personally, he feels ready to face an armed conflict. On the internal level, no one is capable of opposing his decisions. His authority moreover goes beyond the military framework. Member of the top level of the Viet Minh Front, he enjoys an undeniable political prestige; through the numerous clients he has managed to cultivate, he has numerous contacts, in particular in the Ministry of the Interior and the Vietnamese Sûreté. Ambitious, young, energetic, violent, he is at the moment a candidate for dictator."

Vis-à-vis Giap, Ho Chi Minh "played an enigmatic role," the 2e Bureau said. It might be that he really supported the policy of violence and was just letting Giap take responsibility for carrying it out, so that he would be able to disavow it in case of defeat. Yet he seemed eager for détente. Everything was being kept ready to resume the armed struggle, but "certain documents" indicated that it would not be set in motion "unless a serious incident took place in Hanoi." In conclusion: "All the military preparations have been put in place in order to provoke a general state of hostility throughout Indochina, based on however small an incident. Spurred on by its chief, Vo Nguyen Giap, the Vietnamese Army, which constitutes the extremist and anti-French section of the regime,[101] is ready to take the plunge. But it remains to be discovered to what extent President Ho Chi Minh will let the Army take over from the civilian authorities and launch a struggle that may have serious consequences for the future of his government."[102]

The SEHAN continued to provide intelligence on the Vietnamese military preparations, indicating among other things that Giap intended to instill fear into French civilians.[103] It also on December 7 reported that a meeting of the Viet Minh Struggle Front had been held three days earlier. A certain "Le Van Nhanh"—an unknown alias—had made a distinction between the policy of the government and of the front. The government wanted peace to avoid the spilling of blood and consolidate its position. The Viet Minh Struggle Front was, by contrast, firmly resolved to fight and would go beyond the government's orders if the military situation demanded it. Three days later, the SEHAN conveyed that Ho and Giap no longer left each other's side and were living in a state of constant alert. It held that Ho Chi Minh preferred that the tension be reduced peacefully; more time was needed to digest the political results obtained, but in case of rupture, he would certainly rally to the cause of those fighting the French troops. The SEHAN also learned that Giap had given the order to complete all military preparations by December 12, that the buildings of the Ministry of National Defense would have to be emptied by that time, and that a new section of death squads, including many common criminals, had been formed on Giap's orders.

Other special services intercepted the exchange of telegrams between Hanoi and the Vietnamese authorities in the south. Le Duan, who would lead the Vietnamese Communist Party as secretary-general from 1960 to his death in 1986, and was political commissar in Nam Bo in 1946, reportedly radioed Hanoi on December 8 that "only a protracted general war can resolve the question of Vietnam's sovereignty." Shortly afterward, according to these intercepts, Hanoi instructed Nguyen Binh to launch a general attack on all French positions as of December 12. According to a later report, this order had been given by Pham Van Dong, "special delegate of President Ho Chi Minh for the south," but if this was the case, then the order could not have come from Hanoi. Dong had already gone south and was now operating in Quang Ngai. Intelligence files are always full of dubious claims, amid more reliable information. A series of orders, signed Binh and dated from December 14 to 17, ordered all fighting units in Nam Bo to "resume their activities and attack the enemy in order to oblige him to respect our interests." At first, a general attack against Saigon-Cholon was said to have been decided upon. Then apparently it was canceled.[104] It is difficult to say whether the intelligence reports reflected a really existing confusion on the Vietnamese side or if it was the intelligence services themselves that were confused.

Moret estimated, on December 8, that 70 percent of Hanoi's population had already been evacuated and that the government was preparing itself feverishly for the worst: "The ostentation that it brings to this makes it likely that it is 'playing poker' against us. But well-informed people generally think that if it is driven to use force, it will accept this eventuality. No retreat seems possible any longer, and if the French command leaves the Annamite leaders in the dead end where they have placed themselves, without making substantial concessions, then they will go to war." Moret was, with good reason, anxious about the French civilians in Hanoi:

> The problem of protecting the civilian population is not simple. The military author-ities will see to this to the extent possible, of course, but on the other hand, many [French civilian] men have been armed by us. It must be recognized that the inter-weaving of French and Annamite houses that characterizes Hanoi city makes it prob-lematic for an army that cannot disperse its effort and that will be finding important obstacles on its axes of advance, to ensure the protection [of the civilians]. The first moments in an armed phase of the current crisis may cause losses among the French population, and no one is oblivious to the fact that the plan of the Annamite com-mand includes the capture of as many hostages as possible.

On December 10, Moret summoned the heads of the eight sectors where the French civilians lived and expressed a desire that they concentrate the population. Moret drew up an evacuation plan for 400 civilians, but hesitated to carry it out, since it would likely entail looting, housing problems, and perhaps violent incidents, and because it could not go undetected and would therefore be exploited in Vietnamese propaganda. In the evening, he discussed the plan with Sainteny, but the military command considered it premature: "If the situation gets worse, I'll take up the ques-tion again," Moret concluded.[105] This seems strange in light of the fact that an intelligence report had warned of a likely Vietnamese general attack on Decem-ber 12. That day, guerrilla activities intensified somewhat in Cochinchina, but in Tonkin, it passed without any significant disturbance. The French assumed that the attack had been called off, possibly because the Vietnamese leaders were waiting for the French National Assembly to designate Bidault's successor. Sainteny dis-cussed the Vietnamese government's apparent change of mind and how this might relate to political developments in France. Articles in the French press indicating a possible reversal of French policy might have influenced the Vietnamese. Ho Chi Minh was at any rate adopting a moderate approach, said Sainteny, and little seemed to indicate that the government was ready to initiate fighting. A later report estab-lished by Sainteny's staff about all the incidents occurring between the French and the Vietnamese in the streets since the barricades had been put up noted that the Vietnamese liaison officers had done everything possible to prevent such incidents from spreading.[106]

According to a SEHAN informer, a plenary meeting of the Vietnamese govern-ment, held on December 14 around 6 p.m., adopted a twin strategy of waiting for the new French government to take a position and pushing preparations for military resistance in all areas. Christmas Day was seen as a possible date for an attack. Two opinions stood against each other in the government, the informer said. Nam and Giam remained moderate and wanted to reach an arrangement with France. Giap, the military, and the other ministers were, however, in favor of a *politique de force*. General Quang Trung, who was incorrectly said by the SEHAN informers to be the president's chief of staff, reportedly agreed with Giap. Another French intelligence service had been speculating only two weeks earlier that the real commander of the Vietnamese garrison in Hanoi was Hoang Quoc Viet, operating under the name Quang Trung, but neither Hoang Quoc Viet nor the real Quang Trung were actually in Hanoi at this stage. Quang Trung had gone south.[107]

According to the SEHAN, Ho Chi Minh himself was completely unable to make up his mind. Yet another intelligence unit, the 2[e] Bureau of the Navy, made the following assessment of the president's attitude: "He seems ready to discuss our demands in order to prevent a rupture, provided that their form is modified, since the current terms are deemed too humiliating to be accepted publicly. This point of view has, by the way, only been expressed in conversations, which the president has been keen to keep strictly private. His attitude seems to be to want to drag things out, in the firm hope that the change of government in France will bring about a reversal of our policy in Indochina."[108]

In an unofficial report to Saigon on the situation in Hanoi as of December 15, an anonymous author, whose advice was probably taken seriously by Pignon, since he filed it together with other important documents, said there was little chance that the Vietnamese command would order its troops to open fire in Hanoi. Several serious incidents had given it opportunities to do so. "According to the view of everybody, it is [therefore] in our interest to take the initiative in the operations."[109]

On December 15, the local resistance committee at Dong Da (close to Hanoi) met with Tran Huy Lieu. A French informer who was present reported that Tran Huy Lieu had just come from a meeting with Ho Chi Minh. Someone asked Lieu if China might intervene. He answered that the rumors of an impending Chinese intervention might not be without foundation, yet he thought this improbable. China would not want to move troops into Vietnam as long as there were French troops there. Still, the prospect of Chinese intervention might in itself have a positive effect. The fear that both the French and the Chinese had of getting into war with each other might be exploited the same way it had been utilized in March, in order to prevent an open conflict. Lieu believed that the political situation in the world might become more favorable later for the cause of Vietnam's quest for independence. If a conflict were to break out at present, then Indochina would become a vast battlefield and "we would regret that we had been unable to control our temper."[110]

By December 15, it may be assessed that Ho and at least some of his advisors still believed that it *might* be possible to avoid a full-scale war. They knew that Giap had a plan to attack the French in Hanoi, and to hold parts of the city as long as possible, but they only wanted to let him do so if it could be ascertained that the French were about to take the initiative themselves.

If there is any accuracy in what the SEHAN informer reported, Tran Huy Lieu was right also to consider the international aspects of the problem. One of the reasons why the French government was reluctant to let d'Argenlieu and Valluy go all the way down the line they had chosen and break completely with the Viet Minh, was its concern about international repercussions. Yet this concern had been considerably reduced. Franklin D. Roosevelt was long gone. Chiang Kai-shek had withdrawn all of his troops, and in his capacity as U.S. President Harry Truman's envoy to China, General George C. Marshall had not been able to prevent the Guomindang from fighting it out with Mao's Red Army. The French also knew that America was reluctant to put pressure on France in Asia, since this might turn France against the United States in Europe and help fuel the French Communist Party's propaganda machine. Paradoxically, the French Communist Party and the United States both wanted France to make concessions to Vietnamese nationalism, but neither was prepared to push for this in public, giving priority to the French political scene and the French role in an increasingly divided Europe.

A SILENCED AMERICAN

The day Sainteny met Ho in Hanoi, Valluy received a modestly distinguished guest in the high commissioner's palace in Saigon. In order to impress him and give him a false sense of being welcome, Valluy took the unusual step of taking him out to inspect the high commissioner's guard of honor, something heads of state do when welcoming other heads of state. In this case, an interim high commissioner did it for a foreign ministry section chief—but that ministry was the U.S. Department of State. Also present at the inspection were the other members of the triumvirate that ran French Indochina in November–December 1946: the political schemer Pignon and the financial controller Gonon. If d'Argenlieu had been there, the guest would no doubt have been received on a warship and treated to a salute from Navy big guns.

Abbot Low Moffat headed the Southeast Asia Division in the Department of State. Like his boss, John Carter Vincent, director of the Office of Far Eastern Affairs, Moffat belonged to a circle of enlightened U.S. diplomats who knew something about Asia, and thus did their country the service of preventing it from engaging too heavily in trying to save Chiang Kai-shek's moribund regime. Hence they became victims of Senator Joseph McCarthy's vitriolic attacks in the 1950s against the un-American sin of thinking before acting. Moffat was strongly preoccupied by the dangerous rise of communism in Asia, but also convinced that the only way of countering it was to accommodate the national aspirations of the Asian peoples. Moffat rated Indochina as a strategically important territory and did not trust the ability of France, whose major interests were in Europe and North Africa, to protect it. He wrote a number of internal memorandums criticizing French intransigence, which, he said, would push the Indochinese into the arms of the communists. Moffat had convinced himself that France should be made an offer it could not refuse: Anglo-American mediation in Indochina. His boss, John Carter Vincent, had taken up the idea in September, only to see it rejected by the State Department's European Office and top leadership, so in October, Vincent had made it clear that the United States would intervene diplomatically in Indochina only if asked to do so by the parties directly involved.[111] The French would never ask the United States to get involved, however, and before going to Saigon, Moffat again argued, both in the Department of State and vis-à-vis the British Foreign Office, that it was urgent to offer mediation.

D'Argenlieu and Valluy were probably not aware of Moffat's personal views, but they were not exactly happy to receive a visitor from a country that, without even asking de Gaulle's opinion, had imposed the onerous Chinese occupation on northern Indochina. The high commissioner bowed, however, to the French Foreign Ministry's insistence that one could not refuse to receive a representative of the United States, and that Moffat moreover was not on a mission with a specific aim.[112] The French ambassador in Washington also emphasized that Moffat had contributed personally to the agreement reached with Thailand on November 17 to return the Cambodian and Laotian provinces taken from French Indochina in 1941.[113]

Moffat expressed a strong desire to visit Tonkin, where Sainteny was dismayed by the idea of having to receive one of "these American tourists." The commissioner had unpleasant memories of Archimedes L. Patti, a U.S. intelligence officer of Greek-Sicilian heritage who in cooperation with local Chinese authorities had delayed Sainteny's departure from Kunming to Hanoi for several days after the Japanese surrender on August 15, 1945, and subsequently, on September 2, had dressed up in his best uniform to hear Ho denounce French colonialism, quoting the U.S. Declaration of Independence of 1776. Moffat was allowed to come to Hanoi, but Sainteny demanded that he should under no circumstances see Haiphong.[114] When he arrived in Saigon, Moffat had actually not yet heard about the French conquest of Haiphong—a good illustration of how little the international press had written about it. Not a single journalist had visited the city after its destruction, and the Western press, communist newspapers included, had mostly just reprinted the official news bulletins from the AFP and AP, which generally referred to the massacre perpetrated there by the French as an incident provoked by the Vietnamese.

Moffat stayed ten days in Indochina, from December 2 to 12, and was in Hanoi for three days, from December 6 to 8. Letters he wrote to his wife give a fascinating glimpse into the climate among key figures in the weeks before the outbreak of war.[115] Moffat was struck by the quality of the top French leaders in Saigon, Pignon in particular, but he found the quality of the lower-rank French administrators deplorable. Dr. Thinh's mediocre successor as Cochinchinese president, Le Van Hoach, also did not make an indelible impression. Desperately troubled by the visit of such a distinguished visitor, Hoach called U.S. Consul Reed "Monsieur l'Ambassadeur" and seemed to think that Moffat was the secretary of state.

The situation in Hanoi shook Moffat deeply. This was the first time in his life he had been to a place so thoroughly marked by a psychosis of war. He was distressed to discover that in three days, he managed to raise a hesitant responding grin from just one single child. Both parties told him that his presence was contributing to a momentary détente, since it would mean a loss of face if hostilities broke out in the presence of a high-ranking visitor. The cocktails and receptions given in his honor allowed Morlière and Nam, Lami and Giap, Sainteny and Giam to converse amicably around glasses of wine. Sainteny and Morlière felt it strange to offer toasts to men who might, at any time, become their mortal enemies. Moffat saw nothing wrong in trying to reconcile enemies and launched himself into an improvised speech in French, toasting "Monsieur Talleyrand Sainteny." The comparison was surely meant as a reference to the skills Talleyrand had displayed during the peace conference in Vienna in 1814–15, and not to his earlier contributions to Napoleon's subjugation of Europe.

Moffat deliberately sought out the key Vietnamese leaders. He did not warm to Giap; he had always been disconcerted by men with deadpan faces, he confided to his wife. Giap seemed to him to be the "ideal" intelligent communist leader, a prototype, even a caricature. Giap admitted to him that the Vietnamese would not perhaps win a confrontation with France, but in any event, the French would not win either, since the Vietnamese armed forces would always be able to continue the fight. Even with their tanks and planes and guns, the French would therefore be beaten eventually. Moffat and U.S. Vice-Consul O'Sullivan asked him if he did not fear the heavy loss of human life. Giap replied that it was necessary to make sacrifices, sacrifices, sacrifices. He stated emphatically, however, that Vietnam would not make the first move. Many years later, on June 23, 1997, another American, former U.S. Secretary of Defense Robert McNamara, came to meet Giap in the Vietnamese Government Guest House, the former Résidence supérieure du Tonkin, Ho's presidential palace in 1945–46. On McNamara's mind were thoughts similar to those that had preoccupied Moffat and O'Sullivan in 1946. Could the war have been avoided? Had it been worth all the sacrifice? McNamara spent a full hour in the same room as Giap, but he never got to talk to him. Giap gave a lecture instead about the will of the Vietnamese people to resist: We fought because we had to fight. If necessary we would have been willing to fight for a hundred years. Because of our determination, we achieved our national independence almost a hundred years earlier than we might otherwise have done. There had been, he admitted, some friends who said the Vietnamese could not win; he did not want to name them. However, he himself had always been convinced that the Vietnamese people could win. The United States, just like France before it, had made a strategic error when it intervened in Vietnam, Giap said in 1997. The winners of the war were the Vietnamese people and also all the progressive, peace-loving people in the world, including the progressive, peace-loving people in the United States who had opposed the war. This was not what McNamara had wanted to hear. He was searching for specific mistakes, mistakes the avoidance of which could have shortened or limited the suffering that the war had entailed. But the man with the deadpan face was consistent to the end. Moffat and McNamara got the same basic answer.[116]

Moffat liked Giam much better, but the latter made a blunder many leftist politicians make when meeting an American for the first time. He thought Moffat, as a representative of the world's leading capitalist power, would be looking for investment opportunities and military bases. So he held out the enticement of juicy opportunities that American enterprises would find in Vietnam if it became independent, and hinted that the United States might be able to take over the French strategic base at Cam Ranh Bay. This was not what Moffat wanted to hear. The negative consequences that a colonial war might have for the economic, social, and political well-being of France were the State Department's main concern. Moffat and Vincent were also concerned about the stability of Asia, important for the reconstruction of Japan. Thus Moffat was interested to see the French and Vietnamese get on with each other, not to arrange for U.S. companies or the U.S. Navy to take over French assets. To impress Moffat, Giam should rather have spoken about the Vietnamese determination to respect French property and take care of French business interests. It is possible that Giam realized his mistake and dropped a word to President Ho, for he chose a different approach when Moffat came to see him.

On his own initiative, Moffat paid a visit to Ho Chi Minh. Sainteny was furious when he heard about this, because it was not a part of the agreed program. Sainteny had been given the mission to push Ho into a corner where he would have to choose between a confrontation and an agreement on French terms. Moffat's visit could frustrate this mission, he thought, by puffing up Ho's pride and making him believe in miracles. Ho, who had fallen ill after the Haiphong massacre, received the U.S. representative in bed. He spoke with a faltering voice about the friendship and admiration he felt for the United States and for the Americans he had known in the jungle during their common war against Japan. They had treated the Annamese as equals. He spoke of his desire to build up Vietnam in cooperation with the French so that his people might be better off, and said they wanted the freedom to seek friends among other countries along with France so as to secure the capital needed to develop the country. France was now too poor to provide sufficient capital on its own. He knew, he said, that the United States did not like communism, but that was not his aim. If he could secure Vietnam's independence, this would be enough for his lifetime: "Perhaps fifty years from now [1996] the United States will be communist . . . and then they will not object if Vietnam is also." Ho Chi Minh's English was a little hesitant, but Moffat got his message, "a smiling and friendly 'Don't worry.'" Ho ended by stressing his desire for peace, notwithstanding that he did not feel that Vietnam could bow to the most recent French demands.

Our main source for Moffat's visit is the letters he sent to his wife, which were published in 1972, in connection with the U.S. Senate's inquiry into the roots of the Vietnamese tragedy.[117] If these letters had been the only source available on the meeting between Moffat and Ho, then we would have to conclude that Moffat himself said nothing, except expressing a hope for a peaceful settlement. D'Argenlieu's intelligence services, however, soon learned from a Vietnamese source that Moffat had expressed a "desire" that Vietnam appeal to the United Nations. This led the French foreign minister to ask the State Department if this was U.S. policy. While still in Southeast Asia, Moffat was asked from home about the French allegations. He denied having expressed any such desire.[118] If so, this was probably just as well, because when he returned from Hanoi to Saigon on December 9, a telegram from his boss John Carter Vincent was waiting for him, which had no doubt been seen, perhaps even instigated, by the State Department's European Office. It instructed Moffat to avoid giving any impression that the United States intended to interfere with French Indochina policy, saying: "Any publicity would be unfortunate."

Yet Vincent was keen to see an agreement negotiated between France and Vietnam. The State Department had just instructed the U.S. ambassador to Paris, he said, to warn the French government against an intransigence that could not but serve the interest of the extremists, who would take advantage of it to burn their bridges with the West. Vincent would like to know the strength of the noncommunist nationalists and reminded Moffat of "the well-known past of Ho Chi Minh as an agent of international communism."

Moffat answered that the Vietnamese government was clearly in the hands of a small group of communists, who most likely were in indirect contact with Moscow and directly with Yenan (Mao's wartime capital). But he thought the Hanoi leaders were above all nationalists, using the techniques and discipline of the communists in their fight for national independence, and that they were willing to postpone the realization of a communist society. He had reached this conclusion after his conversations with Pignon and Ho Chi Minh. Moffat further emphasized the importance of the French presence in Indochina to the defense of Western interests in Asia. He perceived threats, not only from Moscow, but even more from "future Chinese imperialism." The indispensable French presence could only be maintained at the price of an agreement with the Vietnamese government. He did not think there would be any all-out war, since both parties wished to avoid it, but he nonetheless suggested in conclusion that the United States should offer its "neutral good offices."[119] This proposal did not get any support in Washington, however, where the top-level diplomats and other makers of foreign policy were determined to avoid disturbing the U.S. relationship with France.

The Vietnamese had actually grasped the principal reason for American and British nonintervention early on. Instructions from the Administrative Committee in Nam Bo, dated October 17, 1946, asked rhetorically why the United States and Great Britain had turned their backs on the Vietnamese revolution. The answer was brief: "They have agreed to include France among the great powers to get it to side with them." The Nam Bo section of the Indochinese Communist Party also later asked the same question, and answered: "Internationally, France is one of the great powers in the U.N.—because of its privileged position in Europe, the powers all compete for its favor."[120]

DITHERING

To disentangle the complex web of action and inaction that triggered the outbreak of war on December 19, 1946, one needs to view the chronology of events in Hanoi, Saigon, and Paris in combination, as Philippe Devillers does in *Paris Saigon Hanoi: Les archives de la guerre, 1944–1947*, a documentary volume edited by him and published in 1988. The tragedy played out simultaneously in three places. French decision-makers performed on all three stages, with varying degrees of communication and coordination among themselves. Although the actual events took place in Hanoi, the key decisions were taken by the actors in Saigon, but in constant fear of being overruled, held accountable, or thrown out by the squabbling fools in Paris. This was why the Saigon actor-manager d'Argenlieu spent the whole crisis backstage in the metropolis, struggling to save himself and his Indochinese Federation from any direct contact between Paris and Hanoi. Saigon's vacillation between open belligerence, provocations, waiting games, subtle pressures, and the laying of traps in the four weeks from the Haiphong massacre to the fateful night of December 19, 1946 reflected, not only their expectations concerning the behavior of the Vietnamese government in Hanoi, but even more their need to thwart any harmful intrusion from their own government in Paris.

Pignon wrote on December 17: "It is easy to see that the situation was notably influenced, I would even say commanded, by the metropolitan political situation shaped by November 10. . . . There is no doubt that the results of the elections to the metropolitan National Assembly created premature hopes and illusions in the Hanoi leadership, which would prove perilous."[121] Pignon's point was a valid one, that the victory of the French Left created false hopes among Vietnamese leftists. This danger was reflected in Pignon's own anxiety. The French elections inspired the Vietnamese leaders to think that they might hold on to their capital and reopen negotiations with France in January 1947, as stipulated in the modus vivendi agreement. For the French leaders in Saigon, this was what they feared most, because it would once more boost the local and international legitimacy of the Viet Minh and its republic.

The four weeks from November 23 to December 19 correspond to four distinct phases in the evolution of Saigon's tactics. In the first week up to November 30, Saigon thought, and probably hoped, that a general conflict would evolve as a direct result of what had happened at Haiphong and Langson and the November 28 ultimatum. During this period, Sainteny was retained in Saigon. In the second week, from December 1 to 7, Valluy and Pignon prepared to move on two fronts: troops from Haiphong were to push gradually forward toward Hanoi in order to open and secure the main road, while Sainteny held talks with the Vietnamese leaders. The troop movements would provoke reactions, which could be used as a pretext for a police action against the extremists in the government and the Tong Bo. In the third week, from December 8 to 14, Saigon demurred and postponed both the reopening of the road and the police action. In the fourth week, from December 15 to 19, Saigon urged Sainteny and Morlière to adopt a tougher line. This led to serious incidents in Hanoi on December 17 and 18, which were used by the French to justify new demands, put forward on December 18 and on the morning of December 19.

During the first week, the newly elected French National Assembly had not yet held its first meeting, and no one knew who would lead the next French government. The Cominindo met on November 23 and 29, and Bidault's coalition cabinet met for the last time on November 28. Bidault formally resigned that day, but he continued as a leader of a caretaker government. The Cominindo meetings did not publicly revoke the modus vivendi agreement, as d'Argenlieu had wanted, but gave a green light for using force against the guerrillas based in the south and seemed to accept what Valluy had done in Haiphong. Representatives of the most important ministries drafted a set of secret instructions for d'Argenlieu, but could not agree on them at the November 29 meeting, so the instructions were not ready until December 10, in the third week. It was still unclear who the next French premier would be, but on December 12, the socialist veteran Léon Blum, who had not taken part in the preparation of the instructions, took it upon himself to form a new cabinet and was elected premier by the National Assembly. After abortive talks with the leaders of the PCF and the MRP, Blum realized that he would be unable to put a coalition together and formed an all-socialist cabinet instead on December 16, retaining Marius Moutet as minister for Overseas France. On December 17, reflecting complex negotiations among all the political parties and a general appreciation of the need to overcome the cabinet crisis so that the newly adopted constitution of the French Fourth Republic could enter into force, Blum's cabinet won a vote of confidence of the National Assembly, with only two representatives dissenting. On the following day, Bidault handed over the keys to his offices to Blum, who, like his predecessor, combined the premiership at the Hôtel Matignon with responsibility for foreign affairs at the Quai d'Orsay. On the evening of December 18, a couple of hours before the following day's sunrise in Vietnam, Blum's cabinet met for the first time.

The first phase in Saigon's dithering thus corresponds to a period during which Bidault's cabinet was assuring the high commissioner of its full support; the second and third phases were during Bidault's caretaker government, when the outcome of the political crisis was unknown. And the fourth week of subtle pressures and the laying of traps coincided with Blum taking office.

Let us summarize the communication between Paris and Saigon during the four weeks of wavering. The first reaction from Paris to Valluy's occupation of Haiphong was a telegram of approval from d'Argenlieu, who declared that Valluy's instructions to Morlière were in accord with French government policy as defined at the meeting of the Cominindo on November 23.[122] D'Argenlieu also sent Valluy a summary of the proceedings, which had been read by Moutet as well as by Army Minister Michelet and approved by Bidault. It authorized Valluy to disregard the cease-fire in Cochinchina and "reduce agitation by force."[123] D'Argenlieu assured Valluy that he would have a free hand militarily and urged him to further increase his vigilance.[124] Valluy conveyed the good news to the French commissioners in Saigon, Nha Trang, and Hanoi on November 27. He told them that further instructions would arrive from Paris after the next Cominindo meeting on November 29. In the meantime, they should let their action be inspired by Bidault and Moutet's firm declarations of support. Valluy also urged them to let the firm position of the French government be known through "calculated indiscretion."[125] The reassuring messages from Paris must have inspired the "ultimatum without deadline" that Valluy ordered Morlière to give Giap on November 28. However, the ultimatum did not lead to any violent Vietnamese response, and the Cominindo meeting on November 29 did not please Valluy and d'Argenlieu as much as the previous one. It did not adopt the promised government instructions, and Admiral Barjot was asking inquisitive questions. Thus the situation remained unclear on November 30, when Valluy took his decision to send Sainteny to Hanoi.

Sainteny's clumsy attempts to provoke a split between Vietnamese moderates and extremists characterized the second week. The other element in Saigon's approach was the planned push west along the Haiphong–Hanoi road, which had been cut at several places. On December 5, Morlière declared himself ready to start clearing the road as soon as reinforcements arrived in Haiphong.[126] Sainteny, however, warned that this might lead to a general conflagration and proposed that the operation be postponed until the precise position of Paris was known.[127] When he received this warning, Valluy had just learned from d'Argenlieu that the second meeting of the Cominindo had confirmed Valluy's position, but that no public declaration could be expected from Bidault's caretaker government.[128] Valluy thought this was sufficiently reassuring to ignore the warning from Sainteny and instructed him to demand of the Vietnamese government both the reopening of the Haiphong–Hanoi road and the removal of all blockhouses, barricades, and mines in Hanoi. To make himself clear, Valluy added that once Sainteny received the order to "open the essential road by force, you cannot but conform to it."[129] This admonition was addressed to the political commissioner, not the military commander. By December 5–6, Valluy was thus preparing for a clean break. He sent two long telegrams to Paris warning that war was imminent, asking for a firm government declaration, and emphasizing the positive effect that a firm position in the north would have on the political climate in Cochinchina. In the first cable, he declared that Morlière's failure to implement legitimate and even indispensable local countermeasures could not be tolerated much longer. It was indispensable that the Haiphong–Hanoi road be opened in a matter of days, and if it had to be done by force, the chance of localizing the conflict would be minimal: "It is my duty to warn the government of the almost inevitable rupture that the hatred and insincerity of the Hanoi government are leading us to." The only way of perhaps precluding the rupture would be to deprive the extremist elements of their last hope by issuing a government declaration affirming the determination of France to intensify its military effort and reestablish peace and order.[130] In the second cable, the interim high commissioner commented on the recent formation of a new Cochinchinese cabinet, to succeed that of the deceased Dr. Thinh. Its success would depend on the French approach to Vietnam. If the northern crisis could be handled without France retreating, the fear in the south of "Vietnamese elements" could be reduced. The new, more vigilant Cochinchina policy would then bear fruit, and the population would recover the spirit of self-defense needed to resist the rebels and quell them, with French support.[131] These two telegrams were more candid than d'Argenlieu would have wanted. Valluy cannot have trusted the admiral's ability to cover his actions in Paris. Valluy's alarmist messages most likely led to heated discussions in Paris on Saturday, the 7th.

On Sunday morning December 8, Valluy suddenly changed tack and instructed Sainteny to defer action.[132] This was the same day Admiral Barjot completed his second memorandum, criticizing Valluy for diverting the French military effort from south to north. In a set of new instructions issued that Sunday, Valluy asked Sainteny and Morlière to avoid a generalization of the conflict until reinforcements had arrived from France, which they would do by January 15. In response to this "unexpected moderation," Morlière wrote his report of December 12, warning against the illusion that the peace could be preserved after the recent events. He must have been keen to avoid becoming the scapegoat if war broke out.[133] The need for reinforcements cannot have been the real reason for Valluy's sudden U-turn. He had just been arguing that it was urgent to start military operations, because the planned repatriation of experienced French troops in January would make the military situation worse, not better. What else could explain his sudden change of heart? The presence of Abbot Low Moffat perhaps. As we have seen, Moffat told his wife that his presence was regarded as a deterrent by both sides. He thought, however, that the reasons for the sudden lull in the crisis were "to be sought elsewhere."[134] He was undoubtedly right, for Moffat arrived in Saigon on December 3 and was in Hanoi on December 6. Valluy's moderation only transpired on December 8. The only imaginable cause for Valluy's change of tack would seem to be a negative reaction from Paris to his December 6 cables. Someone high up must have got cold feet. It has not so far been possible to find any trace in the archives of immediate reactions from Paris to Valluy's alarmist messages,[135] but they could have been conveyed by telephone. On Wednesday, the 11th, Laurentie drafted the unsent telegram referred to above for Moutet, and on the 12th, Bidault himself disapproved of Valluy's course of action in the personally signed cable that was also cited above.[136]

Whether the outgoing premier was sincere or writing for the record is uncertain. Suffice it to say that Bidault's message must have shocked d'Argenlieu and Valluy, just when they learned that the Jewish socialist Blum, a man loathed by French conservatives for his pacifism, would form the next cabinet, with almost unanimous support from the French National Assembly. Valluy would later give a vivid, but rudimentary, account of Saigon's disarray and the many telegrams he exchanged with d'Argenlieu and the Cominindo. D'Argenlieu reproached him, he reveals, for having sent information directly to Bidault.[137] Few commanders are happy to take responsibility for actions that are not derived from explicit orders from above. For Valluy, it was not at this stage enough to trust d'Argenlieu. He sent the chief of the high commissioner's special military staff, Colonel Louis Le Puloch, by plane to Paris in order to sound out the government and find out if there was any policy. This was right after Le Puloch had seen Sainteny and Morlière in Hanoi. The colonel presented his views to a meeting of the "Consultative Cominindo," assembling officials from the most important ministries on Saturday, December 14. Le Puloch recommended immediate military action, emphasizing the need to open the Haiphong–Hanoi road, and declared that the Vietnamese army would have to be regarded as an adversary. He estimated French military forces to be strong enough to control both Haiphong and Hanoi, reestablish communications between the two cities, and drive the Vietnamese government from its capital. Ho Chi Minh's government would then be unable to survive, because it would lose the financial basis necessary to maintain a military fighting force. According to Le Puloch, it was necessary to seize the occasion to obtain the fulfillment of the military clauses laid down by General Morlière in the demands of November 28.[138]

This raised strong objections from the young secretary-general of the Cominindo, Pierre Messmer, who said it would create an impossible political situation if France were to maintain a badly disguised indirect rule in the south while limiting its presence in the north to a few big cities. The only solution to the Cochinchinese problem was one in which the government in Hanoi took part. At the tactical level, Messmer advised seeking a provisional arrangement with Ho Chi Minh and trying to bring about a split between his and Giap's factions. The discouraging experiences with the autonomous government in Cochinchina showed it would be unwise just to make Ho disappear. Le Puloch replied that it would be difficult to obtain the desired split in the Vietnamese leadership, since Giap controlled both the Army and the police and had "practically removed Ho Chi Minh from power." Messmer warned against negative reactions from French and international public opinion and stressed that if new incidents were to occur, the fault should not be on the French side. Le Puloch concluded the discussion by insisting that the actual military situation in Tonkin was favorable and that an instant effort, if the government so decided, could lead to a favorable settlement before the spring. It would be desirable to start military operations before the planned troop relief in January.[139]

When Le Puloch returned to Saigon, he must have realized that Paris would not tolerate another Haiphong, but with Messmer's words ringing in his ears—"if new incidents were to occur, the fault should not be on the French side"—he might assume that if only the adversary fired the first shots, then even a Blum government would have to rally behind the flag. If the new French cabinet were given time to get to work, however, the French cause in Indochina might be irreparably damaged. Ho Chi Minh would then have an opportunity to tell everyone what France had done in Haiphong. There was little time left to set out traps and get Giap to take the bait.

ENTER BLUM

Léon Blum was a man of great moral integrity. His Jewish background, antimilitarism, and vast political experience had made him both one of the most insulted and respected politicians of the French Third Republic. In his political career, he was, like most politicians, often obliged to renounce his ideals and adjust to the necessities of the hour. During World War I, his antimilitarist credentials made him suitable for mobilizing the French working class to die in the trenches. His well-known concern for socialist unity made him the most convincing spokesman for the minority that remained in the Section française de l'Internationale ouvrière (SFIO) after the left-wing majority—including the young Ho Chi Minh—broke away at its Tours Congress in 1920 to form the Section française de l'Internationale communiste (SFIC), joining the Leninist Third International, or Comintern, and becoming the French Communist Party. In the 1930s, Blum's skeptical attitude to socialist participation in cabinets of the capitalist state contributed to making him the unquestionable leader of the Popular Front government, and his friendship with the leaders of the Spanish Republic invested him with the moral authority to defend the French policy of nonintervention in the Spanish Civil War. The contrast between what Blum wanted to do and what circumstances forced him to let happen is unmistakable.

From the safe house outside Hanoi where he secretly took refuge at the time, Ho Chi Minh sent a stream of appeals to Paris after the Haiphong debacle. On November 27, Saigon forwarded a personal appeal from Ho to Bidault, begging for the cessation of hostilities in Haiphong and Langson.[140] On December 6, Ho appealed on the radio to the French National Assembly and the French government, asking them to order the French troops to return to the positions they had held before November 20.[141] His appeal was published by *Le Populaire* on December 9, just as the president of the French National Assembly was entrusting Léon Blum with forming a new government. Blum indirectly answered Ho's appeal in an article published in *Le Populaire* on December 10. The difference between Blum's public message and the secret governmental instructions Moutet signed that same day illustrates the duplicity characterizing the French Left's approach to decolonization. The PCF solved the problem with calculated silence, the SFIO with noisy hypocrisy. Yet Léon Blum was not himself a hypocrite. His tragedy was his sincerity, which made him useful to those needing to wash their hands of responsibility. In Blum's December 10 article, he went directly to the core of the problem, expressing his fear that France might go to war:

> The French government now has only two options. Either take back all or part of Indochina by force of arms; or see to it that the agreement concluded last March with Vietnam has force, consistency, and durability *[vertu, consistance et durée]*. Either make use of military constraint or reestablish friendship and confidence. That is the sole choice, and let me add that I do not think it is possible to have any hesitation about which choice to make. . . . No, there is but one means, one only, to preserve the prestige of our civilization, our political and spiritual influence in Indochina, and also those of our legitimate material interests: that is sincere agreements on the basis of independence, confidence, friendship. . . . The general policy must be decided by Parliament. Neither the military authorities nor the civilian *colons* in Indochina must decide, but the government in Paris. And when I say government, I do not mean any of these interministerial committees, who have not been more successful in the Indochinese than in the German case, but the cabinet and the responsible minister. The new government will face the problem from its very first hours. Among all the reasons for pushing forward its formation, we should add this one.[142]

Blum's article made a resounding impression in Paris, Saigon, and Hanoi, and his use of the word "independence" was highly controversial. Two days later, on December 12, Blum was formally entrusted by the National Assembly, by 575 votes out of 583, to form the next French government, which went on to win a vote of confidence in the Assembly on December 17, with 544 votes to 2. In the debate preceding the December 12 vote, Blum's friend the Radical politician Edouard Herriot made an oblique reference to the controversial article in *Le Populaire*, saying that because of "certain articles in the press that have worried us," his own small party, the Rassemblement des gauches, had only reluctantly agreed to vote for Blum. Moutet, another of Blum's close friends, interrupted Herriot: "There are some moments when silence is a requirement for the action itself.... I can tell you that the policy carried out at the moment is not a policy of abandonment, *and* is not of a nature, despite everything, that will engage France in the adventures that some may desire [outcry in the Assembly], but that the country, of this I'm sure, could not sustain either intellectually or materially."[143] Moutet's certainty as to the French incapacity to sustain a military adventure would soon be shattered.

The opposition parties kept the silence demanded by Moutet on December 12 and voted in favor of Blum, but that same day, the MRP issued a brochure on the Indochinese question demanding that the "French government, unanimously and in solidarity, with the support of public opinion as a whole, demonstrate its will to make the French presence in Indochina respected." On the same day, Ho Chi Minh issued a protest to the French government against the deployment of French reinforcements in Da Nang, in contravention of the April 3 accords. This could not but stimulate the fear that a new French use of force was under way, Ho claimed. Valluy forwarded Ho's protest to Paris, saying that this was "yet another example of the well-known intention of President Ho Chi Minh to correspond directly with the French government, and circumvent the French authorities in Indochina.... In fact, it's in our interest to stress the preeminence of federal power in every way possible."[144]

This contradicted what Blum had written in *Le Populaire*. Blum had said that the new government and its responsible minister would have to confront the Indochinese problem in its very first hours. Yet the cabinet could not start functioning before Blum had put it together. First, he needed time to consult the MRP and PCF and conclude on the impossibility of forging a coalition. On December 14, while Le Puloch was quarreling with Messmer, Blum had not yet formed his government. Yet he discussed Indochina with Moutet and d'Argenlieu, and took the fateful decision to overrule the advice of his Socialist Party and keep d'Argenlieu on as high commissioner.[145]

Why? There is every reason to think that Blum and Moutet both wanted to get rid of the admiral; indeed the director of the Asia–Oceania Department in the Ministry of Foreign Affairs had gone so far as to tell the U.S. ambassador on December 3 that d'Argenlieu's replacement might prove desirable.[146] Let us guess that the MRP made it a condition for supporting Blum's government that d'Argenlieu keep his post. On December 13, *L'Aube* reported that the MRP deputies had gathered and expressed their "desire to see a continuation of the work of Premier Georges Bidault with relation to the French Union and the overseas provinces." The French communists do not seem to have lifted a finger to oust the anticommunist admiral. On December 13, *L'Aube* had emphasized that before voting for Blum, all the speakers in the Assembly had underlined how serious the Indochinese question was, "with the exception of M. Duclos." The leader of the communist parliamentary group Jacques Duclos was one of the most talkative of all the National Assembly's members when it met on December 12, and also at its subsequent meeting on December 17, but in line with his party's policy, he never mentioned Indochina.[147]

After his audience with Blum on December 14, d'Argenlieu remarked dryly to the press: "I shall go back to Saigon,"[148] which he did four days later. Moutet gave a much longer statement that day: "When we are accused of practicing a policy of abandonment, this is not justified. Abandonment is not peace. Firmness is not necessarily war. Between the two there are political means." When asked if d'Argenlieu disagreed, Moutet replied, tongue in cheek, that he was under the impression that the admiral had never expressed any disagreement with the policy that they were carrying out together. He added that he would himself be prepared to go to Indochina if he were given full authority to issue an appeal for peace and concord and ask the Vietnamese to stop spilling their blood and respect French interests.[149]

On December 17, Blum had his list of ministers ready, and his all-socialist minority cabinet was able to win its vote of confidence in the National Assembly and assume power the following day. It was an interim government, meant to govern the country until the new French constitution entered into force on December 25 and a more broadly based government could be established. In the debate preceding the vote on December 17, two speakers asked Blum how he would handle the situation in Indochina. He answered that this would require a special debate at a later stage. Maurice Schumann of the MRP then insisted: "a transitory government cannot have the authority to break the continuity of a policy. . . . Continuity, this also means continuity of the French presence in all the territories of the Union." Schumann alerted the new government to "certain words or certain silences encouraging a certain defiance or certain acts overseas that risked spilling the blood of Frenchmen and of France's friends."[150] By "certain silences" he meant Duclos, while "certain words" referred to Blum's December 10 article in *Le Populaire*.[151] These admonitions from the MRP leader were meant to tie Blum's hands. Yet d'Argenlieu and Valluy must have lived in constant fear of being held accountable for the Haiphong massacre.

When Bidault turned over the keys to the Hôtel Matignon and Quai d'Orsay on the afternoon of December 18, he and Blum talked for an hour and a half.[152] They did not know that Ho Chi Minh had sent a new peace proposal to Sainteny three days earlier. Ho Chi Minh had read Blum's article in *Le Populaire*, and then learned that Blum would head the next French government. This was the straw he had been waiting for a chance to grasp at. He wrote a long letter to Blum on December 15 with precise peace proposals. The Vietnamese government would guarantee the resumption of normal economic life in the cities, abolish all protective measures, and reopen communications between Hanoi, Haiphong, and Langson. In return, the French should withdraw their troops to the positions they had held before November 20, pull out the reinforcements they had sent to Da Nang, and cease all military operations in Cochinchina and southern Annam. The two sides should jointly set up the mixed commissions envisaged in the modus vivendi agreement.[153] To sum up, he wanted to expunge the past few weeks from the record and return to the modus vivendi agreement. His message was handed over to Sainteny for transmittal to the French government on December 15. On the following day, Hoang Minh Giam told the gist of it to U.S. Vice-Consul O'Sullivan, who at once reported it to Washington, which in turn informed the U.S. ambassador in Paris, Jefferson Caffery.[154] Caffery thus knew what Ho had proposed by the morning of December 18, while Prime Minister Blum got the proposals only two days later. A two-day delay can make a huge difference.[155]

What had Sainteny done with Ho's letter? Saigon would claim to have received the message by *valise* (official airmail) on the morning of December 18, in which case, Valluy could just as well have brought it personally to Saigon, since he flew north to have a meeting with Sainteny in Haiphong on December 17. Sainteny, however, probably transmitted Ho's message by telegraph to Saigon already on December 15. There is a telegram on file that day from Sainteny to Pignon. The file does not include the text of the message itself, but contains a long commentary from Sainteny alerting Saigon to the efforts of the "Annamite government" to contact Blum personally. He was transmitting "this official telegram, addressed to President Blum," Sainteny declared, but the Vietnamese government might try to use other channels as well. Sainteny then asked Pignon to forward Ho's message to Messmer in Paris. On December 16, Pignon did forward Sainteny's *warning* to Messmer, but not Ho's message. He told Messmer that the message Sainteny was referring to in his warning was a telegram of congratulations to the SFIO in Paris from the Vietnamese Socialist Party, which had been cabled from Saigon on December 14. When he received Sainteny's warning on the afternoon of December 16, Messmer thus still did not know of Ho's proposals. He distributed Sainteny's warning to d'Argenlieu and Moutet, but not to Blum.[156]

Saigon transmitted Ho's message to Paris on the morning of December 18, but with such low priority that it was circulated in Paris only two days later. Moreover, before sending it, Saigon wrote a long commentary, refuting all of Ho's proposals. Saigon also added its own warning to Paris against the Vietnamese government's "maneuvers," consisting of attempts to communicate directly with the French government.[157] Saigon's deliberate attempt to undermine Blum's ability to form his own opinion should be judged against the background of his insistence in *Le Populaire* that the decisions on Indochina should be taken by the cabinet and responsible minister in Paris and not by the military authorities, civilian colonists, or the Comanindo.

The successful effort by Pignon, Valluy, and Sainteny to prevent direct contact between the top leaders of France and Vietnam is a textbook example of how a bureaucracy can obstruct the decision-making process of its political leaders.

On December 18, having waited three days for an answer, Ho Chi Minh wrote a new appeal, proposing that a French parliamentary delegation be sent to Vietnam.[158] Although unaware of Ho's attempts to approach him, Blum made his own attempt to contact Ho. After taking over Bidault's keys, he went directly to his first cabinet meeting, which decided to send Moutet on a mission to Indochina. Then Blum went with Moutet to the Ministry of Overseas France at 27 rue Oudinot, and wrote his own message to the Vietnamese president, informing him that Moutet would go to Indochina, together with d'Argenlieu, in order to "clear up the misunderstandings" standing in the way of an immediate application of the modus vivendi agreement, reestablish confidence, and put an end to hostilities.[159] The message was marked "Urgent" and "Top Priority" and was dated December 18, 10 p.m. In Hanoi, it was early morning on December 19. Those who could sleep were still asleep, but none of the main Vietnamese leaders spent the night inside the city; they were spread out in the surrounding villages.

THE LAST DAYS

December 17 had been a day of fateful decisions in Hanoi, Haiphong, and Saigon. Sainteny's staff wrote a summary of all the incidents that had taken place in the streets over the past few weeks, confirming that the Vietnamese liaison office had done everything possible to prevent them from escalating.[160] Sainteny was in Haiphong at a meeting that had started the day before. Those present were Valluy, Morlière, Dèbes, and Barrière, the local navy commander. No one seems to have taken any minutes, but Barrière noted that they had conducted "an overview of the political and military situation in Tonkin." According to Devillers, Valluy's attitude at the meeting may be summarized as follows: "The *Nhacs* [a pejorative term for peasants, derived from the Vietnamese *nha que*] want a brawl. They'll get it!"[161] Little else is known about the meeting, except that Valluy decided to postpone the opening of the Haiphong–Hanoi road once again. Instead of advancing toward Hanoi, Dèbes's troops were ordered to widen the occupied zone around Haiphong. Valluy also foresaw a need for two defensive maneuvers: the evacuation of Phu Lang Thuong with the help of troops moving up from Bac Ninh, and with troops from Hanoi reinforcing Bac Ninh; and the evacuation of the small garrison at Vinh, in north-central Vietnam, with help from the Navy. These operations would be launched on December 21. The aim was no doubt to concentrate the French forces before the expected confrontation and to secure French control of the "strategic base" of Haiphong. Valluy returned to Saigon in the afternoon.

In Paris, d'Argenlieu was preparing his return to Saigon, after having given up any hope he might have had of getting clear government instructions. He concluded that his only option was to apply his policy of firmness locally, on the spot, on the basis of an interpretation of instructions received from the outgoing government. Before paying a farewell visit to General de Gaulle at Colombey-les-Deux-Eglises, he noted in his diary: "A Blum cabinet is announced, entirely SFIO. It presents itself to the Chamber today. Hypothesis: it'll hold and might last five weeks. Thus, instead of speaking clearly and firmly on the Indochinese problem, this will be the parlance of the recent article [Blum's in *Le Populaire*], with hardly any modification. What shall we do over there? An official line, firm and clear, stressing the disregard of the agreements (chiefly on the military level, hostages, destruction . . .). It remains for firmness on the spot to liberate us from this Vietnamese dictatorship, this drug. Draw the basis for this action, 'using all means . . ., from the last instructions of Georges Bidault."[162]

Meanwhile, in Hanoi and Saigon, the Sûreté chiefs, André Moret and Pierre Perrier, were on the verge of giving up the expectation—or hope—that the Vietnamese might begin the hostilities. Perrier gave Pignon a note on December 17: "I don't think the Vietnamese command has the intention of starting the conflict in Hanoi. Several serious incidents have given it the chance, but it has not seized it. Still, it seems that we cannot much longer let the adversary continue to bar roads, cut down trees, deploy mortars on rooftops, place machine guns here and there in the city, and cut all our communications with the outside. Everyone agrees that we cannot but gain from taking the initiative in the operations ourselves."[163]

Pignon had not gone with Valluy to Haiphong, where the military situation was in focus, but instead wrote a candid report to Paris. The future of Indochina, he said, could not be viewed with confidence "until the day when the team currently in power in Hanoi has disappeared." No sincere agreement could ever be reached with the Viet Minh party; it was "unthinkable." It would be futile to place further hope in the personality of Ho Chi Minh. He was more able and measured than his younger partners, but his aims were those of the Viet Minh Tong Bo. Any reshuffling of his cabinet "could only be a trap." Only the elimination of the Viet Minh party would permit a return to peace. The origin of the Indochinese problem was not in Cochinchina, but in Tonkin, in the fact that the Viet Minh party was in power there. A great number of Annamites knew that this totalitarian party was the obstacle to the prompt and peaceful realization of their national aspirations: independence and the unification of the three *ky*. To destroy the Viet Minh or weaken it to an extent obliging it to come to terms was precisely the condition for the maintenance of France in "the position of preeminence and of major nation that she must keep in relation to all the associated countries."[164]

We do not know whether or not Pignon and Perrier gave new instructions to Moret in Hanoi, but he was informed by one of his informers that during a meeting in the Vietnamese cabinet, Ho Chi Minh, Vo Nguyen Giap, and Pham Van Dong had decided to move the government to Thai Nguyen or Sontay and leave Hanoi without a fight. They were said to have imposed their point of view on the Tong Bo, which did not want to evacuate Hanoi until the Viet Minh's Tu Ve fighters had perished under its rubble.[165]

We have only scant knowledge of what was said at the French meetings in Haiphong and Hanoi that Tuesday, but abundant information on what happened in the streets of Hanoi. Again the French and Vietnamese narratives do not quite converge. When it seems impossible to judge which is the most reliable, they will simply be juxtaposed. Two days earlier, the French liaison in Hanoi had demanded that three specific barricades be removed. The SEHAN subsequently picked up the news that on December 16, the Tu Ve and the assault groups had for the first time received orders to shoot back if they came under attack. Until then they had been told just to shoot in the air.[166] When the Vietnamese did not remove the barricades in question, the French dismantled one of them on the morning of December 17. The Vietnamese did not resist, and that afternoon, they voluntarily removed the other two. At another place, however, there was shooting at 0945 hours between a group of Tu Ve, who were setting up a new barricade, and a French military vehicle driving along the road.[167] According to the French, the Tu Ve opened fire on the car and killed two French soldiers. The Tu Ve post was subsequently "destroyed," the quarter searched, and weapons seized.[168] The Vietnamese claimed that the first shots had been fired from the car.[169] At 0950 hours, the French sentry in the mixed guard at one of Hanoi's two electric plants killed his Vietnamese partner. The electricity workers responded with a strike,[170] but they resumed work at 1300 hours. At 1545, a French police sergeant was killed by a sniper. The blockhouse he shot from was, according to the French version, "destroyed." In the Vietnamese version, the whole quarter came under heavy French fire, and the inhabitants were barely permitted to collect their dead and injured.[171] The French liaison demanded that another barricade near Morlière's office be removed before the next day.[172]

The Vietnamese claimed that more than fifty people were killed or wounded during December 17, and that the premeditation and initiative were entirely on the French side.[173] The French noted in their internal report that the Vietnamese government had shown a desire to avoid incidents, but that its orders were not always obeyed.[174] This remark was omitted when Saigon forwarded the information to Paris.[175]

After having come back from Haiphong, Sainteny discussed the situation with the foreign consuls. O'Sullivan warned Washington afterward that the situation was "drifting aimlessly and dangerously." The Vietnamese government gave some evidence of awaiting developments in Paris, but had reacted negatively to the news that d'Argenlieu would return. O'Sullivan was under the impression that neither side wanted war, but he deemed the situation to be "literally powder keg which may explode at any time."[176]

In the early morning of December 18, about one hundred French paratroopers searched houses belonging to Vietnamese presumed to be responsible for the murder of a fellow paratrooper six days earlier. Thirty Vietnamese were killed during the search. One French soldier was also killed.[177] At 1100 hours, French workers began to dismantle a barricade close to Morlière's headquarters in the presence of a Vietnamese liaison officer. To the officer's embarrassment, someone fired from a neighboring house, wounding a French worker in the stomach.[178]

The incidents in Hanoi on December 17 and 18 made the front page of most French newspapers on December 19. While Le Figaro and Le Monde only reproduced the official news bulletins, L'Aube dramatized the events by writing that 300 Vietnamese, armed and trained by the Japanese, had attacked a French unit.[179] In the same issue of the MRP newspaper, the party leader Maurice Schumann stated that respect for agreements required one not just to observe them, but also to "make them observed." Le Populaire emphasized the cabinet's decision to send Moutet to Indochina, where in cooperation with Ho Chi Minh, he would work out the modalities for an effective application of the modus vivendi agreement. L'Humanité found it curious that the new incidents were occurring just as the French cabinet crisis was about to be resolved and wondered aloud if someone was acting with the purpose of "dividing the French on a difficult and painful question in order to carry out certain domestic political operations."[180] Franc-Tireur launched a frontal attack on d'Argenlieu and his "camarilla," who were "confronting the Paris government with a fait accompli."[181]

At noon on December 18, Sainteny reported from Hanoi that the attitude of the Vietnamese government was in flux. Until then, it had been unwilling to open hostilities, but Hoang Huu Nam had "tacitly admitted" in private talks that the government was about to be outflanked by certain extremist elements.[182] The attitude of the French was not in flux. They applied stronger and stronger pressure on their adversary. Before noon, the Vietnamese liaison received a letter from the French announcing that they would occupy the buildings of the Finance Department and the Ministry of Communications, since a French car had been shot at from these. Sainteny asked Morlière to occupy the two buildings, which he did without meeting any resistance. The same letter also demanded that a number of additional barricades be removed. If not, the French command would feel obliged to clear the roads on its own.[183] The Vietnamese would call this "the first ultimatum."

That same day, a French liaison officer, Major Jean Julien Fonde, wrote a letter that the Vietnamese would call "the second ultimatum," complaining that the Vietnamese police was not performing its duties and stating: "The French command has asked me to let you know that if these shortcomings persist, it will take charge of the maintenance of order in Hanoi from December 20, 1946, at the latest." This threat, which seems to have played a significant role in the deliberations and decisions of the Vietnamese leaders that evening and the following day, was addressed to Hoang Huu Nam.[184] He immediately replied that the police were "courageously" continuing to do their work, and the French should not use the problems encountered as a pretext to strike a blow at the Vietnamese government's right to police its territory, a right derived from Vietnam's "sovereignty as a free state."[185] According to Vietnamese radio, Nam also objected to the French removal of barricades and declared: "At the moment when the formation of the French cabinet allows hope for a peaceful and friendly solution to the crisis that was provoked by the bloody incidents of Langson and Haiphong, any act that risks endangering the situation must be carefully avoided."[186] Giap affirms in his memoirs that the Standing Bureau of the Central Committee of the Party met on December 18 in a village in Ha Dong province, not far from Van Phuc, where Ho Chi Minh had his secret headquarters. Ho had moved out of Hanoi on November 26 and stayed most of the time in various safe houses out of range of French artillery. From December 3 to December 19, he occupied a house in Van Phuc; then he moved to Xuan Duong.[187] According to the memoirs of Vu Ky, who served as Ho's secretary from August 1945 until the president's death in September 1969, and who later became director of the Ho Chi Minh museum in Hanoi, the men who came to see Ho Chi Minh and seek his advice at night were Truong Chinh, Le Duc Tho, and Vo Nguyen Giap.[188] Together they formed what in Vietnamese history books is called the Standing Bureau of the Party. Perhaps it was also conceived of as such at the time. At the crisis meeting on December 18, Ho Chi Minh allegedly declared that the French were entering into a new phase. The period of détente was over. The more concessions one made, the more the enemy exploited them to impede Vietnamese rights. The Vietnamese people could not return to slavery. The resistance would be long, fierce, and arduous, but certainly victorious.[189] This is what Giap claimed later that Uncle Ho had said. Vu Ky's memoirs do not mention any such meeting on December 18.

There are no French intelligence reports from any meetings at Van Phuc or in Ha Dong. The French do not seem to have been aware of Ho's whereabouts, but the SEHAN received information on December 18 that secret orders had been distributed during the night to administrative committees in the various blocks of the city, which were repeated orally to the inhabitants of each house. Families who had not evacuated the town were asked to stock enough food and water for forty-five days. Women, children, and the elderly would all be obliged to leave the capital, but at least one young man *(thanh nien)* should be left in each house as a guard. Each *thanh nien* would receive three grenades, which would cost 2.50 piasters per unit. The orders also described how to construct barricades and defined the penalties to be imposed on those who did not do their duty. Any action, before being executed, should be approved by superior authorities. Those guilty of taking initiatives by themselves that could harm the public order or the policy of the government would be punished with extreme severity. The orders concluded: "The government asks the population to help it to the extent possible to prevent any incidents, keep calm, and be ready to fight when President Ho Chi Minh gives the order."[190] The Vietnamese Sûreté was reported to have ordered its staff to stock as much water as possible in the houses it was responsible for. This last order also mentioned a deadline for having stocked all this water: "5 p.m. tomorrow."[191]

The troops, the Sûreté, and the population were thus ready to fight, but at the same time the Vietnamese government continued to try to prevent incidents in the streets and to stay in touch with the French authorities. Ho Chi Minh was still apparently searching for arguments to postpone the planned attack, so that he could have time to ascertain Blum's intentions. According to Vu Ky, Ho stayed up late in the night of December 18–19 to draft his famous call for national resistance; copies of the handwritten draft (fig. 8, ch. 6) are exhibited in the main Vietnamese museums, and it has been reproduced in numerous books.[192]

To infer from the events of the following day, it seems likely that the decision for a two-pronged initiative was made by the Vietnamese leaders on December 18: first, carry out the last preparations for a surprise attack against the French in the evening, thereby forestalling the French onslaught that, with reference to the deadline set in Fonde's "ultimatum," could be expected on December 20; second, avoid any incidents in Hanoi during the day, contact the French to sound them out concerning their intentions, and if possible obtain guarantees allowing postponement of the surprise attack until Blum's intentions were known.

One should never infer intentions from actions. There is often a wide discrepancy between what people decide to do and what they actually do. In order to find out what Giap, Ho, Le Duc Tho, Truong Chinh, and the other Vietnamese leaders' intentions were on December 18, we need access to documents written that day. The problem is that such sources are not yet accessible, even to Vietnam's own historians. This is why it must be permitted here to state, just as a hypothesis, that Ho and the Standing Bureau agreed on such a two-pronged plan. When people in Hanoi went to bed on December 18, the next day was still an open page in history. It might have been the day when Ho and Blum got in touch, Giap calmed his troops, tension died down around the barricades, Moutet packed his bags, and d'Argenlieu vented his frustration to his pilot in Tunisia. Instead, it was the day when Giap and Ho fell into the French trap.

6

Who Turned Out the Lights?

In January 1947, the French got hold of an order from Vo Nguyen Giap to all Vietnamese military units to "destroy the daily order of December 19 immediately, with all appendices."[1] Something went awry that day. What happened on December 19, 1946, still belongs on the shadowy side of history. Not only the Vietnamese, but the French as well, have had something to hide.

At 2003 or 2004 hours—this we know—electricity and the water supply were cut off in the city. A few minutes later, Vietnamese assault units attacked French civilians in their private houses and took some two hundred hostages. Many civilians had been armed by the Sûreté, and some of them tried to defend themselves. From twenty to thirty French citizens were killed, some of them burned or mutilated in horrible ways. These excesses were subsequently exploited to the maximum by French propaganda, which depicted Ho and Giap as directly responsible for the murder of French citizens.[2] The Hanoi killings boosted the French myth of a generic Far Eastern xenophobic savagery, which had found expression in the Japanese execution of all the French survivors after the battle for Langson on March 11, 1945, the rampage at the Cité Héraud in Saigon on September 24, 1945, where 120 Frenchmen were killed, and now the atrocities in Hanoi. Someone coined the term "Tonkinese Vespers" to denote the December 19 events, alluding to the "Sicilian Vespers" in Palermo on Easter Monday and Tuesday, March 30–31, 1282, when a local aristocratic plot unleashed an insurrection against the domination of the French prince Charles of Anjou. Amid cries of "Death to the French," the revolt soon spread over the entire island, and more than 4,000 French were massacred. Just as Charles had learned not to trust any Sicilian aristocrat, the horrifying fate of the French civilians in Hanoi constituted a powerful argument against ever again dealing with the Viet Minh.

During the first one and a half hours of the fighting, the Tu Ve forces held the initiative, firing from many places, while the French hostages were marched out of Hanoi. A train was moved into a position where it hampered the movement of French vehicles, and roads were mined. Jean Sainteny's car struck a mine, and he was badly wounded. Giap's regular army, positioned at the outskirts of the capital, never entered Hanoi to join the fighting. Its mission was, it seems, to protect the leadership and hold itself in reserve. Around 2130 hours, the French were ready to launch their counterattack. In the following evening, after the first twenty-four hours of fighting, the French had taken control of the whole European part of the city. All the defenders of the presidential palace had been killed by 4 p.m., and the tricolor been hoisted over Ho Chi Minh's office. Neither the president nor any of the other main leaders, however, were apprehended. They had not been in the city when the war broke out.

During the night from December 19 to 20, the other French garrisons in the north also came under attack. The greater the distance from Hanoi, the later in the night it happened.[3] Only at Hai Duong and Vinh, whose small French garrisons Valluy had intended to evacuate in a surprise operation on December 21, were the attackers able to overrun the French and take prisoner the survivors. In the late evening of December 20 and the early morning of December 21, a speaker read out on the radio the appeal that Ho Chi Minh had drafted on the night of December 18–19: "Fight with all the means at your disposal. Fight with your arms, your picks, your spades, your sticks."[4] In the Sino-Vietnamese quarter of Hanoi, fighting dragged on through January and February. The French refrained from employing artillery in the manner of Colonel Dèbes, so the Vietnamese were able to continue their resistance for two months before they found the situation untenable and managed to pull their remaining troops out across the Red River. Eight years then passed before a peace agreement was reached at Geneva, allowing Giap and Ho to return to their capital. The first unit to enter, on October 9, 1954, was the Thu Do (Capital) regiment, made up of those who had fought the French in Hanoi during December 1946–February 1947.

The outward chronology is well established, but a number of puzzles remain. Why did the Vietnamese choose to fight? What can explain the contrast between the sudden attack at 8 p.m. on December 19 and two conciliatory letters that had been sent to the French earlier in the day? Why was the attack executed in such a haphazard manner? Why didn't the troops surrounding Hanoi take part in the fighting? Why wasn't Ho Chi Minh's appeal broadcast when the attack started, but only much later? And what about the almost inexplicable delay in the attack on the other French garrisons?

INTERPRETATIONS

The first official Vietnamese explanation had been prepared before the event. On a poster proclaiming martial law, the year, month, date, and time (2000 hours) were filled in by hand. It was put up in Hanoi the same evening and was prefaced by the following statement: "Official order: Compatriots of the Capital: The French troops have opened the hostilities in Hanoi."[5] Before dawn on December 20, a French counterposter was ready, introducing the official French interpretation, which would dominate the whole Western press: "Proclamation: Viet Minh has treacherously started hostilities, adopting the tactics of the Japanese *coup de force* of March 9, 1945. The Viet Minh government is on the run. French authorities find themselves obliged to reestablish order . . . "[6] It is worth noting that the Vietnamese government had already been downgraded to the *Viet Minh* government.

General Morlière felt sure that the attack had been carried out in accordance with a "premeditated plan," prepared by the Vietnamese military on orders from the government. He even claimed that the attacks on all the French garrisons had been simultaneous.[7] Commissioner Sainteny, in hospital, declared that this "beautiful country, Vietnam, has been the prey of downright bandits, who have at last, while we were waiting, thrown off their mask and revealed the degree of their barbarism."[8] Léon Pignon was not happy with Sainteny's reference to the French "waiting," and he ordered that this statement not be published. Another of the wounded Sainteny's utterances was more appropriate: "I have been hit as one of the first by the blows of an unspeakable treason, even though I offered Vietnam nothing but my loyalty." This was immediately transmitted to Paris, and Saigon asked for international dissemination of these words "from the mouth of the man who signed the March 6 agreement."[9]

Interim High Commissioner Valluy assured Paris on December 21 that the conflict had started with a surprise attack ordered by responsible Vietnamese authorities. He also repeated Morlière's misinformation about the "simultaneousness" of the attacks and used this as proof of premeditation.[10] U.S. Vice-Consul O'Sullivan felt sure that the attack had been planned by the Vietnamese government. His telegrams to Washington, which were sent in the clear, were intercepted by the French in Saigon, translated and sent to Paris in order to convince the French government that Hanoi was not a new Haiphong.[11]

An analysis Pignon wrote on December 23 corresponds closely to what would become the French official version. After stating that the attack had been based on a premeditated plan, modeled on the Japanese coup of March 9, 1945, he added four important points. First, the attack had been preceded by a number of ploys to make the French believe that relations were improving, including friendly letters from Ho Chi Minh to Sainteny and from Hoang Huu Nam to Morlière, as well as attempts by Vietnamese liaison officers to get the French commander to furlough the French troops who were confined to barracks and allow them out on the town. Second, the purpose of these ploys was to ensure complete surprise: the Vietnamese had intended to massacre the French soldiers while they were dispersed in cinemas and restaurants. Third, the ploys were at first successful, and the French command actually decided to furlough the troops that evening, but after an alarming report from a spy, Morlière hastily called the soldiers back to the barracks, saving them from suffering the fate of the French civilians. Fourth, the Vietnamese ploys demonstrated that the whole Vietnamese government, including the letter writers Ho Chi Minh and Hoang Huu Nam, had wished to wipe out the French garrisons: France was facing a united bloc determined to eliminate the French presence in Indochina. Pignon hoped that this would enlighten French and international public opinion as to the real nature of the Viet Minh.[12] Pignon's interpretation would form the basis for the standard Western version of the outbreak of war. For many years, it shut out rival explanations. Its simplicity, its logical structure, and the alluring image of the lone spy who saved the lives of several hundred French boys enabled Pignon's scenario to survive in spite of all the evidence it could not explain.

Ironically, Vietnamese accounts of December 19 tend to confirm Pignon's analysis. President Ho Chi Minh gave his first public interpretation in a radio speech on December 25, holding the French responsible for the outbreak of hostilities. They had handed over an "ultimatum" on December 19, demanding French control of the police. When the Vietnamese refused, "fighting broke out," Ho said.[13] If Associated Press translated the radio speech correctly, Ho's words were surprising. It is normal to accuse the adversary of having opened fire. By saying just that fighting "broke out," Ho more or less admitted that his side had taken the initiative. He was no more specific in a memorandum he signed on December 31, which was meant to prove French responsibility for the outbreak of war. He mentioned three French "ultimatums," two on December 18, one on December 19, but described the attack itself without apportioning blame: "General attack started abruptly in the evening of December 19, and by nightfall, the final preparations were almost complete *[la tombée de la nuit, presque les derniers préparatifs sont accomplis]*." Even in this meticulously compiled and generally reliable memorandum, which is a precious source for this book, Ho does not go beyond stating in general terms that the French had "started and wanted" the conflict *(déclenché et voulu par les colonialistes français)*.[14] French communists would later repeatedly ask their Vietnamese comrades for the truth about December 19, but got only evasive answers.[15]

In 1948, Vietnam's official delegation in France published a booklet in English, blaming the outbreak of war squarely on the French: "Hostilities which broke out on the evening of December 19th were not started by the Vietnamese, but by the French under the pretext that the Vietnamese were going to attack them." Later standard Vietnamese accounts of national history claim that President Ho Chi Minh, realizing the inevitability of war, gave an agreed-on signal to the whole people to resist. In his *Vietnam: A Long History,* which has been published in numerous editions in Hanoi, Nguyen Khac Vien pretends that Ho Chi Minh appealed to the nation to resist on December 19. He quotes the appeal and concludes: "The war of resistance, until then limited to the south, spread across the country." The problem is that Ho's appeal was not actually broadcast until the following day.[16]

Vuong Thua Vu, commander of the special Hanoi zone in December 1946, wrote an article three years later with the promising title "The Truth about December 19 in Hanoi."[17] He devoted seven and a half pages to military background information, six to the heroic struggle of the following two months, and half a page to the outbreak of the fighting itself. This half page says that the Tu Ve forces gathered in the City Hall to declare themselves ready. Then, at 2003 hours, French soldiers provoked incidents and occupied public buildings, obliging the Vietnamese troops to defend themselves. This flawed account could only strengthen the credibility of the French scenario, which was also reinforced by a radio speech made in December 1949 by the former leader of the August 1945 revolution in Saigon, and later prominent Vietnamese historian, Tran Van Giau, who seemed to indicate that the Vietnamese had initiated the fighting three years earlier. Shortly after this speech, which was monitored by the French and used in their propaganda, he lost his position as a minister in the DRV cabinet.

The Vietnamese must have had some reason for avoiding going into the details of the outbreak of fighting on December 19. This could mean, of course, that the French were right. However, if a unanimous party leadership, including Ho Chi Minh, had decided on the attack, why would the party leaders wait so many years before admitting it? One would expect them then to have been proud to tell how the Party had planned and carried out its decision. And if the attack had been the result of well-thought-out decision, an explanatory public statement would surely have been prepared in advance and used in Vietnamese propaganda immediately afterward. There must have been something else that the Vietnamese have wanted to conceal, something more shameful than a devious hoax. The course of events suggests that something went wrong that fateful day on the Vietnamese side.

Pignon's interpretation was accepted and reproduced by almost all of the French press. Only two French journalists looked for alternative explanations, Léon Boutbien in *Franc-Tireur* and Philippe Devillers in *Le Monde.*[18] Boutbien rejected the idea that France had been faced by a united determined bloc and claimed that the Vietnamese leadership had been divided. Vo Nguyen Giap was the leader of the extremists who ordered the killing of the French civilians. Hoang Huu Nam and Hoang Minh Giam were moderates, and Ho Chi Minh was an "enigmatic figure." At some point, the extremists had assumed power from behind the scenes. The government was incapable of retreating, and Ho Chi Minh had let himself be dragged along in order not to lose authority. Philippe Devillers, who had returned to France before the outbreak of war, after eleven months on Leclerc's and Valluy's staff, also pointed to internal disagreements in the Vietnamese leadership, but did not see Giap as the extremist. Giap had long been instrumental in maintaining a relaxed atmosphere in Tonkin between the French and the Vietnamese, but he had then come under pressure from more extreme elements. French Cochinchina policy and the refusal to make any concessions to Hanoi had strengthened the hand of the extremists. In December, French actions had exasperated the Vietnamese so much that the extremists came out on top. In Devillers's view, treating the Viet Minh as a united bloc—lumping Viet Minh moderates and uncompromising enemies of France together—was a dangerous error.

Neither Boutbien nor Devillers was in a position to question the details of Pignon's official version, but in 1947, the French journalist Jean Bidault (not related to the premier) anonymously published an anti–Viet Minh pamphlet, probably based on inside information from one of the French intelligence services. He differed from the official French version on one essential point: when Morlière confined his troops to barracks in the afternoon of December 19, Giap's scheme was foiled. The Vietnamese plan had been to carry out an all-out attack at a time when 1,200 French soldiers were on furlough in Hanoi's restaurants and cafés. When Morlière recalled the troops to barracks and (perhaps) deployed armored vehicles at the road junctions that the Vietnamese troops would need to pass in order to get into the city, Giap could no longer count on the calculated effect of surprise. He therefore tried to call off the whole operation, but his order canceling it did not reach all the Tu Ve units, and at 2000 hours, they carried out their part of the plan. This could explain why the relatively disciplined Vietnamese Army troops around Hanoi remained passive while the Tu Ve took action, and also why the other French garrisons were only attacked much later.[19] In 1952, when Devillers published his Histoire du Viêt-Nam de 1940 à 1952, he took Jean Bidault's point into account, but added that the Tu Ve might deliberately have ignored the cancellation order.[20]

Jean Bidault's revision was important, but the idea that Ho Chi Minh and Hoang Huu Nam wrote conciliatory letters in the morning with the purpose of deceiving the French was left unchallenged. When General Yves Gras published his Histoire de la guerre d'Indochine in 1979, he left open the question of whether or not there had been "treachery on the part of Ho Chi Minh and Giap" or if they had been unable to halt "their [only] too well established mechanism of aggression."[21] What if Nam and Ho's letters were genuine attempts to reduce the tension, with the aim of postponing Giap's attack until Ho had heard from Blum? Could the attack have been canceled *before* Morlière recalled his troops to barracks? What if it had been the news that the French troops had been recalled to barracks and that armored vehicles had been placed at strategic points that led the Vietnamese to decide that the time had come to fight anyhow? Determining whether the two conciliatory letters were a hoax, or if they reflected a last, sincere attempt to avert hostilities, requires an hour-by-hour account of the day, when everything was, in Devillers's words, "bizarre, illogical, even suspect."[22]

HOAX OR HOPE?

At sunrise, Viet Minh newspapers came fresh from the printer in Hanoi for the last time in eight years. *Cuu Quoc* protested "energetically against the fact that the representatives of France in Vietnam had intentionally prepared their offensive in Hanoi in order to extend the hostilities while French Prime Minister Léon Blum and Mr. Moutet were advocating sincere Franco-Vietnamese cooperation." *Dan Thanh* appealed to France's new premier, Léon Blum, to "put an end to the machinations of the colonialists, who were about to complete their effort to drag the two peoples to their death. But he has to act quickly if he wants to get there in time."[23]

In the early morning, the Vietnamese troops around Hanoi were put on a state of alert, and the commanders both there and in the other war zones received a secret order that would later, in accordance with Giap's orders, be destroyed, but turned up again in the new, more complete memoirs Giap published when he was nearly ninety. The order came in three portions. First the following text was sent out at 0900 hours: "The French aggressors have issued an ultimatum [calling for] disarming our army, self-defense, and public security. Our government has rejected this ultimatum. Therefore, within the next twenty-four hours,[24] the French aggressors will definitely open fire. Instructions from the Center: All must be prepared!" This was followed by an order signed by Vo Nguyen Giap himself:

> The motherland is in danger! The time to fight has arrived!
> Per instructions from President Ho and the government, and as minister of national defense and commander in chief, I order the entire Vietnamese national army and self-defense forces, in center, south, and north, to stand up as one man.
> You must rush to the front, kill the aggressor, save the nation.
> Give your life in battle, fight to the last drop of blood!
> Exterminate the French colonialist gang.
> Be resolved to fight.

The third portion was a flash message that was sent out in the early afternoon. It was not sent to the south, but to all those zones in the north that included a French garrison: 1 (Langson), 2 (Sontay, Yen Bai, Lao Cai), 3 (Haiphong, Hai Duong, Mong Cai), 4 (Vinh), and 11 (Hanoi), and also to the southern city of Da Nang, where there was a strong French force. All recipients were requested to make sure that the order would be in the hands of the zone and front commanders before 0930 on December 19: "The freight arrives at 1800 hours December 21, 1946. The freight's registration no. A+2 and B-2. Pay attention and pick up the freight at the exact time." The "freight" was the attack against the French forces. In accordance with a system agreed at a military conference on December 13, the recipients should add two hours to the time given (A+2) and subtract two days from the date (B-2). This meant they should attack at 2000 hours on December 19.[25] All Vietnamese military units were thus ordered on the morning of December 19 to do something they subsequently did not do, but that the French would claim they had done, namely, attack simultaneously at 2000 hours.

At 1100 hours, some of Giap's regular troops had taken up positions between the Red River and the Great Lake in Hanoi, from where it would be possible to attack the Hanoi Citadel, where the bulk of the French forces were concentrated.[26] The commanders of the death squads in the city itself were ordered to prepare for their missions. In an order signed by commissar Le Hong, they were told to count the dead, injured, and survivors after the engagement and report to the command in the village of Gia Quat Ha, east of the Red River.[27] According to his order, the signal for attack would be given in an incredibly complicated way: "preparation signal: green rockets; assault signal: red rocket, followed by three explosions made by three grenades; signal given tonight (19/12.46) at 1845 hours."[28] Military discipline would be ruthlessly enforced by execution: "retreat: death; misinterpretation of the orders: death; fomentation of plots: death." Although the three penalties would seem identical, the second must have made a more chilling impression than the others, for it is not—even with the benefit of hindsight—easy to interpret Le Hong's order. He announced that two signals would be given, one green and one red. Then he gave the exact time for the signal, without saying which of the two signals he meant. Now the suicide squads could, of course, wait till 1845 hours and see if there were several green or just one red rocket. For the historian, who has (fortunately) no chance to replay the events, it is more difficult, but since we know that Giap had ordered the attack to take place at 2000 hours, we must assume that the rockets Le Hong planned to send up at 1845 were green (unless Le Hong used "1845" as a code for 2000).

While the squads prepared for their missions, specially assigned groups were making ready to attack French civilians in their houses, seize arms and ammunition, and take the civilians out of Hanoi as hostages.[29] Meanwhile, the situation in the streets was improving. Vietnamese policemen suddenly appeared all over, busily demonstrating that they were capable of ensuring law and order. Vietnamese workers resumed their work in the Citadel, after having been on strike, and mixed Franco-Vietnamese military patrols resumed their rounds.[30] Sainteny, at his office, was made aware of the Vietnamese preparations by a SEHAN report giving the content of a Vietnamese order, dated December 17, to all neighborhood committees, instructing them to make final preparations for war and ensure that the population was "ready to fight when President Ho Chi Minh gives the order."[31]

At 9:30 a.m., following instructions Ho Chi Minh had sent with his secretary Vu Ky, Hoang Minh Giam asked Sainteny for an appointment in the afternoon, but the latter refused to see him until the next morning.[32] Giam had been asked by Ho Chi Minh to deliver a short letter, which he now instead sent by courier. This conciliatory letter was either a hoax, meant to ensure the surprise effect of the attack in the evening, or a last-minute attempt to reach an accommodation so that the attack could be postponed while Ho waited for Blum to answer his many appeals: "Commissioner and dear friend. The atmosphere has become more tense these past [few] days. This is really regrettable. While waiting for Paris's decision, I count on you to search with Mr. Giam for a solution that can improve the climate."[33] Sainteny did not reply. Instead, he sent a much cooler letter of his own to Ho, warning that if the murderers of a French civilian were not arrested and imprisoned within forty-eight hours, he would investigate himself and do what was needed to prevent such crimes in the future. This letter does not seem to have reached Ho.[34]

Morlière wrote to Nam that morning, reiterating five demands he had first presented orally at the end of the previous day: (1) removal of all barricades and termination of all hostile preparations; (2) disarming the "undisciplined and irresponsible" Tu Ve; (3) release of all arrested French citizens; (4) cessation of the "incendiary propaganda campaign"; and (5) strict cooperation of all institutions responsible for maintaining order.[35] If Morlière had already presented these demands to Nam the day before, then it might explain that the secret orders Giap sent out to all military zones at 8 a.m. already referred to Morlière's "ultimatum" and its demand that the Tu Ve be disarmed. The Vietnamese would later refer to Morlière's letter as "the third ultimatum."

Now, none of the three "ultimatums" were, strictly speaking, ultimatums. An ultimatum sets a deadline for accepting a set of specific demands and threatens forceful action if this is not done. If one issues an ultimatum, and the demands are not accepted, it is essential to carry out the threat once the deadline has passed. If the deadline passes and nothing happens, it leads to a loss of credibility. Dèbes's ultimatum on November 23 is a case in point. It contained a set of specific, albeit highly unrealistic, demands, and Dèbes was more than ready to carry out his threats. This made French threats so immensely credible that the Vietnamese may have overinterpreted the letters they subsequently received in Hanoi. The "first French ultimatum" in Hanoi on December 18 had demanded that barricades be removed and threatened that the French would do this themselves if the Vietnamese did not do it, but there was no deadline indicating when the threat would be effectuated. "The second French ultimatum," signed by Liaison Officer Fonde, did set a deadline for the Vietnamese police to resume their functions and secure law and order. If this did not happen, the French would take responsibility for securing law and order in Hanoi from December 20 at the latest. This "deadline" seems to have made a strong impression on the Vietnamese, and it may have contributed significantly to their fateful decision. Morlière did not attach any precise deadline to his "third French ultimatum," and also did not make any clear threats.[36] Instead, Morlière concluded his letter quite amiably: "The French authorities are prepared to make an urgent joint study of how to implement these measures, which are indispensable to the avoidance of any further incident and would greatly facilitate the establishment of a sincere and durable cooperation." One could see a threat in the words "indispensable for the avoidance of any further incident," and the Vietnamese surely did. But Morlière's threats were neither specific nor attached to any deadline. Now the Vietnamese leaders could not, of course, know that the French government had told d'Argenlieu's and Valluy's emissary Le Puloch in no uncertain terms that it would not tolerate a repetition in Hanoi of what had been done in Haiphong. If there were to be fighting, the initiative should come from the other side. The French authorities in Indochina could not therefore issue any genuine ultimatum. What they could do was apply steadily mounting pressure in the hope of inducing the Vietnamese government to take action.

If Sainteny and Morlière's letters had been the only French response to the Vietnamese overtures, it would have been difficult for anyone on the Vietnamese side to argue that the attack should be further postponed. Giap would have stepped with both feet into the trap that the French had set up, and the war would probably have started with a coordinated Vietnamese attack. Giap could not just look passively on while the French started to disarm the Tu Ve. However, the French also sent out two conciliatory signals that day. Just as they had done the previous morning, Vietnamese liaison officers tested the waters by asking their French contacts if the French troops would be confined to their barracks in the evening.[37] Furloughed French soldiers in the city would be exposed to danger. After December 19, Pignon thus interpreted the Vietnamese request as an attempt to lure the French into a situation where many French soldiers could be killed while on furlough. But signaling goes both ways. To furlough the French troops would be a sure way of telling the Vietnamese that the French were not on the verge of launching a coup of their own. So when Sainteny and Morlière decided to let 1,200 soldiers off in the evening, and informed the Vietnamese of their decision, the Vietnamese leaders may have seen this as a sign that they still had time to wait and see what Blum's new government would do. Sainteny explains in his memoirs that furloughing the soldiers was a "maneuver" with the double aim of either relaxing tensions or obliging the Viet Minh to "show its hand."[38]

Where did the Vietnamese leaders stay? Giap tells in his recent memoirs that his headquarters were in Van Phuc village in Ha Dong, eleven kilometers from Hanoi. Shortly before the Vietnamese attack at 2000 hours, Sainteny reported that Ho had come back to the capital after some days' absence.[39] French intelligence later reported that Ho, Giap, and other cabinet members had left Hanoi again in the afternoon, several hours before the attack,[40] but Ho would state in a letter to Blum on December 23 that he had still been in his residence when the French troops attacked and had only escaped by a miracle.[41] This was surely a lie. The truth is that

Ho did not go to Hanoi at all, but stayed in Van Phuc. On the morning of December 19, he wrote yet another letter to Blum, as well as one to Vincent Auriol, the Speaker of the French National Assembly. Ho told the two French socialists that he had asked his compatriots to stay calm despite the many provocations. This he had done because of his love for France and his confidence in Blum and Auriol: "But for how long will I have to suffer seeing my compatriots being killed before my eyes? I address to you once again this urgent appeal. In the highest interest of our two countries, I beg you once more to put a stop to the provocations and the bloodshed."[42] Vu Ky was charged with bringing these letters into Hanoi, along with Ho's short letter to Sainteny. After handing them over and seeing Hoang Minh Giam, Vu Ky returned to Van Phuc at 1230 hours, where he informed President Ho of Sainteny's refusal to see Giam. Ho walked back and forth for a while, frowning, then approached the table where his draft appeal was lying, and, according to Vu Ky's later published diary, said very clearly: "Hah! We'll fight [Hu! Thi danh]."[43] What this seems to indicate, if true, is, first, that the order Giap had sent in the morning did not represent a definitive decision to launch the attack. Ho had not yet thrown the dice. Second, however, Ho's remark shows that he now thought he had to take the gamble. We do not know if Ho and Giap could communicate with each other at 1230 hours, but according to Giap's biographer Tran Trong Trung, it was now, after Sainteny had refused to see Giam, that Giap issued his second, coded order to attack at 2000 hours.[44]

Meanwhile, inside Hanoi, Hoang Huu Nam answered Morlière's "third French ultimatum" in his capacity as Defense Minister Giap's delegate: "I have referred the matter to the minister of national defense. He has charged me to answer that he will submit your proposals to the weekly meeting of the cabinet tomorrow, Friday, December 20, 1946. In the meantime, he has given orders to avoid all misunderstandings. He hopes that, on your side, the necessary orders will also be given to avoid any aggravation of the present situation."[45] Nam thus claimed that Giap had given orders to "avoid all misunderstandings," while the order that Giap was sending out in the early afternoon to all regional party chiefs and commanders was actually to get ready to attack at 2000 hours.[46]

Two and a half hours later, at 1430 hours, according to Vu Ky, four members of the Standing Bureau of the Party—Ho Chi Minh, Truong Chinh, Le Duc Tho, and Vo Nguyen Giap—met at Van Phuc. Morlière's new demands and Sainteny's refusal to see Giam must have been arguments in favor of carrying out the planned attack. Morlière's suspension of the confinement of French troops to the barracks may have represented an extra temptation. This would make it possible to seek out French troops and kill them individually or in small groups. On the other hand, the fact that some 1,200 French troops would spread out in the bars and restaurants also indicated that the French were not after all on the verge of launching a coup—unless, of course, the lifting of the restriction to barracks was a ruse.

FIGURE 7. No photographs were evidently taken when the leading Vietnamese communists, Truong Chinh, Le Duc Tho, Vo Nguyen Giap, Ho Chi Minh—and perhaps others—
met secretly at Van Phuc in Ha Dong, outside Hanoi, in the afternoon of December 19,
1946. In official party history, the four men are said to have constituted the Standing
Bureau of the clandestine Indochinese Communist Party. That claim is reflected in this
drawing from a 2007 Vietnamese picture book about Truong Chinh. Courtesy Vietnam
News Agency Publishing House, Hanoi.

While these matters were probably discussed at Van Phuc, another piece of news
arrived that might have tipped the balance in favor of keeping the peace. At 1400
hours, the French Information Service learned from Radio Saigon that Blum's cabinet had decided to send Moutet on a special mission to Indochina, news it immediately passed on to its Vietnamese counterpart. Second Assistant Minh, very impressed, gave an assurance that he would at once inform the members of his
government.[47] We do not know if this news reached the four men at Van Phuc, who
agreed, according to Vu Ky, to maintain the decision to launch nationwide resistance that evening. After adding five words suggested by Le Duc Tho, the meeting
approved the text of Ho Chi Minh's appeal, instructed Truong Chinh to finalize
instructions concerning the conduct of a national resistance strategy,[48] and gave
Giap authority to carry out the planned attack. In Hanoi, the signal would be a black-
out caused by sabotage of the Yen Phu power station. And the main signal to the

national resistance would be announcement of the president's call to arms on the national radio.[49]

The question here is whether the decision of members of the Standing Bureau at Van Phuc was irrevocable, or Giap still had the authority to call off the attack if new evidence should emerge concerning the French government's intentions. After 1515 hours, when the meeting ended, President Ho returned to his safe house and started preparing to move to another one. Vu Ky's account of December 19 ends with Ho instructing him to help move to a new safe house at Xuan Duong. Vu Ky's account seems quite reliable, since it builds on his personal diary, with entries every day. The original diary itself, however, was not included in the holdings of the Ho Chi Minh Museum's library when Vu Ky died in 2005. Instead, it seems to have been taken to the Party archives, which remain inaccessible to researchers.[50]

Devillers claims, on the basis of a French intelligence report, that Giap summoned the most important military commanders at Bach Mai, just outside Hanoi, at 1600 hours, that is, after the Standing Bureau's meeting at Van Phuc.[51] This is confirmed by Giap himself and by his biographers. Present at Bach Mai were the intelligence boss Tran Quoc Hoan, representing the Communist Party; Chief of Staff Hoang Van Thai, who was responsible for all cipher communications; and the commander of the 11th Military Zone, Nguyen Van Tran.[52] According to Giap's most recent biographer and also Giap's memoirs, Giap spent the rest of the evening inspecting troops in the capital, and left in the direction of Ha Dong before the hour struck. All the time, he was calm and seemed satisfied (yen tam).

At least one source, however, distorts the general picture of a determined leadership preparing for action. At 1645h, the unit of the soldier with the diary, Ngo Van Chieu, received orders to cancel an attack it had been assigned to take part in. Chieu noted that the attack should now not be carried out "under any pretext" unless there was a written or verbal order from Giap personally, or from one of his two direct assistants. The troops should under no circumstance provoke the French troops who were on furlough in the city.[53] This seems confusing, since it runs counter to the decision made, according to Vu Ky, at Van Phuc just two hours earlier.

Over at the French headquarters, when Morlière received Nam's letter about giving orders to "avoid all misunderstandings," he was just about to change his mind concerning his earlier decision to furlough his troops.[54] At some point in the afternoon, the French command received information that Vietnamese troops had been massed outside Hanoi and that there were plans for an attack the same evening.[55] One of these reports came from a Eurasian spy whose French name was Charles Eugène Fernand Petit.[56] According to Jean Bidault, Petit had been told in the morning that the attack would take place that evening, although he had not heard exactly when. Petit managed to convey this information to the Sûreté a little before 1800 hours. This is confirmed by a statement Petit made under oath to a French judge in February 1947, when he introduced himself as "inspecteur de la Sûreté," working in a counterespionage unit. With the help of a letter of introduction from Viet Minh leaders living in France, he had managed to infiltrate the Tu Ve group in his neighborhood. He had first been told that an attack would take place on Christmas Eve, but on the morning of December 19, he learned from his neighborhood Tu Ve, just as Bidault says, that the attack would be for "tonight." For security reasons, he waited until the evening before conveying this news to the Sûreté, but managed to do so a little before 1800 hours. When he returned to his Tu Ve group, Petit was told by the commander of his unit: "Prepare yourself. It will be this evening at 2000 hours that we attack the French. Go and take up your position of combat!" He first went home to see his Viet wife and inform her that he was leaving for his country *(part pour la patrie)*. Telling this to the French judge, he emphasized that when referring to his country, he had meant France. Then he returned to his Tu Ve group and found an excuse for taking a few minutes off. His commander told him that if he didn't return, his wife and children would suffer (which they later did). Petit now went directly to Colonel Lami, Morlière's second in command. Since the time was now approaching 2000 hours, Colonel Lami recommended that he stay with him rather than go back to his unit. That was how Petit came to take part in defending Lami's home against his Tu Ve comrades.[57]

There are two oddities in this story. First, that Colonel Lami chose to stay home if he expected an attack at 2000 hours. Would he not be needed at his headquarters? Either he did not take Petit's warning seriously or Petit came too late to give Lami time to take any precautionary measures. The other oddity is the timing. If the hours given by Petit are correct, then none of his two reports could have influenced Morlière's decision to recall the troops from furlough, which happened before 1700 hours.[58] In Petit's first report, a little before 1800 hours, he did not know the timing of the attack, but the French had apparently received other information indicating that it would be for 1900 hours.[59] There is some indication that it might have been Trocard's SEHAN, and not Moret's Sûreté (controlling Petit) that provided Morlière with the intelligence that led him to order the troops back to barracks.[60] But SEHAN may have expected the attack earlier than 2000 hours. When nothing seemed to happen at 1700, 1800, or 1900 hours, the French may have concluded that it would not be for that night; there had been several false alarms in the previous weeks. In that case, it would not perhaps have been irresponsible if Colonel Lami and Commissioner Sainteny went home for supper. Then Petit came to Lami's house, well after 1900 hours, and according to his own account informed the French colonel that the Tu Ve would go into action at 2000 hours.

Petit never mentioned any cancellation order. This could either mean that the order to attack was never canceled or that Giap canceled only the regular army's participation in the attack. Perhaps, on discovering that the French had blocked certain intersections with armored vehicles, Giap decided not to risk his main troops in the fighting, but let the Tu Ve go on with their part of the attack as planned. This would explain why Ngo Van Chieu's regular army unit received a cancellation order, but not Petit's Tu Ve. However, it is also conceivable that Giap tried unsuccessfully to hold back the Tu Ve. Jean Bidault credits Petit with having saved French troops from massacre, but this is clearly a myth. Morlière recalled the French troops to their barracks an hour before Petit delivered his first report. The Petit story seems to have done duty as a legend in the French intelligence community, "proving" that secret services sometimes serve a useful purpose.[61]

The news that the French soldiers and officers were being recalled from the streets may have arrived at the Vietnamese headquarters just as efforts were being made to explain to the Tu Ve command, and to all military units, that the attack would be postponed.[62] How would Giap and the Tu Ve react now? What about Ho? Would they not all have felt that they had been taken for a ride? Had Morlière fooled them in saying he would furlough his troops? They may have feared that the French coup was under way anyhow. Giap would write three decades later in his memoirs: "Dusk fell. . . . It was reported that not a single French soldier was to be seen in the restaurants, bars or streets. And enemy armored cars began to push out and stood blocking some crossroads."[63]

DEFIANCE OR BUNGLING?

We have established that the conciliatory letters written by Nam and Ho, and also the Vietnamese request to know if the French troops would be furloughed, may well have resulted from a genuine hope of establishing contact with Léon Blum's new French government before something irrevocable was done. Ho and Nam were not necessarily as cynical as Pignon and Jean Bidault would have it. The next question is why the Vietnamese attack happened at 2000 hours, if the Vietnamese leaders wanted to give Blum a chance to intervene. Was it because of Tu Ve defiance, or did Giap commit his life's biggest blunder?

When we approach 2000 hours, the chronology of events is so complex that we must first examine it from the French side, then the Vietnamese. To recall the troops to barracks, as decided at 1700 hours, was not a radical measure in view of the mounting evidence of a planned attack. Did Morlière really believe that the Vietnamese were about to take action, and did he prepare for combat? On this point, the sources are contradictory. Ho Chi Minh included as an appendix to his memo of December 31 a note from a Vietnamese liaison officer stating that, at 1830 hours, the Vietnamese police reported French armored cars at five sensitive spots.[64] Jean Bidault gives the same information and adds that the armored cars were blocking the roads that Vietnamese troops outside Hanoi would have to use to penetrate the city.[65] D'Argenlieu refutes this, claiming that Ho Chi Minh's allegations were "manifestly wrong." There had been only two armored cars in the city that evening, following the customary itinerary of the mixed patrol.[66] D'Argenlieu's report aimed both to establish the culpability of Ho Chi Minh and the incompetence of Morlière, and this double aim may have influenced his interpretations, although the Vietnamese police might perhaps have observed the same two circulating cars in five different places. An appendix to d'Argenlieu's report categorically affirms that the French in Hanoi were caught by surprise, and that the troops were in their barracks instead of at the prescribed alert positions.[67] And d'Argenlieu is not our only source here. A report from U.S. Vice-Consul O'Sullivan and a copy of one of the first reports going from Hanoi to Saigon after the initial attack support d'Argenlieu's contention. O'Sullivan states that the first French elements—primarily armored cars, half-tracks, and jeeps—began to move into the city from the various cantonments at 2020 hours, seventeen minutes after the electricity had been cut off. The "inexperienced troops manning these vehicles added to the confusion by shooting almost indiscriminately at anything which moved," O'Sullivan noted.[68] This is consistent with a late-night report from Hanoi to Saigon that the French intervention had begun at 2020 hours. Until 2130 hours, the streets were relatively calm, but then combat started and soon intensified.[69] This means that the French counteroffensive did not happen until one and a half hours after the Vietnamese attack. Le Figaro also wrote on February 1, 1947, that the troops had neither been ready to fight nor tactically positioned.[70]

With such contradictory information, it is difficult to assess the degree of French preparedness. The Vietnamese police's detailed information on the five strategically positioned armored cars, confirmed by Jean Bidault, seems convincing. French armored cars were probably blocking the main approaches to the city, yet the French command was taken by surprise at 2000 hours. What if the French had expected the attack to take place earlier? Perhaps they took protective measures in the late afternoon, when the troops were sent back to their barracks, but relaxed their vigilance when nothing seemed to happen. Perhaps the armored cars were at the crossroads at 1830 hours, but not at 2000 hours. Then Ho Chi Minh, Jean Bidault, and d'Argenlieu would all be right. Would it have been irresponsible of Morlière to lift some of his protective measures after 1900 hours? Not if he and Sainteny had received reliable information that Giap had canceled his attack. After 2000 hours, the fact that Giap's regular forces were not taking part in the fighting may have confused the French. The French commanders knew that their adversary had several battalions on the outskirts of the city, and they may in the first phase of the fighting have given priority to taking up defensive positions to thwart a major attack, which never came. Morlière probably needed some time to understand that the Vietnamese main forces would not go into action. Then he set his own offensive plan in motion. Thus the fighting only really began at 2130 hours. This marked the start of the long-planned French "coup d'état." In less than twenty-four hours, the French took full control of all public buildings and strategic points in the city and laid siege to the Chinese and Vietnamese quarters. In the following weeks, the Tu Ve fighters would really need the water they had stocked.

If Morlière was taken by surprise at 2000 hours, the same was certainly true of Sainteny. In a cable sent from Hanoi at 1700 hours, he emphasized Ho's "extremely amiable" letter and only mentioned in passing that "other information" had warned of a great attack that evening.[71] When journalists and inexperienced historians discover that decision-makers received advance warnings of dramatic events such as the Japanese attack on Pearl Harbor or the German Operation Barbarossa, they often blame leaders for having failed to heed the warnings. It is easy to forget that in real life, most advance warnings concern events that never happen. It is infinitely more difficult for a real-life decision-maker than for a later historian to separate correct from erroneous warnings. The telegrams Sainteny sent to Saigon on December 19 between 1800 and 1930 hours were in no way alarming. One was about Ho's amiable letter. The other expressed the desire Sainteny shared with d'Argenlieu that the Commissioner of the Republic should as soon as possible reinstall himself in the Governor-General's Palace, given the "extremely favorable circumstances." Sainteny asked Valluy to urgently reconsider his order to defer this symbolic act for a variety of reasons: the exposed character of his current residence; the inconvenience of having to move around so often in a troubled city; the utility of carrying out this operation before the return of Admiral d'Argenlieu, so that he would not be seen as responsible; the excellent effects obtained through the recent reoccupation of the Direction des Finances on the mentality of the Vietnamese population; and the need to avoid scandalizing Minister for Overseas France Moutet when he came. There would never be a better moment, and no serious reactions were to be expected. So, just a little before 2000 hours, Sainteny asked for permission to up the ante even more in the next few days.[72]

When the water and electricity were cut off at 2000 hours, Sainteny was either at home or on his way home. In his memoirs, he claims to have heard the clock of the Yersin hospital strike eight before he left his office. Just as he got in his car, at 2004 hours "exactly," he heard an explosion and saw all lights go out.[73] The sources are not in full agreement as to the exact time the electricity was cut off. One French telegram from Hanoi said 1955 hrs,[74] while a later Vietnamese account says: "At exactly 2003 [hours] on December 19, 1946, electric lights in the sky over Hanoi suddenly went out."[75] In spite of the darkness, Sainteny apparently drove all the way home, because half an hour later Morlière sent an armored car to fetch him at his residence. Around 2100 hours, this car struck a mine. Sainteny, injured and under Vietnamese fire, agonized while waiting to be saved by a half-track.[76] French military confusion during the first hour and a half after 8 p.m., and the fact that Sainteny drove home instead of staying in his office, are facts pointing in the same direction: in spite of all the warnings, the French did not expect an attack at 2000 hours. "Confirmed information indicates Hanoi garrison completely surprised 19 evening," Dèbes informed Valluy directly two days later as evidence of Morlière's incompetence.[77]

What happened on the other side is even more confusing. Although Giap provides an elaborate strategic argument in his memoirs to demonstrate that everything his forces did on December 19 and during the following days and weeks was exactly what he had planned they should do, it seems more likely that only some parts of a general attack plan were carried out. And these operations were conducted in a haphazard manner. The only effective action at 2000 hours was a number of vile attacks on the homes of French civilians by Tu Ve squads (including recently released common criminals), which took some 200 hostages and killed and mutilated 20–30 members of the families who chose to resist. The other Tu Ve operations were purely obstructive: cutting off water and electricity, blocking crossroads with trams and a road with a train, placing mines in the streets, and aimlessly firing mortars and antiaircraft guns. There was no attempt to attack French military forces in their cantonments, and half-hearted attempts to destroy the vital Long Bien bridge (Pont Doumer) and attack the Gia Lam airfield both failed miserably.[78]

Was all this meant as a cover for the taking of hostages? Why didn't the battalions on the outskirts move into the city? Did the Vietnamese leadership vacillate at the last moment? Giap does provide answers to some of these questions in his memoirs. He claims that the regular troops outside the city were needed for the protection of the government and for future operations. A force that is inferior in arms and equipment can never win a battle in a city. It was therefore best to leave just one battalion in Hanoi to defend the indigenous quarter for as long as possible, tie down enemy forces, and set an example of inventiveness and bravery for the rest of the nation to emulate. This is what Giap says, and it seems convincing. But Giap does not admit any of the confusion that is evident from other sources, and he hardly mentions how ill-timed his attack was. To take military action and commit heinous crimes against civilians on December 19, 1946, just as Blum had taken office in Paris and Moutet was preparing to go to Hanoi, was a strategic blunder of enormous proportions, perhaps the biggest political and diplomatic mistake Ho and Giap made in their entire lives. It was the finest gift they could have given the French triumvirate in Saigon: the world's best excuse for breaking with the DRV once and for all, at the cost of only a few French military losses. The big question is then: Did Giap and Ho bungle it themselves? Or did someone in their ranks force their hands?

Since Giap, shortly after the outbreak of war, ordered all military units to destroy the daily order of December 19 with all its appendices,[79] digging into the details of December 19 has been almost taboo in Vietnam. What was Giap's personal role? Did he decide to attack because he anticipated an imminent French coup? Did he try to cancel his operation when he realized that the French were not attacking after all? Did he then fail to stop the Tu Ve? Did they defy an order to cancel the attack because they were afraid the government would bow to French demands for their disarmament? Did anticommunist nationalist infiltrators incite the Tu Ve to plunge into war, perhaps in collusion with French clandestine agents? Before examining these possibilities, let us take a look at the Vietnamese decision-making hierarchy:

Level 1: President Ho Chi Minh, assisted by his personal secretary, Vu Ky.

Level 2a: The party organization: General Secretary Truong Chinh and Le Duc Tho.

Level 2b: The Army: Defense Minister and Commander in Chief Vo Nguyen Giap, working in tandem with the security boss, Tran Quoc Hoan, and Hoang Van Thai. In communications with the French, Hoang Huu Nam, the chief of the Vietnamese Liaison Office, operated as Giap's special delegate.

Level 3: Hanoi military sector under the command of the recently appointed Vuong Thua Vu, who operated under the authority of Hanoi's Resistance Committee, with the following members: Nguyen Van Tran (chair), Vuong Thua Vu (deputy chair), Tran Do (political commissar), Tran Quoc Hoan, Khuat Duy Tien, Dang Viet Chau, Tran Duy Hung, and Le Quang Dao.[80]

Beneath this level again were the various military units, the National Guard, the militia forces (Tu Ve), and the police.

If recent Vietnamese publications are to be trusted, the highest collective authority was the Standing Bureau of the Central Committee of the Party, led by Truong Chinh, and the meeting at Van Phuc from 1430 to 1515 hours was key. As already mentioned, the French intelligence services do not seem to have been aware of the Standing Bureau at all. They thought the top leadership was the Viet Minh Tong Bo, and Truong Chinh and Le Duc Tho do not seem to have been on their radar screen. A SEHAN report claimed that Giap and Ho never parted company in the critical days of December, in order to ensure full coordination of political, diplomatic, and military concerns. This is wrong. As we have seen, Giap was in Hanoi several times, notably on December 19 after the Van Phuc meeting, while Ho Chi Minh stayed in his safe house, and Giap's military headquarters was located in a different place from Ho's.

A little before December 19, the SEHAN received reports of an internal conflict in the Vietnamese Army, with former officers of the colonial army, trained in French methods, opposed by younger officers trained under Giap. The latter were often the sons of veteran party members who had been recommended to undergo training at the recently formed military academies. A study by Giap in April 1947 entitled "Our Liberation War—Strategy and Tactics" denounced "certain people" who were opposed to the strategy of protracted guerrilla warfare on grounds that the Viet Minh did not yet have regular troops able to sustain a guerrilla struggle, and that because the country was so much smaller than China, it would in any case be extremely difficult to apply the Maoist strategy in Vietnam, where the enemy would be able to take control of all the cities and communication routes, thus paralyzing resistance. Moreover, these "certain people" argued, given the enemy troops' potential range of action and the backwardness of the Vietnamese economy, it would be extremely difficult to create a national army on the tactical level. ICP General Secretary Truong Chinh was working with some of the same issues in an organizational directive for the Indochinese Communist Party that was issued on December 22, 1946. It called for a protracted resistance struggle of the whole nation against the reactionary colonial French aggressors, establishing an alliance with the French people against the reactionary colonialists, and establishing solidarity with the Cambodian and Lao peoples and all oppressed peoples in the French Union. The party should protect the people and win the hearts and minds of the people. The aim should be to make the enemy hungry, thirsty, lame, blind, deaf, mute, tired, and bored. The resistance struggle would have three stages, first one of contention *(phong ngu)*, in which the major cities might have to be abandoned, after first having offered violent resistance, then one of equilibrium *(cam cu)*, where the enemy would continually suffer losses, and finally the counteroffensive *(phan cong)*. One can easily imagine that in December 1946, the more tradition-bound military officers may have wanted to engage their forces in a real battle for Hanoi, while Giap and Truong Chinh wanted to keep them in reserve for a protracted armed struggle. In his directive, Truong Chinh distinguished several stages in the struggle and said of the first: "The defensive stage: We may indeed have no choice but to temporarily evacuate the big cities after having fought decisive battles there. (N.B.: We must continuously harass the places that we have temporarily abandoned)" (Giai doan phong ngu: Co the van bat dac do phai tam thoi bo nhung thanh thi lon sau khi khang chien quyet liet o do. [Chu y: Phai luon luon quay nhieu nhung noi tam bo]).[81] Decisive battles—did Giap perhaps seriously consider the possibility of engaging more of his regular forces in the battle for Hanoi?[82]

The Vietnamese military forces in Hanoi included:

- At least four army battalions positioned around Hanoi and one army battalion inside the city defending public buildings, above all, the presidential palace. The unit defending Ho's residence fought bravely on the night of December 19–20, and all of its members were killed.
- Death squads with special tasks, such as to destroy armored cars, probably with Le Hong as political commissar, who is likely to have reported to Tran Quoc Hoan. They played an active part in the operations at 2000 hours. A French witness saw a red signal rocket.[83]
- Tu Ve militia forces, led by a Central Executive Committee, consisting of about 3,500 men, organized in sections and companies in each city neighborhood. They executed sabotage missions and engaged in much ineffective shooting during the evening of December 19. Some of the militiamen had been trained by deserters from the Japanese Army, and they were probably

responsible for taking the French civilian hostages.[84] According to Giap, the commander of the Tu Ve was Le Trung Toan.[85]

We may now return to the key question: at which level was the ultimate decision taken? Did Giap launch the attack because he misconceived French immediate intentions, or did the Tu Ve disobey orders to cancel? Let us first examine arguments supporting the hypothesis that the Vietnamese leaders tried in vain to cancel the attack once they learned that Blum was sending Moutet on a peace mission.

First, Giap and Ho's public appeals for general resistance came after the fighting had begun, not as a signal to attack, as the Van Phuc meeting had decided. Hence the other French garrisons in the north were attacked only later, so the effect of surprise was lost. If Giap had always been fully determined to attack at 2000 hours, then he would probably have been able, in consonance with the order he had sent out that morning, to get his commanders to attack all the French garrisons simultaneously. The failure of the army to catch the French by surprise in other places than Hanoi indicates that the orders they received are likely to have been ambiguous. Giap issued a public order to all military units to fight on all fronts, but this order was only announced well after 2000 hours.[86] Devillers says 2130 hours, just when the French counterattack was beginning in Hanoi.[87]And why was Ho Chi Minh's appeal, the text of which had been approved at the Van Phuc meeting, not read out on Radio Bach Mai until the next day?

We should take a closer look at Ho Chi Minh's appeal and the circumstances surrounding its launch. There are three oddities: The first concerns the text itself, which refers to a desire for peace, instead of immediately urging the people to fight:

Compatriots all over the country!

As we desire peace, we have made concessions. But the more concessions we make, the more the French colonialists press on, for they are bent on reconquering our country.

No! We would rather sacrifice all than lose our country. Never shall we be enslaved! Compatriots! Stand up!

Men and women, old and young, regardless of religious creed, political affiliation, and nationality, all Vietnamese must stand up to fight the French colonialists and save the Fatherland. Those who have rifles will use their rifles; those who have swords will use their swords; those who have no swords will use spades, hoes, or sticks. Everyone must endeavor to oppose the colonialists and save his country!

Members of the army, the self-defense corps, and the militia!

The hour for national salvation has struck! We must shed even our last drop of blood to safeguard our country.

Even if we must endure the greatest hardships in our war of resistance, with our determination to face all sacrifices, we are bound to win.

Long live independent and unified Viet Nam!

Long live the victorious Resistance!

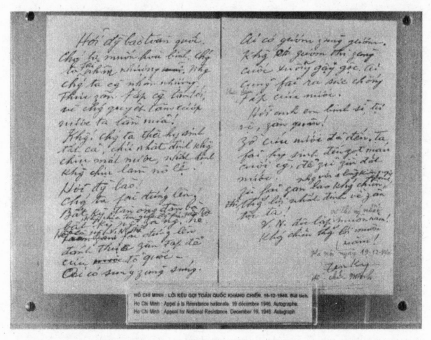

FIGURE 8. Handwritten draft of Ho Chi Minh's famous appeal, dated December 19, 1946: "Fight with your arms, your picks, your spades, your sticks!" Courtesy Ho Chi Minh Museum, Hanoi.

Why did Ho include the first three paragraphs instead of just starting with "Compatriots! Stand up!"? It is as though he were arguing with himself, or seeking to justify his action. This is the first oddity. The second is that Ho never signed the appeal. The entire manuscript is in his handwriting, but the five words suggested by Le Duc Tho at the Van Phuc meeting were added by Truong Chinh in his handwriting, and he also added Ho's signature. According to specialists in Hanoi, it is clear that Ho Chi Minh's signature is written in Truong Chinh's hand. The third oddity is that the appeal was not read out on the radio until the following day. Hence it is dated December 20 in Ho's Collected Works.[88] The sources differ as to when exactly the appeal was broadcast. Devillers claims only on December 21. The French reported to Paris on December 21, however, that Radio Bach Mai had been silent for twenty-four hours, from December 19 to December 20, and that Ho Chi Minh's appeal had been broadcast during the evening of December 20 and again the next morning. Giap's biographer Tran Trong Trung asserts that Giap listened to Ho's appeal on the radio at Tay Mo village in the morning of December 20.[89] The national Vietnamese radio was located at Bach Mai, the same place as Giap's military headquarters. Why was not the appeal broadcast at 2000 hours on December 19 as a signal to attack everywhere at the same time, as the Van Phuc meeting had decided it should? Technical problems, say Hanoi's historians.

Perhaps.

It may be added that the staff of Viet Minh's main journal, *Cuu Quoc*, assumed on December 19 that it would come out as usual the following day. The French later discovered a copy of *Cuu Quoc* dated December 20 with a proclamation from the Viet Minh Committee in Hanoi speaking only of *preparations* for struggle: "The decisive time has come! The Viet Minh front in Hanoi invites its compatriots to remain calm and form the closest possible union, and to prepare themselves even more effectively to rise up once the government's order is received."[90]

The next complicating issue is the regular army's behavior. The battalion inside the city defended public buildings and prepared for a protracted defense of the indigenous and Chinese quarters together with the Tu Ve. Why didn't the regular forces stationed at the city's outskirts take part in the attack at 2000 hours? The strict order received by Ngo Van Chieu to only carry out personal orders from Giap or his two assistants shows that Giap did not fully trust his subordinates. Perhaps the actions of the more disciplined regular army reflect Giap's intentions better than the actions of the Tu Ve. What did the regular army do inside and outside Hanoi after 2000 hours? The first French report to Saigon only said that electricity had been cut off and "V.M. action" started.[91] In the next telegram, electricity had been cut off and fire from Vietnamese mortars and automatic weapons had "begun everywhere simultaneously."[92] A telegram on December 21 added that units of the regular army in the building of the Compagnie Yunnan (inside Hanoi) had opened fire on the Central Liaison Office from 2005 hours.[93] This means, if true, that at least one army unit did open fire before the French troops counterattacked, but such an attack could have resulted from a spontaneous local initiative. Ngo Van Chieu noted in his diary that about fifty young fellows passed by his post at 1830 hours and one of them shouted: "It will be soon, comrade. The victory is ours. Long live President Ho!" A little later, Ngo Van Chieu saw other Tu Ve fighters leave a house armed with hunting guns, one with an enormous saber. He was afraid they might defy orders and asked the commander of his regiment what to do. The answer was: "What do you want to do? Fire at them?"[94] At 1920 hours the commander of the neighboring unit told Chieu that the French troops had been called back to their barracks, and that he thought "it will be for tonight." So forty minutes before the electricity was cut off, at least some of the regular troops had not received any new orders since the order to cancel the attack. Ngo Van Chieu's unit received new orders at 1950 hours. They said it should go round the city and take up a position on the road to Haiphong.

Third, the Tu Ve were poorly organized. They were the result of a merger of the Viet Minh and the VNQDD's self-defense groups, imposed by Giap at the end of

August. An undated Vietnamese report, captured by the French after December 19, concluded that the Tu Ve in Hanoi was "a complex, undisciplined, uncontrollable organization, difficult to reorganize. But with help from the Viet Minh groups, we should expect to be able to rally it to our cause."[95] The great majority of the Tu Ve combatants had no military training. Group and section commanders had been through two training sessions each, of two and three days respectively. A meeting of Hanoi's Resistance Committee on October 18 decided to improve the quality of the training. Hanoi was divided into seven neighborhoods *(khu),* each of which was to select three men to go through a basic course. Then these would be expected to train 100 of their fellow combatants. The main task of the Tu Ve was to defend their own neighborhood. Their principal role was thus defensive, but each *khu* was also expected to recruit enough members to man one death squad, and they would be trained in guerrilla methods and certain offensive operations, notably the destruction of armored vehicles. In a document presented to a regional Viet Minh meeting on October 24, 1946, only 217 Tu Ve fighters were said to be Viet Minh members.[96] In a circular to local Tu Ve commanders dated December 12, they were asked to report on the morale, ideas, and desires of the Vietnamese serving under them, and on whether any of these were "reactionaries," that is, adherents of the China-oriented opposition.[97]

Some of these "reactionaries" saw a Franco-Vietnamese confrontation as the only way to get rid of the Viet Minh and hoped for a Sino-American intervention that would oust the French and the communists at the same time. Moret, the Sûreté boss in Hanoi, noted on December 9 that the upper classes "while contemplating the prospect of war in Hanoi with dread, had come to hope it would come promptly, since this would be their only way to survive." In the weeks before December 19, the French established contact with several anticommunists in Hanoi and Hue. According to a later report from Sainteny, they comprised two tendencies: "the VN-QDD–Dai Viet tendency of a quite narrow nationalism, and who were difficult to approach, and the Catholic-monarchist tendency, whose nationalism was more subtle." The latter were divided into a left-wing faction (Nguyen Manh Ha); a traditional, monarchist, and relatively pro-French faction (Nguyen De, Tran Van Ly); and a violently nationalist faction, which, if it eluded French control, "could turn against us" (Ngo Dinh Diem). Sainteny said Ngo Dinh Diem had placed himself at the junction of all the various tendencies opposing the Viet Minh, and he gave him a "code name" (Jacob), toying with the idea that Diem might play some kind of role in a Hanoi free of the Viet Minh, contending that "the threads of almost every intrigue that is knit . . . either come from him or pass through him."[98]

The VNQDD–Dai Viet tendency had been in decline. Dai Viet leaders such as the former Japanese collaborators Tran Van Lai, Dao Trong Kim, Pham Khac Hoe, and Hoang Xuan Han were taken into protective custody by the French after December 19. The top VNQDD leaders, such as Vu Hong Khanh, who had signed the

March 6 agreement with Ho Chi Minh and Sainteny, and the former minister of foreign affairs Nguyen Tuong Tam, had taken refuge in China, Khanh already in July, but Tam apparently as late as November. But some VNQDD activists remained in Hanoi. In the absence of their leaders, they "see us as their last hope," Sainteny said. As early as October, two VNQDD representatives (Tran Trong Dung, Pham Gia Do) had "found the way to the Commissariat of the Republic."[99] There was also another important actor in Hanoi: Nghiem Ke To, who had served as undersecretary of foreign affairs at the time when Nguyen Tuong Tam was foreign minister. From March to July 1946, Tam and To ran the DRV's diplomacy. In April, with President Ho's approval, they sent former emperor Bao Dai on his fruitless mission to China to try to persuade Chiang Kai-shek to keep some of his troops in Vietnam. When the Chinese withdrew all their forces, To stayed behind. In October, after having narrowly escaped an attempt on his life, he went underground, with a Chinese passport, using the name Ly Hai Kwang. The French files do not say whether he was able to communicate with Nguyen Tuong Tam in Nanjing.[100] On December 19, immediately after the opening of hostilities, Nghiem Ke To was arrested by the French Sûreté, who had had him under surveillance for a long time, but he refused to play any political role in French-occupied territory. Sainteny complained in January that To just wanted to be a simple Chinese citizen. Still, Nghiem Ke To would reappear later as the main leader of a much reduced VNQDD.[101]

Pignon may have had Nghiem Ke To in mind when he affirmed on December 17 that the VNQDD was operating clandestinely in Hanoi, and was infiltrating the Tu Ve with the intention of setting it against the French "in order to create difficulties for the VM leaders."[102] Sainteny and Morlière were just then launching a propaganda campaign to set the regular Vietnamese Army against the Tu Ve,[103] which Morlière followed up on December 19 by demanding that the Tu Ve be disarmed. Hoang Huu Nam's answer to Morlière promised that this would be discussed by the Vietnamese cabinet the following day. Could the Tu Ve have feared being deceived by their government? Their commanders had been informed through Giap's order in the morning that the government had rejected a French demand that they be disarmed. Giap said in his order that the French could be expected to start disarming the militia within the next twenty-four hours. What would the Tu Ve leaders have thought when they heard that Ho and Giap were ready to discuss the French demands? Might they have decided to defy a cancellation order from Giap?

One more troubling fact seems to indicate that the attack did not follow a preset plan: on December 19, the clerks in the government office in Hanoi (the Office of the Northern Region, Bac Bo Phu) continued their normal work, filed documents as late as 1800 hours, and did not seek to destroy even quite sensitive files (which can thus be studied today in the French colonial archives in Aix-en-Provence).[104]

Who ordered the water and electricity to be cut off on December 19? Ngo Van Chieu wrote in his diary that at 2000 hours, the Tu Ve guarding the electric plant "gave the alert."[105] Could someone have infiltrated the Tu Ve guarding the electric plant? The Tu Ve had been infiltrated by the VNQDD, were poorly organized, and were under threat of being disarmed. These three factors could have made it difficult to make them obey an order to postpone the planned assault. Still it seems far-fetched to imagine that a network of infiltrators, with or without French support, would on their own initiative have been able to signal "an alert" setting off all the shooting, mining, killing, and kidnapping that happened immediately after 2000 hours.

By now we have exhausted the arguments for the hypothesis that Giap tried to cancel the attack but failed. There are many troubling facts, but none of them would be accepted as proof in a court of law. Let us turn to evidence indicating that the attack resulted after all from a conscious decision among the top Vietnamese leaders (Ho Chi Minh, Truong Chinh, Le Duc Tho, Vo Nguyen Giap) at their afternoon Van Phuc meeting. The hypothesis is then that Giap did not try to cancel the attack, but dutifully followed the Van Phuc decision in spite of the news that Blum had decided to send Moutet on a peace mission to Hanoi.

First, this is what Vietnamese historians claim today, and what Giap himself asserts in his memoirs. His version is accepted in virtually all the most recent literature, both in Vietnam and abroad. However, we cannot take it for granted that Giap and Vietnam's military and party historians are telling the truth, the whole truth, and nothing but the truth. It just seems natural that their preferred narrative is one in which the party and the military commander were in full control, where everyone agreed with one another and did everything according to plan.

Second, Hanoi's post office knew by 7 p.m. that the attack was going to happen. In an internal Vietnamese letter dated December 23, the "war commissar" at Hanoi's central post office (whose task may have been to alert others by telegraph once fighting had started) said he had been warned of the attack a little after 7 p.m. by the political commissar of the local section of the National Guard.[106] If the National Guard commissar was acting on Giap's orders, this would mean either that Giap never wavered or that he changed his mind several times.

Third, French actions in the late afternoon renewed the fears of an imminent French coup. Starting around 5 p.m., the French soldiers and officers, who had started to spread out through the city, disappeared from the streets again. When he learned this, Giap may have thought that when he said that the French troops would be furloughed, Morlière had been hoodwinking his representative, Hoang Huu Nam. And he may have received this news just as he was trying to convince his men that still more patience was needed; Uncle Ho would need yet another respite to find out what the new French premier would do. Giap was not the kind of man given to panic, but he may have feared that the French were trying to outfox him. Not long after the French troops had been recalled to barracks, Giap received reports that French armored cars had been observed at five strategic locations, and also that a group of French residents in the Hôtel Métropole, who had been reported by the maids to keep guns concealed under their beds, were taking up positions in a restaurant opposite Ho's residence.[107] This news or rumor may have given him the idea that the French were on the verge of taking action, either to disarm the Tu Ve or arrest the Vietnamese leaders. If Giap convinced himself at some point between 1830 and 2003 hours that the French might be about to attack, he may have decided, in order not to lose the initiative, to order his troops into action after all, even at the cost of launching a badly coordinated operation. He may simply have decided to go with what seemed to be the flow of history, rather than making a futile attempt to alter its course. Giap would then have changed his mind twice: in the morning and early afternoon, he had planned to attack; in the late afternoon (upon learning that Blum would send Moutet, and of Morlière's promise to furlough the French troops that evening), he balked; and in the evening (when the French soldiers were recalled to barracks and French armored cars took up strategic positions), he once more decided to proceed with the attack. Regardless of whether Giap wavered or not, it thus seems that he is telling the truth in his memoirs in taking responsibility for the historical plunge:

> The signal for the attack would be the cutting [off] of electricity, followed by cannon fire from the Lang fortress, situated at the periphery [of the city]. We would in this way benefit from the darkness. This was not easy to accomplish. In fact, under the military convention, the Yen Phu electric plant was guarded by a mixed Vietnamese-French patrol. We had secretly to introduce a quantity of explosive material shortly before the time set [l'heure H]. If the enemy had discovered it, he would have used this as a pretext to occupy the plant and take the initiative to attack us throughout the city.[108]

Here, however, the historian Giap misreads his former adversary the same way that the commander Giap may have misunderstood French intentions on December 19. The French needed a much better pretext if they were to launch an all-out attack of their own. They could not use the mere discovery of a plot to introduce explosives into the power plant as a pretext, since their government had forbidden them to take the initiative in the fighting. *They needed Giap to take the initiative.*

The waterworks and electric power station played crucial roles in setting off the attack, especially the Yen Phu plant; the sudden darkness at 2003 hours was noted by everyone. We know from the previous chapter that French intelligence had got hold, well before December 19, of a Vietnamese plan saying a general attack would be initiated by cutting off the water and electricity supply. We also know that Valluy's operational planners in Saigon had planned to cut all telephone lines in Hanoi in the opening phase of the coup they were preparing, either by cutting the lines mechanically or by boosting the electricity (although the latter method would do lasting damage).[109] Both the Yen Phu power plant and the waterworks were situated between Truc Bach Lake and the Red River, north of the Citadel. This was the area where the French launched their most spectacular barricade removal in the days preceding December 19.

One of Moret's Sûreté reports provides a precise description of what happened when the war broke out: "December 19, 1946. At 2000 hours, the Viet Minh blew up the exciter [excitatrice] of the turbine at the electric power station and cut the water supply for the whole city." The Sûreté added more details in another report: three bombs or explosive charges had gone off in the electric power station "after a Vietnamese sabotage of the alternators, into which acid had been poured." How did the Viet Minh get access to the power plant and find out how to sabotage it?

The power station was managed jointly by a French and Vietnamese director and had long been protected by a mixed Franco-Vietnamese guard. In the morning of December 17, a serious incident took place, in which the French sentry killed his Vietnamese colleague. The workers at the plant went on a protest strike, but they subsequently resumed their work at the insistence of the Vietnamese government. On December 19, according to Giap's memoirs, the workers at the power plant, who were members of the self-defense group there, and operated under a leader named Giang, "marvelously succeeded in blowing up the generators at the predetermined time."[110]

After December 19, the Vietnamese power plant director, Hoang Van Ngoc, was arrested by French military police, after having been denounced by his French co-director, Cavalin. Unfortunately, we do not know what the accusation was, but the Sûreté boss, Moret, intervened to obtain Hoang Van Ngoc's release, citing his "anti–Viet Minh" sentiments and praising him for having rendered precious services to the Sûreté. To lend weight to his words, Moret—who, at Pignon's instigation, later received a special promotion for his "vigilance" in December 1946—added: "Mr. Pignon knows about it." The French electricity director, Mr. Cavalin, was unhappy that his Vietnamese co-director was not punished, and he apparently decided to take the law in his own hands. On December 23, he brought a French employee with him to the Vietnamese director's home, and shot Hoang Van Ngoc in the throat, wounding him.[111] Perhaps this was just a private quarrel, but it seems suspicious in light of the essential role the electric plant had played four days earlier. One wonders if the crime committed by the anti–Viet Minh Vietnamese director of the power plant was to shut his eyes, in collusion with the French Sûreté, and allow Giap's agents to bring in their explosives. If he allowed his plant to be sabotaged, this anticommunist Vietnamese director might actually have rendered a precious service to both Giap and Pignon at the same time. Such action may also have pleased the noncommunist nationalists who wanted the French and the Viet Minh to fight each other to clear the way for noncommunist nationalism.

In the end, however, it was the communists who triumphed. Eight years later, when returning to Hanoi after the victory at Dien Bien Phu and the signing of the

Geneva agreement, one of the first places Giap visited in the capital was the Yen Phu electric power plant: "I shook the hands of the workers for a long time ... who, on the night of December 19, 1946, had blown up the generators, giving the signal for the general attack."[112]

FAIT ACCOMPLI

Even today we do not have sufficient evidence to draw a final conclusion as to whether the attack was made in defiance of the high command's orders or if General Giap and President Ho, or just Giap, tried to withdraw the attack order at some point after 1600 hours, and then went back on their cancellation and reordered the action at some point after 1700 hours. Giap and Ho were clearly under pressure from below. Among the Vietnamese youth, there was a widespread urge to fight the French, take revenge, and liberate the fatherland. The enigma of what happened on the Vietnamese side from 1700 to 2000 hours will perhaps never quite be resolved.[113]

If the responsibility for the ultimate decision remains shadowy, it is clear that the whole top leadership knew that an attack had been prepared. Giap says in his memoirs that alternative courses of action had been considered. A Japanese advisor had suggested infiltrating a commando into the Citadel and attacking Morlière's headquarters directly. This was dismissed as too risky, and Giap did not yet have a sufficiently trained unit for such daring special missions. The option of withdrawing from the city without a fight and organizing a counteroffensive from bases in the hinterland had been chosen by all Vietnamese resistance leaders in the past, whenever there had been a Chinese attack on Thang Long (Hanoi). This option was seriously considered, but it would mean losing a chance to set the people a heroic example. Giap considered it important, he says in his memoirs, that Hanoi take the lead in the national resistance. Although there was no prospect of winning a battle for Hanoi, where the French had concentrated substantial and well-equipped forces, by taking the initiative and then defending the Sino-Vietnamese sections of the city for as long as possible before withdrawing, the Vietnamese forces in the capital would provide the Vietnamese younger generation with a heroic example. This would facilitate the task of building a strong army from the rear. Fighting in the national capital itself, might also enhance the internal legitimacy of the DRV in Vietnam and make it more shameful for "traitors" to set up an alternative government in collaboration with the French. The French would also probably have considered a defensive withdrawal as a voluntary abdication, abrogating all previous agreements, and have looked for more manageable local representatives to deal with. These are some of the reasons given by Giap for the choice he made before issuing the fatal order on the morning of December 19. In this way, the battle-tested hero sought to make sense of what he had done when he was young.[114] In his account, everything went according to plan, and he hardly mentions the diplomatic aspects of the struggle for national independence. There were not many options left to the Vietnamese government in December 1946. It had been driven into a corner by the French occupation of Haiphong and Langson and the pressures applied by Sainteny and Morlière. But it had one option that Giap's military brain does not seem to have considered. The government could have chosen to remain in place in Hanoi, wait a little longer for Blum to make his policy known, receive Moutet in Hanoi and present him with good reasons for replacing d'Argenlieu as high commissioner. Ho Chi Minh is likely to have understood this opportunity, as are Hoang Minh Giam and Hoang Huu Nam. Until December 19, Ho resisted the pressure for military action, refusing to let himself be trapped. On December 19, he either lost control of himself or of his men, and stumbled.

The French in Indochina were playing with fire. They steadily escalated the pressure on Ho Chi Minh, while at the same time agitating the Vietnamese population through propaganda, provocations, and reprisals in the streets. The purpose was to either force Ho to make a clean break or to provoke a split between "moderates" and "extremists." Pignon and d'Argenlieu chose the first option and won. With some encouragement from Valluy, Sainteny gambled on the second option, hoping to save his friend Ho for France. Sainteny was the bait in the French trap, and he was devoured. But the trappers in Saigon were not just up against the Vietnamese, they were also seeking to entrap their own government in Paris. It was a race against time, to prevent the new French premier from interfering with the progress toward war. When the lights went out in Hanoi, a personal message to President Ho Chi Minh bearing the signature of Prime Minister Léon Blum was lying on Valluy's desk in Saigon. Valluy let it remain there for as long as he dared before fulfilling his duty and transmitting it to the addressee. In the morning of December 20, Valluy informed Paris that he had been on the verge of transmitting Blum's message to the Vietnamese president when he got the tragic news from Hanoi. He would now "in any case . . . nevertheless, in spite of the events" try to reach the addressee. Ho got the message from a messenger who carried it through the lines, and immediately wrote a reply. Sainteny, however, did not find this reply worthy of being forwarded to the French premier, and suggested that Ho should be so informed.[115]

Blum saw d'Argenlieu in his Paris office on the morning of December 19, before the admiral took off for Tunis and Cairo on his way back to Saigon. The socialist veteran laid out for the Gaullist admiral his humanitarian philosophy concerning the future of the French Union. The high commissioner, reassured by the support he had got from de Gaulle two days earlier and unmoved by Blum's lofty ideas, assured him of his complete agreement. This, at least, is what Blum told the press afterward.[116] Paris was informed of the events in Hanoi only around noon on December 20, twenty-three hours after the event (given the seven-hour time difference).[117] Blum at once smelled a rat, and urgently ordered Valluy to negotiate a suspension of hostilities "if it is possible without compromising the position of the troops and of French civilians." He had this order signed by Chief of Staff Alphonse Juin. He also informed Valluy that Moutet would arrive shortly in order to "try and prevent the definitive outbreak of hostilities." Juin asked Valluy for precise information about what had happened and what had motivated the French occupation of public buildings on December 18. At the same time, Valluy was asked to forward a new telegram to Ho, signed both by Blum and Moutet, pleading with the president to terminate hostilities on his side. Blum and Moutet assured Ho Chi Minh of their desire to keep the peace and apply past agreements, if only it could be done fairly. But no violation of the agreements would be tolerated.[118]

While the order to Valluy and the message to Ho were transmitted to Saigon, Moutet declared in the National Assembly that the government would defend French interests by peaceful means if possible, but would refuse to let anyone impose anything on it with violence. Vincent Auriol, the Assembly's Speaker, who would soon be elected the first president of the French Fourth Republic, read out a message of sympathy for the French combatants, which an MRP deputy was proposing to adopt. Blum intervened to say that while he was not opposed to adopting the message, the lack of precise information from Hanoi left some hope that the events might be less serious than feared. He did not mention either his order to Valluy to negotiate a suspension of hostilities or his telegram to Ho Chi Minh.[119] Not a single French communist or socialist deputy voted against the message of sympathy for the Frenchmen fighting the Democratic Republic of Vietnam, which was adopted unanimously, a notable example of nationalism trumping ideology.

Before Valluy received the order from Blum to seek a suspension of hostilities, the general had already done the opposite. He instructed Morlière to take "energetic action" against the Vietnamese forces, reopen the Haiphong–Hanoi road, and take full control of all traffic between the two cities. In defiance of the military instructions d'Argenlieu had received from the French government on December 10, Valluy now also reduced the French military capability in southern Indochina by sending reinforcements to Haiphong, while also demanding that ten more battalions be dispatched urgently from France.[120] When Valluy received his government's orders, he decided to ignore them and tell Paris why:

> I honestly don't see how I can obtain a suspension of fighting. We have lost contact with the VN government, which is undoubtedly in the view of all French and foreign observers [a word missing] the aggression. It seems that for the sake of French prestige, the request for a suspension of fighting should come from that government ... Yet, if it proves impossible for General Morlière to reach President Ho, I am prepared to make the text of the message from "Monsieur Président Blum" known over Radio Saigon. I feel obliged, however, to draw the attention of the government to the very serious consequences that this would have on the morale of the troops, engaged in a hard struggle, and of the French civilians, who are strongly affected by the assassinations perpetrated on their fellow citizens with a savagery and a perfidy

that will be related to you elsewhere. I add that even indigenous public opinion would not understand.[121]

This was followed by a stream of messages to prove the "premeditation" of the attack. Blum now resigned himself to his fate; in the afternoon of December 23, Juin assured Valluy that the previous instructions had been due to lack of information.[122] That same evening, Blum made a new declaration in the National Assembly, stating that he had been disappointed in his hopes for more reassuring news. He now emphasized that the "necessary orders had been given without any wavering and without any delay," meaning Valluy's orders, not his own. Blum confirmed that France had been obliged to face violence and assured that the French in Indochina and "friendly peoples" could count unreservedly on the vigilance and resolution of his government. He then again brought up the themes he had emphasized in his conversation with d'Argenlieu, focusing on his principled rejection of colonialism: colonial possessions would be justified only the day they cease to be such.[123] These avowals aroused no excitement either in the Assembly or the press. Blum's views were well known. The main point now was that he had loyally stood up for France in the immediate conflict at hand.

In the late evening of December 23, an unanimous Assembly—including all its communist and socialist members—decided to allow the government to transfer funds from one part of the defense budget to another so that reinforcements could be sent to Indochina.[124] The press as a whole praised Blum. Pierre Courtade said in the communist mouthpiece L'Humanité that Blum's statement had been "perfectly reasonable." The premier had pointed out "the only possible solution: negotiations as soon as peace and order have been restored." Franc-Tireur highly appreciated Blum's anticolonialist statements, while Robert Verdier in Le Populaire evoked the "unjust destiny," which had confronted Blum's new government with severe responsibilities. The same concern for the socialist veteran's unjust destiny motivated a comment by Alain Guichard in L'Aube: "Even if it is impossible to subscribe to everything that the head of government affirms, his sincerity and the struggle inside him between the hard realities and his old pacifist dreams give reason for sympathy."[125]

Among the French in Saigon, there were sighs of relief. Plans were being laid for taking Moutet on a tour of the Indochinese Federation, with stopovers in Vientiane and Phnom Penh, and thwarting any idea he might have of wanting to see Ho Chi Minh. Meanwhile, almost recovered from his wounds in the Hanoi hospital, Sainteny could not quite forget the sympathy he had come to feel for the Vietnamese president. One week after he was wounded, he wrote to a friend in Saigon about his desire to know why the Viet Minh leaders had suddenly decided on a suicidal policy. Who had wanted it, and who had been against it? Had Ho Chi Minh enjoyed any freedom of action? Perhaps they had suddenly realized that time was running out, he speculated, since every false move would have the effect of improving the French position. Sainteny found it difficult to believe that Ho had himself been party to such an act of insanity, and he felt almost certain that the president had been working under severe constraint. He wondered if he would ever find out what had happened.[126]

Sainteny would meet Ho again, as the first French representative to the Democratic Republic of Vietnam after the fall of Dien Bien Phu and the Geneva accords in 1954. He would also serve as host for the first secret talks between Henry Kissinger and Le Duc Tho in Paris on August 6, 1969, three weeks before Ho Chi Minh died on September 2, 1969, Vietnam's Independence Day. When Sainteny himself died in 1978, three years after Vietnam's final unification, he had still not found out what happened on the day Giap took the bait.

7

If Only . . .

Historical events change the fate of individuals as much as nations. During the first twelve days of the French Indochina War, the father of the Vietnamese historian Duong Trung Quoc took part in the fighting in Hanoi. On December 31, he was killed near Long Bien bridge. Until recently, I had no idea that my Vietnamese colleague had been so personally engaged in the tragedy of 1946, but in July 2007, after we had known each other for almost twenty years, Quoc suddenly asked if I knew what his name meant. It does not mean "Duong the Chinese," he explained, "although 'Trung Quoc' means 'China.' My 'Trung Quoc' has a different sense. It means 'Duong Loyal to the Nation.' When my father said farewell to my grandmother in December 1946, he told her that if he became the father of a son, his name should be Duong Trung Quoc. I was born on June 2, 1947."

This book revises the history of the origin of the First Indochina War on two main points. First, the signing of the Franco-Vietnamese agreement of March 6, 1946, recognizing Vietnam as a "free state," did not result from any temporary pragmatic, liberal, or moderate ascendancy among French colonial decision-makers. As of late February and early March, France was ready to launch a military reconquest of northern Indochina to follow up its reconquest of the south, if the negotiations with Ho Chi Minh's government should fail. But the French sailed into a Chinese trap. Peace was imposed by China, which forced the two parties to sign a deal on terms neither really wanted. Chiang Kai-shek's government told France to sign the agreement or else risk international war. The Chinese also leaned heavily on Ho Chi Minh. He too signed under Chinese constraint. When the agreement was signed, none of the signatories genuinely intended to implement it faithfully. In the following months, however, a constituency was built both in France and Vietnam for a "policy of accords" that might perhaps have preserved the peace.[1]

Second, the outbreak of war on December 19 was not a premeditated and well-coordinated Vietnamese act of aggression, with simultaneous attacks on all French garrisons in the north, as some recent accounts, both Vietnamese and Western, say. To be sure, it was the Vietnamese who opened fire, just after 8 p.m.; the attack was in accordance with elements of a premeditated plan; and it probably followed a decision taken by the Standing Bureau of the ICP at a meeting that same afternoon. But the attacks on the other French garrisons came only later, and they did not take the French by surprise. Something went wrong at the Vietnamese headquarters that day. Either the leaders were not in control of their forces or they made a momentous blunder—or both. The Vietnamese militia took the offensive just when Léon Blum's new French government had decided to send Minister for Overseas France Marius Moutet on a peace mission to Hanoi. Thus Giap saved High Commissioner d'Argenlieu and General Valluy from what they feared most: a resumption of talks between the French and Vietnamese governments over their heads. Regardless of whether or not Giap ordered or authorized the attack at 8 p.m., or just lost control, he fell into a French trap made in Saigon.

Was the outbreak of war inevitable? Hardly. As of 1946, the great powers, China, Great Britain, the United States, and the Soviet Union, wanted France to show restraint and cooperate with Vietnam. Ho Chi Minh and Léon Blum shared the same wish. Once Blum was elected French premier, the two leaders tried their best to get in touch with each other and prevent the feared outbreak of hostilities. If the timetables of December 19 had been slightly different, if French Commissioner Jean Sainteny had replied positively to Undersecretary for Foreign Affairs Hoang Minh Giam's request for a meeting in the morning, if General Morlière had stuck to his decision to furlough his troops, if the message Blum had sent Ho the day before had not been withheld in General Valluy's Saigon office, if Minister of Defense Vo Nguyen Giap had kept his head, or if someone had prevented the Van Phuc electric power station from being sabotaged, then people in Hanoi might not have heard Ho's call to fight with sticks and spades the following day. The imminent arrival of Moutet's peace mission would instead have been the subject on everyone's lips.

Georges Bidault's outgoing government had made clear to Admiral d'Argenlieu and General Valluy on December 14 that they must not be at fault in any new incidents,[2] so Giap's fear of an imminent French attack was unfounded. He could not know it at the time, of course, but we now know that the French would *not* have launched any major attack if the Vietnamese had kept calm. If Ho had been informed earlier of Blum's decision to dispatch Moutet to Hanoi, he might have persuaded

Giap to wait. The DRV had everything to gain from a chance to alert Blum's government to the French violations of the March 6 and September 14 agreements, and Ho had systematically prepared to do so by drafting a memorandum with seventy-six incriminating appendices.[3]

The question of whether or not the outbreak of war was avoidable invites two additional questions, one small and one big. How and by whom could the outbreak of war have been prevented? And to what extent would this have changed Vietnamese and world history? While the second question calls for a counterfactual analysis of the First and Second Indochina Wars as a whole, the first one relates only to the events analyzed in this book. This concluding chapter will skip the larger question and focus on the might-have-beens in 1946, while at the same time examining what happened in the immediate aftermath of December 19. The aim is to identify the actors who might have changed history.

THE GREAT POWERS

By December 1946, China was no longer in a position to prevent war between France and Vietnam. The withdrawal of its occupation troops from May to September removed China's leverage. China, Britain, and the United States had all been relieved to see France and Vietnam sign the March 6 accords. The Foreign Office and the State Department had worried that France might break its engagements and enter into a costly war. France would be acting against its own best interests in doing so, they thought, since it did not have sufficient resources to wage a colonial war. After the Chinese withdrawal, the United Kingdom and United States had more leverage than China, since France depended on them for arms and equipment, but they did not want to antagonize France by threatening sanctions. U.S. President Harry S Truman had not inherited his predecessor's urge to liberate Indochina from France, and the State Department's European Office warned against doing anything that might offend French amour propre.[4] This is why the early December warnings from the head of the State Department's Southeast Asia Division, Abbot Low Moffat, went unheeded in Washington.

The conflict between Moffat and the Europe-focused leaders of the State Department had a British parallel. The young C. M. Andersson, who handled French Indochina in the Foreign Office, was critical of French intransigence, but his suggestions for action were ignored.[5] The British assistance in pacifying southern Indochina during September 1945–February 1946 had caused much criticism throughout the Commonwealth. Supreme Allied Commander Southeast Asia Lord Louis Mountbatten had been exasperated when France seemed about to go to war in March, and he had sighed with relief when the March 6 agreement was signed,[6] but when the policy of agreement was undermined, the British government did not interfere.

Chiang Kai-shek's government also had to tread carefully, since it did not want to set any precedent for international mediation in its conflict with the Chinese communists; yet, shortly before December 19, the Chinese ambassador to the United Kingdom proposed a joint intervention by Britain, China, and the United States to the British Foreign Office. And on December 24, 1946, the Chinese ambassador in Paris approached his British colleague with a proposal to instruct the British, American, and Chinese consuls in Hanoi to intervene with a view to arriving at a cease-fire. The Foreign Office discussed the Chinese proposals and informed the Chinese embassy that any intervention was thought unwise, and that the United States was taking "a similar line to our own."[7] This was correct. On December 23, Director John Carter Vincent of the Office of Far Eastern Affairs in the State Department warned his superiors that "given the present elements in the situation, guerilla warfare may continue indefinitely."[8] Then Undersecretary of State Dean Acheson, who directed U.S. foreign policy during the absences of Secretary of State James Byrnes, invited the French ambassador, Henri Bonnet, to a meeting. His purpose was not, in Bonnet's words "to embarrass us or to affect us in the defense of our interests in Indochina." He just mentioned the availability of U.S. good offices, an offer Bonnet promptly declined. Bonnet interpreted the meeting as an expression of American goodwill, linked to the State Department's fear of provoking an upsurge of anticolonialism in American public opinion that might compromise U.S. interests in Europe.[9] He was right. The main reason for the U.S. and British hands-off policy was not that Ho Chi Minh was a communist, but the need for French support in Europe. Washington was far more concerned by French than by Vietnamese communism.

Abbot Low Moffat was still in Southeast Asia when the war broke out in Hanoi. On December 19, he asked for permission to return to Washington in order to make his case for mediation.[10] He was instead instructed to participate in an innocuous conference in Batavia (Jakarta). In late December, while there, he impressed on a Dutch colleague that the Indochinese impasse could only be resolved through American mediation, and complained that his government was turning a deaf ear to his arguments. The Dutchman reported what Moffat had said to the French. This led to French diplomatic representations in Washington, obliging Moffat's colleagues to explain. They vowed to a French diplomat that Moffat had never said what he was supposed to have said, and the Frenchman declared himself satisfied. This was exactly what he had wanted to hear. In diplomacy, unlike in science, a transparent lie is often preferable to an inconvenient truth.[11]

In January 1947, while pitched battles were being fought in the indigenous quarters of Hanoi and Hue, the State Department studied Ho Chi Minh's documentation of how France had sabotaged the March 6 and modus vivendi agreements. Acheson adopted a hands-off approach, but when George C. Marshall, with his experience in China, took over as secretary of state, he decided to instruct U.S. Ambassador Jefferson Caffery to tell the French foreign minister that it might be impossible to prevent an Indochina debate in the UN Security Council if France did not show more generosity. On February 3, 1947, after listening to the U.S. ambassador's concerns, the incoming foreign minister in the socialist Paul Ramadier's coalition government, Georges Bidault, promised that France would indeed be generous, and he let Caffery know that d'Argenlieu's days in Saigon were numbered. Washington promptly returned to its polite silence.[12]

So, whereas China lacked the power to prevent the war, the United Kingdom and the United States did not want to risk adverse French reactions. The Soviet Union had the same priority. Moscow was primarily concerned with its relationship to France and kept clear of any open support of Ho Chi Minh.[13] The Soviet Foreign Service, however, also had a "Moffat." Ambassador to France Alexander E. Bogomolov had followed French Indochina policy and was better informed on the subject than anyone in the Soviet capital. In 1945, Bogomolov had expressed himself in favor of establishing an international trusteeship for Indochina, something Franklin Roosevelt had often proposed, but he had been instructed by Moscow that this was not Soviet policy. In October 1945, Bogomolov forwarded a telegram from President Ho to Stalin, explaining that France had forfeited its sovereignty in Indochina through collaboration with Japan, and that Vietnam was upholding its right to independence. The Soviet leaders read and discussed the telegram, but decided to leave it unanswered. In January 1947, the French ambassador to Moscow was told by Foreign Minister Vyacheslav Molotov that "he hoped France and Vietnam would come to an agreement satisfying both parties," without reestablishing a regime of "colonial domination." But Molotov said nothing about bringing up the matter in the UN Security Council.[14] The Soviet leaders did not take up the cause of their Vietnamese comrades until Mao's victory in the Chinese Civil War, when Stalin reluctantly agreed to invite Ho Chi Minh to Moscow.[15]

To sum up, the importance of France for the postwar settlement in Europe immunized it from great power interference in Indochina. Only Chiang Kai-shek's China proposed to do something, and it could not do it alone.

D'ARGENLIEU, PIGNON, AND VALLUY

French High Commissioner Georges Thierry d'Argenlieu and his two main advisors, Commissioner of Political Affairs Léon Pignon and Supreme Commander General Jean-Etienne Valluy, had sufficient power to prevent the Indochina War, but no intention of doing so. They had come to see it as desirable, and it was they who brought it about by transforming a customs conflict in Haiphong into a major military operation, and then pressuring Ho Chi Minh to change his government. Their problem was that their own government in Paris had made clear, after the Haiphong massacre, that France must not be at fault if any further incidents were to occur. They could not take decisive military action in Hanoi unless the adversary took the initiative. D'Argenlieu was in Tunis on his way back from France when he learned of the Vietnamese attack. He arrived in Saigon on December 23, convened his federal cabinet, and affirmed that the initiative and responsibility for the attack belonged "exclusively and manifestly to the Hanoi government. . . . The federal government unanimously rejects the idea of resuming negotiations with the current Ho–Giap team." D'Argenlieu expressed his satisfaction with the turn of events, noting in his diary that the "flight" of the Vietnamese government "liberates us from obligations that the Comnindo itself has recognized as dangers— Mr. Moutet in particular. . . . Personally, I have since September 1945 faithfully executed the policy of agreement in Indochina. It has borne fruit everywhere, except with the Hanoi government. It's over [C'est fini]."[16] What comes out clearly in Frédéric Turpin's superbly researched study De Gaulle, les gaullistes et l'Indochine, 1940–1956 is that d'Argenlieu received constant backing for his policy of firmness from General de Gaulle himself after he had left the French government on January 20. De Gaulle also strongly supported d'Argenlieu in his disagreements with General Leclerc. De Gaulle criticized Leclerc for having waited so long to reoccupy northern Indochina. He supported d'Argenlieu in trying to prevent Ho Chi Minh from being invited to France for negotiations in summer 1946. During the conference at Fontainebleau, de Gaulle contacted Prime Minister Bidault to make sure he did not bow to Vietnamese demands. He strongly supported d'Argenlieu's policy in November–December, receiving him regularly at Colombey-les-Deux-Eglises, and notably urged d'Argenlieu not to give up his post when the government sought to replace him.[17] On December 17, d'Argenlieu saw de Gaulle for more than three hours at Colombey, and de Gaulle told him that as far as Indochina was concerned, d'Argenlieu, not the government, represented France.[18]

After this encounter, d'Argenlieu noted in his diary that since Blum's new government could not be expected to clarify matters, the only remaining possibility was "local firmness" (fermeté sur place) so as to "deliver ourselves from this dictatorship and this Vietnamese drug."[19] After he learned of the December 19 events, d'Argenlieu hoped that they marked the end of both the March 6 accord and the modus vivendi agreement. Back in Saigon, he told the British consul on December 25 that as soon as France had established firm control of the main centers in the north, a new Annamite government would be formed. The French had several contacts outside of Ho Chi Minh's government, and the possibility of reinstalling Emperor Bao Dai should not be overlooked. Shortly afterward, Pignon told the British consul that any republican solution in Vietnam would be either communist or fascist, so it was better to restore the monarchy. Bao Dai, however, was not even in Vietnam, and he was not keen to return there. He lived in Hong Kong, on a French subsidy. From December 20 to 29, he visited Guangzhou, where he met with some noncommunist Vietnamese who were busy setting up a "government in exile," but on returning to Hong Kong, he declared himself disappointed with the trip.[20]

Who else could the French recruit as collaborators? It is not easy for an occupying power to build an alternative leadership for a people that already has leaders, no matter how undesirable they may be. U.S. Vice-Consul James O'Sullivan discussed this problem in a report to Washington. He found the field extremely limited. The leaders of the Viet Nam Nationalist Party (Viet Nam Quoc Dan Dang, or VNQDD) were in China and had little support in Tonkin. The Catholics had few leaders, and they disagreed among themselves. Ngo Dinh Diem was a possibility, but he was "very nationalistic"; to get his support, the French would have to yield more than they had given Ho Chi Minh. O'Sullivan saw the return of Bao Dai as just a remote possibility, and found it more likely that Ho Chi Minh would once again become acceptable to the French as an interlocutor.[21] This was what d'Argenlieu was most keen to prevent. He pleaded with the French government to publicly exclude any future contact with Ho.

Léon Pignon, d'Argenlieu's policy advisor, agreed. He had always looked for ways to draw key Vietnamese leaders into voluntary cooperation, which he thought it possible to achieve through "psychological shocks." The way to provoke such shocks was to take drastic political initiatives. Pignon had been instrumental in drafting de Gaulle's declaration of March 24, 1945, but he regretted that de Gaulle had waited so long to make it. Since the offer to establish a democratic Indochinese Federation with a high degree of autonomy for its constituent parts came after the Japanese coup of March 9, 1945, and Bao Dai's proclamation of a Japan-sponsored state of Vietnam, France seemed to be acting under pressure. The declaration was thus not the intended positive shock, but instead provoked adverse reactions.[22] The same was true of the March 6, 1946, agreement. It had been signed under pressure. Pignon had taken part in negotiating it, as advisor to Sainteny in Hanoi. He also took part in the June–August negotiations at Fontainebleau, south of Paris, contributing actively to their failure.[23] From October 1946, he used the services of the Sûreté to cultivate relations with Vietnamese anticommunists, aiming to set up a new leadership around Bao Dai. In a December 17 report, Pignon asserted that the future of Indochina could be considered with confidence once the current team in Hanoi had disappeared: "Our objective is clearly fixed: to move the quarrel that we have with the Viet Minh party over to the interior Annamite level."[24]

After December 19, Saigon was in an optimistic mood. Pignon laid out a strategy for putting together a new temporary Vietnamese leadership, and he was disappointed when the main noncommunists refused to go along.[25] He considered it vital, in preparing the ground for new leaders to emerge, to remove any illusion that France might ever talk to Ho Chi Minh again. To reopen negotiations with Ho would lead to the loss of all French influence in Indochina, he claimed, and subsequently to the disintegration of the whole French empire.[26] Yet it was necessary to acknowledge the existence of strong nationalist sentiments and reconsider the two stumbling blocks in the 1946 negotiations: the unification of the three *ky* and the question of independence. On these points, Pignon did not agree with d'Argenlieu; he wanted it made known—so as to attract new partners—that France would fulfill its obligations under the March 6 agreement.

Pignon's recommendations in January 1947, which built on his efforts since October, were strikingly similar to the policy he would adopt as high commissioner in 1948–50.[27] At the Pau Conference in 1950, it was he who organized the liquidation of the Indochinese Federation, conceived in the government declaration of March 24, 1945, which he himself had drafted. He replaced it in 1950 with a short-lived structure of three associated states. As early as the end of 1946, Pignon had wanted to provoke a "psychological shock" by publicly endorsing Vietnam's national unification, scrapping the Indochinese Federation, and arranging for the return of Bao Dai. The French government of Paul Ramadier, who succeeded Blum on January 22, 1947, agreed more with Pignon than with d'Argenlieu. When Ramadier presented his new tripartite government to the French National Assembly, he stated that in future, France would face representatives of the "Annamite people" and would "not fear to see realized, if this were the wish of the population, the union of the three Annamite countries, nor refuse to allow Vietnam independence."[28] D'Argenlieu's and Pignon's visions were at odds, but they agreed on the need to break with Ho Chi Minh once and for all. Pignon's and the French socialists' views on the question of Vietnamese unity converged, but the socialists (Moutet and Ramadier) were ardent republicans, did not fancy a monarchic solution, and would not rule out the possibility of talking to Ho Chi Minh once again.

The third member of the Saigon triumvirate, General Valluy, had until October been a source of moderation, since he understood the limitations of French military capabilities. His mood changed, however, and he personally took the most drastic decisions of all in November. How could he act so recklessly? The result was to spread his forces thinly and expose them to the danger of protracted, "dirty" counterinsurgency warfare. And he knew it. Why did he give up his initial preference for concentrating on Cochinchina? Why did he not follow through with his plan to withdraw from Langson—even from Hanoi—and concentrate his forces in the strategically important Haiphong region? Why was Admiral Barjot the only prominent French senior officer who continued to insist on Cochinchina's primacy? Part of the explanation is the exasperation—indeed, a "psychological shock"—felt by the French in Saigon when the southern rebels proved their loyalty and discipline in implementing the cease-fire on October 31, and when the Cochinchinese president took his own life. The reaction was to look for some drastic remedy and to seek comfort in vague hopes that the Viet Minh edifice might crumble if only France displayed sufficient determination. Valluy conceded later that his biggest mistake had been to underestimate the adversary.[29] In November 1946, he recalled, something that until then had been taboo, was suddenly thinkable: "using force no longer seemed doomed to failure. . . . One could certainly win, and a different government, without the Viet Minh clique, might come to an understanding with us."[30] What he was actually saying here was that by force of circumstances, he and other French decision-makers had succumbed to wishful thinking.

The Saigon triumvirate bore the main responsibility for the outbreak of the Indochina War. They had wanted it, and they pushed for it.

MORLIÈRE AND SAINTENY.

What about the Frenchmen on the front line in Hanoi—the hapless Morlière and the pragmatic Sainteny? They did not want to break with Ho Chi Minh. Morlière thought he was faithfully carrying out his government's policy by cooperating with the DRV. Sainteny played a subtle game of trying to provoke a split in the Vietnamese leadership through a series of calculated provocations. Both followed instructions from the war party in Saigon, and neither had any direct contact with government circles in Paris. They were both insecure in their judgments. On December 12, 1946, Morlière flirted, like Valluy, with the illusion that if the DRV were to suffer a clear military defeat, the Vietnamese people might grow weary and seek new leaders who would listen to the "voice of reason." After December 19, however, Morlière became his old self again and warned emphatically against the road France was taking. Even if many "Annamites" were hostile to the Viet Minh, he said, they still lined up behind Ho Chi Minh. France was not just fighting the Viet Minh, but the entire population, or most of it. Morlière recommended renewed talks with Ho Chi Minh and a negotiated cease-fire. Then a date for the referendum on the unification of the three ky should be fixed. After the referendum, there should be general elections to representative assemblies in all three Indochinese countries. If France continued down its present road, this would lead to the rapid loss of Indochina as a whole.[31] No one listened to Morlière. He was a voice crying in the wilderness. His only consolation would be that history proved him right.

During the December crisis, Sainteny plunged deep into wishful thinking, much deeper than Valluy. He expected the Viet Minh's recent edifice to come tumbling down at its first serious defeat, and he assured the U.S. vice-consul that it would be possible to find new, independent leaders to form a government.[32] On December 26, he imagined that the eyes of the Vietnamese had been opened at last. France would now be able to elicit cooperation from unexpected quarters if it could only convince people that the Viet Minh leaders had been ousted for good. To achieve this aim, Sainteny favored a pincer movement to deliver a decisive blow to the "Hanoi government."[33] Sainteny had played a crucial role in negotiating the March 6 agreement, and in his later memoirs, this was what he wanted remembered. He had less reason to be proud of his role in December, when the Saigon triumvirate used him as the bait in their trap.

BIDAULT

The most powerful of all French politicians in 1946 was Georges Bidault, prime minister, foreign minister, and chair of the Cominindo until Léon Blum took over on December 18, and then foreign minister again from January 22, 1947. He was also powerful in the month he was out of government, since Blum depended on parliamentary support from the Christian Democrats. Could Bidault have set history on a different course? He had the power to do so, and he could easily have got socialist and communist support for a peace policy. But his main concern was not peace, but the integrity of the French empire. Bidault avoided any direct contact with the Vietnamese president, protected d'Argenlieu against those who wanted to replace him, and refused to make any substantial concessions to Vietnamese nationalism.[34] He was committed to the French empire—or union—as a whole. A "policy of abandonment" in Indochina could encourage nationalism in other colonies. If a link in the imperial chain were allowed to break, the empire as a whole might disintegrate. At the crucial Cominindo meeting on November 29, 1946, the day after Bidault had resigned, so that he was continuing just in a caretaker capacity, Bidault's key argument was: "There is a local problem, which concerns Indochina, and a general problem, which concerns the French Union. They cannot be separated. We must not do anything in Indochina that may serve as a precedent, especially as regards Morocco or Tunisia."[35] Well into the Indochina War, Bidault would continue to oppose moves to grant Vietnam independence, even as part of the "Bao Dai solution."[36] In 1954, Bidault tried to save French Indochina by getting the United States to intervene militarily in the battle for Dien Bien Phu. In agreeing to an international conference on Indochina at Geneva, his hope was to make China and the Soviet Union abandon their support for the DRV. Only after a cabinet crisis, in which Bidault lost power, did a new government, led by Pierre Mendes-France, arrive at a deal in Geneva. After his fall from power, Bidault stuck to his principles, and in May 1958, when the MRP refused to support his attempt to form a government in defense of French Algeria, and his old nemesis de Gaulle returned to power, he finally broke with his party. When de Gaulle gave up Algeria in 1962, Bidault joined the political underground and was forced to go into exile. He lived on until 1983.

In March 1949, speaking of the responsibility for the outbreak of war two and a half years earlier, the socialist Oreste Rosenfeld said: "If we truly want to determine who was responsible, I do not hesitate to say that the great responsibility falls on the government of 1946, which let its high commissioner formulate a policy contrary to government policy. You know very well that the high commissioner,

M. Georges Thierry d'Argenlieu, appointed by General de Gaulle, had exorbitant powers in Indochina. He was not even under the authority of the Minister for Overseas France, but directly under [that of] the premier and so of the government. . . . The great responsibility of the government of M. Georges Bidault and [Vice-Premier] M. Maurice Thorez was that it lacked the authority to prevent Admiral d'Argenlieu from following a policy contrary to that of the French government."[37]

Rosenfeld was right to assume that the war was a "fait accompli" made in Saigon, but his statement is nevertheless somewhat misleading. While it is true that d'Argenlieu had exorbitant powers, it is not true that he carried out a policy that was contrary to any well-defined governmental position or strategy. Bidault's failure was not his inability to impose his views on Saigon, but his unwillingness to let French Indochina policy be influenced by his socialist and communist ministers. He preferred to leave Indochina in the hands of d'Argenlieu rather than let Moutet or Thorez decide. Bidault said in early 1947 that one of the main reasons why the MRP wanted to serve in coalition governments with the SFIO and PCF was to prevent the loss of Indochina.[38] The normal procedure when important decisions were made was for d'Argenlieu first to make a proposal. The Comonindo then either approved or delayed its decision. When no decision was forthcoming, d'Argenlieu went ahead and implemented his plans. Then the government normally approved what he had done, although there were sometimes complaints. These were not directed against the content of d'Argenlieu's policy, but against the timing and the lack of coordination with political events in France. Marius Moutet tried to augment the power of his ministry, but Bidault protected d'Argenlieu, and kept the Comonindo out of the colonial ministry's hands.

Hence it is unlikely that a stronger or more decisive French government could have prevented the war, as long as it was led by Bidault. The problem was the lack, not of strength, but of will. If the MRP had done better in the French general elections on November 10, and Bidault had not been compelled to resign, his government would have been stronger. Then Valluy might have received the permission he sought for taking control of the road from Haiphong to Hanoi already in early December, perhaps in conjunction with the planned "police action" against the Hanoi government. The election of Léon Blum instead reopened the possibility of Franco-Vietnamese negotiations, and this probably delayed the war's outbreak. Since Bidault feared the political consequences of being seen as responsible for provocative French actions just before leaving the premiership to Blum, he tried to wash his hands of the matter by telling Valluy that nothing in the general's previous messages had indicated that the situation was as alarming as he was now indicating.[39] As long as Bidault was in power, there was no basic disagreement between the leader of the French government and the high commissioner, but this changed when Léon Blum took over. Blum was indeed confronted with a "fait accompli," but one not just of Saigon's making. Bidault had also played his part.

BLUM

Could Léon Blum have changed history? When he took over from Bidault on December 18, he had the will and desire to prevent war. He immediately wrote a peace message to Ho Chi Minh, thus breaking with Bidault's principle of letting d'Argenlieu take care of all substantial communication with the Vietnamese government, and Blum decided at his first cabinet meeting to send Moutet to meet Ho. But the war party in Saigon sabotaged his policy by delaying the transmission of the letters Blum and Ho sent to each other. Perhaps Blum should have appealed directly to Ho over the radio. This could have prevented the war. Blum could also have made known his intention to dismiss d'Argenlieu on December 14, before his government was formed, but then he might not have won the vote of confidence in the National Assembly on December 17. When he learned of the outbreak of hostilities, Blum's first reaction was to order Valluy to arrange for a cease-fire, but the widespread indignation at the "premeditated Vietnamese aggression" made it impossible to impose this order on Saigon. The war was instead imposed on Blum. On December 22, when appearing at the inauguration of *Le Populaire's* Christmas tree, the old socialist wept and complained to the editor: "Have you heard the news from Indochina? . . . Again it has to be me who does it. . . . I did not deserve this."[40]

THE FRENCH COMMUNIST PARTY

What about the Parti communiste français (PCF)? It was well represented in Bidault's government, its leader, Maurice Thorez, serving as vice-premier. The communists were as concerned about French greatness as de Gaulle and the MRP, but they drew different conclusions from their concern. They believed that Syria and Lebanon had been lost because de Gaulle's provocative policy had given Britain and the United States an excuse for stabbing France in the back. Paradoxically, the PCF wanted to treat the French colonies just as liberally as the United States did, but in order to keep them away from U.S. influence. The PCF feared that the French disaster in the Near East would repeat itself in the Far East, and that Sino-American interference would entail the loss of Indochina. On the basis of this fear, which in the following decade proved well founded, the French communists favored cooperation with the DRV, but they also urged the Vietnamese to be patient and to refrain from demanding independence immediately. While the French Right believed that French greatness depended on a firm anti–Viet Minh policy, the communists felt that the French Union would fail to gain support if France did not make concessions to Asian nationalism. For tactical reasons, however, the French communists refrained from publicly voicing their liberal policy vis-à-vis France's colonies, which they felt was politically hard to defend. Rather, they did all they could to avoid giving the impression that the PCF was unpatriotic.

The December 19 attack, and the emotions it provoked in the French National Assembly, placed the PCF in a difficult situation. Its own mouthpiece first reproduced the news without comment. In the National Assembly, the communist members hesitated when asked to support a motion of sympathy for the French soldiers. This led *Le Monde* to publish a front-page article under the insulting headline "The return of Doriot."[41] The late communist leader Jacques Doriot had turned fascist after being expelled from the PCF in 1934, founded the extreme right-wing Parti populaire français in 1936, and later fought for the Nazis. *L'Humanité* replied by emphasizing that the communist deputies had actually voted in favor of the message of sympathy.[42] It also now offered an interpretation of the December 19 events: they were part of a plot to prepare the way for de Gaulle's return to power. The fighting was fratricidal, and the war had only started in the brains of the reactionaries. December 19 was not war, just another incident. If fighting continued, foreign powers would sooner or later interfere in the internal affairs of the French Union. On December 24, *L'Humanité* gave full support to Léon Blum, saying he had pointed out the only possible way: "Negotiations as soon as peace and order have been reestablished."[43] Negotiations did not take place until 1954, however, when the French communists had long been out of power. As vice-premier in the Bidault and Ramadier governments in 1946–47, Maurice Thorez was unable to implement his colonial policy, and in May 1947, the communists were thrown out of the French government.

LECLERC

In order to succeed, the protagonists of the policy of agreement would have needed support from someone with prestige in the armed forces. The most promising candidate was General Philippe Leclerc de Hauteclocque. In late 1946 and early 1947, the French socialists wanted him to take d'Argenlieu's place. Leclerc has since often been portrayed as a "liberal," a "moderate," or "pragmatic," someone who would have followed a conciliatory course if he had got the chance. Could Leclerc have made a difference? Probably not. When he ordered Sainteny, on March 5, to sign an agreement with Ho Chi Minh almost at any cost, it was because he feared an immediate two-front war against both Chinese and Vietnamese forces. If it had not been for the Chinese, he might well have tried to crush the revolution in the north as he had done in the south, in order to allow France to negotiate from a position of strength. He was also concerned about being militarily overextended, however, and might have decided just to take Haiphong and Hanoi and leave the rest of the north to its fate.[44] In August 1946, during the Fontainebleau conference, Leclerc toyed with the idea of breaking off relations with the Hanoi government, letting Tonkin be, and concentrating the French effort on Cochinchina. This would give France a chance to pacify Indochina gradually by making sure that the French-controlled areas thrived while the rest was being asphyxiated economically.[45] If France controlled the Cochinchinese rice basket and rubber plantations, and a few strategic positions in the north, the Vietnamese would in time be compelled to give up their recalcitrance, Leclerc—and Valluy—thought.[46]

In December, Leclerc criticized d'Argenlieu and Valluy. He shared Admiral Barjot's concern that French forces would be spread too thinly. When Prime Minister Blum learned of the December 19 attack, he decided to send Leclerc to Indochina on a mission of inspection, in addition to Moutet. Blum was planning to replace d'Argenlieu with Leclerc. He reportedly told his cabinet that although Leclerc did not belong to "our political friends," he was an "honest and loyal officer" and was aware of the military difficulties of "a new colonial expedition." Blum also reminded his socialist ministers of Leclerc's "legendary conflict" with d'Argenlieu. He asked Leclerc to negotiate with the Vietnamese government as soon as the military situation allowed it, in consultation with Moutet.[47] Leclerc accepted the mission, but he made no attempt to contact the Vietnamese government and did not consult with Moutet. Once having appraised the situation in Saigon, he recommended that Blum send reinforcements.[48] He praised the French military effort, but drew attention to some serious political problems, notably in Cochinchina.[49]

In Hanoi, Leclerc was greeted by a radio message from Ho Chi Minh, who said: "An equitable peace can still be obtained. I speak to you from heart to heart, because it has been very painful for me to see the young French and the young Vietnamese, the flower of the two countries, furiously killing each other."[50] Leclerc did not reply, but he issued a New Year message to the French troops: "France has already understood that the Army is equal to its task, and you can count on me to emphasize it. The country prays for you."[51] Leclerc did not see Ho Chi Minh. Instead, he looked into Morlière's military record, concluded that he had failed to prepare properly for the confrontation, and recommended, in consultation with Valluy, that he be replaced.[52] On January 6, Morlière was summoned to Saigon. He caught the first available plane and arrived the same day. This was sooner than expected, and also not really convenient, since Moutet was still there. Morlière met the minister and told him about his conflict with Valluy in November–December. Moutet asked Morlière to go back to Hanoi, write a formal report, and wait for the government's decision.[53] However, since Blum's government hoped to persuade Leclerc to take d'Argenlieu's place, it did not see it as opportune to oppose Leclerc's recommendations. On February 4, Morlière was therefore officially replaced by Colonel Dèbes, the butcher of Haiphong. Dèbes was killed in an air crash a month later. Morlière lived to be an old man.

Leclerc's mission report of January 13, 1947, was read attentively in official French circles, and has often been quoted since. The editors of The Pentagon Papers would praise Leclerc for having emphasized that no purely military solution was possible, and that a political solution was necessary. However, when Leclerc said "political

solution" in his report, he did not mean with Ho Chi Minh. Leclerc thought along
the same lines as Pignon. And the only really concrete proposal he made in his report was to increase the strength of the French expeditionary forces from 40,000
to 115,000. The stronger the military effort, the easier it would be to reach a political solution, which would consist in "opposing to the existing Viet Minh nationalism one or several other nationalisms."[54] Although Leclerc did not, like d'Argenlieu, exclude the possibility of renewed talks with Ho Chi Minh, there is nothing
in his attitude to indicate that he would, in a position of authority, have opted for
a return to the March 6 and September 14 agreements. On the other hand, if the
French government had dismissed d'Argenlieu *before* December 19, this would most
likely have dissuaded the Vietnamese from launching their attack, since it would
have sent a strong signal of a change in the government's policy and thus opened
the way to negotiations.

MOUTET

Marius Moutet, minister for Overseas France continuously from January 1946 to
October 1947, in the governments of Gouin, Bidault, Blum, and Ramadier, was the
only Frenchman left with both the power and the desire to prevent the Indochina
War. His resignation in October 1947 marked a hardening of French policy. Only
then did the French government dismiss any prospect of resuming talks with Ho
Chi Minh and authorize Valluy to launch Operation Lea, aiming to capture or kill
the Viet Minh leaders.

Moutet had not been instrumental in bringing about the March 6 agreement,
but he was relieved when it was signed, and he was the one who prevented the
Fontainebleau conference from ending in total wreckage by signing the modus
vivendi agreement of September 14. There is no doubt that Moutet disapproved
of d'Argenlieu's style and exorbitant powers, and that he wanted to put Indochina
under firm control of the government in Paris. Nevertheless, he did not pick a fight
with the MRP to get d'Argenlieu replaced, and he authorized—indeed, encouraged—the establishment of the autonomous Cochinchinese Republic. Moutet
played a leading role in preparing the instructions given to d'Argenlieu on December 10, 1946, which rejected the idea of granting full independence to any of
the Indochinese states. Moutet always insisted that France should follow a "policy
of agreement," as opposed to a "policy of abandonment."[55] His mistake was to allow d'Argenlieu to go back to Saigon. If he and Blum had insisted on d'Argenlieu's
replacement, and if the MRP had agreed, war could have been avoided.

Moutet's next chance came when Blum asked him, on December 18, to go immediately to Indochina, with a mandate to meet Ho Chi Minh. However, once he
arrived in Saigon on December 25, he came under pressure to desist from his mission. When Moutet left France, the socialist mouthpiece *Le Populaire* called him

"the peace messenger."[56] When news arrived of Moutet's public statements in Saigon, it was the MRP's *L'Aube* that used the term "peace messenger," asserting that the socialist Moutet now more than ever deserved the epithet.[57] U.S. Ambassador Jefferson Caffery informed Washington that many had been skeptical about sending a "man of Moutet's age and temperament" to Indochina. The advocates of a firm policy feared that he would make new concessions to Ho Chi Minh, while the conciliatory school were afraid he would come under the influence of the colonialists in Saigon.[58] The latter were confirmed in their apprehensions. Moutet did not see anyone in Vietnam to whom he could make concessions. Instead of going directly to Hanoi, he let himself be taken on a tour of Saigon, Phnom Penh, and Vientiane, and the local French officials withheld information about Ho's arduous attempts to set up a meeting. However, this cannot be blamed solely on d'Argenlieu. Moutet's denunciations of the Viet Minh came so soon and were so strongly worded that they must have reflected a conviction. Moutet cannot have fully shared Blum's desire for peace, yet it seems Blum had confidence in him. This confidence was shared even by the leftist newspaper *Franc-Tireur*, which on December 14 had urged Blum to keep Moutet on as minister. When the French cabinet met on December 26, Blum assured his colleagues that Moutet and Leclerc would prevent d'Argenlieu from taking any harmful action. Moutet would be his direct representative, with the right to make decisions on the spot, and Leclerc would be Moutet's military advisor.[59]

Moutet never saw Leclerc in Indochina. They followed different itineraries, and Moutet did not arrive in Hanoi till January 2. He stayed for less than two days, seeing nobody. His declarations of friendship with the Cochinchinese, the Cambodians, the Laotians and the "Montagnards," interspersed with indignant remarks about the ignoble December 19 attack in Hanoi, were delightfully reported in the centrist and conservative French press. On the Left, *L'Humanité* was disappointed, *Le Populaire* ironical, and the *Franc-Tireur* sardonic. When the French cabinet met on December 31, the young socialist minister Guy Mollet asked Blum what on earth Moutet was doing. "I admit that I'm a bit surprised by the silence of my old friend," Blum replied. "You call this silence?" Mollet asked. "Yes, because for my part, I have not yet received anything from him. And what disturbs me most is that it has not been possible to get in touch with Ho Chi Minh."[60] Blum was not telling the whole truth, since he had in fact received a report from Moutet, which characterized the military situation as "good, becoming excellent as soon as the first reinforcements arrive."[61]

On December 23, Vietnamese radio had announced Ho Chi Minh's urgent desire to see Moutet: "I bid you welcome, since you are at the same time my old friend and the representative of the New France. I wish to see you and look forward to this chance to express my profound attachment to peace and to the collaboration between our two countries, and also to get a chance to present our proposals concerning the reestablishment of good relations between them."[62] D'Argenlieu gave

Moutet a copy of Ho's request, attaching it to a letter of his own, saying: "I allow myself to draw your attention to the extraordinarily grave consequences any direct or indirect contact with any representative of the Hanoi government may have for the future of Indochina."[63] While Moutet was in Hanoi, Ho tried to send a message to him by courier, but the courier "disappeared." In the night between January 2 and 3, one of Moutet's advisors, the French socialist Léon Boutbien, woke up the minister in his bedroom to tell him that Ho was ready to see him. Moutet replied that he would first need a signed request from Ho himself. Boutbien explained that this might be difficult to arrange so quickly, and that two couriers had already been killed. Meanwhile, Ho sent a new message to Moutet through the Chinese consul, but before he could hand it over, Moutet was gone. He got Ho's second message only after returning to France.[64]

Ho had prepared a long memorandum for Moutet, with seventy-six attachments, proving the French responsibility for the failure of the March 6 accords and the modus vivendi agreement. This is the Ho Chi Minh memorandum of December 31, 1946, which has been used extensively in the present study. After Moutet had left, Ho sent copies of the memo through several channels, but the French government received it only on February 4, by which time the U.S. and other governments had been reading it for weeks.[65]

Ho proposed an immediate cease-fire; liberation of prisoners; withdrawal of all troops to the positions defined in the agreements of March 6 and April 3; no further reinforcements from France; and a framework for a definitive treaty, which would include: (a) organizing a referendum in Cochinchina, (b) Vietnamese diplomatic relations with foreign countries, (c) organization of the Indochinese Federation, and (d) definition of Vietnam's place in the French Union. Once a framework had been decided upon, a new Franco-Vietnamese treaty conference should be held in Paris. This was what Ho wanted to discuss. Moutet would have rejected most of it,[66] but there would still have been much to talk about, if both parties agreed to return to the modus vivendi agreement. The task Blum had given Moutet was not impossible.

Why did Moutet go with the tragic flow of history rather than trying to stem it? December 19 got in his way. It was tough to go against the sentiment of the local French population and officials at a time when a number of French citizens had been killed and mutilated, and while French soldiers were engaged in heavy fighting. It was risky to go against national feelings back home. Moutet chose the easy way out, and declared, while in Hanoi, that "before any negotiation, it is today necessary to have a military decision. I deplore this, but one cannot commit such madness as the Viet Minh has done with impunity." After this, Vietnamese radio called him "the war messenger."[67]

When Moutet returned to Paris, Blum had only a few days left as interim premier. His successor, Paul Ramadier, decided to keep Moutet on as minister. Before being elected (investi) by the National Assembly to form the next government, Ramadier made a declaration in which he claimed that war in Indochina had been *imposed on France*. France had not wanted it, still did not want it, and would terminate it as soon as order and security had been restored. In the meantime, France would assume its responsibilities. At this point Bidault, once again foreign minister, interjected from his seat: "Very good!"[68]

As soon as Moutet returned to Paris, he and Blum made a move to boost his power. By a government decree of January 8, 1947, the minister for Overseas France took over the premier's position as chair of the Cominindo.[69] It took until January 21, however, before Moutet informed d'Argenlieu of the change. The old system, Moutet explained, had led to a "dispersion of responsibilities, harmful to sound administrative management."[70] The main point of the reform was to make it possible for the minister for Overseas France to issue direct instructions to the high commissioner, without having to ask any interministerial committee. D'Argenlieu protested vehemently against the January 8 decree. He saw it as a "paradox" that the government would now compromise France's admirable military, financial, and diplomatic effort in this way. To implement the government's decree was impossible, he concluded.[71] When Moutet saw this, he scribbled in the margin of the telegram: "Bravo."

Shortly afterward, d'Argenlieu was summoned to Paris for consultations.[72] In the meantime, he took a controversial new initiative. He expanded the powers of the provisional Cochinchinese government without first asking the French government's approval.[73] This gave Moutet the pretext he needed to realize his long-held dream, and it came at a convenient time, just when U.S. Ambassador Caffery was asking Foreign Minister Bidault to be more generous. Bidault now switched loyalties. He assured the U.S. representative that France would be generous in trying to find a solution and confided that the government had decided to accept d'Argenlieu's resignation. He added that the door would remain open to some sort of settlement, and that d'Argenlieu's recommendation that the government promise never again to deal with Ho Chi Minh had been dismissed.[74] So the same man who, as prime minister, had prevented Moutet from revoking d'Argenlieu's appointment at the time when this could have prevented the war now, when the war was a fact, benefited diplomatically from a decision to finally replace the admiral. The government turned down several of d'Argenlieu's proposals in the hope that he would resign voluntarily. De Gaulle, however, told d'Argenlieu that it was he who represented France, not the government, so he should stay at his post and force the government to dismiss him. In the end, on March 4, the government did just that.[75] So when they wanted to, Moutet and Bidault could defy de Gaulle and his admiral.

Blum, Ramadier, Moutet, and Bidault had struggled for well over a month to find an able and willing successor. They all badly wanted Leclerc for the job. Leclerc was clearly tempted, but turned down two consecutive offers, each time after seeking de Gaulle's advice. De Gaulle told him that to accept an appointment in place of d'Argenlieu would be to "disavow ourselves," and that Leclerc could never count on the necessary backing from the present regime.[76] A civilian bureaucrat, the Radical politician Emile Bollaert, then took upon himself the task. During much of Bollaert's indecisive period as high commissioner, the possibility of reestablishing contact with Ho Chi Minh was left open. Meanwhile, the plan to restore Bao Dai was put on the backburner. When Moutet resigned in October 1947, French policy became more consistent, aiming to realize Pignon's ambition to create a new, French-controlled, nominally independent state, with Saigon as capital. Vietnam was to be divided along social and ideological lines, so that the Franco-Vietnamese struggle could be transformed into a Vietnamese civil war.

In mid-March 1947, Moutet defended his policy in the National Assembly, which was debating a motion to grant substantial war credits. He did not cast any blame on d'Argenlieu, but continued to defend the admiral. Although d'Argenlieu might be reproached for often having moved ahead without waiting for instructions, he could not be accused of having disobeyed orders, Moutet said. When criticized for never having fixed a date for the promised referendum on Vietnamese unity, Moutet took full responsibility for the delay. It was impossible to hold free elections in a state of terror, he claimed. He commented briefly on the occupation of Haiphong, asserting that the Vietnamese had opened fire first, and that France had suffered serious losses. He did not deny, however, that the Haiphong events had been of a "certain gravity."

With regard to December 19, Moutet contended that when they decided to carry out their attack, the Vietnamese leaders had known about Blum's decision to send him on a peace mission. They had taken no notice of this and had hoped to catch the French forces by surprise and wipe out the French soldiers while they were dispersed in cinemas, cafés, and dance halls. Only because of warnings from the remarkable French intelligence service were the French soldiers saved from these "Tonkinese vespers." Moutet quoted from Hoang Huu Nam's friendly letter, sent only hours before the attack. The method of appearing friendly while preparing to strike was very "Far Eastern," Moutet said, obviously referring to Pearl Harbor. Moutet did not hold Ho Chi Minh personally responsible. Extremists had taken over the reins of power while Ho was away in France, he claimed. In response, a conservative politician pointed out that Ho Chi Minh had also sent a friendly letter on the day of the attack. One Assembly member compared Ho to Hitler.

What was it that prevented Moutet from doing what was needed to prevent the Indochina War, or to stop it once it had broken out? The answer remains uncertain. Perhaps he was concerned about his political career.[77] Perhaps he was keen to maintain smooth collaboration with the MRP. Perhaps he felt that he had to take responsibility even for actions he had been unable to control. The historian Martin Thomas has discussed the reasons for Moutet's failure, both in 1946 and in fall 1947, when again he failed to assert himself and lost his post as minister. Thomas offers three explanations. First, there was Moutet's inability to consolidate his personal influence within the coalition cabinets, despite close relations with the socialist premiers Gouin, Blum, and Ramadier. What this means is that Moutet failed to gain the trust of Bidault. Second, there was his lack of authority over the French administration in Saigon. This is clearly true, and the problem was both personal and structural. Moutet failed to get Bidault's support for doing something to stem d'Argenlieu's exorbitant powers. And, third, Moutet was "confounded by the SFIO's failure to define a coherent postwar colonial reformism." Just like the parties of the Center and Right, the socialists were not ready to risk losing imperial control.[78]

Perhaps Moutet's problem was that he simply believed what he said. He was anxious to prevent Cochinchina from falling under communist rule and backed the idea of Cochinchinese autonomy. He was also personally engaged in seeking to protect the ethnic minorities of the central highlands against "Annamite" domination.[79] The key factors in his "policy of agreement" were his personal affinity for Ho Chi Minh and his emphasis on French interests in Cochinchina, rather than Tonkin. These were his main reasons for signing the modus vivendi agreement, but after the October 31 cease-fire undermined French power in Cochinchina, his policy was difficult to pursue. He needed a compromise allowing the Viet Minh to control the north while France continued to dominate the south. In early November, when d'Argenlieu's team decided that this policy was untenable, and aimed instead for a direct confrontation in the north, Moutet was not in control of the Cominindo and also not sufficiently decisive to get d'Argenlieu's appointment revoked. Yet again, if the Vietnamese had not attacked on December 19, if Moutet had gone to see Ho in Hanoi, Moutet would have had a better chance to set history on a different, more peaceful course. As the war intensified in Indochina, Moutet was haunted by a sense of guilt: "I have had this nightmare of bearing a heavy part of the responsibility for what happened in Indochina," he told the French Senate on November 12, 1953.[80] He did not blame d'Argenlieu, who had done his duty. Moutet emphasized at this juncture that he had been the only French politician who had negotiated with Ho Chi Minh, and that Ho had said to him when they met at the airport in June 1946: "You are my oldest friend; I count on you to arrive at a result. I will do what is in my power." On September 18, 1954, after Dien Bien Phu and the Geneva accords, Moutet tried to take comfort in claiming that the fault had not, after all, been his own. His failure had been due to lack of support: "I did all that was in my power to prevent this war," he argued in August 1955. "I could not find any parliamentary opinion or any public opinion ready to support me, not even the instruments needed to bring the negotiations to a successful conclusion, which might perhaps have prevented six years of war and saved hundreds of thousands of lives," he lamented in September 1955.[81]

THE VIET NAM NATIONALIST PARTY

On the Vietnamese side, the anticommunist leaders of the VNQDD and other nationalist factions had little chance of influencing events after their Chinese protec-
tors had left. The DRV suppressed their party organizations and forced their militia forces either to surrender or to merge with the forces controlled by the Viet
Minh.[82] Some of the anticommunist leaders also wanted a Franco-Vietnamese war,
since this might weaken both the French and the DRV and open up new chances
for an alternative national leadership. Some noncommunist leaders lived clandestinely in Hanoi, and Nguyen De, Ngo Dinh Diem, and Nghiem Ke To were among
those who were in some kind of contact with the Sûreté. Pignon played with them.
He had told the French consul in Kunming on December 4 to refrain from harm-
ing the exile leaders: "In particular as far as the VNQDD is concerned, it does not
seem to be in our interest to remember its francophobe character too much at
present."[83] The anticommunist director of Hanoi's electric power plant, who was
under the protection of the French Sûreté, played an enigmatic role when his plant
was sabotaged in the evening of December 19. Once learning of the outbreak of
hostilities, a group of nationalist Vietnamese politicians in Nanjing announced the
formation of a "provisional Vietnamese government" in anticipation of a Sino-
American intervention, and Bao Dai traveled from Hong Kong to Guangzhou on
December 20 to meet with exiled Vietnamese politicians.[84] The "government" in
exile formed in Nanjing on this occasion would never play much of a role, although
some of its members later backed "the Bao Dai solution." Quite curiously, however,
John Carter Vincent, head of the Asia Office in the U.S. State Department, told the
French ambassador in Washington on January 10, 1947, that a party, whose Annamite name was similar to that of the Chinese Guomindang (obviously the VN-
QDD) seemed to have been the real instigator of the opening of hostilities.[85] Did
he know something that no one has yet uncovered? What is certain is that the anticommunist opposition was not a force for peace.

HO AND GIAP

In the DRV, the two main decision-makers were Ho Chi Minh and Vo Nguyen Giap,
although they had to coordinate with the "Standing Bureau" of the officially non-
existent Communist Party. We may never know if Ho and Giap were in agreement
on December 19. No Vietnamese veteran would admit to disagreeing with Uncle
Ho or having failed to carry out his instructions. Ho Chi Minh had also warned the
French on an earlier occasion against thinking that Giap would ever defy his master: "Giap is totally devoted to me; he exists only because I support him; he and the
others cannot do anything without me. I am the father of the revolution," Ho told
General Salan in late May.[86] There are many indications, however, notably in

French intelligence, that Ho Chi Minh, Undersecretary of Foreign Affairs Hoang Minh Giam, and Undersecretary of the Interior Hoang Huu Nam were more patient, keener to exploit the swing to the left in French politics, than Giap.[87]

Giap may have spoken for the rank and file who wanted to retaliate for the Haiphong massacre and preempt a similar French onslaught in Hanoi. Ho knew the French leaders from his stays in France around 1920 and in the summer of 1946. Giap had spent all his life in Vietnam or neighboring China and had devoted himself before the August Revolution to organizing the guerrilla struggle against the French and Japanese and to building up Vietnam's armed forces. His attempts as a negotiator at Dalat in April–May had not been successful, but he had ably organized the repression of the pro-Chinese nationalist parties during Ho's absence in France. By late 1946, he was ready to return to the jungle. So was Ho, if need be. He had warned the French and the West repeatedly that Vietnam's will to resist was ferocious. On November 5, Ho Chi Minh had penned a "Note on Urgent Work at Present" (Cong viec khan cap bay gio), which would be revered later as an expression of "Ho Chi Minh Thought." Anticipating the French assault, Ho spoke of the need for a protracted resistance struggle. The most important thing would be to make sure that the people were determined, he said: "Even if the enemy is driven to almost complete failure, he will, all the same, strive to hit back. For a defeat in Vietnam would lead to a disintegration of all his empire. . . . Even should we have to withdraw from the towns, it will not be important, for the whole countryside will remain in our hands. . . . We can surely fight for several years, till victory."[88]

Ho considered war likely, but not inevitable, and between the signing of the modus vivendi agreement and the outbreak of war, he may have changed his mind several times about whether or not it was possible to maintain his government in Hanoi. His talent for making friends with adversaries might help Vietnam. Much of what he did publicly in November–December 1946, and also in the following months, when he repeatedly called for a cease-fire,[89] testifies to his desire to prevent armed conflict, or at least postpone it as long as possible, while impressing on the French government the need to repudiate the actions of d'Argenlieu. It must have felt strange for Ho to see war with France coming while his comrades were members of the French government. It is curious both that he did not personally sign the draft for the call to arms that he discussed with Giap, Le Duc Tho, and Truong Chinh on the afternoon of December 19, and that Truong Chinh had to sign it for him, and that the appeal was not read on the radio at 8 p.m., as agreed, but only the following day. After the meeting of the Standing Bureau, Ho Chi Minh moved to a safe house thirty-two kilometers from central Hanoi. Unless he could communicate with Giap by telephone, he was then unable to take part in any further decisions. Giap revealed in his 1995 memoir that after the battle for Haiphong, the president had emphasized the need to avoid falling into any French trap: "The

French are waiting for an occasion to attack us. We must seek every means to avoid the outbreak of a generalized conflict. While we are devoting all our forces to preparing for a protracted war, we must absolutely not let ourselves be trapped by the provocative acts of the enemy."[90] When quoting this, did Giap sense that he himself had been trapped?

During the whole of the "Thirty Years' War," 1945–75, Giap served as secretary of the Communist Party's Military Committee, although he shared power over military affairs with others in the 1950s and was sidelined for a long period in the 1960s and 1970s.[91] The battle at Dien Bien Phu in 1954 was the apogee of his life. In his 1997 biography of Giap entitled *Victory at Any Cost*, Cecil B. Currey states, on the basis of his studies and interviews, that "Senior General Vo Nguyen Giap is not a nice person," but he adds that this applies to all famous warriors.[92] Before becoming a general, Giap was a historian, reading all he could find about Vietnam's national history, and about Napoleon Bonaparte. His studies were subsidized by a chief of the French security police in appreciation of the young man's intellect. In the early phase of World War II, Giap left his pregnant wife in Hanoi and clandestinely made his way to China. On returning in 1945, he learned that his wife had been tortured and died in a French prison. His second wife, Professor Dang Bich Ha, whom he married in 1946, is also a historian. And Giap returned to history in his old age. I have met him four times in Hanoi, the last time in December 2005. In September 1992, we discussed December 19. He had familiarized himself with Devillers's and my published work, where I claimed that the French had provoked the outbreak of war, and hypothesized that someone, perhaps infiltrators, had confronted Giap and Ho with a fait accompli. Giap told me right away that I was wrong. We realized, he said, that the war was unavoidable, and on that day, we decided to take the initiative. Giap would later repeat this to other visitors.[93]

Without Giap's decision—if indeed he took it—to unleash the attack at 8 p.m. in the evening on December 19, it is not certain that he would have become the hero of Dien Bien Phu, that his army would have defeated the French, the United States, and South Vietnam and dealt devastating blows in 1979 to the Chinese invaders. Innumerable lives might have been spared. Vo Nguyen Giap's life and achievements are remarkable. He built his army from scratch and took the fateful decision—so he claims—that started a whole string of wars. Finally, after surviving virtually all of his contemporaries, he was able to sit down and write lengthy memoirs, basking in his status as a national hero.

Giap's first set of memoirs were written in the early 1970s, when Vietnam had not yet been reunified, when Party Secretary Le Duan had sidelined him and picked some of his juniors to replace him.[94] Giap started his account with his and Uncle Ho's arrival in Hanoi in late August 1945, shortly after local Viet Minh leaders had seized power from the Japanese, and he ended this first of his published accounts on March 6, 1946:

So, in the extremely confusing and complicated situation at the time, the negotiations between us and the French led to a preliminary accord. This was the first international treaty that the DRV signed with a foreign country. . . . On behalf of our people, President Ho expressed to the people of the world our sincere aspiration for peace—a genuine peace—in independence and freedom. And since we could not have peace now because of the greed and blind actions of imperialism, this was a moment of compromise to prepare for a protracted resistance, which we believed would bring victory.[95]

Giap's next account ended on December 19, 1946, with three little dots, just at the brink of the essential:

Dusk fell. The whole city was unusually quiet. It was cold and dry. The houses seemed to shrink back and to be standing warming themselves in the yellowish electric light. Outwardly, the city seemed to grow lazy in the cold and go to bed early. But beneath this calm surface, line upon line of surging wave was ready to rise. All the combatants were present at their posts. It was reported that not a single French soldier was to be seen in the restaurants, bars or streets. And enemy armored cars began to push out and stood blocking some crossroads . . .[96]

Not a word about his own decisions, just the yellowish electric light, waiting to be cut off so that the surging waves of war could rise.

Giap published much about the triumph at Dien Bien Phu, but it took until the 1990s before he once more delved into the origin of the Vietnamese tragedy. This time he discussed the inevitability of December 19 in a new detailed memoir, a three-volume narrative, written with the assistance of Colonel Huu Mai, that covers the whole war against France, ending with Uncle Ho's and Giap's triumphant return to Hanoi in October 1954. This memoir is more reflective, less emotional, not as puffed up as the ones he wrote in the 1970s. And Giap goes right to the heart of the matter in a subchapter titled "War or Peace." First, he cites a question he had received from the daughter of General Leclerc: "Could the war between France and Vietnam have been avoided?"[97] It is to Giap's credit that he raises the question. After wars have broken out, it is always tempting to consider them inevitable. Sainteny, for instance, would say in 1973 that "after the Haiphong affair, the chain of events was irreversible."[98] For Giap, who bore so much responsibility, not only for the decision to start the fighting, but for all the death and suffering during all of Indochina's wars, it must have seemed almost unbearable to consider the possibility that this tragedy might have begun with a misunderstanding. In the 1970s, Giap took it for granted that the wars had been inevitable.[99] Vietnam would never have won independence and unity without its wars of resistance. He had organized and led the nation in a struggle imposed on it by the French and Americans. Uncle Ho had also realized the inevitability of an armed confrontation when he returned to Hanoi after signing the modus vivendi agreement.[100]

There are two ways of contemplating a war's inevitability, which often lead to opposite conclusions. One may, on the one hand, examine the aims of the parties and ask whether a win-win solution or a viable compromise was possible. This method tends to confirm the thesis of inevitability, because it is the maximum, not the minimum, aims that leave the most visible traces in the historical sources. Written texts and declarations are dedicated to explaining and promoting maximum goals, while decision-makers find it preferable to keep their bottom lines to themselves. They may even be unaware of them; when leaders are truly eager to avoid or get out of a war, they may well go beyond what they themselves imagined to be their bottom line.

The other way of considering the question of inevitability is to examine the precise circumstances of the war's outbreak, ponder the elements of coincidence, and consider what would have had to be different in order to produce a different outcome. When using this method, the historian may easily gain the impression that the war could very well have been prevented, and will thus tend to explain it in terms of bad choices, unfortunate circumstances, or outright "folly."[101]

The first chapter of this book tends to confirm the inevitability thesis by showing how the new French and Vietnamese republics, each with its own ambitious reform plans, clashed in Indochina. The two adversaries were both dissatisfied with the March 6 accord, which China had forced upon them; they both saw it as a stepping-stone to something better. When China withdrew its forces, it seemed obvious that an open conflict would result from the sheer incompatibility of aims. However, chapter 6, on the lights being cut off in Hanoi, conveys the impression that if circumstances had differed just a little, Indochina's subsequent history might have been different.

How did the aging Giap tackle this problem? He does not immediately dismiss the idea that the war might have been avoided, but cites the two Western historians Devillers and Tønnesson, who have persistently asked who started the war. They remain perplexed, he says, since they have found that Ho Chi Minh did all he could to avoid war, and yet the "young Vietnamese army and the self-defense units were the first to open fire." The end of World War II had marked the beginning of the Cold War, leading the imperialist powers to increase their repression of popular insurrections, Giap explains. Since Vietnam was the first Third World country to install a Communist Party government, it became a target of encirclement. The war of imperial reconquest actually started long before December 19, with the French coup in Saigon on September 23, 1945, and the ensuing resistance struggle in the south. It is true that a cease-fire was obtained in the modus vivendi agreement, Giap admits, but he had realized when he met d'Argenlieu in Dalat in April that it would be "difficult" to avoid war. Then, in November, came the French attacks on Haiphong and Langson, and the situation in Hanoi worsened. President Ho had nonetheless done everything possible to try to "halt the generalization of the conflict or at least delay its outbreak."[102] The armed forces were ordered to maintain strict discipline and not to let themselves be provoked. On December 13, an extraordinary meeting was held near Hanoi, with all the main Vietnamese military commanders present. They adopted a plan of action and agreed on the codes to be used in the final order to attack. The French "ultimatum" of December 18, threatening to assume responsibility for the security of Hanoi by December 20, reminded Giap of the Haiphong ultimatum a month earlier, when the French had inevitably called the shots because of the shortness of the deadline. It was essential to prevent the capital from succumbing to a similar surprise: "This would be a heavy responsibility in face of history."[103] This was why the party's Standing Bureau, meeting at Van Phuc on December 19, decided to employ the codes agreed upon six days earlier, and send out the order to attack at 8 p.m. It seemed possible at the time, says Giap, that this was too late, since the French ultimatum might allow them to take the initiative already the next morning.

The problem with this account is that the French were not about to attack, and that the December 16 request was not really an ultimatum. The French government had made it clear that the French forces must not take the initiative in any further serious incidents. D'Argenlieu, Valluy, and Pignon therefore needed Giap to make the first move. Giap could not know this at the time, but when publishing his memoirs in 1995, he knew: "The researchers will certainly find proof in the archives of the Indochina War," he writes, "showing that General Valluy and his political advisor Léon Pignon, the two who held responsibility for the Expeditionary Corps at the time, needed to generalize the conflict in the north of Vietnam immediately in order to confront the recently formed socialist government of Léon Blum with a fait accompli."[104] So far, so good, the historians have caught Giap's attention with their findings in the archives; but then, rather than admitting that he fell into a trap, Giap skirts the issue: "However, don't forget the role of d'Argenlieu, that obstinate defrocked monk. And don't forget the anticommunist Harry Truman, Franklin Roosevelt's successor as the leader of the free world." There were people in the French government who foresaw the somber perspectives of a war against Vietnam, Giap concedes, but their voices fell on deaf ears: "Imperialism still believed in the possibility of easily defeating the weak nations with the use of armed force."

Then Giap evokes Uncle Ho and reminds us that even after December 19, the president did not give up his hope of reviving the peace. Ho never missed any opportunity of trying to restore peace for the good of the two peoples: "However, the fire of war cannot be extinguished unilaterally." With this sentence, Giap washes his hands of any contamination by historical scholarship and reverts to his familiar position: "In this context, the events of the night of December 19, 1946, as well as the Vietnam War, turn out to have been inescapable."[105]

NOTES

INTRODUCTION

Epigraph: Herbert Butterfield, *History and Human Relations* (London: Collins, 1951), 9.

1. Butterfield, *History and Human Relations*, 20.

2. Gabriel Kolko, in *Anatomy of a War: Vietnam, the United States, and the Modern Historical Experience* (New York: Pantheon Books, 1985), 36, and *Century of War: Politics, Conflicts, and Society since 1914* (New York: New Press, 1994), 342, is one of the few to have appreciated the political importance of the famine that reached its apex in March–April 1945 in preparing the ground for the revolution that followed. The communists capitalized on the famine in organizing a movement to "break open the rice stores to avert famine." By March 1945, the famine had claimed "a minimum of one million and perhaps as many as two million lives—or up to one-fifth of Tonkin's population," Kolko says. However, on the basis of a thorough examination of demographic statistics, French colonial and Vietnamese government archives, David G. Marr has concluded that one million seems the more credible estimate: David G. Marr, *Vietnam 1945: The Quest for Power* (Berkeley: University of California Press, 1995), 104; David G. Marr, "Beyond High Politics: State Formation in Northern Vietnam, 1945–1946," in *Naissance d'un Etat-Parti: Le Viêt Nam depuis 1945*, ed. Christopher E. Goscha and Benoît de Tréglodé (Paris: Les Indes savantes, 2004), 29.

3. This is based on Micheal Clodfelter, *Vietnam in Military Statistics: A History of the Indochina Wars, 1772–1991* (Jefferson NC: McFarland, 1995), 33; Clodfelter, *Warfare and Armed Conflicts: A Statistical Reference to Casualty and Other Figures, 1500–2000*, 2nd ed. (Jefferson NC: McFarland, 2002), 675–81; and Anthony Clayton, *The Wars of French Decolonization* (London: Longman, 1994), 74. The account follows the estimate made by Bethany Lacina. See Bethany Lacina and Nils Petter Gleditsch, "Monitoring Trends in Global Combat: A New Dataset of Battle Deaths," *European Journal of Population* 21, no. 2 (2005): 145–66. Jacques Dalloz, *Dictionnaire de la guerre d'Indochine, 1945–1954* (Paris: Armand Colin, 2006), 194, sets the figures higher, at 500,000 on the side of the DRV and 100,000 for the French.

4. Bethany Lacina, "Monitoring Trends in Global Combat: A New Dataset of Battle Deaths, Documentation of Coding Decisions I, Uppsala/PRIO Data." www.prio.no/sptrans/ 671630282/Documentation_PRIO-UCDP.pdf (accessed January 4, 2009), 430–35. A much higher estimate, 3.8 million for the period 1955–2002, is given in Ziad Obermeyer, Christopher J. L. Murray, and Emmanuela Gakidou, "Fifty Years of Violent War Deaths from Vietnam to Bosnia: Analysis of Data from the World Health Survey Programme," *British Medical Journal* 7659 (June 28, 2008): 1482–86. This estimate, which is probably exaggerated, is based on interviewing a representative sample of Vietnamese about the deaths of their siblings.

5. Stein Tønnesson, "The Vietnam Peace" (paper presented at the International Studies Association convention, New York City, February 15–18, 2009).

6. Anthony Short, *The Origins of the Vietnam War* (London: Longman, 1989), 326.

7. Dixee R. Bartholomew-Feis, *The OSS and Ho Chi Minh: Unexpected Allies in the War against Japan* (Lawrence: University Press of Kansas, 2006), 288–99.

8. Vo Nguyen Giap, *Chien Dau trong vong vay* (Hanoi: Nha Xuat Ban Quan Doi Nhan Dan, 1995), 22, and *Mémoires, 1946–1954*, vol. 1: *La résistance encerclée* (Fontenay-sous-Bois: Anako, 2003–4), 27.

9. Alain Ruscio, *La guerre française d'Indochine* (Paris: Editions Complexe, 1992), 92.

10. See the different interpretations in Bernard B. Fall, *The Two Viet-Nams: A Political and Military Analysis* (London: Pall Mall, 1963), 77; Ellen J. Hammer, *The Struggle for Indochina, 1940–1955* (Stanford: Stanford University Press, 1954), 187–91; and Philippe Devillers, *Histoire du Viêt-Nam de 1940 à 1952* (Paris: Seuil, 1952), 353–57.

11. Lloyd C. Gardner, *Approaching Vietnam: From World War II through Dienbienphu* (New York: Norton, 1988), 75, refers to the Fall/Hammer difference, but is himself closer to Fall than to Hammer-Devillers. Pierre Brocheux and Daniel Hémery, *Indochine: La colonisation ambiguë, 1858–1954* (Paris: La Découverte, 1995; 2nd ed., 2001), 351, 397n 55 (in the 2001 ed., 350, 399n 68), think Devillers and his disciple Tønnesson have been proven wrong by the Vietnamese "admission of guilt." The present book results from a struggle with the version of December 19 presented in Vo Nguyen Giap, *Chien Dau trong vong vay*, 43–45, and *Mémoires*, 1: 29, 40–42.

12. King C. Chen, *Vietnam and China, 1938–1954* (Princeton: Princeton University Press, 1969); Lin Hua, *Chiang Kai-shek, de Gaulle contre Hô Chi Minh: Viêt-nam, 1945–1946* (Paris: L'Harmattan, 1994); Lin Hua, "The Chinese Occupation of Northern Vietnam," in *Imperial Policy and Southeast Asian Nationalism*, ed. Hans Antlöv and Stein Tønnesson (Copenhagen: NIAS; London: Curzon Press, 1995), 144–69.

13. Jean-Claude Devos, *Inventaire des archives de l'Indochine: sous-série 10 H (1867–1956)*, 2 vols. (Vincennes: SHAT, 1987), is a useful guide to this file.

14. Frédéric Turpin, *De Gaulle, les gaullistes et l'Indochine, 1940–1956* (Paris: Les Indes savantes, 2005).

1. A CLASH OF REPUBLICS

1. Stein Tønnesson, "National Divisions in Indochina's Decolonization," in *Decolonization*, ed. Prasenjit Duara (London: Routledge, 2004), 253–77.

2. Martin Thomas, "The Colonial Policies of the Mouvement républicain populaire, 1944–1954," *English Historical Review* 476 (April 2003): 381.

3. U.S. Department of State, Interim Research and Intelligence Service, Research and Analysis Branch: R&A No. 3336, "Biographical Information on Prominent Nationalist Leaders in French Indochina," USNA. Full or partial biographies of Ho Chi Minh in Western languages have been written by Jean Lacouture, Jean Sainteny, Nguyen Khac Huyen, Charles Fenn, David Halberstam, William Warbey, Douglas Pike, Daniel Hémery, Pierre Brocheux, William J. Duiker, and Sophie Quinn-Judge. William J. Duiker, *Ho Chi Minh* (New York: Hyperion, 2000) is now the standard work on the subject, although Duiker relies too much on official Vietnamese narratives. Daniel Hémery, *Ho Chi Minh: De l'Indochine au Vietnam* (Paris: Découvertes Gallimard, 1990), Pierre Brocheux, *Hô Chi Minh: Du révolutionnaire à l'icône* (Paris: Payot, 2003), trans. Claire Duiker as *Ho Chi Minh: A Biography* (New York: Cambridge University Press, 2007), and Sophie Quinn-Judge, *Ho Chi Minh: The Missing Years* (Berkeley: University of California Press, 2002), are more independent and critical in their judgments.

4. Quinn-Judge, *Ho Chi Minh: The Missing Years*, 194; Duiker, *Ho Chi Minh*, 209; Hémery, *Ho Chi Minh*, 72–73.

5. William J. Duiker, *The Communist Road to Power in Vietnam* (Boulder CO: Westview Press, 1996), 53.

6. Quinn-Judge, *Ho Chi Minh: The Missing Years*, 195–200, 208–11, 216–28.

7. Thong Tan Xa Viet Nam [Vietnam News Agency], *Dong chi Truong Chinh* [Comrade Truong Chinh] (Hanoi: Nha Xuat Ban Thong Tan [Vietnam News Agency Publishing House], 2007).

8. Eric T. Jennings, *Vichy in the Tropics: Pétain's National Revolution in Madagascar, Guadeloupe, and Indochina, 1940–1944* (Stanford CA: Stanford University Press, 2001), 151–61, 167–73.

9. Stein Tønnesson, "Franklin Roosevelt, Trusteeship, and Indochina: A Reassessment," in *The First Vietnam War: Colonial Conflict and Cold War Crisis*, ed. Mark Atwood Lawrence and Fred Logevall (Cambridge MA: Harvard University Press, 2007), 56–73.

10. Stein Tønnesson, *The Vietnamese Revolution of 1945: Roosevelt, Ho Chi Minh and de Gaulle in a World at War* (Oslo: International Peace Research Institute; Newbury Park CA: Sage Publications, 1991), 326–27.

11. The collaboration between the Viet Minh and the OSS is described in many books, notably Archimedes L. Patti, *Why Vietnam? Prelude to America's Albatross* (Berkeley: University of California Press, 1980); Marr, *Vietnam 1945;* and Bartholomew-Feis, *OSS and Ho Chi Minh.*

12. Devillers, *Histoire du Viêt-Nam*, 111.

13. Christopher E. Goscha, "Belated Asian Allies: The Technical and Military Contributions of Japanese Deserters (1945–50)," in *A Companion to the Vietnam War*, ed. Marilyn B. Young and Robert Buzzanco (London: Blackwell, 2002), 37–64: 42–44; Peter M. Dunn, *The First Vietnam War* (London: Hurst, 1985), 149–50, 263, 282, 300, 322, 337, 367; Peter Dennis, *Troubled Days of Peace: Mountbatten and South East Asia Command, 1945–46* (Manchester, UK: Manchester University Press, 1987), 54, 58; Bartholomew-Feis, *OSS and Ho Chi Minh*, 276–77, 291, 300, 385–86; "Notice technique de contre-ingérence politique," No.

635/238./239.5.2./BA. L/00.002/SD, on "Les Japonais en Indochine depuis le 15 août 1945," Paris, Jan. 23, 1947, INF, carton 138-39, dossier 1249, AOM.

14. Alain Ruscio, *Les communistes français et la guerre d'Indochine 1944-1954* (Paris: L'Harmattan, 1985), 89-90; Mari Olsen, *Soviet-Vietnam Relations and the Role of China, 1949-64: Changing Alliances* (London: Routledge, 2006), 1.

15. Vo Nguyen Giap, *Unforgettable Days* (Hanoi: Foreign Languages Publishing House, 1975), 68.

16. Stein Tønnesson, "Filling the Power Vacuum: 1945 in French Indochina, the Netherlands East Indies and British Malaya," in *Imperial Policy and Southeast Asian Nationalism*, ed. Antlöv and Tønnesson, 110-43.

17. The British had lost 40 killed in action themselves and estimated that by mid-January 1946, 1,565 Vietnamese had been killed by French forces, 641 by British, and 550 by Japanese. Clodfelter, *Vietnam in Military Statistics*, 16.

18. On July 27, 1973, Mountbatten claimed the opposite in an interview with Philippe Devillers, one of the authors behind the 1974 film *La République est morte à Dien Bien Phu*, saying, "si j'avais eu l'Indochine entière sous mes ordres, j'aurais tout de suite mis en négociant avec Ho, qui était un homme tout à fait sensé." However, the French would have reacted vehemently if Mountbatten had negotiated directly with Ho. If Mountbatten had been willing to risk French animosity, he could have come to an agreement with the local Vietnamese leaders in Saigon; there were talks between them and the British. Mountbatten's statement no doubt reflects what he thought later that he should have done rather than what he actually would have done at the time. The pro-French actions of Mountbatten's commander in Saigon, General Douglas Gracey, are related in Dunn, *First Vietnam War*.

19. Devillers, *Histoire du Viêt-Nam*, 128.

20. Hoang Tung interview, Hanoi, July 14, 2007.

21. From 1948, the party was revitalized, and its leaders claimed it had actually never been dissolved, just gone underground. For instructions from 1948 to emphasize the role of the party in "individual propaganda" even if its existence should not be mentioned on the radio or in the press, see appendix to "Note sur l'activité du Parti communiste indochinois," HC 4, AOM.

22. For the declaration of the "dissolution volontaire du Parti communiste indochinois," see CP 22, AOM. See also Devillers, *Histoire du Viêt-Nam*, 195, citing a French version of the declaration, published in *La République*, no. 7 (Nov. 18, 1945). In a forthcoming book on Vietnam 1945-50, David G. Marr discusses thoroughly the respective roles and powers of the public administration, the media, the Army, the Viet Minh front, and the nominally dissolved Indochinese Communist Party ("The Organization").

23. The following is based on a French intelligence study from June 1946: "Etude sur le parti Viet Minh en Indochine du Nord," CP 21, AOM. For the DRV's food, property, and fiscal policies, see Marr, "Beyond High Politics."

24. Devillers, *Histoire du Viêt-Nam*, 232.

25. The following is based on a French intelligence report: "SDECE: Notice Technique de Contre-Ingérence Politique," Nov. 28, 1946, AO, MAE.

26. "Toan dan khang chien chi thi cua doan the," Dec. 22, 1946, TBN-75, doc. 48, VNA-I. A copy of this booklet is also exhibited in the Army History Museum in Hanoi. The "Stand-

ing Bureau . . . " in Vietnamese is: "Thuong Vu Trung Uong Dang Cong San Dong Duong." After the outbreak of war in Hanoi on December 19, the French also captured an undated and unsigned typewritten draft for an internal report on the situation of the ICP. It said there were only 208 party members in Hanoi and spoke of lack of respect for the party hierarchy when people of lower stature were assigned leadership roles, whereas comrades with government responsibility turned into "moderates." Le chef de la police et de la Sûreté fédérales (Moret) to various agencies, note no. 604-PS, Jan. 31, 1947, CP-sup. 22, *dossier* "Groupe culturel marxiste & PCF," AOM.

27. "Etude sur les principaux partis . . . annamites," edited by Lieutenant Augier, June 1947, p. 124, DGD 89, AOM.

28. Jean Sainteny, *Histoire d'une paix manquée, Indochine 1945–1947* (Paris: Amiot-Dumont, 1953, reprint, Fayard, 1967), 166. Daniel Hémery, "Paul Mus: Un orientaliste dans la décolonisation" in *Paul Mus (1902–1969)*, ed. David Chandler and Christopher E. Goscha (Paris: Les Indes savantes, 2006), 221–46.

29. Notes by Dang Phuc Thang from a conversation with Paul Mus early 1947, document captured by the 2ᵉ Bureau No. 2283/2, CP-sup. 9, AOM. Vo Nguyen Giap, *Unforgettable Days*, 95.

30. *Journal officiel . . . Assemblée nationale*, session of Mar. 18, 1947, 879.

31. Jean Decoux, *A la barre de l'Indochine, 1940–1945* (Paris: Plon, 1950), 477.

32. For general treatments of French colonial reform, see Paul Mus, *Le déstin de l'Union française de l'Indochine à l'Afrique* (Paris: Seuil, 1954); Henri Grimal, *La décolonisation de 1919 à nos jours* (Brussels: Editions Complexe, 1984); Charles-Robert Ageron, *La décolonisation française* (Paris: Armand Colin, 1991); Catherine Cocquery-Vidrovitch and Charles-Robert Ageron, *Histoire de la France Coloniale*, vol. 3: *Le déclin* (Paris: Armand Colin, 1991). Martin Shipway, *The Road to War: France and Vietnam, 1944–1947* (Providence RI: Berghahn, 1996), thoroughly examines French Indochina policy, 1944–47. Brocheux and Hémery, *Indochine: La colonisation ambiguë* provides a broad historical reflection.

33. Caffery to Secstate, Mar. 13, 1945, FRUS 1945, 6: 300.

34. Devillers, *Histoire du Viêt-Nam*, 144. Shipway, *Road to War*, 59–62.

35. As late as August 1946, the high commissioner stated that the March 24 declaration remained the basis for French policy in Indochina. *Paris-Saigon*, Aug. 14, 1946, 6.

36. Tønnesson, *Vietnamese Revolution*, 314.

37. Georgette Elgey, *Histoire de la IVème République*, vol. 1: *La République des illusions, 1945–1951* (Paris: Fayard, 1965), 101.

38. William I. Hitchcock, *France Restored: Cold War Diplomacy and the Quest for Leadership in Europe, 1944–1954* (Chapel Hill: University of North Carolina Press, 1998); Mark Atwood Lawrence, *Assuming the Burden: Europe and the American Commitment to War in Vietnam* (Berkeley: University of California Press, 2005), 159–60.

39. *Le Populaire*, Dec. 28, 1945, cited from Jean-Pierre Gratien, *Marius Moutet: Un socialiste à l'Outre-mer* (Paris: L'Harmattan, 2006), 231.

40. *Le Populaire*, Dec. 27, 1945.

41. Ibid. The original reads: "On n'improvise pas un gouvernement, une législation, une administration dans un pays hétérogène où l'opinion publique ne peut encore exprimer consciemment ses préférences."

42. Speech at SFIO meeting in La Rochelle, Aug. 18, 1946, Papiers Moutet, PA 28, C3, *dossier* 87, AOM.

43. "Fidèle à sa mission traditionelle, la France entend conduire les peuples dont elle a pris la charge à la liberté de s'administrer eux-mêmes et de gérer démocratiquement leurs propres affaires." The constitution quoted from Alfred Grosser, *La 4ème Republique et sa politique extérieure* (Paris: Armand Colin, 1961), 248.

44. See, e.g., R. E. M. Irving, *The First Indochina War: French and American Policy, 1945-54* (London: Croom Helm, 1975), 21-22.

45. In a meeting with MRP and SFIO National Assembly members in August 1946, Moutet regretted the whole Cominindo system instituted by de Gaulle. Note by Pierre Chevigné (MRP), Aug. 7, 1946, cited in Jean-Pierre Gratien, "Marius Moutet, de la question coloniale à la construction européenne, 1914-1962" (PhD diss., Université de Paris I, 2004), 2: 327.

46. For André Labrouquère's failure as secretary-general April-June 1946, see Gratien, *Marius Moutet: Un socialiste à l'Outre-mer*, 327-30. For Messmer's account of his service as secretary-general, see Pierre Messmer, *Après tant de bataille* (Paris: A. Michel, 1992), 176-81.

47. *Marchés coloniaux*, Mar. 16, 1946, copy in HC 4, AOM.

48. General Valluy, who commanded the French forces in Indochina from July 1946, asked rhetorically in 1967 if there had been any alternative to the policy pursued in 1946: "Peut-être eut-il fallu diriger sur Hanoi, auprès de Ho, un ministre ou un de ces jeunes hommes des cabinets ministériels dont l'idéologie était très voisine de celle du Viet-Minh et qui avaient décidé soit à Dalat, soit à Paris, de tutoyer Giap et Giam." Valluy, *Revue des deux mondes* 5F (Dec. 15, 1967): 515. No wonder Valluy did not name Messmer, for in 1967 Messmer was de Gaulle's minister of defense.

49. Note from Messmer to the "Président du Gouvernement," the "Ministre de la France d'Outremer," and the "Ministre des Armées" on the subject of dissolving the Cominindo, Nov. 11, 1946, AP 3440/5, AOM.

50. Moutet to Haussaire, Jan. 21, 1947, AP 3440/5, AOM.

51. Vo Nguyen Giap, *Unforgettable Days*, 247.

52. Valluy, *Revue des deux mondes*, Nov. 15, 1967, 205, 210.

53. For a lucid discussion of the federal project of 1945, and how it differed from the prewar Indochinese Union, see Daniel Hémery, "Asie du Sud-Est, 1945: Vers un nouvel impérialisme colonial? Le projet indochinois de la France au lendemain de la Seconde Guerre mondiale," in *L'ère des décolonisations: Sélection de textes du Colloque "Décolonisations comparées," Aix-en-Provence, 30 septembre-3 octobre 1993*, ed. Charles-Robert Ageron and M. Michel (Paris: Karthala, 1995), 65-84. See also Tønnesson, "National divisions in Indochina's decolonization."

54. Valluy, *Revue des deux mondes*, Nov. 15, 1967, 209. "Arreté" on responsibilities during the high commissioner's absence, Oct. 30, 1946, CP 13 (2-I), AOM.

55. Jacques Baeyens, "Indo-China," *Asiatic Review* 46 (1950): 1170.

56. In February 1947, d'Argenlieu complained to the French minister of finance that the ministry of Overseas France had never answered his repeated demands for more personnel. D'Argenlieu, letter to Robert Schuman, Feb. 4, 1947, F60 C3024, AN.

57. Devillers, *Histoire du Viêt-Nam*, 172ff. On Mar. 16, 1947, Moutet admitted that in establishing the Cochinchinese Council and the provisional Cochinchinese government, the

French had had to accept those who were willing. *Journal officiel . . . Assemblée nationale,* 881. Statement by French member of the Cochinchinese Council, M. Clogne, to *Paris-Saigon* 42 (Nov. 6, 1946): 7.

58. *Le Monde,* July 14, 1946, quoted in Devillers, *Histoire du Viêt-Nam,* 297.

59. Devillers, *Histoire du Viêt-Nam,* 212; Georges Thierry d'Argenlieu, *Chronique d'Indochine, 1945–1947* (Paris: Albin Michel, 1985), 126–27.

2. THE CHINESE TRAP

1. French Consul Batavia to MAE, Oct. 12, 1946, INF, *dossier* 1424, AOM.

2. Philippe Franchini, *Les mensonges de la guerre d'Indochine* (Paris: Perrin, 2005), 156, notes this.

3. "En ce qui concerne la réunion des trois ky, le Gouvernement français s'engage à entériner les décisions prises par les populations consultées par référendum." *Documents relatifs aux problèmes indochinois* (Paris 1946), "Convention préliminaire franco-vietnamienne du 6 mars 1946."

4. See Devillers, *Histoire du Viêt-Nam,* 207; Marilyn B. Young, *The Vietnam Wars, 1945–1990* (New York: Harper, 1991), 14; Robert D. Schulzinger, *A Time for War: The United States and Vietnam, 1941–1975* (Oxford: Oxford University Press, 1997), 25; Gary R. Hess, *Vietnam and the United States: Origins and Legacy of War* (New York: Twayne, 1998), 35; Brocheux, *Hô Chi Minh,* 167–70; Peter Worthing, *Occupation and Revolution. China and the Vietnamese August Revolution of 1945,* China Research Monograph 54 (Berkeley: Institute of East Asian Studies, University of California, Berkeley, 2001), 113, 136; and Lawrence, *Assuming the Burden,* 127–29, esp. 150. By contrast, Stanley Karnow, in his bestseller *Vietnam: A History* (New York: Penguin Books, 1984), 153, emphasizes the linkage between Leclerc's "gunboat diplomacy" and the signing of the accord, which had little to do with any moderation or liberalism among French decision-makers.

5. Two authors who have grasped the role of the Chinese in compelling France to sign the March 6 accord are Laurent Césari, *L'Indochine en guerres, 1945–1993* (Paris: Belin, 1995), 42–43, and Martin Shipway, in *Road to War,* 166, 174. Shipway notes that the French "would inevitably be caught in a Chinese-laid trap," and remarks that although the accords were hailed as a triumph for French liberalism, they were "fatally compromised by the fact that they emerged from crisis, with the result that, at bottom, they suited no-one."

6. Turpin, *De Gaulle, les gaullistes et l'Indochine 1940–1956,* 183–90.

7. Devillers, *Histoire du Viêt-Nam,* 205–26; Turpin, *De Gaulle, les gaullistes et l'Indochine 1940–1956,* 195–215; René Le Gendre, "Genèse, déroulement, suites immédiates de l'incident franco-chinois du 6 Mars 1946, à Haïphong" (in seven parts), T735, SHAT, 1992; Lin Hua, *Chiang Kai-shek, de Gaulle contre Hô Chi Minh;* Worthing, *Occupation and Revolution,* 113–81. David G. Marr's forthcoming book on "Vietnam 1945–50" will discuss political developments on the Vietnamese side thoroughly.

8. A plan for the reoccupation of the north, with a coordinated landing at Haiphong and capture of Hanoi by parachute troops, had been drafted already the previous fall but rejected as too risky. At that time, moreover, the troops needed for the northern operation were still heavily engaged in suppressing the revolutionary forces in the south, and the 3rd DIC had

not yet arrived. It took over responsibility for the south when the 9th DIC sailed north on March 1, 1946. For the earlier reoccupation plan, see Devillers, *Histoire du Viêt-Nam*, 207.

9. Leclerc to Juin, Feb. 20, 1946, cited by Gilbert Bodinier and Philippe Duplay, "Montrer sa force et négocier: Le général Leclerc et la négociation annamite," in *Leclerc et l'Indochine 1945-1947*, ed. Guy Pedroncini and Philippe Duplay (Paris: Albin Michel, 1992), 189.

10. Bodinier and Duplay, "Montrer sa force et négocier," 190.

11. Leclerc sent Repiton-Préneuf several times to Hanoi to consult with and convey instructions to Sainteny. Sainteny, *Histoire d'une paix manquée*, 173. See also Devillers, *Histoire du Viêt-Nam*, 208. Devillers was a member of Leclerc's staff at the time.

12. Philippe Devillers, ed., *Paris Saigon Hanoi: Les archives de la guerre, 1944-1947* (Paris: Gallimard/Julliard, 1988), 155-57. See also Brocheux, *Hô Chi Minh*, 167-68.

13. Jean Sainteny, *Histoire d'une paix manquée*, 173.

14. See Irving, *First Indochina War*, 15.

15. Secstate to Caffery, No. 564, Feb. 4, 1946, *FRUS, 1946*, 8: 23.

16. Sainteny in interview for the film *La République est morte à Dien Bien Phu* (1973). The editors of Vincent Auriol, *Journal du septennat, 1947-1954*, vol. 1: *1947* (Paris: Armand Colin, 1970), say that a "certain legend" had presented Leclerc as a great liberal (733, note 32). This legend is reflected also in American literature, e.g., in *The Pentagon Papers: The Defense Department History of United States Decisionmaking on Vietnam*, vol. 1 (Boston: Beacon Press, 1971), 21-22.

17. Bodinier and Duplay, "Montrer sa force et négocier," 182.

18. Valluy, *Revue des deux mondes*, Nov. 1, 1967, 22ff.

19. Turpin, *De Gaulle, les gaullistes et l'Indochine, 1940-1956*, 210.

20. "Note pour le Général Salan rédigée par l'état-major du général Leclerc" (Feb. 27, 1946), printed in *1945-1946: Le retour de la France en Indochine. Textes et documents*, ed. Gilbert Bodinier (Vincennes: SHAT, 1987), 213.

21. Ensure "la relève des troupes chinoises par les troupes françaises . . . dans le courant de Mars," "Opération Bentré, Ordre Général no. 9, Commandement Supérieur des FFEO, Etat Major, 3è Bureau," No. 1705-3/OP, 10H1136, SHAT.

22. Ibid.

23. Bodinier and Duplay, "Montrer sa force et négocier," 184-85.

24. Salan had brought up the need to rearm the troops in the Citadel with the Chinese government already in January, even writing a special memo to Chiang Kai-shek about the matter. Worthing, *Occupation and Revolution*, 120. For the plan to send in parachutists and arm the troops in the Citadel so that they could protect the French civilian population, see also Sainteny, *Histoire d'une paix manquée*, 177.

25. On the repercussions of the March 6, 1946 agreement, see Sûreté report No. 1713, Hanoi, Mar. 17, 1946, CP 130, s/d. "Accord 6 mars," AOM.

26. The cargo would include 46 machine guns, 440 pistols and revolvers, 1,500 rifles and carbines *(fusils et mousquetons)*, and 659 Sten guns, of which 300 were designed for an (unspecified in the document) special mission. "Note de service" No. 386/3-OP, Mar. 6, 1946, signed Lajoine for Salan, 10H2513, SHAT.

27. "Plan d'action" No. 2 (with a map of Hanoi), Commandement supérieur des troupes françaises en Extrême Orient, Troupes de Chine et d'Indochine du Nord, Commandement

des troupes de Hanoi, 2ème Section, No. 111-3-OPS, drafted in February 1946, one copy signed in Hanoi, February 15, and another (revised) on March 1 by Lt. Col. Lefebvre d'Argence, commander of the troops in Hanoi, for General Salan and the Hanoi units, 10H2513, *dossier* "Plan d'action des troupes de Hanoi," SHAT.

28. Comrep Hanoi à Haussaire, No. 410, Mar. 6, 1946, 1MiF2, AOM.

29. The high commissioner's special military staff *(état-major particulier)* admitted that this would be difficult. "Réoccupation du Tonkin," No. 47/EMP-3, Saigon, Feb. 12, 1946, 10H162, *dossier* 3, SHAT.

30. Bodinier and Duplay, "Montrer sa force et négocier," 192.

31. JSM Washington to Cabinet Offices, JSM 178, Feb. 1, 1946, FO371/53958/F1889/8/61, PRO.

32. Lawrence, *Assuming the Burden*, 115.

33. Ibid., 122. Dennis, *Troubled Days of Peace*, 179. Dunn, *First Vietnam War*, 355.

34. For documentation of the British concern and its negotiations with the CCS in Washington, see FO371/53959-61; FO 959/6/S/79/190-193/46; WO 203/6209, 6216 and 6258, PRO; and the folder "Indo-China (Dec. 16, 1944)," RG165, ABC384, Sec. 1-B (filed in 1-C), USNA. See also Lawrence, *Assuming the Burden*, 113-14.

35. Meiklereid to FO, rept. to SACSEA and Paris, No. 49, Feb. 21, 1946, FO371/53959/F2882/8/61 (also in WO 203/6216), PRO.

36. The head of Leclerc's 2e Bureau, Lieutenant-Colonel Repiton Préneuf, understood the difference between the situations in Tonkin and Cochinchina, and that it would be infinitely more difficult to pacify the north. Undated instructions, signed Repiton Préneuf, *dossier* "Tonkin. Opération Bentré," 10H601, SHAT.

37. Leclerc said it himself in the report to de Gaulle he wrote in Saigon on March 27: "il était indispensable de trouver un gouvernement annamite, si imparfait soit-il, en place à Hanoï et n'ayant pas pris la brousse." Rapport sur "le problème d'ensemble de notre rétablissement en Indochine depuis le 20 Octobre 1945 jusqu'au 25 Mars 1946," signed by Leclerc in Saigon, Mar. 27, 1946, Archives Sainteny, 1SA4, *dossier* 3, FNSP.

38. Memo from Valluy to Bidault, Feb. 3, 1946, F60 C3024, AN.

39. D'Argenlieu, *Chronique d'Indochine*, 173.

40. Leclerc to Juin and d'Argenlieu, Feb. 14, 1946, Tel. 933, AOM; reprinted in *1945-1946: Le retour de la France en Indochine*, ed. Bodinier, 208-9.

41. D'Argenlieu to Sainteny, Feb. 20, 1946, AN, F60 C3024.

42. D'Argenlieu later spoke of the "menace" of the referendum, which he claimed had been introduced at the very last minute of the negotiations. D'Argenlieu memo, Apr. 26, 1946, F60 C3024, AN.

43. Moutet to Haussaire, No. CI/00903, Mar. 3, 1946, EA, *carton* 39, *dossier* B-605, MAE.

44. Moutet to Haussaire, RB/No. 187/CI/00.901, Mar. 3, 1946, EA, *carton* 1 and 39, *dossier* A-112 and B-605, MAE.

45. Lin Hua, *Chiang Kai-shek, de Gaulle contre Hô Chi Minh*, 223.

46. The French military negotiator in Chongqing, Colonel Jean Crépin, tried to warn the high commissioner as early as February 26 that France would depend urgently on strong Chinese support. This telegram was not received in Saigon (after repetition) until March 1. Crépin to Haussaire No. 51/SC, Feb. 26, 1946, 1MiF2, AOM.

47. Salan had already mentioned this proposal during a visit to Chongqing in early February, but had met a cold shoulder. Etat-major particulier du haut commissaire, Saigon, "Pièce de renseignements sur la mission du général Salan à Tchungking," Feb. 12, 1946, 10H162, *dossier* 3, SHAT.

48. "Résumé chronologique des événements, conversations, entretiens qui se sont déroulés et des accords qui ont été signés entre autorités françaises et chinoises au mois de mars 1946," ed. Délégation militaire en Indochine du Nord du haut-commissaire (hereafter cited as "Chronological Summary of Events"), HC 270, AOM. See also Turpin, *De Gaulle, les gaullistes et l'Indochine, 1940–1956*, 201–10, who refers to another copy of the same document in EA 11, MAE. In spite of Crépin's arguments, the Chinese continued to find excuses for not sending the instructions that the French demanded to the Chinese commanders in Hanoi and Haiphong. Crépin thus had to admit on March 4: "Vice-Ministre a ... reconnu qu'aucun ordre n'a été envoyé malgré toutes les assurances données. ... Je dois voir de toute façon Général Chin mais j'ai peu d'espoir d'en rien obtenir car il semble maintenant dépassé et peu disposé à prendre une initiative quelconque." Milfrance Chungking to Haussaire No. 75/SC, Mar. 4, 1946, 13h15, received Mar. 5, 1946, 00h00, 1MiF2, AOM. See also Crépin's testimony in *Leclerc et l'Indochine*, ed. Pedroncini and Duplay, 167–73.

49. Carton de Wiart to Mountbatten, W. 2358, Mar. 3, 1946, WO 203/6216, PRO.

50. Note on General Valluy's presentation, sent under cover of letter No. 8456 from the Comenindo (de Langlade) to French Prime Minister Gouin, Feb. 3, 1946, *dossier* "fév. 46–fév. 47," s/d. "Comité de l'Indochine Février 1946," EA, *carton* 9, *dossier* A-298 "Chine," MAE.

51. Salan to Lu Han, No. 334/3-OP, Mar. 3, 1946, EA, *carton* 8, *dossier* A 298-06, MAE.

52. "Le libérateur de Paris [Leclerc] et son état-major s'engagèrent donc délibérément dans une opération qu'ils savaient pouvoir comporter de graves risques d'incidents. Leclerc, impatient, jouait, comme à son habitude, son va-tout au culot. La méthode avait fait ses preuves. ... A Haiphong, elle échoua." Turpin, *De Gaulle, les gaullistes et l'Indochine, 1940–1956*, 208.

53. "As the Chinese occupation command came to realize that a Franco-Vietnamese agreement was necessary for peace in Indochina, it began to push its own government to ensure that a satisfactory political agreement between the French and Vietnamese precede a French return. The occupation authorities would cling doggedly to this position throughout the discussions on the troop exchange." Worthing, *Occupation and Revolution*, 132–33 (for the different perspectives of the command in Hanoi and the central Chinese government in Chongqing, see p. 123).

54. Lin Hua, *Chiang Kai-shek, de Gaulle contre Hô Chi Minh*, 234–51. Leclerc wrote at the end of March 1946: "Ce qu'on appelle 'l'incident d'Haïphong' est lumineux. ... En réalité, il ne s'agit nullement d'un incident, mais bien d'un combat contre un Général chinois prévenu en excellente liaison avec nous et ayant parfaitement préparé son attaque." Report on "le problème d'ensemble de notre rétablissement en Indochine depuis le 20 Octobre 1945 jusqu'au 25 Mars 1946," signed by General Leclerc in Saigon, Mar. 27, 1946, Archives Sainteny, *carton* 1SA4, *dossier* 3, FNSP.

55. Devillers, *Histoire du Viêt-Nam*, 224. Through secret intelligence, the French knew exactly where General Wang had stocked an enormous amount of munitions, meant to be shipped and sold on the international market, so in response to the Chinese artillery fire,

they blew up the munitions depot, thus causing Wang a huge financial loss. Philippe Devillers, oral communication, July 2, 2007.

56. Bouffanais (Kunming) to Meyrier (Chongqing), Feb. 28, 1946, EA, *carton* 11, *dossier* A 298–26, MAE. For Lu Han's bribe, see also Dunn, *First Vietnam War,* 353, and the testimony of Henrie Lamarque in *Léon Pignon, 1908–1976: Un homme de coeur au service de l'Outre-Mer français: Témoignages et documents* (Paris: Academie des sciences d'Outre-Mer, 1988), 34. Lamarque claimed to have seen a Dakota aircraft arrive with 60 million piasters in 100-piaster bills.

57. Colonel Crépin held this view at the time: "Le Généralissime . . . n'est donc pas au courant des difficultés actuelles. Ceci confirme définitivement notre impression que toutes nos difficultés sont dues à la mauvaise volonté des militaires qui n'obéissent pas pour le moment aux ordres du généralissime." Milfrance Chongqing to Haussaire, No. 77/SC, Mar. 5, 1946, 0930hZ [Z = Zulu time, i.e., GMT] (could not be deciphered in Saigon and was therefore repeated on March 7), 1MiF2, AOM. Lin Hua seems to agree with Crépin.

58. Worthing, *Occupation and Revolution,* 133–35.

59. "Entrevue du 3 mars 1946 avec Monsieur Tch'eng Tch'ang," No. 467/BL, EA, *carton* 10, *dossier* 298–15, MAE.

60. Ma Ying talked about "complications avec les éléments annamites. S'il y a 'bagarre' il y aura des troubles, l'ordre et la sécurité seront compromis, il y a lieu de rechercher une solution pour parer aux difficultés pouvant survenir du fait de ces troubles." Salan answered that there "existe évidemment des possibilités de 'bagarre', mais au fur et à mesure de notre arrivée nous prenons à notre charge la responsabilité de l'ordre et de la sécurité et à partir de ce moment nous assurerons ordre et sécurité avec tous nos moyens. Il y aura peut-être un peu de flottement au début, mais il disparaîtra rapidement, et il n'y a pas de raison pour qu'il y ait de grosses difficultés." And he added: "Par ailleurs des pourparlers existent avec le gouvernement annamite et il n'est pas impossible que nous ne devenions amis avec eux. . . . Quand vous partirez, l'accord avec les Annamites sera sans doute signé, ainsi la situation sera clarifiée." When the Chinese said the agreement ought to be signed in advance of the French landing, Salan replied: "Nous travaillons activement à cela." Chronological Summary of Events, app. 17, "Conférence franco-chinoise tenue le 4 Mars et le 5 Mars 1946 au palais du Gouvernement général de Hanoï"; HC 270, AOM; and EA, *carton* 8, *dossier* A298–06, MAE.

61. Cominindo (de Langlade) to Haussaire, No. CI/00903, Mar. 3, 1946, AI 36, MAE, as quoted in Turpin, *De Gaulle, les gaullistes et l'Indochine, 1940–1956,* 212.

62. D'Argenlieu to Leclerc, No. 75/5C, Mar. 4, 1946, cited by Bodinier and Duplay, "Montrer sa force et négocier," 194.

63. " . . . si, facteur principal, le gouvernement continue à nous appuyer, nous réussirons à doubler ce cap . . . il me parait juste de prévoir pendant quelques jours des hauts et des bas dans l'appréciation de l'action maintenant engagée. Je vous demande donc de ne pas vous étonner si mes communiqués demeurent purement objectifs et froids." D'Argenlieu to Moutet, No. 3976F, Mar. 4, 1946, 0340h, EA, *carton* 36, *dossier* 15, MAE.

64. Lin Hua, *Chiang Kai-shek, de Gaulle contre Hô Chi Minh,* 235.

65. Salan to Leclerc, No. 375/3/OP, Mar. 5, 1946, cited by Bodinier and Duplay, "Montrer sa force et négocier," 195.

66. Chronological Summary of Events, app. 19, "Compte rendu d'entrevue du 5 mars 1946 entre délégués chinois et français."

67. Lecomte, handwritten letter to Sainteny, Archives Sainteny, *carton* 1SA4, *dossier* 2, FNSP. See also Devillers, *Paris-Saigon-Hanoi*, 146–47, and Sainteny, *Histoire d'une paix manquée*, 178n1.

68. Salan to Haussaire, No. 374/3-OP, Mar. 6, 1946, 0h50, Chronological Summary of Events, app. 10b. "Entrevue avec le Général Salan au matin du 11 mars à 9h30," annex 2 to the report of "mission au Tonkin du 10 au 13 mars" by the head of the high commissioner's military staff (EMP), Saigon, Mar. 13, 1946, 10H162, *dossier* 3, SHAT.

69. Sainteny himself considered these concessions as minor. Sainteny to Leclerc, Mar. 5, 1946, Fonds Leclerc, CI/46.47/27/002, cited by Bodinier and Duplay, "Montrer sa force et négocier," 192. D'Argenlieu, however, thoroughly disliked this military annex, as did the French chiefs of staff. See "Accord complémentaire de Hanoi du 7 mars 1946," undated memo with comments from Admiral d'Argenlieu, 10H162, *dossier* 3, SHAT; and "Observation sur l'accord annexe à la Convention du 6 mars," EMGDN, no signature, 10H162, *dossier* 3, SHAT. Salan does not seem to have immersed himself in the negotiations with the Vietnamese, not even when military matters were brought up. He left the talks in the hands of Sainteny, assisted by Léon Pignon. According to a report Pignon wrote later, it was not until almost 6 p.m. on March 5 that the military question was discussed. Pignon underlined in his report that during the negotiations with the Chinese there had been pressure to get the Annamites and French to arrive at an agreement. And the Chinese "voulaient être les gérants de cette accord." Pignon thought therefore that the fact the convention was signed only by the French and Annamites represented a "defeat" for the Chinese. "Exposé de M. Pignon du mercredi 12 mars," 10H162, *dossier* 3, SHAT.

70. Ibid.

71. SEHAN report, "Le Viet Minh et les Chinois," probably written by Lt. Col. Trocard, signed Hanoi, Apr. 8, 1946, Archives Sainteny, 1SA4, *dossier* 3, FNSP.

72. Foreign Minister Nguyen Tuong Tam had left Hanoi at the critical moment and could therefore not sign the Convention. Thus he was later free to criticize it. Devillers, *Histoire du Viêt-Nam*, 232.

73. Haussaire to Defnat Paris, No. 404F (for the attention of Moutet), Mar. 6, 1946, 0940hZ, 1MiF40, AOM.

74. Devillers, *Histoire du Viêt-Nam*, 234.

75. Vo Nguyen Giap's long defense of the accords was published in the Hue newspaper *Quyet Chien*, Mar. 8, 1946. Devillers, *Histoire du Viêt-Nam*, 229–31, gives a summary.

76. Nguyen Khac Vien, *Vietnam: A Long History* (Hanoi: The Gioi, 1999), 251.

77. Devillers, *Histoire du Viêt-Nam*, 242.

78. Speech by d'Argenlieu, Mar. 9, 1946, HC 4, AOM.

79. "Bulletin spécial d'informations No. 16 concernant l'Indochine du Nord" (summary of comments in Vietnamese media, 10–16 Mar., 1946), CP 13 (1), AOM.

80. Inter-service Mission (Saigon) to SACSEA No. 1.384, Mar. 11, 1946; and French Liaison Mission to HQ SACSEA, Mar. 29, 1946, WO 203/6216, PRO. Rapport de la Sûreté No. 1713, Hanoi, Mar. 17, 1946, on the repercussions of the March 6, 1946, agreement, s/d. "Accord 6 mars," CP 130, AOM.

81. Chen Jian, *Mao's China and the Cold War* (Chapel Hill: University of North Carolina Press, 2001), 123–24.

82. General Valluy, memo to Prime Minister Bidault, Feb. 3, 1946, F60 C3024, AN. Viet Minh circular, Mar. 3, 1946, captured in 1947 by the French Sûreté, BR No. 675/PS, CP 17 (14), AOM.

3. MODUS VIVENDI

1. The modus vivendi agreement was dated September 14, but Ho and Moutet signed only after midnight, so strictly speaking the agreement should be dated September 15. Laurent Césari, *L'Indochine en guerres, 1945–1993* (Paris: Belin, 1995), 49; Shipway, *Road to War*, 218; Lawrence, *Assuming the Burden*, 152.

2. Sainteny, *Histoire d'une paix manquée*, 209.

3. SESAG, "Renseignements divers recueillis à Haiphong," Saigon, May 3, 1946, CP, AOM.

4. Raoul Salan, *Mémoires: Fin d'un empire*, vol. 1: *Le sens d'un engagement, juin 1899–septembre 1946* (Paris: Presses de la Cité, 1970), 347. We cannot trust Salan's accuracy when he quotes conversations, because he wrote his memoirs only in the late 1960s. However, when he cites documents, we must assume that the quotations are correct.

5. Salan, *Mémoires*, 1: 343.

6. D'Argenlieu to Cominindo. No. 421F, rec'd Mar. 9, 1946, F60 C3024, AN.

7. Salan, *Mémoires*, 1: 353.

8. The report was reproduced in full in Sainteny, *Histoire d'une paix manquée*, 244ff. In the first edition of Sainteny's book (printed Oct. 15, 1953), it was called "Lettre du général Leclerc au général De Gaulle." In the next edition (printed Nov. 30, 1954), it was cited as "Rapport du général Leclerc," and de Gaulle's name was omitted.

9. "Lettre du général Leclerc au général De Gaulle," as reprinted in Sainteny, *Histoire d'une paix manquée*, 244ff.

10. Pignon started to write his memoirs but was prevented by illness from completing them. After his death, his widow, Elise Pignon, solicited the help of her husband's former colleagues and friends, leading to the publication in 1988 of *Léon Pignon 1908–1976: Un homme de coeur au service de l'Outre-Mer français: témoignages et documents* (Paris: Academie des sciences d'Outre-Mer, 1988), which reveals some of his thinking. For a detailed examination of Pignon's role in French Indochina policy, see Daniel Varga, "La politique française en Indochine (1947–50): Histoire d'une décolonisation manquée" (PhD diss., Université d'Aix–Marseille I, 2004).

11. Leclerc, letter to Maurice Schumann, June 8, 1946, reproduced in Georgette Elgey, *Histoire de la IVème République*, vol. 1: *La République des illusions, 1945–1951* (Paris: Fayard, 1965), 161–62.

12. A summary of Leclerc's lecture was sent to all French diplomatic stations on Aug. 8, 1946, AO, MAE.

13. Part of Leclerc's final report is reproduced in Claude Paillat, *Dossier secret de l'Indochine* (Paris: Presses de la Cité, 1964), 93–94, and the whole report can be found in Auriol, *Journal du septennat*, 1: 661–64, app. 1, as well as in *Leclerc et l'Indochine*, ed. Pedroncini and Duplay, 379–82.

14. Sainteny, *Histoire d'une paix manquée,* 167.

15. Memo from d'Argenlieu, Apr. 26, 1946, F60 C3024, AN.

16. D'Argenlieu to Cominindo No. 1149F, July 30, 1946, AN, F60 C3024; EMGDN, Bulletin d'études No. 40 (a 22-page summary of proposals from the second Dalat conference), AO, MAE.

17. Minutes and other essential French documents from the unsuccessful negotiations in Dalat and Fontainebleau may be found in EA, *carton* 32–36, MAE; and in CP 246 and CP 301, AOM. Useful analyses of the negotiations can be found in Henri Azeau, *Ho Chi Minh, dernière chance: La conférence franco-vietnamienne de Fontainebleau, juillet 1946* (Paris: Flammarion, 1968); Patricia Sockeel-Richarté, "La conférence franco-vietnamienne de Fontainebleau (juillet–août 1946)," *Espoir* 35 (July 1981): 54–64; Jacques Valette, "La conférence de Fontainebleau (1946)," in *Les chemins de la décolonisation de l'empire français 1936–1956,* ed. Charles-Robert Ageron (Paris: Centre national de la recherche scientifique, 1986), 231–50; and Micheline Schlienger, *Vers l'éclatement du conflit franco-vietnamien* (Paris: Mare & Martin, 2005), 140–73; and David Marr's forthcoming "Vietnam 1945–50."

18. In January 1947, Pignon remarked that Ho Chi Minh had been more popular in the south than in the north. Pignon report No. 276CP/CP/Cab, Jan. 21, 1947, CP-sup. 18, AOM.

19. Devillers, *Histoire du Viêt-Nam,* 244. This was one of the reasons for Leclerc's March 15 telegram to d'Argenlieu.

20. Ibid., 324.

21. Reed to Secstate, dispatch No. 113, Oct. 24. 1946, DF851G.00/10–2446, USNA.

22. Haussaire to EMGDN No. 841/EMHC, Oct. 1, 1946, Tel. 933, AOM.

23. Leclerc report Jan. 8, 1947, in Auriol, *Journal du septennat,* 1: 661–64; and in *Leclerc et l'Indochine,* ed. Pedroncini and Duplay, 379–82.

24. Leclerc report Jan. 8, 1947, in Auriol, *Journal du septennat,* 1: 661ff. Leclerc had a personal interest in exaggerating the April figure, since he had then been responsible, and of minimizing the figure in January, when he had been out of command for six months. What Leclerc fails to mention, is that the decline of French control in the south began in March–April, four months before he left his command, and largely because he moved his best units north.

25. Draft reply to a parliamentary question from Mr. Driberg, signed in FO Jan. 26, 1946. FO371/53958/F1759/8/61, PRO.

26. Devillers, *Histoire du Viêt-Nam,* 253, 258.

27. "Rapport sur la situation politique intérieure de l'Indochine au 10 janvier 1947," 8, signed Pignon, Jan. 21, 1947, CP-sup. 18, AOM.

28. Salan, *Mémoires,* 1: 401.

29. Nguyen Binh's original name was Nguyen Phuong Thao. He took the name Nguyen Binh ("Nguyen the Peacemaker") when joining the Viet Minh in 1945. For his biography, see Christopher E. Goscha, "A 'Popular' Side of the Vietnamese Army: General Nguyen Binh and the Early War in the South (1910–1951)," in *Naissance d'un Etat-parti,* ed. Goscha and de Tréglodé, 325–54.

30. Instructions to Nam Bo from the minister of propaganda (Tran Huy Lieu), early September 1946, appendix to a memo from d'Argenlieu to the session of the Cominindo on Nov. 23, 1946, F60 C3024, AN.

31. Impression from examination of the daily military reports in AOM.

32. Haussaire to FOM, No. 857/EMHC, Oct. 7, 1946, Tel. 933, AOM.

33. Haussaire to EMGDN, No. 817/EMHC, Sept. 19, 1946, Tel. 933, AOM. EMGDN endorsed the proposal and asked the Cominindo to decide accordingly by letter of Sept. 23, 1946, F60 C3024, AN.

34. Haussaire to EMGDN, No. 816/EMHC, Sept. 19, 1946, Tel. 933, AOM. The telegraph operators in Paris were not very good at writing Vietnamese names. Those in Washington were no better at writing French. Probably thinking he was Vietnamese, they once called d'Argenlieu "Dar Gen Lieu."

35. D'Argenlieu to Cominindo, No. 1703F, Oct. 26, 1946, Tel. 937, AOM.

36. Devillers, *Histoire du Viêt-Nam*, 318.

37. Under the command of Generals Crépin and Morlière, the French forces in Hanoi seem to have tolerated, if not openly supported, the repression of the nationalists. See Paul Mus, *Sociologie d'une guerre* (Paris: Seuil, 1952), 52–53; Institut franco-suisse d'études coloniales [Jean Bidault], *France et Viet-Nam: Le conflit franco-vietnamien d'après les documents officiels* (Geneva: Editions du Milieu du monde, n.d. [1947]); and notably François Guillemot, "Au coeur de la fracture vietnamienne: L'élimination de l'opposition nationaliste et anticolonialiste dans le Nord du Viêt Nam (1945–1946)," in *Naissance d'un Etat-parti*, ed. Goscha and de Tréglodé, 175–216. Bidault speaks of the ironic destiny that led to French officers helping the Viet Minh crush the opposition, leaving the Vietnamese to Viet Minh's totalitarianism. Guillemot, 215, speaks of Franco–Viet Minh "collusion."

38. Pignon in interview with Jean Lacouture, Mar. 30, 1973 for the film *La République est morte à Dien Bien Phu*.

39. Frédéric Turpin, "Le Mouvement républicain populaire et la guerre d'Indochine (1944–1954)," *Revue d'histoire diplomatique* 110 (1996): 159.

40. Paul Isoart, "L'élaboration de la Constitution de l'Union française: Les Assemblées constituantes et le problème colonial," in *Les chemins de la décolonisation de l'empire français 1936–1956*, ed. Charles-Robert Ageron (Paris: Centre national de la recherche scientifique, 1986), 15–32.

41. Bidault to d'Argenlieu, Mar. 29, 1946, quoted by Sockeel-Richarté, "La conférence franco-vietnamienne de Fontainebleau." She does not tell where she found the document, but she had access to d'Argenlieu's personal archives. The letter is not mentioned in d'Argenlieu, *Chronique d'Indochine*.

42. FOM to Haussaire, Apr. 19, 1946, Tel. 910, AOM.

43. Devillers, *Histoire du Viêt-Nam*, 258–59. This memo has not been found in AOM, but the archives from this period are incomplete.

44. Labrouquère to Haussaire, May 15, 1946, Papiers Moutet, PA 28, *carton 3, dossier 83*, AOM.

45. Moutet to Haussaire, May 15, 1946, PA 28, *carton 3, dossier 83*, AOM.

46. In a personal letter to d'Argenlieu dated Aug. 19, 1946, Moutet claimed that neither he nor Bidault had been informed. D'Argenlieu had in fact spoken of the forthcoming conference in a cable sent on July 22, but Moutet did not receive his copy of this telegram before the news of the planned conference was publicly known in Paris on July 26. Papiers Moutet, PA 28, *carton 3, dossier 82*, AOM.

47. D'Argenlieu memo, Aug. 2, 1946, signed in Dalat, F60 C3024, AN; also in AO, MAE.

48. Elgey, *Histoire de la IVème République*, 1: 164.

49. Baudet in personal letter to Clarac, Aug. 21, 1946, AO, MAE.

50. Moutet to d'Argenlieu, Aug. 19, 1946, Papiers Moutet, PA 28, C3, d.82, AOM.

51. Bulletin AFP No. 413, Nov. 6, 1946, CP 13, AOM.

52. "Note de Moutet a/s de la conférence de Fontainebleau," Aug. 8, 1946, EA, *carton* 36, *dossier* 15, MAE.

53. Devillers, *Histoire du Viêt-Nam*, 302.

54. Moutet to d'Argenlieu, Aug. 19, 1946, Papiers Moutet, PA 28, C3, d.82, AOM.

55. Memo signed by d'Argenlieu at Dalat, Aug. 2, 1946, P60 C3024, AN and AO, MAE.

56. Moutet to d'Argenlieu, Aug. 19, 1946, Papiers Moutet, PA 28, C3, d.82, AOM.

57. Bidault to d'Argenlieu, typed Sept. 21 and sent Sept. 25, 1946, Tel. 914, AOM. Copies of this telegram were not distributed to other officials in Paris.

58. Jean Sainteny, *Histoire d'une paix manquée*, 209-10.

59. The source for this information is a telegram from three of the French negotiators (Gonon, Pignon, and Torel) to d'Argenlieu, telling him that the French proposal was to be discussed between the prime minister and Ho Chi Minh the same day. Gonon, Pignon, and Torel to d'Argenlieu No. 65 CP, Sept. 14, 1946, 1800hZ, Tel. 914 and Tel. 915, AOM.

60. The full French text can be found in Sainteny, *Histoire d'une paix manquée*, 248-52, and in *1945-1946: Le retour de la France en Indochine*, ed. Bodinier, 287-91. *Vietnam: A History in Documents*, ed. Gareth Porter (New York: Meridian, 1981), 48ff., has been consulted for the quotations in English.

61. On board were also 100 Vietnamese workers and 1,586 Vietnamese soldiers *(tirailleurs)*, who were being repatriated after serving France in World War II, Cominindo to Haussaire, Sept. 28, 1946, Tel. 914, AOM.

62. Ho Chi Minh to delegation on *Pasteur*, Sept. 15, 1946, Tel. 914, AOM.

63. Pham Van Dong to Hoang Minh Giam, Sept. 19, 1946, Tel. 937, AOM.

64. Cominindo to Haussaire No. CI/02810, Sept. 27, 1946, Tel. 914, AOM.

65. Messmer to d'Argenlieu personally, Sept. 20, 1946, Tel. 914, AOM.

66. "Rapport mensuel (octobre 1946) de la Sûreté féderale," No. 3278 (signed A. Moret), Oct. 27, 1946, PCE 8, AOM.

67. During the Fontainebleau conference, there had been radio contact between the Vietnamese delegation and the Hanoi government. SDECE report, July 18, 1946, AO, MAE.

68. *Elections et référendums des 13 oct., 10 et 24 nov. et 8 déc. 1946. Résultats par département et par canton (France métropolitaine et France d'Outre-mer)* (Paris: Le Monde, 1947), 249. Haussaire to Paris No. 1741F, Nov. 2, 1946, Tel. 938, AOM.

69. Reed to Secstate, No. 411, Oct. 19, 1946, DF851G.00/10-1946, USNA.

70. Haussaire to Cominindo No. 1628F, undated, Tel. 937, AOM.

71. *Franc-Tireur*, Oct. 15, 1946, 3.

72. Vo Nguyen Giap, *Unforgettable Days*, 338.

73. Sainteny, *Histoire d'une paix manquée*, 210.

74. Vo Nguyen Giap, *Unforgettable Days*, 332.

75. "S'il a signé, affirmera plus tard Ngo Dinh Diem, c'est par peur d'être arreté et envoyé à l'île de la Réunion." Elgey, *Histoire de la IVème République*, 1: 165.

76. Ho Chi Minh to VN govt., Sept. 16, 1946, Tel. 914, AOM.

77. Ho Chi Minh to VN govt., Sept. 19 and 26, 1946, Tel. 937, AOM.

78. For an account of the journey based on interviews with the crew, see Georges Chaffard, *Les carnets secrets de la décolonisation* (Paris: Calmann-Lévy, 1965), 11ff.

79. Captain of the *Dumont d'Urville*, report, quoted in a note from EMGDN (2nd section) to MAE, Dec. 23, 1946, AO, MAE.

80. Ho Chi Minh to Moutet, Sept. 19, 1946, Tel. 937, AOM.

81. Ho to Bidault, received in Paris Oct. 12, 1946, Tel. 933, AOM.

82. Comonindo to Haussaire, Oct. 26, 1946, Tel. 938, AOM.

83. Haussaire to Comonindo, No. 1483F, Sept. 25, 1946, Tel. 937, AOM; Comonindo to Haussaire, No. C.I./02879, Oct. 5, 1946, Tel. 914, AOM; Haussaire to Moutet, no number, copy in Paris dated Oct. 14, 1946, Tel. 937, AOM.

84. Tran Ngoc Danh, the brother of a former secretary-general of the Indochinese Communist Party, was in fact an opponent of Ho Chi Minh's within the ICP, and would later criticize Ho in communication with the leaders of the Soviet Union for nationalist, right-wing deviationism. Christopher E. Goscha, "Courting Diplomatic Disaster? The Difficult Integration of Vietnam into the Internationalist Communist Movement (1945–1950)," *Journal of Vietnamese Studies* 1–2 (2006): 59–103.

85. D'Argenlieu to Comonindo, No. 1789F, copy in Paris dated Nov. 11, 1946, Tel. 938, AOM.

86. Messmer to d'Argenlieu, Oct. 26, 1946, enclosure to ibid.

87. "Instructions aux sections V.N. à Hanoï," Sept. 23, 1946, CP-sup. 8 (1), AOM. "Instructions du directeur de la propagande au *Trung Bo* (Hai Trieu)," Sept. 24, 1946, Notice SDECE, Nov. 28, 1946, AO, MAE.

88. Jean Sainteny in 1973 interview with Jean Lacouture for the film *La République est morte à Dien Bien Phu.*

89. D'Argenlieu to Comonindo, No. 50.721–50.733/106, Mar. 27, 1946, Tel. 933, AOM.

90. Salan, *Mémoires,* 1: 353. Salan was the officer who accompanied Ho Chi Minh.

91. Haussaire to Comonindo, Cabinfor 671, Oct. 19, 1946, Tel. 937, AOM.

92. D'Argenlieu to Comonindo (for the attention of Moutet), Oct. 19, 1946, Tel. 937, AOM.

93. O'Sullivan to Secstate, No. 94, Oct. 24, 1946, DF851G.00/10-2446, USNA.

94. Ho Chi Minh, *Selected Works,* vol. 3 (Hanoi: Foreign Languages Publishing House, 1961), 71ff.

95. Draft memorandum from Pignon "Action du front Viet-Minh contre les partis d'opposition (Octobre 1945–Novembre 1946)," No. 4562/CP/AP, Dec. 17, 1946, CP-sup. 21 and CP 247, AOM. See also Guillemot, "Au coeur de la fracture vietnamienne," 198–99.

96. David Marr analyzes the construction of the DRV state and army in "Beyond High Politics: State Formation in Northern Vietnam, 1945–1946," and in "Creating Defense Capacity in Vietnam, 1945–1947," in *The First Vietnam War,* ed. Lawrence and Logevall, 74–104, and treats these topics thoroughly in his forthcoming book on "Vietnam 1945–50." For an earlier account, largely based on Vietnamese published sources, see Greg Lockhart, *Nation in Arms: The Origins of the People's Army of Vietnam* (Sydney: Asian Studies Association of Australia in association with Allen & Unwin, 1989).

97. Note from Pignon to Moutet, Dec. 30, 1946, EA, *carton* 59, *dossier* C-303, MAE.

98. *Hien Phap nuoc Viet-nam Dan Chu Cong Hoa,* undated printed copy in *dossier* 572, file DRV 1945–54, "Affaires intérieures," VNA-I (also in Museum of Revolution, Hanoi). A contemporary French translation can be found in CP-Sup. 5, AOM. The latter also includes

French-language minutes from the second session of the Vietnamese National (or Constitutive) Assembly, Oct. 28–Nov. 10, 1946. A thorough analysis of Vietnamese constitution-making in 1945–46 may be found in chapter 2 of David G. Marr's forthcoming book on "Vietnam 1945–50."

99. *Hien Phap nuoc Viet-nam Dan Chu Cong Hoa*, Museum of Revolution, Hanoi.

100. The following persons were elected as members of its Standing Committee, ten of whom belonged to the Viet Minh: Bui Bang Doan, Ton Duc Thang, Ton Quang Phiet, Pham Ba Chuc, Duong Duc Hien, Hoang Minh Chau, Phan Thanh, Nguyen Dinh Thi, I Ngo Ong, Cung Dinh Quy, Duong Van Du, Tran Huy Lieu, Tran Van Cung, Hoang Van Hoa, and Nguyen Van Luyen.

101. The commission had the following members, seven of whom, including the first four on the list, belonged to the Viet Minh: Nguyen Thi Thuc Vien, Ton Quang Phiet, Nguyen Dinh Thi, Tran Duy Hung, Do Duc Duc, Cu Huy Can, Huynh Ba Nhung, Tran Tan Tho, Nguyen Van Hach, Dao Huu Duong, Pham Gia Do.

102. "La constitution de la République démocratique du Viet Nam" (a 27-page French study of Vietnamese constitution-making), CP-sup. 4, AOM, p. 5.

103. Moutet to Haussaire, Sept. 21, 1946, Papiers Moutet, PA 28, C3, d.83, AOM.

104. Haussaire to Cominindo, Cabinfor 640, Sept. 22, 1946, Tel. 937, AOM.

105. Devillers, *Histoire du Viêt-Nam*, 301. Devillers was present when the declaration was made.

106. Moutet to Haussaire, Sept. 21, 1946, Papiers Moutet, PA 28, C3, d.83, AOM.

107. "Communiqué de la Commission Permanente à tous les secrétaires Municipaux et provinciaux-Délégués de la Nation," Oct. 28, 1946. It is unclear to which organization this Standing Committee belonged, the DRV National Assembly, the Viet Minh or other, but the circular was reproduced in French translation as doc. 16 in "Réponse au Mémorandum vietnamien 'sur les manoeuvres colonialistes depuis le 6 mars 1946 et les origines de l'actuel conflit franco-vietnamien'" (hereafter cited as "d'Argenlieu memo, Feb. 11, 1947"), a memorandum with fifteen appendices, consisting of twenty-four documents, sent by d'Argenlieu to FOM on Feb. 11, 1947, copies in EA, *carton* 41, *dossier* B-608, and *carton* 56, *dossier* 247, s/d. XVIII, MAE, also in AO, MAE and DF851G.00/2–2047, USNA.

108. Pignon to de Lacharrière, No. 1082E, Nov. 21, 1946, 1MiF44, AOM.

109. Haussaire to Cominindo, No. 1613F, Oct. 15, 1946, Tel. 937, AOM.

110. Haussaire to Cominindo MP/No. 517, copy in Paris dated 21 Oct. 1946, Tel. 937, AOM.

111. Haussaire to Prési. Paris, No. 1740, 1 Nov. 1946, 1MiF44, AOM. On November 19, Giap told U.S. Vice-Consul O'Sullivan that the French were "not releasing political prisoners save symbolically, although he said there is some freedom of press in Saigon." O'Sullivan to Secstate, No. 108, Nov. 19, 1946, DF851G.00/11–1946, USNA.

112. The DRV media are analyzed in David Marr's forthcoming book on "Vietnam 1945–50."

113. Comrep Hanoi to Haussaire, No. 273, Oct. 22, 1946, 1MiF5, AOM.

114. Haussaire to Prési. Paris, Nov. 26, 1946, 1MiF44, AOM.

115. Reed to Secstate, No. 421, Oct. 24, 1946, DF851G.00/10–2446, USNA.

116. "Cochinchine—Depuis le 30 Octobre o heure, situation calme sur ensemble secteurs." Haussaire to EMGDN, Nov. 1, 1946, Tel. 933, AOM.

117. Haussaire to Cominindo, Nov. 3, 1946, Tel. 938, AOM.

118. Beziat to FOM, Nov. 9, 1946, Tel. 933, AOM. This complaint is also mentioned in Reed to Secstate, No. 438, Nov. 9, 1946, DF851G.00/11–946, USNA.

119. "Mémorandum—Faits postérieurs au 30/10/1946," enclosure to Ho Chi Minh to d'Argenlieu, No. 852-VP/CT, Nov. 11, 1946, CP 8, AOM (VN files, captured in Hanoi 1947); "Mémorandum récapitulatif des actes contraires au modus-vivendi du 14/9/46," enclosure to letter from Ho Chi Minh to the French premier, Nov. 17, 1946, CP 8, AOM.

120. Appendix to memo from d'Argenlieu to the Cominindo session on Nov. 23, 1946, F60 C3024, AN. "Mémorandum récapitulatif des actes contraires au modus-vivendi du 14/9/46," appendix to letter from Ho Chi Minh to Léon Blum, Dec. 17, 1946, CP-sup. 8, AOM.

121. "Once again the enemy was surprised and embarrassed to find that we were in full control of South Viet Nam." Vo Nguyen Giap, *Unforgettable Days*, 335. "L'éxécution stricte de la cessation du feu au jour et à l'heure fixés par les chefs rebelles fournit la preuve de l'organisation et de la discipline des bandes rebelles qui tendent de plus en plus à s'assimiler dans la clandestinité à des troupes régulières." Valluy to EMGDN, No. 1902/3/T/, Nov. 22, 1946, Tel. 933, AOM and 4Q78, *dossier* 3, SHAT. Moutet used the same words in an interview with "l'agence P.F.A." on Nov. 27, 1946, Papiers Moutet, PA 28, C3, d.87, AOM.

122. Report from the "Cabinet du Général TFIN" concerning "Notre action en Indochine du Sud du 30 octobre au 25 décembre," Dec. 28, 1946, app. 6 to "Note sur l'Examen…," June 1947, CP 21, AOM.

123. O'Sullivan to Secstate, No. 96, Oct. 25, 1946, DF851G.00/10–2546, USNA.

124. "Nous vous répétons aussi que du moment qu'aucun ordre précise n'est donné par le Gouvernement, aucun organisme (liaison comprise) n'est autorisé à appliquer lui même le Modus Vivendi." Chief of the central liaison office to liaison chiefs in eleven towns, No. 2006/TV, Hanoi, Oct. 30, 1946, app. 2 to memo "Le Modus Vivendi et le Vietminh," CP 8, AOM.

125. Gonon, Pignon, and Torel to d'Argenlieu, No. 65CP, Sept. 14, 1946, Tel. 914, AOM.

126. It has not been possible to locate these instructions in the French archives, but Moutet announced that they would be prepared in his letter to d'Argenlieu on Sept. 21, 1946, Papiers Moutet, PA 28, C3, d.83, AOM. D'Argenlieu referred to the military instructions in a telegram to FOM on October 31, and Valluy in a telegram on November 19.

127. Haussaire to FOM, Oct. 31, 1946, Tel. 933, AOM.

128. Haussaire to Comrep Hanoi, Nov. 11, 1946, 1MiF44, AOM. "Compte rendu vietnamien des conversations avec le général Nyo du 9 au 13.11.46 et lettre de Hoang Huu Nam au général Nyo," Nov. 19, 1946, CP-sup. 8, AOM (Vietnamese files captured in 1947). Wilson to Meiklereid, Nov. 23, 1946, FO959/11/243/3635/46, PRO.

129. "Réponse au télégramme général Nyo du 9. J'estime qu'il y à intéret à gagner du temps." Haussaire to Comrep Hanoi, Nov. 11, 1946, 1MiF44, AOM.

130. Vietnamese summary of the Nyo talks, Nov. 9–13, 1946; Hoang Huu Nam, letter to General Nyo, Nov. 19, 1946, both in CP 8, AOM (Vietnamese files, captured in 1947).

131. Devillers, *Histoire du Viêt-Nam*, 325.

132. Tran Buu Kiem (secretary-general), Pham Ngoc Thuan (deputy chairman), and Ung Van Khiem (commissar of the interior), instructions signed Oct. 17, 1946, CP-Sup. 8 (2), AOM.

133. D'Argenlieu to Cominindo, No. 1726F, Oct. 29, 1946, Tel. 937 (RG/No. 536), and 1MiF43, AOM. Haussaire to Comrep Hanoi, No. 1007F, Oct. 29, 1946, 1MiF43, AOM.

134. Cominindo to Haussaire, No. 1903/CI/3110, Nov. 2, 1946, CP 13, AOM.

135. Cominindo to Haussaire, No. CI/03285, Nov. 25, 1946, AO, MAE. Haussaire to Comrep Hanoi, No. 1899E, Nov. 27, 1946, 1MiF44, AOM.

136. Prési. Paris to Haussaire, No. 1903/CI/3110, Nov. 2, 1946, CP-sup. 13 (2-2), AOM.

137. D'Argenlieu to Morlière, No. 10341E, Nov. 6, 1946, 1MiF44, AOM. Morlière, letter to Ho Chi Minh, No. 161/CAB.CIV, Nov. 7, 1946, CP-sup. 8, AOM.

138. President Ho Chi Minh to high commissioner (through Morlière), Nov. 9, 1946, CP-sup. 8, AOM.

139. High commissioner to President Ho Chi Minh (through Morlière), Nov. 12, 1946, CP-sup. 8, AOM.

140. President Ho Chi Minh to high commissioner, Nov. 14, 1946, in Comrep Hanoi to Haussaire, No. 462, Nov. 15, 1946, 1MiF5, AOM.

141. Comrep Hanoi to Haussaire, No. 478, Nov. 17, 1946, CP-sup. 13 (3-III), AOM.

142. High commissioner to President Ho Chi Minh (through Morlière), Nov. 20, 1946, CP-sup. 8, AOM (VN files).

143. "Renseignements" from 2ème Bureau (Keller), Nov. 7, 1946, CP-sup. 13 (1), AOM.

144. SDECE, "Notice technique de contre-ingérence politique," Nov. 28, 1946, AO, MAE. In 1947, the British consul found three kilograms of Vietnamese documents in Hanoi, some which showed that they had prepared themselves seriously for negotiating in the mixed commissions. Saigon examined the documents and concluded: "Comme les Anglais en Birmanie, nous avions en somme le droit de payer et de nous en aller." Study on "Les positions Vietminh concernant l'application du Modus Vivendi," CP-sup. 8, AOM (where the most important Vietnamese documents are also found).

145. "Instructions pour la constitution des commissions mixtes prévues par le modus vivendi du 14 septembre," Saigon, Oct. 17, 1946, EA, carton 38, dossier "Application," MAE. SEHAN BR No. 3729, Oct. 28, 1946, EA, carton 39, dossier B-605, MAE. "Renseignements du 2ème Bureau" (Keller), Nov. 7, 1946, CP-sup. 13 (1), AOM. SDECE "Notice technique de contre-ingérence politique," Nov. 28, 1946, AO, MAE. Comrep Hanoi to Haussaire, No. 311, Oct. 26, No. 366, Nov. 4, and No. 451, Nov. 13, 1946, 1MiF5, AOM.

146. D'Argenlieu to Cominindo, No. 1785F, Nov. 7, 1946, Tel. 938 and 1MiF44, AOM.

147. Haussaire to Cominindo, No. 1837F, Nov. 16, 1946, AOM, 1MiF44. See also Valluy, letter to Ho Chi Minh, No. 3095, Nov. 16, 1946, CP-sup. 8, AOM (VN files).

148. Haussaire Paris to Haussaire Saigon, Nov. 21, 1946, 1MiF5, AOM.

149. De Lacharrière to Valluy, No. 673-678, Nov. 22, 1946, 1MiF5, AOM.

150. Haussaire to Comrep Hanoi, No. 1890E, Nov. 23, 1946, 1MiF44, AOM.

151. Haussaire to Cominindo, No. 1628F, Oct. 16, 1946, Tel. 937 and 1MiF43, AOM.

152. Léon Pignon 1908-1976: Un homme de coeur au service de l'Outre-Mer français (cited n. 10 above), 44.

153. Haussaire to Cominindo, Oct. 19, 1946, Tel. 937, AOM.

154. D'Argenlieu to Défense nationale (for Bidault and Juin only), Oct. 19, 1946, reproduced in 1945-1946: Le retour de la France en Indochine, ed. Bodinier, 300-302.

155. Haussaire to Cominindo, No. 679CH, Oct. 26, 1946 (three telegrams under the same number), Tel. 937, AOM.

156. D'Argenlieu to Cominindo, No. 1703F, Oct. 26, 1946, Tel. 937, AOM. D'Argenlieu's use in this text of the words "L'ambassadeur" (for Morlière) and "Gouvernement" (for himself) was no doubt ironical. While he clearly perceived himself as leading a federal government, he did not of course want to concede any independent status to the government of Ho Chi Minh.

157. Reed to Secstate, No. 428, Oct. 31, 1946, DF851G.00/10–3146, USNA.

158. Haussaire to Cominindo, Nov. 1, 1946, Tel. 938, AOM.

159. Haussaire to Cominindo, Nov. 3, 1946, Tel. 938, AOM.

160. D'Argenlieu to Cominindo (for the attention of the Minister for Overseas France), Nov. 6, 1946, Tel. 938, AOM.

161. Haussaire to Cominindo, No. 1824F, Nov. 16, 1946, Tel. 938, AOM.

162. Haussaire to Cominindo, No. 1853F, Nov. 19, 1946, Tel. 938, AOM.

163. Minutes from the plenary session of the "Assemblée de Cochinchine," Oct. 31, 1946, EA, carton 48, dossier C-223, MAE.

164. Ibid.

165. The demand was made with twenty-three votes in favor and three abstentions. Ibid. See also Haussaire to Cominindo, No. 1795F, Nov. 8, 1946, 1MiF44, AOM.

166. David G. Marr, Vietnamese Anticolonialism, 1885–1925 (Berkeley: University of California Press, 1971), 39.

167. "Le président Thinh a certainement voulu dépouiller l'injustice des attaques dont il était l'objet et auxquelles l'application du modus-vivendi allait donner encore plus de liberté d'expression." Haussaire to Cominindo, No. 1800F, Nov. 10, 1946, Tel. 938, AOM.

168. "Procès-verbaux des séances de l'Assemblée de Cochinchine le 31.10.46," Haussaire to Cominindo, No. 1795F, distributed in Paris Nov. 11, 1946; "Note relative à la séance du Conseil de Cochinchine le 7.11.46," AFP Service spécial outre-mer, No. 63, No. 5, Nov. 12, 1946; Haussaire to Cominindo, No. 1917F, Nov. 29, 1946, EA, carton 48, dossier C-223, MAE; Haussaire to Cominindo, No. 697, Cabinfor, Nov. 13, 1946, EA, carton 30, dossier B-263, MAE. Haussaire to Cominindo, No. 1800F, Nov. 10, 1946, Tel. 938, AOM. Handwritten note on the last page of the draft instructions from d'Argenlieu to Valluy, Nov. 13, 1946, 10H162, SHAT.

169. "Or la loyauté avec laquelle de part et d'autre fut appliqué le 'modus vivendi' signé entre M. Ho Chi Minh et Marius Moutet enlève peu à peu toute raison d'être et toute autorité à ce pseudo-gouvernement. Le suicide de son président va sans nul doute en hâter la disparition." Le Populaire, Nov. 11, 1946.

170. D'Argenlieu had good reason to fear a change in the French government's approach to Vietnam. In a lecture about French colonial policy later that same month, the director of political affairs in the Ministry of Overseas France, Henri Laurentie, listed the likely "Associated States" as Morocco, Tunisia, Cambodia, and Vietnam. "Conférence du Gouverneur Laurentie—King's College, Londres 28 Novembre 1946," CP 295, dossier C, AOM.

171. D'Argenlieu's words were "recourir à une action de force directe contre le gouvernement de Hanoi." See the next chapter for further discussion and source references for these important instructions.

4. MASSACRE

Epigraph: COMAR Haiphong to Saigon, No. 30.693–94, Nov. 23, 1946; italics added.

1. Comrep Hanoi to Haussaire, No. 698, Dec. 4, 1946, 1MiF5, AOM.

2. Nguyen Binh apparently tried to launch a military offensive in December, but failed. The concentration on the political field in November, and on internal conflict between him and the political leader Pham Van Bach, caused problems. "Notre action en Indochine du Sud du 30 octobre au 25 décembre," note dated Dec. 28, 1946, CP 21, AOM; "Directives du gouvernement vietnamien," covering the period from Oct. 31, 1946, to Jan. 15, 1947, signed by BCR chief Barada on Dec. 13, 1946, and Jan. 31, 1947, CP 15(1), AOM.

3. D'Argenlieu to Bidault and Juin, No. 429/EMP/3, Oct. 19, 1946, 4Q78, *dossier 7*, SHAT, and EA, *carton 36, dossier 15*, MAE. Juin, "Note d'avis," No. 540 DN/S.COL, Oct. 23, 1946, 4Q80, *dossier 1*, SHAT. Devillers, *Paris-Saigon-Hanoi*, 231–34; *1945–1946: Le retour de la France en Indochine*, ed. Bodinier, 300–302.

4. Valluy, *Revue des deux mondes*, Dec. 1, 1967, 363, was the first to cite this "lettre 2949 du 25 octobre adressée à tous les Commissaires": "Mettons-nous en mesure de répondre éventuellement dès janvier 47 à une reprise des hostilités par une action de force visant à neutraliser politiquement et moralement le gouvernement de Hanoi et à faciliter ainsi la pacification du Sud."

5. "Etude préliminaire concernant l'exécution d'un coup de force au Tonkin," No. 4310/3-OP-S, enclosure to Valluy to d'Argenlieu, No. 4309/3-OP-S, Nov. 9, 1946, 10H162, SHAT. The full text of this study is reproduced as an appendix to Turpin, *De Gaulle, les gaullistes et l'Indochine, 1940–1956*, 602–24.

6. D'Argenlieu, letter to Valluy, Nov. 13, 1946, 10H162, SHAT. Reproduced in full, dated Nov. 12, from 10H165, *dossier 1*, SHAT, in *1945–1946: Le retour de la France en Indochine*, ed. Bodinier, 315–17. Excerpts, also dated Nov. 12, in Devillers, *Paris-Saigon-Hanoi*, 240–41. Cited, dated Nov. 11, by Valluy, *Revue des deux mondes*, Dec. 1, 1967, 363.

7. Ibid.

8. D'Argenlieu, *Chronique d'Indochine*, 339.

9. The order was sent from Saigon at 12.58 (local time) and the report on the situation in the south at 6.12 (French time). This means that they were sent with only fourteen minutes' interval. The order bears No. 1903/3/T and the report No. 1902/3/T. This proves that these two sources are remnants of the same action, and the statements in the report are likely to have been a major motive for the order (of which Valluy only informed Paris the next day). For the order, see Morlière, report No. 3687/3, Dec. 4, 1946, CP 7, AOM. For the summary, see Valluy to EMGDN No. 1902/3/T, Nov. 22, 1946, 06H12, Tel. 933, AOM.

10. Valluy to EMGDN, No. 1902/3/T, Nov. 22, 1946, 06H12, Tel. 933, AOM.

11. Bidault to d'Argenlieu No. C.I./02975, Oct. 17, 1946, Tel. 914, AOM.

12. Reed to Secstate No. 440, Nov. 13, 1946, DF851G.00/11–1346, USNA.

13. See *Le Populaire*, Nov. 15, 1946.

14. Valluy demanded that a severe sanction, "telle que le rappel immédiat, soit prise contre Monsieur NOFGEV [de Norjeu], Directeur de l'A.F.P." Valluy to Cominindo, No. 1824F, Nov. 15, 1946, Tel. 938, AOM.

15. Reed to Secstate, No. 439, Nov. 11, 1946, DF851G.00/11–1146, USNA.

16. "Memorandum of the Viet-Nam Government on the Origin of the Present Franco Vietnam Conflict" (with seventy-six documents attached), originally intended to be handed to Minister for Overseas France Marius Moutet in late December 1946. When Ho failed to meet Moutet, the memo was sent through various channels to the French and U.S. governments in January 1947. Copies are in EA, *carton* 41, *dossier* B-608, in *carton* 43, *dossier* C-112, and in *carton* 56, *dossier* 247 s/d. XVIII, MAE, in AO, MAE, and in DF851G.oo/4-2447, USNA (hereafter cited as "Ho Chi Minh memo, Dec. 31, 1946"). The reference here is to doc. 4, "Directives No 1 du General Leclerc."

17. Salan, *Mémoires*, 1: 358.

18. Ho Chi Minh memo, Dec. 31, 1946, doc. 5, "Directives No 2 du General Valluy." The Vietnamese were able to quote Leclerc's and Valluy's orders after having found them during the fighting in Haiphong in late November. D'Argenlieu memo, Feb. 11, 1947, written in response to Ho Chi Minh memo, Dec. 31, 1946, does not contest the authenticity of these documents, which is also confirmed in Valluy to Moutet, EA, *carton* 57, *dossier* 304, MAE ("réponse à la note no. 355, 7.2.47 du ministre," EA, *carton* 43, *dossier* C-110, MAE). When Pierre Cot quoted Valluy's order in the French National Assembly on March 18, 1947, he was interrupted by Moutet, who cited the first part of the order (omitted in Ho Chi Minh memo, Dec. 31, 1946), which mandated avoiding any incident. On this basis, Moutet insisted that Valluy's order had been of a "caractère préventif et défensif qu'on reprocherait sans doute à nos chefs de ne pas avoir respecté s'ils s'étaient laissé eux aussi, surprendre." But he admitted that it had been "très maladroit d'employer ces termes de 'scénario de coup d'Etat,'" *Journal officiel . . . Assemblée nationale*, session of Mar. 18, 1947, 872.

19. Reed to Secstate, No. 122, Apr. 27, 1946, *FRUS, 1946,* 8: 38.

20. According to the French, the incident started with a Vietnamese ambush. The French reacted by occupying several important buildings in the town (northeast of Hanoi). Bac Ninh was not included on the list of French garrisons in the April 3 convention, so the Vietnamese viewed the continued French presence after the incident as violating the agreement. See reprinted telegram from Saigon to Paris on Bac Ninh incident in Salan, *Mémoires*, 1: 402.

21. Valluy to Juin, Aug. 29, 1946; Juin to the Army minister (signed Fassy), No. 440 DN/S.COL, 4Q80, *dossier* 1, SHAT.

22. "Extraits du rapport mensuel du Conseiller Militaire," No. 999/CAB, signed Valluy, Sept. 10, 1946, 10H163, *dossier* 1, SHAT.

23. From July to August, the commander of the French forces in the north was Colonel Jean Crépin, who had played an essential role in negotiations with the Chinese in the run-up to March 6.

24. Valluy in *Revue des deux mondes*, Dec. 1, 1967, 368–69. Chaffard, *Les deux guerres du Vietnam*, 33ff. Raoul Salan, *Mémoires*, vol. 2: *Le Viêt-minh mon adversaire, octobre 1946–octobre 1954* (Paris: Presses de la Cité, 1971). Vo Nguyen Giap, *Unforgettable Days*, 318. "Note sur la situation en Indochine," signed Morlière, Feb. 10, 1947, author's copy.

25. Jean Ferrandi, *Les officiers français face au Vietminh, 1945–1954* (Paris: Fayard, 1966), 83. I thank Gilles de Gantès for information on the relationship between Dèbes and Valluy, based on their private correspondence from 1946.

26. This order, signed by Dercourt, is in attachment 2 to dispatch No. 12 from O'Sullivan to Secstate, Dec. 1, 1946, DF851G.oo/12-146, USNA. O'Sullivan had got a copy from

the Vietnamese. The authenticity of the order is confirmed in a telegram from Haussaire to EMGDN, Dec. 5, 1946, Tel. 933, AOM.

27. "Rapport de quinzaine du 16 au 31 janvier 1947," signed Sainteny, DGD 75, AOM.

28. In July 1946, d'Argenlieu had instructed the French services in Hanoi to follow the opposition closely for the purpose of eventually using it in the service of French interests. D'Argenlieu to Comrep Hanoi, July 22, 1946, CP 13, AOM.

29. Devillers, *Histoire du Viêt-Nam*, 327.

30. Bruce Lockhart, *The End of the Vietnamese Monarchy* (New Haven CT: Council on Southeast Asia Studies, Yale Center for International and Area Studies, 1993), 166–67.

31. Bouffanais (Kunming) to Meyrier (Nanjing), May 7, 1946, BR No. 21.1–3135/SD from DEC, May 13, 1946, BR No. 21.1–3278/SD from DEC, June 6, 1946, EA, *carton* 62, *dossier* C-707 "Bao Daï," MAE. Devillers, *Histoire du Viêt-Nam*, 327. Haussaire to Diplomatie Paris, No. 1482F, Sept. 25, 1946, Haussaire to Cominindo, No. 1529F, Oct. 3, 1946, Haussaire to Cominindo, No. 1569F, Oct. 9, 1946, and Haussaire to Comrep Hanoi, No. 986E, Oct. 24, 1946, 1MiF43, AOM. Cominindo to Haussaire, RG/No. 1728/C.I./02870, Oct. 4, 1946, Tel. 915, AOM. Fransulat Hong Kong to Haussaire, Oct. 26, 1946, 1MiF43, AOM. Memorandum ("directives générales de notre action politique)," Saigon, Oct. 28, 1946, signed d'Argenlieu, EA, *carton* 52, *dossier* "Après le 15 août 1945," MAE.

32. Haussaire to Diplomatie Paris, No. 1482F, Sept. 25, 1946, 1MiF43, AOM; Haussaire to Cominindo, No. 1529F, Oct. 3, 1946, 1MiF43 and Tel. 937, AOM; Cominindo to Haussaire, RG/No. 1728/C.I./02870, Oct. 4, 1946, Tel. 915, AOM; Haussaire to Cominindo, No. 1569F, Oct. 9, 1946, 1MiF43 and Tel. 937, AOM; Haussaire to Comrep Hanoi, No. 986E, Oct. 24, 1946, 1MiF43, AOM; Fransulat Hong Kong to Haussaire, Oct. 26, 1946, 1MiF5, AOM.

33. Turpin, *De Gaulle, les gaullistes et l'Indochine 1940–1956*, 190–94.

34. "Note de Mr Marius Moutet a/s de la Conférence de Fontainebleau," Aug. 8, 1946, EA, *carton* 36, *dossier* 15, MAE. Personal message from Moutet to d'Argenlieu, Aug. 19, 1946, EA, *carton* 42, *dossier* C-101, MAE.

35. Note from Pignon to Messmer No. 3598/CP-Cab, Oct. 5, 1946, EA, *carton* 37, MAE. "Echos de la. . . ." Pignon to Laurentie, Oct. 25, 1946, EA, *carton* 36, *dossier* 15, MAE. Pignon to Messmer (copy of letter to Laurentie), Oct. 25, 1946, Papiers Bidault, 457AP 127, *dossier* "octobre et novembre 1946." Mathivet to Messmer, Oct. 26, 1946, EA, *carton* 35, *dossier* 505–1, MAE.

36. Personal note from Laurentie to Moutet, Oct. 21, 1946, EA, *carton* 36, *dossier* 15, MAE.

37. Ibid. and Laurentie to Moutet, Nov. 27, 1946, EA, *carton* 36, *dossier* 15, MAE. "Projet d'instructions pour le Haut Commissaire," Papiers Bidault, 457AP 127, *dossier* "octobre-novembre 1946," AN.

38. Daniel Varga, "La politique française en Indochine (1947–50): Histoire d'une décolonisation manquée" (PhD diss., Université d'Aix–Marseille I, 2004), 124–25, analyzes Pignon's reasoning. For a specific study of the DRV's repression of the nationalist parties, seeking to evoke the history of the losers, see Guillemot, "Au coeur de la fracture vietnamienne," an essay based on his thesis *Révolution nationale et lutte pour l'indépendance au Viêt-Nam: L'échec de la troisième voie Dai Viet* (Paris: Ecole pratique des hautes études, 2003).

39. Bao Dai was even less remarkable as an autobiographer than as head of state. Several sections of his 1980 memoirs, *Le dragon d'Annam* (Paris: Plon, 1980), are drawn more

or less directly from Philippe Devillers, *Histoire du Viêt-Nam de 1940 à 1952* (Paris: Seuil, 1952).

40. "Rapport mensuel de la Sûreté fédérale," No. 3278, signed A. Moret, Oct. 27, 1946, PCE 8, AOM.

41. "Bulletin de renseignements . . . Source: très sure," No. 99/DAPA/S from Comrep Hanoi to Haussaire, Nov. 12, 1946, CP 6, AOM.

42. MAE to Ambafrance Nankin, June 19, 1946, AP 3441/3/3, AOM; Cominindo to Haussaire, No. CI/02645, Sept. 9, 1946, Tel. 915, AOM. The French Foreign Ministry criticized d'Argenlieu for his attitude with regard to Chinese authorities and interests. Diplomatie to Haussaire, No. CI/02712, Sept. 14, 1946, Tel. 915, AOM.

43. Devillers, *Histoire du Viêt-Nam*, 286.

44. Leclerc to Valluy No. 2043-CE/CAB, June 17, 1946, CP 7(5a), AOM.

45. Valluy to Leclerc/Longeaux, July 5, 1946, CP 7(5a), AOM.

46. Vietnamese note on "les agissements des autorités françaises en matière douanière" captured by the French after the outbreak of war, CP 8(5), AOM.

47. Colonel Domergue, report to Valluy, No. 2051/A/SECT, Jan. 14, 1947, AP 3441/7, AOM.

48. Commandant Camoin, report, No. 318/LFVN, Haiphong, Sept. 19, 1946, CP 7(4), AOM.

49. Ibid., 5, 3.

50. D'Argenlieu to Cominindo, No. 1314F, rec'd Sept. 5, 1946, Tel. 937, AOM.

51. There is considerable confusion concerning the date of this circular. If it was issued after the signing of the modus vivendi agreement, it might be seen as violating that. In Ho Chi Minh memo, Dec. 31, 1946, a copy of the circular sent to the Vietnamese government for information on September 24 is enclosed as doc. 52. It carries the No. 257-DNCE and is dated September 19. In an undated protest from interim president Huynh Thuc Khang (doc. 52) reference is also made to the circular of September 19, and explicit protests are expressed against the fact that the circular was issued after the signing of the modus vivendi agreement. A reply from Comrep, dated October 19 (Ho Chi Minh memo, Dec. 31, 1946, doc. 53), affirms that the date September 19 is an error and that the circular was issued under No. 257-DNCE on September 10, thus four days before the signing of the modus vivendi agreement. Attached to Ho Chi Minh memo, Dec. 31, 1946, doc. 54 is another copy of the circular, this time called No. 267-DNCE and dated September 10. A report from the delegate for economic affairs at Morlière's headquarters has a copy of Morlière's circular as appendix 1, called No. 267-DNCE and dated September 9: "Note sur le contrôle de l'importation et de l'exportation dans le port de Haïphong," signed [Robert] Davée, "Délégué aux affaires économiques au Commissariat de la République pour le Tonkin et le Nord-Annam," Hanoi, Nov. 23, 1946, CP 6, AOM (hereafter cited as "Davée report, Nov. 23, 1946"). We consequently have two numbers and three dates for the same circular. It is difficult to decide which one is correct, but a Vietnamese document from October (or November) shows that they accepted September 10 as the date of the circular. "Les agissements des autorités françaises en matière douane," document seized by the French after the battle of Hanoi, CP 8(5), AOM. September 10 is also the date generally referred to in later French documents.

52. Davée report, Nov. 23, 1946, 1. Most of the following is based on this report.

53. "Rapport mensuel de la Sûreté fédérale," No. 3278, October 1946, signed A. Moret, Oct. 27, 1946, PCE 8, AOM.

54. Note from the chief of the police and the "Sûreté Fédérale," Saigon, Oct. 30, 1946, CP 7(1), AOM.

55. Davée report, Nov. 23, 1946, app. 3; Ho Chi Minh memo, Dec. 31, 1946, doc. 54.

56. Morlière to Haussaire, No. 254, Oct. 29, 1946, 1MiF5, AOM.

57. Davée report, Nov. 23, 1946, 8.

58. Morlière to Haussaire, No. 1.033 S/CAB/AE, Nov. 4, 1946; Davée report, Nov. 23, 1946, app. 6.

59. Sûreté, Saigon, "Note d'information" to Comafp, Dircab, and Cominf, Nov. 24, 1946, CP 7(4), AOM.

60. Ho Chi Minh to high commissioner, Nov. 11, 1946, AO, MAE. Ho Chi Minh asked d'Argenlieu to forward his protest to Bidault. It was mentioned by Le Monde, Nov. 19, 1946. The cold, arrogant style of this letter is similar to that used by the French (above all, d'Argenlieu) in messages to the Vietnamese government, but very different from the intense, personal style of Ho Chi Minh.

61. Orders No. 350TV, Oct. 13, No. 380, Oct. 21, No. 369, Oct. 31, and No. 62TVT, Nov. 13, 1946, 2ème Bureau docs No. 2.138/2, 2.136/2, 2.137/2, 2.141/2, CP7, AOM.

62. Order No. 1197-VPM-NVC, Nov. 14, 1946, 2ème Bureau doc. No. 2.134/2, CP 7, AOM.

63. Dèbes, report to Morlière, No. 422/A/Sect, Nov. 20, 1946, CP 7(4), AOM.

64. Morlière to Haussaire, No. 646–47, Nov. 18, 1946, CP 7(5b), AOM.

65. Haussaire to Cominindo, No. 1865F, Nov. 21, 1946, 1MiF44, AOM. Turpin, De Gaulle, les gaullistes et l'Indochine 1940–1956, 287–88.

66. Declaration to AFP, Nov. 27, 1946, Papiers Moutet, PA 28, C3, d.87, AOM.

67. Marr, "Beyond High Politics," 28–37.

68. Vietnamese note, October–November, on "les agissements des autorités françaises en matière douanière," CP 8(5), AOM (VN files captured by the French in the battle for Hanoi).

69. French intelligence later discovered that Vietnam on some occasions in the spring of 1946 had bought weapons through a Chinese general, paying with opium and rice. "Trafic d'armes entre Chinois et V.M. Source: Informateur annamite bien placé," Sûreté fédérale du Tonkin No. 383/RG, Hanoi, Jan. 19, 1947. For equivalent information, see Devillers, Histoire du Viêt-Nam, 286. A French intelligence report on "economic counterinterference" dated Jan. 9, 1947, said that the Vietnamese army desperately needed gas. SDECE, "Notice technique de contre-ingérence économique," Jan. 9, 1947, Papiers Moutet, PA 28, C7, d.158, s/d.5, AOM.

70. Note No. 4718 CP/CAB/SD, Dec. 28, 1946, CP 7(5b), AOM.

71. Haussaire to Comrep Hanoi, No. 1890E, Nov. 23, 1946, 0445hZ, 1MiF44, AOM.

72. Report No. 4231/CP-Cab on "la campagne économique anti-française," Nov. 23, 1946, CP 154, AOM. See also SDECE "Notice technique de contre-ingérence économique," No. 2526/ . . . /SD, Jan. 9, 1947, Papiers Moutet, PA28, carton 7, dossier 158, s/d. 5, AOM. EMGDN, "Bulletin d'études no. 48," Dec. 8, 1946. Morlière to Haussaire, No. 1033 S/CAB/AE, Nov. 4, 1946, Davée report, Nov. 23, 1946, app. 6. Morlière to Haussaire, No. 646–47, Nov. 18, 1946, CP-sup. 7(5b), AOM.

73. Davée report, Nov. 23, 1946, 1.

74. Ibid., 10.

75. Mus, *Viet Nam: Sociologie d'une guerre*, 73.

76. Valluy in *Revue des deux mondes*, Dec. 1, 1967, 364–65.

77. SDECE, "Notice technique de contre-ingérence economique," No. 2526/237/231.S.2. M.00.004/SD, Jan. 9, 1947, Papiers Moutet, PA 28, C7, d.158, s/d.5, AOM.

78. EMGDN, Bulletin d'études, No. 48, Dec. 8, 1946, author's copy.

79. Dèbes, report to Morlière, No. 422/A/Sect, Nov. 20, 1946, CP 7(4), AOM. Bull. d'inf. No. 162/EM/2, signed Nougarède, Nov. 21, 1946, and countersigned by Barrière, Nov. 24, 1946, UU-TB-17, SHM. Barrière to "Vice-amiral cdt. les forces navales d'Extrême Orient et le contre-amiral commandant la Marine en Indochine," No. 457/Cdt, Nov. 22, 1946, UU-TB-17, SHM. French translation of report by Le Van My, probably captured during the conquest of Haiphong, AO, MAE. Le Van My's report shows that he was not afraid only of the French, but also of his own troops, who accused him of treason, since he worked with French liaison officers in trying to stop hostilities. *Le Peuple*, no. 68 (Nov. 23, 1946), author's copy. Ho Chi Minh memo, Dec. 31, 1946, doc. 55, s/d.3. When the same information is to be found in both the Ho Chi Minh memo and *Le Peuple*, this is hereafter called "the Vietnamese version."

80. Le Van My's report probably served as a basis for the Vietnamese version, but only partially. Information from Saigon to Paris relied heavily on the Dèbes report to Morlière No. 422/A/Sect, Nov. 20, 1946, CP 7(4), AOM, which served as basis for the version printed in d'Argenlieu memo, Feb. 11, 1947, app. 11. Morlière's report of Jan. 10, 1947, is also based on the Dèbes report: General Louis-Constant Morlière, "Rapport sur les événements politiques et militaires en Indochine du Nord, au cours du dernier trimestre 1946," Jan. 10, 1947, reproduced in Georges Chaffard, *Les deux guerres du Viêt-nam de Valluy à Westmoreland* (Paris: Table ronde, 1969), 36–58 (hereafter cited as "Morlière report, Jan. 10, 1947"). Also close to the Dèbes version are Vice-Consul O'Sullivan's reports to Washington, i.e., O'Sullivan to Secstate, dispatch 9, Nov. 23, 1946, DF851G.00/11–2346, and O'Sullivan to Secstate, dispatch 12, Dec. 14, 1946, DF851G.00/12–1446, USNA. The account in Devillers, *Histoire du Viêt-Nam*, 332ff., reads like a summary of the Dèbes report; the same is true of Fonde, *Traitez à tout prix*, 283–84. Vo Nguyen Giap, *Unforgettable Days*, 373, briefly recounts the Vietnamese version.

81. Devillers, *Histoire du Viêt-Nam*, 332.

82. Morlière report, Jan. 10, 1947, 39. Ferrandi, *Les officiers français face au Vietminh*, 85.

83. Untitled document on the premeditation of the December 19 attack, written by French counterespionage, probably early 1947, EA, *carton* 30, *dossier* B-236, MAE. Morlière report, Jan. 10, 1947. For Jumeau's role, see also Morlière's note on the "affaire Pho Ba Hung," EA, *carton* 41, *dossier* "P.11 . . . P.18," MAE. On Jumeau in 1951, see Devillers, *Histoire du Viêt-Nam*, 332.

84. Dèbes, report to Morlière, No. 422/A/Sect, Nov. 29, 1946, CP 7(4), AOM. The Vietnamese version only says the car was stopped and does not mention that anyone was injured. The Le Van My report has a lot about cars and bicycles going back and forth, but does not mention the particular incident with the car.

85. Morlière report, Jan. 10, 1947, 40.

86. Dèbes, report to Morlière, No. 422/A/Sect, Nov. 20, 1946, CP 7(4), AOM. A draft report from Saigon to Paris on November 22 said the Vietnamese "troops" were responsible

for the affair, but in the final telegram to Paris, "troops" was replaced by "authorities." Haussaire to Cominindo (signed Giard), No. 1878F, Nov. 22, 1946, 1200h, 1MiF44, AOM.

87. Vo Nguyen Giap, letter of protest to Morlière, Nov. 21, 1946, Ho Chi Minh memo, Dec. 31, 1946, doc. 55, s/d.2.

88. Documentation on BFDOC in UU-FT-1, SHM. See also note No. 3672/2, Aug. 2, 1946, 4Q43, dossier 3, SHAT.

89. Dèbes, report to Morlière, No. 422/A/Sect, Nov. 20, 1946, CP 7(4), AOM, 5.

90. Morlière report, Jan. 10, 1947, 40.

91. Ibid., 39–40. The message to Morlière is also printed in Morlière report, Dec. 4, 1946, app. 3, CP 7, AOM. This report is a collection of the most important telegrams from Saigon to Hanoi, Saigon to Haiphong, and Hanoi to Haiphong (only downwards in the hierarchy), Nov. 20–26, 1946. Most of the telegrams are also quoted in Morlière report, Jan. 10, 1947.

92. Comrep Hanoi to Haussaire, No. 513, 0905hZ, and No. 514, 1215hZ, Nov. 20, 1946, CP 13 (3-I), AOM.

93. O'Sullivan to Secstate, dispatch 12, Dec. 14, 1946, DF851G.00/12-1446, USNA.

94. Morlière report, No. 3687/3, Dec. 4, 1946, app. 1, CP 7, AOM.

95. Col. Lami to Morlière, No. 127/DAPA, Nov. 23, 1946, EA, carton 41, dossier "P.11 ... P.19," MAE.

96. Morlière report, Jan. 10, 1947, 42.

97. Valluy to Morlière, No. 1901/3.T, Nov. 21, 1946, 19.05 local time. Morlière report, Dec. 4, 1946, CP 7, AOM.

98. Haussaire to Cominindo, SSS Saigon 0083 220, Nov. 21, 1946, 1240hZ, Tel. 938, AOM.

99. Valluy to EMGDN, No. 1898/3.T, Nov. 21, 1946, 1410hZ, Tel. 933, AOM and 4Q78, dossier 4, SHAT.

100. Morlière to Dèbes, No. 3506/3, Nov. 22, 1946, 08.45 local time. Morlière report, Dec. 4, 1946, CP 7, AOM.

101. Morlière to Valluy No. 3511/3, Nov. 22, 1946, 09.55 local time. Morlière report, Jan. 10, 1947, 43.

102. Valluy to Morlière, No. 1903/3.T, and to Dèbes, No. 1904/3.T, Nov. 22, 1946, 12.58 local time. Morlière report, Dec. 4, 1946, CP 7, AOM, and Morlière report, Jan. 10, 1947, 44.

103. Valluy to Morlière, No. 1907/3.T, Nov. 22, 1946, 19.20 local time. Morlière report Dec. 4, 1946, CP 7, AOM.

104. Col. Lami, letter to Dèbes, Haiphong, Nov. 22, 1946, author's copy, and D'Argenlieu, Chronique d'Indochine, 354.

105. Dèbes to president of the Haiphong Administrative Committee, No. 461/I-SECT, Nov. 22, 1946. Morlière report, Dec. 4, 1946, app. 5, and Pignon report, Dec. 10, 1946, app. 9, both CP 7, AOM. The essential part is also in Ho Chi Minh memo, Dec. 31, 1946, doc. 55, s/d.8.

106. Dèbes report to Morlière, No. 422/A/Sect, Nov. 20, 1946, CP 7(4), AOM (annexe No. 13: Dèbes to "Président du Comité administratif de Haïphong," No. 461/R-SECT, Nov. 22, 1946; annexe No. 15: "Président du Comité administratif" Nguyen to Dèbes, No. 1239/BVT, Nov. 23, 1946; annexe No. 16: Dèbes to "Président du Comité administratif de Haïphong," No. 463/A/Sect, Nov. 23, 1946; annexe No. 17: "Président du Comité administratif" Nguyen to Dèbes, No. 1240/U/B/B, Nov. 23, 1946). Comrep Hanoi to Haussaire No. 565, Nov. 23, 1946, 1115hZ, 1MiF5 and CP-sup. 13 (3), AOM. "Bulletin d'information sur

les 'opérations de la journée du 23 Novembre 1946,'" signed Nougarède, Nov. 23, 1946, UU-TB-17, SHM. Comrep Hanoi to Haussaire, No. 565, Nov. 23, 1946, 1115hZ, 1MiF5 and CP 13(3), AOM says the bombing started at 10.05. Ho Chi Minh memo, Dec. 31, 1946, doc. 55, s/d. 3, says 10.06, while O'Sullivan to Secstate, dispatch No. 12, Dec. 1, 1946, DF851G.00/12-146, USNA, says "10.13 or 10.30."

107. Pierre Voisin in *Le Figaro*, Jan. 21, 1947, 3.

108. Haussaire to Ambafrance Nankin (repeating No. 630 from Comrep Hanoi), Dec. 3, 1946, 1MiF44, AOM.

109. The French said the convoy was attacked by Vietnamese forces. The Vietnamese said the last cars in the convoy fired on some houses at the northern end of "Pont des Rapides." VN liaison report, Aug. 4, 1946, Ho Chi Minh memo, Dec. 31, 1946, doc. 23.

110. Morlière to Ho Chi Minh (signed Lami) No. 47/DAPA, Oct. 20, 1946, CP 7, AOM. Ho Chi Minh memo, Dec. 31, 1946, docs. 25-31 show convincingly that the French troops were recruiting "auxiliaries."

111. Ho Chi Minh memo, Dec. 31, 1946, docs. 56-57.

112. Lt. Col. Sizaire, report, No. 6291/3, Nov. 30, 1946, CP 1, AOM.

113. Folder entitled "Affaire de Langson entre le 21 et le 30 novembre 1946" and documents captured by the French during the fighting, 4Q43, *dossier* 1, SHAT.

114. Ibid.

115. Comrep Hanoi to Haussaire, No. 663, Nov. 21, 1946, 0245hZ, CP-sup. 7, AOM.

116. Giap to Morlière, Nov. 21, 1946, Ho Chi Minh memo, Dec. 31, 1946, doc. 56.

117. Lt. Col. Sizaire, report, No. 6291/3, Nov. 30, 1946, CP 1, AOM.

118. Cororient Hanoi to Cororient Saigon, No. 3610/3, Nov. 23, 1946, 0235hZ, CP 13 (3-II), AOM.

119. Lt. Col. Sizaire, report, No. 6291/3, Nov. 30, 1946, CP 1, AOM.

120. Comrep Hanoi to Haussaire, No. 610, Nov. 27, 1946, 1225hZ, 1MiF5, AOM.

121. Haussaire to Comrep Hanoi, No. 967 EMHC, Nov. 28, 1946, 0940hZ, 1MiF44, AOM. "Note de service" No. 3639/3, Nov. 30, 1946, 4Q43, *dossier* 1, SHAT.

122. Note No. 4369/CP-Cab from Pignon to Valluy and Sainteny, Nov. 30, 1946, CP 7, AOM.

123. Ibid. "Rapport de quinzaine du 1er au 15 Janvier 1947," signed Sainteny, DGD 75, AOM.

124. Clayton, *Wars of French Decolonization*, 55; Ruscio, *Guerre française d'Indochine*, 148-50. Dalloz, *Dictionnaire de la guerre d'Indochine*, 46.

125. Giap to Morlière, Nov. 21, 1946, Ho Chi Minh memo, Dec. 31, 1946, doc. 56.

126. O'Sullivan to Secstate, dispatch No. 9, Nov. 23, 1946, DF851G.00/11-2346, USNA.

127. Col. Lami, undated report, probably Nov. 18, 1946, app. 1 to Pignon report, Dec. 10, 1946, CP 7, AOM.

128. "Marine Haïphong, registre des messages clairs," No. 23, UU-TB-2, SHM.

129. O'Sullivan to Secstate, dispatch No. 12, Dec. 1, 1946, DF851G.00/12-146, USNA. Ho Chi Minh memo, Dec. 31, 1946, Morlière report, Jan. 10, 1947, 45-46. Valluy in *Revue des deux mondes*, Dec. 15, 1967, 510-11.

130. "There was no time to evacuate the civilian population which had, however, probably in large measure, already left the city." O'Sullivan to Secstate, dispatch No. 12, Dec. 1, 1946, DF851G.00/12-146, USNA.

131. Comar Haiphong to Comar Saigon, No. 50693–94, Nov. 23, 1946, 18h52G, UUTB-17, SHM. Cororient Hanoi to Cororient Saigon, No. 3.529/3, Nov. 23, 1946, 1130hZ, CP-sup. 13 (3-II), AOM. O'Sullivan to Secstate, dispatch No. 12, Dec. 1, 1946, DF851G.00/12–146, USNA. Ho Chi Minh memo, Dec. 31, 1946. Morlière report, Jan. 10, 1947. Valluy in *Revue des deux mondes*, Dec. 15, 1967, 510.

132. Ho Chi Minh memo, Dec. 31, 1946, doc. 55, s/d. "Incident de Haiphong," p. 3: "Le 25-11-46 … à 10h06 … la population civile vietnamienne et chinoise évacuée précipitamment vers Kien-An, bombardée par l'avion française." Valluy, *Revue des deux mondes*, Dec. 15, 1967, 508: "La population annamite semble avoir évacué la ville et s'être réfugiée à Kienam [sic]." O'Sullivan to Secstate, Nov. 24, 1946, DF851G.00/11–2446, USNA: "this village, which apparently is the headquarters of the Vietnamese Army."

133. Valluy to Morlière, No. 1915/3.T, Nov. 24, 1946, 1235hZ: "Vous occuperez définitivement Kien An"; Valluy to Morlière, No. 1918/3.T, Nov. 24, 1946, 1810hZ. Morlière report, Dec. 4, 1946, CP 7, AOM: "j'estime en raison de tension politique qu'il est préférable pour l'instant de ne pas occuper Kien An." Morlière to Valluy, No. 3.561/3 (probably error for 3.261/3), Nov. 25, 1946, 0335hZ, CP 13 (3-II), AOM: "Estime opération sur Kien An exigerait effectifs importants, généraliserait sûrement un conflit qui a déjà tendance à s'étendre et ne présente en définitive qu'intérêt secondaire"; Cororient Hanoi to Cororient Saigon, Nov. 25, 1946, 1515hZ, CP 13(3-II), AOM: "M'abstiendrai évidemment de toute action sur Kien-An."

134. Comrep Hanoi to Haussaire, No. 271, Nov. 25, 1946, 1040hZ, CP 7, AOM: "Vice-Consul Etats-Unis et Consul Grande-Bretagne reçus amicalement aujourd'hui seize heures par Général Morlière qui les a renseignés sur situation. Bombardement Kienan par Français toujours formellement démenti." Haussaire to Comrep Hanoi, No. 962 EMHC, Nov. 26, 1946, 0830hZ: "Comar Haiphong a rendu compte par télégramme 30.693–94 du 23 18h50G [local time]: 'Mission de la Marine parfaitement éxécutée notamment tirs *Savorgna de Brazza* sur Kienam [sic] et un village désigné.'"

135. Sûreté fédérale, Haiphong, Note No. 495, Nov. 29, 1946, CP 7, AOM: "D'autre part, on signale, ceci n'a pu être vérifié, que les bombardements de Kien-An et des agglomérations environnantes auraient fait de nombreuses victimes, ainsi que le mitraillage des routes aux environs de la ville." See also O'Sullivan to Secstate, dispatch No. 12, Dec. 1, 1946, DF851G.00/12–146, USNA.

136. Haussaire to Cominindo, signed Giard, No. 1965F, Dec. 5, 1946, 1130hZ, CP 2(3), AOM. A slightly different version can be found in EA, MAE. The Quai d'Orsay dutifully conveyed the lies to all French diplomatic stations, even adding that the order not to use artillery except as the last resort had been "strictly" observed. Circulaire No. 110F, Dec. 7, 1946, CP 13(2), AOM.

137. Valluy, *Revue des deux mondes*, Dec. 15, 1967, 507.

138. Comrep Hanoi to Haussaire, No. 698, Dec. 4, 1946, 1600hZ, 1MiF5, AOM.

139. Valluy, *Revue des deux mondes*, Dec. 15, 1967, 511. Moret, Sûreté fédérale, Tonkin, report No. 4271, Dec. 9, 1946, CP 13(1), AOM, said that the Vietnamese side had reported 800 dead and wounded (including 400 civilians) in the first fighting on November 20—that is, before there was any bombing—and that the Vietnamese losses on November 26 "se monteraient à 10 ou 12 00 tués. Ce chiffre étant donné sous toutes réserves."

140. Paul Mus wrote in *Témoignage chrétien*, Aug. 12, 1949 what he had heard from Admiral Roger Battet: "'Pas plus de 6000 tués, en ce qui concerne le tir du croiseur sur les colonnes de fuyards civils . . .' m'a dit l'amiral Battet, commandant des forces navales, en mai 1947, à Saigon." The probable reason why 6,000 has become the conventional figure (cited also in Clodfelter, *Vietnam in Military Statistics*, 17), is that Devillers quoted Mus in *Histoire du Viêt-Nam*, 337.

141. Gen. Yves Gras, *Histoire de la guerre d'Indochine* (Paris: Plon, 1979), 148n1.

142. For documentation on the amount and nature of the naval fire, see the registry of telegraphic messages between the vessels and the naval HQ in Haiphong, UUTB-2, SHM, and the files of each vessel, UU-Y-111–417, SHM.

143. O'Sullivan to Secstate, No. 144, Dec. 18, 1946, DF851G.00/12–1846, USNA.

144. Pignon à Dronne, Nov. 29, 1946, CP 216, AOM: "les Vietnamiens ont subi des pertes encore non précisées, mais qui se chiffrent certainement par milliers." In the draft of his memoirs, written many years later, Pignon insisted that he had not been informed in advance of Valluy's orders to Dèbes. See *Léon Pignon: Une vie au service des peuples d'Outre-Mer*, 55.

145. "Une information du 2ème Bureau de l'Etat-major des TFEO signale que les pertes vietnamiennes à Haiphong et Langson atteindraient 10.000 tués et blesses." Chef du Bureau fédéral de documentation (Schlumberger) to Comafp and "le Chef du Service de l'Information Fédérale," Dec. 13, 1946, CP 7(1), AOM.

146. "Des tués et blessés de Hanoi s'ajoutent aux 3.000 victimes de Haiphong." Ho Chi Minh to Blum and Auriol, Dec. 19, 1946, Ho Chi Minh memo, Dec. 31, 1946, doc. 76.

147. Valluy, *Revue des deux mondes*, Dec. 1, 1967.

148. For Morlière's protest against being replaced by Dèbes, "un Officier supérieur que je considère comme le responsable No 1 de la tragique situation actuelle en Indochine," see Morlière, "Note au sujet du Colonel Dèbes," Paris, Feb. 10, 1947, EA, *carton* 41, *dossier* "Notes du Général Morlière 1947," MAE.

149. Salan, *Mémoires*, 1: 27–28.

150. Valluy, *Revue des deux mondes*, Nov. 1, 1967, 15.

151. Michelet (who left the MRP and joined de Gaulle's RPF in 1947), interview with Irving, Apr. 25, 1967. Irving, *First Indochina War*, 141.

152. Azeau, *Ho Chi Minh dernière chance*, 226.

153. This view is expressed in Irving, *First Indochina War*, 141.

154. Jacques Dalloz, "Le MRP et la guerre d'Indochine," *Cahiers de l'Institut d'histoire du temps présent* 34 (1996): 57–76. Turpin, "Le Mouvement républicain populaire et la guerre d'Indochine (1944–1954)." Thomas, "Colonial Policies of the Mouvement républicain populaire, 1944–1954."

155. Edward Francis Rice-Maximin, "The French Left and Indochina, 1945–1954" (PhD thesis, University of Wisconsin, 1974); Martin Thomas, "French Imperial Reconstruction and the Development of the Indochina War," in *First Vietnam War*, ed. Lawrence and Logevall, 130–51; Gratien, *Marius Moutet: Un socialiste à l'Outre-mer*.

156. Alain Ruscio's study *Les communistes français et la guerre d'Indochine, 1944–1954* uncovers the tactical concerns leading the PCF to tone down its support for the Viet Minh, in order to defend its position as a coalition partner with the MRP and the SFIO. See also d'Argenlieu's famous account of how the PCF's leader Maurice Thorez told him in February

1946 that if he had to he should hit hard ("s'il faut cogner, cognez et cognez dur"), because the French colors had to come first: d'Argenlieu, *Chronique d'Indochine*, 168.

157. After his trip to Paris in May 1946, the anti–Viet Minh Cochinchinese politician Nguyen Van Xuan reported that Thorez had affirmed "que le Parti Communiste n'entendait en aucune façon être considéré comme le liquidateur éventuel des positions françaises en Indochine et qu'il souhaitait ardemment voir le drapeau français flotter sur tous les coins de l'Union Française." Devillers, *Histoire du Viêt-Nam*, 269. During a visit to Indochina in November 1946, the French Foreign Ministry official Jacques Boissier nonetheless exaggerated strongly in telling U.S. Vice-Consul O'Sullivan that the PCF had been "more colonialist than other French groups" at the Fontainebleau conference. O'Sullivan to Secstate, No. 106, Nov. 11, 1946, DF851G.00/11-1146, USNA. Frédéric Turpin claims that Lozeray behaved disloyally to France at Fontainebleau, providing information to the adversary about French negotiating positions, and that both he and Thorez pleaded the DRV's case. Turpin, *De Gaulle, les gaullistes et l'Indochine, 1940–1956*, 254, 265.

158. Michael A. Moutschen was fatally wounded in an incident near Hanoi on February 7, 1947.

159. See Haussaire to Ambafrance Nanking, Bangkok, Manila, and Cairo, and Fransulat Singapore, Canton, Shanghai, Hong Kong, and Calcutta, No. 138G, Dec. 28, 1946, 1MiF44, AOM.

160. *Le Populaire*, Nov. 11, 1946. *Le Monde*, Nov. 17-18, 1946.

161. Some of the newspaper headlines are indicative. *Le Figaro*, Nov. 23, 1946: "De nouveaux incidents au Tonkin. Les éléments vietnamiens multiplient les agressions contre les Français. De nombreux morts." *L'Aube*, Nov. 22, 1946: "Une agression vietnamienne dégénère en bataille rangée." *Le Monde*, Nov. 23, 1946: "Les Viet-Namiens tirent sur les Français à Haiphong."

162. *Le Monde*, Nov. 24-25, 1946.

163. *L'Humanité*, Nov. 23, 1946.

164. *Franc-Tireur*, Nov. 25 and 26, 1946.

165. *L'Humanité*, Nov. 26 and 27, 1946.

166. *L'Humanité*, Nov. 29, 1946.

167. *Le Populaire*, Dec. 19, 1946.

168. The members were Georges Bidault (MRP), who chaired the committee, Marius Moutet (SFIO), who was deputy chair, Edmond Michelet (MRP, minister of armies), Charles Tillon (PCF, aviation minister), Robert Schuman (MRP, finance minister), General Alphonse Juin (chief of staff), Henri Ribière (chief of the intelligence service SDECE). The Comindo also had the right to invite others to its meetings, and Alexandre Varenne (Radical, minister without portfolio), who had been governor-general of Indochina, 1925–28, took part regularly in its deliberations.

169. D'Argenlieu, memo to the Cominindo session of Nov. 23, 1946, AN, F60 C3024.

170. Valluy to EMGDN, No. 1898/3.T, Nov. 21, 1946, 1410hZ, Tel. 933, AOM. This telegram was circulated on Nov. 22, 1946, but Tillon was not on the distribution list.

171. Cororient, Saigon, to EMGDN, No. 1906/3.T., Nov. 23, 1946, 1533hZ, Tel. 933, AOM. Tillon was not on the distribution list of this telegram either.

172. Immediately after the meeting, Messmer cabled Valluy that there had been a long

debate between Moutet, Michelet, and Tillon. He did not mention Bidault's statement and made no mention of what had been said. Messmer to Haussaire, No. 2043, Nov. 23, 1946, 1930hZ, Tel. 915, and 1MiF5, AOM.

173. There exist two summaries of Bidault's statement, one written by his secretary-general (Segalat), which was typed on the basis of a handwritten note and probably approved by Bidault, and one written by d'Argenlieu for transmittal to Valluy, which says it was approved by Bidault. The wording is slightly different in the two versions, the conclusion differing as follows. Segalat: "le gouvernement a le devoir de faire respecter tous les droits de la France par tous les moyens y compris la force." D'Argenlieu: "Le Haut Commissaire a le (droit) d'y (faire respecter) l'ordre et la loi par tous les moyens contre qui que ce soit." The parentheses are in the original. Segalat's note can be found in F60 C3024, AN, d'Argenlieu's in Haussaire Paris to Haussaire, Saigon, No. 200C, Nov. 25, 1946, 1630hZ, 1MiF5, AOM.

174. This is from d'Argenlieu's summary in Haussaire Paris to Haussaire Saigon, No. 200C, Nov. 25, 1946, 1630hZ, 1MiF5, AOM, but d'Argenlieu had announced to Valluy that it had been seen (vu) by Moutet and Michelet and that it would not be cabled Saigon before Bidault had approved it. Haussaire Paris to Haussaire Saigon, Nov. 25, 1946, 10h16Z, 1MiF5, AOM.

175. Haussaire Paris to Haussaire Saigon, Nov. 25, 1946, 10h16Z, 1MiF5, AOM.

176. Moutet, statement to the press, PA 28, C3, d.87, AOM.

177. Haussaire to Cominindo, No. 2038F, Dec. 17, 1946, 0330hZ, Tel. 938, AOM.

178. EMGDN, Bulletin d'étude, No. 46, Paris, Nov. 30, 1946 (written by Barjot), author's copy. A part of the statement cited was quoted in Franc-Tireur, Dec. 27, 1946. Barjot may have been wrong (he was wrong on other points regarding lack of information from Saigon), but I have found no reports on the import-export controls before the information contained in Haussaire to Cominindo, No. 1865F, Nov. 21, 1946, 1MiF4, AOM. This telegram also gives the impression that no information had been provided earlier.

179. The November 22 instructions were quoted in extenso in Cororient Saigon to EMGDN, No. 1906/3.T, Nov. 23, 1946, 1533hZ, Tel. 933, AOM.

180. Haussaire to Prési. Paris, No. 1909F, Nov. 27, 1946, 1030hZ, rec'd Nov. 28, 16h55Z, Tel. 938, AOM. It is not known when Ho Chi Minh handed this protest to the French.

181. E.g., Haussaire Paris to Haussaire Saigon, Nov. 25, 1946, 1016hZ, 1MiF5, AOM: "J'approuve entièrement les instructions que vous avez données au General Morlière. Elles sont dans la ligne des dispositions Gouvernementales."

5. THE FRENCH TRAP

1. Comrep Hanoi to Haussaire, No. 584, Nov. 25, 1946, 1220hZ, CP 13(3-I), AOM.

2. Franc-Tireur, Dec. 20, 1946. The Spanish word camarilla, literally, "a small room," is used to denote a group of secret, often scheming, advisors, a cabal or clique.

3. Valluy to Morlière, No. 1928/3.T, Nov. 26, 1946, 11h30G, rec'd 14.10, Morlière report, Dec. 4, 1946, CP 7, AOM. See also Morlière report, Jan. 10, 1947, 47.

4. Valluy and Pignon to d'Argenlieu, Nov. 23, 1946, 11h40, EA, carton 36, dossier 15, MAE. The governor-general's palace, French Hanoi's biggest and most prestigious public building, had served as the Chinese occupation forces' headquarters until June, and then been repaired so that it could once more house the main French authority in the north.

5. Valluy to Morlière, No. 1929/3.T, Nov. 26, 1946, 12.00 G, Morlière report, Dec. 4, 1946, CP 7, AOM.

6. Morlière to Valluy, No. 3578/3, and Valluy to Morlière, No. 1931/3.T, Nov. 27, 1946, 11.30. Morlière report, Jan. 10, 1947, 47–48. For assurance from Paris, see chapter 4, n. 181.

7. The ultimatum and the subsequent correspondence between Giap and Morlière are attached to Morlière report, Dec. 4, 1946, and Pignon report, Dec. 10, 1946, both CP 7, AOM.

8. O'Sullivan to Secstate, No. 127, Nov. 30, 1946, 1 p.m., DF851G.00/11–3046, USNA.

9. L'Humanité, Dec. 3, 1946.

10. O'Sullivan to Secstate, No. 127, Nov. 30, 1946, 1 p.m., DF851G.00/11–3046, USNA. By March 1947, the French estimated that only some 15,000 out of a normal population of 180–200,000 Vietnamese remained in Hanoi. Report Walrand signed Mar. 3, 1947, sent with letter HC Cab 3658 from Hanoi to Saigon, Mar. 11, 1947, EA, carton 40, dossier 607–01, MAE.

11. Comrep Hanoi to Haussaire, No. 645, Nov. 30, 1946, 1147hZ, CP 13(3-I), AOM.

12. Inspector Gayet, report, Nov. 10, 1946, Papiers Moutet, PA 28, C7, d.158, s/d.9, AOM.

13. Haussaire to EMGDN, No. 846/EMHC, Oct. 4, 1946, Tel. 933, AOM.

14. Inspector Gayet, report, Oct. 10, 1946, Papiers Moutet, PA 28, C7, d.158, s/d.8, AOM.

15. Barjot (in the name of Juin) to Moutet, Oct. 25, 1946, Papiers Moutet, PA 28, C7, d.158, s/d.8, AOM. See also Hugues Tertrais, La piastre et le fusil: Le coût de la guerre d'Indochine, 1945–1954 (Paris: Comité pour l'histoire économique et financière de la France, 2002), 42–43.

16. Haussaire to EMGDN, Nov. 27, 1946, Tel. 933, AOM.

17. Devillers, Paris-Saigon-Hanoi, 257–58.

18. Haussaire to EMGDN, No. 978/EMHC, Nov. 30, 1946, 0735hZ, Tel. 933 and 1MiF44, AOM, and EA, MAE.

19. Defnat to Haussaire, No. 733/EMG/DN/AD-JT, Dec. 1, 1946, 2201hZ, 1MiF5 and CP 13(2), AOM.

20. FOM (Moutet) to Haussaire, Dec. 1, 1946, 1215hZ, Tel. 915, AOM.

21. Haussaire to EMGDN (for communication to d'Argenlieu and Moutet), no number, Dec. 5, 1946, 2328hZ, Tel. 933, AOM.

22. Dec. 4, 1946, Morlière report, CP 7, AOM.

23. Haussaire to Comrep Hanoi, No. 1001 EMHC, Dec. 7, 1946, 03h55Z, 1MiF44, AOM.

24. Handwritten note in CP 7, dos. "Haiphong à M. Riner," AOM.

25. Handwritten copy for the typists. Pignon report, Dec. 10, 1946, CP 7, AOM.

26. "Rapport sur les incidents de Haïphong et de Langson du 20 au 28 novembre 1946," Nov. 28, 1946, with conclusion signed by Barjot, Nov. 29, 1946, Papiers Bidault, 457AP 127 dossier "octobre–novembre," AN. Also reproduced in EMGDN, Bulletin d'études, No. 46, Nov. 30, 1946, 4Q77, dossier 5, SHAT.

27. Note on the "situation actuelle en Indochine" by General Leclerc, Paris, Dec. 5, 1946, 10H163, SHAT. See also note appended to "Note historique sur la situation au Tonkin ayant conduit aux opérations du 20 au 30 novembre 1946," Paris, Dec. 4, 1946, 4Q77, dossier 3, SHAT. Part of the background for Leclerc's note was that, as inspector general of the French forces in North Africa, he had opposed a decision to transfer a parachute battalion to Indochina. Turpin, De Gaulle, les gaullistes et l'Indochine, 1940–1956, 304.

28. EMGDN, Bulletin d'études, No. 48, Dec. 8, 1946, author's copy.

29. Note from General Leclerc on the "situation actuelle en Indochine," Paris, Dec. 5, 1946, 10H163, SHAT. "Rapport sur les incidents de Haïphong et de Langson du 20 au 28 novembre 1946," Nov. 28, 1946, with conclusions signed by Barjot, Nov. 29, 1946, Papiers Bidault, 457AP 127, *dossier* "octobre–novembre," AN. EMGDN, Bulletin d'études, No. 46, Nov. 30, 1946, 4Q77, *dossier* 5, SHAT. "Note historique sur la situation au Tonkin ayant conduit aux opérations du 20 au 30 novembre 1946," Paris, Dec. 4, 1946, *dossier* 3, 4Q77, SHAT.

30. Jean Rous in interview with Jean Lacouture for the film *La République est morte à Dien Bien Phu*, 1973. *Franc-Tireur* mistakenly attributed the instructions to Morlière instead of Valluy and thus continued to include Morlière in d'Argenlieu's "camarilla." Barjot's "indiscretion" is also the likely reason why I now possess copies of his memos.

31. MAE to sixty-three diplomatic stations, circular No. 97IP, AO, MAE.

32. This summary is based on Segalat's rudimentary notes, which may be open to interpretation, F60 C3024, AN.

33. Typed summary, based on Segalat's notes, F60 C3024, AN.

34. D'Argenlieu to Valluy, No. 42/DC, Dec. 3, 1946, CP 13(2-2), AOM.

35. *Le Populaire*, Dec. 8, 1946.

36. "Projet de décret déterminant les attributions du Haut Commissaire de France pour l'Indochine," EA, *carton* 27, *dossier* B-101, MAE.

37. "Bidault redoutait une rupture dans son Parti." Moutet in a statement to the SFIO "Comité directeur," Jan. 27, 1947. The minutes of this meeting are attached to Gratien, "Marius Moutet, de la question coloniale à la construction européenne," 3: 675–83.

38. According to the British ambassador in Paris, Indochina played an important role in the negotiations preceding the formation of the new French government. Cooper to Bevin, No. 1133, Dec. 30, 1946, FO371/63451/F53/5/86, PRO.

39. Governmental instructions to High Commissioner d'Argenlieu, Dec. 10, 1946, signed Bidault, Moutet, and Michelet, EA, *carton* 27, *dossier* B-1 ("Affaires réservés Thierry d'Argenlieu"), MAE. Drafts for the instructions, one version dated November 29, and a later one with Moutet's handwritten revisions, are in EA, *carton* 27, *dossier* B-101, MAE, where there is also a "résumé analytique de la question indochinoise" (a note made by Moutet, which served as basis for the ministry's work on the drafts) and also a draft for a governmental declaration. The revised version of the government instructions given to the new high commissioner, Bollaert, in March 1947 is in EA, *carton* 42, *dossier* C-102, MAE. Other draft copies may be found in Papiers Bidault, 457AP 127 *dossier* "octobre–novembre 1946," AN. The governmental instructions of December 10, 1946 have received far too little attention in studies of French colonial history. A notable exception is Shipway, *Road to War*, 257–58.

40. Lawrence, *Assuming the Burden*, 103, 148. "Tout problème n'est pas financier mais le devient un jour." Tertrais, *La piastre et le fusil*, 23–24.

41. Tertrais, *La piastre et le fusil*, 404.

42. Valluy, *Revue des deux mondes*, Dec. 15, 1967, 527.

43. The proposals of the EMGDN and the high commissioner are attached to *bordereau* No. 56-OC from the "direction du cabinet du Haut Commissariat," Paris, Dec. 3, 1946, Papiers Bidault, 457AP 127, AN.

44. "Résumé analytique de la question indochinoise," cited n. 39 above.

45. Instructions to High Commissioner d'Argenlieu, Dec. 10, 1946, cited n. 39 above.

46. "Qu'il [Ho Chi Minh] comprenne qu'en fait nous considérons maintenant comme essentiel qu'il soit débarrassé des éléments extrêmistes de son gouvernement . . . " Moutet to Haussaire, not sent, EA, *carton* 27, *dossier* B-101, MAE, and Papiers Bidault, 457AP 127, *dossier* "décembre 1946," AN.

47. Valluy warned of the "caractère presque fatal de la rupture à laquelle nous entraînent la haine et la mauvaise foi du Gouvernement de Hanoï." Bidault commented: "Je désire toutefois marquer que j'ai été surpris des termes de votre télégramme précité qui font subitement état d'une situation alarmante que rien ne laissait prévoir dans vos communications précédentes." Haussaire to Cominindo, No. 1001/EMHC, Dec. 6, 1946, 0440hZ, Tel. 938 and 1MiF44, AOM. Bidault to Valluy (countersigned by Messmer), No. CI/03466, Dec. 12, 1946, Tel. 915, AOM and EA, *carton* 27, *dossier* B-106, MAE.

48. *La France et le problème indochinois* (leaflet issued by the MRP's Service d'outre-Mer, Dec. 12, 1946), dos. "Documentation Indochine 1946, écrite en 1946," AN.

49. Sainteny's memoirs were published in 1953 under the title *Histoire d'une paix manquée* [History of a Missed Peace]. They are well written but conceal the most central aspects of Saigon's policy and his own role in December 1946. Sainteny reproduced approximately the same account in *Face à Ho Chi Minh* (Paris: Seghers, 1970).

50. "Jean Sainteny, à nouveau dépeché à Hanoi, y arrive trop tard pour éviter le 19 décembre 1946, le déclenchement de la guerre d'Indochine dont il est pratiquement la première victime." Sainteny, *Histoire d'une paix manquée,* the jacket.

51. Haussaire to Cominindo, No. 1530F, rec'd Oct. 5, 1946, Tel. 937, AOM.

52. Valluy, *Revue des deux mondes,* Dec. 15, 1967, 513.

53. D'Argenlieu to Cominindo, Oct. 29, 1946, Tel. 937, AOM. D'Argenlieu to Cominindo, No. 1744F, Nov. 2, 1946, 1MiF44, AOM. Cominindo to Haussaire, No. CI/03112, Nov. 4, 1946, Tel. 915, AOM.

54. Haussaire Paris to Haussaire Saigon, No. 5, undated in Nov. 1946, CP 13(2–2), AOM.

55. Haussaire to Cominindo, No. 1924F (signed Valluy), Nov. 30, 1946, 0505hZ, Tel. 938, AOM.

56. "Affirmer notre volonté de ne rien céder de nos positions essentielles anciennes et nouvellement acquises mais si une rupture devait intervenir en laisser soigneusement l'initiative à nos partenaires en prenant toutes précautions pour ne pas être surpris par les événements." Haussaire to d'Argenlieu, No. 1938F, Dec. 3, 1946, CP 2(3), AOM.

57. Ibid., and Note No. 4369/CPCab (signed Pignon) to Valluy and Sainteny, Nov. 30, 1946, CP 7, AOM.

58. Comrep Hanoi to Haussaire, No. 650, Dec. 1, 1946, 1125hZ, 1MiF5, AOM.

59. Comrep Hanoi to Haussaire, No. 655, Dec. 2, 1946, 0435hZ, 1MiF5, AOM. In July 1947, Ho Chi Minh actually did undertake a government reshuffle. The purpose then was both to ensure broad support for the war of resistance and to increase the chance that the French would reopen talks. Devillers, *Histoire du Viêt-Nam,* 400–401.

60. Sainteny, *Histoire d'une paix manquée* (1953), 209.

61. Letter from Association Viet-Nam France, Hanoi, Dec. 3, 1946 (signed Nguyen Manh Ha), CP 2(9), AOM.

62. Sainteny, *Face à Hô Chi Minh,* 112. Valluy and Pignon to d'Argenlieu, Nov. 23, 1946, EA, *carton* 36, *dossier* 15, MAE.

63. Cf. the statements made by d'Argenlieu's diplomatic advisor Achille Clarac on Dec. 6, 1946, to the British consul in Saigon. Meiklereid to Bevin, No. 156, Dec. 10, 1946, FO371/53970/F18207/8/61, PRO, and "Note du 6.12.46," FO959/14, PRO.

64. Vu Ky, "Nhung chang duong truong ky khang chien nhat dinh thang loi" [The Protracted Resistance Will Certainly Be Victorious], *Lich su Quan su* [Military History] 12 (1988): 72–82.

65. Sainteny, *Histoire d'une paix manquée* (1953), 217 and the rest of the literature say this was Giam. Sainteny to Valluy (personally), No. 670, Dec. 3, 1946, 1930hZ, 1MiF5, AOM, however, says Giap. On this point, Sainteny's later memory is probably more reliable than the contemporary document, since the French telex operators may easily have typed a "p" instead of an "m."

66. Sainteny to Valluy (personally), No. 670, Dec. 3, 1946, 1930hZ, 1MiF5, AOM.

67. Vo Nguyen Giap, *Unforgettable Days*, 391. Statement by Giam summarized in Comrep Hanoi to Haussaire, No. 721, Dec. 6, 1946, CP 13(3-III), AOM.

68. The journalist asked Sainteny about the message to Paris, and Sainteny replied: "c'est à la suite de l'entretien que j'ai eu, mercredi dernier avec le president Ho-Chi-Minh, que j'ai décidé, sur la demande du Président de la République du Viet-Nam, de faire connaître à Paris la position vietnamienne. Comme je l'ai indiqué à M. Giam, j'en attends encore la réponse ... c'est à Paris, aux responsables de la politique française en Extrême-Orient d'estimer si la question doit être ou peut être reconsidérée." *Paris-Saigon*, Dec. 11, 1946. Saigon was unhappy with this interview and twice asked Sainteny to disclaim parts of it. Sainteny refused, although claiming that his ideas had been distorted by the journalist (Dranber). Comrep Hanoi to Haussaire, No. 859, Dec. 17, 1946, 1100hZ, and No. 915 (2), Dec. 18, 1946, 0320hZ, CP 13 (3-I), AOM.

69. French summary of Vietnamese attitudes in "Annexe de la note quotidienne No. 270," probably written Dec. 20, 1946, CP 14(5), AOM.

70. O'Sullivan to Secstate, Nos. 133 and 134, Dec. 5, 1946, 1 and 6 p.m., DF851G.00/12–546, USNA.

71. Sainteny to Haussaire, No. 709/H, Dec. 5, 1946, 1425hZ, 1MiF5, AOM.

72. Sainteny, "Rapport de quinzaine du 15 au 30 novembre 1946," No. 1274/S/BP (signed Sainteny), Dec. 10, 1946, CP 18, AOM.

73. Morlière report, No. 440/CAB-S, Dec. 12, 1946, EA, *carton* 39, *dossier* B-602, MAE.

74. Sainteny warned in the "Rapport" cited in n. 72 above: "il ne faut pas nous leurrer et croire que notre retrait de secteurs économiques particuliers et des concessions raisonables suffiront à assouvir les revendications vietnamiennes: C'est le début d'une offensive générale dans le but de nous évincer totalement de l'économie du pays, prélude à une éviction dans tous les autres domaines." This is the only passage in Sainteny's report that was underlined in Pignon's office.

75. Morlière report, No. 440/CAB-S, Dec. 12, 1946, EA, *carton* 39, *dossier* B-602, MAE.

76. Ibid. (with comments by Sainteny and Pignon). Note No. 71 D/C from Haussaire to Paris, Dec. 17, 1946, 4Q1, *dossier* 3, SHAT. Morlière report, Jan. 10, 1947, 57. See also "Note sur la situation en Indochine," Feb. 10, 1947, EA, *carton* 41, *dossier* "Notes du général Morlière 1947," MAE.

77. Brocheux, *Hô Chi Minh*, 93; Quinn-Judge, *Ho Chi Minh: The Missing Years*, 71, 81–85, 315–16.

78. Interview with Professor Tran Thanh, Institute of Ho Chi Minh Thought, Hanoi, Nov. 25, 1993.

79. Cecil B. Currey, *Victory at any Cost: The Genius of Viet Nam's Gen. Vo Nguyen Giap* (Washington DC: Potomac Books, 1997), 24–31.

80. For a discussion of the methodological problems faced by historians working with intelligence sources, see Stein Tønnesson, "La difficulté d'utilisation des archives des services secrets: Le cas de l'Indochine lors de la Seconde Guerre mondiale," *Renseignements & opérations spéciales* 2 (2000): 61–70.

81. SEH replaced SRO ("Service de renseignements opérationnels"), which was organized in December 1945 by Lieutenant-Colonel Trocard, UU-FT-1, SHM. In addition to BFDOC, the high commissioner also had a "Bureau central de renseignements" (BCR), which was responsible for counterespionage. On Sept. 20, 1986, Alexandre de Marenches, who directed the French intelligence service SDECE from 1970 to 1981, stated in *Le Monde*: "Durant la guerre et à la Libération, des éléments venus d'un peu partout, qui n'avaient pas bien fusionné, se mêlaient et s'entremêlaient (in the French intelligence services). Il y avait des chapelles, des représentants des différents partis politiques, voir des groupuscules qui pouvaient, comme au Moyen Age, dépendre d'un certain nombre de personnalités de l'époque. Tout cela manquait d'un bon amalgame. Le service souffrait de ce que j'ai appelé 'le millefeuille': les gens s'occupaient surtout à se bagarrer entre eux."

82. *Léon Pignon: Une vie au service des peuples d'Outre-Mer,* 40, 42.

83. MAE to Lisbon No. 737, signed Philippe Baudet, Dec. 20, 1946, AO, *dossier* 179, MAE. Meiklereid to Hong Kong S.117 "chiffré no. 9," Jan. 30, 1947, FO959/14/238/205/47, PRO. Bousquet told the newspaper *Sud*: "A Haïphong, j'ai été le témoin de leur désarroi; les ministres vietnamiens n'ont pas pu dominer l'indiscipline de leurs militaires. Ils auraient voulu arrêter la bataille. Ils n'ont pas pu. A Hanoï, il régnait une véritable hantise. J'ai quitté la ville avant le 20 décembre mais je sais que le Viêt-minh vivait dans une atmosphère de panique." *Sud*, April 15, 1947, clipping, app. 5 to Haussaire to FOM, No. 5675/CAB, Aug. 12, 1947, EA, *carton* 61, *dossier* C-605, MAE.

84. D'Argenlieu to Bidault, Moutet, and Michelet, No. 1703F, Oct. 26, 1946, Papiers Bidault, 457AP, *dossier* "octobre–novembre 1946," AN. Trocard "fréquentait des 'Marxistes'": Valluy, *Revue des deux mondes*, Nov. 15, 1967, 204.

85. Sûreté director Pierre Perrier to Pignon, No. 8035/SG, Oct. 18, 1946, CP 138, AOM. Valluy, *Revue des deux mondes*, Nov. 15, 1967, 204. Valluy to Haussaire, No. 5362/2 ("Projet de coordination des services spéciaux en Indochine"), Nov. 6, 1946, 10H266, SHAT. Order signed by Valluy, Dec. 10, 1946, on the creation of a BFDOC branch in Hanoi, UU-FT-1, SHM. Haussaire to Cominindo, No. 2130F, Dec. 30, 1946, EA, *carton* 42, *dossier* C-101–5, MAE, and 4Q78, *dossier* 4, SHAT.

86. "Que resterait-il maintenant de l'armée vietnamienne si l'on avait écouté Giap quand il voulait partir en guerre il n'y a pas si longtemps contre les occupants chinois?" Moret to DirSurFe, No. 3968, Nov. 28, 1946 (with two appendices), PCE, *dossier* "Renseignements 1946," AOM. The rest of the paragraph is based on SEHAN Bulletins de renseignements (BR) No. 3504, Oct. 12, 1946; 3539, Oct. 14, 1946; 3639, Oct. 21, 1946; 3696, Oct. 24, 1946; 3706, Oct. 25, 1946; 3722, Oct. 26, 1946; 3802, Nov. 2, 1946; 3812, Nov. 4, 1946; 3829, Nov. 6, 1946; 4016, Nov. 25, 1946; 4030, Nov. 26, 1946, EA, *carton* 40, *dossier* B-607–6, MAE.

87. Fifteen of the first proofs can be found in d'Argenlieu memo, Feb. 11, 1947, app. 3. The same fifteen documents and several other proofs can be found among the remnants from Pignon's office in the Conseiller politique (CP) files, AOM.

88. Vo Nguyen Giap, *Mémoires*, 1: 31–32.

89. An AP report estimated the number of arrested at 1,400, but this was probably an exaggeration. *L'Aube*, Dec. 5, 1946.

90. Duong Trung Quoc, ed. *"Thu do huyet le" (Hinh anh Ha Noi hai tuan trang khoi lua— mua dong 1946–1947)* (Hanoi: Nha Xuat ban Lao Dong—Xa Hoi, 2006).

91. Where the archives were used for editing Ho Chi Minh memo, Dec. 31, 1946.

92. Vo Nguyen Giap, *Unforgettable Days*, 402. This is confirmed in the Morlière report, Jan. 10, 1947, 51.

93. There were five battalions, or 2,500 troops, in the Hanoi area according to Colonel Vuong Thua Vu, "La vérité sur le 19 décembre 1946 à Hanoï," appendix in Léo Figuères, *Je reviens du Viet Nâm libre* (Paris: J. London, 1950), 184. The French estimated the regular Vietnamese army, concentrated around Hanoi, to number 30,000. Report from the Sûreté in Hanoi (Moret), Dec. 9, 1946, CP 13(1), AOM.

94. Ngo Van Chieu, *Journal d'un combattant Viet-Minh: Traduit et adapté par Jacques Despuech* (Paris: Seuil, 1955), 106. Despuech says in his foreword that the diary contradicts well-established French information about December 19, but that he wished to present it as it was. On this point, the diary has therefore presumably not been "adapted."

95. Revue de la presse, Dec. 3, 1946, CP-sup. 22, AOM. "Annexe 2 au rapport Walrand," Mar. 5, 1947, EA, *carton 40, dossier B-607–01,* MAE.

96. "Ton général presse V.N. ce matin un peu moins violent. Nombreux passages censurés. Nam hier soir dans conversation a fait état difficultés services censures V.N. qui seraient débordées par ultra violence tons journaux." Comrep Hanoi to Haussaire, No. 746, Dec. 8, 1946, 2025hZ, CP 13(3-III), AOM.

97. SEHAN BR No. 4082, Dec. 1, 1946, EA, *carton 40, dossier B-607–06,* DEC to Messmer, Dec. 2, 1946, EA, *carton 39, dossier B-602,* untitled document on the premeditation of the attack on December 19, 1946, with summaries of captured and intercepted documents, EA, *carton 30, dossier B-236,* MAE.

98. Intercepted telegram from Nguyen Binh to Vo Nguyen Giap, Dec. 8, 1946, *dossier* "Renseignements Viet Minh," 10H602, SHAT, cited by Goscha, "A 'Popular' Side of the Vietnamese Army," 341.

99. Moret report AM/je/7, No. 4271, Dec. 9, 1946, CP 13(1), AOM.

100. Sainteny to Haussaire, No. 83 (probably error for 823 or 830), Dec. 14, 1946, 1305hZ, CP 13(3-I), AOM.

101. This was a simplistic or inaccurate assessment. The militia forces were certainly more impatient and anti-French than the Army, and it is by no means clear that Giap was more "extremist" or "anti-French" than the top party leaders Truong Chinh and Le Duc Tho, whose roles were largely ignored by the French intelligence agencies.

102. BR No. 7 from 2ᵉ Bureau TFEO, No. 5816/2, Dec. 2, 1946, CP 181, AOM.

103. SEHAN BR No. 4254, Dec. 14, 1946, and No. 4266, Dec. 16, 1946, EA, *carton 40, dossier B-607–06,* MAE.

104. "Pièce no. 16" (Le Duan to Comité exécutif), EA, *carton 39, dossier B-604,* MAE. SE-

HAN BR No. 4248, Dec. 13, 1946, EA, *carton* 40, *dossier* B-607-06, MAE. Order signed Nguyen Binh No. 1674/QS, Dec. 15, 1946, appendix No. 3 to Torel report, Apr. 3, 1947, EA, *carton* 59, *dossier* C-325, MAE. "Notre action en Indochine du Sud du 30 octobre au 25 décembre," report dated Dec. 28, 1946, EA, *carton* 52, *dossier* "Le modus vivendi," MAE.

105. Moret to Dirsurfe, No. 4271, Dec. 9, 1946, and No. 4307, Dec. 10, 1946, PCE, *dossier* "Renseignements 1946," AOM.

106. SEHAN BR No. 4152, Dec. 7, 1946, Nos. 4184 and 4189, Dec. 10, 1946, EA, *carton* 40, *dossier* B-607-06, MAE. Sainteny to Haussaire, No. 820, Dec. 13, 1946, 1400hZ, and No. 83 (mistake for 823 or 830), Dec. 14, 1946, 1305hZ, Comrep Hanoi to Haussaire, No. 872, Dec. 17, 1946, CP-sup. 13 (3-I), AOM. Navy BR No. 250 EM2, signed Doignon, Saigon, Dec. 15, 1946, DGD 65, AOM.

107. SDECE, "Notice technique de contre-ingérence politique," Nov. 28, 1946, AO, MAE.

108. BR No. 250 EM2 from the Navy staff headquarters (signed Doignon) on the situation in Hanoi on December 15, copy made in Saigon, Dec. 23, 1946, DGD 65, AOM.

109. Unsigned report on the "Situation à Hanoi au 15 décembre 1946," CP 13(1), AOM.

110. SEHAN BR No. 4280, Dec. 16, 1946, and No. 4289, Dec. 17, 1946, EA, *carton* 40, MAE. Report from a French spy, dated Dec. 17, 1946, "Notice technique de contre-ingérence politique. Ingérences chinoises en Indochine," No. 2528/23.9.5.2/V./BAK.00026/SB, ex. No. 19, Paris, Jan. 10, 1947, Papiers Moutet, PA28, C7, d.158, s/d.4, AOM.

111. Lawrence, *Assuming the Burden*, 49, 98-101.

112. Haussaire to Diplomatie Paris, No. 1606F, Oct. 14, 1946, 1MiF43; Bonnet to d'Argenlieu, Nov. 11, 1946, Prési. Paris to Haussaire, No. 1998/CI/3215, Nov. 18, 1946, 1MiF5 and Tel. 915; Haussaire to Comrep Hanoi, No. 392/Cab.Mil., Nov. 28, 1946, 1MiF44, AOM. Allen to Meiklereid, Dec. 4, 1946, FO371/53968/F17052/8/61, PRO. Allen Minutes, Nov. 29, 1946, Note from Graves, Dec. 4, 1946, and Lambert Minutes, Dec. 7, 1946, FO371/53969/ F17656, F17748, and F17458/8/61, PRO. Lawrence, *Assuming the Burden*, 144.

113. After U.S. mediation, Thailand agreed on October 14, 1946, to give back the Cambodian and Laotian provinces it had annexed in 1941, after a brief Franco-Thai war. This removed the danger of a new war with Thailand, which might have dissuaded France from seeking a confrontation with the Viet Minh. The Franco-Thai treaty was signed on November 17, and a French mission arrived without incident in Battambang on November 25. The actual reoccupation was undertaken December 7-15. Pignon, "Note d'orientation no. 7," No. 4602 CP/CAB/SD, Dec. 20, 1946, *dossier* C-307, *carton* 59, EA, MAE.

114. Sainteny to Haussaire, No. 671, Dec. 3, 1946, CP-sup. 13(3-I), AOM. Sainteny to Haussaire, No. 836, n.d., and No. 842, Dec. 14, 1946, MAE. Sainteny, *Histoire d'une paix manquée* (1953), 67-72, 95; Patti, *Why Viet Nam?* 151-53, 248-53.

115. Abbot Low Moffat, letters to his wife, in U.S. Congress, Senate, *The United States and Vietnam, 1944-1947* (a staff study prepared for the use of the Senate Committee on Foreign Relations) (Washington DC: GPO, 1972), app. 2.

116. Stein Tønnesson, "The Meeting That Never Was," *NIAS-Nytt*, [Nordic Institute of Asian Studies, Copenhagen, newsletter], no. 3 (1997).

117. U.S. Congress, *United States and Vietnam*, 39-41. See also Lisle Abbott Rose, *Roots of Tragedy, the United States and the Struggle for Asia, 1945-1953* (Westport CT: Greenwood Press, 1976).

118. Note dated Feb. 1, 1947, MAE. As early as in October 1946, the Vietnamese government had written a memorandum to the UN, but it does not seem to have been sent. Moret to Dirsurfe, No. 3188, CP 128, AOM.

119. Reed to Secstate, No. 479 (from Moffat), Dec. 12, 1946, DF851G.00/12-1246, USNA, also quoted in Mark Philip Bradley, *Imagining Vietnam and America: The Making of Postcolonial Vietnam, 1919–1950* (Chapel Hill: University of North Carolina Press, 2000), 144. See also Secstate to Reed, No. 305 (for Moffat), Dec. 5, 1946, DF851G.00/12-546, USNA; MAE to AmbaFrance Washington, Jan. 3, 1947, citing a telegram from Haussaire dated Dec. 31, 1946; and d'Argenlieu to Cominindo, Jan. 27, 1947, MAE.

120. French translation of "instructions de la section des Affaires courantes du Comité exécutif du Nam Bô" No. 2.698/2, Oct. 17, 1946, CP-sup. 8(2), AOM. "Compte rendu d'une séance plénière du PC de Nam Bô (Cochinchine)," Feb. 27–28, 1947, captured in Vinh, 2ᵉ Bureau Note No. 30711/2, June 21, 1947, CP-sup. 22, *dossier* "Le PCI," AOM.

121. Pignon report No. 4579/CP-AP, Dec. 17, 1946, AO, MAE.

122. D'Argenlieu to Valluy, Nov. 25, 1946, 1016hZ, 1MiF5, AOM.

123. D'Argenlieu to Valluy, No. 20DC, Nov. 25, 1946, 1630hZ, 1MiF5, AOM.

124. D'Argenlieu to Valluy, No. 26DC, Nov. 26, 1946, 1445hZ, 1MiF5, AOM. D'Argenlieu to Valluy and Pignon, Nos. 27–28–29, Nov. 26, 1946, 0700hZ, 1MiF5, AOM.

125. Valluy to Lorillot No. 180C and to Morlière No. 1900E, Nov. 27, 1946, 0950hZ and 1000hZ, 1MiF44 and CP 13(2-I), AOM.

126. Morlière to Haussaire and Cororient Saigon, No. 3685/3, Dec. 5, 1946, 0405hZ, 1MiF5, AOM.

127. Comrep Hanoi to Haussaire, No. 698, Dec. 4, 1946, 1600hZ, CP 2(6), AOM.

128. D'Argenlieu to Valluy, No. 42/DC, Dec. 3, 1946, 1930hZ, CP 13(2-2), AOM.

129. Valluy to Sainteny, No. 11372, Dec. 5, 1946, 0915hZ, CP 13(2-1), AOM.

130. Haussaire to Cominindo, No. 1001/EMHC, Dec. 6, 1946, 0440hZ, Tel. 938, and 1MiF44, AOM. Meiklereid to FO No. 373, Dec. 9, 1946, FO371/53969/F17611/8/61, PRO; "Note d'orientation," Dec. 9, 1946, signed Valluy, EA, *carton* 41, *dossier* "P.11 ... P.18," MAE.

131. Haussaire to Cominindo, No. 431/CAB.CIV, Dec. 6, 1946, 1130hZ, Tel. 938, AOM.

132. Haussaire to Comrep Hanoi, No. 1011/EMHC, Dec. 8, 1946, 0630Z, Tel. 938 and 1MiF44, AOM.

133. Morlière report, Jan. 10, 1947, 52.

134. Moffat, letter extracts in U.S. Congress, *United States and Vietnam*, app. 2, 38.

135. Unfortunately there is a lacuna from December 6 to 31 in the microfilmed secret telegram file of AOM.

136. For Moutet's unsent telegram, see n. 46 above. For quotations from Bidault to Valluy (countersigned by Messmer), Dec. 12, 1946, Tel. 915, AOM, see n. 47.

137. Valluy, *Revue des deux mondes*, Dec. 15, 1967, 514.

138. Summary of the December 14, 1946 meeting, probably made by Quai d'Orsay's representative: "Note sur la situation militaire en Indochine, 14 décembre 1946," PS/GM Asie-Océanie, AO, MAE.

139. Ibid.

140. Haussaire to Cominindo, No. 1909F, Nov. 27, 1946, 1030hZ, AO, MAE.

141. This message, dated December 6 and broadcast on December 8 is quoted in Mess-

mer to Moutet, Dec. 11, 1946, and reproduced as appendix to Tran Ngoc Danh to Messmer, Dec. 10, 1946, EA, *carton* 38, *dossier* "Application," s/d. "Déclaration," MAE. Devillers, *Histoire du Viêt-Nam,* 349.

142. Léon Blum, "En Indochine," *Le Populaire,* Dec. 10, 1946.

143. *Journal officiel . . . Assemblée nationale,* session of Dec. 12, 1946, 74.

144. Ho Chi Minh to Haussaire and président du Conseil, Dec. 12, 1946, CP-sup. 8, AOM, and Ho Chi Minh memo, Dec. 31, 1946, app. X, doc. 60. Valluy to Moutet, No. 3179/Cab, Dec. 17, 1946, forwarding Ho Chi Minh to "Président du Gouvernement de la République française," No. 1077 VP/CT, Dec. 14, 1946, EA, *carton* 39, *dossier* B-605, MAE.

145. *Le Populaire,* Dec. 6 and 15–16, 1946.

146. Caffery to Secstate No. 5921, Dec. 3, 1946, *FRUS 1946,* 6: 65.

147. *Journal officiel . . . Assemblée nationale,* session of Dec. 12, 1946, 74–75. "Documentation sur la question indochinoise," MRP Overseas Service, Dec. 12, 1946.

148. Michel-Morin in *Le Populaire,* Dec. 6, 1946. "12 H 5: Sortie de l'amiral [from Blum's office, Dec. 14, 1946]. Très sec: 'Je repars pour Saigon,'" *Le Populaire,* Dec. 15–16, 1946.

149. Declaration by Moutet to *France Soir,* quoted in *Journal de Saigon,* Dec. 16, 1946, clipping in PCE, AP 49, *dossier* "Ho Chi Minh années 1941–1946," AOM.

150. *L'Aube,* Dec. 18, 1946.

151. Schumann alerted the government to "certaines paroles ou certains silences encourageant au-delà des mers, certains défis ou certains actes qui risquent de faire couler, eux aussi, le sang des Français et des amis de la France." *Journal officiel . . . Assemblée nationale,* session of Dec. 12, 1946, 103–4.

152. *Le Monde,* Dec. 20, 1946.

153. Haussaire to Comindino, No. 2062F, Dec. 18, 1946, 1030hZ, Tel. 938, AOM.

154. O'Sullivan to Secstate, No. 140, 7 p.m. Dec. 16, 1946, rec'd Washington, 11.07 a.m. Dec. 17, repeated to Paris, 4 p.m. Dec. 17, DF851G.00/12–1646, USNA.

155. It has been asserted that Blum only received it on 23 or 26 December, but the copy made by Messmer's Comindino secretariat is dated Dec. 20, 1145h, and Blum was on the circulation list. Moreover, Blum referred to the proposals in a telegram to Ho Chi Minh that same evening.

156. Sainteny to Haussaire, No. 891, Dec. 15, 1946, 1120hZ, 1MiF44, AOM. This telegram was forwarded to Paris with the following addendum: "Le message en clair de référence vous a été retransmis samedi soir 14 décembre sous le No. 760CH." Haussaire to Comindino (no number), Dec. 16, 1946, 0420hZ, Tel. 938, AOM. This was either a mistake or a lie. 760CH was a message of congratulations from the section of the French Socialist party SFIO in Hanoi (signed Hoang Minh Giam and Pham Tu Nghia) to SFIO Paris. This was dispatched from Hanoi in the morning of December 14 at 0220hZ, and cannot have been the subject of Sainteny's warning in the evening of December 15 at 1120hZ. For the congratulation message, see Tel. 938, AOM where, unfortunately, one of the two copies of 760CH is called 750CH.

157. Haussaire to Comindino, No. 2062F, Dec. 18, 1946, 1030hZ, Tel. 938, AOM.

158. Ho Chi Minh memo, Dec. 31, 1946, app. X, doc. 72.

159. Léon Blum to Ho Chi Minh, No. 238/CH/Cab, Dec. 18, 1946, 2200hZ, Tel. 920, AOM.

160. Comrep Hanoi to Haussaire, No. 872, Dec. 17, 1946, 12h30–1240hZ, CP 13(3-I), AOM.

161. *Le Monde*, Dec. 19, 1946, 8; Devillers, *Histoire du Viêt-Nam*, 352. This meeting seems to have gone unmentioned in the whole correspondence between Saigon and Paris, or at least in the part of it on file. Valluy also does not mention it in the articles he published in 1967. An AFP news bulletin published in *Le Monde* said that "dans les milieux officiels français, on ne donne aucune précision sur la visite que le général Valluy a faite hier à Haïphong ainsi que sur les entretiens que le haut commissaire intérimaire a eus avec M. Sainteny et le général Morlière. Le général Valluy est rentré à Saïgon dans l'après-midi." The few details we have managed to locate are from reports written by the naval commander in Haiphong: Barrière to Cdts de la Marine, No. 485/Cdt, Dec. 18, 1946, and No. 494/Cdt, Dec. 21, 1946, UU-TB-17, SHM.

162. D'Argenlieu, *Chronique d'Indochine*, 368.

163. Perrier to Pignon, "Note sur la situation à Hanoï au 15 décembre 1946," Dec. 17, 1946, CP-sup. 13(3–1), and PCE, *dossier* "Renseignements 1946," AOM.

164. Pignon report "sur la situation politique intérieure de l'Indochine," No. 4579/CP-AP, Dec. 17, 1946, AO, MAE.

165. Appendix to Sûreté BQ, Dec. 17, 1946, PCE, *dossier* "Renseignements 1946," AOM. See also transcripts from radio interceptions, sent from Hanoi to Saigon, Jan. 3, 1947, AOM CP-sup. 2(1), AOM, and EA, *carton* 29, *dossier* B-212, MAE. They confirm that the government met on December 17.

166. SEHAN BR No. 4290, Dec. 17, 1946, EA, *carton* 40, dos. B-607–06, MAE. Letters from Hoang Huu Nam to Sainteny and Morlière, dated Dec. 16, 1946, tend to confirm this, EA, *carton* 39, *dossier* B-602, MAE.

167. Comrep Hanoi to Haussaire, No. 862, Dec. 16, 1946, 1130hZ (must be error for Dec. 17), CP 13 (3-III), AOM.

168. Ibid.; Haussaire to Cominindo, No. 2080F, Dec. 21, 1946 (a summary of all incidents up to Dec. 19), Tel. 938, AOM.

169. Nguyen Phien, letter of protest to Captain de Chatillon, Ho Chi Minh memo, Dec. 31, 1946, app. X, doc. 62.

170. Saigon only told Paris that "un incident nait à la centrale électrique où les ouvriers se mettent en grève et un V.N. de la garde est tué." Haussaire to EMGDN, No. 1038/EMHC, Dec. 19, 1946, Tel. 933, AOM. But AFP (*Le Monde*, Dec. 19) confirms the Vietnamese version in Nguyen Phien's letter to de Chatillon, cited n. 169 above.

171. Haussaire to Cominindo, No. 2080F, Dec. 21, 1946, Tel. 938, AOM. D'Argenlieu memo, Feb. 11, 1947, 35. Nguyen Phien, letter to de Chatillon, cited n. 169 above.

172. Comrep Hanoi to Haussaire, No. 862, Dec. 16, 1946, 1130hZ (must be error for Dec. 17), CP 13 (3-III), AOM.

173. Nguyen Phien, letter to de Chatillon, cited n. 169 above.

174. Comrep Hanoi to Haussaire, No. 862, Dec. 16, 1946, 1130hZ (must be error for Dec. 17), CP 13 (3-III), AOM.

175. Haussaire to Cominindo, No. 2080F, Dec. 21, 1946, Tel. 938, AOM.

176. O'Sullivan to Secstate, No. 147, Dec. 18, 1946, 0900h, DF851G.00/12–1846, USNA.

177. Haussaire to Cominindo, No. 2080F, Dec. 21, 1946, Tel. 938, AOM. Surprisingly, these events are not mentioned either in Ho Chi Minh memo, Dec. 31, 1946 or in Giap's memoirs. Giap, who may have based his account on the Ho Chi Minh memo, even says that

"on the morning of December 18, the city seemed quiet." Vo Nguyen Giap, *Unforgettable Days*, 410.

178. Haussaire to Cominindo, No. 2080F, Dec. 21, 1946, Tel. 938, AOM. D'Argenlieu memo, Feb. 11, 1947, 36. This event is not mentioned in the Vietnamese versions either, but that is more understandable.

179. *L'Aube*, Dec. 19, 1946.

180. *L'Humanité*, Dec. 19 and 20, 1946.

181. *Franc-Tireur*, Dec. 20, 1946.

182. Comrep Hanoi to Haussaire, No. 873, Dec. 18, 1946, 0500hZ, CP 13 (3-III), AOM.

183. De Chatillon to Bui Quy No. 5032-IH, Dec. 18, 1946, Ho Chi Minh memo, Dec. 31, 1946, doc. 64: "... faute de quoi, le commandement local français se verra dans l'obligation de procéder à ce déblaiement par ses propres moyens." Haussaire to Cominindo, No. 2080F, Dec. 21, 1946, Tel. 938, AOM. The Vietnamese liaison answered in the following day that "pour éviter l'aggravation irrémédiable de la situation le poste vietnamien n'a pas cru utile de réagir" against the occupation of the buildings, but "le prétexte invoqué dans ce cas est de pure invention: ni la liaison, ni aucune autorité vietnamienne n'a jamais été saisie de cette gratuite histoire de coups de feu tirés de ce local." Nguyen Phien to de Chatillon No. 4284-EL, Dec. 19, 1946, Ho Chi Minh memo, Dec. 31, 1946, doc. 65. For Sainteny's active role in undertaking these measures, by contrast to Morlière's more cautious approach, see d'Argenlieu, *Chronique d'Indochine*, 374.

184. Fonde to Nam, No. 1536, Dec. 18, 1946, Ho Chi Minh memo, Dec. 31, 1946, doc. 68. D'Argenlieu memo, Feb. 11, 1947, 37.

185. "Nous ne pensons pas qu'il soit question pour les troupes françaises d'y trouver un prétexte afin de porter atteinte à notre droit qu'exerçait la police, droit qui relève de la souveraineté de l'Etat libre du Viet-Nam." Nam carefully used the expression "free state" from the March 6 agreement. Nam to Fonde No. 2389-TU, Dec. 18, 1946, Ho Chi Minh memo, Dec. 31, 1946, doc. 68-B. Fonde tells in his memoirs that he went to see Giap on the morning of December 18, before writing his "ultimatum." He even quotes at length from what Giap is supposed to have said to him, and these statements have since been quoted by many authors. However, the detailed reports Fonde wrote at the time, principally "Compte-rendu des activités de la liaison pour la période du 15 au 20 décembre 1946," Dec. 20, 1946, signed Fonde, DGD 75, AOM, do not mention any such meeting. Given Fonde's professionalism at the time, which would require of a junior officer that he report to his superiors on a meeting with the adversary's commander in chief and defense minister, one wonders if the meeting took place at all. For the alleged meeting, see Jean-Julien Fonde, *Traitez à tout prix* (Paris: Plon, 1971), 312 and Jean-Julien Fonde and Jacques Massu, *L'aventure Viêt-minh* (Paris: Plon, 1980), 137.

186. French notes from Vietnamese radio, Dec. 16, 17, and 18, sent to Saigon Jan. 3, 1947, CP 2(1), AOM.

187. Oral information from the director of the Ho Chi Minh Museum, Hanoi, July 2007.

188. Vu Ky, *Thu ky Bac Ho ke chuyen* (Hanoi: Nha Xuat Ban Chinh Tri Quoc Gia, 2005), 29. This chapter in Vu Ky's collection of essays builds closely on Vu Ky, "Nhung chang duong truong ky khang chien nhat dinh thang loi."

189. Giap, *Unforgettable Days*, 413.

190. SEHAN BR No. 4303, Dec. 19, 1946, EA, *carton* 40, *dossier* B-607-06, MAE.

French translations of orders to stock water and make other preparations can be found in CP 8(4), AOM.

191. Dao Xuan Mai to Sûreté staff, No. 9982-CA.VP, Dec. 18, 1946, French trans. in PCE, *dossier* "Renseignements 1946," AOM.

192. Vu Ky, "Nhung chang duong truong ky khang chien nhat dinh thang loi," 79.

6. WHO TURNED OUT THE LIGHTS?

1. Information obtained Jan. 12, 1947 (*valeur:* B/1 [document of unclear origin (B) deemed by the intelligence agency BCR to include highly reliable information (1)]), "Directives du gouvernement vietnamien du 15.12.46 au 15.1.47," 8, BCR No. 378/1000/B.3, Jan. 21, 1947, CP 15(1), AOM.

2. In early January, Paris asked Saigon to send photos that could be used to justify French policy to foreign countries. Cominindo to Haussaire, No. CI/050, Jan. 8, 1947, AO, MAE. An attempt to repudiate French exaggerations of Vietnamese savagery can be found in a series of four articles by Paul Mus in *Témoignage chrétien*, Aug. 12 and Nov. 18, 1949, Jan. 6 and Feb. 10, 1950.

3. Hai Duong was attacked at 2230, Phu Lang Thuong at 0130, Bac Ninh and Vinh at 0200, Hue at 0230, and Pont des Rapides at 0300h.

4. This text is based on Haussaire to Prési. Paris, No. 431CAB/MIL, Dec. 21, 1946, 1320hZ, 1MiF44, AOM. The text in Ho Chi Minh, *Selected Works*, 3: 81, dated Dec. 20, 1946, differs slightly.

5. "Cong-lenh Dong bao thu do! Quan Phap da khoi han o Ha-noi," CP 8(4), AOM. There is a French translation in d'Argenlieu memo, Feb. 11, 1947, app. 3, doc. 7.

6. Comrep Hanoi to Haussaire (no number), Dec. 19, 1946, CP 13(3-I), AOM.

7. Morlière to Haussaire, No. 3841/3, Dec. 20, 1946, 0145hZ, CP 13(3-II), AOM.

8. Comrep Hanoi to Haussaire, No. 929, Dec. 21, 1946, 0845hZ, CP 13(3-II), AOM.

9. Haussaire to Cominindo, No. 767, Dec. 20, 1946, 1000hZ, Tel. 938, AOM.

10. Valluy to EMGDN, No. 2072/3.T, Dec. 21, 1946, Tel. 933, AOM. Haussaire to EMGDN (no number), Dec. 21, 1946, 1352hZ, Tel. 933, AOM.

11. O'Sullivan to Secstate, Nos. 149 and 150, Dec. 20 and 21, 1946, DF851G.00/12-2046 and 851G.00/12-2146, USNA. Haussaire to Cominindo, Nos. 2074F and 2103F, Dec. 21 and 23, 1946, Tel. 938, AOM.

12. Pignon and Longeaux to Prési. Paris, No. 2102F, Dec. 23, 1946, 1005hZ, 1MiF44, AOM.

13. News from the AP correspondent in Saigon, as published by *Le Monde*, Dec. 29–30, 1946.

14. Ho Chi Minh memo, Dec. 31, 1946, 8–9.

15. See, e.g., a message from Ho Chi Minh to the French communist journalist l'Hermitte, intercepted by French intelligence on April 23, 1947, CP 15(1), AOM. L'Hermitte had asked for the truth about December 19. Ho just reminded him of Aesop's fable "The Wolf and the Lamb," which makes the point that the strongest is always right.

16. *Causes of the Conflict between France and Viet-Nam*, a booklet signed June 1, 1947, by Tran Ngoc Danh, president, delegation in France of the DRV (Paris: Viet-Nam Delega-

tion in France, 1948). Nguyen Khac Vien, *Vietnam: A Long History*, 255-56. See also Hac Hai, "L'an I de la République Démocratique du Viêtnam," *Etudes vietnamiennes* 7 (1965): 50.

17. Col. Vuong Thua Vu, "La vérité sur le 19 décembre 1946 à Hanoï," appendix in Figuères, *Je reviens du Viet Nâm libre*, 181-94.

18. *Franc Tireur*, Jan. 16, 17, 18, 19, 22, 24, and 27, 1947. *Le Monde*, Jan. 7, 1947.

19. Institut franco-suisse d'études coloniales [Jean Bidault], *France et Viet-Nam: Le conflit franco-vietnamien d'après les documents officiels* (Geneva: Editions du Milieu du monde, n.d. [1947]), 47-48.

20. Devillers, *Histoire du Viêt-Nam*, 355.

21. Gras, *Histoire de la guerre d'Indochine*, 154.

22. Devillers, *Histoire du Viêt-Nam*, 353.

23. *Cuu Quoc* protested "énergiquement contre le fait que les représentants de la France au Viêt-nam ont intentionnellement préparé leur offensive à Hanoï pour étendre les hostilités au moment même où le premier ministre français Léon Blum et M. Moutet préconisent la coopération sincère franco-vietnamienne." *Dan Thanh* appealed to Léon Blum to "mettre fin aux machinations des colonialistes qui sont en train de faire leurs efforts pour entraîner les deux peuples à la mort. Mais il faut qu'il se hâte s'il veut encore arriver à temps," "Revue de la presse vietnamienne du 19/12/46," note No. 7421/DOC from Dirinfor Saigon, Dec. 28, 1946, DGD 75, AOM.

24. The text does not actually say "within the next" twenty-four hours, but that twenty-four hours will pass before the French attack, but the meaning must have been "within twenty-four hours."

25. Vo Nguyen Giap, *Chien Dau trong vong vay*, 26 (French translation in Giap, *Mémoires*, 1: 29), referring to *Lich su Bo Tong Tham Muu trong Khang Chiên chong Phap* [History of the General Chiefs of Staff during the Resistance against the French Aggression] (Hanoi: Ho Tong Tham Muu, 1997), 109. For an English translation of these orders, see *Essential Matters: A History of the Cryptographic Branch of the People's Army of Viet-Nam, 1945-1975*, trans. and ed. David W. Gaddy (Fort George G. Meade, MD: Center for Cryptologic History, National Security Agency, 1994), 13. See also Tran Trong Trung, *Tong Tu Lenh Vo Nguyen Giap* (Hanoi: Nha Xuat Ban Chinh Tri Quoc Gia, 2006), 216.

26. Ngo Van Chieu, *Journal d'un combattant Viet-Minh*, 105-6.

27. The order was found by the French after the battle and was included in d'Argenlieu memo, Feb. 11, 1947, app. 3, doc. 2. The first French translation, which was sent from Hanoi to Saigon on January 20, 1947, is in CP 8(4), AOM. This led to a request from Saigon to Hanoi on January 25 for a photograph of the original document. No such photograph has been found in the CP files. Le Hong is a pseudonym that was used by Hoang Minh Chinh, so this could be him.

28. French translation in CP 8(4), AOM: "6. Signal de préparation: fusées vertes. 7. Signal d'assaut: fusée rouge, suivie de 3 explosions provoquées par 3 grenades. 8. Signal donné cette nuit (19/12.46) à 7 heures moins le quart." The translation in d'Argenlieu memo, Feb. 11, 1947, differs slightly.

29. Fernand Petit, the spy who warned the French command of the planned attack, statement to Paul Mus, *Témoignage chrétien*, Jan. 6, 1950.

30. Fonde, *Traitez à tout prix*, 313.

31. SEHAN BR No. 4303, Dec. 19, 1946, EA, *carton* 40, *dossier* B-607–06, MAE. Comrep Hanoi to Haussaire, No. 907, Dec. 19, 1946, 1200hZ, CP-sup 13(3-I), *sous-dossier* "Décembre 1946," AOM.

32. Comrep Hanoi to Haussaire, No. 907, Dec. 19, 1946, 1200hZ, CP 13(3-I), AOM. Ho Chi Minh memo, Dec. 31, 1946, 7 (USNA version) and 8 (AOM version). Sainteny, *Histoire d'une paix manquée*, 223.

33. Ho Chi Minh memo, Dec. 31, 1946, doc. 75. O'Sullivan to Secstate, written December 29, 1946, and sent as dispatch No. 13, April 1947, DF851G.oo/4–1847, attachment 3, USNA. Devillers, *Histoire du Viêt-Nam*, 354.

34. Sainteny, *Histoire d'une paix manquée*, 222–23. The letter is reproduced as app. 11, 256–57.

35. Morlière to Nam, No. 464-CAB, Dec. 19, 1946. Ho Chi Minh memo, Dec. 31, 1946, doc. 69. O'Sullivan to Secstate cited n. 33 above, attachment 1. In Moutet's March 18, 1947, statement to the French National Assembly, he quoted from the introduction and the conclusion of Morlière's letter (which were quite friendly) but omitted the demands. *Journal officiel . . . Assémblée nationale*, sess. of Mar. 18, 1947, 879. Vu Ky says the "ultimatum" was received at 2415h. This might explain that the secret orders sent out to all military zones in the morning referred to Morlière's "ultimatum" with its demand for the disarming of the Tu Ve. Vu Ky, "Nhung chang duong truong ky khang chien nhat dinh thang loi," 78.

36. Giap claims in his memoirs that Morlière's "ultimatum" set the morning of December 20 as deadline for disarming the Vietnamese forces in Hanoi. Vo Nguyen Giap, *Chien Dau trong vong vay*, 26; Giap, *Mémoires, 1946–1954*, 1: 29. However, there is no such deadline in the letter Morlière sent on December 19.

37. Comrep Hanoi to Haussaire, No. 928, Dec. 21, 1946, 1930hZ, CP 13 (3-I), AOM. O'Sullivan to Secstate cited n. 33 above.

38. Sainteny, *Histoire d'une paix manquée*, 223–24.

39. Comrep Hanoi to Haussaire, No. 907, Dec. 19, 1946, 1200hZ. CP 13(3-I), AOM.

40. Annexe de la Note quotidienne No. 270, CP 14(5), AOM.

41. Ho Chi Minh to Blum, Dec. 23, 1946, Ho Chi Minh memo, Dec. 31, 1946, doc. 76-B. This letter probably never reached Blum. The allegation that Ho had narrowly escaped was repeated later by Tran Ngoc Danh as proof that the French had been responsible for the outbreak of war: "Hostilities which broke out on the evening of December 19th were not started by the Vietnamese, but by the French under the pretext that the Vietnamese were going to attack them. How can any other explanation be supported now that it is known that even President Ho Chi Minh himself, together with his guard, had difficulty in making his way out of burning Hanoi, under a rain of bullets and shells?" (*Causes of the Conflict between France and Viet-Nam*, cited n. 16 above).

42. Ho Chi Minh memo, Dec. 31, 1946, doc. 76.

43. Vu Ky, *Thu ky Bac Ho ke chuyen*, 49–50.

44. Tran Trong Trung, *Tong Tu Lenh Vo Nguyen Giap*, 216–17.

45. Nam to Morlière, No. 2396/TU, Dec. 19, 1946, reproduced in Haussaire to Cominindo, No. 2106, Dec. 24, 1946, Tel. 938, AOM. According to Morlière, Nam's letter did not reach him until 1800 hours: Morlière to Haussaire No. 406/Cab, Dec. 12, 1946, EA. *carton* 40, *dossier* B 607–04, MAE. O'Sullivan to Secstate cited n. 33 above, attachment 2.

46. Vu Ky, "Nhung chang duong truong ky khang chien nhat dinh thang loi," 81.

47. Comrep Hanoi to Haussaire, No. 927, Dec. 21, 1946, 0640hZ, CP 13 (3-III), AOM. News forwarded to Paris in Haussaire to Comindo, No. 2083F, Dec. 22, 1946, Tel. 938, AOM. Moutet would be particularly shocked by the fact that the Hanoi leadership had known he would come when they launched the attack, and Pignon claimed Ho had attacked because he did not dare to meet Moutet. "Rapport sur la situation politique intérieure de l'Indochine au 10 janvier 1947," Saigon, Jan. 21, 1947, CP 18, AOM. The head of the Asia section in the French Foreign Ministry, Philippe Baudet, informed thirty-seven French diplomatic stations that there were two reasons for the sudden Vietnamese decision to attack: (1) Morlière's decision to furlough the French troops; (2) the news that Moutet would come. MAE to thirty-seven diplomatic stations, Jan. 28, 1947, AO, MAE.

48. Truong Chinh most probably already had the text ready. The printed version of these instructions were first dated "12-12-1946," but the date was later changed by hand to "22-12-1946." *Toan dan khang chien: Chi thi cua doan the*, doc. 48, TBN-75, VNA-I (Hanoi: Standing Bureau of the Central Committee of the ICP, 1946).

49. Vu Ky, "Nhung chang duong truong ky khang chien nhat dinh thang loi," 81. Vu Ky, *Thu ky Bac Ho ke chuyen*, 51.

50. Information obtained in Hanoi, July 2007.

51. Devillers, *Histoire du Viêt-Nam*, 355, gives time and place for the meeting at Bach Mai, referring to "renseignements ultérieurs parvenus à l'Etat-Major." In 1966, Joseph Buttinger concluded, on the basis of Devillers's account, that Giap's order to cancel the operation could not have been motivated by French defense measures, since the meeting at Bach Mai was held several hours before the French carried out these measures. Joseph Buttinger, *Vietnam: A Dragon Embattled*, vol. 1: *From Colonialism to the Vietminh* (London: Pall Mall, 1967), 661n80.

52. Tran Trong Trung, *Tong Tu Lenh Vo Nguyen Giap*, 215.

53. Ngo Van Chieu, *Journal d'un combattant Viet-Minh*, 106.

54. There is some confusion as to when Morlière received Nam's letter. Fonde, *Traitez à tout prix*, 313 says that he got the letter "vers 16 h." O'Sullivan to Secstate cited n. 33 above, 3–4, says Morlière received it at 1130. Devillers, *Histoire du Viêt-Nam*, 355, and Haussaire to Comindo, No. 242, Dec. 21, 1946, and No. 2106, Dec. 24, 1946, all say 1830. Could Fonde have kept the letter for one or two hours before handing it over to Morlière?

55. O'Sullivan to Secstate cited n. 33 above. Morlière report, Jan. 10, 1947, 53.

56. There is no information on Petit's intelligence either in d'Argenlieu memo, Feb. 11, 1947, or in the CP files, AOM. The only relatively precise published account of Petit's actions is in Institut franco-suisse d'études coloniales [Bidault], *France et Viet-Nam*, 46–50.

57. Testimony under oath ("Affidavit") by Petit to Walrand, "Procureur général près la Cour d'Appel de Hanoï," Feb. 10, 1947, EA, C.40, *dossier* B-607–01, MAE.

58. "A 17 heures Général Morlière recevant rapports inquiétants décida au dernier moment les consigner à nouveau." Comrep Hanoi to Haussaire, No. 930, Dec. 21, 1946, 0900hZ, CP 13(3-III), AOM. The same hour is given in Fonde, *Traitez à tout prix*, 314, Sainteny, *Histoire d'une paix manquée*, 224, and O'Sullivan to Secstate cited n. 33 above. *Procureur général* Walrand, who undertook a judicial enquiry into the events of December 19, says Morlière

recalled his order to furlough the soldiers "avant 17 heures": Report Walrand signed Mar. 3, 1947, sent with letter HC Cab 3658 from Hanoi to Saigon, Mar. 11, 1947, EA, *carton 40, dossier 607-01*, MAE.

59. "A 17 heures des renseignements (dernier délai donné pour les évacuations—mise en place des postes d'attaques) laissaient prévoir l'agression pour 19 heures"; "Exposé chronologique des événements ayant amené l'éclatement du conflit franco-vietnamien (fin 1946)" No. 37/SP/BFDH, Hanoi, Jan. 7, 1947, signed Sainteny, DGD 75, AOM.

60. Morlière report, Jan. 10, 1947, only speaks of "renseignements obtenus en partie de source personnelle," but the well-connected French journalist Pierre Voisin wrote in *Le Figaro*, Jan. 21, 1947: "La surprise n'a pas joué, grace notamment aux remarquables services du colonel Trocard." See also Salan, *Mémoires*, 2: 37. A report from Sûreté chief Moret gives another reason for Morlière's decision at 1700 hrs to cancel the furlough: The rapidity with which Hoang Huu Nam had responded to the French request earlier in the day for barricades to be removed: "La rapidité même de la réponse, après une période d'atermoiements et d'insolences, mettent en garde le Commandant des Troupes contre un piège destiné à la mettre en confiance pour accorder 'quartier libre.' Ces troupes serons donc consignées." BR No. 260/PS, signed Moret Jan 7, 1947, and sent to Comafpol as No. 441/sg1, Jan. 14, 1947, CP 113, *dossier* "M. Giraudon," AOM.

61. Douglas Porch, *The French Secret Services: From the Dreyfus Affair to the Gulf War* (New York: Farrar, Straus and Giroux, 1995), 299.

62. The Tu Ve section meetings were customarily held between 1700h and 1900h. Tu Ve documents from December 1946 in "Bulletin de renseignements," No. 2853/PS from Sûreté Hanoi, Apr. 26, 1947, CP 17(14), AOM.

63. Vo Nguyen Giap, *Unforgettable Days*, 416.

64. Ho Chi Minh memo, Dec. 31, 1946, doc. 70: "à la rue Lo-Duc, à la rue Mongrand, à l'Hopital de Lanessan, à la rampe d'accès au pont Long-bien, devant le Commissariat du IIe arrondissement."

65. Institut franco-suisse d'études coloniales [Bidault], *France et Viet-Nam*, 47.

66. D'Argenlieu memo, Feb. 11, 1947, 37.

67. Ibid., app. 3, "Note . . . ".

68. O'Sullivan to Secstate cited n. 33 above.

69. Comrep Hanoi to Haussaire (no number), dated Dec. 20, 1946, stamped in Saigon at 0700h, CP 13(3-III), AOM.

70. *Le Figaro*, Feb. 1, 1947: "on ne leur avait fait prendre ni les dispositions de combat ni les positions tactiques." However, the same Voisin had written ten days earlier: "Les 1200 hommes éparpillés en ville se retrouvèrent à huit heures du soir l'arme au pied, et lorsque la coupure de l'électricité, signal convenu, déchaina un conflit longuement et minutieusement préparé, la 9e DIC réagit aussitôt avec la vigueur et l'efficacité que l'on pouvait attendre de cette magnifique et glorieuse unité." *Le Figaro*, Jan. 21, 1947.

71. Comrep Hanoi to Haussaire, No. 907, Dec. 19, 1946, 1200hZ, CP 13(3-I), AOM, and EA, C.40, *dossier B-607-04*, MAE.

72. Ibid. and Comrep Hanoi to Haussaire, No. 903, Dec. 19, 1946, 19h30G (local time), EA, C.40, *dossier B-607-04*, MAE.

73. Sainteny, *Histoire d'une paix manquée*, 224.

74. One report from Hanoi said 1955 hours: "Dix neuf heures cinquante cinq ville plongée brusquement dans obscurité totale." Comrep Hanoi to Haussaire (no number), dated Dec. 20, 1946, stamped Saigon, 0700h, CP 13(3-III), AOM. Some later reports said it happened *exactly* at 2000h.

75. *Essential Matters*, 14.

76. Comrep Hanoi to Haussaire, No. 941, Dec. 21, 1946, 2240hZ, CP 13(3-III), AOM.

77. Dèbes to Valluy (Comar Tonkin to Comar Saigon, No. 50823–24), Dec. 21, 1946, "Registre des Messages Secrets," UUTB-8, SHM.

78. Vo Nguyen Giap, *Mémoires*, 1: 45.

79. "Directives du gouvernement vietnamien du 15.12.46 au 15.1.47," 8, BCR, No. 378/1000/B.3, Jan. 21, 1947, CP 15(1), AOM.

80. Six of them (all except Tran Do and Le Quang Ba) had been appointed by a decree of Sept. 11, 1946, signed by Giap. On October 7, Nguyen Van Tran (a key member of the Northern Region Administrative Committee) resigned and announced that he would be replaced by "the Hanoi commander, colonel Le Quang Ba," but Ba went south to join the fight there before December 19 and was replaced as commander by Vuong Thua Vu. French translations of the September 11 decree and Nguyen Van Tran's letter of resignation (documents found by the Sûreté) are in CP 2(1), AOM. For a list of the above persons, see Vo Nguyen Giap, *Mémoires*, 1: 34. See also SEHAN BR No. 3722, Oct. 6, 1946, EA, C.40, *dossier* 607–06, MAE; SDECE "Notice technique de contre-ingérence politique," Nov. 28, 1946, MAE; and SEHAN BR No. 4282, Dec. 16, 1946, CP 128, AOM.

81. *Toan dan khang chien: Chi thi cua doan the* (The Resistance of the Whole People: Organizational Directive) (Hanoi: Standing Bureau of the Central Committee of the ICP, 1946), doc. 48, TBN-75, VNA-I. December 22; first printed with the date Dec. 12, 1946, then corrected to Dec. 22. For the quotation with Vietnamese diacritical marks, see the Glossary.

82. Vo Nguyen Giap, "Notre guerre de libération—stratégie et tactique," Apr. 3, 1947, French translation in TFIN 2ᵉ Bureau BR No. 2788/2, June 11, 1947, CP 128, AOM. There are references to these debates in Vo Nguyen Giap, *Mémoires*, 1: 37–39, and *Unforgettable Days*, 409. See also Vuong Thua Vu, "La vérité sur le 19 décembre 1946 à Hanoï" and "Truong thanh trong chien dau"; and Devillers, *Histoire du Viêt-Nam*, 349.

83. Affidavit of Jean Romain Cuey's testimony, Feb. 12, 1947, to Walrand, "Procureur Général près la Cour d'appel à Hanoï," EA, C.40, *dossier* 607–01, MAE.

84. Vuong Thua Vu, "La vérité sur le 19 décembre 1946 à Hanoï," 185–86.

85. Vo Nguyen Giap, *Mémoires*, 1: 34.

86. The order begins like this: "Le 19-12-46 à 8 heures du soir, les troupes françaises ont pris l'offensive." A printed copy was found by the French on December 30, 1946. BR No. 69/2 from the 2ᵉ Bureau, CP 8(4), AOM.

87. Devillers, *Histoire du Viêt-Nam*, 357. Fonde, *Traitez à tout prix*, 321, also says 2130h, but may have taken this from Devillers.

88. Ho Chi Minh, *Toan Tap*, 4: *1945–1947* (Hanoi: Nha Xuat Ban Su That, 1984), 200–203. An official English translation can be found in Ho Chi Minh, *Selected Writings* (Hanoi: Foreign Languages Publishing House, 1977), 68.

89. Devillers, *Histoire du Viêt-Nam*, 357. Haussaire to Cominindo, No. 2081/F, Dec. 21,

1946, and No. 430/CAB/MIL, Dec. 21, 1946, 2000hZ, AO, MAE and 4Q78, *dossier* 4, SHAT. Tran Trong Trung, *Tong Tu Lenh Vo Nguyen Giap*, 218.

90. "Extraits de presse vietnamienne," BFDOC, Dec. 27, 1946, DGD 62, AOM.

91. Comrep Hanoi to Haussaire (no number), Dec. 19, 1946, rec'd in Saigon at 2200h, probably Saigon time, CP 13(3-I), AOM.

92. Comrep Hanoi to Haussaire (no number), dated Dec. 10, 1946, and stamped in Saigon at 0700h, CP 13(3-III), AOM.

93. Comrep Hanoi to Haussaire, No. 930, Dec. 21, 1946, 0900hZ, CP 13(3-III), AOM.

94. Ngo Van Chieu, *Journal d'un combattant Viet-Minh*, 107.

95. "Le corps de Tu Ve de Hanoï est un organisme complexe, indiscipliné, sans contrôle, et sa réorganisation est difficile. Mais avec l'aide des groupements du Viêt-minh nous pouvons compter le rallier à nous." Undated "Etude sur l'organisation des *Tu Ve Quu Quoc Doi.*" French translation in Moret to BFDOC, Feb. 3, 1947, CP-sup. 2, AOM.

96. Note found by the French in February 1947, No. 1878/SG/I (Sûreté fédérale), CP 21, AOM.

97. "Pour faciliter ma tache, je vous demande m'envoyer un rapport selon le plan suivant: . . . 2. Attitudes des Vietnamiens à votre Service: Moral, pensées, désirs. Sont-ils réactionnaires?" Signed Bo Chi Huy and N. Khuoi, CP 17(14), AOM.

98. "Le désarroi règne dans les classes intellectuelle et possédante qui, tout en envisageant avec effroi la guerre à Hanoï, en sont arrivées à l'espérer promptement comme leur dernière chance de survivre." Moret to Dirsurfe, No. 4271, Dec. 9, 1946, PCE, *carton* "Renseignements 1946," AOM, and CP 13, *dossier* 1 "Activités françaises," s/d. "Décembre 1946," AOM. "Le V.N.Q.D.D.-Dai Viêt au nationalisme encore assez étroit et d'abord difficiles, tendance catholique-monarchiste au nationalisme plus souple. . . . les fils conducteurs de presque toutes les intrigues qui se nouent . . . ou bien partent de lui [Ngo Dinh Diem] ou bien passent par lui." "Rapport de quinzaine du 1er au 15 Janvier 1947," signed Sainteny, att. to Comrep Tonkin and North Annam to BFDOC, Saigon, Jan. 27, 1947, DGD 75, AOM. Just after the outbreak of war, Pignon had asked Sainteny "si l'on ne pourrait constituer un gouvernement sérieux avec les hommes de JACOB [Ngo Dinh Diem]," but had by hand replaced the word *gouvernement* with *comité.* Pignon, letter, to Sainteny, Dec. 20, 1946, Archives Sainteny, 1SA5, *dossier* 4, FNSP. Sainteny reported on December 22 that Diem was "en sécurité Hanoi." Comrep Hanoi to Haussaire No. 948–950, Dec. 22, 1946, 0400hZ, CP-sup. 13, *dossier* "De Comrep," AOM. He quickly realized, however, that neither Diem nor anyone else of importance were willing to compromise themselves through collaboration with France under the circumstances. Diem apparently stayed in Hanoi until April 1947, when accepting a French offer to be flown to Saigon: Déléhaussaire Hanoi to Pignon (réservé) No. 915, Apr. 9, 1947 CP-sup.13 (II), *dossier* "T.O. Comrep Hanoi," AOM.

99. "Sans liaison avec leurs leaders réfugiés en Chine V.N.Q.D.D. et Dai Viêt surnageant cherchent une ultime planche de salut de notre côté, se raccrochant à nous la plupart avec un empressement aimable, quelques uns avec une répulsion à pleine déguisée, tous avec le désir de se compromettre le moins possible sans contre partie substantielle. . . . Il reste par contre bon nombre de personnalités mineures, V.N.Q.D.D. ou tout au plus nationalistes ayant évolué dans l'orbite V.N.Q.D.D.: quelques députés . . . dès le mois d'Octobre avait . . . appris le chemin du Commissariat de la République." "Rapport de quinzaine du 1er au 15 Janvier

1947," signed Sainteny, att. to Comrep Tonkin and North Annam to BFDOC, Saigon, Jan. 27, 1947, DGD 75, AOM. See also "Rapport sur le VNQDD nov.-46 à fin mai-47," No. 1.668, signed Michel, June 6, 1947, CP 143, AOM.

100. SEHAN BR No. 3706, Oct. 25, 1946, EA, C.40, *dossier* 607–06, MAE. Note No. 1878/SG/I from the Sûreté fédérale, citing a note captured in February 1947, CP-sup. 21, AOM. Answer form signed Bo Chi Huy and N. Khuoi, CP-sup. 17(14), AOM.

101. "Rapport de quinzaine du 1er au 15 Janvier 1947," signed Sainteny, att. to Comrep Tonkin and North Annam to BFDOC, Saigon, Jan. 27, 1947, DGD 75, AOM. See also Sainteny, letter, to a friend in Saigon, probably Longeaux, Dec. 26, 1946, CP 18, AOM, and document entitled "Comment le Viêt-minh a su détruire les partis politiques d'opposition," EA, *carton 55, dossier 247, s/d.* I, MAE.

102. Report No. 4562/CP/AP on the "action du front Viet-Minh contre les partis d'opposition," signed Pignon, Dec. 17, 1946, CP 21, AOM.

103. Comrep Hanoi to Haussaire, No. 872, Dec. 17, 1946, 1240hZ, CP 13(3-I), AOM.

104. The GF *(Gouvernement de fait)* file in AOM forms much of the basis for Marr, *Vietnam 1945,* and also for Marr's forthcoming book on "Vietnam 1945–50."

105. Ngo Van Chieu, *Journal d'un combattant Viet-Minh,* 108.

106. "Dans la nuit du 19.12.46—il était alors 19 heures passées, le Commissaire politique de la Section de la Garde Nationale me fit connaître qu'à 20 heures il y aurait bataille." "Le Commissaire à la Guerre du Comité de Protection du Service des P.T.T. de Hanoi Dac Le Hong" to Minister of Public Works Tran Dang Khoa, Dec. 23, 1946, doc. 1746/DAP, Nov. 7, 1947, CP 17(14), AOM.

107. "Aujourd'hui les troupes françaises ont l'intention de nous provoquer et de créer un conflit général. En ce moment les troupes françaises sont en train de prendre position au restaurant se trouvant devant la Présidence. Faites prendre d'urgence toutes dispositions utiles." Circular to the three sections of the company protecting Ho Chi Minh's residence, signed Le Binh, Dec. 19, 1946, d'Argenlieu memo, Feb. 11, 1947, app. 3, doc. 8. This might have been written after 2000h, but the first sentence would then probably have asserted that the French had already offered provocation. It might also have been written in the morning, but then the second sentence would have been different. Le Binh's order was therefore probably written shortly before 2000h. The d'Argenlieu report claims that the troops in the Hôtel Métropole were "5 ou 6 officiers, clients de l'hôtel, non touchés par l'ordre de consigne du quartier."

108. Vo Nguyen Giap, *Mémoires,* 1: 40.

109. "Etude préliminaire concernant l'exécution d'un coup de force au Tonkin," No. 4310/3-OP-S, enclosure to Valluy to d'Argenlieu, No. 4309/3-OP-S, Nov. 9, 1946, 10H162, SHAT. The full text of this study has been published as appendix in Turpin, *De Gaulle, les gaullistes et l'Indochine 1940–1956,* 602–24.

110. Vo Nguyen Giap, *Chien Dau trong vong vay,* 43; Vo Nguyen Giap, *Mémoires,* 1: 41.

111. For the December 17 incident, see: "Compte-rendu hebdomadaire des activités de la liaison du 30 novembre au 7 décembre 1946," signed Fonde, Dec. 7, 1946, DGD 75, AOM. "Un incident naît à la Centrale électrique où les ouvriers se mettent en grève et un V.N. de la garde est tué": Haussaire to EMGDN, No. 1038/EMHC, Dec. 19, 1946, Tel. 933, AOM. AFP confirmed the Vietnamese version of the Dec. 17 incident, saying it was the French guard who had killed the Vietnamese guard: *Le Monde,* Dec. 19, 1946. "M. Pignon connaît la ques-

tion": Unsigned, undated appendix to "note quotidienne no. 270" on the "situation à Hanoï depuis le 12 décembre 1946," 7, CP-sup. 14(5), AOM. Concerning the loss of electricity on December 19: "Journée du 19-12-46. A 20 heures, les Viêt-minh font sauter l'excitatrice de la turbine de l'usine électrique et coupent le courant dans toute la ville": Note from Moret on the situation in Hanoi, Dec. 22, 1946, PCE, *carton* "Renseignements 1946," AOM. "L'action a débuté vers 20 heures par l'explosion de trois bombes ou pétards de dynamite dans la Centrale Electrique de Hanoi, après un sabotage vietnamien des alternateurs dans lesquels de l'acide avait été versé": BR "Attaque vietnamienne de Hanoï," Dec. 23, 1946, PCE, *carton* "Renseignements 1946," AOM. "Les excitatrices de la Centrale électrique ayant été sabotée par des éléments V.N. du personnel": "Exposé chronologique des événements ayant amené l'éclatement du conflit franco-vietnamien (fin 1946)," No. 37/SP/BFDH, Hanoi, Jan. 7, 1947, signed Sainteny, DGD 75, AOM. Moret to Dirsurfe concerning "agression de M. Hoang Van Ngoc, chef annamite de la Centrale électrique par M. Cavalin, directeur français et un de ses adjoints," Dec. 24, 1946, PCE, *carton* "Renseignements 1946," AOM. "Il était constaté à l'U-sine électrique que trois excitatrices avaient été sabotées": Report on the "Action des serv-ices de Sûreté . . . ," enclosed with Dirsurfe Perrier to Comafpol Pignon, No. 10316/SG, Dec. 20, 1946, CP 138, AOM.

112. Vo Nguyen Giap, *Mémoires*, 3: 332. According to Giap's biographer Cecil B. Cur-rey, it was two days after his return to Hanoi on October 10, 1954, that Giap "walked into the power station to discuss technical problems of its operation with French engineers who still manned the installation." Currey, *Victory at Any Cost*, 209.

113. Cf. Turpin, *De Gaulle, les gaullistes et l'Indochine 1940-1956*, 307n3, 308.

114. Vo Nguyen Giap published his memoirs in 1995, when he was eighty-four, and the three-volume French version appeared when he was over ninety. Vo Nguyen Giap, *Mémoires, 1946-1954*, 3 vols. (Fontenay-sous-bois: Anako, 2003-4).

115. Haussaire to Cominindo, No. 424/Cab/Mil, Dec. 20, 1946, 0210hZ, Tel. 938, AOM. Ho Chi Minh to Blum, Dec. 23, 1946, enclosed with Ho Chi Minh memo, Dec. 31, 1946, as doc. 76-b. Note to the high commissioner from Morlière, Dec. 23, 1946, EA, *carton* 40, *dossier* B-607-04, MAE.

116. *Le Monde*, Dec. 25, 1946.

117. Haussaire to Paris, No. 425 Cab/Mil, Dec. 20, 1946, 0200hZ, as registered in Paris at 1230h, Tel. 938 and Tel. 933, AOM. Philippe Devillers, who was at the Cominindo head-quarters in the rue St. Dominique at the time, claims the news arrived before noon. Letter to the author, May 18, 2007.

118. EMGDN to Haussaire from Blum and Juin, No. DN/CAB 264, Dec. 20, 1946, Tel. 933, AOM. The telegram to Ho Chi Minh was also sent separately as DN/CAB 265.

119. *Journal officiel . . . Assemblée nationale*, sess. of Dec. 20, 1946, 196-97.

120. Valluy to EMGDN, No. 6036/2, Dec. 21, 1946, 0545hZ, rec'd 2015hZ, and No. 2072/3.T, Dec. 21, 1946, 1245hZ, rec'd 2010hZ, Tel. 933, AOM.

121. Haussaire (Valluy) to FOM and EMGDN, Dec. 21, 1946, 1350h (GMT), rec'd Dec. 22, 0925h, Tel. 933, AOM.

122. Juin to Haussaire, No. 268 DN Cab, Dec. 23, 1946, 1440hZ, CP 13(2-2), AOM.

123. *Journal officiel . . . Assemblée nationale*, 2nd sess., Dec. 23, 1946, 320-21.

124. Duclos (PCF) accepted this after he had obtained a promise that the government

would submit a report on the budgetary changes before January 31, 1947. *Journal officiel . . . Assemblée nationale*, 3rd sess., Dec. 23, 1946, 360.

125. *L'Humanité, Franc-Tireur, Le Populaire*, and *L'Aube*, Dec. 24, 1946.

126. Sainteny, letter, probably to Longeaux, signed Hanoi, Dec. 26, 1946, CP 18, AOM.

7. IF ONLY . . .

1. I thus disagree with the French writer Philippe Franchini, who with the benefit of hindsight claims in *Les mensonges de la guerre d'Indochine*, 219, that the protagonists of peace on either side were insincere: "En cet automne 1946, proclamer qu'on tient à la paix est un simulacre partagé par les différent protagonistes."

2. At a meeting of Cominindo officials on December 14, 1946 (see pp. 189–90 above), Messmer told the chief of d'Argenlieu's military cabinet, Le Puloch, that "the fault should not be on the French side" if there were further incidents. "Note sur la situation militaire en Indochine, 14 décembre 1946," PS/GM Asie-Océanie, AO, MAE.

3. Ho Chi Minh memo, Dec. 31, 1946.

4. For analyses of how and why Roosevelt's policy was abandoned during spring and summer 1945, while continuing to influence local U.S. actions in China and Southeast Asia, see George C. Herring, "The Truman Administration and the Restoration of French Sovereignty in Indochina," *Diplomatic History* 1 (1977): 97–117; Lawrence, *Assuming the Burden*, 68–81; Tønnesson, *Vietnamese Revolution*, 255–80; and Tønnesson, "Franklin Roosevelt, Trusteeship, and Indochina."

5. Secstate to Amembassy Paris, No. 6643, Dec. 31, 1946, DF851G.00/12–3046, USNA. Minutes to dispatch No. 156 from Meiklereid, FO371/53970/F18207/8/61, PRO. Lord Inverchapel to FO, No. 7372, Dec. 31, 1946, FO371/63451/F18303/8/61–46, PRO.

6. Lawrence, *Assuming the Burden*, 115. Dunn, *First Vietnam War*, 353–57. Dennis, *Troubled Days of Peace*, 179.

7. For China's policy: Stuart (Nanking) to SecState No. 251, Feb. 12, 1947, RG 59, DF 751G.93/2–1247, USA. For Britain's policy: Minutes dated December 17–23, FO 371/53969/F18076/8/61; Cooper to FO, No. 693, Dec. 24, 1946; draft telegram from FO to Cooper, Dec. 31, 1946, FO371/53970/F18303/8/61, PRO. See also Lawrence, *Assuming the Burden*, 165n45.

8. Vincent, memo to Acheson, Dec. 23, 1946, *FRUS, 1946,* 8: 76.

9. Cooper to FO, No. 693, Dec. 24, 1946, FO371/53970/F18303/8/61, PRO. Bonnet to MAE, No. 5315, Dec. 5, 1946, MAE. Bonnet to MAE, No. 5489–96, Dec. 24, 1946, MAE. Lord Killearn (Singapore) to FO, No. 388, Dec. 15, 1946 (on Moffat's ideas), FO Minutes, Feb. 16–23, 1946, FO371/53969/F17972/8/61 and F18076/8/61, PRO. Lord Killearn to FO, No. 6, Jan. 17, 1947, FO371/63452/F1300/5/86, PRO.

10. Foote (Batavia) to Secstate, No. 486, Dec. 19, 1946, DF851G.00/12–1946, USNA.

11. Raux (Batavia) to Haussaire, Jan. 14, 1947, Asie/Indochine, MAE. Memo of conversation between Lacoste, Lacy, and Ogburn, Jan. 28, 1947, DF851G.00/1–2847, USNA.

12. Secstate (Marshall) to Caffery, No. 431, Feb. 3, 1947, and No. 469, Feb. 6, 1947, Secstate to Reed, No. 30, Feb. 7, 1947, DF851G.00/2–47 to 2–747, USNA. Memo from Philippe Baudet, head of the Asia-Oceania section in the French Foreign Ministry, Feb. 10, 1947, EA,

carton 57, *dossier* C-312, MAE: "A l'égard de l'opinion internationale, et dans la mesure où la politique française à l'égard du Vietnam a paru incertaine, . . . le remplacement de l'Amiral d'Argenlieu apparaitra comme un élément favorable."

13. See Philippe Baudet's undated memo from August 1945 "a.s. attitude des principales puissances dans la question de l'Indochine. Plan d'action français," Fonds Bidault 457AP120, *dossier* "Notes récapitulatives," AN; and Ilya V. Gaiduk, *Confronting Vietnam: Soviet Policy toward the Indochina Conflict, 1954–1963* (Washington DC: Woodrow Wilson Center Press, 2003), 3.

14. Copy of Catroux (Moscow) to MAE, Jan. 15, 1947, INF, *carton* 153, *dossier* 1349, AOM. Igor Bukharkin, "Moscow and Ho Chi Minh, 1945–1969" (paper presented to a conference on "International relations in East Asia after World War II," organized by the Department of History, University of Hong Kong, and the Cold War International History Project, Jan. 9–12, 1996); Goscha, "Courting Diplomatic Disaster?"

15. Gaiduk, *Confronting Vietnam*, 5. Chen Jian, *Mao's China and the Cold War* (Chapel Hill: University of North Carolina Press, 2001), 121.

16. D'Argenlieu, *Chronique d'Indochine*, 370. Devillers, *Paris-Saigon-Hanoi*, 311.

17. Turpin, *De Gaulle, les gaullistes et l'Indochine, 1940–1956*, 232–35, 255, 258–59, 269–70, 294n90, 299–300, 304, 310.

18. "Je vous le répète: la France, dans cette affaire, c'était vous! Ce gouvernement n'en était pas un; il ne représentait pas la France." Claude Guy's notes from the meeting, as published in Claude Guy, *En écoutant de Gaulle: Journal, 1946–1949* (Paris: Grasset, 1996). Quoted from Turpin, *De Gaulle, les gaullistes et l'Indochine, 1940–1956*, 300.

19. "Reste la fermeté sur place pour nous délivrer de cette dictature et de cette drogue vietnamiennes." D'Argenlieu, *Chronique d'Indochine*, 368.

20. "Notes d'informations de Yolle" (Hong Kong), No. 9 and 10, Dec. 31, 1946, and Jan. 2, 1947, CP 255, s/d. "Bao Dai," AOM. Meiklereid to Foreign Office, Nos. 405 and 407, Dec. 27, 1946, FO371/53970/F18361/8/61 and 18363/8/61, PRO.

21. O'Sullivan to Secstate, No. 9, Jan. 7, 1947, DF851G.00/1–747, USNA.

22. Shipway, *Road to War*, 128. Hémery, "Asie du Sud-Est, 1945," 69.

23. Shipway, *Road to War*, 205.

24. Note d'orientation No. 9, No. 36/CP/CAS, signed Pignon, Jan. 4, 1947, MAE. Devillers, *Histoire du Viêt-Nam*, 364.

25. Pignon report, No. 276 CP/CAB, Jan. 21, 1947, CP 18, AOM.

26. Note d'orientation No. 9, signed Pignon, Jan. 4, 1947, MAE.

27. "Rapport sur la situation politique intérieure de l'Indochine au 10 janvier 1947," No. 276 CP/CAB, signed Pignon, Jan. 21, 1947, CP 18, AOM.

28. *Journal officiel . . . Assemblée nationale*, session of Jan. 21, 1947, 29.

29. Valluy, *Revue des deux mondes*, Dec. 15, 1967, 523.

30. Valluy, *Revue des deux mondes*, Dec. 1, 1967, 363.

31. "Note sur la situation en Indochine," signed Morlière, Paris, Feb. 10, 1947, EA, *carton* 41, *dossier* "Notes du Général Morlière," MAE. On March 18, 1947, a communist member of the National Assembly quoted from Morlière's note, without mentioning the source. *Journal officiel . . . Assemblée nationale*, session of Mar. 18, 1947, 897. Hammer, *Struggle for Indochina*, 197.

32. "Rapport de quinzaine du 15 au 30 novembre 1946," No. 1274/S/BP (signed Sainteny), Dec. 10, 1946, CP 18, AOM. O'Sullivan to Secstate, Nos. 133 and 134, Dec. 5, 1946, 1 p.m. and 6 p.m., DF851G.00/12-546, USNA.

33. Sainteny to a friend in Saigon (probably Longeaux), Dec. 26, 1946, CP 18, AOM.

34. Dalloz, Dictionnaire de la guerre d'Indochine, 33.

35. Segalat's summary of the Nov. 29, 1946, Cominindo session, F60 C3024, AN.

36. Dalloz, "Le MRP et la guerre d'Indochine," 59. Interview with Bollaert, Oct. 29, 1966, cited in Irving, First Indochina War, 49.

37. Journal officiel... Assemblée de l'Union française, Mar. 9, 1949, 337, quoted by Hammer, Struggle for Indochina, 189.

38. Bidault said this at a party meeting on Feb. 28, 1947. Dalloz, Dictionnaire de la guerre d'Indochine, 33.

39. See above, pp. 161, 189, for discussion of Bidault's telegram to Valluy (countersigned by Messmer) No. CI/03466, Dec. 12, 1946, Tel. 915, AOM, and EA, carton 27, dossier B-106, MAE.

40. Elgey, Histoire de la IVème République, 171.

41. Le Monde, Dec. 22-23, 1946.

42. L'Humanité, Dec. 22-23, 1946.

43. L'Humanité, Dec. 24, 1946.

44. In his Jan. 8, 1947, report, Leclerc said that the French troops had been ordered to occupy Haiphong and Hanoi by force if the March 6 agreement had not been signed. Tertrais, La piastre et le fusil, 40.

45. Leclerc had expressed the same idea on March 7, 1946. Turpin, De Gaulle, les gaullistes et l'Indochine, 1940-1956, 222.

46. Leclerc in lecture to Paris newsmen, summary to all French diplomatic stations, Aug. 8, 1946, AO, MAE.

47. Franc-Tireur, Jan. 1, 1947.

48. Leclerc to FOM No. 8/CAB, Dec. 30, 1946, Tel. 933, AOM. Leclerc to FOM No. 13/CAB, Jan. 2, 1947, repeating No. 2/CAB, Dec. 29, 1946, Tel. 963, AOM.

49. Leclerc to FOM No. 13/CAB, Jan. 2, 1947, repeating No. 2/CAB, Dec. 29, 1946, Tel. 963, AOM.

50. Le Monde, Jan. 4, 1947.

51. Comrep Hanoi to Haussaire, No. 22, Jan. 2, 1947, CP 13(II-Ie), AOM.

52. Haussaire to Cominindo, Jan. 1, 1947, EA, carton 42, dossier C-101, MAE. Valluy, Revue des deux mondes, Dec. 15, 1967, 520. Salan, Mémoires, 2: 48, says Valluy asked Paris to dismiss Morlière with Leclerc's recommendation. The French Foreign Ministry would later explain to the U.S. embassy that Morlière had been dismissed "because he did not take adequate precautionary measures before the Viet-Namese uprising on December 19. Information had been received by the authorities that a revolt was about to take place and it was only three hours before the attack that troops were confined to quarters." Incoming airgram A-286 from Paris, DF 851G.00/2-1347, USNA.

53. Chaffard, Les carnets secrets, 90-91. This probably explains why Morlière's Dec. 4, 1946, report was given to Moutet and Messmer on Jan. 6, 1947.

54. Leclerc, report, Jan. 8, 1947, reproduced in Auriol, Journal du septennat, 1: 661-64.

According to Turpin, *De Gaulle, les gaullistes et l'Indochine, 1940–1956,* 320n80, this document was merely an aide-mémoire, and Leclerc's actual mission report was dated Jan. 13, 1947. Based on a quotation from Leclerc's report omitting the essential parts of it (probably derived from Hammer, *Struggle for Indochina,* 193, who cites a Nov. 22, 1950, statement by Pierre Mendès-France in the French National Assembly), the editors of *The Pentagon Papers* (Gravel ed.), 23, read Leclerc's views as "diametrically opposing" Moutet's. The myth of the liberal Leclerc has been nurtured in France by some of his former officers; see Adrien Dansette, *Leclerc* (Paris: Editions de l'Empire français, 1948), and Fonde, *Traitez à tout prix.* Turpin, *De Gaulle, les gaullistes et l'Indochine,* and *Leclerc et l'Indochine,* ed. Pedroncini and Duplay, offer more nuanced views.

55. Moutet defended the "policy of agreement," after discussing Indochina with Blum on December 15. "Extrait du *Journal de Saigon,*" Dec. 16, 1946, PCE, AP 49, *dossier* "Ho Chi Minh années 1941–1946," AOM. Hémery's "Asie du Sud-Est, 1945," 77, defines Moutet's "policy of agreement" as a prolonged coexistence with the DRV, based on limited agreements, which would, Moutet believed, be susceptible to converge in due course with Ho Chi Minh's independence policy and thus lead to an overall solution acceptable to everyone.

56. *Le Populaire,* Dec. 24, 1946.

57. Maurice Schumann, article in *L'Aube,* Dec. 29–30, 1946.

58. Caffery had met Baudet. Caffery to Secstate, No. 6230, Dec. 23, 1946, DF851G.00/12–2346, USNA.

59. *Franc-Tireur,* Dec. 27, 1946. One of the cabinet ministers must have told a journalist what was said in the meeting.

60. *Franc-Tireur,* Jan. 1, 1947.

61. Moutet to Blum in Haussaire to EMGDN, No. 125 S/P, Dec. 25, 1946, 1530hZ, rec'd Dec. 26, 0625hZ, 1MiF44 and Tel. 933, AOM. See also Moutet to Blum, Le Troquer, and Juin, Dec. 27, 1946, 0302hZ, rec'd Dec. 27, 1510hZ, Tel. 933, AOM, where Moutet asked for four battalions.

62. Comrep Hanoi to Haussaire, No. 37, Jan. 1, 1947, 1015hZ, 1MiF6, AOM. Vo Nguyen Giap, *Mémoires,* 1: 74.

63. D'Argenlieu to Moutet, Jan. 1, 1947, extracts in d'Argenlieu, *Chronique d'Indochine,* 375.

64. Gratien, *Marius Moutet: Un socialiste à l'Outre-mer,* 260. Confidential information from the Chinese embassy in Caffery to Secstate, No. 402, Jan. 30, 1946, DF851G.00/1-3047, USNA. When Moutet finally received Ho's message after returning to Paris, he asked Saigon for the original envelope so that he could find out who was responsible for the delay. Moutet to Haussaire, No. C.I./0174, Jan. 28, 1947, AO, MAE.

65. The most complete version of the Ho Chi Minh memo, Dec. 31, 1946, is in EA, MAE, but there are copies also in AOM and DF851G, USNA.

66. When, one month later, Moutet received Ho's proposals in Paris, he scribbled the following counterproposals in the margin: "faire disparaître toutes les autorités imposées par la terreur par le V.M." Moutet's main concern was to preserve Cochinchina. Papiers Moutet, PA 28 CI, *dossier* 158, *sous-dossier* 7, AOM.

67. *Le Populaire,* Jan. 5–6, 1946. Comrep Hanoi to Haussaire, No. 71, Jan. 6, 1947, CP 13(II-Ie), AOM.

68. *Journal officiel . . . Assemblée nationale,* session of Jan. 21, 1947, 29.

69. *Journal officiel des décrets . . . ,* Jan. 9, 1947. Varet to Haussaire, No. C.I./063, Jan. 10, 1947, Tel. 915, AOM.

70. Moutet to Haussaire, Jan. 21, 1947, AP 3440/S, AOM.

71. D'Argenlieu to R. Schuman, Feb. 4, 1947, F60 C3024, AN.

72. Haussaire to Cominindo, No. 178F, Jan. 25, and 233F, Feb. 4, 1947, AO, MAE. Cominindo to Haussaire, No. C.I./0241, Feb. 8, 1947, AO, MAE.

73. " . . . j'ai . . . utilisé cette procédure qui permettait seule la réalisation d'une réforme jugée souhaitable par tous . . . " D'Argenlieu to FOM No. 260F, Feb. 5, 1947, Tel. 963, AOM.

74. Caffery to Secstate, No. 524, Feb. 6, 1947, *FRUS, 1947,* 6: 69–70.

75. Auriol, *Journal du septennat,* 1: 62. Turpin, *De Gaulle, les gaullistes et l'Indochine, 1940–1956,* 327.

76. After first refusing Blum's request that he go back to Indochina as commander in chief, Leclerc once again refused when asked by Paul Ramadier and Georges Bidault to take over as high commissioner, with full powers. Paillat, *Dossier secret de l'Indochine,* 116; Général Jean Crépin, "Pressions parisiennes: Le refus du général Leclerc de reprendre des responsabilités en Indochine. Témoignage," in *Leclerc et L'Indochine,* ed. Pedroncini and Duplay, 305–8. Turpin, *De Gaulle, les gaullistes et l'Indochine, 1940–1956,* 322–25.

77. Moutet was about to lose his seat in the National Assembly because the Nov. 10, 1946 elections in the Drôme were about to be declared invalid. No one could serve as minister without being a member of either the National Assembly or the Senate. Moutet may have hoped to be elected senator from Pondichéry, and he therefore paid a visit to this tiny French colony in India before returning to France. The attitude in Pondichéry was negative because of Moutet's failure to negotiate peace in Indochina. On Jan. 13, 1947, Moutet was instead elected senator from French Sudan, so he could continue to serve as minister. Undersecretary Gaston Defferre in his ministry asked him to come back to Paris before January 14, "si événements Indochine le permettent," in order to take part in electing the new president of the Senate *(Conseil de la République),* as well as the new president of the Republic. Defferre to Moutet No. 247/CH, Dec. 31, 1946, Tel. 920, AOM.

78. Martin Thomas, "French Imperial Reconstruction and the Development of the Indochina War."

79. For Moutet's career and attitude, see Gratien, *Marius Moutet: Un socialiste à l'Outre-mer.*

80. *Journal officiel, Débats parlementaires, Conseil de la République,* session of Nov. 12, 1953, quoted from Gratien, *Marius Moutet: Un socialiste à l'Outre-mer,* 323.

81. Moutet in statement to the European Council on Sept. 18, 1954, and in *Miroir de l'histoire,* August 1955, both quoted from Gratien, *Marius Moutet: Un socialiste à l'Outre-mer,* 325, 327.

82. Guillemot, "Au coeur de la fracture vietnamienne."

83. Pignon to Fransul Kunming, No. 4401 CP/AP/1, Dec. 4, 1946, CP 13(2–5), AOM.

84. "Notes d'informations" from Yolle (Hong Kong), No. 9, Dec. 31, 1946, and No. 10, Jan. 2, 1947, CP 255 *sous-dossier* "Bao Dai," AOM. "Rapport sur le VNQDD nov.-46 à fin mai-47," No. 1.668, signed Michel, June 6, 1947, CP 143, AOM.

85. The VNQDD had been "le véritable instigateur de l'ouverture des hostilités." Bonnet to MAE, No. 109/114, Jan. 10, 1947, AO, MAE; and Fonds Bidault 457 AP 128, *dossier* 1131-2, "Indochine 1947 1. semestre," AN.

86. Jacques de Folin, "Surprises et inquiétudes à Saigon et à Paris," in *Leclerc et l'Indochine,* ed. Pedroncini and Duplay, 217.

87. Many French authors have wondered if Ho Chi Minh was behind the attack on December 19. Philippe Franchini concludes in *Les mensonges de la guerre d'Indochine,* 252, without basis in any new evidence, that Ho was probably personally responsible.

88. Ho Chi Minh, *Toan Tap* [Collected Works], vol. 4: *1945-1947* (Hanoi: Nha Xuat Ban Su That, 1984), 179-83. Vo Nguyen Giap, *Unforgettable Days,* 417-18, and *Mémoires,* 1: 78.

89. Ho appealed seven times for a cease-fire in the first two and a half months after December 19, but never received an answer. Jean-Pierre Rioux, *La France de la Quatrième République,* vol. 1: *L'ardeur et la nécessité, 1944-1952* (Paris: Seuil, 1980), 171.

90. Vo Nguyen Giap, *Chien Dau trong vong vay,* 33, and *Mémoires,* 1: 34.

91. Merle L. Pribbenow II, "General Vo Nguyen Giap and the Mysterious Evolution of the Plan for the 1968 Tet Offensive," *Journal of Vietnamese Studies,* no. 2 (2008): 1-33.

92. Currey, *Victory at Any Cost,* 317.

93. See Nguyen Thanh, *Hoat Dong Bao Chi Cua Dai tuong Vo Nguyen Giap* (Hanoi: Nha Xuat Ban Ly Luan Chinh Tri, 2005), 166-69.

94. Pribbenow, "General Vo Nguyen Giap and the Mysterious Evolution," 14.

95. Vo Nguyen Giap, *Unforgettable Months and Years,* Data Paper No. 99 (Ithaca NY: Southeast Asia Program, Dept. of Asian Studies, Cornell University, 1975), 101-3.

96. Vo Nguyen Giap, *Unforgettable Days,* 416 (the last page before the epilogue).

97. Vo Nguyen Giap, *Mémoires,* 1: 26.

98. Sainteny in a 1973 interview with Jean Lacouture for the film *La République est morte à Dien Bien Phu.*

99. Vo Nguyen Giap, *Unforgettable Days,* 418: "as soon as he returned from France, President Ho had foreseen the inevitability of a wide-spread war started by the French imperialists."

100. Ibid., 392, 395-96, 413, 418.

101. The role of folly in military decision-making was explored, long before the U.S. invasion of Iraq in 2003, in Barbara W. Tuchman, *The March of Folly: From Troy to Vietnam* (New York: Knopf, 1984).

102. Vo Nguyen Giap, *Mémoires,* 1: 28. Vo Nguyen Giap, *Chien Dau trong vong vay,* 24. What Giap says here builds on an interview he gave to the Vietnamese veterans' journal in 1996, which is summarized in Nguyen Thanh, *Hoat Dong Bao Chi Cua Dai tuong Vo Nguyen Giap,* 166-69.

103. Vo Nguyen Giap, *Mémoires,* 1: 29, and *Chien Dau trong vong vay,* 25.

104. Vo Nguyen Giap, *Mémoires,* 1: 29-30, and *Chien Dau trong vong vay,* 26.

105. Vo Nguyen Giap, *Mémoires,* 1: 30, and *Chien Dau trong vong vay,* 27-28.

GLOSSARY

Vietnamese words in the main text as well as the footnotes do not have the diacritical marks that are used in written Vietnamese (Quoc ngu). The following list provides diacritical marks for the Vietnamese words that appear in the book, first those mentioned in the text and then the bibliographical references.

TEXT

An Nam

Bắc Bộ

Bắc Bộ Phủ

Bắc Kỳ

Bắc Ninh

Bạch Đằng

Bạch Mai

Bảo Đại

Bình Dân Học Vụ

Bộ Chỉ Huy

Bùi Bằng Đoàn

cầm cự

Cam Ly

Cam Ranh

Cao Bằng

Cao Đài

Chu Đức Tính

Chú ý: Phải luôn luôn quấy nhiễu những nơi tạm bỏ

Cờ Giải Phóng

Công-lệnh Đồng bào thủ đô! Quân Pháp đã khởi hấn ở Hà-nội

Công việc khẩn cấp bây giờ

Cù Huy Cận

Cung Đình Quỳ

Cứu Quốc

Đà Lạt

Đà Nẵng

Đạc Lê Hồng
Đại Hùng
Đại Việt
Đại Việt Quốc Dân Đảng (Đại Việt)
Dân Chủ
Đặng Việt Châu
Đặng Xuân Khu (Trường Chinh)
Đào Hữu Dương
Đào Trọng Kim
Điện Biên Phu
Dinh Lập
Đỗ Đức Dục
đoàn thể
Độc lập
Đổi mới
Đồng chí
Đống Đa
Đông Dương
Đông Dương Cộng Sản Đảng
Đồng Minh Hội
Dương Bạch Mai
Dương Đức Hiên
Dương Kinh Quốc
Dương Quốc Thanh
Dương Trung Quốc
Dương Văn Du
Duy Tân
Gia Lâm
Gia Quạt Hạ
Giai Đoạn Phòng Ngự: Có thể vạn bất đắc
    dĩ phải tạm thời bỏ những thành thị lớn
    sau khi kháng chiến quyết liệt ở đó. (Chú
    ý: Phải luôn luôn quấy nhiễu những nơi
    tạm bỏ).
Hà Đông

Hà Hoàng Hợp
Hạ Long
Hà Nội
Hắc Hải
Hải Dương
Hải Phòng
Hiến Pháp nước Việt Nam Dân
    Chủ Cộng Hòa
Hồ Chí Minh
Hồ Tùng Mậu
Hòa Bình
Hòa Hảo
Hoàng Diệu (Hà Nội)
Hoàng Hữu Nam
Hoàng Minh Châu
Hoàng Minh Chính
Hoàng Minh Giám
Hoàng Quốc Việt
Hoàng Văn Hoa
Hoàng Văn Hoan
Hoàng Văn Thái
Hoàng Văn Thụ
Hoàng Xuân Hãn
Hóc Môn
Hội Liên Hiệp Quốc Dân Việt
    Nam
Hòn Gai
Huế
Hừ! Thì đánh
Huỳnh Ba Nhung
Huỳnh Kim Khánh
Huỳnh Thúc Kháng
Khu
Khuất Duy Tiến
Kiến An

Kinh
Lạc Viên
Lai Châu
Lạng Sơn
Lao Động
Lào Cai
Lê Bình
Lê Duẩn
Lê Đức Thọ
Lê Hồng
Lê Quảng Ba
Lê Quang Đạo
Lê Trung Toàn
Lê Văn Hiến
Lê Văn Hoạch
Lê Văn My
Lê Văn Nhanh
Lịch sử Bộ Tổng Tham Mưu trong
   Kháng Chiến chống Pháp
Liên Kiểm
Liên Việt
Lộc Bình
Long Biên
Mai Hắc Đế
Mán
Móng Cái
Mỹ Tho
Nam Bộ
Nam Định
Nam Kỳ
Nghiêm Kế Tổ
Ngô Đình Diệm
Ngô Tấn Nhơn
Ngô Văn Chiếu
Nguyễn Ái Quốc

Nguyễn Bình
Nguyễn Đệ
Nguyễn Đình Thi
Nguyễn Hải Thần
Nguyễn Khắc Huyên
Nguyễn Khắc Viện
Nguyễn Lượng Bằng
Nguyễn Mạnh Hà
Nguyễn Ngọc Bích
Nguyễn Phiên
Nguyễn Sơn
Nguyễn Tất Thành
Nguyễn Thị Thúc Viên
Nguyễn Tường Tam
Nguyễn Văn Hách
Nguyễn Văn Huyên
Nguyễn Văn Kỳ
Nguyễn Văn Luyện
Nguyễn Văn Tạo
Nguyễn Văn Thịnh
Nguyễn Văn Trấn
Nguyễn Văn Xuân
Nguyễn Vũ Tùng
Nhà quê
Nùng
Phạm Ba Chúc
Phạm Gia Đỗ
Phạm Khắc Hoè
Phạm Ngọc Thạch
Phạm Ngọc Thuần
Phạm Quốc Quân
Phạm Tư Nghĩa
Phạm Văn Bạch
phân công

Phan Huy Lê

Phan Mỹ

Phan Thanh

Phan Thanh Giản

Phó Bạ Hưng

phòng ngủ

Phủ Lạng Thương

Quảng Bình

Quảng Ngãi

Quang Phiệt

Quang Trung

Quốc ngữ

Sài Gòn

Sơn Tây

Sự thật

Tân An

Tân Sơn Nhứt

Tây Mỗ

Thái Nguyên

Thăng Long (Hà Nội)

Thanh Hóa

Thanh niên

Thế Giới

Thổ

Thông Tấn Xã Việt Nam

Thủ Dầu Một

Thủ Đô

Thường Vụ Trung Ương Đảng Cộng
   Sản Đông Dương
   (T.V.T.Ư.Đ.C.S.Đ.D.)

Toàn Dân

Tôn Đức Thắng

Tôn Quang Phiệt

Tổng Bộ Việt Minh

Tổng Tư Lệnh

Trần Bửu Kiếm

Trần Đăng Khoa

Trần Độ

Trần Duy Hưng

Trần Huy Liệu

Trần Ngọc Danh

Trần Quốc Hoàn

Trần Tấn Thơ

Trần Thành

Trần Thị Liên

Trần Trọng Dung

Trần Trọng Kim

Trần Trọng Trung

Trần Văn Cung

Trần Văn Giàu

Trần Văn Lai

Trần Văn Lý

Trần Văn Tỵ

Triệu Văn Hiển

Trung Bộ

Trung Kỳ

Trường Chinh

Tự vệ

Tự vệ Cứu Quốc

Ung Văn Khiêm

Vạn Phúc

Việt Kiều

Việt Minh

Việt Nam

Việt Nam Cách Mệnh Đồng Minh Hội

Việt Nam Dân Chủ Đảng

Việt Nam Độc Lập Đồng Minh
   (Việt Minh)

Việt Nam Quốc Dân Đảng
  (VNQDĐ)
Vinh
Vĩnh Thụy
Võ Nguyên Giáp
Vũ Đình Hoè
Vũ Hồng Khanh
Vũ Kỳ

Vũng Tàu
Vương Thừa Vũ
xã hội
Xưa & Nay
Xuân Dương
Yên Bái
Yên Phụ

BIBLIOGRAPHIC REFERENCES

Dương Trung Quốc, ed. *"Thủ đô huyết lệ" (Hình ảnh Hà Nội hai tuần trăng khói lửa—mùa đông 1946–1947)*. Hà Nội: Nhà Xuất bản Lao Động—Xã Hội, 2006.

Hiến Pháp nước Việt-nam Dân Chủ Cộng Hòa. Museum of Revolution, Hanoi.

Hồ Chí Minh. *Toàn Tập.* Vol. 4: *1945–1947.* Hanoi: Nhà Xuất Bản Sự Thật, 1984.

Nguyễn Thành. *Hoạt Động Báo Chí Của Đại tướng Võ Nguyên Giáp.* Hà Nội: Nhà Xuất Bản Lý Luận Chính Trị, 2005.

Thông Tấn Xã Việt Nam. *Đồng chí Trường Chinh.* Hanoi: Nhà Xuất Bản Thông Tấn, 2007.

Toàn dân kháng chiến: Chỉ thị của đoàn thể. Hanoi: Standing Bureau of the Central Committee of the ICP, 1946 (Dec. 22).

Trần Trọng Trung. *Tổng Tư Lệnh Võ Nguyên Giáp.* Hà Nội: Nhà Xuất Bản Chính Trị Quốc Gia, 2006.

Võ Nguyên Giáp. *Chiến Đấu trong vòng vây.* Hà Nội: Nhà Xuất Bản Quân Đội Nhân Dân, 1995.

Vũ Kỳ. "Những chặng đường trường kỳ kháng chiến nhất định thắng lợi." *Lịch sử Quân sự* 12 (1988): 72–82.

———. *Thư ký Bác Hồ kể chuyện.* Hà Nội: Nhà Xuất Bản Chính Trị Quốc Gia, 2005.

Vương Thừa Vũ. *Trưởng thành trong chiến đấu: Hồi ký.* Hà Nội: Quân đội nhân dân, 1979.

BIBLIOGRAPHY

ARCHIVES

Archives nationales de France, Section contemporaine, Paris (AN)

Fonds F60 C3035, Présidence du Conseil

Fonds 457AP, Papiers privés de Georges Bidault

Centre des archives d'outre-mer, Aix-en-Provence (AOM)

Fonds 1MiF, Microfilm des télégrammes du bureau du chiffre

Fonds AP, Direction des affaires politiques du Ministère de la France d'Outre-mer

Fonds CD, Conseiller diplomatique (Saigon)

Fonds CP, Conseiller politique (Saigon)

Fonds DGD, Direction générale de la documentation (Saigon)

Fonds HC, Cabinet du Haut Commissaire (Saigon)

Fonds INF, Indochine nouveau fonds: Ministère de la France d'Outre Mer archives, incorporating Comité interministériel de l'Indochine (Cominindo) files from before January 1, 1945

Fonds PA28, Papiers privés de Marius Moutet

Fonds PCE, Service de protection du Corps expéditionnaire (Saigon)

Fonds S. Eco., Service des affaires économiques (Saigon)

Fonds Tel., Ministère de la France d'Outre Mer, télégrammes, départ et arrivée (Paris)

Ministère des affaires étrangères, Paris (MAE)

Fonds Asie-Océanie (AO), Indochine

Fonds EA (archives of the former Ministry of Associated States (including Cominindo files newer than January 1, 1945)

N.B.: The MAE files have been reorganized since the research for this book was done, so the box numbers cited in the notes no longer apply.

Public Record Office, London (PRO)

File FO371, General Foreign Office file
File FO959, Archives of the British Consulate in Saigon

Service historique de l'Armée de Terre, Paris (SHAT)

Fonds 10H, Military files from Indochina
Fonds 4Q, Archives of the Etat-major général de la défense nationale (EMGDN; chiefs of staff)
Fonds 1K238, Papiers privés de Maréchal Juin

Service historique de la Marine, Paris (SHM)

Série UU, Guerre d'Indochine
Série TT-T38, Marine en Indochine

United States National Archives, Suitland, Maryland (USNA)

Diplomatic Branch, RG69, decimal file 851G.00

FREQUENTLY CITED ARCHIVAL DOCUMENTS

Chronological Summary of Events. "Résumé chronologique des événements, conversations, entretiens qui se sont déroulés et des accords qui ont été signés entre autorités françaises et chinoises au mois de mars 1946." Edited by the "Délégation militaire en Indochine du Nord du haut-commissaire." HC 270, AOM.

D'Argenlieu memo, Feb. 11, 1947. "Réponse au mémorandum vietnamien 'sur les manoeuvres colonialistes depuis le 6 mars 1946 et les origines de l'actuel conflit franco-vietnamien,'" with fifteen appendices, consisting of twenty-four documents. First sent by d'Argenlieu from Saigon to Paris on Feb. 11, 1947, later used as basis for documentation presented by the FOM to the U.S. Embassy in Paris. Copies in EA, C. 41, d. B-608, MAE, and C. 56, d. 247, s/d. XVIII, also in AO, MAE and DF851G.00/2-2047, USNA. (High Commissioner d'Argenlieu's answer to Ho Chi Minh memo, Dec. 31, 1946.)

Davée report, Nov. 23, 1946. "Note sur le contrôle de l'importation et de l'exportation dans le port de Haïphong," signed [Robert] Davée, "Délégué aux affaires économiques au Commissariat de la République pour le Tonkin et le Nord-Annam," Hanoi, Nov. 23, 1946, CP 6, AOM.

Ho Chi Minh memo, Dec. 31, 1946. "Memorandum of the Viet-Nam Government on the Origin of the Present Franco Vietnam Conflict." Memorandum, with seventy-six documents attached, originally intended to be handed over to Minister for Overseas France Marius Moutet. When Ho failed to meet Moutet, the memo was sent through various channels to the French, U.S., and Chinese governments in January 1947. Copies are in EA, C. 41, d. B-608, MAE, in C. 43, d. C-112, and in C. 56, d. 247 s/d. XVIII, in AO, MAE, and in DF851G.00/4-2447, USNA.

Morlière report, Dec. 4, 1946. CP 7, AOM. A collection of the most important telegrams from Saigon to Hanoi, Saigon to Haiphong, and Hanoi to Haiphong, Nov. 20–26, 1946.

Morlière report, Jan. 10, 1947. General Louis-Constant Morlière, "Rapport sur les événements politiques et militaires en Indochine du Nord, au cours du dernier trimestre 1946," Jan. 10, 1947, reproduced in Georges Chaffard, *Les deux guerres du Viêt-nam de Valluy à Westmoreland* (Paris: Table ronde, 1969), 36–58.

ORIGINAL PUBLISHED DOCUMENTS

d'Argenlieu. See "Thierry d'Argenlieu" below.

Auriol, Vincent. *Journal du septennat, 1947–1954.* Vol. 1: *1947.* Paris: Armand Colin, 1970.

Bodinier, Gilbert, ed. *1945–1946: Le retour de la France en Indochine: Textes et documents.* Vincennes: SHAT, 1987.

Causes of the Conflict between France and Viet-Nam. Paris: Viet-Nam Delegation in France, 1948. Booklet signed June 1, 1947 by Tran Ngoc Danh, president, DRV delegation in France.

Constitutions of Vietnam, 1946–1959–1980–1992. Hanoi: The Gioi [The World], 2003.

Devillers, Philippe, ed. *Paris-Saigon-Hanoi: Les archives de la guerre 1944–1947.* Paris: Gallimard/Julliard, 1988.

Foreign Relations of the United States. Diplomatic Papers [cited as FRUS], *1945, The Conference at Berlin (the Potsdam Conference).* Vol. 2. Washington DC: GPO, 1960.

———. *Diplomatic Papers, 1945.* Vol. 6: *The British Commonwealth, The Far East.* Washington DC: GPO, 1969.

———. *Diplomatic Papers, 1946.* Vol. 8: *The Far East.* Washington DC: GPO, 1971.

———. *Diplomatic Papers, 1947.* Vol. 6: *The Far East.* Washington DC: GPO, 1972.

Hien Phap nuoc Viet-nam Dan Chu Cong Hoa [Constitution of the Democratic Republic of Vietnam]. Hanoi, 1946.

Leclerc de Hautecloque, General Philippe. "Rapport au Général de Gaulle 27 mars 1946." In Jean Sainteny, *Histoire d'une paix manquée,* 244–46 (appendix VII). Paris: Amiot-Dumont, 1953.

———. "Rapport de mission en Indochine 8 janvier 1947." In Vincent Auriol, *Journal du septennat, 1947–1954,* vol. 1: *1947,* 661–64 (appendix 1). Paris: Armand Colin, 1970.

Morlière, General Louis-Constant. "Rapport sur les événements politiques et militaires en Indochine du Nord, au cours du dernier trimestre 1946," Jan. 10, 1947. Reproduced in Georges Chaffard, *Les deux guerres du Viêt-nam, de Valluy à Westmoreland* (Paris: Table ronde, 1969), 36–58.

The Pentagon Papers: The Defense Department History of United States Decisionmaking on Vietnam. The Senator Gravel edition. Vol. 1. Boston: Beacon Press, 1971.

Porter, Gareth, ed. *Vietnam: The Definitive Documentation of Human Decisions.* Vols 1–2. London: Heyden, 1979.

———, ed. *Vietnam: A History in Documents.* New York: Meridian, 1981.

Thierry d'Argenlieu, Georges. *Chronique d'Indochine, 1945–1947.* Paris: Albin Michel, 1985.

Toan dan khang chien: Chi thi cua doan the [The Resistance of the Whole People: Organizational Directive]. Hanoi: Indochinese Communist Party, 1946 (December 22).

U.S. Congress. Senate. Committee on Foreign Relations. *Causes, Origins, and Lessons of the Vietnam War: Hearings before the Committee on Foreign Relations.* 92nd Congress, 2nd sess., May 9, 10, and 11, 1972. Washington DC: GPO, 1973.

——. *The United States and Vietnam, 1944–1947* [by Robert M. Blum]. A staff study based on the Pentagon Papers prepared for the use of the Committee on Foreign Relations, U.S. Senate. Study No. 2. Washington DC: GPO, 1972.

NEWSPAPERS

L'Aube (Paris), Nov. 1946–Jan. 1947
Le Figaro (Paris), Nov. 1946–Jan. 1947
Franc-Tireur (Paris), Nov. 1946–Jan. 1947
L'Humanité (Paris), Nov. 1946–Jan. 1947
Journal officiel de la République française (Paris), Dec. 1946–Mar. 1947
Le Monde (Paris), Oct. 1946–Dec. 1946
New York Times, Nov. 1946–Jan. 1947
Paris-Saigon (Saigon), July 1946–Jan. 1947
Le Populaire (Paris), Nov. 1946–Jan. 1947

LITERATURE

Ageron, Charles-Robert, ed. *Les chemins de la décolonisation de l'empire français, 1936–1956.* Paris: Centre national de la recherche scientifique, 1986.

——. *La décolonisation française.* Paris: Armand Colin, 1991.

Antlöv, Hans, and Stein Tønnesson, eds. *Imperial Policy and Southeast Asian Nationalism.* Copenhagen: NIAS; London: Curzon Press, 1995.

Azeau, Henri. *Ho Chi Minh, dernière chance: La conférence franco-vietnamienne de Fontaine-bleau, juillet 1946.* Paris: Flammarion, 1968.

Baeyens, Jacques. "Indo-China." *Asiatic Review* 46 (1950).

Bao Dai, Emperor. *Le dragon d'Annam.* Paris: Plon, 1980.

Bartholomew-Feis, Dixee R. *The OSS and Ho Chi Minh: Unexpected Allies in the War against Japan.* Lawrence: University Press of Kansas, 2006.

Bodinier, Gilbert, and Philippe Duplay. "Montrer sa force et négocier: Le général Leclerc et la négociation annamite." In *Leclerc et l'Indochine, 1945–1947: Quand se noua le destin d'un empire,* ed. Guy Pedroncini and Philippe Duplay, 181–97. Paris: Albin Michel, 1992.

Boudarel, Georges. *Giap.* Paris: Atlas, 1977.

Bradley, Mark Philip. *Imagining Vietnam and America: The Making of Postcolonial Vietnam, 1919–1950.* Chapel Hill: University of North Carolina Press, 2000.

Brocheux, Pierre. *The Mekong Delta: Ecology, Economy, and Revolution, 1860–1960.* Madison: University of Wisconsin, 1995.

——. *Ho Chi Minh.* Paris: Presses de Sciences po, 2000.

——. *Hô Chi Minh: Du révolutionnaire à l'icône.* Paris: Payot, 2003.

——. *Ho Chi Minh: A Biography.* Translated by Claire Duiker. New York: Cambridge University Press, 2007.

Brocheux, Pierre, and Daniel Hémery. *Indochine: La colonisation ambiguë, 1858–1954.* Paris: Editions La Découverte, 1995, 2001.

———. *Indochina: An Ambiguous Colonization, 1858–1954.* Translated by Ly Lan Dill-Klein et al. Berkeley: University of California Press, 2009. Expands and updates the 2001 French edition of *Indochine: La colonisation ambiguë.*

Bui Diem, with David Chanoff. *In the Jaws of History.* Boston: Houghton-Mifflin, 1987. Bloomington: Indiana University Press, 1999.

Bukharkin, Igor. "Moscow and Ho Chi Minh, 1945–1969." Paper presented to a conference on "International Relations in East Asia after World War II," organized by the Department of History, University of Hong Kong, and the Cold War International History Project, January 9–12, 1996.

Butterfield, Herbert. *History and Human Relations.* London: Collins, 1951.

Buttinger, Joseph. *Vietnam: A Dragon Embattled.* Vol. 1: *From Colonialism to the Vietminh.* London: Pall Mall, 1967.

Césari, Laurent. *L'Indochine en guerres, 1945–1993.* Paris: Belin, 1995.

Chaffard, Georges. *Les carnets secrets de la décolonisation.* Paris: Calmann-Lévy, 1965.

———. *Les deux guerres du Viêt-nam, de Valluy à Westmoreland.* Paris: Table ronde, 1969.

Chandler, David, and Christopher E. Goscha, eds. *Paul Mus (1902–1969).* Paris: Les Indes savantes, 2006.

Chen, King C. *Vietnam and China, 1938–1954.* Princeton: Princeton University Press, 1969.

Chen Jian. *Mao's China and the Cold War.* Chapel Hill: University of North Carolina Press, 2001.

Clayton, Anthony. *The Wars of French Decolonization.* London: Longman, 1994.

Clodfelter, Micheal. *Vietnam in Military Statistics: A History of the Indochina Wars, 1772–1991.* Jefferson NC: McFarland, 1995.

———. *Warfare and Armed Conflicts: A Statistical Reference to Casualty and Other Figures, 1500–2000.* 2nd ed. Jefferson NC: McFarland, 2002.

Cocquery-Vidrovitch, Catherine, and Charles-Robert Ageron. *Histoire de la France Coloniale.* Vol. 3: *Le déclin.* Paris: Armand Colin, 1991.

Crépin, Général Jean. "Pressions parisiennes: Le refus du général Leclerc de reprendre des responsabilités en Indochine. Témoignage." In *Leclerc et l'Indochine, 1945–1947: Quand se noua le destin d'un empire,* ed. Guy Pedroncini and Philippe Duplay, 305–7. Paris: Albin Michel, 1992.

Currey, Cecil B. *Victory at Any Cost: The Genius of Viet Nam's Gen. Vo Nguyen Giap.* 1997. Washington DC: Potomac Books, 2005.

Dalloz, Jacques. "Le MRP et la guerre d'Indochine." *Cahiers de l'Institut d'histoire du temps présent,* no. 34 (June 1996): 57–76.

———. *Dictionnaire de la guerre d'Indochine, 1945–1954.* Paris: Armand Colin, 2006.

Dansette, Adrien. *Leclerc.* Paris: Editions de l'Empire français, 1948.

Décolonisations européennes: Actes du Colloque international "Décolonisations comparées." Aix–Marseille: Publications de l'Université de Provence, 1995.

Decoux, Jean. *A la barre de l'Indochine, 1940–1945.* Paris: Plon, 1950.

Dennis, Peter. *Troubled Days of Peace: Mountbatten and South East Asia Command, 1945–46.* Manchester, UK: Manchester University Press, 1987.

Devillers, Philippe. *Histoire du Viêt-Nam de 1940 à 1952.* Paris: Le Seuil, 1952.

——, ed. *Paris-Saigon-Hanoi: Les archives de la guerre, 1944-1947.* Paris: Gallimard/Julliard, 1988.

Devos, Jean-Claude. *Inventaire des archives de l'Indochine: Sous-série 10 H (1867-1956).* 2 vols. Vincennes: SHAT, 1987.

Dommen, Arthur J. *The Indochinese Experience of the French and the Americans: Nationalism and Communism in Cambodia, Laos, and Vietnam.* Bloomington: Indiana University Press, 2001.

Duara, Prasenjit, ed. *Decolonization.* London: Routledge, 2004.

Duiker, William J. *U.S. Containment Policy and the Conflict in Indochina.* Stanford CA: Stanford University Press, 1994.

——. *The Communist Road to Power in Vietnam.* 2nd ed. Boulder CO: Westview Press, 1996.

——. *Ho Chi Minh.* New York: Hyperion, 2000.

Dunn, Peter M. *The First Vietnam War.* London: Hurst, 1985.

Duong Trung Quoc, ed. *"Thu do huyet le" (Hinh anh Ha Noi hai tuan trang khoi lua—mua dong 1946-1947) ["The Capital in Anguish" (Photos of Hanoi During the Two Lunar Months of Heated Battle—Winter 1946-1947)].* Hanoi: Nha Xuat ban Lao Dong—Xa Hoi [Labor and Social Affairs Publishing House], 2006.

Elections et référendums des 13. oct., 10 et 24 nov. et 8 déc. 1946. Résultats par département et par canton (France métropolitaine et France d'Outre-mer). Paris: Le Monde, 1947.

Elgey, Georgette. *Histoire de la IVème République.* Vol. 1: *La République des illusions, 1945-1951.* Paris: Fayard, 1965.

Elliott, David W. P. *The Vietnamese War: Revolution and Social Change in the Mekong Delta, 1930-1975.* 2 vols. Armonk NY: M. E. Sharpe, 2003.

Essential Matters: A History of the Cryptographic Branch of the People's Army of Viet-Nam, 1945-1975. Translated and edited by David W. Gaddy. Fort George G. Meade, MD: Center for Cryptologic History, National Security Agency, 1994.

Faligot, Roger, and Pascal Krop. *La piscine: Les services secrets français, 1944-1984.* Paris: Seuil, 1985.

Fall, Bernard B. *The Two Viet-Nams: A Political and Military Analysis.* London: Pall Mall, 1963.

Ferrandi, Jean. *Les officiers français face au Vietminh, 1945-1954.* Paris: Fayard, 1966.

Figuères, Léo. *Je reviens du Vietnam libre.* Paris: J. London, 1950.

Folin, Jacques de. "Surprises et inquiétudes à Saigon et à Paris." In *Leclerc et l'Indochine, 1945-1947: Quand se noua le destin d'un empire,* ed. Guy Pedroncini and Philippe Duplay, 211-18. Paris: Albin Michel, 1992.

Fonde, Jean-Julien. *Traitez à tout prix.* Paris: Robert Laffont, 1971.

——. "Le jour ou commença la guerre d'Indochine." *Le Monde Dimanche,* Aug. 2, 1981.

——, and J. Massu. *L'aventure Viêt-minh.* Paris: Plon, 1980.

Fourniau, Charles, and Alain Ruscio. "Le monde politique francais, le P.C.F. face au déclenchement de la première guerre d'Indochine." *Cahiers d'histoire de l'Institut Maurice Thorez* 10, 19 (1976): 191-226.

——. "Le déclenchement de la guerre (2ᵉ partie)." *Cahiers d'histoire de l'Institut Maurice Thorez* 11, 22 (1977): 177-216.

Franchini, Philippe. *Les mensonges de la guerre d'Indochine*. Paris: Perrin, 2005.

Gaiduk, Ilya V. *Confronting Vietnam: Soviet Policy toward the Indochina Conflict, 1954-1963*. Washington DC: Woodrow Wilson Center Press, 2003.

Gardner, Lloyd C. *Approaching Vietnam: From World War II through Dienbienphu*. New York: Norton, 1988.

Goscha, Christopher E. *Thailand and the Southeast Asian Networks of the Vietnamese Revolution, 1885-1954*. Richmond, Surrey, UK: Curzon Press/NIAS, 1999.

———. "Le contexte asiatique de la guerre franco-vietnamienne: Réseaux, relations et économie (août 1945–mai 1954)." 2 vols. PhD diss., Ecole pratique des hautes études, Paris, 2000.

———. "Belated Asian Allies: The Technical and Military Contributions of Japanese Deserters (1945–50)." In *A Companion to the Vietnam War*, ed. Marilyn B. Young and Robert Buzzanco, 37–64. Malden MA: Blackwell, 2002.

———. "A 'Popular' Side of the Vietnamese Army: General Nguyen Binh and the Early War in the South (1910–1951)." In *Naissance d'un Etat-Parti: Le Viêt Nam depuis 1945*, ed. C. E. Goscha and Benoît de Tréglodé, 325–54. Paris: Les Indes savantes, 2004.

———. "Courting Diplomatic Disaster? The Difficult Integration of Vietnam into the Internationalist Communist Movement (1945–1950)." *Journal of Vietnamese Studies* 1–2 (2006): 59–103.

Goscha, Christopher E., and Benoît de Tréglodé, eds. *Naissance d'un Etat-Parti: Le Viêt Nam depuis 1945*. Paris: Les Indes savantes, 2004.

Gras, General Yves. *Histoire de la guerre d'Indochine*. Paris: Plon, 1979.

Gratien, Jean-Pierre. "Marius Moutet, de la question coloniale à la construction européenne, 1914–1962." 3 vols. PhD diss., Université de Paris I (Sorbonne), 2004.

———. *Marius Moutet: Un socialiste à l'outre-mer*. Paris: L'Harmattan, 2006.

Grimal, Henri. *La décolonisation de 1919 à nos jours*. Brussels: Editions Complexe, 1984.

Grosser, Alfred. *La IVème république et sa politique extérieure*. Paris: Armand Colin, 1961.

Guillemot, François. "Au coeur de la fracture vietnamienne: L'élimination de l'opposition nationaliste et anticolonialiste dans le Nord du Viêt Nam (1945–1946)." In *Naissance d'un Etat-Parti: Le Viêt Nam depuis 1945*, ed. C. E. Goscha and Benoît de Tréglodé, 175–216. Paris: Les Indes savantes, 2004.

Hac Hai. "L'an I de la République Démocratique du Viêtnam." *Etudes vietnamiennes* 7 (1965).

Hammer, Ellen J. *The Struggle for Indochina, 1940-1955*. Stanford CA: Stanford University Press, 1954.

Hémery, Daniel. *Ho Chi Minh: De l'Indochine au Vietnam*. Paris: Découvertes Gallimard, 1990.

———. "Asie du Sud-Est, 1945: Vers un nouvel impérialisme colonial? Le projet indochinois de la France au lendemain de la Seconde Guerre mondiale." In *L'ère des décolonisations: Sélection de textes du Colloque "Décolonisations comparées," Aix-en-Provence, 30 septembre–3 octobre 1993*, ed. Charles-Robert Ageron and M. Michel, 65–84. Paris: Karthala, 1995.

———. "Paul Mus: Un orientaliste dans la décolonisation." In *Paul Mus (1902–1969)*, ed. David Chandler and Christopher E. Goscha, 221–46. Paris: Les Indes savantes, 2006.

Herring, George C. "The Truman Administration and the Restoration of French Sovereignty in Indochina." *Diplomatic History* 1 (1977): 97–117.

Hertrich, Jean-Michel. *Doc-Lap! (L'indépendance ou la mort!): Choses vues en Indochine.* Paris: Jean Vigneau, 1946.

Hess, Gary R. "United States Policy and the Origins of the French–Viet Minh War, 1945–46." *Peace and Change* 2–3 (Summer–Fall 1975): 21–33.

———. *Vietnam and the United States: Origins and Legacy of War.* Rev. ed. New York: Twayne, 1998.

Hitchcock, William I. *France Restored: Cold War Diplomacy and the Quest for Leadership in Europe, 1944–1954.* Chapel Hill: University of North Carolina Press, 1998.

Ho Chi Minh. *Selected Works.* Vol. 3. Hanoi: Foreign Languages Publishing House, 1961.

———. *Selected Writings.* Hanoi: Foreign Languages Publishing House, 1977.

———. *Toan Tap* [Collected Works]. Vol. 4: *1945–1947.* Hanoi: Nha Xuat Ban Su That, 1984.

Huynh Kim Khanh. *Vietnamese Communism, 1925–1945.* Ithaca NY: Cornell University Press, 1982.

Institut franco-suisse d'études coloniales [Jean Bidault]. *France et Viet-Nam: Le conflit franco-vietnamien d'après les documents officiels.* Geneva: Editions du Milieu du monde, n.d. [1947].

Irving, R.E.M. *The First Indochina War: French and American Policy 1945–54.* London: Croom Helm, 1975.

Isoart, Paul. "L'élaboration de la Constitution de l'Union française: Les Assemblées constituantes et le problème colonial." In *Les chemins de la décolonisation de l'empire français, 1936–1956,* ed. Charles-Robert Ageron, 15–32. Paris: Centre national de la recherche scientifique, 1986.

Jennings, Eric T. *Vichy in the Tropics: Pétain's National Revolution in Madagascar, Guadeloupe, and Indochina, 1940–1944.* Stanford CA: Stanford University Press, 2001.

Karnow, Stanley. *Vietnam: A History.* New York: Penguin Books, 1984.

Kolko, Gabriel. *Anatomy of a War: Vietnam, the United States, and the Modern Historical Experience.* New York: Pantheon Books, 1985.

———. *Century of War: Politics, Conflicts, and Society since 1914.* New York: New Press, 1994.

Lacina, Bethany, "Monitoring Trends in Global Combat: A New Dataset of Battle Deaths, Documentation of Coding Decisions I, Uppsala/PRIO Data." www.prio.no/sptrans/671630282/Documentation_PRIO-UCDP.pdf (accessed January 4, 2009).

Lacina, Bethany, and Nils Petter Gleditsch. "Monitoring Trends in Global Combat: A New Dataset of Battle Deaths." *European Journal of Population* 21, 2 (2005): 145–66.

Lacouture, Jean, *Hô Chi Minh.* Paris: Seuil, 1977.

———. *Léon Blum.* Paris: Seuil, 1977.

La République est morte à Dien Bien Phu. Documentary film directed by Jérôme Kanapa from a scenario by Kanapa, Philippe Devillers, and Jean Lacouture, 1974.

Lawrence, Mark Atwood. *Assuming the Burden: Europe and the American Commitment to War in Vietnam.* Berkeley: University of California Press, 2005.

Lawrence, Mark Atwood, and Fred Logevall, eds. *The First Vietnam War: Colonial Conflict and Cold War Crisis.* Cambridge MA: Harvard University Press, 2007.

Le Couriard, Daniel. "Les socialistes et les débuts de la guerre d'Indochine (1946–1947)." *Revue d'histoire moderne et contemporaine* 31 (April–June 1984): 334–53.

Léon Pignon, 1908–1976: Un homme de coeur au service de l'Outre-Mer français: Témoignages et documents. Paris: Academie des sciences d'Outre-Mer, 1988.

Lin Hua. *Chiang Kai-shek, de Gaulle contre Hô Chi Minh: Viêt-nam, 1945–1946*. Paris: L'Harmattan, 1994.

———. "The Chinese Occupation of Northern Vietnam." In *Imperial Policy and Southeast Asian Nationalism*, ed. Hans Antlöv and Stein Tønnesson, 144–69. Copenhagen: NIAS; London: Curzon Press, 1995.

Lockhart, Bruce McFarland. *The End of the Vietnamese Monarchy*. New Haven CT: Council on Southeast Asia Studies, Yale Center for International and Area Studies, 1993.

Lockhart, Greg. *Nation in Arms: The Origins of the People's Army of Vietnam*. Sydney: Asian Studies Association of Australia in association with Allen & Unwin, 1989.

Marr, David G. *Vietnamese Anticolonialism, 1885–1925*. Berkeley: University of California Press, 1971.

———. *Vietnamese Tradition on Trial, 1920–1945*. Berkeley: University of California Press, 1981.

———. *Vietnam 1945: The Quest for Power*. Berkeley: University of California Press, 1995.

———. "Beyond High Politics: State Formation in Northern Vietnam, 1945–1946." In *Naissance d'un Etat-Parti: Le Viêt Nam depuis 1945*, ed. C. E. Goscha and Benoît de Tréglodé, 25–60. Paris: Les Indes savantes, 2004.

———. "Creating Defense Capacity in Vietnam, 1945–1947." In *The First Vietnam War: Colonial Conflict and Cold War Crisis*, ed. Mark Atwood Lawrence and Fred Logevall, 74–104. Cambridge MA: Harvard University Press, 2007.

Marsot, Alain-Gérard. "The Crucial Year: Indochina 1946." *Journal of Contemporary History* 19, 2 (1984): 337–54.

McAlister, John T., Jr. *Viet Nam: Yhe Origins of Revolution*. New York: Knopf, 1969.

McTurnan Kahin, George. "The United States and the Anticolonial Revolutions in Southeast Asia, 1945–50." In *The Origins of the Cold War in Asia*, ed. Yonosuki Nagai and Akira Iriye, 338–61. New York: Columbia University Press, 1977.

Messmer, Pierre. *Après tant de batailles . . . mémoires*. Paris: Albin Michel, 1992.

Meuleau, Marc. *Les pionniers en Extrême-Orient: Histoire de la Banque de l'Indochine, 1875–1975*. Paris: Fayard, 1990.

Mus, Paul. Articles in *Le Témoignage Chrétien*, Aug. 12 and Nov. 18, 1949; Jan. 7 and Feb. 10, 1950.

———. *Viet-Nam: Sociologie d'une guerre*. Paris: Seuil, 1952.

———. *Le destin de l'Union française de l'Indochine à l'Afrique*. Paris: Seuil, 1954.

Nagai, Yonosuki, and Akira Iriye, eds. *The Origins of the Cold War in Asia*. New York: Columbia University Press, 1977.

Ngo Van Chieu. *Journal d'un combattant Viet-Minh: Traduit et adapté par Jacques Despuech*. Paris: Seuil, 1955.

Nguyen Khac Vien. *The Long Resistance, 1858–1975*. 2nd ed. Hanoi: Foreign Languages Publishing House, 1978.

———. *Vietnam: A Long History*. Hanoi: The Gioi, 1999.

Nguyen Thanh. *Hoat Dong Bao Chi Cua Dai tuong Vo Nguyen Giap* [General Vo Nguyen Giap's Press Activities]. Hanoi: Nha Xuat Ban Ly Luan Chinh Tri, 2005.

Obermeyer, Ziad, Christopher J. L. Murray, and Emmanuela Gakidou. "Fifty Years of Violent War Deaths from Vietnam to Bosnia: Analysis of Data from the World Health Survey Programme." *British Medical Journal* 7659 (June 28, 2008): 1482–86.

Olsen, Mari. *Soviet-Vietnam Relations and the Role of China, 1949–64: Changing Alliances.* London: Routledge, 2006.

Paillat, Claude. *Dossier secret de l'Indochine.* Paris: Presses de la Cité, 1964.

Patti, Archimedes L. *Why Vietnam? Prelude to America's Albatross.* Berkeley: University of California Press, 1980.

Pedroncini, Guy, and Philippe Duplay, eds. *Leclerc et l'Indochine, 1945–1947: Quand se noua le destin d'un empire.* Paris: Albin Michel, 1992.

Porch, Douglas. *The French Secret Services: From the Dreyfus Affair to the Gulf War.* New York: Farrar, Straus and Giroux, 1995.

Pribbenow, Merle L., II. "General Vo Nguyen Giap and the Mysterious Evolution of the Plan for the 1968 Tet Offensive." *Journal of Vietnamese Studies* 2 (2008): 1–33.

Qiang Zhai. *China and the Vietnam Wars, 1950–1975.* Chapel Hill: University of North Carolina Press, 2000.

Quinn-Judge, Sophie. *Ho Chi Minh: The Missing Years.* Berkeley: University of California Press, 2002.

Rice-Maximin, Edward Francis. "The French Left and Indochina, 1945–1954." PhD thesis, University of Wisconsin, 1974.

Rioux, Jean-Pierre. *La France de la Quatrième République.* Vol. 1: *L'ardeur et la nécessité, 1944–1952.* Paris: Seuil, 1980.

Rivet, Paul. "Le drame franco-vietnamien." *Cahiers internationaux: Revue internationale du monde du travail* 6 (1949): 45–66.

Rose, Lisle Abbott. *Roots of Tragedy: The United States and the Struggle for Asia, 1945–1953.* Westport CT: Greenwood Press, 1976.

Ruscio, Alain. "Les communistes, le gouvernement francais et l'Indochine en 1947." *Cahiers d'histoire de l'Institut de recherches marxistes* 13 (1983): 25–40.

———. "Le premier mois de la guerre: Etude sur le déclenchement du conflit franco-vietnamien, novembre–décembre 1946." *Cahiers d'histoire de l'Institut de recherches marxistes* 17 (1984): 15–32.

———. *Les communistes français et la guerre d'Indochine, 1944–1954.* Paris: L'Harmattan, 1985.

———. *La guerre française d'Indochine.* Paris: Editions Complexe, 1992.

———, ed. *La guerre "française" d'Indochine (1945–1954): Les sources de la connaissance. Bibliographie, filmographie, documents divers.* Paris: Les Indes savantes, 2002.

Sainteny, Jean. *Histoire d'une paix manquée: Indochine, 1945–1947.* Paris, Amiot-Dumont, 1953. Reprint. Paris: Fayard, 1967.

———. *Face à Hô Chi Minh.* Paris: Seghers, 1970.

Salan, Raoul. *Mémoires: Fin d'un empire.* Vol. 1: *Le sens d'un engagement, juin 1899–septembre 1946.* Vol. 2: *Le Viêt-minh mon adversaire, octobre 1946–octobre 1954.* Paris: Presses de la Cité, 1970–71.

Sapp, Steven P. "The United States, France, and the Cold War: Jefferson Caffery and American-French Relations, 1944–1949." PhD diss., Kent State University, 1978.

Schlienger, Micheline. *Vers l'éclatement du conflit franco-vietnamien.* Paris: Mare & Martin, 2005.

Schulzinger, Robert D. *A Time for War: The United States and Vietnam, 1941–1975.* Oxford: Oxford University Press, 1997.

Shipway, Martin. *The Road to War: France and Vietnam, 1944–1947*. Providence RI: Berghahn, 1996.

Short, Anthony. *The Origins of the Vietnam War*. London: Longman, 1989.

Sockeel-Richarté, Patricia. "La conférence franco-vietnamienne de Fontainebleau (juillet–août 1946)." *Espoir* 35 (June 1981): 54–64.

Tertrais, Hugues. *La piastre et le fusil: Le coût de la guerre d'Indochine, 1945–1954*. Paris: Comité pour l'histoire économique et financière de la France, 2002.

Thomas, Martin. "The Colonial Policies of the Mouvement Républicain Populaire, 1944–1954." *English Historical Review* 476 (April 2003): 382–411.

———. "French Imperial Reconstruction and the Development of the Indochina War." *The First Vietnam War: Colonial Conflict and Cold War Crisis*, ed. Mark Atwood Lawrence and Fred Logevall, 130–51. Cambridge MA: Harvard University Press, 2007.

Thong Tan Xa Viet Nam [Vietnam News Agency]. *Dong chi Truong Chinh* [Comrade Truong Chinh]. Hanoi: Nha Xuat Ban Thong Tan [Vietnam News Agency Publishing House], 2007.

Tønnesson, Stein. *The Outbreak of War in Indochina, 1946*. PRIO Report no. 3. Oslo: International Peace Research Institute, 1984.

———. "The Longest Wars: Indochina 1945–75." *Journal of Peace Research* 1 (1985): 9–30.

———. *1946: Déclenchement de la guerre d'Indochine: Les vêpres tonkinoises du 19 décembre*. Paris: L'Harmattan, 1987.

———. "A French Decision for War: French and Vietnamese Decision-Making before the Outbreak of the War in Indochina, December 1946." *Vietnam Forum* 12 (Summer–Fall 1988): 112–35.

———. *The Vietnamese Revolution of 1945: Roosevelt, Ho Chi Minh, and de Gaulle in a World at War*. Oslo: International Peace Research Institute; Newbury Park CA: Sage Publications, 1991.

———. "Filling the Power Vacuum: 1945 in French Indochina, the Netherlands East Indies and British Malaya." In *Imperial Policy and Southeast Asian Nationalism*, ed. Hans Antlöv and Stein Tønnesson, 110–43. Copenhagen: NIAS; London: Curzon Press, 1995.

———. "La paix imposée par la Chine: L'accord franco-vietnamien du 6 mars 1946." *Cahiers de l'Institut d'histoire du temps présent*, 34 (1996): 35–56.

———. "The Meeting That Never Was." *NIAS-Nytt* [newsletter of the Nordic Institute of Asian Studies] 3 (1997).

———. "La difficulté d'utilisation des archives des services secrets: Le cas de l'Indochine lors de la Seconde Guerre mondiale." *Renseignements & opérations spéciales* 2 (2000): 61–70.

———. "National Divisions in Indochina's Decolonization." In *Decolonization*, ed. Prasenjit Duara, 253–77. London: Routledge, 2004.

———. "Franklin Roosevelt, Trusteeship, and Indochina: A Reassessment." In *The First Vietnam War: Colonial Conflict and Cold War Crisis*, ed. Mark Atwood Lawrence and Fred Logevall, 56–73. Cambridge MA: Harvard University Press, 2007.

———. "The Vietnam Peace." Paper presented at the International Studies Association convention, New York City, February 15–18, 2009.

Tran Thi Lien. "Les catholiques vietnamiens pendant la guerre d'indépendance (1945–1954) entre la reconquête coloniale et la résistance communiste." PhD diss., Institut d'études politiques, Paris, 1996.

Tran Trong Trung. *Tong Tu Lenh Vo Nguyen Giap [General Commander Vo Nguyen Giap]*. Hanoi: Nha Xuat Ban Chinh Tri Quoc Gia, 2006.

Tuchman, Barbara W. *The March of Folly: From Troy to Vietnam*. New York: Knopf, 1984.

Turpin, Frédéric. "Le Mouvement républicain populaire et la guerre d'Indochine (1944–1954)." *Revue d'histoire diplomatique* 110 (1996): 157–90.

———. *De Gaulle, les gaullistes et l'Indochine, 1940–1956*. Paris: Les Indes savantes, 2005.

Valette, Jacques. "La Conférence de Fontainebleau (1946)." In *Les chemins de la décolonisation de l'empire français, 1936–1956*, ed. Charles-Robert Ageron, 231–50. Paris: Centre national de la recherche scientifique, 1986.

———. *La guerre d'Indochine, 1945–1954*. Paris: Armand Colin, 1994.

Valluy, Jean. "Indochine octobre 45–mars 47." *Revue des deux mondes*, Nov. 1 and 15, Dec. 1 and 15, 1967.

Varga, Daniel. "La politique française en Indochine (1947–50): Histoire d'une décolonisation manquée." PhD diss., Université d'Aix–Marseille I, 2004.

Vo Nguyen Giap. *The Military Art of People's War: Selected Writings of General Vo Nguyen Giap*. Edited by Russell Stetler. New York: Monthly Review Press, 1970.

———. *Unforgettable Days*. Hanoi: Foreign Languages Publishing House, 1975.

———. *Unforgettable Months and Years*. Translated by Mai Van Elliott. Data Paper No. 99. Ithaca NY: Southeast Asia Program, Dept. of Asian Studies, Cornell University, 1975.

———. *Chien Dau trong vong vay [Fighting While Encircled]*. Hanoi: Nha Xuat Ban Quan Doi Nhan Dan [People's Army of Vietnam Publishing House], 1995.

———. *Mémoires, 1946–1954*. Vol. 1: *La résistance encerclée*. Fontenay-sous-Bois: Anako, 2003–4.

Vu Ky. "Nhung chang duong truong ky khang chien nhat dinh thang loi" [The Protracted Resistance Will Certainly Be Victorious]. *Lich su Quan su [Military History]* 12 (1988): 72–82.

———. *Thu ky Bac Ho ke chuyen [Uncle Ho's Secretary Talks]*. Hanoi: Nha Xuat Ban Chinh Tri Quoc Gia, 2005.

Vuong Thua Vu, Colonel. "La vérité sur le 19 décembre 1946 à Hanoï." Appendix in Léo Figuères, *Je reviens du Viet Nâm libre*, 181–94. Paris: J. London, 1950.

———. *Truong thanh trong chien dau: hoi ky [Growing Up in Battle: Memoir]*. Hanoi: Quan doi nhan dan, 1979.

Worthing, Peter. *Occupation and Revolution: China and the Vietnamese August Revolution of 1945*. China Research Monograph 54. Berkeley: Institute of East Asian Studies, University of California, Berkeley, 2001.

Young, Marilyn B. *The Vietnam Wars, 1945–1990*. New York: Harper Perennial, 1991.

Young, Marilyn B., and Robert Buzzanco, eds. *A Companion to the Vietnam War*. Malden MA: Blackwell, 2002.

TEXT: 10/12.5 Minion Pro
DISPLAY: Minion Pro
INDEXER: Barbara Roos
COMPOSITOR: Integrated Composition Systems